Carolyn Miller

Maine Art now

Maine Art now

Edgar Allen Beem
preface by Arthur C. Danto

The Dog Ear Press
Gardiner, Maine

The Dog Ear Press

132 Water Street

Gardiner, Maine 04345

First Edition
10 9 8 7 6 5 4 3 2 1

Acknowledgments: All of the writings in this book by Edgar Allen Beem originally appeared in *Maine Times*, with the exception of the following: "The Uncertain Fate of Langlais' Menagerie", "People and Things Connected", and "Joseph Nicoletti" first appeared in the *Portland Independent;* "Dahlov Ipcar" and "George Delyra" first appeared in *Art New England;* "A Painter of Signs" first appeared in *Down East.*

Library of Congress Cataloging-in-Publication Data

Beem, Edgar Allen, 1949-
Maine art now / Edgar Allen Beem.
p. cm.
ISBN 0-937966-31-2 : $55.00. -- ISBN 0-937966-32-0 (pbk.) : $27.50
1. Art, American--Maine. 2. Art, Modern--20th century--Maine.
3. Artists--Maine--Biography. I. Title.
N6530 . M2B4 1990
709' . 741' 09048--dc20

90-35284
CIP

Cover:

Celeste Roberge
Northern Archives, Rising Cairn, 1989.
Galvanized steel and granite stone, 54 x 58 x 40.
Collection of Runny Mede Sculpture Farm,
Woodside, California. Photo by Jon Bonjour.

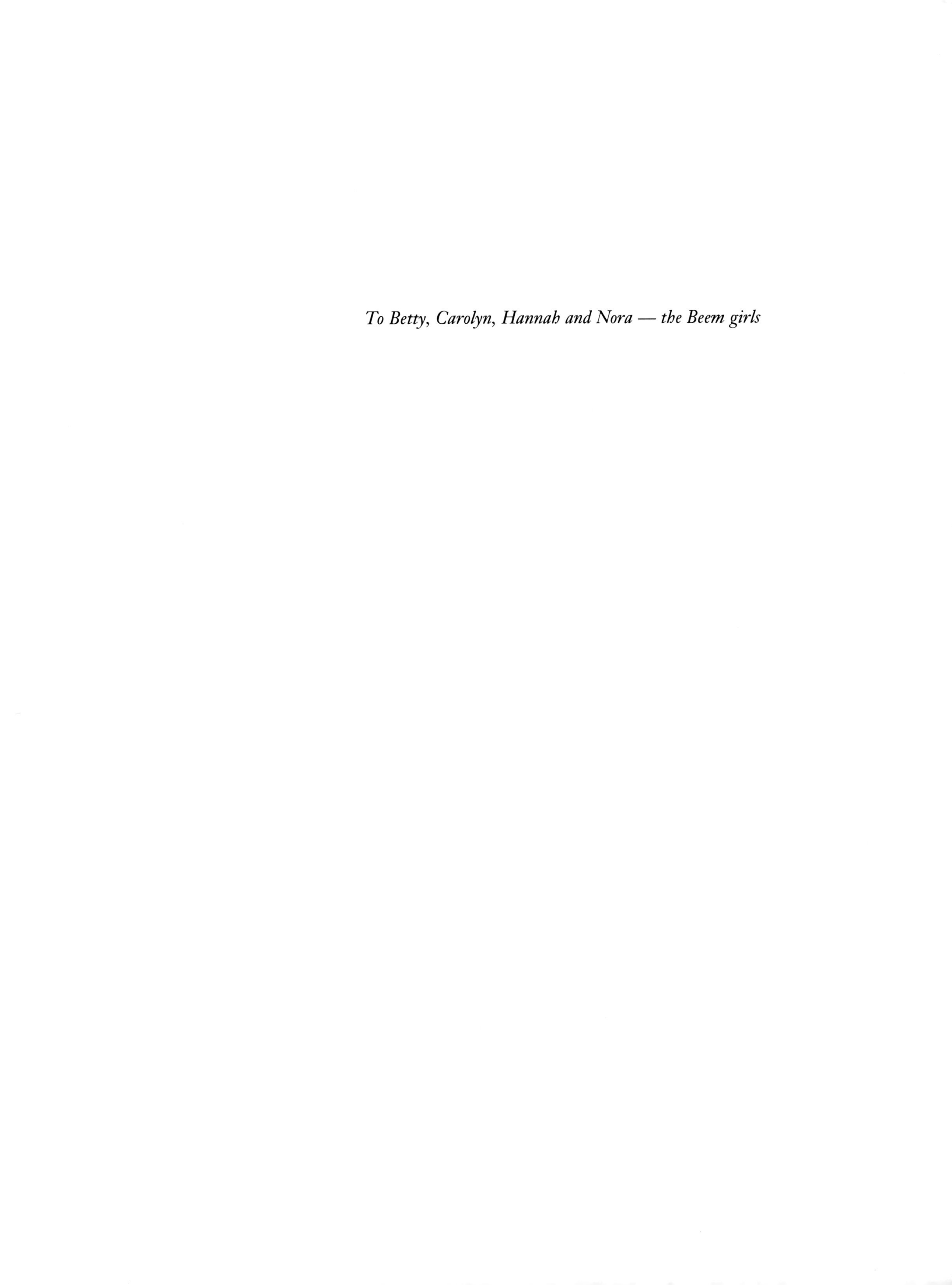

To Betty, Carolyn, Hannah and Nora — the Beem girls

Contents

Maine Art now

Preface & Introduction

Preface

Arthur C. Danto

In *Maine Art Now*, Edgar Allen Beem seeks to drive an emblematic stake through the heart of the expression "Maine Art," that genre of souvenir images of lobstermen, tumbled rocks, pointed firs, bleak islets in sullen waters. Just so, one might seek to redeem "Venetian Art," construed as designating picturesque gondoliers, palazzi reflected in canals, vistas over boated lagoons to shimmering palladian churches, marble bridges over romantic waters. The difficulty is that both these expressions define territories which border on kitsch in one direction, but whose other border overlaps the provinces of high art. Maine Art has at one extreme the nameless daubers of post-card scenery, but at its other extreme there is Marin, Homer, and Hartley, who belong in the company, surely, of Carpaccio, Canaletto, and Guardi, whose subject matter and even treatment differ not so greatly from tacky waterscenes on velvet pillowslips, on canalscapes in ricordi di Venezia albums. Both extremes in each of these genres are artistic responses to the same visual facts, the things that bring visitors to Maine and to Venice, tourists and artists alike, responsive in their own ways to the unmistakable identities of people and *paysage*. The hateful expression "West Virginia Art" requires no such redemption because there is no universal visual wonder that draws all the world to West Virginia, and fires them with the desire to carry away with them images of what brought them there. Putting into pictures what pleasures the eye and stirs the soul is one of the primordial motives of art.

Still, the expression "Venetian Art" does something more than mark off a class of images of Venice, and my sense of the title *Maine Art Now* is that Beem means to elide the tacit "of" in "Maine Art," now read as "Art of Maine," hence art that has Maine as its visual subject. Venetian art was among the glories of world art: it was an art that embodied rather than merely depicted the opulent reality of a Venice that was three-fifths fantasy to begin with, a world of damask and brocade, cruelty and eroticism, pearls and flesh, the ecstasies of Christianity and the crass wealth of the Orient. Not everything that had Venice as its subject was Venetian art in this sense, though it is plain that Carpaccio, Canaletto, and Guardi was Venetian Art as well as Art of Venice. And Marin, Homer, and Hartley, in parity, would belong to Maine Art as well as to the Art of Maine, embodying as well as representing a spirit whose outward signs may well have been lobstermen, tumbled rocks, pointed firs, bleak islets in sullen waters. But the important thing is that something could be

Maine Art without having to be Art of Maine, and, as such and like Venetian art, be among the artistic wonders of the world. The painting of the New York School rarely depicted the great city where it was enacted, but perhaps it embodies the drives that explain the uniqueness of New York. The California School of Diebenkorn embody a California of the soul, whether they represent it or not, though the tableaux of David Hockney perhaps does both. The point is that *Maine Art Now* is a kind of invocative chant for an art that embodies whatever it is that makes Maine Maine, whether it represents Maine or not. As a chant, it is, I think, possibly more a demand than a description—like "Freedom Now!" or "Peace Now!", where the "Now" concedes that we do not have at this moment what we are demanding, where the "Now" is not a temporal indexical, like "Today," as in "The Way We Live Now."

But whether or not the painting and sculpture he is demanding in fact exists, I am certain the spirit it must embody to meet the demand is itself already present in the critical writings of Edgar Allen Beem. Somehow, the very audacity, the preemptive pride, the fierce independence of mind implicit in the ideal is actual in the writing. It is as if Beem were saying that since Maine Writing is actual, Maine Art has to be a true possibility. And like an art which, like that of Venice in its flowering, embodied the spirit of a place with such intensity that it transcended it, Beem's writing goes beyond its locus and its immediate subject, and commands the interest of anyone interested in art, in writing on art, whatever their relationship to Maine, to the Art of Maine, or to Maine Art.

Beem is to be admired for the same reasons, and in consequence of the same virtues that Henry James found admirable in his Americans at a time when the expression "American Art" would have struck Europeans, or worldly Americans themselves, as over-reaching if not oxymoronic. There is in him a directness, an honesty, a clarity of perception, an optimism given tang by skepticism, a journalistic drive for the bare truth, and an intellectual uprightness that, in combination, make him unique in an artworld whose writers stumble about drunk on rot-gut theory, and emit, like squids, inky clouds of pretension and obscurity, of ideology and, finally, of publicity. Beem is astringent, linguistically thrifty, literate, and exact, with a touch of the prophet and of the judge—fine Old Testament virtues in the New England mind at its most characteristic and at its best. And there is, beyond all that, a remarkable fairness. There can be few writers capable of giving, so to speak, equal time to the conservative Hilton Kramer and the radical Lucy Lippard.

So whether or not Maine Art as yet exists, here is an uncontested example of Maine Writing. At the same time, a certain dilemma that would have to face Maine Art is visible in Maine Writing. Beem has as primary audience no doubt those who read him in the *Maine Times*, and who think about Maine and art and Maine Art. Maine Art, like Maine Writing, might be for that audience, but not only for it. Its audience would be everyone interested in art wherever they are. Beem's peers would not just be the art writers of Maine, reviewing the shows as they come up, but the best art writers anywhere. As the art he wants would want to be identified with but not solely identified with Maine, so with him. He is, to be sure, a cultural patriot, but also a man of the wide world.

In view of this dilemma, I suppose one can sympathize with the animus against Maine Art. *Maine Art Now* will be displayed with the Maine books in Maine bookstores, in Portland and Blue Hill, Damariscotta and Lewiston, Ogunquit and Rockland, Bangor and Bar Harbor. There it will be with the volumes of down east recipes, albums of Maine-scenes, books of local verse, compendia of salty proverbs. But it really deserves a place in bookstores everywhere, among the best writing on art by the best art writers there are, at very least as a model of style, a paradigm of good sense, and exemplar of clear thinking about difficult subjects.

Maine: The State of the Art

An Introduction

The history of Maine is fairly impressed with the names of great American artists. Beginning perhaps with Jonathan Fisher's *A Morning View of Bluehill, Sept. 1824*, the Maine landscape and the Maine reality have served as subject and sustenance for a steady stream of painters, sculptors, and photographers—Thomas Cole, Frederick Church, FitzHugh Lane, Winslow Homer, Rockwell Kent, Marsden Hartley, John Marin, Berenice Abbott, Louise Nevelson, Fairfield Porter, Neil Welliver, Eliot Porter, Andrew Wyeth, and more to come.

From the early romantics to the latter-day realists, Maine has been a locus of art making. What is new, however, is the development within the past 25 years of an audience and a market for serious art in Maine. In 1963, when Colby College mounted its landmark *Maine and Its Role in American Art, 1740-1963* exhibition, there was not a single year-round commercial art gallery in Maine. Art, except as preserved in museums, belonged largely to the summer life of the state. Many of the best Maine artists were not Maine residents, but New Yorkers on working vacations. That, too, has changed within our lifetimes.

The somewhat awkward title of the Colby show speaks directly, if unintentionally, to the identity crisis (inferiority complex?) that continues to afflict art and artists in Maine. "*Maine and Its Role in American Art*" asserts a special relationship between the state of Maine and the mainstream of American art history while scrupulously avoiding the provincial connotations which might arise if "Maine" modified "Art," as in "A History of Maine Art" or "Maine Art History." Even as long ago as 1963, "Maine art" was understood as a stigma in ways that other regional labels such as "Hudson River School" or "New York School" are not. "Maine art" had long since become something light and inconsequential—a watery confection of lighthouses and lobster traps, rowboats and fisherfolks.

In calling this collection of articles and reviews *Maine Art Now*, I have gingerly placed the words "Maine" and "Art" next to one another in hopes of taking the first tentative steps toward rehabilitating the term. For Maine art—art made by artists in Maine and often in consequence of the artist being in Maine—has become something much finer than the resort kitsch most often associated with the term.

Beginning perhaps with that major Maine survey retrospective in 1963, artists and audiences in Maine have made steady progress toward full artistic self-consciousness. The 1960s were a time of beginning to take art in

Maine seriously. The 1970s were years of learning to take serious art seriously. And the 1980s have been a decade of looking deeper than ever before into the Maine reality while, at the same time, beginning to look beyond it. Exhibitions of work by artists who have no connection whatsoever to Maine are still rare on the Maine art scene, however.

Those of us who were born here as well as those who have come from away, those who come for the summer, and even those who just come for a visit understand the powerful physical attraction of Maine. The drowned, boreal coast sweeping up from the sand beaches of York County to the wild, bold headlands of Washington County, the shattered islands of Penobscot Bay, the deep fastness of the North Woods, the charmed austerity of whitewashed fishing villages, even the smoky, riverine stench of the paper mill towns add up to a very strong sense of regional identity.

What artists respond to in this raw northeastern land is the aura of authenticity which radiates from a place when Culture is not yet far removed from Nature. Parson Fisher's view of Blue Hill lifted the curtain on a settlement being hacked out of the woods. Cole and Church made the trek down east to Mount Desert in search of the transcendental landscape, an Arcadia where God could be intuited from his breathtaking Creation. Luminists like Lane subordinated the landscape in all its clarity to the divine light which illuminated it. Then tough-minded fellows like Homer and Kent came along to transform places like Prouts Neck and Monhegan into heroic settings pitting Man against Nature.

Always, always there is that undeniable physicality. Abstraction is an urban turn of mind; rural landscapes draw one out. So even those quintessential early modernists of Maine —Hartley and Marin—yoke their vision to the elements. In Marin's watercolors the Maine sea, shore, and sky fairly fracture under the push-pull dynamics of creation. With Hartley, the Maine landscape seems in danger of imploding of its own tension and weight.

"Poor Hartley," wrote Marin to Alfred Stieglitz of Hartley's death in 1943, "alas who is there to take up the brush where he left off with the [Maine Legend]."

Hartley, Maine's prodigal son, was born in the unloveliness of Lewiston, spent most of his life roaming in search of an alternative way to be, and finally settled on the remote fishing village of Corea as his last stop in this life. His embrace of Maine-ness was passionate and his desire to be identified with his native state touching given his cosmopolitan air.

In his 1937 essay, "On the Subject of Nativeness—A Tribute to Maine," Hartley located the essence of nativeness in the natural constancy of rivers flowing to the sea, loons on inland lakes, angles of geese overhead, bear roaming the mountains, gulls in flight.

"The gulls remain the same and the rocks, pines, and thrashing seas never lose their power or their native tang," wrote Hartley.

"Nativeness is built of such primitive things, and whatever is one's nativeness, one holds and never loses no matter how far afield the traveling may be...This quality of nativeness is couloured by heritage, birth, and environment, and it is therefore for this reason that I wish to declare myself the painter from Maine."

A half-century after Hartley's death, it is difficult to imagine any ambitious artist staking a similar claim. Why? Because after World War II, Maine became an aesthetic backwater, a slough of romantic realism, organic abstraction, and dead-end art impulses. Chasing the ghosts of Homer and Hartley and pursuing dreams of Wyeth, a generation of lesser lights arrived to colonize the coast. They made a virtue of backwardness, pandering to the public taste for the picturesque such that Hartley's "rocks, pines, and thrashing seas" became a formula for triteness. And still the sponge-stippled surf beats against Maine's palette-knifed rocks!

It is easy to beat on that group of older Maine artists (now in their sixties, seventies, eighties, and graves) who covered the state with so much stylized and mannered paint, but, in truth, theirs was a healthy enthusiasm for Maine even if it did produce intellectually and emotionally neutral art.

To belittle enthusiasm is a mean-spirited thing, but the distress one feels when art becomes a set of conditioned responses, when artists stop growing, is genuine. And, indeed, art in Maine seems to have experienced a period of no-growth during the 1950s and 1960s. The primary reason for this aesthetic stagnation should be fairly obvious.

Maine is a conservative state, resistant to rapid change. As the mainstream of American art became increasingly reflective and reflexive, examining first the nature of the inner being then the nature of art itself, Maine remained a bastion of representationalism, the artists still content to examine and respond to appearances. One of the few Maine artists to work abstractly in a convincing way was William Kienbusch out on the Cranberry Isles. Pop art didn't get here until a decade after the fact, when Robert Indiana moved to Vinalhaven. Conceptualism and minimalism never really arrived at all.

After drifting for a decade or two on the calm seas of pictorialism, the engine driving Maine art finally got jump-started again in the 1970s. Young artists began arriving from out-of-state, but though they often came in search of a simpler life, they did not leave their visual sophistication behind in the cities. They were not interested in making pretty pictures for the tourist trade.

The degree of change that took place in the nature and character of Maine art during the 1970s and 1980s is suggested by a letter which appeared in the *Maine Times* during the summer of 1988. In the letter a gentleman from Camden complained that he could not find any "beautiful paintings" in Portland galleries to hanging on the walls of his "beautiful, expensive new home in Maine."

"All the paintings are obviously displayed for the delight of the critics," complained the letter-writer, who went on to describe what he saw in Maine galleries as "overly large and for the most part grotesque images" and to report how he and his wife were "repelled by distorted and even ugly forms."

"The local art buying public," concluded the peeved correspondent, "wants paintings that show the beauty of Maine (that is why we are here), not some poor man's idea of New York 'art.'"

Since the gentleman made the point that "Money is not a consideration," it's surprising that someone didn't steer him in the direction of a nice Welliver oil or Wyeth watercolor, either of which could be had for the price of a small Maine house, but neither of which are apt to be available in Portland galleries. Still, if Welliver's woodlands and Wyeth's coastal vignettes don't qualify as "paintings that show the beauty of Maine," nothing does.

As to the charge that Maine painters are producing "some poor man's idea of New York 'art'" (what malicious little quotation marks, those!), it should first be pointed out that some very significant New York art is made in Maine by artists such as Welliver, Alex Katz, Richard Estes, Yvonne Jacquette, Rackstraw Downes, Lois Dodd, and Katharine Porter. All except Porter, a painter of politically-charged abstractions, work firmly within the precincts of realism.

Were one to survey the dominant trends in Maine art in recent years, varieties of realism would still lead the way. Whether made manifest in the painterly mode of J. Thomas R. Higgins and Alfred Chadbourn, the romantic idiom of Thomas Crotty and John Gable, the factual American style of DeWitt Hardy and the late Stephen Etnier, the super-realism of Beverly Hallam and Alan Magee, or the classical orientation of Joseph Nicoletti and Thomas Cornell, representational painting is still king in Maine.

The distorted forms the disaffected gentleman from Camden wrote of suggest that he may have run across some examples of another strong trend in Maine art—the expressionist resurgence that is everywhere in modern art today. Marjorie Moore's bizarre woodland fables, Frederick Lynch's patterned constructions, Janice Kasper's strange little doggy mysteries, even Wendy Kindred's existential androgynes might disturb an eye in search of nothing more challenging than likenesses of local scenery.

Then, too, an unwary viewer in 1988 could easily have come upon some very difficult abstract work of a sort not seen in Maine 20 years ago. Abby Shahn's illuminated color squares, Kathy Bradford's biomorphic and geometric explorations, Johnnie Ross's severely analytic forms, Lisa Allen's bold gestural abstractions, and William Manning's complex constructions are all firmly based on the experience of Maine light, landscape, and life, but not in simple or obvious ways.

The most important development in Maine art during the decade of the 1980s, however, has been the emergence of native Maine artists of real substance and vision. Artists like Dozier Bell, Alan Bray, Anne Gresinger, Eric Hopkins, Celeste Roberge, and Richard Wilson are all sons and daughters of this sea and soil who possess aspects of a truth about Maine that has never before been expressed. It is not always pretty, but it is a new, deep-structured order of the local reality that comes through in their work. They are the best hope we have of rehabilitating the reputation of Maine art.

In the catalogue for *Maine and Its Role in American Art*, Colby College art historian James M. Carpenter wrote that the one thesis of the show that would "stand the test of time" was "that artists who have worked in Maine have felt the impress of a place and that their works, when gathered together, bear witness to this."

As we head wide-eyed into the 1990s, that Maine impress is becoming more obscure and harder to detect in Maine-made art increasingly marked by art history and contemporary cultural influences. To the extent that the best Maine artists participate in the national and international art dialogue, they may be losing their regional identity, but that is not necessarily a bad thing.

Sometimes it becomes necessary to free one's self of the bonds of home. Louise Nevelson, for example, left Maine as soon as she was old enough to be on her own, and ever after she denied that her choice of scrap wood as a medium had anything to do with the fact that her father ran a lumber yard in Rockland.

Maine is, after all, a land of limited horizons. And what Maine can offer a good young artist is equally limited. When an exciting new artist surfaces—usually at the Maine Coast Artists' annual juried show or the All Maine Biennial—the best he/she can hope for locally is a solo gallery show, a few sales to the handful of adventurous collectors in the state, a good review or two, possibly a museum show, and a summer scholarship to the Skowhegan School. All of this can be accomplished in about 18 to 24 months' time, after which the artist's chances of reaching a wider audience depend upon getting into a New York gallery.

My twin goals in assembling these writings into a book, then, are to help some of Maine's best artists find the wider audience they deserve and to challenge a few assumptions about what art in Maine is and can be.

Maine Art Now consists primarily of writings which have appeared in *Maine Times* since I began as the newspaper's art critic in 1981. There are also several earlier pieces from other publications, and except for a few cases, I have elected to let them stand as they first appeared. For though I write in the final frozen days of 1989, the "now"of this collection is the decade of the 1980s.

Edgar Allen Beem
Yarmouth, Maine
December 1, 1989

Artists

1

Representative Maine Artists

An Apology

The first thing I did after I decided to assemble some of my writings on art in Maine into a book was to compile a list of the artists I felt should be included. I have that alphabetical list before me now, and it runs to 239 names from Sigmund Abeles to Valerie Zint. Realizing that to adequately cover the work of 239 artists in profiles and reviews would result in a book of near-biblical dimensions, I made a second and more selective list of 55 artists who absolutely *had* to be included. Even at this, I have failed.

The feature-length pieces gathered here are, then, bio-critical essays on 25 representative Maine artists. I use the word "representative" deliberately, to indicate that I consider the work of the individuals profiled to be exemplary of the ideas and practices operative in modern Maine art generally. This book purports to be about *Maine Art Now*, but as even a casual reader will realize it is just as much about *Maine* Artists *Now*. Though I understand the idealist argument for letting a work of art speak for itself, I confess I am rarely moved by a painting, sculpture, print, or photograph without wanting to know something about the person who created it.

The artists discussed here approach the making of art from a variety of ideological, temperamental, and stylistic directions, but the one obvious thing they all have in common is that they make (or made) art in Maine. It has been my peculiar preoccupation to attempt to discover what, if anything, Maine means to these artists and their art while, at the same time, suggesting what these artists and their art may mean to Maine.

These profiles are arranged informally into groups of my own devising, categorical assignments which the artists themselves might well reject. I apologize in advance both for my rude taxonomy and for the fact that not all of the Maine artists who should be profiled could be.

I have chosen to lead off with the articles on Bernard Langlais and Fairfield Porter because they are among the earliest sustained pieces I wrote on Maine artists and because, in common with the later Stephen Etnier essay, these posthumous pieces (Langlais died in 1977, Porter in 1975, Etnier in 1984) are indicative of some prevalent characteristics in Maine art. In Langlais' sculpture, we see a degree of rugged, spirited humanism that typifies much of Maine life, not just art. In Porter's paintings and prints, we find that painterly approach to realism that America inherited from abroad. And in Etnier's romantic realism, we see Maine in a much more indigenous light.

I also found Langlais, Porter, and Etnier appropriate points of departure, because they are fairly representative of the sociology of Maine art. Langlais was a returned native; Porter, a distinguished summer resident; and Etnier, a summer resident who went native.

Andrew Wyeth, Neil Welliver, Alex Katz, Yvonne Jacquette, Robert Indiana, and Alan Magee are all Maine-connected artists with national and international reputations. The audience and the market for their work may primarily be elsewhere, but a major focus of their lives and their art is in Maine. Had time and space allowed, I would have liked to add similar considerations of Lois Dodd, Rackstraw Downes, and Katherine Porter, artists of equal stature; but perhaps because they have not exhibited extensively in Maine, occasions to visit them have not yet arisen.

The grouping of master photographers Berenice Abbott, Todd Webb, and Eliot Porter is too self-evident to require comment other than to express gratitude and awe that three of America's greatest photographers have worked and walked among us.

The profiles of Beverly Hallam, John Laurent, and Pat and DeWitt Hardy are together both because these are artists with personal and professional connections to the heydays of the Ogunquit art colony and because they are representative of mature Maine artists with well-established regional reputations. I would as well have included longer appraisals of Alfred Chadbourn, John Muench, and William Manning, to name but a few of their peers.

Lisa Allen, Mark Wethli, Marjorie Moore, Carlo Pittore, Paul Heroux, and Wendy Kindred are, to my mind, representative of the talented younger generation of artists who arrived from out-of-state within the past 20 years. Artists such as these, choosing to make Maine their year-round home and not just a summer retreat, established a new level of visual sophistication in Maine art. Today, they form the strong core of art in Maine. They should, of course, be joined by others of their generation—Kathy Bradford, Gary Buch, Tom Higgins, Paul Maddrell, Natasha Mayers, Joseph Nicoletti, Johnnie Ross, Abby Shahn, and more.

The sixth and final grouping of these profiles is meant to be representative of the native Maine artists who have emerged in the past decade. Eric Hopkins, Dozier Bell, and Celeste Roberge are unquestionably among Maine's best and brightest. Were they but accompanied here by Alan Bray, Anne Gresinger, Michael Waterman, and Richard Wilson, *Maine Art Now* would be much more comprehensive.

The Uncertain Fate of Langlais' Menagerie

Bernard Langlais

I miss Blackie Langlais. I never knew the man except through his art, but I miss his presence on the coast and his genius in our midst.

Bernard Langlais died in December of 1977 at the height of his creative powers. He was known widely as a master sculptor who used the native wood of his state to create big-hearted, lively and often humorous pieces which gladdened the eye and the heart. His art was democratic...no, populist...warm and human in a most expansive way. Maine residents probably know him best for his Skowhegan Indian, but the works which he left behind range from small animals and birds to satirical political sculpture and visual puns such as his larger-than-life *Christina* taken from Andrew Wyeth's famous painting. His art was not always intentionally humorous, but wit is a natural part of genius and Blackie Langlais was a genius.

Until two weeks ago, the Samoset Resort in Rockland was graced with this Langlais genius. Samoset commissioned a Langlais sculpture as a fountain when the resort was built. The Samoset is now undergoing design changes which include re-landscaping, and the management of the resort felt that the 24-foot sculpture (which was created out of heavy timber adorned with seabirds and a seal) was out of keeping with the new look. So two weeks ago, they took the sculpture apart and put it in storage. They are looking for a buyer and awaiting an appraisal of the piece's worth. The idea of cutting down the sculpture and dismantling it bothered me. It bothered Mrs. Langlais, too.

"They no longer have a Bernard Langlais sculpture. It no longer exists as such and never will again," Helen Langlais told me. She spoke the words with a determined conviction, sounding out each phrase as though she had repeated it to herself many times. And, of course, she is right. The Samoset Langlais no longer exists and no discerning art appraiser will ever validate it as a Langlais sculpture. It is now only an interesting collection of wood.

What makes the dismantling even more upsetting for Helen Langlais are the memories attached to the piece. She told me that Bernard was happy doing the work and that when it was ready for installation she took a field trip with the first and second graders she teaches at Cushing Elementary School to watch the project's completion. The kids loved it. It was a great day.

"It's almost like having Bernard die all over again," sighed Mrs. Langlais. She made it clear that her husband's art always came first with him. His creations were their children.

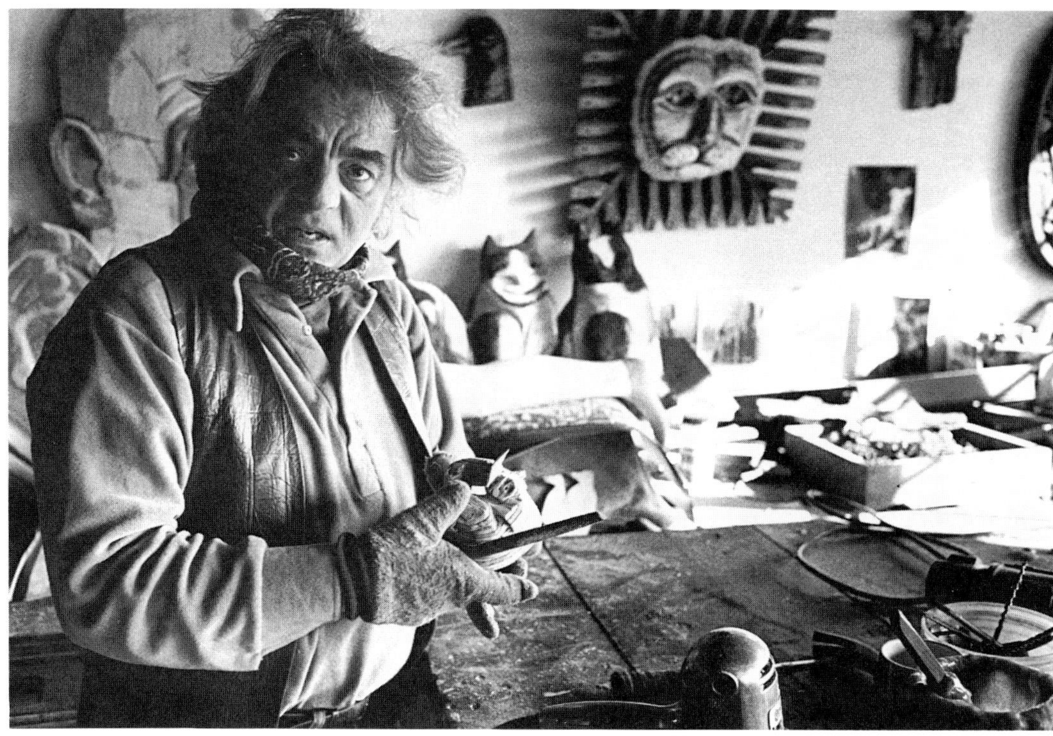

1. *Blackie Langlais at work in his studio, 1972. Photo by Stephen B. Nichols.*

The irony of the matter is that the Langlais sculpture was never paid for. The Samoset developers went through bankruptcy and the debt was legally erased. It should be obvious, however, that even if the present owners of the resort bear no legal responsibility, there is an ethical debt to be paid to the Langlais estate should the piece actually be sold. Funds are needed to maintain and conserve the legacy of brilliant sculptures Langlais created. This means that the works must now support themselves. Revenues from sales must be used to preserve other existing works.

The job of caring for Langlais' estate is a great one and Helen Langlais does not take the job lightly. The sculptures themselves generate problems for her.

To begin with, the Langlais home in Cushing is a wonderland of giant football players, Trojan horses, wild animals, and ingenious figures. They are natural traffic stoppers, and Helen Langlais is constantly faced with strangers wandering about on her property. She envisions the day when the property is given over to a public sculpture garden, but in the meantime, it is her home. One car stopping attracts another and before long, she can neither get into or out of her own driveway, not to mention the obvious undesirability of having strangers peering in windows and snooping about the yard. For this reason, she must discourage visitors. True art lovers will appreciate this and respect her privacy, but the problem persists.

The Langlais estate has not yet been settled, but the inheritance taxes on so much valuable art can be crippling. Mrs. Langlais recently testified on behalf of a bill before the Maine Legislature which would allow the estates of artists to pay taxes to the state in art rather than money.

Pointing to a shed wall which is roughly sketched with paint and adorned with four or five crude wooden bird figures, Helen Langlais says with disbelief, "Can you believe they appraised that at several thousand dollars? Now I have to pay taxes on it. They call that art? It was never finished." Again, she is right, but because it came from Bernard Langlais' hand, it must be art, right? Wrong.

The big job in maintaining the sculpture collection is repairing and weatherproofing the outdoor pieces each year. The winter takes its toll, and already a two-story elephant is listing mortally and a giraffe has collapsed. The snow falls, the ground heaves, and the sun burns down. Mrs. Langlais has had to hire a caretaker, but the expense of keeping the art for the future will be burdensome. Conserving and maintaining the Langlais legacy so that one day it will become a public exhibit might prove to be a natural work project for an art school, but for now, it is Helen Langlais' problem.

When Bernard Langlais died, he was in the midst of preparations for a federal government commission in Idaho. The piece was never executed. In the side yard stands a magical cluster of huge bears which was commissioned for the Philadelphia Zoo. Since the project was completed, the zoo's administration had changed and the bears' fate remains unknown.

And the death of an artist does not mean the death of his works. Helen Langlais has been kept busy arranging exhibits of her husband's works at Hobe Sound, Florida, the Farnsworth in Rockland, the Greenwich, Connecticut, Library, Wingspread Gallery in Northeast Harbor and a retrospective at the Maine Coast Artists Gallery in Rockport. Currently there is a showing of Langlais works in his hometown. The show at the Old Town Museum will run through June and July and there are other exhibits in the works.

Portland residents can see fine examples of Langlais' work at both Casco Bank and the Maine Savings Bank. Casco has his upbeat Portland waterfront and skyline construction and Maine Savings displays one of his screaming wooden hawks. Viewers interested in Langlais works which are still available for sale will find an excellent selection at Frost Gully Gallery on Exchange Street. Shingled, blank-eyed sheep, a marvelous barking dog and Langlais' emblematic lionheads. Bernard Langlais was a Leo, and with his shaggy mane of black-grey hair he was indeed lionine. Helen Langlais smiles. "He did grow to look like a lion, didn't he?"

Sitting in her unique living room filled with plants and art and the collection of "toys" she bought Bernard—delightful wooden airplanes, carved Indians, horses and dogs—Helen Langlais can point with sincere pride to the legislative proclamation mourning the passing of Blackie Langlais. Soon she will meet the most recent recipient of the Bernard Langlais Memorial Scholarship to the Skowhegan School. Her black dog mutters as smoke coughs into the room from a dying morning fire. At one time the sculpture outside shared the grounds with 16 live geese, two ducks, a billy goat, a ram, a donkey, a large spotted pony and an artist. Now that they are all gone, it is quiet in the yard.

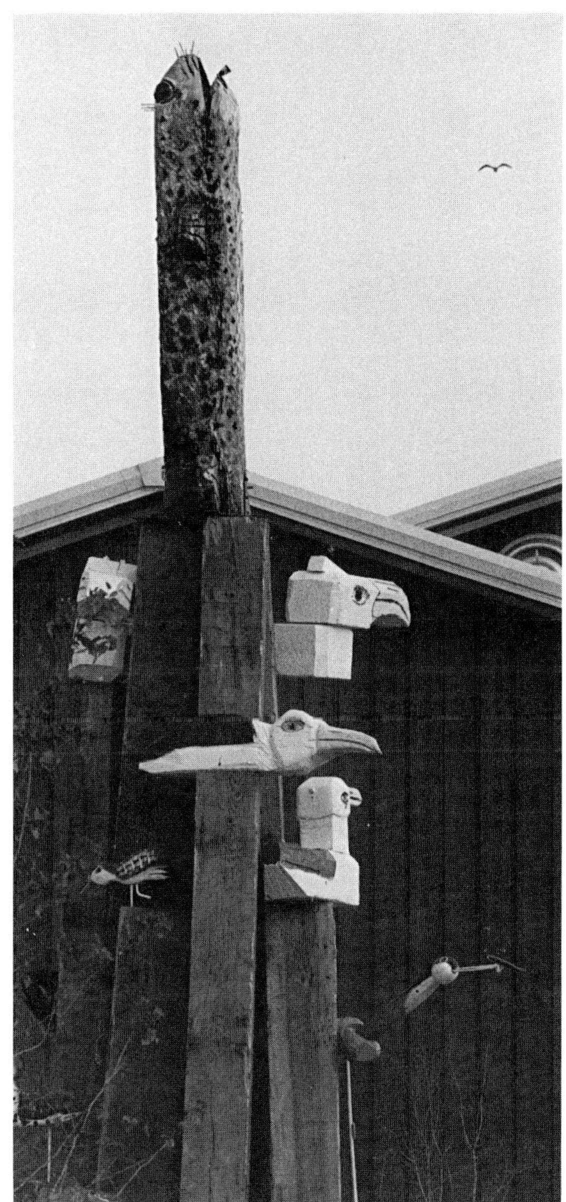

2. *Langlais' sculpture at the Samoset before it was torn down. Photo by Tom Jones.*

Below the house is a small pond. In the pond are two delightful "Bathers"—naked wooden nymphs with newel posts for breasts. It troubles Helen Langlais to think of the things Bernard would have done if he had lived. In the woods behind their house is another pond that Langlais created. Who knows what he had planned for it?

"It was like a cloud of white geese when they crossed the yard," says Helen Langlais, recalling the lively barnyard where her husband worked. "That's no more...but at least they don't chase me anymore." She misses Blackie Langlais, too. But what wonders the man left.

June 15, 1979

People and Things Connected

Fairfield Porter

Until recently I had a lot of miscon-ceptions about Fairfield Porter. I thought of him as summerfolk. Long Island winters and Great Spruce Head summers. Old money, probably politically conservative, possibly too academic, definitely a traditionalist. Fairfield Porter was, in my mind, the dean of new American realism. His representational paintings and prints lent respectability to a style of art that flourished in Maine, but was debunked in the contemporary art capitals of the world.

In addition to being an artist of accomplishment, Fairfield Porter was an articulate critic who contributed heavily to *Art News* and *The Nation*. *Art In Its Own Terms; Selected Criticism 1935-1975* was published by Taplinger this year, and reading Porter's writings forced me to reconsider my hasty judgments.

Porter himself felt that he was stronger as a critic than as a painter. He was definitely a fine and perceptive critic and I believe his self-assessment was correct. This is not to diminish his art, but merely to state that he seems to have possessed an intelligence and an eye which outstripped his abilities. His paintings are very good: his criticism is excellent. But judge for yourself. Barridoff Galleries currently has an impressive selection of Porter's works on exhibit and his writings are available for sale there also. The show will run through September 3rd.

So how mistaken was I? Well, to begin with, the strength of Porter's criticism comes from his refusal to toe any artistic party line. I would have expected him to promulgate a doctrine of representationalism. He does not. In fact, I think it would be very, very difficult to discern Porter's style as an artist from a reading of his writings. He is one of those rare critics who remains open to what is before him. Most critics—art, literary, and music—tend to review their own expectations. They apply preconceived formulas to creative acts. That's the easy way out. If what they encounter doesn't fit into their scheme of things, they dismiss it. Porter refuses to do this. He distrusts systems. He is always on the side of immediacy and vitality in art. His openness to possibilities means that at times his writings become obscure because he has no quick opinions at the ready. He has to get in there and muddle around to discover what he thinks. This is very refreshing.

Now let's banish those other misconceptions of mine. First, politically, Porter flirted with Communism and the social significance of art is never far from his thoughts. Also, Porter was an early and committed opponent of nuclear power. Rackstraw Downes, who wrote the excellent introduction to Porter's criticism as well as the text of the Barridoff catalog, states that Porter seriously considered giving up painting to devote himself full-time to organic farming and anti-nuke activities. So much for the gentleman summerfolk.

If there is a constant theme to Porter's view of art it would be his concern for the opposition of artistic truth to scientific truth. "Art connects us with the material world, from which mathematics, science, and technology separate us. Artistic particularity has no connection with technological generality. The concern of technology is to even out, to bring about that uniformity of nature envisaged by the idealism required by the effective working of its methods. The purpose of technology is in effect, to hasten the process of entropy—in short, to destroy."

In Porter's view, art deals with specifics, it admits of random facts and differences. It creates. Technology, the bastard child of science, deals with generalizations. It demands a closed order.

Pure science may be an art form, but technology is just a mechanical mopping up operation. So just as he distrusts methodology in science, he distrusts it in art.

"One learns from art to recognize and accept diversity for its own sake. One experiences a connection with the deepest part of oneself, and one learns that formality thought up ahead of time is incomplete, and leads away from wholeness."

And so Porter heroically resists a credo in order that he might approach wholeness.

In his own art, Fairfield Porter admits of two primary influences. Downes reports how, in 1938, Porter saw an exhibit of works by Pierre Bonnard and Jean Edouard Vuillard, both of whom might be called intimists for their post-impressionist handling of interior settings. Porter's reaction was strong and immediate. "I looked at the Vuillards and thought 'Maybe it was just a revelation of the obvious, and why does one think of doing anything else when it is so natural to do this?'" His debt to Vuillard should be obvious to anyone who sees Porter's work. Light and color are primary. He trusts his senses.

Porter's other debt is far less obvious. He was an early champion of Willem de Kooning and

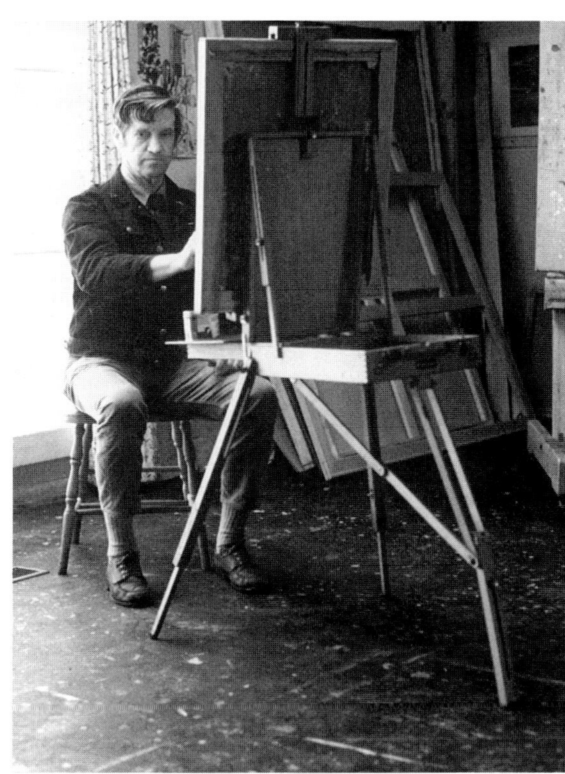

1. *Fairfield Porter. Photo by John Mac Whinnie.*

believed that de Kooning was the best of contemporary American painters. In a 1959 review essay on de Kooning, Porter seemed enraptured when he wrote:

"There is [in de Kooning's painting] that elementary principle of organization in any art that nothing gets in anything else's way, and everything is at its own limit of possibilities. What does this do to the person who looks at the paintings? This: the picture presented of released possibilities, or ordinary qualities existing at their fullest limits and acting harmoniously together—this picture is exalting." Porter concludes this essay by saying, "The vacuum they [de Kooning's paintings] leave behind them is a vacuum in accomplishment, in significance and genuineness. No one else whose paintings can be in any way considered to resemble his reaches his level." This, I think, is a definition of "glowing terms."

Porter's own paintings have such contentment —a range of contemplative stillness that runs from lyric to pastoral to purely intuitive—that it is difficult to find the de Kooning influence. Chased by Vuillard and in pursuit of de Kooning would be an oversimplification, but it might head the viewer in the right direction.

As a critic Porter did his best to be faithful to the work before him, to do it justice. Therefore, he described and tried to communicate between the visual and the verbal by analogy. John Updike, in his literary criticism, is Porter's only peer when it comes to faithfulness to the subject. Still, Porter runs a cautionary vein through his writings that is constantly on guard against easy judgments, formulas and cursory dismissals.

Even in the petty battle between objective and nonobjective, realistic and abstract art, Porter remained above the fray.

"The opposition between 'realism' and 'abstraction' is a misleading one. Both realists and abstractionists think they embody an ideal of art of which each work is the shadow: the realist making a reflection of the world of ideas in the largest sense...Both think that what is real about art exists in the realm of Whitehead's 'eternal objects.'" Porter saw the quarrel as one based on ideals. The title of this 1964 essay is "Against Idealism." What Porter valued above the ideal was the immediate and he said so time and time again. It is against this sense of immediacy that his own works should be judged, and if they fail to achieve greatness it is because Porter the critic set Porter the artist up for a fall.

Again, in his cautionary role, Porter addressed figurative art and those insecure camp followers who would proclaim the human figure exhausted as a fit subject for art today.

"To say that you cannot paint the figure today, is like an architectural critic saying that you must not use ornament, or as if a literary critic proscribed reminiscence. In each case the critical remark is less descriptive of what is going on than it is calling for a following—a slogan demanding allegiance. In this criticism is so much influenced by politics that it imitates the technique of a totalitarian party on the way to power."

The *Fairfield Porter* show at Barridoff was put together largely from works loaned by the Hirshl & Adler Gallery and the Brooke Alexander Gallery, both in New York. The exhibit includes oils, watercolors, pen and pencil drawings and a good selection of Porter's few lithographs. The range of subjects is from figures to seascapes to interiors and still life. Porter often painted in a style—flat fields of luminous color—that translates nicely to lithography and it is interesting to see a painting and a print spin-off in the same room. I think that in many cases Porter was stronger as a printmaker than as a painter. This may be because the prints were generally done later in his career, and so they tend to a consistency that we have no right to expect from paintings done over a lifetime.

Porter's established stature in the contemporary art world is attested to by the values attached to his work. Prices range from a high of $25,000 for the tremendous *Under the Elms* (an oil of green liquid light and beauty containing the figure of a young girl caught in fresh, if even petulant pose), down to a modest three-hundred dollar price for his exceptional prints.

One of the most impressive pieces in the show is his *Lizzie and Bruno* which pictures a young girl (his daughter, I imagine) with a dog at her feet. The canvas and the composition are wonderfully vertical, giving the piece the abundant vitality of adolescent growth, the ungainly grace of shooting up.

Dog At The Door is a well-known painting and one infused with a seductive, summery calm. It depicts a pet dog standing on steps gazing in through the door of a white house and off the picture plane. *Dog At The Door* employs a skillful use of whites and in the litho version of this subject these whites run down into greys. It is a painting which provides the viewer who needs a narrative explanation with a great many story possibilities, but it needs none to succeed.

Porter's seascapes distinguish him and it is easy to see the influence he has had on the present generation of representational painters. He handles the sea magically in terms of light and color while never allowing the scene to become more than the painting. This is where his concern for immediacy and the intuitive trusting of his senses comes in.

I am at a loss to explain or amplify Porter's floral renderings except to say that they are paintings of beautiful things competently done. The large oil entitled *Lichen, Wild Roses and Primroses* begs the clichéd "explosion of color" and is barely contained within its frame.

Portrait of Richard Freeman, the only really straightforward portraiture, shows an aggressive, contemporary young man who seems somewhat

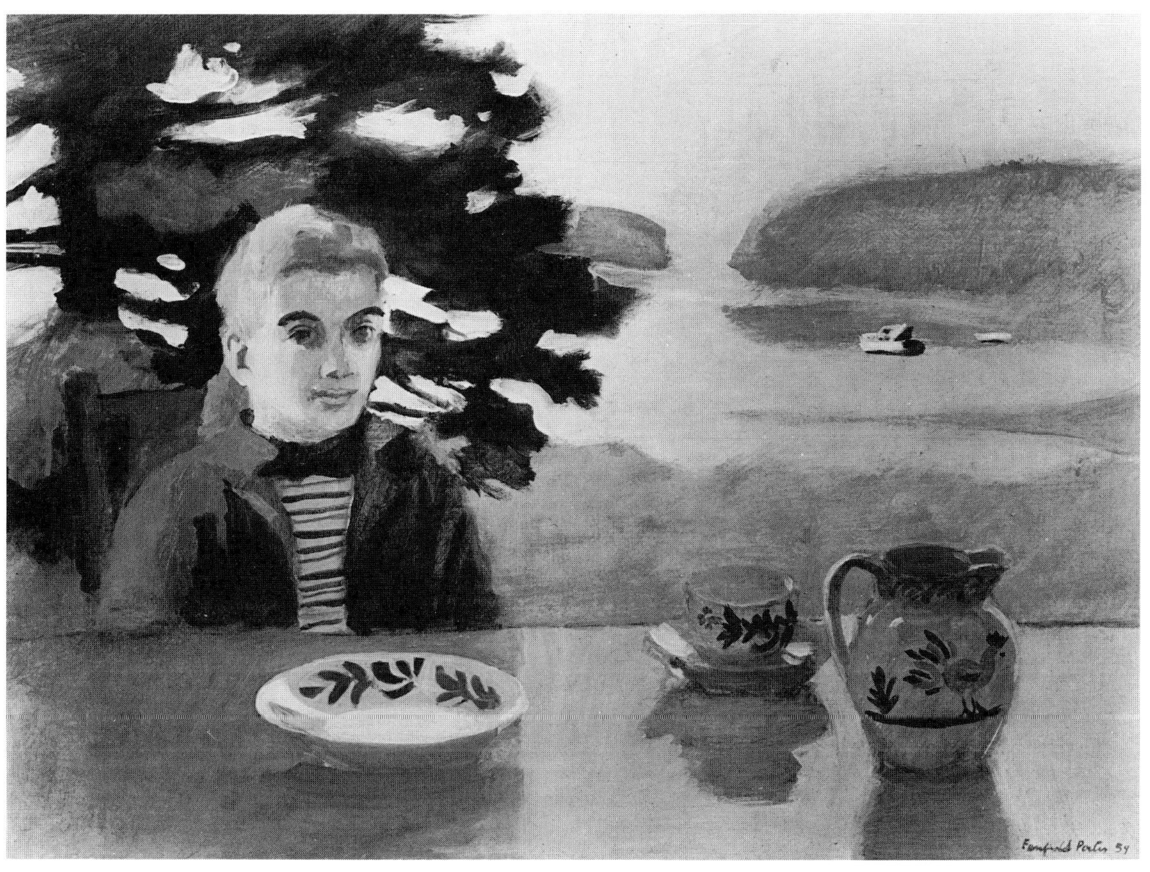

2. *Fairfield Porter,* Breakfast in Maine, *1954. Oil on canvas. Courtesy of the Hirschl & Adler Galleries.*

reluctant to be posed. The styling and subject bring to mind a more refined Raphael Soyer.

My favorite piece in the show is Porter's lithograph, *The Table*. It is an exquisite creation of mannerly composition which manages to remain loose. An oval table top seen from an eccentric angle set with china, it achieves vitality through the tension between imbalance and poise.

Sweeping the eye around the gallery, the viewer is struck by the powerfully subdued nature of Porter's colors—blues and purples and warm sand and flesh tones. He is at his best when he realizes his limitations and exploits them fully. I'm sure he would not have to be told this.

Returning finally to Porter's critical judgment, it was interesting to see what he had to say about photography as an art form. Eliot Porter, the nature photographer, is Fairfield Porter's brother, and it was with obvious delight that he was able to write:

"An expression of the immediacy of experience—for what else is the namelessness of everything—is proper to poetry and natural to photography. I know no photographs that express this so well as the color prints of my brother, Eliot Porter who, like Audubon, is known for his record of the birds of America."

Porter went on to observe that "drawing and painting have a language, but literature and photography are language." And in a review of a 1960 photography exhibition at the Metropolitan Museum entitled "Is Photography An Art?," Porter addressed the question squarely.

"One wonders whether a photograph is art, not so much because of anything inherent in the medium, as because the difference between art and craft, and art or craft and mechanism, is very subtle in photography. This subtlety has mostly eluded the screening organizations and jurors; so if this rather disappointing exhibition proves anything about the artistic nature of photography, it is that among the thousands of photographs taken every year, very few are art." Porter, however, allowed that the same was true of all art forms.

Fairfield Porter was an artist whose social commitment was not manifest in the subject matter or style of his art, but more deeply rooted in the very fact of creating art. In 1961 he wrote: "The morality and the communication inherent in the nature of art is that it makes one aware of the connectedness between people

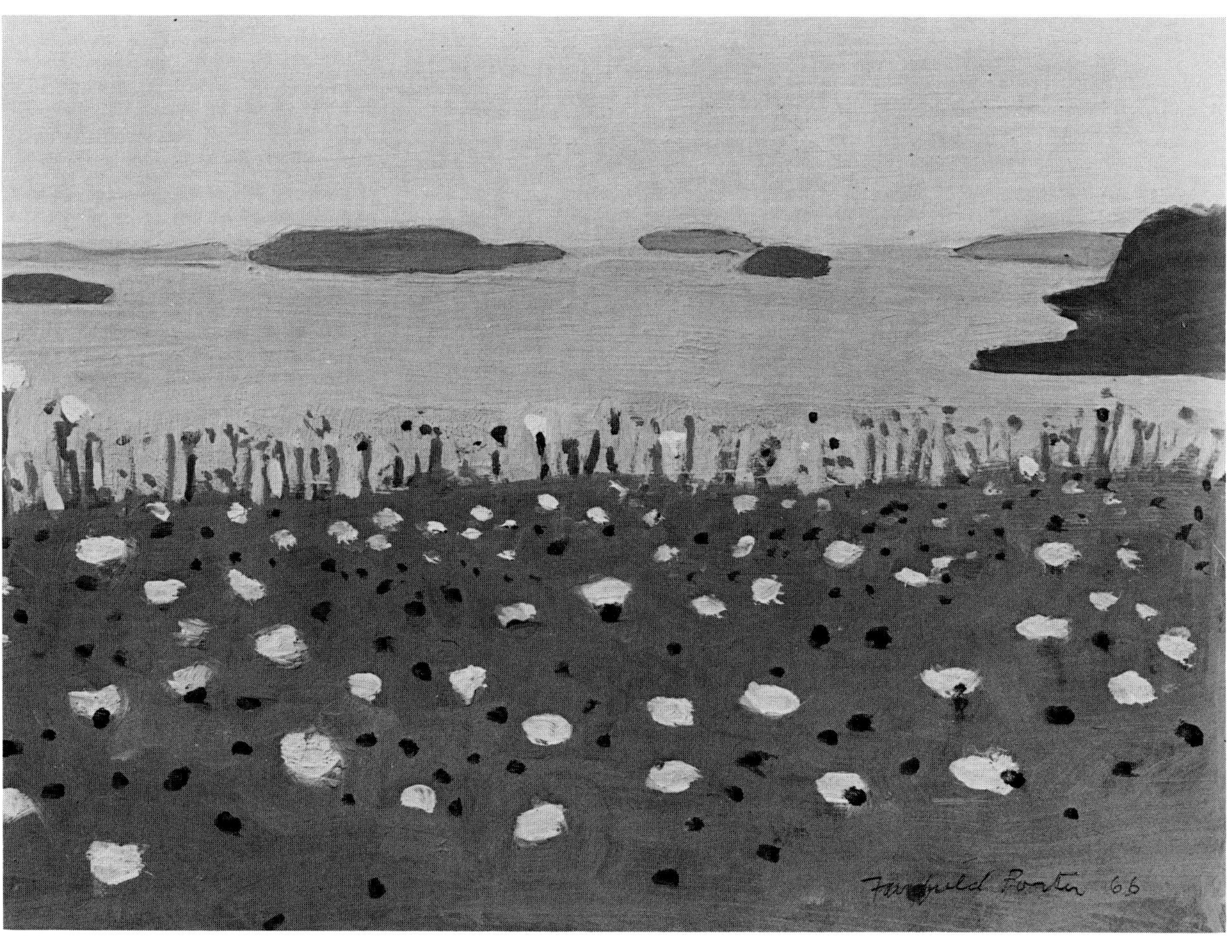

3. *Fairfield Porter*, Islands and Queen's Anne's Lace, *1966. Oil on canvas. Courtesy of the Hirschl & Adler Galleries.*

and between things."

A foe of the technology he saw rapidly outrunning the morality necessary to deal with it, Porter was a true champion of art as truth.

But let Fairfield Porter have the final word. What follows is as clear a statement as I have ever found in answer to that troubled population of art viewers who never seem to know what's going on in what they see. If Fairfield Porter had a credo, it might be this.

"Art has no rules to confine awareness. Because art is concerned with the ineffable—what cannot be translated—it will seem difficult to anyone who believes that explanation is the road to understanding. Artistic understanding comes from confidence in one's intuition."

July 27, 1979

"You should paint what you love"

Stephen Etnier

"I don't pretend to be a great painter," he said. "I'm not a Michael Angelo [sic], no, but I have something. I sell. I bring romance into the homes of all sorts of people."

—W. Somerset Maugham, *The Moon and Sixpence.*

York, Pennsylvania, is a tidy little industrial city far from the sea. Landlocked in Pennsylvania Dutch farm country, the factories of York produce barbells, motorcycles, tractors, turbines, and softball players. The galleries of the Historical Society of York County on historic East Market Street are devoted primarily to the machinery of the city's past—a Conestoga wagon here, a collection of antique autos there. But for six months of 1989 (May 24 to November 22), the featured exhibition at the York historical society is a retrospective of paintings by "York artist" Stephen Morgan Etnier (1903-1984).

Maine art lovers, of course, know this same Stephen Etnier as a popular and prolific "Maine artist"—in the opinion of some, even one of *the* Maine artists.

"Stephen Etnier is a very important Maine artist, far better than we realize," says painter Andrew Wyeth, an old friend who shares Etnier's Pennsylvania-Maine roots. "A lot of people talk about Fairfield Porter, but I think Steve did it earlier and with more snap, more edge. At his best, I think Steve struck a very strong chord for Maine. I love the clarity of his work."

The Etnier we know was a painter of luminous scenes of littoral life along the working coast. Like Winslow Homer, he worked in both Maine and the Caribbean. Like his mentor Rockwell Kent, he was drawn to the landscape of human toil, but unlike Kent, he did not idealize the common man. Indeed, Etnier painted backward from the heroic realism of Kent toward the poetic luminism of FitzHugh Lane. For, ultimately, like his more famous friend Wyeth, Stephen Etnier was romantic.

Today, Stephen Etnier lies in the little country graveyard behind the Elijah Kellogg Church in Harspwell Center. His final resting place is marked by a headstone carved with an image Rockwell Kent created in 1929 as a bookplate for Etnier. The image is that of a strapping young man standing upon the shore carrying a book, a canvas, and pair of oars in his arm. This stone, as fitting and handsome as it is, is Etnier's only memorial in Maine. For despite the fact that Etnier lived and painted in Maine for more than half a century, there have been no memorial exhibitions, let alone a retrospective, since his death. To understand this neglect, it is useful to begin in York, Pa.

Stephen Morgan Etnier was born in York, where his maternal grandfather, S. Morgan Smith, had made the family fortune by inventing the modern washing machine and founding a successful turbine company. The Smith family estate on Windham Hill still occupies the high ground above workaday York. Stephen's father, Carey Etnier, married Susan Smith and eventually took over the Smith turbine company, but Stephen was never cut out to become a captain of industry.

During his and the century's teens, young Etnier drifted from one prep school to another—Haverford School, Hill School, Roxbury School—without distinguishing himself academically. During the Roaring Twenties he furthered his checkered academic career with stops at Yale, Yale Art School, Haverford College, and the Pennsylvania Academy of Fine Arts. At one point, under the spell of Somerset Maugham's 1919 *The Moon and Sixpence*, an idealistic potboiling of the artistic calling loosely based on the life of Gauguin, he sailed off to South America to paint for six miserable months. It seems that the urge to paint, a guilty passion for the manchild of merchant wealth, did not find a real focus until 1927, when Etnier met Rockwell Kent in Philadelphia at a lecture Kent was giving about his recent trip to Alaska.

"When I heard him, it was sort of like the original business of reading *The Moon and Sixpence* because here he was leading a romantic life," Etnier said in a 1973 interview for the Archives of American Art. "I could see that he was a very disciplined individual. So I thought if I went to talk to somebody like that, he would either make me or break me."

"More than twenty years have elapsed since, in pursuance of a letter asking that I take him as a pupil, and in defiance of my answer that I wouldn't, a young man who wouldn't take no for an answer arrived at my door, was invited in, showed me a number of pathetic little daubs that he had perpetrated, and somehow won my consent to take him as a pupil free of charge," wrote Kent in his 1955 autobiography *It's Me O Lord*. "So Steve and Mrs. Steve moved into town; and Steve began to paint. And, surprisingly, before the winter was over he was painting good, creditable, realistic pictures."

That winter of 1927-28 Etnier spent studying with Kent at Kent's Asgaard Farm in Ausable, New York. The following year, 1929, he apprenticed himself to another of his artist-heroes, painter John Carroll. Thus tutored, by 1931 Etnier was ready to try himself out in the big time.

Etnier's first exhibition was a vanity show he paid for himself at the Dudensing Gallery in New York. His work was well enough received, however, that he was invited to show at the gallery later that same year. Thereafter, he showed regularly in New York, for 35 years (1932-1966) at the Milch Gallery and for more than another decade (1966-1980) at the Midtown Gallery.

Susquehanna River (1931), a riverine townscape that is the only painting from Etnier's first Dudensing show included in the York historical society retrospective, shows Etnier following the prevalent manner of Depression realism practiced by Ashcan School masters such as George Luks and John Sloan. Maine audiences familiar with Etnier's mature style of sharp, clear, unbroken realism might be forgiven if they didn't recognize the bold, loose strokes and cartooned renderings of early works such as *Susquehanna River* and the 1934 downtown view of hometown *York, Pa.* as Etnier's work. For despite the fact that Frost Gully Gallery in Portland has represented Etnier for more than 20 years, there has not been a comprehensive consideration of Etnier's art since a 1953 retrospective at the Farnsworth Museum in Rockland.

Stephen Etnier first came to Maine as a child in 1905 when his family began summering at South Harpswell. In 1926, when he married Matilde Gray (Kent's Mrs. Steve), he became a more permanent resident, living in the family's winterized cottage. In 1933, his first marriage having ended in divorce, he married a Barnard College coed named Elizabeth Jay whom he had met at a New York opening. Together, Stephen and Elizabeth Etnier became among the first of the modern age to make the transition from summerfolk to settlers when they purchased an old house on Gilbert Head, Long Island, at the

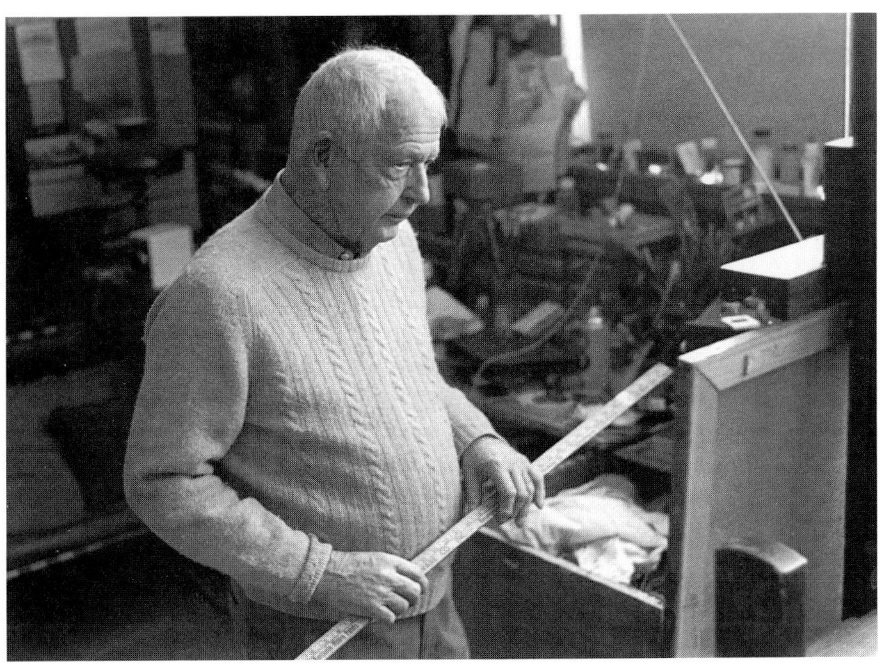

1. *Stephen Etnier at work in his South Harpswell studio. Courtesy of David Etnier.*

mouth of the Kennebec River. Elizabeth Etnier's 1937 bestseller *On Gilbert Head* chronicled the genteel adventures of the highborn couple roughing it on a Maine island, but shed precious little light on Etnier the painter.

Two years later, however, an article in the May, 1939 *Esquire* shed light on Etnier that 50 years later still adds color to our perception of the artist. Entitled "Stephen Etnier: Bad-Boy Artist," the profile is a classic of the sort of hip-hype *Esquire* purveys to this very day.

"Etnier is young and he is handsome, strong and sensitive. He knows how to live and he knows how to work," wrote someone named Harry Salpeter in a ravishing, opalescent prose. "He has a decent respect for the amenities of cosmopolitan life. No one seeing him stripped to the waist and pulling rocks out of the soil of his Maine island could ever guess that this was the champagne-drinking, tea dansant dandy who used to come down from Yale with his silver-topped cane concealed in his overcoat. Even today he has a face and figure that would flutter the dovecote of any young ladies' seminary."

Rich boy, ladies' man, tea-dance dandy, dilettante—the declension was so persuasive that as recently as 1981 *Maine Life* would report that "Etnier overcame a life of indulgence and affluence that would have overwhelmed a lesser man."

True, the young Stephen Etnier lived life in the fast lane. True, Etnier parties at South Harpswell are legendary among survivors. True, too, that his third wife, a beautiful young woman named Jane Pearce who suffered from manic-depression, committed suicide in 1949 after a South Harpswell dinner party. And true that "the amenities of cosmopolitan life" in Etnier's case included fast cars, fast boats, fast planes, and fast women. But what this catalogue of excess fails to note is that Stephen Etnier created his best work after his 1950 marriage to Samuela "Brownie" Rose, the decades of the 1950s, 1960s, and 1970s during which, according to his 1973 American Archives interview, there was "absolutely nothing but a very well regulated peace and quiet, slightly interrupted and improved by having two sons."

Stephen and Brownie Etnier and their sons John and David lived happily for many years in a contemporary house perched atop a cliff at Old Cove in South Harpswell. This idyll, too, ended in divorce in 1983, and was followed by a fifth, brief marriage in Etnier's final year of life. By that time, however, what Stephen Etnier was and would be as an artist was already long established.

The intimation at the outset of this essay that Stephen Etnier has not received proper attention is a view shared by many of his admirers, but the factors contributing to this critical situation are quite various. The first strike against Etnier, however, should be fairly obvious by now.

Painter George Delyra, Etnier's stable-mate at Frost Gully Gallery and his South Harpswell neighbor from 1957 to 1968, suggests that Etnier's inherited wealth prejudices some against his art.

"Steve was rich to begin with," says DeLyra. "By virtue of that, some people got it in their heads that he was an amateur, but that guy worked harder as a painter than anyone I've known except maybe Lonnie Sisson."

Delyra's reference to Laurence Sisson, an extremely popular Maine painter now resident in Santa Fe, raises a further difficulty some have in *seeing* Etnier's art properly. Etnier and Sisson, in company with artists such as Andrew Wyeth, Thomas Crotty, and William Thon, are essentially romantic realists, and the great peril of romanticism is preciousness, the triteness that develops when the bittersweet becomes too sweet, when love becomes sentimentality.

It is extremely difficult to paint traditional Maine images like lighthouses, lobster boats, traps, dories, and fishermen without slipping occasionally down the slippery slope of triviality, but Stephen Etnier was ever on guard against the corny. His weaker work slid toward illustration, but he was his own harshest critic as attested to by the number of times that "Destroyed" is pencilled beneath a photograph of a painting in the ledger albums Etnier kept. And though he was a great one for salvaging pieces from unsuccessful paintings, one of his final requests in this life was that his son David burn a stack of paintings he had left in his studio.

Then, too, Stephen Etnier lived long enough to become old-fashioned, and he certainly suffered with some peculiarly old-fashioned ideas about art. One of these was a Hemingway-esque anxiety that art was not a manly pursuit. It was not until his father met big, burly N.C. Wyeth that Etnier *père* conceded art might not be just for sissies, and Etnier *fils* seems to have inherited that gender doubt.

In a 1938 letter to his father, for example, Etnier confessed that part of his attraction to boats was the macho image of the sailor.

"To you a boat is simply some sort of semi-dangerous plaything," he wrote, "but to me it is a very definite means of holding my self-respect, for it gives me a sense of accomplishment in a man's world which most artists are presumably not members of. I want to be respected by men who know that it is a very real accomplishment to take a boat from here to Florida."

And just a year later *Esquire* quoted Etnier as saying, "The sea makes you masculine and gives you that respect in the masculine world you can't have as a painter."

Etnier's defensiveness about the nature and value of his work could also be misconstrued to mean that he did not take his art seriously. Partly humility, partly the manner of his age, Etnier always referred to himself as a "painter," never an "artist."

"I took up painting with the same practical attitude a doctor or a businessman has toward his career, the attitude of providing something of value to the public," Etnier told *American Artist* in 1956. "People like to enjoy themselves; I try to insure that they will have a good time in my paintings—a Renoir-ish attitude, let us say, rather than a profound preoccupation with the meaning of things."

And in his 1973 American Archives interview, Etnier said of his experience with Rockwell Kent, "I think I can say that there was never any talk about A-R-T. We just wanted things to look the way they are. Actually he's quite abstract if you really look. I still can't think of my pictures as being anything but just pure realism. I've never been in any way, never in any way, have I tried to produce art."

"He wanted to paint paintings that people would find enjoyable," says Etnier's friend, fellow painter, and dealer Thomas Crotty. "The fact that he was a good painter was probably a coincidence. He could have been just as successful without being a good painter. That's the irony of his success. It was always so important to him that he paint something the local lobsterman could relate to, but at the same time a museum curator with an ounce of brains could also relate to. It was an interesting challenge."

Several museum curators have related to Etnier's art, but so far nothing definitive has come of it. Bowdoin College, which gave Etnier an honorary degree in 1969 and to which Stephen and Brownie Etnier gave several paintings including a Wyeth, a Homer, and a

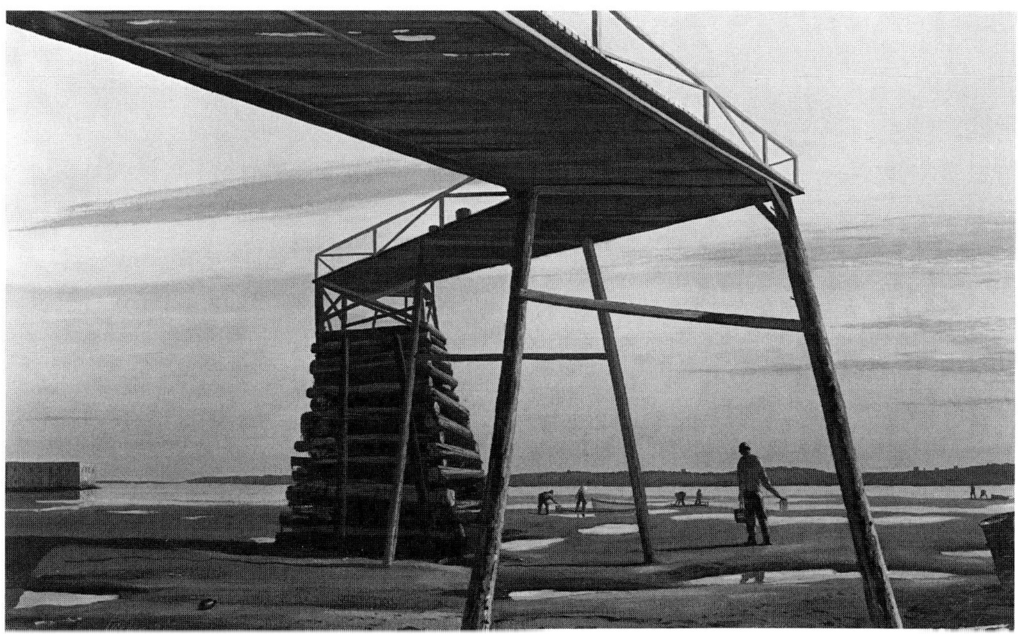

2. *Stephen Etnier*, Under the Pier, *1963. Courtesy of David Etnier.*

Glackens, would seem the logical place for an Etnier retrospective, but under the curatorship of John Coffey (who left Bowdoin last fall for a position in North Carolina), the Bowdoin College Museum of Art was steering a course away from showing Maine art in the belief that several other institutions were performing that function. In particular, Coffey says he felt that an Etnier retrospective was the proper province of the Portland Museum of Art.

Martha Severens, curator of the Portland Museum of Art, says the Portland museum is considering an Etnier exhibition, but that it will not take place until after a retrospective of another "mid-century master," William Kienbusch, is mounted in 1991.

Stephen Etnier's paintings must stand on their own merits, of course, but his Maine importance is not limited to his own art. For one thing, he was a generous man, supportive of other artists both morally and financially. Andrew Wyeth, for instance, recalls how "back when my temperas weren't selling well, Steve arranged to sell a couple for me at very good prices and wouldn't take a commission."

Etnier is also important because of his influence on other Maine artists. Painters Tom Crotty, George Delyra, and Robert Solotaire, for example, all acknowledge a debt to Etnier as a role model. As Etnier said of his role model, Rockwell Kent, "His honesty, simplicity, and dedication to work was contagious."

Bob Solotaire, who saw a great deal of Etnier during the years that he and Etnier were married to sisters (Etnier to Samuela Rose, Solotaire to Pat Rose), considers the older man his mentor.

"On the crassest level," says Solotaire, "Steve was a financially successful painter. He gave me a more sophisticated view of what it means to be a professional."

And in terms of aesthetic influence, Solotaire cites Etnier as the person who persuaded him "to work outdoors" directly from nature and who "made me aware that there is a marvelous equation between paint and reality." That equation—not imitation, but correspondence—is, of course, the essence of creativity.

"The guy was in some ways a painter's painter," says George Delyra. "Artists who respond to paint as paint like Steve's work."

Steve's work. The elements of an Etnier painting are fairly simply to catalog. First, they most often concern the shore. No one in Maine ever lived closer to the sea, literally and figuratively speaking. Second, Etnier's world is the world of dawn. The bloody, buttery quality of light in an Etnier is attributable to the fact that he routinely got up before the sun and sought out the first light of day. This, too, accounts for the calm, flat serenity of the seas in his paintings.

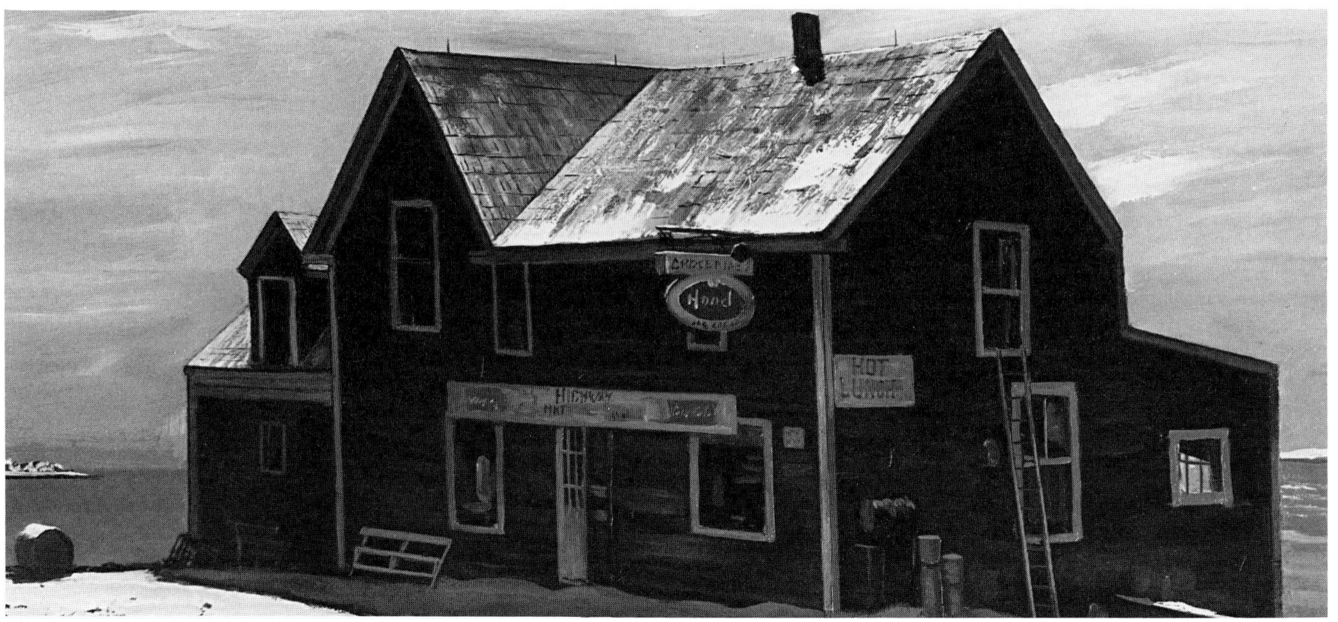

3. *Stephen Etnier,* Store in Winter. *Courtesy of David Etnier.*

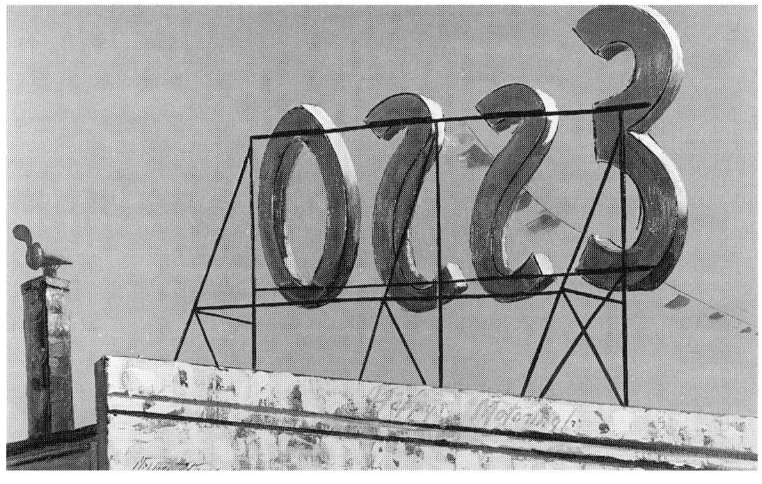

4. *Stephen Etnier,* ESSO, *1959. Courtesy of David Etnier.*

The elements of composition in a prototypical Etnier are most often the man-made and mechanical devices of the working coast: boats, piers, spindles, marker buoys, etc. One of his favorite paintings, *Telecommunications Forward Scatter Site, Nassau* (1960), is a workscape depicting a brace of dish antennae in the Bahamas.

Often, an Etnier painting will feature abrupt vertical elements thrusting into the picture plane and up from the dominant horizontal. *Port of Call* (1955), a European snapshot view of a town square imaginatively transported to the West Indies in Etnier's studio, is a good example of his penchant for vertical thrust and his allegiance to Rockwell Kent's dictum, "Occupy your corners!"

Ultimately, what we have in a good Stephen Etnier oil is a place and time lovingly preserved under varnish. Peaceful, serene, and sad.

"One of the qualities in his paintings that is so wonderful," says Bob Solotaire, "is that sadness. You get a very strong sense of things passing, of things that aren't going to be around anymore."

Love and death, the two arms with which the romantic embraces the beauty of this world.

"The only reason I paint is because this, I think, is wonderful and I want other people to know that it's wonderful," Stephen Etnier once said of Maine. "You should paint what you love."

June 23, 1989

The Brave New Landscape

Neil Welliver

Down a steep ravine in Montville, Neil Welliver has set up his easel midstream in the shallows just below where Bartlett Stream slows momentarily to a deep pool. Each spiked leg of the wooden tripod rests firmly on its own stone; Welliver stands on a fourth. He is a short, powerful, white-haired man with dark mustache, dog-brown eyes, and good balance. Dressed uniformly in khaki suntans, Welliver looks more like a misplaced merchant mariner than one of this country's foremost painters, but when he begins to apply paint to canvas, he will erase all doubt.

Neil Welliver will be 54 years old on July 22. His 53rd year has been a good one. He is at the height of his powers. His career has taken off. Fame and fortune, which have been gathering on the horizon for several years now, have begun to arrive. There is every indication that Welliver will fall heir to the mantle worn by Winslow Homer, Marsden Hartley, and John Marin. Neil Welliver, *the* Maine painter.

In January, a major retrospective closed in Richmond, Virginia, after a tour of six American museums. Assessing the exhibition, *Time* magazine art critic Robert Hughes wrote, "Welliver's huge painting of the Maine woods...is among the strongest images in modern American art." In February, *Neil Welliver, Recent Paintings* was featured at New York's powerhouse Marlborough Gallery. The Marlborough show prompted *New York Times* art critic Grace Glueck to call Welliver "one of our most accomplished realist painters." Moreover, the Marlborough exhibition all but sold out...14 of 15 works...at $35,000 to $40,000 a painting (though after the gallery and the government take their cuts, Welliver is left short of being a rich man).

In April, it was announced that Welliver had been awarded an $18,000 Guggenheim fellowship. A book on his art is the works. Riding this crest of acclaim and accomplishment, Welliver will take next year off from his teaching duties at the University of Pennsylvania in order to paint full time. As he stands in Bartlett Stream, he has his back to all this. He is still suffering jet lag from a European trip which took him to West Germany, where he attended the opening of the Joseph Albers museum in Bottrop (and, as a strong anti-nuker, found himself caught on the wrong side of anti-missile protests aimed at Vice-President George Bush, who was speaking at the museum opening), and to England, where he looked over Marlborough's London gallery in preparation for a show next March. It is good to be back in the woods.

A good year, then. A Guggenheim. A

retrospective. Height of his powers. Time to paint. "Among the strongest images in modern American art." A book. Critical success. Commercial success. What does it all mean?

"It means," says Welliver, "that when they come to assess this period in painting they will have to look at my paintings...and that's all it means. The work will have to stand on its own, because I'll be deep under by then.

"I find it curious," he says, "to read that I'm now one of the best painters in the United States. Dear God, when did that happen? It happened so slowly that it was hardly discernible to me."

Living in Lincolnville, Maine, for the past 21 years, Welliver has been too far removed from the locus of art activity to engineer a career for himself. But then, he's no careerist. His obsessions, he says, are with painting and seeing, not fame and fortune. But if he seems puzzled as to how he got to the top, he is clear about why.

"I think," he says, "that I see more than other people do. I knew even when I was a child that I saw more than others saw."

The evidence of his paintings suggest that by "seeing more" Welliver does not mean that he sees in more detail. He is not a photorealist or super-realist obsessed with minutes. He is a painterly realist obsessed with the big picture. He "sees more" by looking longer and deeper, by living with, possessing and being possessed by his subject...Maine.

Welliver first came to Maine 21 years ago at the invitation of fellow painter Alex Katz, a summer resident of Lincolnville. In search of unspoiled landscapes, Welliver had been trying out life in Canada, but his "lousy French" betrayed him. He didn't want to be the gringo the rest of his life, so he jumped at the prospect of spending a few days in Lincolnville with Katz.

"But I realized I was in the right place when I hit China Lakes and Palermo," says Welliver. Not only did the landscape seem "right," but so did the people he met. "The people seemed sane to me. Like they hadn't lost their marbles yet. I love Maine people. They may be the only people who still have ingenuity."

Ingenuity, and something equally if not more precious to Welliver...privacy.

Through painter Lois Dodd, Welliver located a secluded old 106-acre grass farm—no plumbing, no heating, no electricity—which he purchased for $2,500. For eight years he summered at the farm before deciding to move to Maine permanently. Over the years, as paintings have sold and land has become available, Welliver has added to his holdings so that today he has some 1,200 acres.

Welliver's world in Lincolnville is a shipshape, self-contained little world flowing down one side of Gould Hill along a mile of the Duck Trap River through Tunk Woods and over Briggs Meadow. It is acre after acre of field and forest, peat bog and beaver flowage, sugarbush and pasture pine.

"The land," says Welliver, "is central to my interests." The land is his inspiration and his subject matter. He buys it not to possess, but to protect.

The Welliver homestead is located in a clearing two miles down a dirt road, the entrance to which is guarded by a sheep farm owned by Welliver's brother-in-law. He is further insulated by friends like filmmaker (*Titticut Follies*) Fred Wiseman and law professor Joe Goldstein who have purchased neighboring properties.

Welliver's home is a long, low, rambling, weathered farmhouse culminating in an attached barn which serves as his studio. Welliver shares this home with his wife Sheila, a West Highland terrier named Steiff, and three of his five sons—Eli, 13, Ethan, 8, and John, 1. Two older sons—Silas, 25, and Titus, 20—live in New York City pursuing careers in music and theater.

The farm is home, and Welliver's base of operations. During the academic year, he journeys to Philadelphia for three days every two weeks to teach painting at the University of Pennsylvania Graduate School of Fine Art.

Surrounding the house are a separate storage barn, a studio for Sheila (who is also a painter), coops and pens for chickens and geese, a skating pond, a swimming pond, an ample garden, a long row of swallow boxes, a 108-foot windmill, five huge cones of firewood containing eight cords each, and, a mile or so back in the woods, a sugarhouse and a guest cottage.

Shipshape and self-contained. A great place

to become snowbound. The stark New England interior of the Welliver house is appointed with home computer, video cassette recorder, stereo, piano, and billiards table. Since Marlborough Gallery sends a truck to Lincolnville to pick up Welliver's huge paintings of the Maine woods (typically measuring eight feet square), it seems entirely possible that the artist could go into permanent retreat, never to be seen again.

But Neil Welliver is a man who values his privacy, not a recluse. Unlike many other artists who settle or summer in Maine, he takes an active part in local affairs. Recently, he served on the local school board and helped engineer Lincolnville's withdrawal from the area school administrative district. And there was also a time when Welliver was known to pick a mean bluegrass banjo on Belfast radio. A self-proclaimed "eco-freak and a sorehead about it," Welliver has also supported the Nature Conservancy and Safe Power for Maine. He directs particular wrath at the nuclear power industry as the ultimate despoilers of the land.

"Nuclear power," he insists, "is most appalling because one does, after all, have a responsibility to future generations. We are leaving [radioactive] residue for thousands of years in order to solve a very, very short-term problem in human terms. Each generation generates its own garbage, but to generate garbage for hundreds of centuries is absolutely immoral."

Welliver's home in Lincolnville, with its easy overlay of nature, culture, and agriculture, is worlds away from the New York art scene, with its tense undercurrent of influence, ego, and artifice. The contrast between Neil Welliver, the distinguished gentleman in Ivy League blue blazer surrounded by friends and admirers at his Marlborough opening, and Neil Welliver, the rather disheveled fellow with a pinch of Skoal between his cheek and gum, is as marked as the contrast between a Welliver oil enshrined on West 57th Street and a Welliver oil propped up against the barn wall.

In years past, Welliver shared his barn studio with swallows, and in order to keep their droppings off his paintings he was forced to turn all of his canvases to the wall. One day years ago he received a telephone call from art collector and patron Joseph Hirschhorn

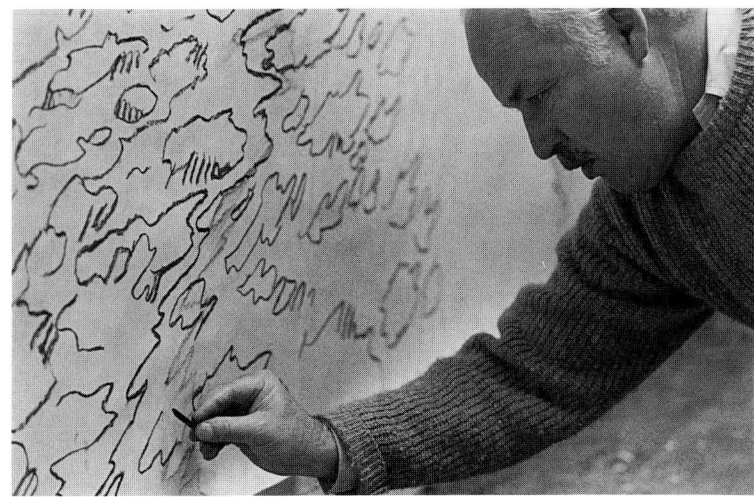

1. *A detail from the drawing which is one stage in the unique process Welliver uses to create his large paintings. Photo by Stephen B. Nichols.*

(Hirschhorn Museum and Sculpture Garden, Washington, D.C.) who had purchased some paintings from a Welliver show at Tibor De Nagy Gallery.

"Welliver," complained the millionaire collector, "there's pigeon shit all over the back of these paintings."

"That isn't pigeon shit, you city hick," the artist replied abruptly. "That's swallow shit."

After a good laugh, the two men agreed that the canvases would have to be re-stretched.

Today, there are no swallows in the barn. Screening covers the opening where the barn doors have been pulled back to reveal a rustic spartan interior filled primarily with light and space. A woodstove, couch, and mongrel chairs stand in one corner. Small oils and studies are propped upon the wall. A handsome cabinet for prints and drawings stands in a far corner. There is a rolling palette the size of a desk, its top covered in puddles of pigment like shallow volcanoes of color. Beside it a table stacked high with boxes of Windsor-Newton oil paints—Naples yellow, Sevres blue, cadmium yellow, talens green light, Rembrandt green, permalba white, and ivory black.

Beneath a huge skylight that was once a window in the John Hancock Tower stands Welliver's most recently completed painting. It quietly proclaims itself the apex of Welliver's achievements to date and all but demands museum acquisition.

The image of the untitled painting is of a bend in Kendall Brook between Pitcher Pond and the Duck Trap River. It is a winter scene, a symphony in black, white and greys, the normally vivid Welliver landscape now hushed and softened, seen through a screen of white marks.

"It isn't a snow painting," points out eight-year-old Ethan, "it's a snowing painting." The snowing painting is both a departure for Welliver and a logical extension of his visual and painterly concerns.

"The excitement of it for me," says Welliver, "is to have that much action and silence together."

The importance of Welliver's painting to modern American art lies partly in the middle ground it occupies (along with the work of such artists as Alex Katz, Fairfield Porter, Philip Pearlstein, and Jack Beal) between abstraction and pure realism. Welliver is concerned both with the abstract notion of the integrity of the painting as paint-on-canvas and with keeping faith with the real world of appearances. Push a Welliver landscape slightly in the direction of more generalization and you have abstract marks on canvas. Push the same landscape slightly in the direction of more specificity and you tip the scale in favor of photo-real illusion. Welliver's best paintings are both deep and flat at the same time, leading poet-critic Mark Strand to refer to them as "terrestrial Pollocks."

The importance of the snowing painting to Welliver's development is that it introduces a new element of motion which is both optical and illusory. The viewer is forced to "see through" a filter of white marks (snow) which is both painterly, calling attention to the overall flatness of the canvas edge-to-edge, and phenomenal, obscuring vision the way falling snow does.

Few, if any, artists paint the way Welliver does. Which is not to say he is not widely imitated. He is. But Welliver's process is unique.

Welliver begins by executing a small oil painting directly from nature. Then, if he can see a "big picture" in the small oil, he may elect to either do a slightly larger version or go to a large eight-foot square format.

To realize a big picture, Welliver first makes a freehand drawing in charcoal on signwriter's paper. This drawing blows the basic design of the image up to full-size. The drawing is then traced with a toothed pounce wheel; the perforated drawing is taped over a prepared canvas, and using a small bag of charcoal dust, the artist transfers the generalized drawing from paper to canvas. The transferred lines which form the structure of the painting are then sprayed with a fixative and Welliver is ready to paint.

Again, unlike any artist he can think of, Welliver paints strictly from top down, completing each area as he goes. The progress of the Welliver painting is somewhat analogous to the drawing down of a window shade. When a painting is half done, it is literally half done...the top half.

Welliver says that painting an area at a time forces him to think differently about painting. Since he never goes back to layer or paint over, he must "constellate" colors rather than physically change them if he wants to adjust an area.

"Every painting is a battle from top to bottom," he says. "When I'm finished, I sign my name and duck out the bottom. I go out of here every night on my knees."

The painting of snowfall on Kendall Brook was a particularly grueling battle because of the tedious, exacting requirement of placing thousands of snowflake marks at proper intervals as Welliver progressed down the canvas. (The snowflakes were not simply painted on afterwards.) But the Kendall Brook painting is special to Welliver for another reason.

"I painted that exact same spot on Kendall Brook once before," he explains, "but that painting burned in the fire."

The fire.

On January 31, 1975, the Welliver home caught fire and burned to the ground. No one was hurt, but a small fortune in paintings (Welliver could only recoup the cost of materials) was destroyed.

"It was kind of like an erasing of tracks in a way," says Welliver of the fire. "I should have burned some of those paintings myself."

But the fire which erased much of Neil Welliver's artistic past was only one in a series of events which befell him in 1975 and 1976. In October, 1976, Welliver's second wife, Polly, mother of Ethan and Eli, died suddenly at age 37. Polly's death came only months after the couple had lost their one-year-old daughter, Ashley, to sudden infant death syndrome (crib death).

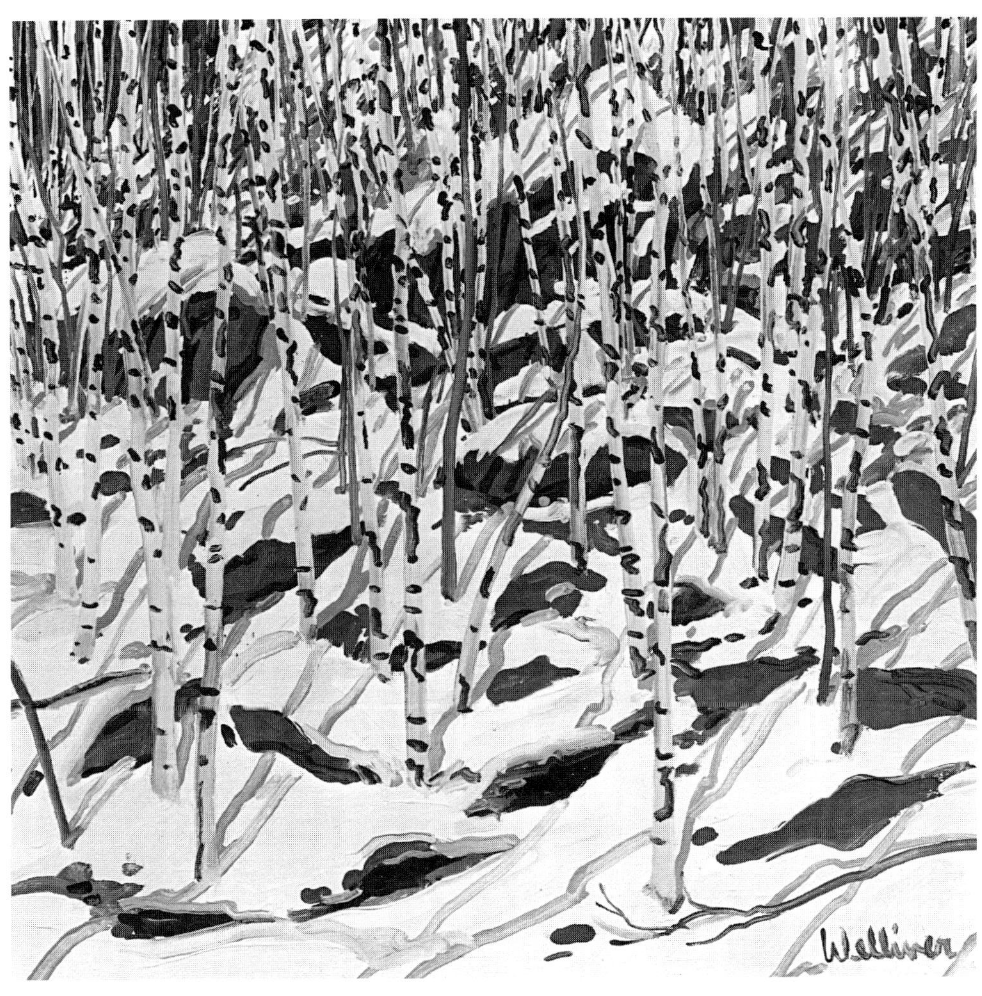

2. *Neil Welliver,* Old Avalanche, *1979. Oil on canvas. Courtesy of the Marlborough Gallery.*

It would not be unreasonable to expect that a series of losses such as Welliver experienced would have visibly affected his art, but there are no overt signs of suffering in Welliver's paintings. Did he then manage to harden himself against the pain of loss?

"No," says Welliver, "you can't do that. You can't allow yourself to become hard. You have to remain open." He was able to endure the loss of a home, a child, and a wife because, says Welliver, "I didn't take it personally."

Welliver is not talking about indifference. His grief was deep and personal. But Welliver is a realist. Death is not a judgment. Loss is not a punishment. He accepts...and yet, there is a strong sense that Neil Welliver has developed responses to the major influences on his life and his art which are restorative.

In response to the fire, Welliver went out and found a nearly identical farmhouse six miles away. It took 12 carpenters a year to systematically disassemble the replacement house, move it, and reassemble it on the burned-out site. The restored house is a few feet longer than the original, but for all practical purposes, Welliver says, "It's it. Some people don't even know there was a fire."

Born in the lumbering town of Millville, Pennsylvania, Welliver was raised by his mother and grandparents. As though in response to a split family, he became a prodigious father.

"I'm crazy about kids," Welliver says. "My children provide me with endless pleasure and endless wonderment. One of the best things about having children is that it really slices hard into one's selfishness."

Welliver describes his own Pennsylvania boyhood as "a real Huck Finn rural life."

"I graduated at the bottom of my high school class of 21," he says, "because I never paid attention. I just wasn't interested, so I played hookey all the time. My real education was the privilege of reading whenever and whatever I wanted."

Welliver says his major entertainment expenses are still the book bills he runs up at the

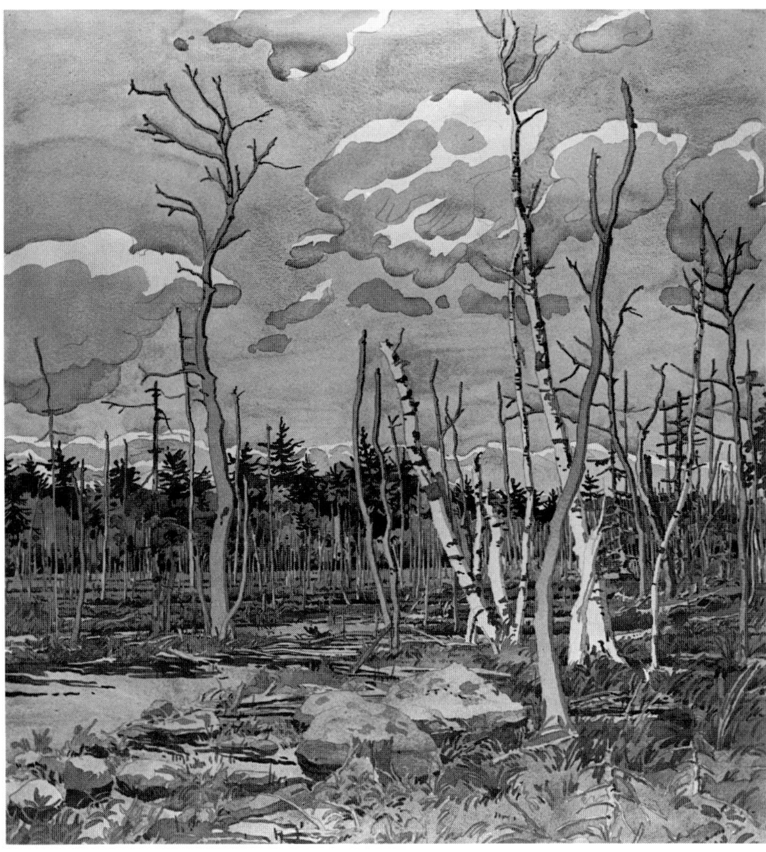

3. *Neil Welliver,* Moose Horn, *1977. Watercolor on paper, some pencil. Courtesy of the Bowdoin College Museum of Art.*

Owl and the Turtle bookstore in Camden. His reading interests run heavily to poetry, philosophy, and sciences.

The idyllic Huck Finn life came to a screeching four-lane halt when, Welliver explains, "a couple of big expressways were put through and that was the end of it."

As though in response to the violation of his childhood homeland, Welliver has become the passionate protector and painter of the land, new land, Maine land.

"The geography of Maine is diagrammatic," he says. "It's new land. Pennsylvania is old land. Here there is incredible clarity. The land is very clear and very primal."

Welliver received a Bachelor of Fine Arts degree from the Philadelphia Museum College of Art in 1953. In Philadelphia he was taught by and large to paint academicized Winslow Homers.

"I didn't run into real education," says Welliver, "until I met Joseph Albers. Fortunately, by then I was 27, old enough to foul his aggressiveness."

Welliver received his MFA from Yale in 1955. His principal mentor was Albers, master color theoretician of the Bauhaus famous for his *Homage to the Square* series. From Albers, Welliver got a thorough grounding in the empirical dynamics of color relations, a grounding that shows everywhere in his painting today. Welliver says Albers called him "my prodigal protégé" because, as Welliver indelicately puts it, "Albers never liked my work worth a shit." Welliver left Yale painting nudes, and nudes were anathema to Albers.

In an interview Welliver did with Albers for *Art News* (January 1966), however, Albers strongly admonished art students to "stay off the bandwagon."

"To follow me," said Albers, "follow yourself." Neil Welliver got the message.

"My painting," he explains, "comes out of painting that is totally unlike it. I've painted my way through Albers, Gorky, Klee, de Kooning, but these things have been erased."

Four years out of Yale when *Art in America* magazine nominated Welliver along with some 200 other young artists as "New Talent, 1959," he was painting fleshy nude abstractions in the broadbrush manner of de Kooning. Through the mid-1960s he worked his way into a brand of domestic realism (picnics, weddings, family groups) that painter-critic Fairfield Porter liked

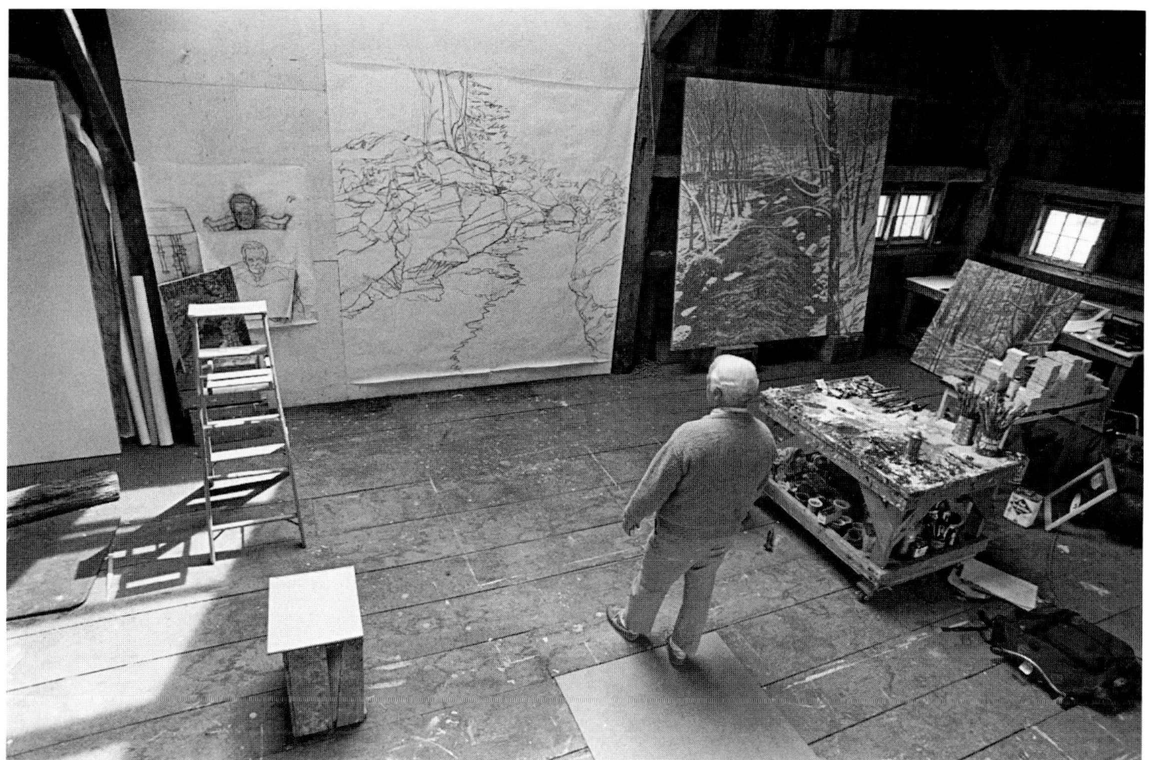

4. *Based on the small oil, behind the ladder, Welliver inspects his large freehand drawing on signwriter's paper. The drawing will then be used to transfer the image to canvas. Photo by Stephen B. Nichols.*

to refer to as "good-natured expressionism." Schooled in the abstract '50s and apprenticed into the Pop '60s, Neil Welliver did not really come into his own artistically until he banished the figure from his landscapes. The figure, often in the form of a female nude literally in nature, partially submerged in a woodland pool, continued to intrude on the landscape until the early 1970s.

Welliver is often referred to as a colorist because of the luminous quality of his very specialized palette and because he does not simply reproduce local color but establishes his own color relations. But color is seductive, and Welliver's use of color is more seductive than most. Below the level of the allure of color, the best Welliver landscapes vibrate at a frequency finely tuned between art and nature. It is this frequency—the intervals between marks, the degree of generalization and specificity—that distinguishes a Welliver, not color.

Several of the strongest Welliver paintings, in fact, share at least three distinct characteristics. The figure is gone. The angle of vision is locked in below the horizon. And color is minimal. The dynamics of a Welliver oil are best revealed when color is vague and subtle.

"It always stuns me when people talk about the exactitude of my painting," Welliver says as he stands knee-deep in abstraction with realist boots on. "If they mean exact description, they're using the word in the loosest possible sense. In my paintings, it's always a matter of interval."

Some viewers say they find Welliver landscapes cool, soulless, even formulaic. A paint-by-numbers label is sometimes hung on his work, but Welliver says he has never heard this criticism outside of Maine. But the cool impersonality of Welliver's landscapes is an achievement, not a weakness. What Welliver has achieved is the brave new landscape, nature stripped of the artist's ego, personality, and emotions, but possessed of the residue of intelligence. Welliver captures the rationale of chaos, consciousness in the wilderness.

Welliver's visions of Maine which are "among the strongest images in modern American Art" are rarely seen in Maine.

"I've never really had sales in Maine," Welliver says. "Colby College was given an oil [*Duck Trap*, 1972] by Alex Katz and Bowdoin College bought a large watercolor [*Moose Horn*, 1977]. There's money here to buy painting, but no one's buying. Then, of course, I never sold a painting in Philadelphia either until the Pennsylvania Academy bought one in 1975."

From time to time a painting may appear at

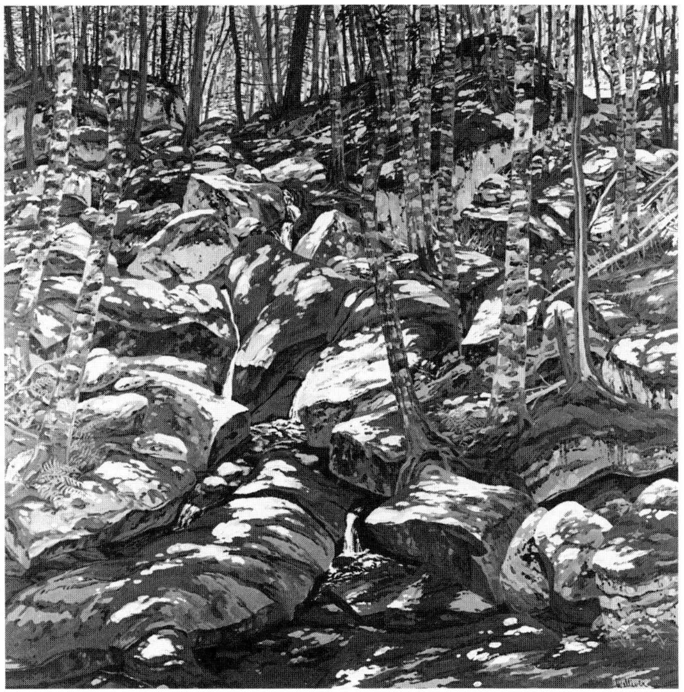

5. *Neil Welliver,* Fractured Light, *1980. Oil on canvas. Courtesy of the Marlborough Gallery.*

Artfellows in Belfast or Maine Coast Artists in Rockport, but Welliver is most often represented in Maine in prints and reproduction. The traveling *1966-1980* retrospective, consisting almost entirely of Maine images, did not come to Maine because there was not a museum space capable of handling so many large canvases. The only signs of Welliver's presence in Lincolnville Center are four posters advertising Welliver exhibitions at Fischbach Gallery in New York, which hang behind yellow plastic above the grease pit at Dean & Eugley's garage.

Maine is where Welliver makes his home, not his living. The market is elsewhere. The inspiration is here.

"Most of my paintings are done within rifle range of home," Welliver says. "What I find in the woods is endless surprise...endless surprise. If my work changes, that's why. I would think I'd paint my life out here. I can't imagine it running dry. But I would have no hesitation about pulling up stakes and leaving Maine if it ever did dry up for me."

Maine dry up? Not likely. For Neil Welliver has begun to change the way we see Maine land. It is increasingly difficult for artists to paint the Maine woods without imitating, so powerful is the Welliver animus. The woods are Welliver's.

"My love for the woods is a complete passion," he says. "I don't look out the window and think 'how beautiful,' I want to be *in* it."

And so Neil Welliver has bushwacked down to Bartlett Stream for a third and final day of painting. He has retrieved his palette from beneath a ledge where it has lain hidden overnight and he has placed his unfinished oil on the portable easel.

For the next four and a half hours, stopping only briefly to eat half a steak and cheese sandwich, he will stand in midstream gazing into the dim greyness of a rock ledge, slowly, carefully placing paint until all remaining whiteness is submerged in oil. He is not creator, but restorer. Man alone in nature, intelligence resident in the wild. His activity here is silent, unobtrusive, benign. When he is done, he will take care to erase his tracks, wiping away the few errant drops of paint that fall upon the rocks. When he is gone, all that will remain will be a faint waft of turpentine...and then that too will be gone.

"I've spent my entire adult life painting. I know a good deal about painting. I know the history of art cold...or at least as cold as I need to know it. But I'll tell you something. I could tell you everything that can be said about painting...not information, now, but critically...in 15 minutes. The rest is ineffable."

July 22, 1983

The Art of the Common Man

Andrew Wyeth

"A man I have painted ever since I was 12, Walter Anderson, died today," Andrew Wyeth told me. "He was 63. We grew up together."

Walter A. Anderson, 63, died July 31 at Penobscot Bay Medical Center "after a long illness." His obituary in the August 4th *Rockland Courier-Gazette* reported that he was born September 10, 1923, in Cushing, son of Augustus and Estelle Hussey Anderson. With the cruel impartiality with which obituaries reduce our lives to a few factual cinders, Anderson's life was rendered in three sentences.

"Mr. Anderson attended schools at Port Clyde and Cushing and was a U.S. Army veteran. He had been employed as a crewman aboard several fishing draggers. He was also the subject of several works by artist Andrew Wyeth."

Andrew Wyeth is now 70. When he dies, his lengthy obituary will probably not contain the line, "He also painted several pictures of fisherman Walter Anderson." Though the two men were friends from childhood, the famous painter will always have a starring role in the life of the local fisherman, while the fisherman will always be a walk-on in the life of the great man. Such are the unfair judgments of history.

On Friday, July 31, I had telephoned Andrew Wyeth to ask if he might find time to talk about his art. This seemed an opportune time to profile Maine's and America's most famous artist, since his headline-making pictures of *Helga* were being shown at the National Gallery in Washington simultaneously with *An American Vision: Three Generations of Wyeth Art* at the Corcoran Gallery. But as I proposed topics for discussion—his extraordinary, artistic family, his personal and professional relationship to Maine, Helga, the difficulty many critics have with his art—Wyeth, in a telephone voice that contained the harsh cackle of a witch, dismissed them all. "It's been done," he complained repeatedly and rightly. What he'd really like to talk about was his friendship with Walter Anderson, a man whom, by his own estimation, he had painted at least 100 times. No one had ever written about Walter Anderson. If I would go to Chadds Ford, Pennsylvania, and Washington, D.C., to see the paintings, then we could talk.

Chadds Ford, Pennsylvania, where Andrew Wyeth was born on July 12, 1917, seems at first glance to be little more than a residual farm-country crossroads in the process of being eaten up by suburban sprawl creeping south from Philadelphia and north from Wilmington. The center of town is the intersection of Routes 1 and 100, the four corners occupied respectively by a Sunoco station, a restaurant called Hank's

Place, the Chadds Ford Inn, and an unlikely looking board-and-batten building that houses the post office and a WAWA convenience store. But as Wyeth fans know, Andrew Wyeth does not paint WAWA stores. The local Ramada Inn may feature a Wyeth Room and a new condo project may call itself Painters' Crossing, but Andrew Wyeth inhabits and evokes a world apart.

Turn off Route 1 onto Route 100 and you are suddenly transported via a narrow, winding lane 200 years into the past, into the Brandywine River valley of revolutionary America. Down this lane Wyeth lives in a stony 18th-century compound consisting of an old mill, miller's house, and granary surrounded by water meadows. The hills, the meadows, and the square, spare Germanic architecture of this historical oasis are so recognizably Wyeth Country that they might as well be covered with tempera. One intuits, however, that this picturesque Chadds Ford is becoming fashionable, that residence here may soon be more a matter of affluence and aesthetics than agriculture and ancestry.

Andrew Newell Wyeth was born in this Chester County valley because his father, Newell Convers Wyeth, beloved illustrator of such classics as *Treasure Island* and *The Last of the Mohicans*, came to nearby Wilmington, Delaware, from Needham, Massachusetts, in 1902 to study with famed illustrator Howard Pyle and eventually settled in rural Chadds Ford. Andrew's son James Browning Wyeth was born here in 1946. The rich farmland of the district, then, supports a dense overlay of American art and Wyeth family history. Conservator of this regional complexity is the Brandywine River Museum, part of the Brandywine Conservancy.

Popularly known as "The Wyeth Museum," the Brandywine River Museum is indeed the repository of the Wyeth family's personal collection, but it is also dedicated to preserving both the art and landscape of the Brandywine River valley. The museum had its genesis in 1967 when Hoffman's grist mill, a venerable brick structure on the banks of the brown and sleepy Brandywine, was threatened by a proposed tank farm. With the aid of the Wyeths and other concerned local citizens, Hoffman's grist mill was born again in 1971 as a museum and conservancy. In 1984, the old mill was expanded; with a $3.6 million annual budget and 180,000 visitors a year, the Brandywine River Museum is, in the words of public relations director John Sheppard, "the fastest-growing small museum in America."

The day I visited, the first floor gallery of the museum was devoted to local landscapes by such artists as Thomas Doughty, Asher B. Durand, and Jasper Cropsey. The second-floor gallery contained a selection of works by the Wyeth clan. But I found what I was looking for on the third floor in a gallery devoted exclusively to the work of Andrew Wyeth. Here were the images of Walter Anderson I had come to see.

In the 1974 watercolor *Watch Cap*, the earliest image on view, Anderson already seems old, though he would have been 51 at the time. There is something frail, delicate, even broken about the being beneath this weathered exterior. Gaunt and watchful, Anderson seems more hermit than seadog, his unkempt hair and grizzly blond beard suggesting dereliction. But while the big forms of the composition are Anderson's upper torso, hawkish head, and signature watch cap, the focus of the picture is his resolute, fixed gaze, a function of the ghostly white that is all that shows of his eye. In the 1982 watercolor *Davis Straits*, Wyeth uses one of his favorite enigmatic poses, portraying his old friend back-to, again looking out to sea, again bundled against the elements in heavy coat and knit cap. On another wall is a 1976 dry brush study for *Sea Boots*, a rather romantic portrait of Anderson's boots, which are as tattered and torn as he appears to be. But the revelations in the gallery are a pair of watercolor studies for *Adrift*, the 1982 tempera of Anderson lying in a drifting dory that is among Wyeth's finest paintings. The sketches provide a tantalizing glimpse of the working-out of a bizarre idea. Returning to *Watch Cap* and *Davis Straits*, I came to think that what Walt Anderson was gazing at out to sea was his own fate, an apparition of himself alone and adrift in the world.

Somehow, these images of Walter Anderson seem strangely out of place here, dislocated. Anderson is a man of the sea. His image belongs not to stony 18th-century Chadds Ford, but to the wooden 19th-century coastal town of Cushing, Maine, the north pole of Andrew Wyeth's tightly circumscribed little world. But in a sense, Chadds Ford and Cushing (the two worlds of the 1976 exhibition *The Two Worlds of Andrew Wyeth* at the Metropolitan Museum of Art in New York) are extensions of the same magical world of the imagination that Wyeth has created for himself. In the summer, he and his wife, Betsy, simply exchange their 18th-century mill in Pennsylvania for their 18th-century home in Maine, and Wyeth keeps on painting. The environmental and preservation concerns the Wyeths support through the Brandywine Conservancy are mirrored in Maine by their support for the Island Institute. And while Maine does not have a "Wyeth museum" as extensive as that in Chadds Ford, the Farnsworth Museum in Rockland has long maintained an identity as the Wyeths' summer gallery.

Actually, Maine almost had an official Wyeth gallery back in the early 1970s when motion picture magnate Joseph E. Levine, producer of such films as *The Graduate* and *Lion in Winter*, purchased the Olson house of Wyeth's most famous painting, the 1948 *Christina's World*, and attempted to turn it into a museum. That venture died in its infancy, however, when neighbors in Cushing complained about the traffic the gallery was creating. Ironically, Joseph E. Levine, who donated his Wyeth collection to the Greenville (South Carolina) Country Art Museum, died at age 84 on the same day that Walter Anderson died.

Andrew Wyeth's sustained obsession with the people of the places he inhabits—Karl Kuerner and his wife, Anna, in Chadds Ford; Christina Olson and her brother Alvaro in Cushing—led to two distinctive bodies of work that have been referred to as his Chadds Ford "novel" and his Cushing "novel." His elemental visions of these two barren, bloodless, provincial worlds occupied him for decades, the Olsons from 1940 until 1969, the Kuerners from 1946 until 1978. Given the tragic dimensions of these extended family sagas (told in portraits, landscapes, and still lifes), it is not surprising that Wyeth sought lyrical relief as he completed both "novels." In both cases, he found this release in the bodies of

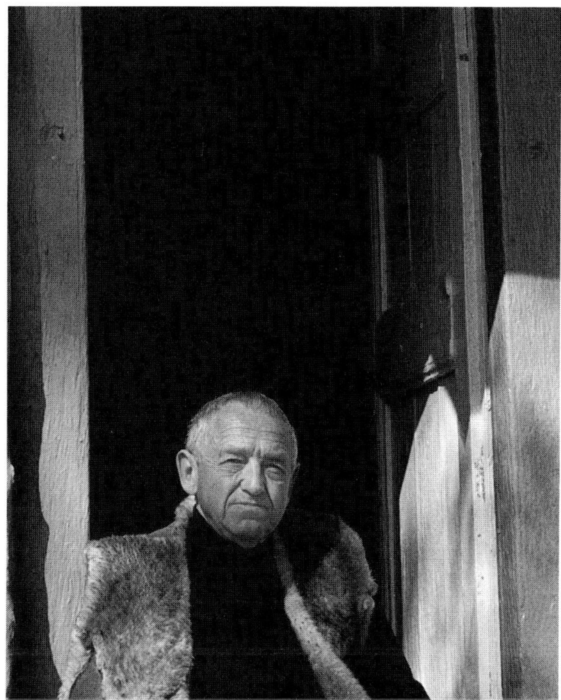

1. *Andrew Wyeth. Photo by Peter Ralston.*

young women. With the Olsons in decline, Wyeth executed a series of portraits of the teenaged Siri Erickson between 1968 and 1972. As the Kuerners' lives ebbed away, he turned to his "secret" obsession with painting Helga Testorf, the Prussian beauty who worked on the Kuerners' farm. The Siri and Helga portraits form life-affirming epilogues to Wyeth's long, sad "novels" of rural American life.

Casual viewers and even some inattentive critics tend to see Wyeth's work as romantic, bucolic, even idyllic, but such a reading misses the essence of Wyeth. Andrew Wyeth's art is Gothic in the literary sense: barbaric, offensive to classical tastes, wild, natural, authentic. Look sometime at *The Kuerners*, Wyeth's remarkable 1971 portrait of Karl and Anna—he gazing out a window as he cradles a deer rifle pointed directly at his wife, she with her head swaddled against her constant headaches. Look at all the portraits of Christina Olson, her man-handsome face twisted and ugly; at Wyeth's depiction of Alvaro, her big-beaked brother. The poetry of these lives is bleak, desperate stuff. The characters in Andrew Wyeth's "novels" step directly out of the frank, brutal prose of Carolyn Chute's fiction—*The Kuerners of Chadds Ford, Pennsylvania*; *The Olsons of Cushing, Maine*.

Walter Anderson, too, belonged to what we have lately come to refer to as "the real Maine." The reason Wyeth's late pictures of Walter

Anderson evoke a broken man is that Anderson was, literally, a broken man, a fisherman beached, his body crushed several years ago when he became entangled in a dragger winch. His neck was broken. His back was broken. A rib punctured his lung. In time, the pneumonia that killed him would be complicated by these old injuries. The real Maine is a harsh and dangerous place, its symbolism simple and direct. When Walter Anderson died, a friend honored his memory by emptying a six-pack into Port Clyde Harbor. Wyeth country.

"Walter was my connection to Maine," Wyeth had told me. "Out of him came Christina and all the others. But Walter was not a character to me. He was my own age. He was an American Indian who had Finnish blood. He was a remarkable-looking, towheaded boy who grew up to be a stalwart man."

Andrew Wyeth and Walter Anderson met in the 1920s when the Wyeth family first began summering in Maine. Walter's mother was then working as a cook at The Wavenock, the hotel in Port Clyde where N. C. Wyeth and his family first stayed before they purchased a summer home. Andy and Walter became fast friends, the younger local boy introducing the summer kid to the pleasures and the lore of the sea, taking him out in his mother's dory to pick mussels, dig clams, and fish. Yet despite their lifelong friendship and Anderson's frequent appearance in Wyeth's art, little mention is made of Walter Anderson in the voluminous documentation of all things Wyeth. Even Gene Longsdon's 1971 hero-worshipping hymn to the common man, *Wyeth People*, does not mention Anderson. One of the few references to be found to this fast friendship is in a letter N.C. Wyeth wrote to his daughter Ann from Port Clyde in 1938.

"Andy has worked steadily on his tempera painting," his appreciative father reports, "and all I have to do is turn my head to the right to see him and his panel silhouetted against the sky. Walter, his man Friday, is hunched up beside him mixing color, preparing egg, and whatnot.

"This noon Walter visited the surrounding traps and brought in 14 lobsters, cooked them, besides baking potatoes, etc., and we had the finest feast of sweet lobster meat I ever expect to have!"

In the summer of 1938, the fledgling painter had just turned 21 and his "man Friday" was not yet 15. Three years later, Wyeth would paint the teenaged Anderson with gun and birds in *Coot Hunter*, a picture now owned by the Art Institute of Chicago and painted in the loose, wet watercolor style of the artist's youth. Six years later, in 1944, Wyeth would paint Walter leaning confidently against a dory in *Young Fisherman and Dory*, a watercolor currently on display at the Farnsworth in Rockland. This is Walter Anderson the "stalwart man," a golden-haired buck in new sea boots, his future still ahead of him, his back not yet broken. In the photo files at the Farnsworth, there are also two later portraits of Walter Anderson of unknown provenance, one apparently a watercolor, the other perhaps a dry brush sketch. These images show a handsome, middle-aged Anderson, still strong and hardy, still clean-shaven, but now more pensive. The journey from the promise of youth in *Young Fisherman and Dory* to the desuetude of age in *Adrift* has begun.

Walter Anderson's mother, now 84 and confined to a nursing home, told me recently that folks have told her that "Walter put Andy Wyeth on the map" with the 1944 *Young Fisherman and Dory*, but, in fact, Andrew Wyeth made his spectacular art world debut in October, 1937, with a sold-out watercolor show at the Macbeth Gallery in New York. At the time, Wyeth was just 20 years old. The Boston opening of the *Helga* show at the Museum of Fine Arts in October will coincide with the 50th anniversary of Wyeth's singular artistic career, a career marked by extraordinary popular success and deeply divided critical opinion.

The late Fairfield Porter, himself a realist painter with Maine connections and a critic with generous sensibilities, did not like Wyeth's work, but wasn't sure exactly why. "I think the reason is that there's something he communicates to me that is disagreeable to me," Porter once said in an interview, "something from him that I dislike. In him." Hilton Kramer has called Wyeth "just an illustrator." And Paul Richards of the *Washington Post* has said Wyeth's art "has nothing to do with serious

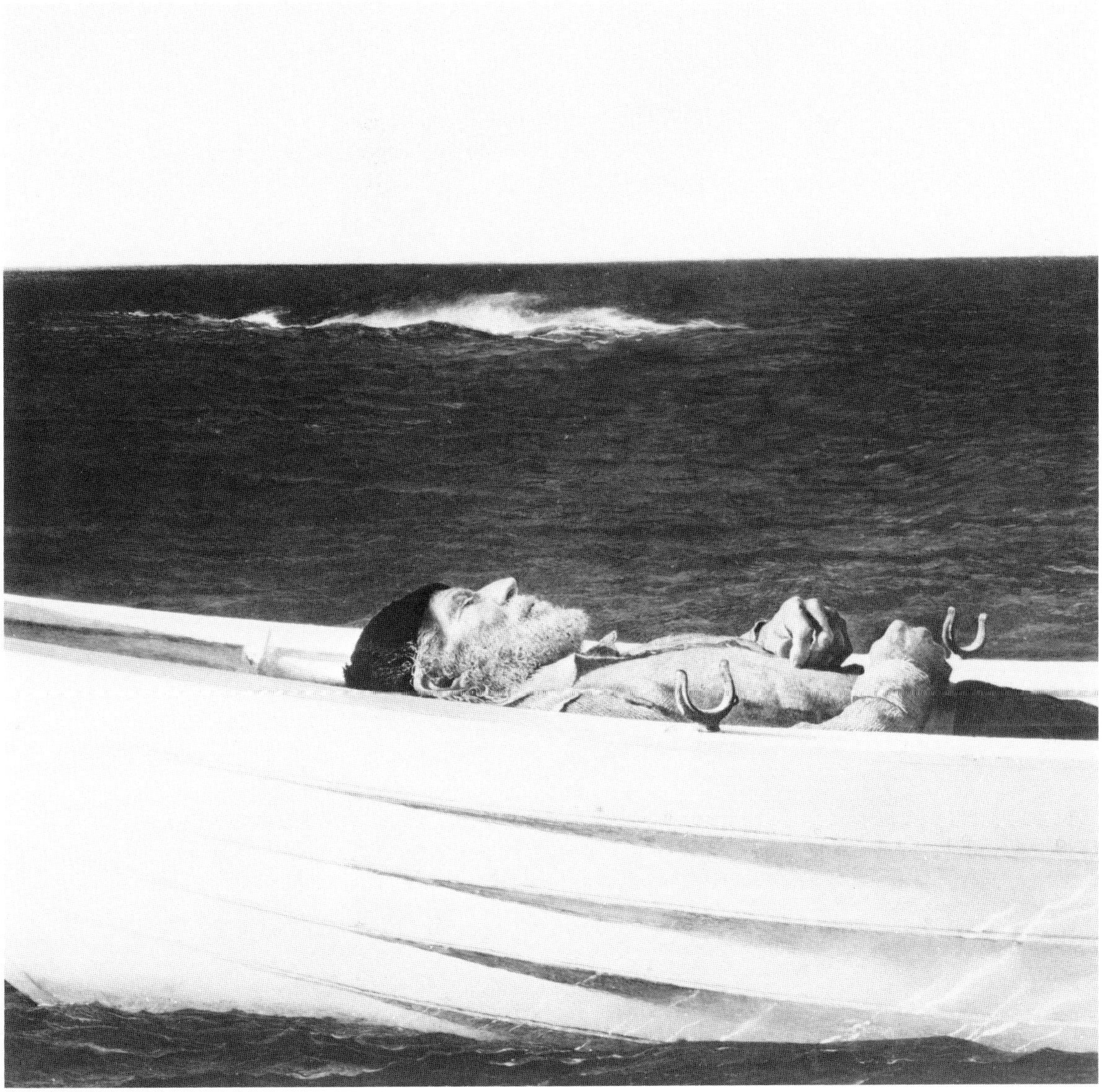

2. *Andrew Wyeth,* Adrift, *1982. Tempera on panel. Courtesy of Mr. & Mrs. Andrew Wyeth.*

artistic expression."

All the media hype surrounding last summer's revelation of Wyeth's *Helga* suite naturally invited the special wrath of many critics. Jack Flam of the *Wall Street Journal*, pronouncing Wyeth's world "a dry and cliché-ridden one," found the *Helga* pictures produced "boredom . . . Indeed," wrote Flam, "you come away from this show with the impression that Andrew Wyeth is not so much a latter-day Winslow Homer as he is a tougher and more interesting version of Norman Rockwell." And Charles Giuliano, anticipating the arrival of *Helga* in Boston for *Art New England*, wrote, "Helga is really little more than the Donna Rice of the art world as seen through the eyes of America's greatest living nineteenth-century artist."

Helga hit the front pages last August during what the press traditionally regards as the "silly season," the slow news period of the year when most newsmakers are on vacation. It was an irresistible story and the media had a field day with it. America's most famous artist had executed a series of 240 works (4 temperas, 9 dry brush paintings, 63 watercolors, and 164 pencil drawings) of a sensuous Pennsylvania neighbor between 1971 and 1985 and had kept them a secret from everyone, including his wife. Now a big collector had bought the whole cache for a reported $10 million. Sex, scandal, secrecy, celebrity, money—*Helga* had everything going for it. Never mind that the sale of the *Helga* pictures to Leonard E. B. Andrews had been reported almost a year earlier in local papers. Never mind that several of the *Helga* pictures had been exhibited in recent years. Never mind that most major artists hoard their work until they are ready to show it. Never let the facts get

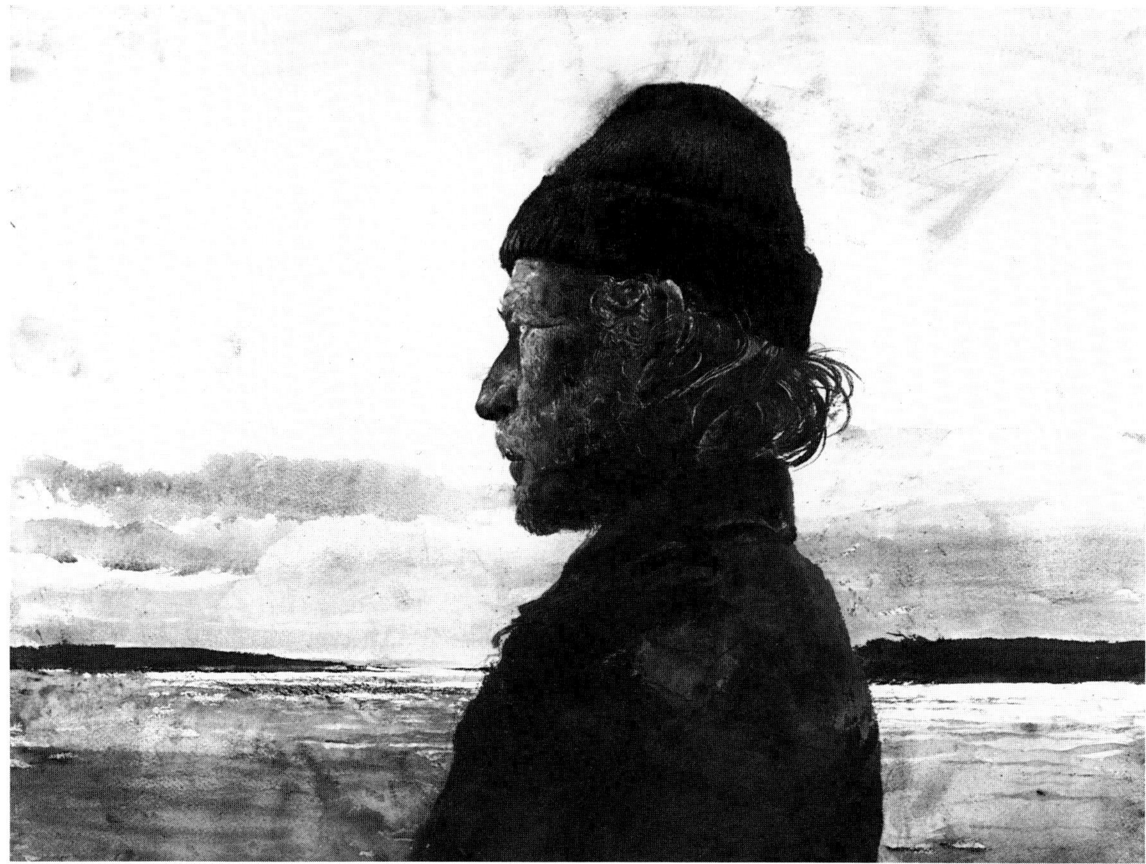

3. *Andrew Wyeth,* Watch Cap, *1974. Watercolor. Courtesy of Mr. & Mrs. Andrew Wyeth.*

in the way of a good story.

The curious thing to me as I wandered through the seven galleries the National Gallery devoted to *Helga* this summer was the politeness with which the pictures were received by the general public. On the one hand, the crush of gallery-goers with whom I saw the *Helga* show seemed to appropriate a personal relationship with Wyeth. As I strained to eavesdrop on people's comments, the word I heard over and over was "he." He does this, he does that, see how he uses that. What the public was commenting on was not the scintillating story behind the pictures, but the technical aspects of their execution—the handling of light and space, the modulation of color and texture, etc. I came away thinking that ordinary people, left to their own devices, can figure things out pretty nicely, thank you. One young lady even made the novel observation that Helga Testorf "looks just like Louise Lasser," which, of course, she does.

But the most salient comment I overheard in the National Gallery came from a disembodied female voice that observed, "He paints better than he draws." Actually, several critics have commented on this fact, often in an attempt to discredit Wyeth's talent. Surely, many of Wyeth's early drawings of Helga fail utterly to capture likeness and many preparatory pencil and watercolor sketches have awkward passages, but what this points out to me is the great difficulty with which the artist achieves his final product. Who said it was supposed to be easy, anyway?

Obviously, one of the things that the public values in the art of Andrew Wyeth is precisely the evidence of hard work that goes into its making. Work, after all, is a cornerstone of the American ethic. Art that looks as though it could have been achieved effortlessly, mechanically, or, worse, accidentally, offends the average viewer. And here we have the fundamental distinction between the two cultures of American art, cultures I have come to think of as the Worlds of the Two Andys—Wyeth and Warhol. Wyeth, the country boy, is respected almost everywhere except in New York. Warhol, the late warlock of Gotham, is respected almost nowhere else.

Assailing Wyeth's most adamant critics, Theodore Wolff of the *Christian Science Monitor*, a critic very friendly to representational art, wrote, "It seems never to occur to them that a deeply committed artist of genuine talent and substance could turn his or her back on any or all modernist or post-modernist approaches without batting an eyelash." Wolff concludes that Wyeth "could easily end up as one of America's most highly acclaimed 20th-century painters." Of course, Andrew Wyeth already is one of America's most highly acclaimed 20th-century painters. It's just that Wyeth's acclaim is democratic while the "serious" art world is a dictatorship.

When I was first married in 1972, my mother gave me a reproduction of *Christina's World.* It was the first "art work" to hang in my new Portland apartment. At the time, I regarded Andrew Wyeth as America's greatest living artist and *Christina's World* as his masterpiece. Like so many others, I made the obligatory pilgrimage to Cushing. On the way, I stopped by Bernard Langlais' sculpture farm, also in Cushing. My perception began to change, my tastes and appreciations to evolve away from Wyeth. Five years later, I had become sophisticated enough to repudiate Wyeth as a hack pandering to public nostalgia. Now, after another five years, I like to think that I have achieved an even higher plane of perception from which it is possible to be critically appreciative of both Wyeth and Warhol. Indeed, I have come to think of Andrew Wyeth as the exception that proves the rule, an artist set apart. Often I can judge the progress of others' artistic awareness by where they stand on Andrew Wyeth. Loving his art uncritically is Art Consciousness One. Detesting his art is Consciousness Two. Being able to discriminate between good Wyeths and bad Wyeths is Consciousness Three.

The final stop on my journey in quest of Consciousness Three (with the spirit of Walter Anderson as my guide) was at the Corcoran Gallery of Art hard by the Reagan White House where I took in the so-called "international show." *An American Vision: Three Generations of Wyeth Art* was organized by the Brandywine River Museum and traveled to Leningrad and Moscow before coming to Washington this summer. The N. C., Andy & Jamie Show is

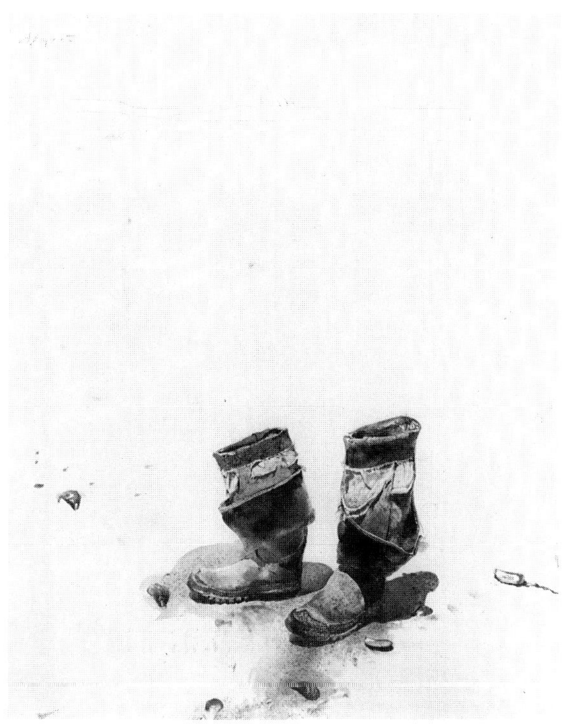

4. *Andrew Wyeth,* Study for Sea Boots, *1984. Dry brush. Courtesy of Mr. & Mrs. Andrew Wyeth.*

currently on its way to Dallas and from there to Chicago, Tokyo, and Cambridge, England. It will come home to Chadds Ford in September 1988.

In general, *An American Vision* persuaded me that N. C. Wyeth was a brilliant illustrator and a far more "modern" painter than his son; that Andrew Wyeth has, in the grudging words of *Time* critic Robert Hughes, "moments of vision"; and that Jamie Wyeth was a far better painter in his twenties than he is in his forties. Essentially, the generational differences are a matter of texts. N. C. Wyeth was a straightforward illustrator. Someone else supplied the text, he supplied the picture. Andrew Wyeth supplies both text and pictures. Jamie Wyeth supplies pictures without texts. This, it seems to me, is why Andrew makes greater claims on our attentions than either his father or his son.

For me, the revelation of Andrew Wyeth's greatness and weakness came in contemplating the paired images of Walter Anderson in *Adrift* (1982) and Karl Kuerner in *Spring* (1978). Hanging toe-to-toe, Walter to the left, Karl to the right, these deathly images show Wyeth attempting materially and imaginatively to resolve the lives of old friends and perhaps, by extension, his own. Walter Anderson, man of the sea, is disposed of at sea, set adrift in a white dory. Karl Kuerner, man of the soil, is returned to earth, his body melting away in a patch of rotting show on hillside pasture. *Adrift* is a brilliant painting, while even Thomas Hoving, the P. T. Barnum of American art, recognizes in his catalogue essay that *Spring* is "trite."

"So much more effective, indeed a world apart in its ability to capture one's attention and imagination, is the perverse, ambiguous, chilling statement about death in *Adrift*, a tempera painted in 1982," continues Hoving. "What is this? A suicide, a burial, or a Maine fisherman simply lying back in his dory in the afternoon sun? The painter refuses to resolve our questions, and in dismissing them, reaches our emotions in a compelling way."

What is this? The anticipation of death in *Adrift* is there for all to see, but a close friend of the artist's told me recently that when Wyeth and Walter Anderson were boys one of their favorite summer pastimes was to lie down in the bottom of a dory and just drift. Time and tide...*Adrift*, then, may represent Andrew Wyeth's most successful visual fusion of innocence and experience. Hard work, Gothic in its implications, great art.

Epilogue: "Andrew Wyeth is on the phone."

Upon returning from Washington, I telephoned Andrew Wyeth and made an appointment to talk with him about Walter Anderson. A few days before the appointed interview, I was working in the yard when the phone rang. My mother, who was visiting at the time, answered the call.

"Andrew Wyeth is on the phone," she called out the back door.

I knew instinctively that Wyeth was calling to cancel. And, yes, something had come up, something he was sure I would understand later when he was able to tell me about it. For now, however, the interview was off. I was neither surprised, nor greatly disappointed. My mother, of course, was greatly impressed.

September 18, 1987

Style as Content

Alex Katz

Alex Katz, one of America's most celebrated realist painters, first came to Maine in 1949 as a student at the Skowhegan School of Painting and Sculpture. Since 1954 he has lived and worked each summer in Lincolnville, but in all those 30 years he has never had a major exhibition in Maine.

"I thought it was pretty weird," confesses Katz, "but I was never asked."

Maine is notoriously slow—both out of a respect for privacy and a certain natural reserve—to recognize and accept anything... people, ideas, trends..."from away," but let the record show that in the summer of 1985 Maine embraced Alex Katz as her own. Katz has finally been asked...by just about everyone.

Now through September 15, the Farnsworth Art Museum in Rockland is featuring twelve major Maine works by Katz. In a collaborative effort, Colby College and Bowdoin College are presenting (through October 6) *Alex Katz: An Exhibition Featuring Works from the Collection of Paul J. Schupf.* Schupf, a New York businessman, is Katz's primary collector. Colby is showing some 30 large paintings and studies from the collection; Bowdoin a selection of 22 small paintings and studies. (The majority of the works at the Farnsworth came from Marlborough Gallery in New York.) And, finally, this fall the O'Farrell Gallery in Brunswick will be presenting an exhibition of prints and drawings by Katz.

This flurry of Maine shows might be regarded as an off-Broadway warmup for two major Alex Katz retrospectives in New York. In the fall, the Brooklyn Museum is staging a Katz print retrospective. And in March of 1986 Alex Katz will be the recipient of that jewel in any artist's crown...a major retrospective at the Whitney Museum.

"The Colby show," says Katz, "will really be a piece of the Whitney show."

The focus of all this institutional attention is an art characterized by Alex Katz's distinctive style of figurative realism—flat, clean, seemingly effortless, cool (some even say impersonal). The typical Katz subject is a friend (often an artist) or a family member whose likeness is both glamorized and generalized (comparisons are often made to billboard figures), reduced to essentials, but (important to Katz) presented in a very specific light. Katz's highly individualistic and instantly recognizable style has made him one of the stars of the realist revival, linking his name with those of artists like Philip Pearlstein, Jack Beal, Alfred Leslie, and (closer and closer to home) Fairfield Porter and Neil Welliver.

Welliver, in fact, first came to Maine in the

early 1960s to visit Katz and ultimately settled just up the road from his old friend. Comparing and contrasting the two artists is (at least in Maine) unavoidable. Where Welliver is the complete country boy, living year-round in Maine and avoiding the New York scene at all cost, Katz is the consummate New Yorker, his sensibilities fine-tuned to the contemporary cultural scene. But what Neil Welliver is to landscape painting, Alex Katz is to figure painting...The Great Purifier.

Alex Katz is a slight, dark, intense man who turned 58 on July 24. His dominant aspect is a natural scowl compounded in its brooding by cruel, pouting lips. A smile crosses his face often and easily, but it flashes instantaneously and seems to come from far away...like heat lightning. And though he is intimately aware of everything important that is happening with contemporary art, Katz is surprisingly inarticulate discussing art. (He explains Neil Welliver's extremely articulate conversation by pointing out that his neighbor is a teacher and he is not.) He seems most comfortable when he can say things that he has said before...and that he knows have impact. Mention his close friend Francesco Clemente, the hot young master of neo-expressionist eroticism, for instance, and Katz is pleased to be able to say, "Clemente is the best painter to come out of Italy since de Chirico." But then there is no reason to expect an artist's verbal confidence to match his visual confidence.

Born in Brooklyn and raised in Queens, Katz studied commercial art at Woodrow Wilson Vocational High School and served in the U.S. Navy before attending Cooper Union from 1946-49. Upon graduating from Cooper Union, he received a scholarship to the Skowhegan School. He liked what he saw in Maine and quickly made it his second home.

"It's like originally [Maine] was a place I could paint landscape," says Katz. "The light here is very beautiful. I guess it was just chasing the beautiful. It's as beautiful here in August as anyplace in the world."

In 1954, Katz and artist Lois Dodd purchased a small, rundown Lincolnville farmhouse together and in 1963 Katz purchased Dodd's interest. He settled in Lincolnville because he was drawn to the terrain between Liberty and Camden.

"I figured I liked inland better than the shore...for looks," Katz says. "It hadn't been tramped over by a lot of artists."

In a charming way, Katz might be described as house-proud, as though his Lincolnville summer retreat were a little bit of country that a city boy has managed to claw away from nature. If the Slab City Road had a center line, it would be exactly the color of Katz's Lincolnville farm...bright yellow.

Of his house's immodest hue, Katz says, "It sort of ran away. I started out trying to get an authentic buttermilk yellow, but after awhile it seemed like any yellow looked good."

The yellow farmhouse is trimmed in forest green and surrounded by lupines, lilies, and greenery. Attached to the front door is a little cut-out cat's head (with cat's-eye marbles for eyes) left there by artist Philip Guston. The interior of the house is stark and cool, breathing an air of wintery abandon. Attached to the little house is a barn which, until this summer, served at Katz's summer studio.

Alex Katz's new studio is a spacious, airy affair on the reedy shore of secluded Coleman Pond. Designed by architect Frank Kawasaki (of the University of Pennsylvania faculty where Neil Welliver also teaches), the studio successfully synthesizes Japanese temple design (specifically, the Katsura Temple) with New England barn architecture. Against the walls of the raw new studio are large blank canvases, some primed with the lead white that gives Katz the hard surface he likes to work on. Both because of all the exhibitions and because Alex Katz is very successful (his major works selling in the $65,000 range), there are no old paintings hanging around. It is a space pure with potential.

"I used to come here," says Katz of his working environment in Maine, "to open myself up and find new things. Then I'd develop the new ideas in New York. I don't know, but it may have turned itself around now."

Ths summer Katz has brought ideas from New York to work out in Maine. He says he may attempt some woodland variations on a theme he has visually articulated in some of his

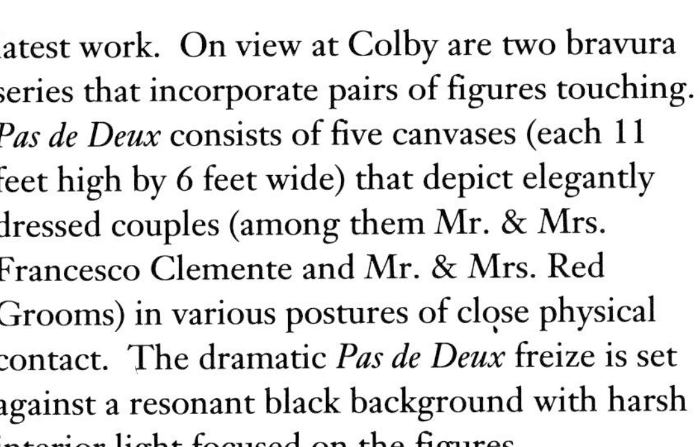

latest work. On view at Colby are two bravura series that incorporate pairs of figures touching. *Pas de Deux* consists of five canvases (each 11 feet high by 6 feet wide) that depict elegantly dressed couples (among them Mr. & Mrs. Francesco Clemente and Mr. & Mrs. Red Grooms) in various postures of close physical contact. The dramatic *Pas de Deux* freize is set against a resonant black background with harsh interior light focused on the figures.

In brilliant contrast to the formal darkness of the *Pas de Deux* series are the four 10-foot canvases that make up *Eleuthera*, a series depicting young women in bathing suits and bathing caps bathed in the glare of the tropical light of the Bahamian island from which the paintings take their title. The *Pas de Deux* suite suggests a formalwear spread from GQ; *Eleuthera* features designer swimwear by Norma Kamali. Clearly, Alex Katz's subject is Style, but one must be very precise when discussing the relationship of Style to the art of Alex Katz.

Readers of Katz's interview with poet Mark Strand in *The Art of the Real* (C.N. Potter, 1983) may be taken aback by the artist's statement, "I'd like to have style take the place of content, or the style be the content." This may sound like a formula for shallowness, but one must understand what Katz means by style. "To me," Katz continues, "there's an enormous difference between something that's stylized and something that has style. Stylized is like a cheap way to make handwriting identifiable. Whereas style is a much broader thing. It covers more ground...I think of style as being a conscious choice. Everything you do in your life ends up the next day with your making a choice. It's one thing built on the next. One's behavior is determined by one's previous behaviors. I think that has to do with style."

What Alex Katz means by Style might better be described as the personal core, the constant that makes an act, a look, one's own. Katz has often said that he feels viewers and critics tend too often to dwell on the formal and social aspects of his art when what is important to him is appearance.

"I think if there is an emotional content to my work, it's not the center of what it's about," says Katz. "I think of my work as layered. That's

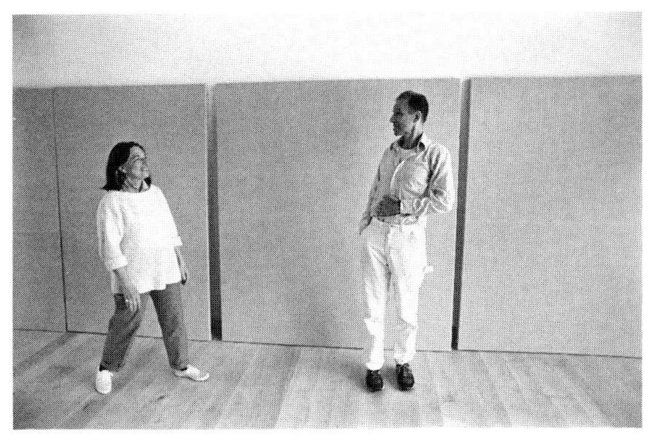

1. *Alex and Ada Katz display style, movement and light. Photo by Christopher Ayres.*

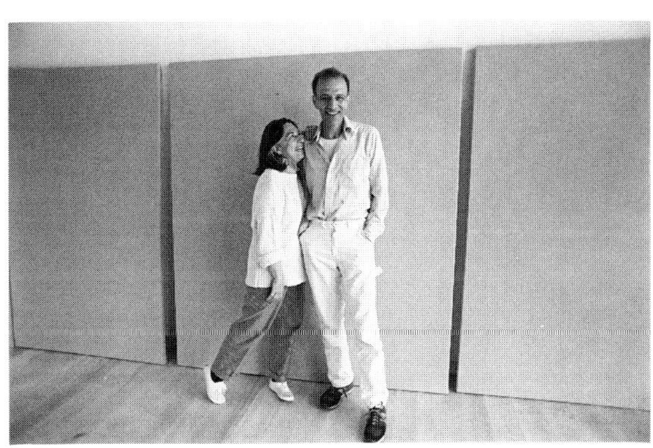

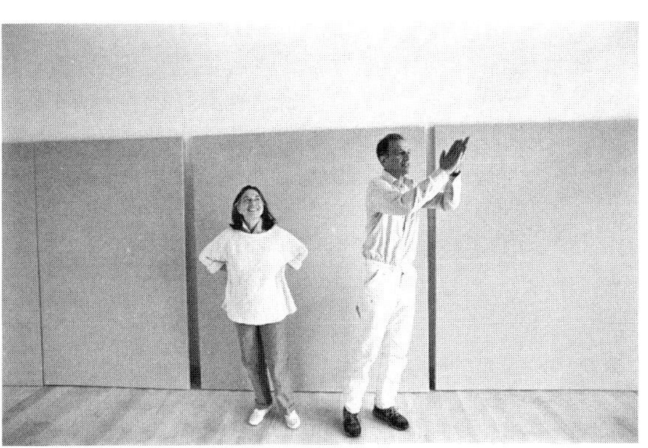

one of the layers, but not one of the important ones. Subject matter, form, content, and expression are unimportant things in one of my paintings. Style, light, and movement are the important things...the things that interest me."

The quality of light in a Katz painting is ultimately what differentiates it from the work of any other artist. He repeatedly stresses that while the details of his subjects may be generalized, the light is very specific...and therefore the most "real" aspect of the painting. Whereas most realists (particularly true of the Luminists) pursued light as radiant energy, and more painterly realists (like Neil Welliver) tend to treat light as a liquid (dripping over the surface images), Alex Katz uses light as though it were a

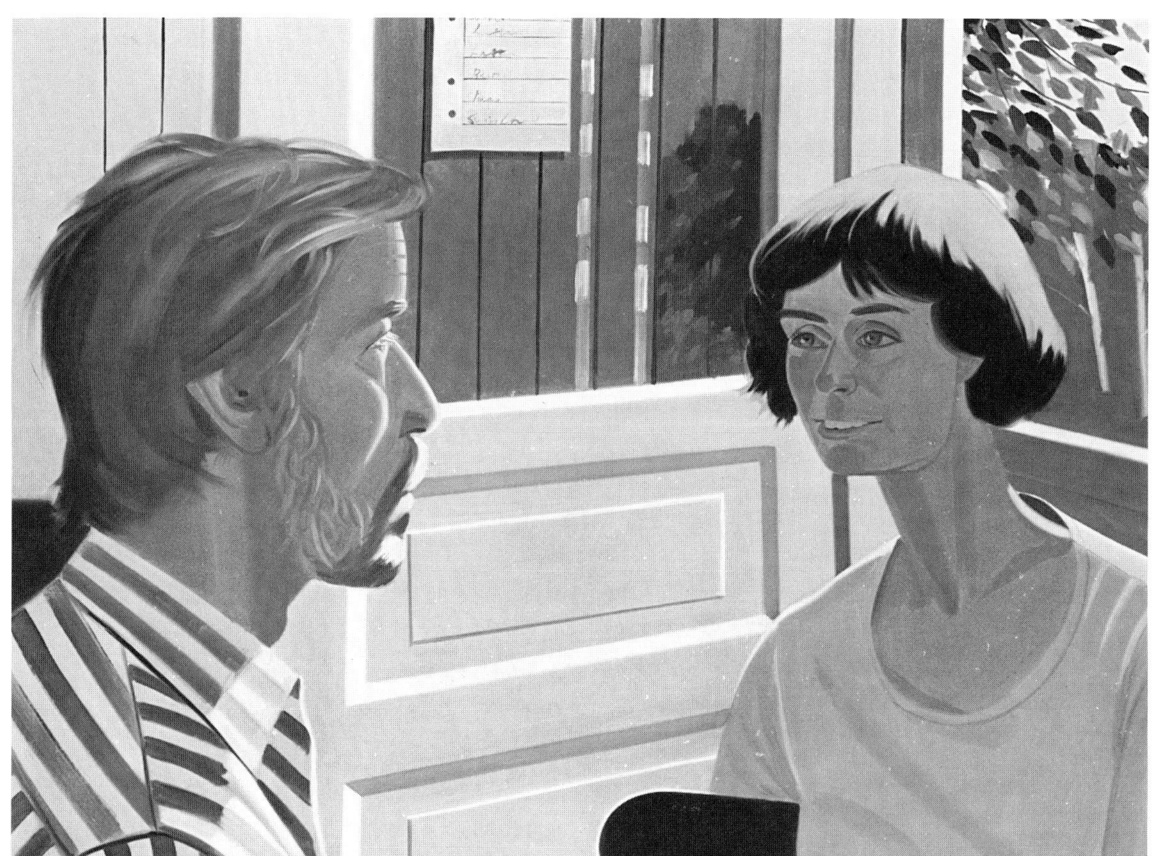

2. *Alex Katz,* Rudy and Yvonne, *1977. Oil on canvas. Courtesy of the Marlborough Gallery.*

solid. Solid Light...it accounts for the familiar flatness of any Katz image. Look at any Katz portrait and you see light applied to faces as though it were pancake make-up.

In the harsh glare of *Eleuthera*, this principle of light as solid entity is concretized. Katz paints the reflected glare off the Caribbean waters in little white squares, hot ice cubes dancing over the surfaces of the bathers.

Katz is most successful when he paints subjects he knows well, and in many cases this has meant his son Vincent and his wife Ada. Ada Katz, in fact, may be the most painted and most recognized woman in contemporary art, the subject of more than 80 paintings.

Prepared to meet Ada only by her symbolic painted image, most people expect a much larger woman...possibly haughty, aristocratic, cool and aloof. In person, Ada Katz is even more beautiful than her husband's images of her classic Mediterranean beauty suggest. Where Alex Katz is sometimes remote, Ada Katz is always right there...open, unguarded, friendly.

Born Ada Del Moro, Ada Katz was working as a research biologist at the Sloan-Kettering Institute for Cancer Research when she met Alex Katz at a New York opening in 1957. They have been married since 1958, and in that time Alex Katz has transformed his wife's image into a universal symbol of womanhood.

Though he was talking about a bust of Nefertiti at the time, Katz's statements quoted in Irving Sandler's *Alex Katz* (Harry N. Abrams, 1979) aptly apply to the place Ada Katz occupies in his own art:

"It is a specific woman. It is a beautiful woman. It is realism. It is an aristocrat. It is elegancè. It is mother. It is queen. It is power. It is a god. It is steadfast and unchanging and therefore security. It is fleeting beauty. It is the unattainable. The style enables the image to move gracefully from one idea to another."

Being the most recognizable living image in contemporary art would seem to be a heavy burden to bear, but Ada Katz, who for the past five years has been active with New York's Eye & Ear Theatre, shrugs the burden off lightly.

"I think if I made that kind of identification with the paintings," says Ada, "I would go nuts. I don't get emotionally involved with them in that sense."

It is best that she not become emotionally attached to her husband's paintings, if only because they are generally destined for the homes of collectors and the galleries of museums.

"I don't feel at this point," explains Katz, "that I have the right to keep anything of my own. I don't think you can really own a work of art anyway. We're all custodians for it."

Pressed for his own personal favorite among his works, Katz hedges, but, pressed by Ada, admits that one of the few major paintings he has hung onto is *Walk*, a painting of him, Ada, and son Vincent on the shore of Coleman Lake...his family occupying the view from his new studio. Unfortunately, *Walk* is not part of any of the Maine exhibitions, though a preliminary study for the painting is among the small pieces on view at Bowdoin.

The process by which Katz achieves the apparent effortlessness of his large canvases is a study in concealed effort. Most paintings begin with pen and ink sketches. Based on the sketches, Katz may execute a small preliminary oil, to establish formal and tonal harmonies. These small oils are then translated into enlarged drawings so that (in a technique learned from Neil Welliver) the image can be transferred to primed canvas by tracing the large drawing with a pounce wheel.

"From beginning to end the process might take three weeks," says Katz, "but the final painting may be done in one day. The final painting is real quick. What you see on the surface is what's there."

In addition to his distinctive oil paintings and prints, Katz is also well-known for his cut-outs, two-dimensional stand-up figures often lifted from the paintings. These days, most Katz cut-outs are painted on aluminum blanks, but the original cut-out (*Helen and Bernard Langlais*, 1959) was the result of excising the figure from a canvas and mounting them on wood. In this, Katz seems to have prefigured Pop art, popping images out of his paintings into the real space of the gallery. Katz never became identified with Pop art, but he credits the movement with increasing his own audience.

"I think Pop art did a lot for making figurative painting a negotiable idea in contemporary painting," says Katz. "Before Pop art I don't think people took any figuration seriously as a modern art thing. There was a conservative modernism that wouldn't allow figurative art in the 1950s. I think now it's wide open. You can do whatever you want to do. It definitely increased my audience."

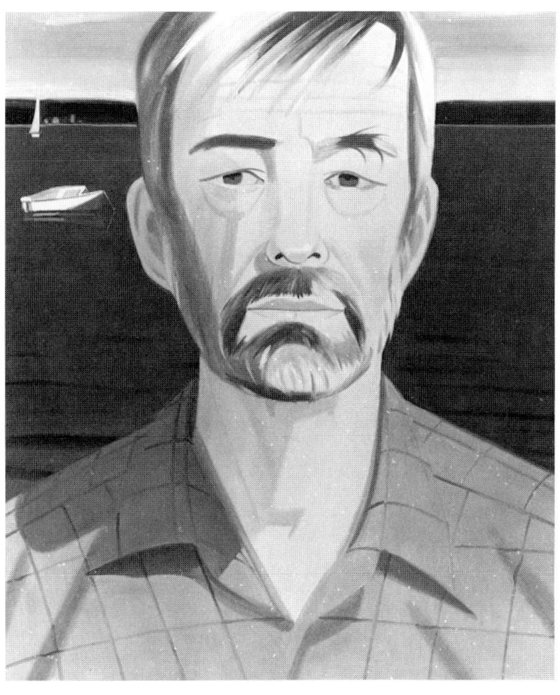

3. *Alex Katz,* Rudy, *1980. Oil on canvas. Courtesy of the Marlborough Gallery.*

Though Alex Katz is closely identified with the new realism (representational painting that has learned the lessons of abstraction), he has managed to escape precise pigeonholing. When it is suggested that art history may one day come to consider his art in a category (both geographical and aesthetic) with Fairfield Porter and Neil Welliver, he replies testily, "I don't know what art history is going to do...and I don't give a damn."

Alex Katz has created an art that so far defies categories. He has articulated no credo and accepts no aesthetic dogma. His art is his own.

"I'd swap a dogma for a good painting any day," says Katz with a sureness of tongue that seems to indicate he has used these words before. "When you're making a painting, you're just a desperate man...a beggar begging you'll come out of it alive. You'd be a fool to stick to your dogma."

July 19, 1985

A View from Above

Yvonne Jacquette

The countryside west of Belfast is a working landscape of fields and farms and forests. It is close enough to the coast to pick up the radiant sea light of Penobscot Bay, but far enough inland to retain its agrarian qualities. The art lover knows this land. It is Neil Welliver country. (He owns the wilder aspect of this landscape.) It is Alex Katz country. (He owns the more cultured aspects of the area, populating it with billboard likenesses of the artists and intellectuals who summer here.) It is Rackstraw Downes country. (To him belongs the working landscape of gravel pits, construction equipment, and commercial docks.) And it is Yvonne Jacquette country. She owns the air rights.

Yvonne Jacquette laughs when it is suggested that she took to the air a dozen years ago in order to find room to paint in this heavily staked-out artistic terrain. Her laugh acknowledges the partial truth of the proposition that she was forced aloft in search of her own vision. When she first came to this landscape more than 20 years ago, Yvonne Jacquette was an unknown artist, distinctly in the shadow of the more accomplished painters in the area like Welliver, Katz, and Fairfield Porter. Today, however, she casts her own shadow as an internationally known artist famed for her aerial visions of countryside and cityscape alike.

Yvonne Jacquette first came to Maine in 1963 with her husband, the filmmaker-photographer-painter Rudolph Burckhardt. That summer, the couple came to Lincolnville to visit Alex and Ada Katz. The Maine landscape made such a strong impression on them that they returned the following summer, renting a house with artist Red Grooms and his wife Mimi. Then, in 1965, Jacquette and Burckhardt purchased a 70-acre farm near Lawry Pond in Searsmont with poet and dance critic Edwin Denby. The natural and artistic terrain of this corner of Maine had a profound impact on Jacquette.

"Being here," says Jacquette, "made me look at light much more intensely, not just at landscape. And I liked the community that we came up among and into. It was a very interesting and supportive group of artists...Alex and Neil and Fairfield and Rudy were strong teachers for me, since I'm younger. The experience of going around to their studios, seeing their work in progress, and having them talk about my own work was better than graduate school."

Considering the nexus of important contemporary representational painters around Lincolnville, it seems possible that art historians will some day delineate a "Lincolnville School" of painterly realism, citing (and perhaps inventing) lines of aesthetic communion and influence.

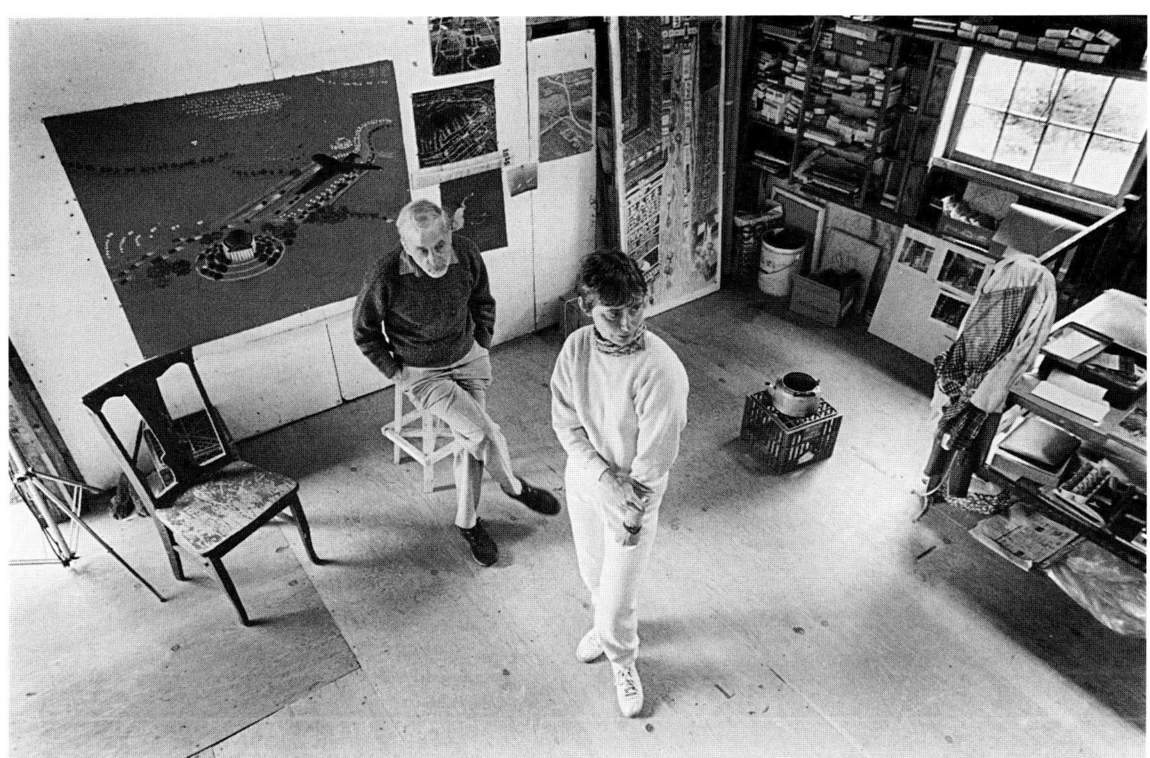

1. *Yvonne Jacquette and Rudy Burckhardt in their studio. Photo by Scott Perry.*

This possibility does not seem all that far-fetched to Rudy Burckhardt.

"It might make a good subject for study," says Burckhardt of the Lincolnville connection, "certainly not any more made up than abstract expressionism. People make up art history just to do something. Making these connections makes people more secure. I think this Maine colony of artists would be just as good."

"Everybody that we knew [in Maine] at first was involved with perceptual experience," says Yvonne Jacquette. "Only Kathy Porter is an abstract painter. In the '60s, there was a totally different attitude in New York than there is now. There was a very strong minimal and Pop viewpoint, and still something of abstract expressionism. Why none of these viewpoints was important to any of us is interesting. It seems to me the reason is that we were all here looking at a new place with new eyes."

The viewpoint that was important to Jacquette was the aerial viewpoint, a lofty perspective she developed from the ground up. Though Jacquette is by no means the first or only artist to employ a bird's-eye perspective, she is the artist most closely identified with it in a contemporary idiom. She began her ascent modestly enough by first executing paintings of interiors, looking at the intersecting and overlapping planes formed by open doors and corners where walls meet ceiling. From there she moved on to a series of paintings inspired by the pressed tin patterns on the ceiling of her New York loft. Then, in the habit of looking up, she began a series of cloud paintings, viewing the sky from the vantage point of the ground, often looking at the same small patch of sky day after day and recording the changes on canvas. The ground-based cloud paintings gradually gave way to cloudscapes as viewed from airplanes. Then one day while flying in a cloudless sky, Yvonne Jacquette looked down and discovered the aerial landscape. That was about 1974 and she has been refining her visions from on high ever since. (As a curious side note, one of Jacquette's first jobs after graduating from the Rhode Island School of Design in 1956 was drafting catalog illustrations of helicopter engines.)

Perhaps the best-known Jacquette aerial in Maine is the three-panel mural she created in 1980 for the post office and federal building in Bangor. Entitled *Autumn Expansion*, the Bangor mural consists of three different views of the land across the road from her Searsmont farm. The rough-cut serial nature of the shifting fall scene owes something to her husband's filmmaking aesthetic.

Rudy Burckhardt, a Swiss-born artist 20 years his wife's senior, is a celebrated experimental

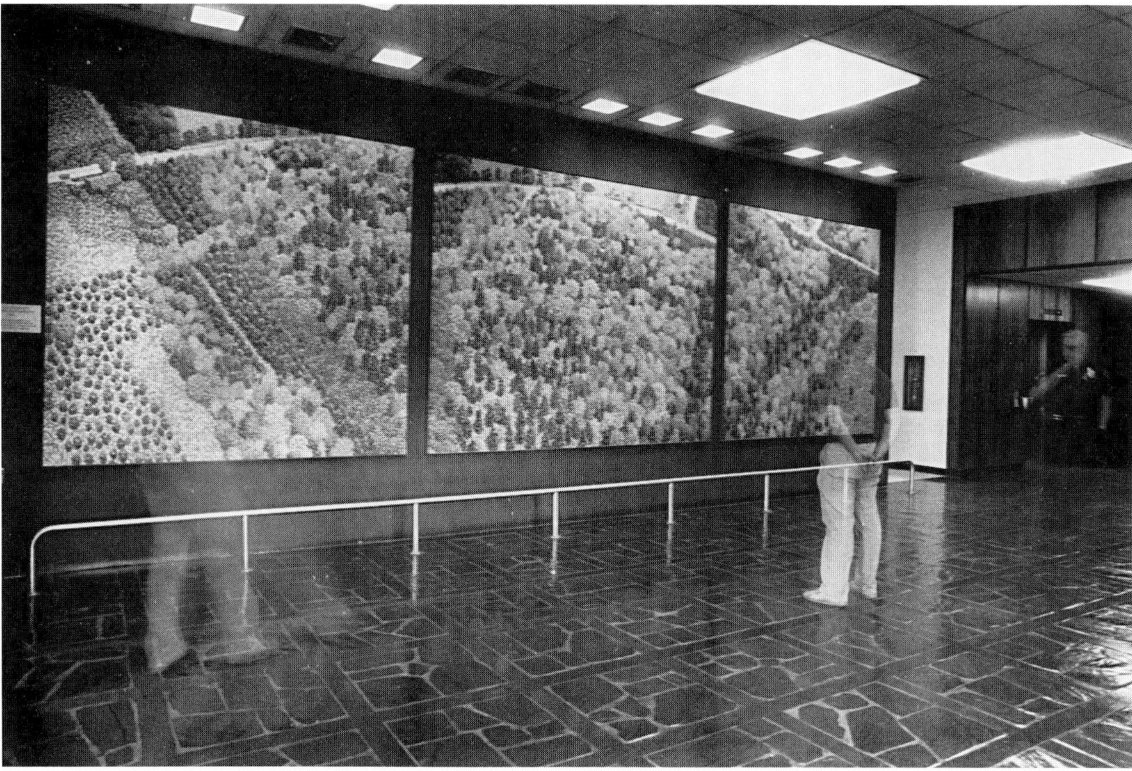

2. *Yvonne Jacquette's autumn landscape in the federal building in Bangor. Photo by Scott Perry.*

filmmaker. More cinema poet than entertainer, Burckhardt made his living for many years photographing art for New York galleries, but he is better known as the creator of more than 60 art films ranging in length from 2 to 45 minutes. Last week, the Portland Museum of Art featured an evening of Burckhardt's films, and next February, the Museum of Modern Art will devote 12 evenings to a Burckhardt retrospective.

While Yvonne Jacquette (like many of the other artists working in the Searsmont-Lincolnville area) has appeared in several Burckhardt films, the couple's closest collaboration was the film Burckhardt made documenting his wife's work in *Autumn Expansion*. Burckhardt does not normally film documentaries, however.

"All terms like 'script,' 'director,' and 'producer' don't apply to my films," says Burckhardt. "It's like who is 'producing' Yvonne's paintings. My films are one-man things."

Jacquette finds a sympathetic sensibility at work between her art and her husband's.

"I always think of my work as a little primitive, not technically refined and unbelievable. Rudy's filmmaking is primitive in that way, too. It's not smooth and slick in any way. It has an authentic feeling."

Jacquette has refined her process of creation, however. She begins a painting by flying over an area and making immediate pastel sketches of what she sees. She often takes photographs as well, the drawings and photographs serving as her notes as she elaborates (and sometimes invents) details back in the studio. Unlike her neighbors Welliver and Katz, who both use a pounce-wheel tracery method to enlarge preliminary works via cartoon into large paintings, Jacquette projects slides of her pastel studies onto canvas in order to outline her major works.

In Maine, Jacquette likes to fly with pilot Floyd Watts out of the Belfast Airport, but she also sketches from commercial airliners and on sightseeing flights. Most of her chartered sketching trips last no more than one hour or so.

"Normally, I circle an area," she says, "but after an hour of circling I'm usually dizzy and confused."

The distinctive look of an Yvonne Jacquette painting is part perspective, part aesthetic choice, and part physiology of vision. She has long suffered from problems of eyesight connected with being farsighted and doing close-up work. Today, she wears bifocal lenses over soft contact lenses to help correct the problem, "so when I'm painting, I have lots of help."

Her vision problems affect her art in so far as

"I couldn't, or wouldn't, do a refined, close-focus kind of painting. Because I'm farsighted, I think it's more comfortable for me to look long distances."

Maine audiences can currently (through August 24 at Bowdoin's Walker Art Gallery) get a close look at some of Jacquette's most recent paintings and drawings in *Tokyo Nightviews*, a collaborative exhibition between Bowdoin College and the Brooke Alexander Gallery in New York. Jacquette's Brooke Alexander show was sold out, with prices ranging as high as $60,000 for one painting. By comparison, the federal government got a bargain on the Bangor mural, acquiring three major pieces for just $40,000.

The four major oil paintings and seven pastel drawings of *Tokyo Nightviews* owe their genius to a family excursion Jacquette took in 1982 with Rudy Burckhardt's son Jacob, who is married to a Japanese woman. Struck by the colorful spectacle of Tokyo nightlife, the brilliant neon billboards glaring into the night of the city, the streets and highways teeming with cars and pedestrians, Jacquette resolved to return to Japan to paint. She got her chance in May of last year when she was invited to exhibit by the Seibu Department Store in Tokyo. (Japan has a tradition of art galleries in department stores.)

The *Tokyo Nightviews* are remarkable chiefly for the dramatic contrasts between the deep green-black gloom of night and the screaming electric colors of the city billboards. Color is always a function of light in a naturalistic painting, but in Jacquette's Tokyo paintings the colors *are* lights. And because most western viewers (indeed Jacquette herself) cannot read the Japanese graphics, these paintings and drawings are pure visual experiences, the pattern and intensity of the lights lending the surfaces an abstract quality in the absence of linguistic meaning.

Jacquette was particularly pleased that the Museum of Modern Art acquired her favorite painting, *Shinjuku Pleasure District, Tokyo II*, 1985, from the Brooke Alexander show. The painting is the artist's favorite because "the structure of the darks and the structure of the brights work together best" in this particular painting. As a personal aside, Jacquette also notes that one of the figures down in the rainy Tokyo street is Jacob Burckhardt returning to Jacquette's hotel with some late-night sushi.

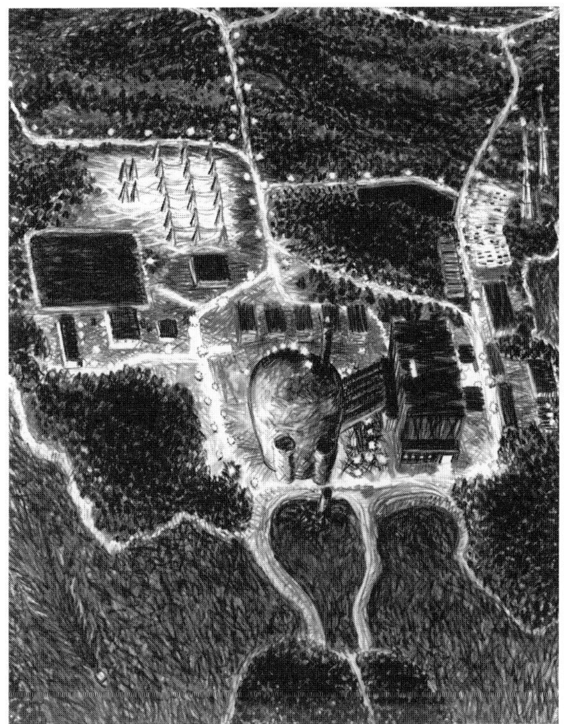

3. *Yvonne Jacquette,* Maine Yankee Nuclear Plant, IV. *Charcoal on synthetic vellum. Courtesy of the Bowdoin College Museum of Art.*

Jacquette's nocturnes began in 1979, just about the time she was commissioned by the General Services Administration to execute the Bangor project. Her original idea had been to paint a night view of Bangor for the federal building, and she had gone so far as to fly over the city to make sketches before she was forced to scrap that idea. When she saw how dark and cramped the post office lobby was, she knew she would have to do something bright, thus the foliage display of *Autumnal Expansion*.

Jacquette's foray into night painting occurred during a period when her great friend and summer housemate Edwin Denby was hospitalized in New York. When Denby complained that Jacquette should be working instead of spending every evening at his bedside, Jacquette began sketching during her visits, her first nightview being that of the East River seen from University Hospital. Edwin Denby elected to end his life last year in Searsmont after suffering with a lengthy illness. The personal tragedy associated with the inspiration of the night paintings adds a depth of feeling to Jacquette's nightviews.

Just as Neil Welliver sorts out and purifies the apparent chaos of nature, Jacquette finds order in the bewildering urban labyrinth. And just as Alex Katz simplifies and generalizes details in his quest to conquer likeness with personal style, Jacquette reduces the random assault of the city to a gently pulsing whole made up of countless fillips of color. This summer she is devoting herself to executing four large paintings (conceived as one piece) in which she sets the parameters of Times Square through depictions of four sign fragments. The Times Square paintings are the New York counterparts to the Tokyo nightviews, but because the advertising graphics are familiar—TWA, Midtown Liquor, Coca-Cola, Panasonic—these paintings read in more of a Pop idiom than the Japanese paintings. It takes an effort of will (both on the artist's part and the viewer's) to see beyond the meaning of these words and letters to their purely visual impact. Yet, in subtle and not-so-subtle ways, Yvonne Jacquette's work is always culturally loaded.

These are modern paintings and they have modern sensibilities. In a high-rise, airborne society, we consider aerial perspectives normal. Superficially, these are just very pretty pictures of a reality we all know, the world as seen from skyscrapers and airplanes. But, like many people, the artist had to overcome a fear of flying in order to accomplish these paintings. The residual, often unspoken anxiety that underlies a society which places so much blind trust in technology speaks quietly through Jacquette's art. Her art is not vertiginous, but it is jittery and precarious. Often it is informed by events, knowledge, doubts, and dreads not expressed directly.

In 1984, for example, Jacquette was commissioned to do a painting for the American Medical Association headquarters in Washington, D.C. That painting, done from the vantage of the Washington Monument, shows the illuminated dome of the Jefferson Memorial, a portion of the Bureau of Engraving (Jacquette is also an accomplished printmaker), the inflated bubble of a tennis court, and a stretch of bridge over the Potomac. In the middle ground (which in a Jacquette painting is midair) is the dark silhouette of an airliner gliding ominously below the eye level achieved atop the monument. Yes, this is the same stretch of bridge where a doomed jetliner, overloaded and burdened with ice, plunged into the icy river a few years ago. Jacquette is now working on a second version of this D.C. painting in which she has adjusted the position of the plane to even greater effect. The image elicits a shudder of recognition.

Beauty pregnant with the possibility of tragedy is a subtext of many Jacquette paintings. It is the main text of a series of aerial views she has done in recent years of nuclear power plants. Jacquette is an avowed anti-nuke sympathizer, but her attraction to nuclear plants is more than political. She traces some of her interest in industrial structures in the landscape to the influence of Rackstraw Downes, the consummate artist of the workscape who summers in nearby Morrill. From Downes, Jacquette discovered "I like the way things fit together that you don't normally think of as fitting together, the man-made and the nature making something new."

The Bowdoin College Museum of Art first became interested in an Yvonne Jacquette show back in 1983 when it acquired a charcoal drawing of the Maine Yankee nuclear plant. It is hard to see beyond the political and social implications of a nuclear power plant glowing in the dark to the neutral beauty of the thing-in-itself, but Jacquette tries.

"I don't really think I could have any effect," says the artist of her nuclear pieces as agents of change. "I'm really doing it for myself. I'm really interested in the mixed thing of something wonderful and something horrible being together in the same thing."

Though she initially approached the Maine Yankee dome as something horrible, she ultimately came away with a transcendent experience.

"In the end," she says, "I saw how beautiful the site was. If you didn't know what was going on, you'd say it was an interesting patch of land, full of color. The density of all that is fantastic."

July 25, 1986

A Painter of Signs

Robert Indiana

If you take the state ferry *Governor Curtis* out of Rockland, you will arrive fifteen miles and one hour-and-a-half hours later at the spruce-furred and quarry-pocked island of Vinalhaven. As you make your way up from the ferry dock into the village, you will be sure to notice the former Odd Fellows Hall, a large, weathered Victorian structure, the facade of which has been boxed in temporarily with three tiers of plywood. The street-level tier is painted a deep barn red. The second tier is unpainted wood which has not yet silvered in the salt sea air. And the top tier is an incongruous robin's-egg blue. In other words, you can't miss it.

As you approach the building, you may see a rather rakish figure, a middle-aged man, dressed somewhat like a highwayman of old in boots, leather vest, and jaunty snap-brimmed cap, suddenly appear from a small door in the red plywood, propelled into the street by a Great Dane and a little Tasmanian shepherd on leashes. The Odd Fellows Hall is known as the Star of Hope. The Great Dane is called Casso, after Picasso. The Tasmanian goes by the name of Cleon. And the master of all three is the world-famous artist Robert Indiana.

Whether you know the name Robert Indiana or not, chances are you know his most famous work. Indiana, along with Andy Warhol, Roy Lichtenstein, Claes Oldenburg, Tom Wesselman, and James Rosenquist, was one of the stars of Pop art (so-called because of the artists' wholesale adoption of popular culture images and commercial art techniques) in the 1960s. In 1965, Indiana originated his LOVE design, which very quickly escaped the world of fine art to enter the mainstream of society as a true sign of the times.

Born Robert Clark in New Castle, Indiana, in 1928, the artist studied at the Art Institute of Chicago (1949-1953) and, following a year of study in Edinburgh, Scotland, arrived on the New York art scene in 1954. In the mid-1950s, Indiana discarded his family name and adopted the name of his home state. As the artist himself explains the change, "When I became Indiana, my work became Indiana. It was a well-timed coincidence, let's say."

Becoming Indiana meant that the artist evolved his mature style of painting, a style characterized by impersonal, mechanical designs which employ words, numbers, and geometric figures in bright, hard-edged colors. The introduction of words into his paintings, which so distinguishes Indiana's style, came about as a result of his finding a set of brass ship chandler's stencils in a Manhattan waterfront loft. The discovery of those stencils was pivotal in

Indiana's career. The instantly recognizable style that resulted from that discovery served the artist well, and his star rose through the decades of the 1960s and 1970s.

Today, Indiana's place in art history seems assured, his works are represented in major museums all over the world, and, in 1977, he executed the design for what has to be one of the world's largest paintings—*MECCA*, the floor of the Milwaukee Exposition Convention Center Arena, home court to the Milwaukee Bucks of the National Basketball Association.

Despite all of his success, however, Robert Indiana, at fifty-three, allows himself but two extravagances—time and space. Time is purchased at the expense of companionship, through self-imposed isolation on Vinalhaven. Space takes the form of the cavernous Odd Fellows Hall, a sail-loft studio on Carvers Harbor, and an additional building used to house his artistic overflow. But, luxuries of time and space aside, Indiana's material possessions are relatively meager. For instance, he still drives the only vehicle he has ever owned, a ten-year-old yellow and white VW van, named Denise after the owner of his New York gallery, Denise René. He also allows himself a liberal supply of outsized White Owl cigars and the constant company of two dogs and ten cats, which he babies unashamedly.

Robert Indiana first came to Maine in 1953 on a scholarship to study at the Skowhegan School of Painting and Sculpture. Of his Skowhegan experience, Indiana says, "It was the most beautiful summer of my life—up to that point."

At Skowhegan, Indiana studied fresco painting with Henry Varnum Poor and created two murals, one of Pilate washing his hands and the other a protest against the Korean War. The frescoes were eventually destroyed when the school's fresco barn burned.

"I hated to see the barn go," says Indiana, "but I was glad to see those frescoes go."

Indiana has maintained his Skowhegan ties as a long-standing member of the school's board of governors, and it was through the Skowhegan School that, in the summer of 1969, he met famed *Life* photographer Eliot Elisofon, who introduced him to Vinalhaven. On a visit to Elisofon's Crockett Cove summer home, Indiana first saw the derelict Odd Fellows Hall and immediately fell in love with it. Within two weeks, Elisofon had purchased the Star of Hope and began renting it to Indiana as a seasonal studio. Following Elisofon's death, Indiana bought the building from the photographer's estate. Thus, from 1970 to 1977, Indiana visited Vinalhaven each fall, making a concerted effort not to become identified as a summer person. Then, in 1978, after twenty-four years in New York City, Indiana moved to Vinalhaven on a permanent basis.

One has to wonder whether such an exotic bird, a world-famous artist, might not face insurmountable obstacles in penetrating a tight-knit island community, but Indiana, who maintains a low profile, says he knew exactly what he was getting into when he made the decision to move.

"The thing to remember about Vinalhaven," he says, "is that it is not Monhegan. It is not a summer art colony; it is a working island. There isn't any real appreciation or feeling for the artist here. When Marsden Hartley was here in 1938, the kids threw stones at him. But Hartley was only a summer visitor, and I'm here permanently. Remember, I'd been coming here almost ten years before I moved, so I was fully aware of the nature of the island. Islanders don't want to be overrun with tourists and artists, and I respect that attitude. It protects me as well as the island. I'm a private person, so it works both ways."

In his life and in his art, Robert Indiana says he works "very much by the magic of coincidence," and the fact that Marsden Hartley spent time on Vinalhaven figures prominently in Indiana's presence on the island. He does not object when it is suggested that he is obsessed with Hartley's life and work.

"The most compelling thing in my being here on the island is my involvement with Hartley," he admits. "Hartley is Maine's most famous native artist, but his name doesn't mean anything here. I've always been a champion of the underdog, so I'd like to help focus attention on Hartley and his achievement. After all, he was one of the first American abstract artists… though no one seems to pay attention to that."

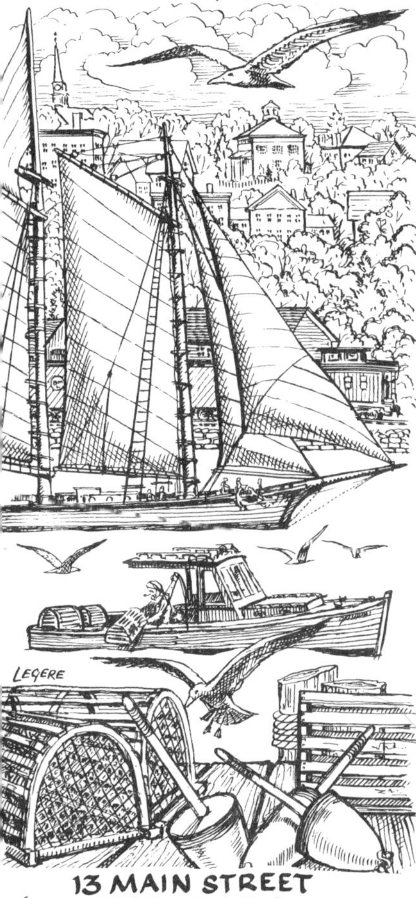

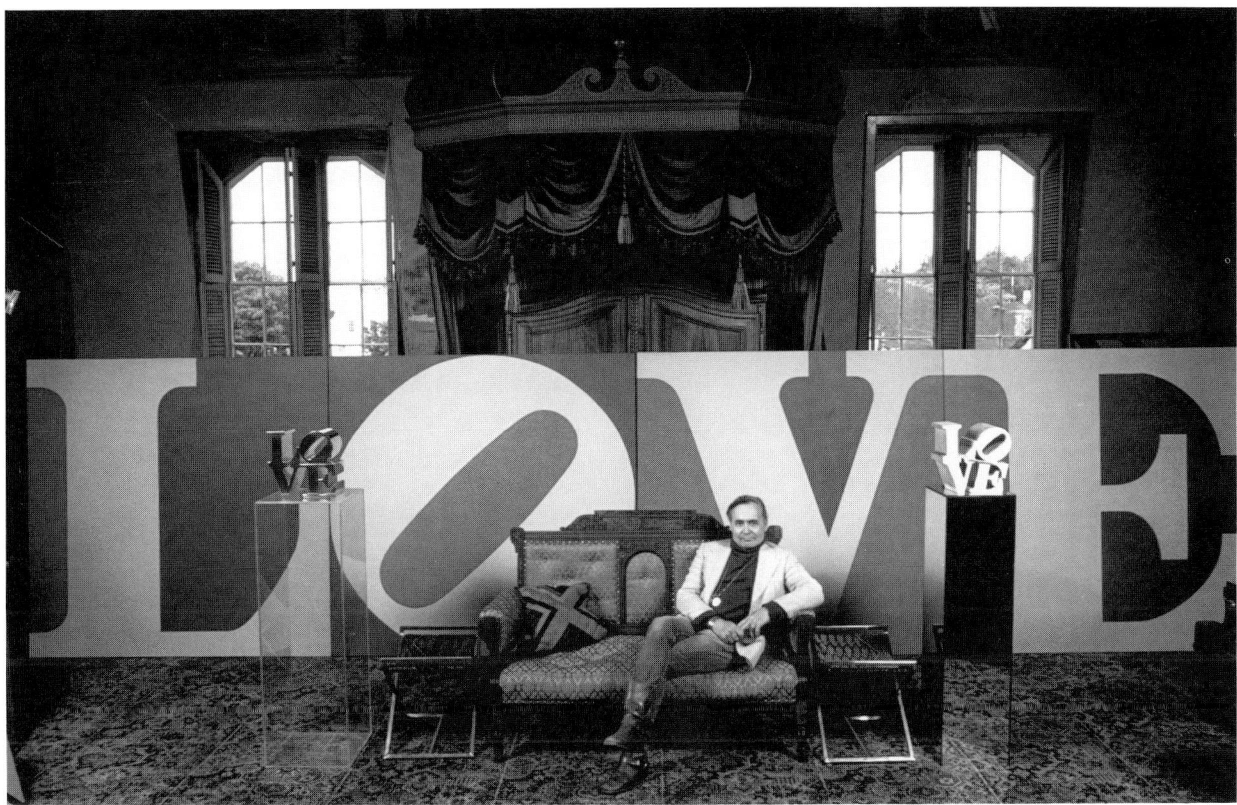

1. *Robert Indiana at home in the former Odd Fellows Hall known as the Star of Hope. Photo by Kip Brundage.*

Indiana finds a great affinity between his art and Hartley's. The connection is particularly evident between Indiana's cryptic *Autoportraits* —a series of annual geometric compositions which incorporate names, dates, and places important to his life—and Hartley's Berlin abstractions of 1914-15. Both sets of works are symbolic portraits of a deeply personal nature made apprehensible to the public through the iconography of letter, number, and pattern.

"My manner is different from Hartley's," says Indiana. "I'm hard-edge coming from a geometric background, but our works deal with the same thing—the fabric of people's lives. Hartley was rooted enough in the native idiom that he was able to achieve the ruggedness and grandeur of the Maine landscape in his paintings."

Though Robert Indiana is universally categorized as a Pop artist, like all serious artists he resists classification. His one acknowledged influence is his friend, the painter Ellsworth Kelly, who introduced him to hard-edge color abstraction. If he is to be labeled at all, it is as a hard-edged painter that he prefers to be known.

"It is much safer to generalize about the abstract expressionists than about Pop art," Indiana insists. "The abstract expressionists knew one another, drank together, and discussed their art. The Pop artists didn't. Pop just sort of happened."

Indiana calls himself "the least Pop" of all the Pop artists and feels that Andy Warhol, having come from a background as a successful commercial artist and having consistently employed images of consumerism in his work, is really the only true Pop artist.

"I've never advertised anything in my art," he says. "Most of my works are celebrations of something. My style comes more from road signs than from commercial advertising."

Since moving to Maine, Indiana has found it difficult to find time to paint, and, looking around his labyrinthian Star of Hope studio-home, it is easy to see why.

"I'm still unpacking from that horrendous move," Indiana says, without exaggeration.

In New York, Indiana occupied a five-floor, nine-studio building on the Bowery. It took two vans twelve trips to transport everything from the Bowery to Vinalhaven.

On the ground floor of the Star of Hope, Indiana has installed his voluminous library and a temporary painting studio. The library is the authoritative Robert Indiana archive, chock-full with every magazine, newspaper, and book that has ever mentioned him or his art. One shelf contains twenty black loose-leaf notebooks cataloging the activities of each year of his career. Across the room is an impressive display of art journals which have featured his work. Attached to a column in the middle of the library is the old blue and white street sign from his first New York address on Coentis Slip. The library is currently being used as the primary research center for the definitive book on Robert Indiana to be published sometime next year by Harry N. Abrams, Inc.

Because the stove in his sail-loft studio produces ash, which tends to settle over his paintings (Indiana works on the floor), he has thus far been working across the foyer from his library in a temporary studio, already jammed to the rafters with older works and art supplies.

The steep, central staircase that leads to the second-floor living quarters is lined with a set of Indiana's famed number prints (each based on a painting), odd numbers on one wall, even on the other. The numbers correspond to the ten stages of human life as represented in an 18th-century print, *The Ten Ages of Man, The Life and Age of Man, Cradle to Grave*, which hangs in Indiana's living room, the former Odd Fellows card room.

The card room-living room features remnants of the secret society's past—a wall of numbered wooden lockers, the linked-ring Odd Fellows emblem symbolizing Friendship and Truth linked by Love, a spray of American flags—living side by side with Indiana's personal keepsakes and mementos: high-school watercolors, photos of friends (such as one of Indiana and Ellsworth Kelly riding bicycles on Wall Street), and an 1890 *Harper's Weekly* view of Coentis Slip. In this spacious, cluttered room it is possible for even ten cats to go unnoticed.

Across the hall, in what was the Odd Fellows ballroom, Indiana has his print room, hung with his *Decade* prints and furnished with two mammoth banks of print drawers. Also prominently displayed is a large black and white photograph of the Brooklyn Bridge. The bridge figures as one of Indiana's well-loved coincidences in that his first studio looked out on the bridge, and he now lives on the island that supplied the granite for the bridge's twin towers. Next year, on the occasion of the Brooklyn Bridge's 100th anniversary, Indiana will be designing a poster of the bridge, which is one of his recurring themes.

The stairs to the third floor are lined with Indiana's *Polygons*, a series of unique prints which celebrate both numbers and their corresponding plane geometric figures. Looking back down the stairs, one notices hanging above the second-floor landing Lowell Nesbitt's photo-grey painting of the Odd Fellows Hall facade.

On the third floor, in the grand salon, Indiana has stored and displayed his own collection of his work. In the middle of the great hall hangs an ornate steamboat-gothic chandelier of gilded iron and on each of the four walls is a tasseled canopy, which once covered the four Odd Fellows thrones. The Victorian fussiness of the grand salon contrasts markedly with the clean, colorful, contemporary lines of Indiana's paintings and sculpture.

The contents of the grand salon will be exhibited this summer (July 16-September 26) as *Indiana's Indianas* at the Farnsworth Museum in Rockland.

"What the Farnsworth show is all about," says Indiana, "is that I'd like to establish the fact that I'm here in Maine. So far I've just been hiding out, but I'm really not a recluse."

Every indication is that *Indiana's Indianas* should be one of the most ambitious and important exhibitions the Farnsworth has ever mounted. Indiana and Farnsworth director Marius B. Peladeau began planning for the show over two years ago, on the occasion of the museum's major Louise Nevelson retrospective.

According to Indiana, "The Farnsworth show will be practically my entire collection of my own work. Because I set a policy early on to keep a major work from each year, these works represent the nucleus of all my other retrospectives."

The catalog for *Indiana's Indianas* lists almost fifty works, ranging from the 1972 oil, *LOVE WALL*, which measures twelve feet on a side, to a collection of the artist's early "herms," wooden beams taken from many demolished warehouses on the New York waterfront and stenciled with words, prefiguring Indiana's later word-paint-

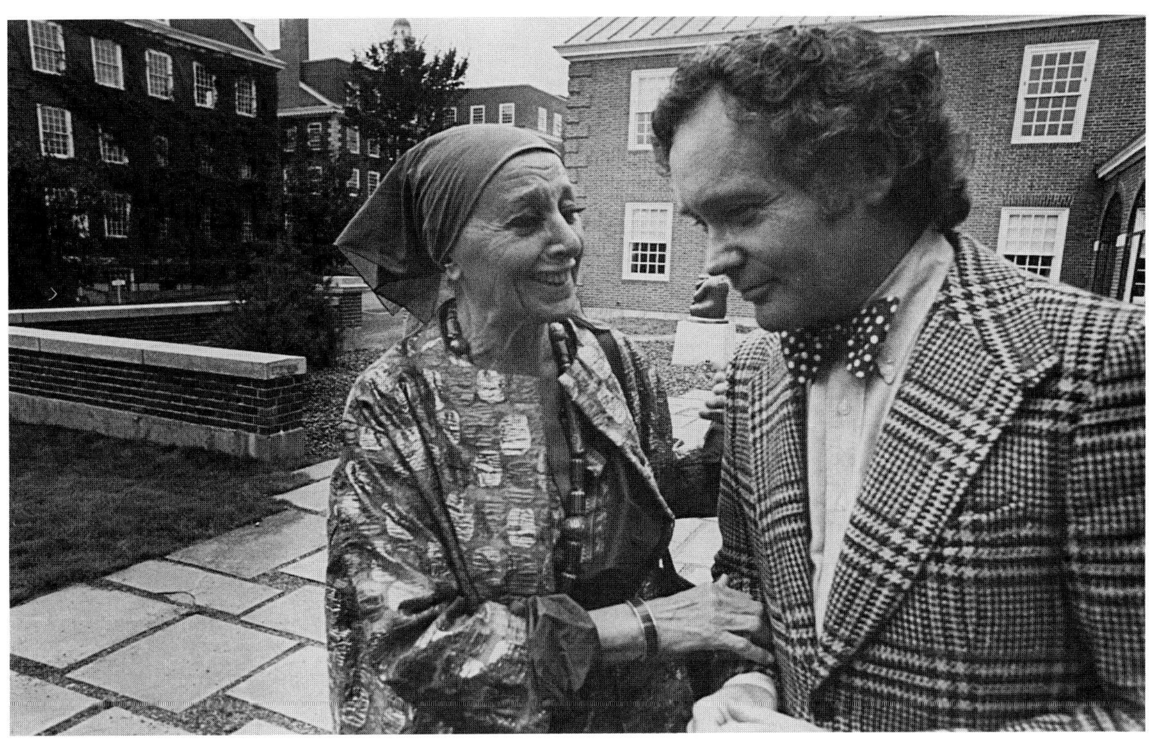

2. *Robert Indiana and Louise Nevelson exchanging a few words on the campus of Colby College, September, 1973. Photographer unknown.*

ings and word-sculpture.

Peladeau and novelist-art critic Martin Dibner have provided the show catalog with a discerning text made all the more insightful for the fact that Robert Indiana, unlike many contemporary artists, is not interested in mystifying his audience. He is exceptionally generous about sharing information and meanings in his works, meanings which could not possibly be fathomed otherwise.

For example, in writing about one of Indiana's best-known word-paintings, *EAT/DIE*, Dibner admits, "Frankly, I'm puzzled by what *EAT/DIE* is supposed to be telling me." As Dibner reports, Indiana explained to him that his mother's dying words were, "Did you have something to eat?" Hence, *EAT/DIE*. Coincidentally, the 1973 article on Robert Indiana in *Current Biography* explains the painting by reporting that Indiana's father dropped dead after eating breakfast. That, says Indiana, is perfectly true, but *EAT/DIE* was painted long before his father died. Coincidence.

As Dibner points out, "Coincidence is a phenomenon to which Robert Indiana pays rapt attention, attaching as much significance to it as to the visible elements of his compositions." Therein lies one key to any understanding of Robert Indiana and his art. Indiana is primarily a designer. Even unfriendly critics concede that he is a flawless one. He divines design everywhere in nature and in his own life. Temperamentally, he is a fatalist. In his art he seeks to acknowledge and cement these perceived and intuited connections visually and symbolically. Thus, one of his most recent constructions, entitled *Bay*, employs a beam from the area near his Coentis Slip studio, iron wheels from his Bowery studio, and a nautical metal ring from his Vinalhaven sail-loft studio. In art, as in life itself, all things are connected.

Of course, like all good system builders, Indiana is not above forcing connections and creating coincidences. When he found that the post office next door did not have a Box I, his sense of symbolic order must have been slightly disturbed. The postmistress obliged Indiana's penchant for order by painting out the tail of the letter J on Box J to create Box I for him.

Indiana has thoroughly documented his first ten years on Vinalhaven in a series of ten emblematic silk-screens known as *Decade: Autoportraits, The Vinalhaven Suite*. *The Vinalhaven Suite* is a consummation of the art of personal symbology, encoding the major events of each year in the artist's life in semaphoric designs that flash information through words, numerals, color, and geometry. The 1977 entry, for example, is entitled *Tiptoe Mt.* after one of Vinalhaven's larger hills. It incorporates the

word "MECCA" for the Milwaukee arena project; the word "Casablanca" in exotic reference to the White House, where Indiana visited President Jimmy Carter and later painted his symbolic portrait; and the name "San Antonio", the home of Indiana's major American collector, the site of his basic training in the Air Force, and, coincidentally, one of the cities which played host to his 1978 traveling retrospective.

The Vinalhaven Suite will not be part of the Farnsworth exhibition (there are no prints in the show), but four of the major *Decade* paintings chronicling Indiana's 1960s, which inspired the print series, will be. Indiana is also allowing the Farnsworth to publish a special edition of 125 prints based on his painting, *Decade: Autoportrait, 1969* to help defray the cost of the exhibition. The 1969 work features the first reference to Vinalhaven, including the use of the name Penobscot Bay and the three-linked Odd Fellows symbol.

Indiana's four years on Vinalhaven have been among the busiest in a twenty-year career dating from his first major New York exhibition. One of his most ambitious projects, a series of ten polychromed aluminum numbers, each eight feet high and four feet deep, is currently being fabricated according to his design for installation in the reflecting pool of the Indianapolis Museum of Art. Still, he is yet to produce his first major Maine paintings, which he says will be a series in homage to Marsden Hartley.

"When I get my life back in order," says Indiana, "I have got to do Maine paintings and I want to."

The grandeur of the Maine landscape and the quality of light in Maine have been known to convert even the most ardent nonrepresentational painter to realism, and Indiana confesses he feels the pull. He says he sees his work becoming looser and freer.

"It's very possible I might get back into realism," he allows, "but I'll still be Indiana."

Indiana also confides that he harbors a dream of having his *LOVE* logo carved into the living rock of Vinalhaven. Realistically, however, he doubts that islanders would take kindly to the idea of creating a permanent tourist attraction.

The visual seduction of the island can be irresistible. Throwing open the double doors of his sail-loft studio, Indiana reveals a glorious view of Carvers Harbor—work boats, fish huts, and three mallard ducks.

"This is my winning thing here on the island," he says enthusiastically. "With this view one day I may be painting lobster boats. This is eternal. People will always enjoy this. The nice thing is when an artist is able to see it the way Hartley saw it...and perhaps one day I shall myself."

The view from Robert Indiana's studio reinforces the initial impression one gets from the ferry. The spruce-clad island seems so permanent, anchored to the bedrock, enduring; while the presence of man, the modest homes and working watercraft, seem fragile and transient, as though one great wind or one great wave might wipe the island clean of all human traces.

"One compelling argument for becoming an artist," Robert Indiana is saying, "is that the one thing that survives and endures is Art. That is a tremendous incentive. It makes the struggle worthwhile."

August, 1982

Alan Magee and his Perfect Stones

Alan Magee

"A dazzling New Realist Painter," proclaimed the headline over John Canaday's art review in the December issue of *Saturday Review*. Canaday, for many years *The New York Times*'s leading art critic and a respected art historian, was sounding the trumpet for Alan Magee and the arrival of "new realism." The occasion for the article was Magee's recent sold-out showing at New York's prestigious Staempfli Gallery. To hear Canaday tell it, he had discovered this brilliant new talent, a "newcomer" and "unknown," but his glowing account of Alan Magee's entrance into the inner circle of the art world really says more about John Canaday and the New York art world than it does about Alan Magee and his art.

Alan Magee and his wife, Monica, live in a charming little gambrel-roofed house in Cushing, overlooking a frozen St. George River. Canaday's recognition of Magee's genius merely confirms what many people in the land already knew: the best and most important art in America is not necessarily being created in New York City. New York may still be the administrative capital of the American art scene, but the real work is being done everywhere.

At 33, Alan Magee is a boyish young man with bangs and a full beard. He could easily be mistaken for an art student rather than the successful illustrator and critically acclaimed painter that he is. He is modest in discussing his own talents and generous in explaining how he works and how he achieves the stunning, illusionistic realism in his paintings of beach stones and drawings of his wife Monica's braided hair. And while hardly an overnight success, Magee is one of those rare creative exceptions to the rule who has never really had to face rejection.

Educated at Tyler School of Art and Philadelphia College of Art, Alan Magee ventured to New York in the late '60s and very quickly became a successful illustrator.

"It was easier back then," Magee explains modestly. "You could just walk in and talk to any art director. Nowadays, if they know you're an art student, they'd have you leave your portfolio and maybe, if you're lucky, somebody would look at it."

Magee feels that one of the reasons access was easier only a decade ago was that most publishers were independents. Now they are all parts of conglomerates. He also notes that he entered the field at a time when photography was just giving way to graphic arts in the illustration field.

Most readers, whether they know it or not, have probably seen Magee's illustrations. He did the paperback covers for Yukio Mishima's *Sea of Fertility* tetralogy, Lawrence Durrell's *Alexandria Quartet*, and 45 Agatha Christie mysteries, as well as scores of others.

Magee's illustration style is totally different than his painting style. In his book covers and magazine work he tends to produce slick, surreal designs aimed at immèdiate, eye-catching impact. But, of course, that's the name of the game in commercial work: get the viewer's attention.

"You know they do market studies on every paperback cover," Magee says. "I did one Agatha Christie [*And Then There Were None*, known in England as *Ten Little Indians*] that sold 250,000 copies." On the strength of that success, Magee was commissioned to do 40-odd more. Ordinarily, Magee begins by reading the books he is commissioned to illustrate, but in the case of the Christie mysteries he just couldn't bring himself to plow through them.

"I had friends read them and write synopses for me. Finally, the publisher began providing me with outlines."

Readers will also know Magee's illustrations from the cover of *Time* magazine. He had been doing covers for *New York* magazine, and when the art director for that publication moved to *Time*, he took Magee along with him. He has done six or seven covers for *Time*, but only two have been used. News breaks often preempt planned cover stories, but his covers for "How Gay Is Gay?" (April 23, 1979) and "The Computer Society" (February 20, 1978) made it to the front.

While I was talking to Magee he received a nervously awaited phone call from New York. *Time* had accepted his cover design for a story on San Francisco molecular geneticist Herbert Wayne Boyer.

"They liked it. They really liked it," Magee said with obvious relief after he hung up the phone. I was surprised that he was surprised.

Alan and Monica Magee moved to Maine from Pennsylvania in 1976 to settle in Camden. This past October they moved to the Cushing home, but Magee maintains his painting studio in Camden.

"I've always tried to keep illustrating separate from my painting," he explains. So there is a spatial distance as well as an aesthetic distance between his two pursuits. His critical and financial success with his paintings now means that he could stop illustrating if he so desired, but he has no such plans.

"I kind of like it," he confesses.

It also seems somehow odd that an artist of Magee's caliber, both as an illustrator and a painter, would be appearing on the cover of next month's *Down East* magazine, but, again, Magee feels this says more about the expanding and improving taste of regional publications than it does about his work. He also confides that having lived and worked in Camden had a lot to do with *Down East*'s commissioning a cover.

Magee's paintings of stones, inspired by the beaches at Pemaquid and Owls Head, might easily be called "photo-realism," but Magee is more comfortable with "new realism."

"I don't generally work from photographs," he explains, but his paintings are of such intense, clear and heightened realism that, in reproduction as well as original, they do have a photographic exactness about them.

I got the feeling when I read John Canaday's article that he might have been scouting to fill a weak spot in the super-realism lineup, and even Magee agreed there might be something to that. Chuck Close represents super-realism in the portrait field, and Richard Estes (who summers in Maine) celebrates elaborately reflected urban scenes. Adding Alan Magee to this all-star outfield now means that natural forms are equally represented.

But unlike Close and Estes, who tend to work in mechanical, grid-transfer manners, Magee achieves his illusive realities by much freer means. As he explains himself in his program from the Staempfli show:

"In painting the stones I have gradually developed the view that it is not appropriate or satisfying to realistically copy existing stones. I try to get closer to the elements which fascinate me; the rhythms, flowing patterns and natural marks that give stone forms their wild precision. By using methods of dripping and flowing paint, and by employing a great variety of unusual tools for applying paint, I attempt to restage these natural occurrences on the canvas in order to better experience and present this part of

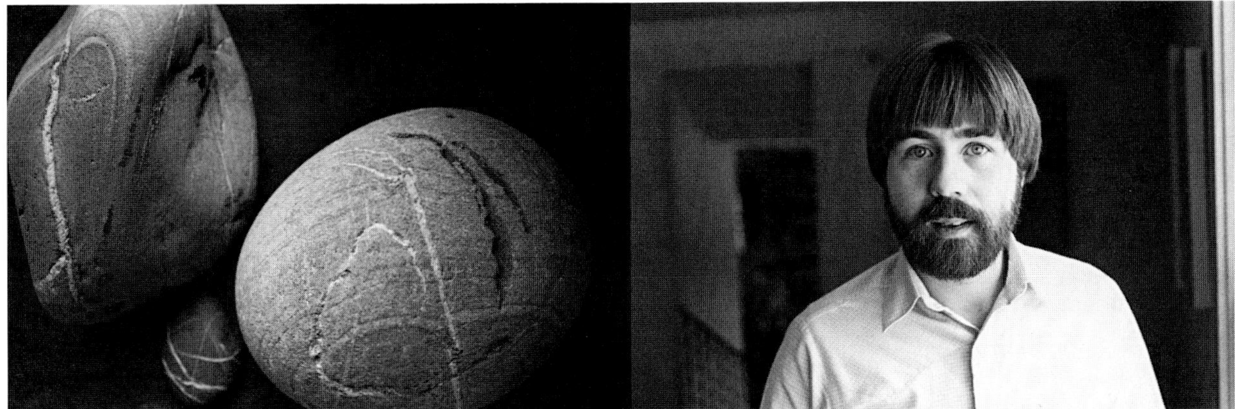

1. *Alan Magee with one of his favorite subjects: a group of stones. Photo by Stephen B. Nichols.*

nature."

Working in acrylics, Magee first roughs out crude forms and then works up specific surfaces and textures through the use of such "unusual tools" as toothbrushes, Saran Wrap and window-cleaning squeegees. It is only in the latter stages of creation that the works take on the highly rendered and refined quality of the finished product. Stippling, spattering, dripping, pouring and flowing paints mean that Magee's stone paintings are not ultra-realistic reproductions of stone arrangements, but painterly renditions of compositions which are entirely transformed.

Nor is it lost on Magee that he is using the very material of stone to produce his stone paintings. Graphite is used in the drawings and mineral pigments in the paintings.

"Red oxide makes excellent rust," he laughs.

John Canaday pointed out that some observers have called Alan Magee a "new Wyeth," but Canaday is quick to dispel the notion in a way which praises Magee and disparages Andrew Wyeth. Magee thinks that it is a shame that critics have such a hard time accepting Wyeth's genius. Wyeth, who is a Cushing neighbor of Magee's (though Magee says he met the celebrated painter only once when he was 15), was an early influence on Magee. A Japanese exhibition poster of Wyeth's work hangs in Magee's home studio, along with posters of Richard Estes and Wayne Thibault. Outside the bathroom hangs a Norman Rockwell reproduction, and Magee grins sheepishly when I notice it. Serious artists aren't supposed to like Norman Rockwell, but Alan Magee has an open and generous appreciation of all manner of art.

"Working so long in illustration, you tend to take a slightly different view of what art can encompass than if you simply stay in a fine art community," he says. "I don't mind doing birthday cards for friends, for example."

It at first seems strange when Magee says that he was inspired in high school toward art by the designs and drawings of customized cars by "Big Daddy" Roth and "Mouse Studios," but when you think about the fresh, illusionistic style of his work now, you begin to understand how a fresh and lively art form, no matter how lowly, might have impressed a shaping mind.

"It was just that [the cars] were such a change from still-life arrangements of two lemons," Magee says. "Of course, now I like the lemons, too."

Indeed, the new directions that his work is taking include a move toward studies and arrangements of isolated vegetable and mechanical forms. Dictated by the new subject matter, Magee is beginning to experiment with oil paints. He finds them more suited to vegetable colors and textures, and this new interest has propelled him toward the super-realist oils of Ralph Goings, famous for his pickup trucks and diners.

Magee never seems more enthusiastic than when discussing how materials and tools work, and when he describes how oils might be used in creating a painting of butternut squash he becomes positively animated.

Looking at Alan Magee's work it is often difficult to remember what you are seeing. His purified realism is so startling that it can be anesthetic. He flashes slides of earlier works on his studio wall and there appears a large stone sitting on a white pedestal. Surely this is a slide of a piece of sculpture. But, no, it is a slide of a painting of a stone on a pedestal. Another slide shows the painting *Stones and Islands*. A stone

on a pedestal set in front of a painting of stone islands. I look around for the painting of the islands in the studio. It's not there.

"That painting only exists in this painting," Magee directed me back to the slide projection. Only with sustained perceptual effort can the mind and eye follow.

"Is it hard to do?" I finally have to ask naively.

"Your first impression is that it must be very hard to do, very technical, but really it's very natural and very easy when everything is working well," Magee insists. Easy for Alan Magee is what he means.

Another direction that Magee's painting is taking is toward larger and more abstracted forms. He shows me a slide of a painting of a large rock marbled with quartz. The foreground is anchored by a band of small stones and pebbles. Then he flicks to a slide which appears to be a detail from the larger rock, but it is an entirely different painting. Simply by restricting his focus he has succeeded in transforming a realistic painting of a stone form into an abstraction based on natural patterns. The quartz formation takes on the look of a Pollock drip painting.

Until recently Magee has preferred to work life-sized for the sake of preserving the illusion, but now he is headed toward enlargements—but not, he insists, to the point of sensationalizing the image.

"Working on a larger-than-life scale just enables me to focus in on detail, like the wrinkled top of a rotting pear, which would be too compressed for much detail if done life-size."

One of the most remarkable recent works is a highly rendered arrangement of two disembodied carburetors. Sitting side by side, one turned toward the other, they convey the nostalgic feeling of a 19th-century portrait. Then Magee shows me a slide of the first carburetor he drew. This lone, exquisite image admits the viewer to the process of creation by tapering off from polished refinement to simple line drawing. It is a bravura performance.

"What I like about the new realism is the human connection," says Magee, "knowing that there is a human being behind the work." Allowing the process of creation to leave its traces provides this humanness.

Despite his successes, Magee has remained admirably resistant to over-inflated estimations of the significance of his work. Referring to his stunning drawings of paint tubes, which he says in his show program "have become personal symbols" along with Monica's braids, Magee relates how others have seen tremendous social and psychological revelations in his spatial arrangements and color selection.

"Obviously, spatial relations are crucial, but I don't know what they mean. I don't want to know."

One of the hallmarks of acceptance in the art world is museum acquisition of an artist's work, and Magee reports that the Los Angeles and San Francisco museums have purchased his work. But there has not yet been enough time, nor are there that many Alan Magee paintings on the market for major museums to have selected. It seems likely that will come next.

But if museums have yet to respond, collectors already have, and Alan Magee's work has another distinction. It has been stolen. Magee's very first stone painting, a watercolor done on Block Island in which he was more inclined to draw details exactly, was stolen from a collector's truck somewhere between Dallas and Nashville. A dubious distinction, but then the art market in times of inflation can become rapaciously bullish. If you have some capital on hand, you can either buy a new Volvo or an Alan Magee painting. I'd have to say that what with oil prices and maintenance, the painting would be the better investment.

Alan Magee is a quiet and likable man. I found it to his everlasting credit that when he was commissioned to do a *Time* cover of J.R. Ewing, he had not yet heard of the insipid *Dallas* character. Fortunately, or unfortunately, *Time* did not use Magee's J.R.

Finally, Alan Magee is quite serious about stones. There is an arrangement of skull-sized stones on his hearth. Individual stones are set about the studio discreetly. There are pebbles in a shallow dish full of water on the kitchen table. And, illusively, the soapdish in the bathroom is full of palm-size stones. The top stone is actually the soap.

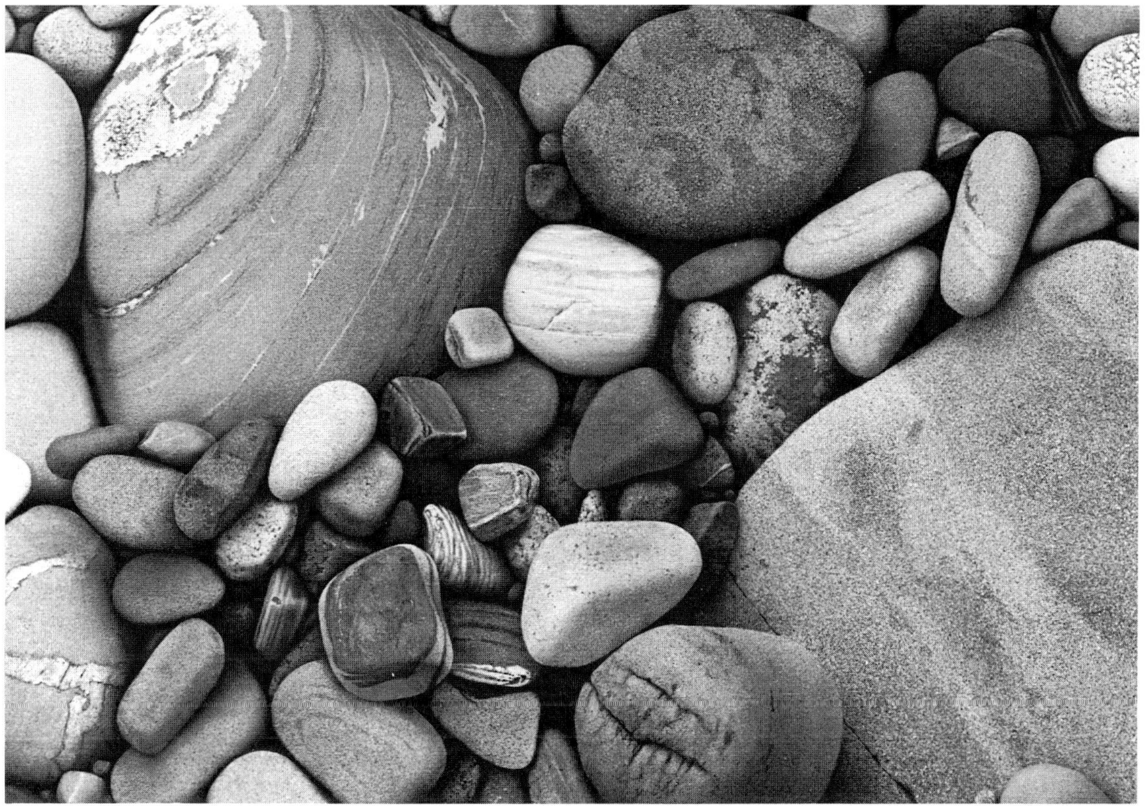

2. *Alan Magee,* Stones VI, *1979. Acrylic on canvas. Courtesy of the artist.*

The Staempfli program again:

"The natural arrangement of the smooth rounded shapes and subdued colors which I find on the beach possess an arbitrary perfection; there is something monumental and profound about them."

So, then, would Alan Magee ever consider using the actual stones in his art? Say as elements of construction or to sculpt?

"Oh no," he rejects the suggestion. "They're really perfect as they are."

"Arbitrary perfection." One might say the same of Alan Magee's paintings.

February 6, 1981

A Belief in the Present

Berenice Abbott

No, she is not working at the moment. Not now.

"It's just a question of energy," she says. "There's no limit to the things I'd like to do. It's purely and entirely energy. With energy there would be a lot of projects."

Berenice Abbott is clearly tired as she sits talking in her snug little cabin on the quiet shores of Lake Hebron. She has not been well this past year, but then her health has never been robust. Financial worries have been wearing her down, but then she has never really been free of the wolf at the door. Still, at 86, Berenice Abbott continues to manifest the fierce independence of spirit that helped make her one of the most important photographers of the 20th century.

Perhaps ironically, Berenice Abbott does not like to be photographed herself. She watches the photographer warily as she talks. The look in her eyes is not the nervous look of the hunted, however; it is the defiant look of the predator at bay, the hunter become prey. Perhaps she does not like to be photographed because she, better than anyone, knows what the camera sees.

It cannot help but see her age. It sees a white-haired woman, but there is a residual boyishness about Berenice Abbott that would keep all but complete fools from calling her an old lady. She looks today the way one imagines Olympic marathoner Joan Benoit will look at 86—small, tired, plucky, proud, American.

What the camera cannot see is that Berenice Abbott is still the same woman who photographed the intellectual communities of Paris and New York in the 1920s, the same woman who chronicled for all times the transformation of New York City from urban America to international metropolis in the 1930s, the same woman who saved French master photographer Eugene Atget from obscurity, who pioneered the art of scientific photography, who even in the 1960s was busy documenting the rural life of her adopted state of Maine, the same woman.

What the camera cannot see are Berenice Abbott's accomplishments, which Hank O'Neal, in his text for *Berenice Abbott, American Photographer* (McGraw-Hill, 1982), called "wider ranging than anyone else's in the history of American photography." What the camera cannot see is, in the words of art critic John Canaday, "that Berenice Abbott is one of an eminent group who can properly be called classicists, in the sense of the word that connotes adherence to traditionally authoritative standards of form, balance and restraint, standards that she herself took part in establishing."

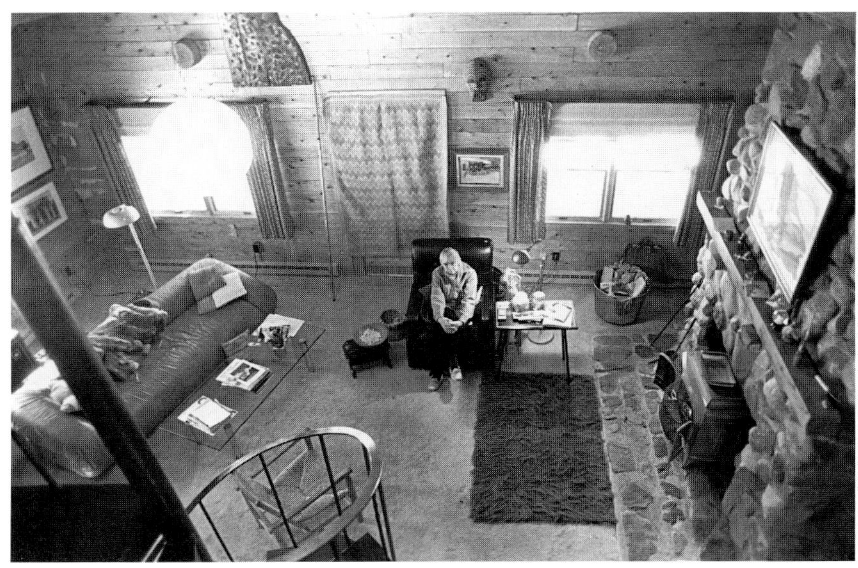

1. *Berenice Abbott seated in her cabin on the quiet shores of Lake Hebron. Photo by Christopher Ayres.*

Berenice Abbott was born in Springfield, Ohio, on July 17, 1898. She attended Ohio State University briefly, but quickly became disenchanted with provincial academic life. In 1918, therefore, she traveled to New York with the idea of becoming a journalist. There she fell in with the bohemian artists and nonconformists of Greenwich Village, people like poet Edna St. Vincent Millay, artist Marcel Duchamp, writer Djuna Barnes, critic Malcolm Cowley, and most importantly, photographer Man Ray. Her interest turned from journalism to sculpture.

In 1921, disenchanted with America, she moved with the Lost Generation to Paris.

"The truth of the matter is," she says, "you have to take terrible chances in life. At the time I went to Europe I was in a desperate situation. I was a very poor girl and I knew I had to make it on my own. I bought a one-way ticket to Paris. I figured I might as well starve there as starve here. I shudder when I think of it now...but I'm glad I went."

For two years Abbott struggled in Paris as an artist and model. But one of the major turning points in her professional life was taking a job as assistant to her old friend Man Ray. Though best known today for his "Rayograph" photograms, at the time Man Ray had a growing portrait business in Paris and was troubled with know-it-all assistants. He wanted someone to assist him who knew absolutely nothing about photography and Berenice Abbott filled the bill.

"I never expected to learn photography and go out and become a photographer," says Abbott. "But I just took to printing naturally. It was like a miracle. [Man Ray] was amazed. I was surprised. I think if I had realized how much money you need to really to do it, I'd never have been a photographer. I never had the lenses I needed."

From Man Ray's darkroom, Berenice Abbott gradually emerged into the light. She began taking portraits of her own. Her association with Man Ray ended when art patroness-collector Peggy Guggenheim came to his studio and requested a sitting with Abbott. By 1926, Abbott was ready for her first solo exhibition, a show which included portraits of James Joyce, Jean Cocteau, Andre Gide, Djuna Barnes, and bookseller Sylvia Beach.

Between 1926 and 1931, Abbott devoted herself primarily to portrait photography both in Paris and New York. These portraits are straightforward formal and casual poses, strong on composition yet always deferring to personality. With Abbott, the subject always comes first. It is a tenet of her artistic faith. Edna St. Vincent Millay manfully emerges from the blackness dressed in a suit and tie, worried or distracted by something invisible beyond the frame. Her fragility and fearfulness contrast as markedly with her attire as her illuminated figure contrasts with the black space around it. There is Abbott's famous photograph of James Joyce slumped in a chair, his face expressionless, his eyes all but glazed, as though overcome by the emptiness of a world he overfilled with fiction.

But the strongest, most stark portrait of all is the ghostly gray evocation of the aging photog-

rapher Eugene Atget, a topcoated spectre who seems to be slipping into the past even as he is captured in the fleeting here and now. Abbott first saw the work of Atget while working for Man Ray. Atget's simple, direct approach to photography and his faithfulness to his subject—30 years of quietly chronicling Paris and environs—would remain the primary influences on Abbott's own work.

In 1928, Abbott acquired the some 1,500 glass plates and 8,000 prints that constituted Atget's life work and began the long campaign to bring his work to the public. *A Vision of Paris*, pairing Atget's images with Marcel Proust's prose, appeared in 1963. *The World of Atget*, with text by Abbott, was finally published in 1964. And in 1968, the Museum of Modern Art purchased the Atget Collection.

In 1929, Abbott returned to America and began her 10-year campaign to chronicle the visual intensity and vital humanity of New York City. Portraiture was left behind. For one thing, she could not afford a skylit studio. For another, Abbott was obsessed by the city.

"To photograph New York City," Abbott wrote in her 1935 grant application to the Federal Art Project, "means to seek to catch in the sensitive and delicate photographic emulsion the spirit of the metropolis, while remaining true to its essential fact, its hurrying tempo, its congested streets, the past jostling the present."

The Museum of the City of New York exhibited 110 of Abbott's New York prints in 1937, and her book *Changing New York* was published in 1939. The works in this monumental New York series have become classics of modern photography, Abbott's selective eye unfailingly picking out jarring views, pictures too full, dizzying, sometimes disorienting, but ultimately clear. The New York pictures are often witty—a giant revolver (advertising a gunsmith) pointing at the police station—but their real subject is change. Her view of the art deco Greyhound bus terminal smack in front of McKim, Meade & White's doomed classical Penn Station portrays one age brashly supplanting another.

With *Changing New York*, Berenice Abbott's reputation was established, and it was and is a reputation founded on a rock-hard philosophy of photographic realism.

"The greatest influence obscuring the entire field of photography," she wrote in the important 1951 essay "It Has To Walk Alone," "has, in my opinion, been pictorialism. But first let me define it: pictorialism means chiefly the making of pleasant, pretty, artificial pictures in the superficial spirit of certain minor painters. What is more, the imitators of these superficial qualities are not aware of the true values for which painting strives. Photography can never grow up if it imitates some other medium. It has to walk alone; it has to be itself."

Chief among the "arty" photographers imitating painting was, in Abbott's opinion, Alfred Stieglitz. Her own sympathies lay with "straight" and documentary photographers like Nadar, Atget, Lewis Hine, Walker Evans, Ansel Adams, Margaret Bourke-White, and Lisette Model.

"You have to have a philosophy in back of your photographs," Abbott says today, "what's important, what's significant and what isn't. I'm a realist. I believe in the present."

In 1941, Abbott published *A Guide to Better Photography*. In 1949, she published *Greenwich Village Today and Yesterday*. And during 1953-54 she undertook to photograph U.S. Route One from Key West, Florida, to Fort Kent, Maine, but by 1956 gave up on trying to get the Route One pictures (still among her least-known works) published. But after *Changing New York* in 1939, Abbott's most persistent photographic efforts were in the field of science.

"I sort of have to have a subject," she says. "I spent 20 years trying to get into science work. By the time I got in I was getting old and I was afraid they wouldn't take me. But I had three years of, to me, very exciting work. Oh, I could have done so many things in science."

Abbott's highly innovative science photographs—multiple exposures of bouncing and revolving balls, the patterns of iron filings in magnetic fields, the structure of soap bubbles—illustrated principles of physical science, but also maintained their integrity as strong photographic compositions. Many were poorly reproduced in the 1960 textbook *Physics*. Throughout the 1960s they continued to appear in science books by E.G. Valens.

Abbott's work with scientific photography also led, indirectly, to her settling in Maine. She had visited the state in the mid-1950s while documenting Route One. Then, while working at Harvard University, she met Margaret Bennett, a woman from Guilford. Through Bennett she discovered that an old home (a circa 1810 stagecoach inn) in Blanchard was for sale "dirt cheap." Abbott purchased the old inn on a whim in 1956. Over the next 10 years she gradually made improvements to the Maine house and by 1966, Abbott's move to Maine was complete.

"I just sort of fell in love with Maine," says Abbott, who has since moved to her log cabin four miles away and is presently trying to sell the big Blanchard village home. "It was the first place I ever wanted to live outside the city."

The move to Maine was partly motivated by health considerations. In 1962 Abbott had part of a lung removed, and the Maine environment seemed healthier than the closed confines of New York.

"I think it was the air," says Abbott. "I got out of Manhattan and the darkroom...the dust and dirt and airlessness. Here the air is like champagne, only better."

In 1968, Abbott's love affair with rural Maine resulted in *A Portrait of Maine*. And if the Maine pictures lack the visual drama of *Changing New York*, it may be due in part to the fact that Abbott insisted on remaining true to her subject—the drab, often colorless life of small-town Maine in transition. Her images of working Maine are anti-heroic, realistic, at odds with the romanticized images of Maine as Vacationland paradise. Indeed, nature photography is one of the few areas that Abbott has never fully explored.

"I never had the courage to tackle nature," she says. "I don't know anyone who's ever done it outside of making pretty pictures. It's so complicated."

Yet one of the unrealized projects the photographer would undertake given sufficient energy is an exploration of "the mechanics of nature"—principles of science as revealed in nature.

Abbott has also steered largely clear of color photography.

"I don't really care for color photography," she says. "I had a couple of jobs where I had to do color photography commercially and they came out all right, but I don't like it. Color photographs tend to become fussy and crowded. The color isn't always very good. There's too much color and too little space."

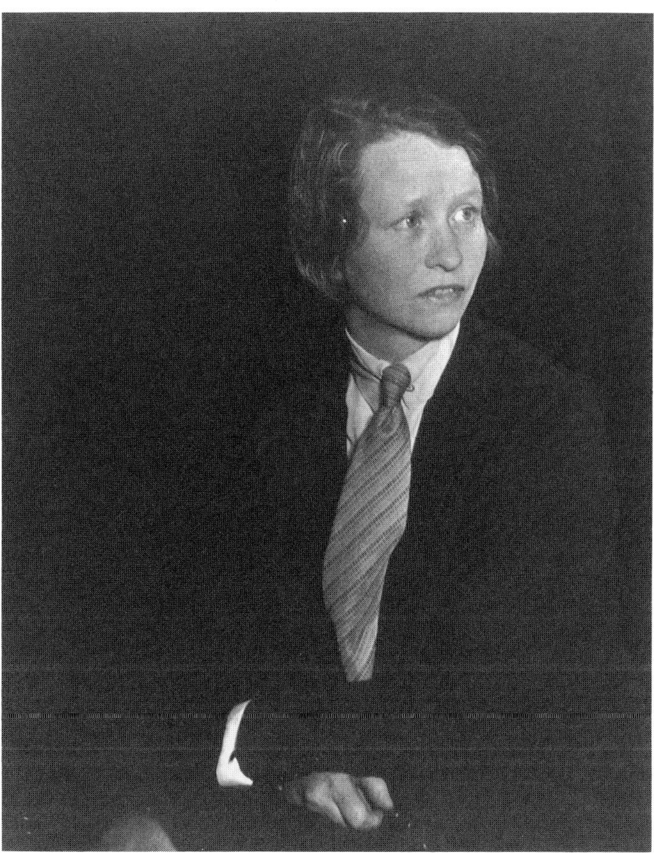

2. *Berenice Abbott,* Edna St. Vincent Millay. *Photograph. Courtesy of Berenice Abbott/ Commerce Graphics, Ltd, Inc.*

Her last project before her recent spate of ill health and low energy concentrated on the disappearance of the traditional country store.

"I did some," she says, "but I didn't like them. I realized I didn't get through to what I wanted. That's the first time that ever happened to me. It's very sad to see the country stores go."

But if Berenice Abbott never takes another photograph, her position in the history of photography is secure. She has made her mark as an independent eye, and as an independent woman she has been an inspiration to the present generation of women artists. And make no mistake about it, being a woman was a definite handicap in her career.

"Oh, yes," Abbott says, "I'd never get certain jobs. I would love to have done the Olympic Games, but they wouldn't have dreamed of sending a woman over. I'd never get the same money [as a male photographer]. I'd be called in on tough jobs others couldn't do and I'd get

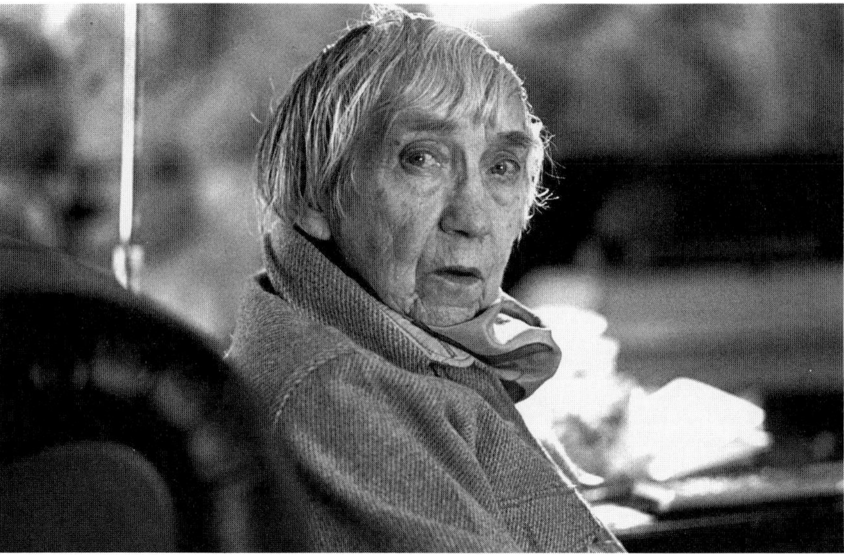

3. *Berenice Abbott in Maine. Photo by Christopher Ayres.*

paid half."

Her entry into the male-dominated field of science was hampered because she was a woman and when she came to Maine she was unable to get a bank loan because she was a woman, but Abbott managed to overcome this handicap on her own.

"I was surprised," she says, "when all the feminist movements started. I was amazed really. It didn't exist when I was functioning. I was always a liberated woman. I never understood what the big thing was. Self-confidence? Why didn't they have self-confidence? But until there is a real equality of opportunity, I don't think we'll really be civilized."

But today Berenice Abbott has other worries. For one thing, she has never made the kind of money one might expect a world-famous photographer to make.

"When I worked," she explains, "photography wasn't considered anything. It didn't come alive until the 1960s as far as getting a price for it."

Recently, Abbott sold her entire collection to Parasol Press in New York, but the retirement nest egg she had planned on seems to have disappeared.

"The federal income tax is absolutely ruining me," she complains. "They've taken over half. I've had a whole year of agony over it."

She talks only half-humorously of learning to fish the lake in order to eat. As she sits in her cabin surrounded by nibbles—containers of popcorn, pistachios, sunflower seeds—Berenice Abbott is tired, worried, unable to work, pessimistic about world affairs. And she has the realist's curse. She cannot be content to rest on her laurels. (There is not a Berenice Abbott photograph in sight.) What's important is now.

"I've accomplished about 1/20th of what I could have," she insists. "I'm no success...far from it. I got a little bit through, that's all."

March 29, 1985

Historian with a Camera

Todd Webb

There are photographers in Maine more famous...Berenice Abbott and Eliot Porter come first to mind, but if Todd Webb is not so well-known it is not because he lacks for accomplishments or because his work does not measure up. Todd Webb is a world-class photographer. And if his name is not a household word, it may just be, as one colleague suggests, that Todd Webb is simply not pushy enough. Todd Webb is a quiet man with a lucid eye, but over the past 40 years he has quietly established an enduring place for himself and his work in the history of photography.

Todd Webb was born in Detroit, Michigan, in 1905, the son of a doctor who turned to pharmacy because he could not stand the sight of blood. He came late to photography, having first engaged in a meteoric career as a stock broker. It was a pretty wild life for a young man in the bull market of the 1920s.

"When I was 23," says Webb, "I was making $100,000 a year." But unless one thinks him a crass braggard, he quickly adds, "Of course it was really all on paper."

When the stock market crashed in 1929, Webb says, "I was relieved. I lost everything I had and went prospecting for gold in California." Not aggressive by nature anyway, Webb thinks that his early financial success may have further tempered his appetite for fame and fortune. "I had my money splurge early," he says. "I think that really affected me. I've never really had any great urge since to get ahead."

From 1930 to 1933, Webb prospected for gold in the California deserts, averaging about 50 cents a day selling his gold finds to dentists for fillings. For a time he found steadier work with the U.S. Forestry Service, but that job ended in 1933 when the New Deal inaugurated the Civilian Conservation Corps. Webb then returned to his native Detroit where he found work with Chrysler Motors.

At work Webb eventually joined the Chrysler Camera Club along with his great friend, Harry Callahan, today one of America's foremost photographers. Both men also became active in the Photo Guild of Detroit, an involvement that would eventually prove crucial in their careers.

"What got me into photography," says Webb, "there was a vogue in the 1930s of people going into strange places and making films and then coming back and lecturing about them. Richard Haliburton was probably the best known. Well, I'd been to a few of these lectures and I thought that was kind of what I wanted to do."

"We were both just nuts about photography when we got started," says Harry Callahan. "We talked about it all the time and we did it all the time. At two in the morning, if Todd got excited about something, he'd call up and we'd talk."

In 1941, Ansel Adams, the grand master of American photography, came to Detroit to teach a 10-day workshop, and both Webb and Callahan attended.

"That was the real beginning for both Callahan and myself," says Webb.

"Ansel Adams hit me quicker than he did Todd, I think," says Callahan. "For me it was a totally freeing experience. When he came, everything about it was just right. I was just ripe for him."

In the summer of 1942, still inspired by Adams' example and teachings, Webb decided to head for Rocky Mountain National Park in Colorado to photograph mountains. Harry Callahan and his wife, Eleanor, went along for the ride.

"Todd and I were friends so I just went along," says Callahan of the western trip. "The photographs that Ansel had made of close-ups of plants I figured I could photograph anywhere. I had no need for spectacular mountains, but as it turned out, I wasn't able to photograph anything at all."

Todd Webb, however, must have photographed mountains until his eyes popped out of his head. After the Callahans left for New York, Webb stayed on alone to shoot more mountains. When he finally decided to return, he drove straight through and headed directly to the darkroom when he got home. It was late at night and extremely hot, Todd recalls, but he couldn't wait to see the visions he had captured. As the first prints emerged from the soup, he exclaimed to himself, "Oh boy, look at those snow-capped peaks." Then another, "Oh boy, look at those snow-capped peaks." And another. And another.

"Pretty soon," says Todd, "I was so sick of snow-capped peaks that I threw most of the pictures away. I was disgusted with myself for trying to be Ansel Adams. It was right then that I learned that it's not where or what you photograph, it's what comes out of you that counts."

For the next three months, Webb restricted himself to photographing his own house and yard, just to make sure the lesson took.

The lesson Webb learned from his Ansel Adams overdose was "be yourself." Today, it is easy to see how that lesson infused Webb's work with his own personality...for it is his personality, more than anything else, that distinguishes his work.

Todd Webb is a gentle man, modest, unassuming, even shy at times. His wife, Lucille, is bright, quick, elfin, and sharp when need be. She provides the snap in their marriage. For the past five years the Webbs have lived in an old house in Bath surrounded by Todd's photographs...photographs taken all over the world from bases in places like New York, Paris, and Santa Fe. The Webbs have lived and traveled the world, but Todd, at least, has somehow managed to escape becoming worldly.

"Todd is such a gentle person," says photographer Juris Ubans of the University of Southern Maine. Ubans exhibited Webb's work in Gorham in the fall of 1980. "He has such a great sense of humor, but he's reticent, shy really. I think his photographs are like that too...not pushy."

From 1942 to 1945 Webb served as a Navy photographer in New Guinea and the Philippines. While in the South Pacific he corresponded regularly with Alfred Stieglitz, the father of modern photography. Webb had met Stieglitz in New York shortly after joining the Navy. When he was discharged in 1945, Webb naturally gravitated to New York and to Stieglitz. Soon he was wandering the streets of Manhattan looking for pictures to make.

"Webb," said the aging Stieglitz, "when it rains, why don't you come in and talk to me."

Artist Georgia O'Keeffe, Stieglitz's widow, once told Lucille Webb that Todd reminded the master of himself as a young man photographing the streets of New York.

In New York, Webb began photographing doorways, lamps, bridges, streetcars, church fronts, almost anything except people. "Todd Webb is a photographer of places—places shaped by the lives of men," Peter Pollack writes in his monumental *The Picture History of Photography*. But men and women rarely appear in Webb's work.

"Todd has always been sensitive about people

asking why aren't there any people in your photographs," says Harry Callahan. "But Todd would take a picture of something like brooms leaning up against a wall and say, 'Can't you see the people sweeping with those brooms?' He tries to make you feel the people without there being people in the photograph. He gives evidence of people. His photographs are taken when the body is still warm."

Others who know Todd say that he just would never be comfortable sticking a camera in someone's face. Just as he does not intrude on his pictures, he does not intrude upon his subjects. His own explanation of his depopulated pictures is even more to the point.

"When I started working in New York I only had a 5 x 7 view camera. I love people, but I couldn't photograph people with the big machine, so I got into doorways, signs, symbols of people. I try to make photographs of people without any people in them."

Through Alfred Stieglitz, Webb's work came to the attention of the Museum of the City of New York. In September, 1946, at the age of 41, Webb had his first exhibition—165 of his New York pictures were shown at the museum. The show was not only a critical success, it also launched Webb's career.

First, *Fortune* magazine sent a telegram (Webb had no phone) asking Webb to photograph the traffic congestion in the city. Then Roy Stryker sent a telegram with an offer of more work.

During the Depression, Roy Stryker had become the director of the Farm Security Administration photography project, which had employed photographers like Ben Shahn, Dorothea Lange, Gordon Parks, and Walker Evans to chronicle poverty in America. But in 1946, Stryker was in the midst of running the Esso Public Service File for Standard Oil of New Jersey. The photography file was meant to improve Esso's public image, and between 1943 and 1950, Stryker spent more than $1 million and employed a dozen photographers making 67,000 black and white photographs and 1,000 color slides of American life. In May, 1983, 200 of these photographs were the subject of a show entitled *Roy Stryker: USA, 1943-50* at the International Center of Photography in New York.

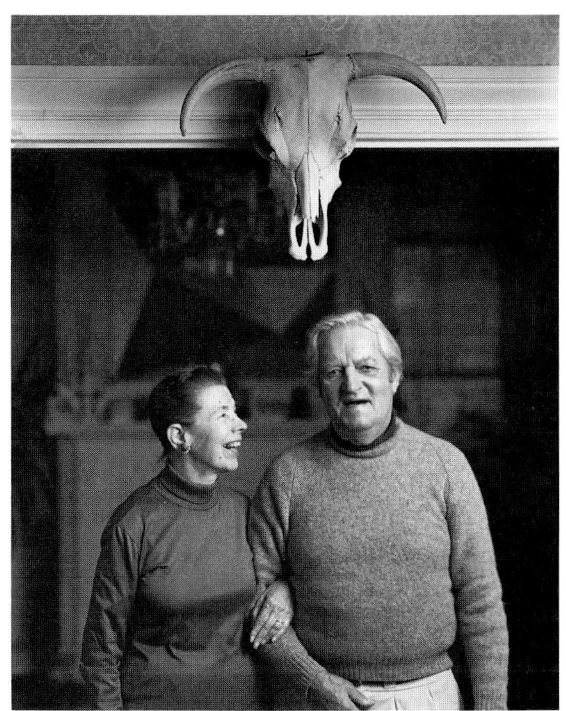

1. *Lucille and Todd Webb beneath a skull which was a present from their friend Georgia O'Keeffe. Photo by Stephen B. Nichols.*

Stryker kept Webb busy for a few more years with assignments like the opening of the Portland-to-Montreal pipeline in 1947 and the filming of Robert Flaherty's *Louisiana Story*.

In 1948, Webb spent several months roaming the English countryside photographing for a New York agency. Then, in 1949, he was sent to Paris where he fell in love...with a city and a woman. Todd and Lucille met in Paris in April, 1949, and were married in the 14th Arrondisement in September, 1949. From 1949 to 1952, they lived in Paris while Todd worked on assignment for picture magazines documenting the effects of the Marshall Plan and the rebuilding of Europe.

When the Webbs returned to New York in 1953, Todd found that he was out of touch with the job market and had difficulty getting assignments.

"That's when I went on my history binge," Todd explains.

In 1955 and 1956, Webb received back-to-back Guggenheim grants to enable him to undertake a project to document the overland pioneer trails west. Using old pioneer diaries, he followed the trails west on foot, hitchhiking, and finally on a motorscooter. These experiences and the photographs Webb took along the way became the basis of two books, *Gold Strikes and Ghost Towns* (1961) and *The Gold Rush Trail and the Road to Oregon* (1962).

The Guggenheim projects established a major theme in Webb's work.

"I think Todd is basically a historian," says Lucille Webb. "He sees things he thinks will disappear and he makes a record of them."

The eminent photography historian Beaumont Newhall, writing in the preface to a small catalog of Webb's photographs published by the Amon Carter Museum in Fort Worth, Texas, seconds Lucille's opinion and amplifies it.

"Todd is an historian with a camera," Newhall writes. "...He has been classified as a documentary photographer, but to me this is not accurate, although his photographs are undeniably documents. The documentary photographer is more sociologist than historian: he seeks with his camera to point out needs for improving social conditions. Todd records what moves him, what fascinates him; he photographs that which defines the character of a place."

From 1956 to 1960, Webb was contracted to photograph the United Nations General Assembly and also documented the work of U.N. organizations like the World Health Organization. In 1958, he spent eight months photographing the emerging African nations south of the Sahara Desert.

In 1961, the Webbs, who had often spent vacations visiting with Georgia O'Keeffe in New Mexico, moved from New York to Santa Fe. They remained in Santa Fe for 10 years, during which time Todd wrote his two Guggenheim books and did the architectural photography which became two other books, *Texas Homes of the 19th Century* (1965) and *Texas Public Buildings of the 19th Century* (1974). In Santa Fe, Lucille operated a bookstore for 10 years.

Ten years in the Southwest seemed enough.

"We'd gotten all the juice out of it," says Lucille.

"I wear places out photographing them," adds Todd.

In 1971, the Webbs sold home and business and took up residence in an 11th-century house in Provence, France. In 1974, their wanderlust took them to Bath, England, where they lived for a year. While in England, Lucille became ill and the Webbs decided to return to the United States. They wanted to be somewhere close to New York City, but not too close. Friends from New York had moved to Portland, and sent them Chamber of Commerce brochures advertising the liveability of the city...and the excellent health care facilities.

In August, 1975, the Webbs moved to Portland, coming to Bath five years ago after their Portland apartment was sold.

"It's lucky for us we're as old as we are," says Todd. "Otherwise, we'd be about to leave Maine now."

The Webbs are by no means settled in, however. In 1979, Todd was awarded a National Endowment for the Arts grant which allowed them to travel to Ireland, Spain, and Portugal. And if Lucille hadn't injured a hip, the Webbs would have undertaken a trip to Italy this year. And though a cataract operation somewhat curtailed Todd's photographing in 1983, he has been busy printing and making plans for several projects he cannot discuss yet.

Dealing with Todd Webb's work in words puts one on thin ice. He refuses to intellectualize something that is essentially a visual experience. Harry Callahan shares this nonverbal approach to photography.

"I think [Todd's] photographs, or at least the ones he has done for himself outside of commercial assignments, are strictly intuitive," says Callahan. "I don't think you can really relate some fabulous intellectual business to it."

For instance, in *The Art of Photography: Image and Illusion*, author Gene Markowski reproduces Webb's 1946 photograph, *First Spiritualist Physic Science Church, Harlem*, a straightforward picture of a storefront church, and analyzes it in terms of how Webb has flattened the picture plane. In response to this kind of close analysis, Todd says, "I can't tell you what I was thinking about when I took that photograph, but he can."

Webb says he fears that too many of the young people coming out of photography schools today are talkers rather than photographers. His own approach to his art is simple and direct.

"Oh, I just have to photograph," Webb says. "When I go out I have no ideas in mind. I go out and see what moves me. I don't have to have a plan to photograph and I don't have to

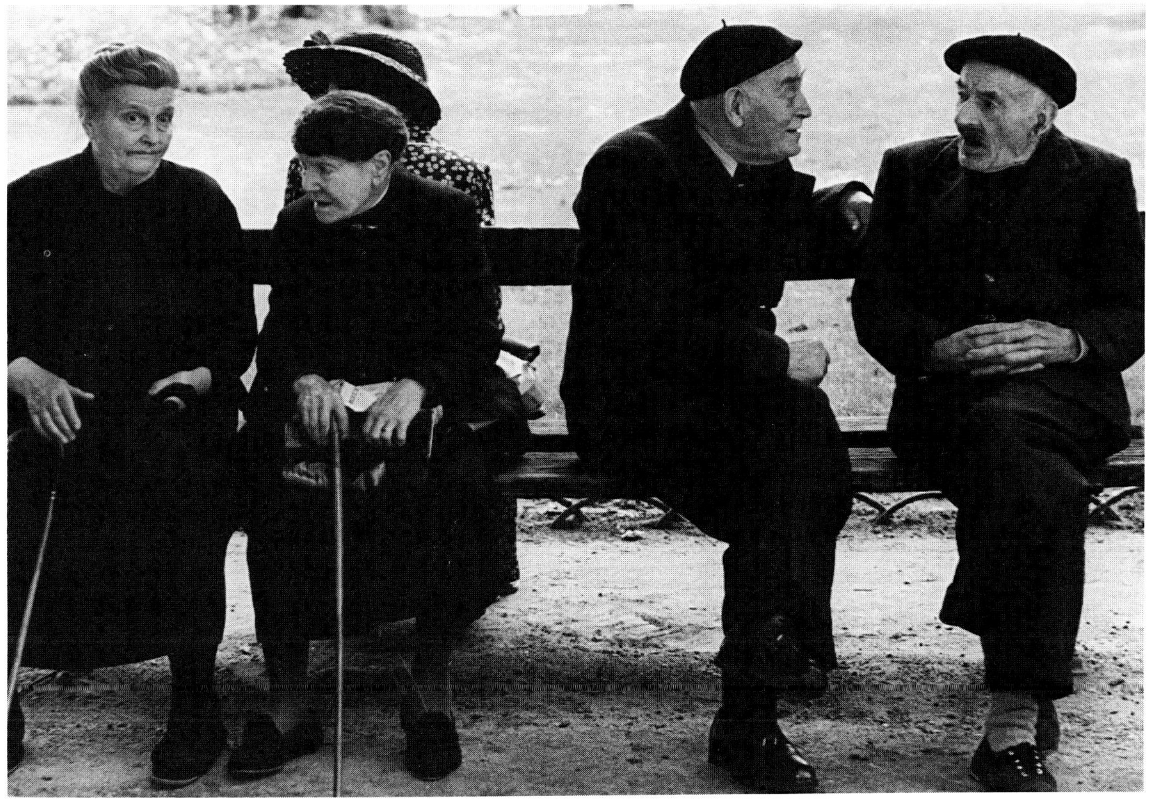

2. *Todd Webb,* Luxembourg Gardens, Paris, *1949. Photograph. Courtesy of the artist.*

have anything to say. I'm not much of a cause guy. I just like to go out and see."

Rose Marasco, a photographer who teaches at both the Portland School of Art and the University of Southern Maine, studied privately with Webb a few years ago as part of a master's degree program. Marasco values Webb's walk-around-and-see-where-your-eye-leads-you approach to photography. Though her own work is as difficult, manipulated, and experimental as Webb's is simple, pure, and classical, Marasco believes Webb's approach keeps one open to the world. She, like many young photographers in the state, has been inspired by Webb's work and example.

"A good teacher," says Rose Marasco, "provokes a lot of questions and provides examples. Todd's joy in doing it...the very basic desire to keep making photographs...excites me. To see an artist in his later years still growing and working hard inspires me."

For himself, Webb finds inspiration not only in recording the world around him, but also in the work of photographers he values.

"Walker Evans is my favorite photographer," Todd says with very little hesitation. "He's my prince."

"He's my second favorite photographer," says Lucille with even less hesitation.

January 6, 1984

The Father of Color Photography

Eliot Porter

Although Eliot Porter gave up medical research almost 50 years ago to pursue photography, his manner and bearing are such that it would be easy to call him Dr. Porter. At 86, he still possesses the natural nobility of a bright schoolboy. He is handsome, fastidious, obviously well-born, well-bred, and well-educated—lightly patrician. A small, dry man with short, pewter hair and gold-rimmed spectacles, he walks cautiously, aided by a cane, across the gravel drive between his home and his studio. It is a clear, mild winter day in rural Tesuque, the small town just north of Santa Fe where Porter has lived since moving to New Mexico in 1946. Tall cottonwoods and Chinese elms sway gently above the adobe compound. The interior of the studio is spacious, cool, airy, and organized, as much the workplace of a scientist as that of an artist.

Given the vitality of the man and the volume of his work, it comes as something of a surprise when Porter says, "I'm not doing any photography now. I've given away all my cameras." Age? No, illness. "I can't photograph anymore," he explains. "I have ALS."

As he talks, Porter folds his hands in his lap to still the tremblings of amyotrophic lateral sclerosis, the nerve disorder (popularly known as Lou Gehrig's disease) which has curtailed his brilliant career. But while he is no longer making photography, Eliot Porter's *oeuvre* continues to grow as a lifetime of images issues forth from his Tesuque archive in the form of portfolios, books, and exhibitions. From where he sits, Porter surveys an entire wall of well-ordered, carefully labeled folio boxes, each containing perhaps 40 photographs.

From his library of some 6,000 prints, Martha Sandweiss of the Amon Carter Museum in Fort Worth and Eleanor Morris Caponigro, designer of many of Porter's photographic books, have selected 128 prints for inclusion in *Eliot Porter*, a retrospective exhibition celebrating and summarizing Porter's contributions to the history of photography. To accomplish this daunting task, the two women hired a hall in Santa Fe and pored over Porter's life's work until they had a representative sampling of images spanning 50 years, from a 1936 black and white New Hampshire landscape to a 1985 color print of graffiti in Macao.

"I went down and watched once or twice," says Porter of the selection process, "but they didn't care for that much. They wanted to be left alone."

The *Eliot Porter* photographs include pictures taken all over the globe, from New England to New Mexico, Iceland to Antarctica, but the

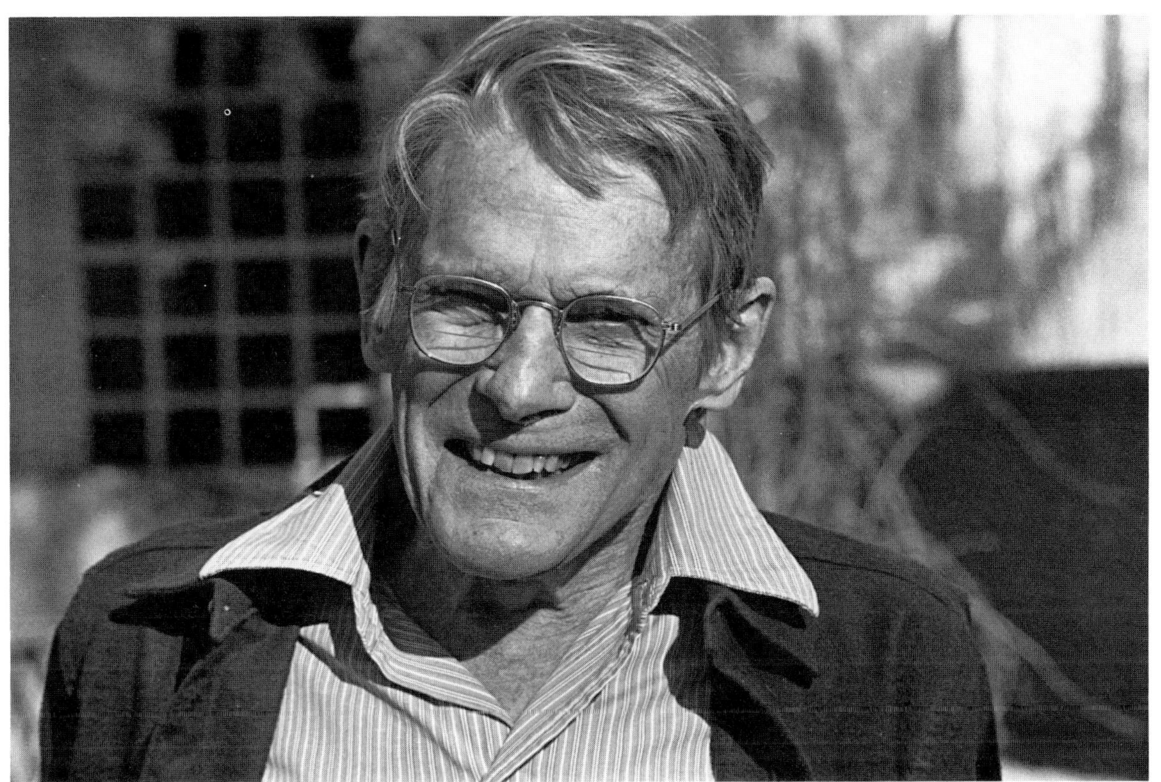

1. *Eliot Porter, the father of color photography. Photo by Christopher Ayres.*

location most favored in the exhibition (28 prints) is Maine, the Maine coast in particular, and even more specifically Great Spruce Head Island in Penobscot Bay. The Porter family has owned Great Spruce Head since 1912, and Eliot Porter summered there from the time he was 11 until two years ago. Happily, the Bowdoin College Museum of Art, which stepped in when the Portland Museum of Art was unable to take the show, will host *Eliot Porter* (April 15 to June 5), thus affording Maine viewers an opportunity to assess and enjoy the work of one of the state's most distinguished summer residents and one of the country's most distinguished photographers.

Eliot Porter is a pivotal figure in the development of modern photography. Janet Russek and David Scheinbaum, Porter's dealers in Santa Fe, refer to him as "the father of color photography." For while color photography had been around in one form of another for almost a century before Eliot Porter took it up, he was the first major photographer to concentrate on color photography, as John Szarkowski, head of the department of photography at the Museum of Modern Art, explains.

"I think one might say," says Szarkowski, "that Eliot Porter was the first photographer of high ambition—artistic ambition—who regarded his photography in color to be more important than what he'd done in black and white...and that's not an uninteresting fact. If you applied the old 'burning house' test of freshman philosophy—if your house were on fire, what would you save?—to all of the photographers of his generation, Eliot is the only one who would have saved his transparencies. Eliot was really a pioneer in that he didn't consider color to be a second-class citizen."

Until well into the 1960s, black and white photography reigned in the world of art photography with an air of classical orthodoxy. Serious photographs were black and white photographs. The photographers of Porter's generation—great artists such as Berenice Abbott, Ansel Adams, Walker Evans, Aaron Siskind, Paul Strand, Minor White, Todd Webb, and Edward Weston—all did their most important work in black and white. Ansel Adams, in fact, was actively opposed to color photography, as Eliot Porter discovered firsthand in 1961 when he and other members of the Sierra Club were invited to Adams' California home. The occasion was a celebration of the Sierra Club's decision to publish Porter's first book, the now-classic *In Wildness Is the Preservation of the World*, in which Porter's color photographs were paired with excerpts from Thoreau's journals.

As Porter writes in the text of *Eliot Porter*,

when he unpacked his photographs, Adams "would not look at them and left the room. He had a strong aversion to color photography, maintaining that color had no legitimate place in the art of photography, and that it degraded the medium. Amplifying his views later, he explained that color photography was too literal to be an art form, that it was not possible to practice it interpretively, and therefore that it was not creative, whereas the interpretive possibilities of black and white were unlimited."

Great artists often suffer such defensive myopia as a condition of genius, but toward the end of his life, Adams apparently found room in the pantheon of photography for color. In one of the last interviews he did shortly before his death in 1984, for instance, Adams named Eliot Porter (along with younger color photographers Joel Meyerowitz and Mary Ellen Marks) as one of the contemporary photographers he admired most.

Porter's own views on the black-and-white-versus-color debate are situational.

"Some subjects," he says, "are better in black and white, but close-ups of nature—subjects like things in the woods, the forest floor, lichen—are almost meaningless in black and white. Many kinds of landscapes, though, are better in black and white. I think Ansel Adams' black and white landscapes, for example, are incomparable."

Porter does, however, maintain something of a purist line, preferring so-called "straight" photography to manipulated photographs.

"A lot of mixed media, while I'm not saying I dislike it, I don't like the way it's practiced in some cases. I don't like contrived photography or hand-painted photographs. I don't believe in coloring negatives either."

Porter's preference for color photography developed as a natural outgrowth of photographing birds, an interest he first acquired as a boy shooting gulls and terns around Great Spruce Head, first with a Brownie, then a Kodak camera, and finally a Graflex, the naturalist's camera of choice. The birds of his summer youth, however, were all shot in black and white. Color did not appear until Porter took up photography full-time in 1939.

Eliot Furness Porter was born December 6, 1901, in Winnetka, Ill., the second of five children (Nancy, Eliot, Edward, Fairfield and John) of James Foster Porter and Ruth Wadsworth Porter. His father was an architect of independent means and liberal inclinations, and the Porter children were raised in a genteel, humanist tradition to respect truth, honesty, and duty. Eliot's early interest in natural history and science was encouraged by his father, who had studied biology at Harvard before taking up architecture at Columbia. At Harvard, Eliot Porter studied chemical engineering, earning his B.S. in 1924. Following graduation, he entered the Harvard Medical School, taking his M.D. in 1929. For the next 10 years, he worked as a medical researcher at Harvard. In 1939, however, his life took a dramatic turn.

While working as a scientist at Harvard, Porter renewed his childhood interest in photographing nature. In 1930, his brother Fairfield, a painter, introduced Eliot to Alfred Stieglitz. Porter showed his photographs to the great man periodically, but it was not until 1938 that Stieglitz judged Porter ready. "You have arrived," Stieglitz announced upon seeing black and white prints Porter had made during a trip to Europe. "I want to show these."

From December 29, 1938, to January 18, 1939, Porter exhibited 29 prints at Stieglitz's An American Place in New York. Encouraged by this validation of his talent, Porter decided to leave medical research to devote himself to photography. That very summer, while photographing birds in Maine, he also made the fateful switch to color, having been persuaded by a publisher that color photographs were necessary for bird identification. With the past as prologue, Porter found that his scientific background eased the transition from black and white silver prints to dye-transfer color prints.

"Chemistry was what photography was all about," he explains. "So when I found it necessary to make color prints, it wasn't difficult for me."

The color photographs that made Eliot Porter famous are distinguished by a number of features that define Porter's photographic style. Patricia Caulfield neatly summarized some of these features in a 1967 interview she did with Porter for *Natural History* magazine.

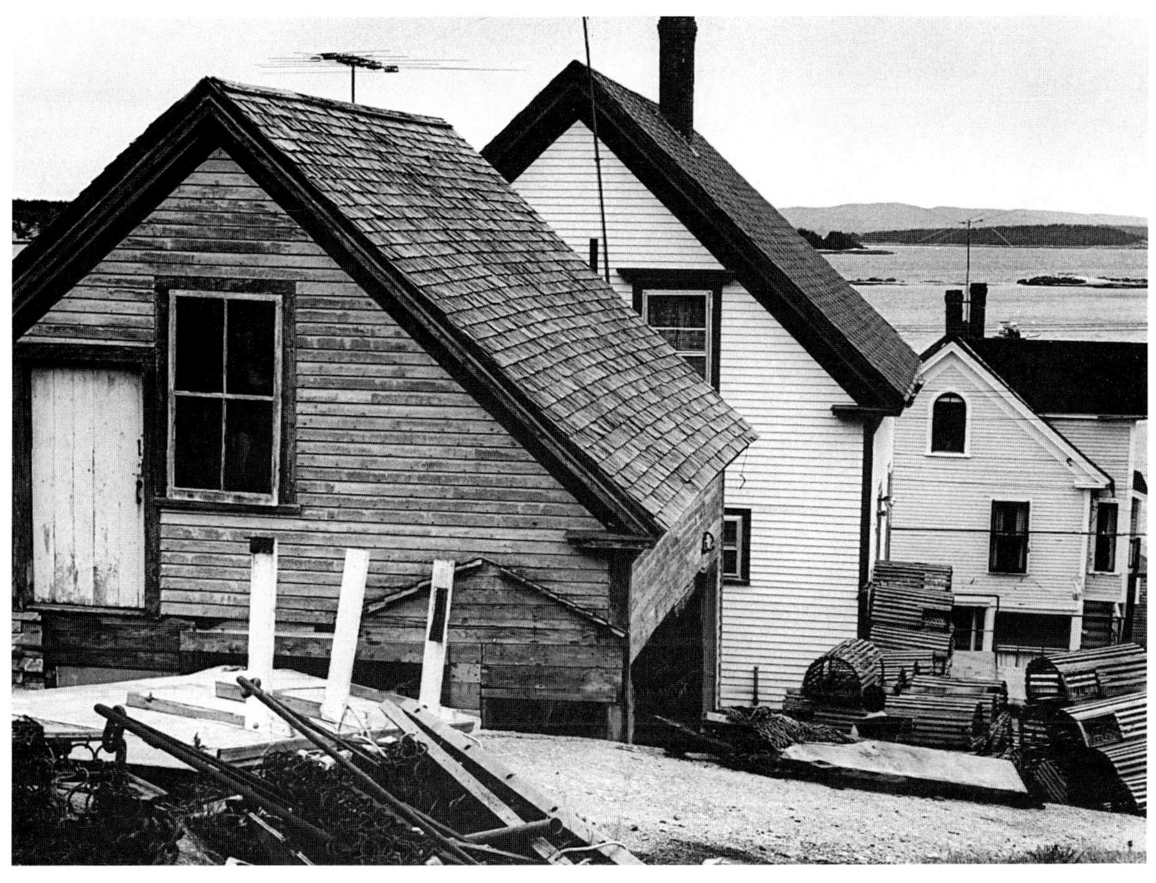

2. *Eliot Porter,* Houses and harbour, Stonington, Maine, *1974. Dye-transfer print. Courtesy of the artist.*

"First," Caulfield wrote, "his pictures lack scale. Second, he rarely includes horizon lines or sky. Third, his camera is more often pointed down than up. Fourth, he uses foregrounds, not as frames for backgrounds, but in complex relationships with backgrounds, both grounds occupying the entire picture area."

In making this last statement, Caulfield was really only saying that everything in a typical Eliot Porter photograph is in focus, a characteristic his work shares with that of the f64 group (photographers such as Adams, Weston, and Imogen Cunningham who preferred the small f64 aperture setting in order to achieve greater detail). To Caulfield's stylistic inventory, one need only add that Porter most often photographed natural subjects in natural color and that human beings rarely appear in his photographs. The human population of the 128 prints in *Eliot Porter* is four—Earl Brown of Eagle Island, Maine, in a 1939 silver print; a pair of Chinese girls in a 1981 color print; and a Mexican lad holding a branch of birds from 1956.

"I have photographed people," says Porter, "but, yes, I had a reputation for never photographing people. In 1956, though, I went to Mexico and photographed Mexicans everywhere. When I was in the Galapagos Island [in 1966], I sailed to Ecuador and photographed native Indians there. I also photographed people extensively in China [in 1980]. I was always interested in the natural scene, so I photographed the relation between people and nature. You can't photograph a landscape in Maine without showing the influence of humans."

When people appear in Porter's photographs, they tend to be the native and natural people of the region, more human specimens than personalities. Both this clinical approach to humanity and the relative absence of human figures add up to photographs which are physically beautiful, yet very cool and dispassionate. Like painter Neil Welliver, Eliot Porter is the human presence in his art.

"I had a scientific upbringing," says Porter, "so I guess I looked at nature in a detached, objective way."

This scientific upbringing, the influence of a father who was a Darwinian agnostic, is one Porter shared with his late brother Fairfield, the

realist painter and celebrated art critic. But while Eliot took after his father, Fairfield had his own interests.

"Fairfield was an artist from the time he was born," says his brother. "It was that way of looking at the world that influenced him most. Father and Fairfield didn't have a lot in common. He wasn't ever sure Fairfield was serious. Fairfield and I didn't have much in common either until I started doing photography entirely, and then we would both be photographing and painting on the island. Later in life we established a more sympathetic relationship."

Critics and commentators sometimes strain to find similarities between the paintings of Fairfield Porter and the photographs of Eliot Porter, but aside from overlapping subject matter (Great Spruce Head Island) and a preference for the intimate over the grandiose, the contrasts are more interesting and obvious than the similarities. Fairfield was a poet of the domestic, painting a summery world where people seem always to be on vacation; while Eliot is an explorer of the wild, photographing a natural world which always seems to be vacant. Where Fairfield generalized in a painterly way, Eliot is always quite specific and very precise. Their different sensibilities did not, however, keep the Porter brothers from appreciating each other's art.

Writing in *The Nation* in 1960, Fairfield Porter observed, "An expression of the immediacy of experience—for what else is the namelessness of everything—is proper to poetry and natural to photography. I know no photographs that express this so well as the color prints of my brother, Eliot Porter who, like Audubon, is known for his record of the birds of America." Fairfield then went on to write of Eliot's work, "These photographs make wonder the natural condition of the human mind. Have you ever seen before the redness of grass, the blueness of leaves, the orange cliffs of autumn, the two circles of sunflower blossoms, or a kerosene lamp against the sun in a window? Or that where a tree has fallen, it seems to have fallen with intention? There is no subject and background, every corner is equally alive."

Philip Ferrato, writing in the catalogue essay for *The Porter Family*, a 1980 exhibition at the Parrish Art Museum in Southampton, N.Y., of works by Fairfield Porter, Eliot Porter, painter Aline Porter (Eliot's wife), and sculptor Stephen Porter (Eliot and Aline's son), argued that Fairfield and Eliot Porter both stressed the "same importance of physical integrity, visual aspect and color over subject." To bolster his argument for fraternal aesthetic linkage, Ferrato cited Eliot Porter's statement in *Intimate Landscapes* (a companion book to the 1979 Porter exhibition at the Metropolitan Museum of Art) that "I do not photograph for ulterior purposes...I photograph for the thing itself—for the photograph—without consideration of how it may be used."

Porter's rejection of his "nature photographer" label was no doubt genuine, but it should not be taken to mean that "how" Porter makes a photograph is necessarily more important than "what" he photographs. His chosen subject is nature's wildness and his agenda is to save and preserve it. That intention (ulterior purpose?) is clearly documented in books ranging from *In Wildness Is the Preservation of the World* (1962) and *The Place No One Knew: Glen Canyon on the Colorado* (1963) to *Forever Wild: The Adirondacks* (1966), *Appalachian Wilderness: The Great Smoky Mountains* (1970), and *The Tree Where Man Was Born* (a book about East Africa with Peter Matthiessen, 1972). It was not until the 1980s, with the world alerted to a raft of environmental concerns, that Porter allowed himself the luxury of pure travel books—*The Greek World* (1980), *All Under Heaven: The Chinese World* (1983), *Eliot Porter's Southwest* (1985), *Maine* (1986), and *Mexican Churches* (1987). A book of his photographs of the West is scheduled for publication in the fall, and there are also plans to publish books of his photographs on Iceland, Egypt, and Mexico.

That the thrust of Eliot Porter's photography was once as much toward conservation as toward art is undeniable. In 1961, for example, Porter took a raft trip down the Colorado accompanied by painter Georgia O'Keeffe, photographer Todd Webb, son Stephen, and Stephen's fiancee. (Stephen Porter and painter Katherine Porter, a Maine resident, have since married and divorced.) As Webb, who lived in Santa Fe from 1961 to 1971 before moving to

Maine in 1975, recalls, "Eliot was trying to stop the dam [the Glen Canyon dam which created Lake Powell] when it was almost built. He wanted to save the river." As far as Webb was concerned, the Colorado River was just "a dirty creek." He much prefers man-made Lake Powell. Porter was eventually able to persuade the Sierra Club to oppose construction of the dam, but the opposition came too late to prevent the damming and flooding of 100 miles of the canyon under hundreds of feet of water.

To art historians, however, this 1961 river journey might hold non-environmental interests. The senior artists on the trip, it seems, performed true to form. O'Keeffe, the formalist, spent much of her time searching for interesting rocks to add to her collection. Porter, the conservationist, photographed the river and the canyon. And Webb, an historian with a camera? Well, as Porter recalls, "Todd spent most of his time photographing O'Keeffe."

While Eliot Porter's photographs have been widely exhibited in museums all over the country, there is a persistent notion, not altogether unfounded, that he has not yet been accorded the status in greatness of, say, an Ansel Adams. As Douglas Davis, reviewing the Amon Carter retrospective for *Time*, noted recently, "Despite their fragile beauty, the color photographs of Eliot Porter have never quite won over the critics, academicians and curators who write histories and mold reputations." In a certain sense, Porter's own achievements may weigh against him as an artist, if critics view him as 1) a color photographer, 2) a nature photographer, and 3) a photographer focused on books. All or one of these standings can be grounds in some minds for withholding full critical acclaim.

Prices of Porter photographs—which range from $800 for an 8 x 10 black and white to $2,500 for a 16 x 20 color print—are modest considering his status as the father of color photography. But what these prices reflect far more than diminution of Porter's importance is the fact that for the same amount of money you'd have to spend on a painting by an emerging artist, you can own a photograph by a great photographer.

What Maine viewers should know, if they don't already, is that Eliot Porter is a great photographer. But while his photographs have been exhibited frequently in Maine (at Bowdoin in 1965, Colby in 1969, Orono in 1977 and 1979, the Farnsworth in 1980, Maine Photographic Workshop in Rockport in 1982, and most recently at Gould Academy earlier this year), Eliot Porter is still probably best-known in Maine as the author-artist of *Summer Island*, the book Peter Cox (former owner-editor-publisher of *Maine Times*) referred to back in 1968 as "undoubtedly the best book there is about Maine."

In *Summer Island*, Porter observes Great Spruce Head as closely and carefully in prose as in pictures. *Maine*, published 20 years after *Summer Island*, lacks this tight, personal focus and suffers somewhat by comparison. Sitting in Tesuque, Porter notes that he prefers the writing in *Summer Island* but the photographs in *Maine*. His judgment is sound.

Like his photographs and his person, Eliot Porter's prose is clean, clear, perceptive, and unadorned—empirical. And when all is said and done, it is the clarity with which Eliot Porter views the world that distinguishes his art as much as his color. His is a clarity even a child will respond to. So how to account for this amazing clarity? Scientific upbringing? Artistic taste? Photographic technology?

"I don't know," says the artist. "I always thought what I photographed was very obvious. But if you mean by clarity that people can understand it, that's fine."

April 15, 1988

Blowing Up Flowers

Beverly Hallam

Late in the afternoon the marine sunlight on the York coast slants in low over the distant treetops and penetrates the vertical blinds of Surf Point, an imposing seaside home massed of sunbleached cedar cubes. The penetrating light casts long shadows across the austere whiteness of the dining room and illuminates a tableau of orange flowers isolated before the window in four crystal cruets. This is the moment painter Beverly Hallam waits for, that brief passage of time when the low, raking sun creates its drama of shadow and light, shimmering reflections and floral glow. This is the time to work.

Since she began working on her floral series in 1981, Beverly Hallam has produced an exquisite bouquet of spectacular flower paintings, most seen in just this post-meridian light and just this elegant interior. Lilies, tulips, pansies, hibiscus, irises, even naked stalks of Egyptian onion are blown up larger-than-life and captured within luminous prisons of louvered light, mirrored reflection, and patterns of glassy refraction. After years of working in more abstract styles and experimenting with a variety of mediums, Hallam has reached the height of her powers with these tightly rendered, realistic floral acrylics. Her flower paintings have been shown one or two at a time in Maine since the early 1980s, but now they have been gathered together in an exhibition currently making its way from Midtown Galleries in New York to Hobe Sound Galleries North in Portland (June 28 to July 23) by way of the Francesca Anderson Gallery in Boston (through June 26). *Beverly Hallam, The Floral Image* is, in effect, the coronation of an artist who has been a mainstay of the Ogunquit art scene for almost 40 years now.

Judging solely from the ultra-chic formality of her imagery, one might expect Beverly Hallam to be a stylish resortocrat, one of those lock-jawed garden club matrons who rule Maine summer colonies, but the creator of these gracious floral visions is, in fact, a hardy, pink-faced woman, an industrious worker from a long line of industrious folk going back to the lacemakers of Nottingham. A great-great-grandfather was a builder of church steeples. A grandfather invented a machine to put tips on shoelaces. An uncle designed the modern-day traffic light.

"I'm very mechanical," says the artist. "I got that from my father."

Edwin F. Hallam, an engineer with the giant General Electric plant in Lynn, Mass., designed turbines for submarines and was among the first and youngest licensed radio operators in the

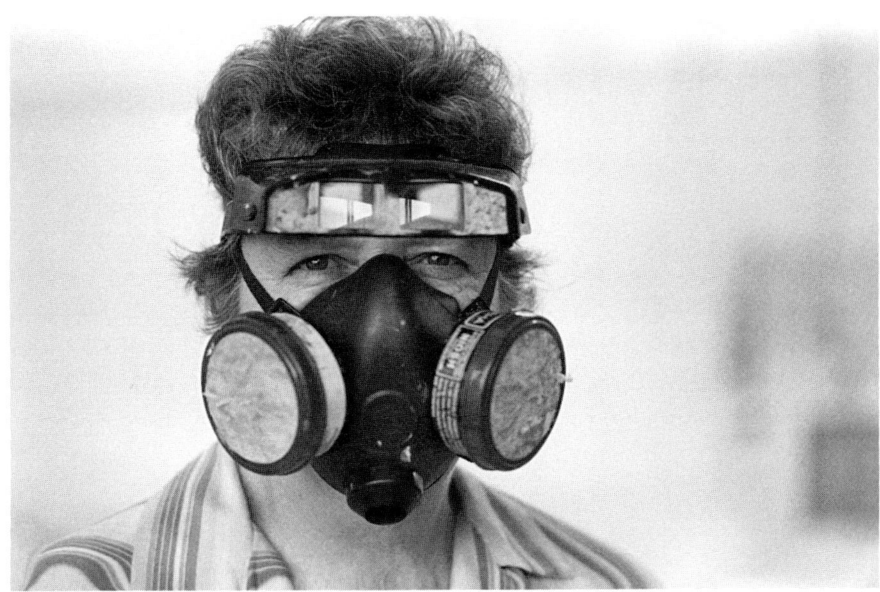

1. *Beverly Hallam, a portrait of the artist as airbrush alien. Photo by Christopher Ayres.*

U.S., his license signed by Guglielmo Marconi, inventor of the wireless.

Hallam's inherited mechanical aptitude serves her well in her new paintings, for the process of their making is surprisingly mechanized. But then Beverly Hallam has never been intimidated by technology.

A Beverly Hallam painting typically begins in the flower garden behind her studio where she grows, among other flora, a wide variety of lilies ranging in color from almost white to almost black. Once a subject has been cultivated and picked, it is brought into the house and arranged, a circular dining table serving as the stage for Hallam's theater of light. When the sun slips down toward the horizon, the artist photographs the arrangement from various angles. Hallam is an instinctive, self-taught photographer.

"If I raise a fantastic lily," she says, "I take a picture of it. I just can't help it."

Her color photographs serve as preparatory notes for the painting to come. Studying the photographs, she finally selects one to execute in acrylics, but it will be some time yet before she actually applies paint to canvas. First she must decide how large to make the painting and, that determined, she will begin the laborious process of transferring the image from a color slide to a prepared canvas. This she accomplishes by projecting the slide onto the canvas which has been covered with a frisket, a masking layer of thin paper. Using a black felt-tip waterproof pen, she then draws the projected image directly on the frisket. Sounds like cheating, but then artists have been using projections since the invention of the camera obscura and the camera lucida.

With the floral image outlined on the frisket, Hallam next spends hours taking out lines with a Q-tip dipped in alcohol, simplifying and editing reality and altering the structure of shadows. When she is satisfied with the composition, she is ready to begin keyholing, cutting away small sections of the frisket with an Exacto knife. The actual painting of the picture is, then, a stenciling process using an airbrush to spray on thin mists of acrylic color.

"I only cut what I'm about to spray," the artist explains, "and I can only work on one painting at a time, because I have to keep the whole painting in my memory. I never see the painting uncovered until the very end."

Hallam refers to the final removal of the by-now tattered and taped frisket, the moment when the finished painting is revealed to her for the first time, as "the facelift."

Aesthetic by-products of this creative process are the photographic abstractions Hallam makes by photographing details of her work-in-progress. What emerges in these photographs are images of peeled, patched, and painted surfaces as raw and richly textured as the finished paintings are polished and sublimely slick. Hallam has her detail abstractions printed in Cibachrome, but she works from Kodak color enlargements while painting because the Kodak prints are better suited to the translucence of flowers.

"I can't work from Cibachrome prints," she says, "because they're so color-saturated. They're Wagnerian."

Hallam's fascination with process and materials, the manipulation of reality, came early in life. Born in 1923, she grew up in suburban Lynn, where her girlhood hobby was magic. Her interest in illusions resulted in frequent trips to Howe's Rubber Store to purchase and then master magic tricks. Even today, the artist occasionally performs sleight-of-hand stunts at parties, but her more earnest interest in illusions and how they work goes directly into her art. The greatest compliment another artist can pay Beverly Hallam is to ask, "How did you do that?"

As a high-school student in Lynn, Hallam studied art with Anne Carleton (1878-1968), a late American impressionist, herself a student of Ogunquit art colony founder and Lynn native Charles H. Woodbury (1864-1940). Anne Carleton, however, favored her male students and did not take much notice of young Hallam until Beverly announced her intention to apply for admission to the Massachusetts College of Art. Furious with Hallam at first for not telling her that she was serious about art, Carleton then proceeded to give Beverly a crash course in how to pass the entrance test.

Hallam's decision to enter Mass Art resulted from a chance encounter with a Lynn neighbor, Allison Macomber ("He had a great influence on my life.") One day, Beverly noticed Macomber out in his yard pouring a white substance into molds. Curious about what her neighbor was up to, she discovered that the white stuff was plaster of Paris and that Macomber was designing silverware. Until she met Macomber, Hallam had planned to become a photographer after high school.

"I wanted to go to New York and be Margaret Bourke-White," says Hallam. "Photography seemed to be something a woman could do and it was very glamorous to me."

Beverly Hallam attended Mass Art from 1941 until 1945, graduating with a degree in art education. For the next four years she taught art at Lasell Junior College before returning to Massachusetts College of Art in 1949, this time as a member of the faculty. Nineteen forty-nine was also the first year Hallam summered in Ogunquit, the Maine art colony and beach resort where she settled year-round in 1963 after leaving Mass Art to pursue her own art.

Hallam's first Ogunquit home was Stonecrop, the unique barn board studio erected on Shore Road in 1923 by Grace Morrill, one of Charles Woodbury's protégés. Once she had winterized Stonecrop to live in, she moved her studio to the Perkins Cove cottage previously occupied by actor-painter-chef J. Scott "Jack" Smart, star of the popular radio program "The Fat Man." For the past 14 years now Hallam has lived and worked at Surf Point, the contemporary shorefront home she shares with Jack Smart's widow and her great friend, Mary-Leigh Smart.

Beverly Hallam and Mary-Leigh Smart first met when Smart, a long-time supporter of the Barn Gallery in Ogunquit, asked Hallam to give a lecture there.

"I said no," recalls Hallam, "but you just don't do that with Mary-Leigh. She just kept talking, so finally I said yes."

The lecture Hallam gave was on the use of polyvinyl acetate, a quick-drying milk-based paint emulsion. Hallam was among the first painters to master the new medium and she is credited with introducing it to the Ogunquit colony. Today, artists everywhere know polyvinyl acetate by its more common name—acrylic.

Beverly Hallam has always been a relentless experimenter with both materials and styles. From 1952 until 1967, she worked primarily in acrylic, often adding mica talc, tissue paper, and glazes to her painting to create textured works inspired by seashore life. From 1958 until 1978, she created abstract and landscape monotypes using gelatin rollers and elements of collage. She first began using the airbrush in conjunction with her monotypes in order to add atmospheric detail. In her realist florals, she has married the airbrush techniques learned from the monotypes with her natural interest in photographing flowers. This spirit of innovation and material experimentation, Hallam believes, is rooted in her work as an art teacher.

"I think I was born with a good sense of composition and design. That's always been my strength," she says. "Then I taught a course at the Massachusetts College of Art, my favorite course, called Fundamentals. My job was to introduce all the junior art education students to art materials—anything that you can create a work of art with. I even had them using paper clips. What I was doing was giving them a vocabulary, teaching them to use materials, to experiment."

Anyone who knows Beverly Hallam's earlier work—organic abstractions characterized by a dashing spontaneity and fluency—might find it strange to see her at work today. Hunched over before a canvas, welder's goggles protecting her eyes, airgun in hand, she could as easily be an industrial laborer as an artist—Rosie the Riveter incongruously transported to an airy seaside studio.

"The spontaneous way of painting is the most fun," Hallam admits. "It's the natural way for me to work. It's relaxing, fast, no worries. But now it's all hard work. The fun is in the preparation. The taking of the picture is the most emotionally creative moment, taking the picture and then the facelift."

The shift from abstraction to realism entailed not only a new way of working, but also the mastery of a whole new visual vocabulary, no small feat for a serious, mature artist. In effect, Beverly Hallam learned a new language in her sixties. One is tempted to say it was the language of photo-realism, but Hallam doesn't think she speaks that language.

"I'm not really a photo-realist," says Hallam. "I'm not that painstaking. I don't know what I am, but I've never gone with the tide."

Indeed, the only painting in the *Floral Image* exhibition that truly qualifies as photo-realism is *Birds of Paradise* (1987), a vase of those exotic blossoms surrounded by irises and set against a painting by Hallam's Midtown-Hobe Sound gallery mate Gary Buch. The painting is photorealist principally because the focus and depth of field are those of the camera, not the human eye. Buch's background painting is blurred, as are the feathery greens which project into the foreground, leaving only a narrow band of middle ground sharply in focus.

In terms of floral subject matter, Hallam's acrylics speak directly to some of Carolyn Brady's watercolors, but stylistically Hallam is closer to Audrey Flack, a contemporary intimist who also uses an airbrush.

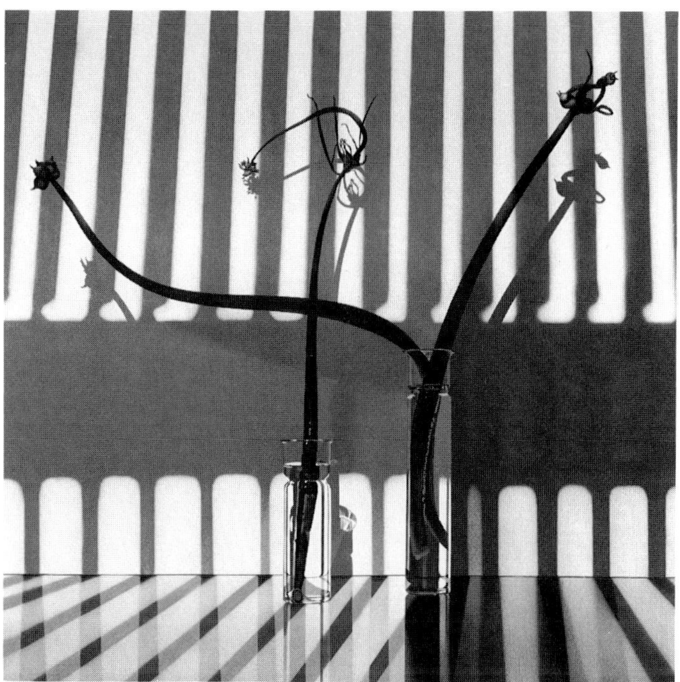

2. *Beverly Hallam,* Egyptian Onions, *1988. Acrylic on canvas. Courtesy of the Midtown Galleries, Inc., New York. Photo by Douglas Armsden.*

"I think they look sprayed," Hallam says of Flack's paintings. "She doesn't use many masks. I try to make my work look not sprayed. I like more variation than having everything look soft."

True, Hallam's floral still lifes have an almost mechanical sharpness and precision about them. They are also so finely and thinly sprayed that the image seems one with the surface weave of the canvas. But perhaps Hallam's niftiest visual sleight of hand is the trick she plays with size and scale. For example, on *Orange Prince* (1985), the orange blossoms in the four crystal cruets appear to be as large, lush, and showy as peonies, but they are in fact dainty little pansies. The illusion is one of misdirection. The glass surface upon which the cruets sit appears to be a coffee table, but it is really a small mirror. In the absence of other visual cues, the eye reads the real table (Hallam's circular dining table) as the floor.

Despite the complexity of her methods, however, Beverly Hallam ultimately has a very simple goal in creating her elaborate illusions.

"I'm old-fashioned, I guess, but I would like everything I do to be pleasing," she says. "It's not that I don't like what young artists are doing today; I do like some of the way-out stuff that's dark and exciting and turbulent, but I don't

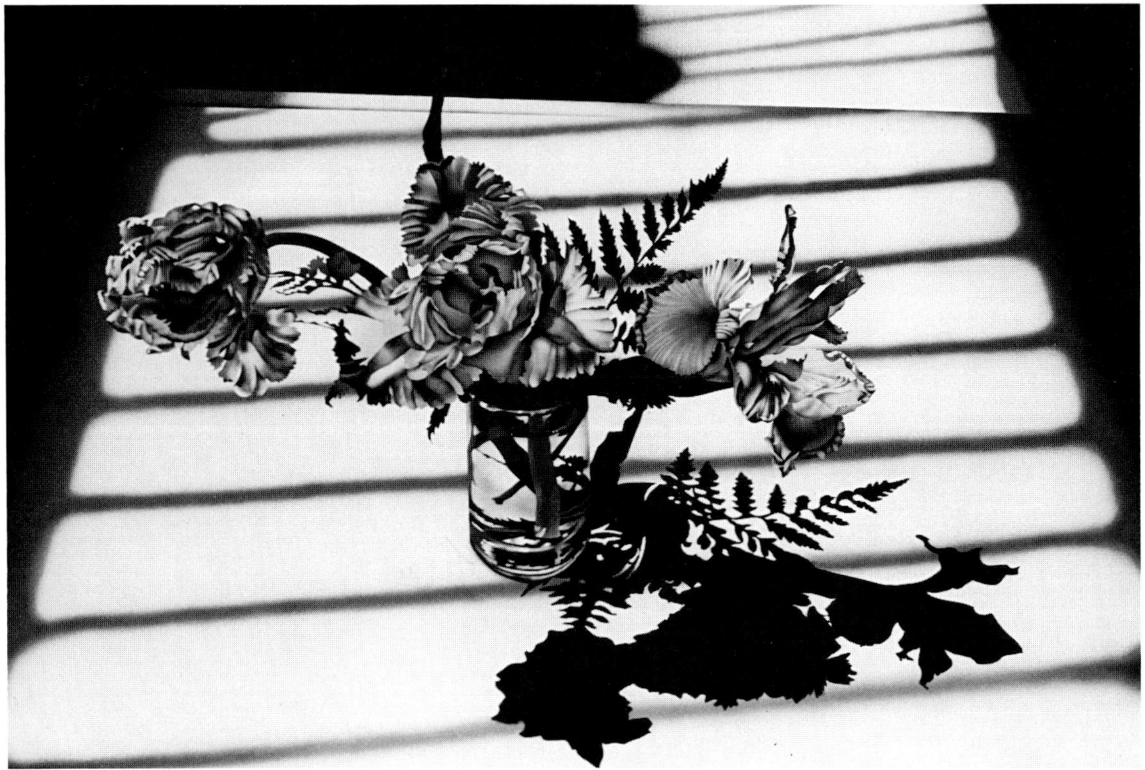

3. *Beverly Hallam,* Parrots, *1985. Acrylic on canvas. Courtesy of the Midtown Galleries, Inc., New York. Photo by Nathan Rabin.*

know if I'd like to live with it. For myself, I have to get great pleasure from my art. It has to make me happier. I would like people to have this feeling too, to add something pleasant to their day."

Beverly Hallam is a survivor and she has survived as an artist the same way the flora and fauna of Earth survive, by adapting. Looking back over the aesthetic terrain she has covered, she can appreciate the irony of where she finds herself today.

"I was brought up with the idea that Braque was a great artist, that you never puncture the picture plane, and you never bring a photograph into a painting studio," laughs Hallam. "Now look what I'm doing!"

June 24, 1988

Favorite Son

John Laurent

As he approaches his 63rd birthday, John Laurent has every right to be satisfied with his life. A casual, charming, cultured yet crusty man with a closely cropped gray-white beard, Laurent projects the image of the gentleman farmer and veteran sport fisherman that he is. Of course, John Laurent is also one of Maine's best and best-known painters, a part of the Maine art scene virtually all his life. And on the eve of his retirement after 30 years teaching at the University of New Hampshire, that school has mounted a 30-year retrospective which serves as a visual autobiography.

John Laurent was born in 1921 in Brooklyn, N.Y., one of two sons of the celebrated modernist sculptor Robert Laurent. His childhood was one rich in art and artists, both in New York and Ogunquit, where his father was a key figure in the Maine summer art colony.

"I was lucky," he says, reflecting on his childhood from the comfortably cluttered confines of his studio in the barn of the York farm he has inhabited since 1969. "I grew up with all the New York superstars. The majority of our family friends were artists." He mentions first some of his father's closest friends, lesser-known artists, but the Laurent household also attracted artist friends like Bernard Karfiol, Walt Kuhn, Gaston Lachaise, William Zorach, Alexander Calder, and David Smith. "So I grew up exposed to all their stuff," Laurent continues, "but I never thought I'd be an artist. I was more interested in the outdoors, forestry, veterinary medicine. For a long time I thought I might become a forest ranger or a vet. It wasn't until I graduated from prep school and did so poorly in chemistry that I knew veterinary medicine would be out for me."

The summer after he graduated from prep school, he came across a Syracuse University catalogue which listed a new degree in public school art education. Having drawn all his life, the young Laurent thought that might be for him.

After two years at Syracuse, Laurent became disillusioned when he found himself making papier-mâché dolls with yarn hair. When World War II broke out, therefore, he quickly joined the Navy, where he kept drawing and sending his sketches home to his father.

Most of Laurent's formal art training came after the war when he finished an art degree, went to Paris for a year, and taught art at Virginia Polytechnical Institute.

Nineteen fifty-four was a watershed year for Laurent. In that year he completed graduate work at Indiana University, got married (Nancy Laurent was a sculpture student of his father's), and took a position as a lowly art instructor at the University of New Hampshire. Accepting the New Hampshire position was largely motivated by the artist's desire to return to Maine.

John Laurent—30 Years, the New Hampshire retrospective, picks up the fledgling artist in the mid-1950s after his return to New England. The early paintings, like *Boats in Bottles* (1955), show a young Laurent heavily under the influence of Bauhaus master Paul Klee. The quirky quality of line that recurs in Laurent's work to this day can be traced to his early infatuation with Klee. An exquisite Klee watercolor drawing (picked up in Zurich many years ago for $90 by Laurent's father) hangs in the living room of the York farm.

"I remember the first major showing of Klee that I saw," says Laurent. "It blew my brain."

In a 1956 review, *Art News* cited the "Cubist hieroglyphics" (the Klee influence) and the "light but athletic palette" (derived both from Klee and Mexican painter Rufino Tamayo) in what it described as "a sparkling one-man debut."

From the experimental Klee-Tamayo period, Laurent entered what some have called his "somber period," characterized by a dramatic isolation of subjects against dense, dark backgrounds. Paintings like *Still Life* (1963) present objects as stiffly posed as Federalist portraits, as dramatically lit as Old Master paintings.

In 1962, *Art News* noted this stylistic change by reporting that Laurent's "bleak still-lifes and landscapes suggest a conflict between the desire to paint traditional subjects and the desire to include elements of modernity—which he does in background treatment, in paint handling, and in a sometimes unexplained starkness."

But John Laurent can easily explain the starkness and the conflict of the paintings from his "somber period." The starkness is the Walt Kuhn influence. The conflict was his own.

Robert Laurent showed the drawings his son sent home during the war to his friend, the painter Walt Kuhn.

"Is this guy serious?" Kuhn asked Laurent père. "If he is, when he comes back I can help him."

Thus, between 1946 and 1949, John Laurent studied under Kuhn both in New York during the winter and Ogunquit during the summer.

"Kuhn was certainly the biggest influence on my life," says Laurent. "Everything he told me turned out to be true. When I talk to my own students, it's just stuff he told me."

Kuhn was a stern master, seeking to turn the young Laurent away from the "charm" and "tossed salad" of French art and back toward the authority of masters like Rembrandt and Velasquez. The somber mood of Laurent's early 1960s paintings, then, is the Old Masters filtered through Kuhn.

"Kuhn was a tough SOB," says Laurent, "but his bark was worse than his bite. But I can understand why he never got his due as an artist. If he didn't like something, he'd tell you right to your face. He didn't pull any punches."

Kuhn's distaste for French painting was such, in fact, that Laurent feared telling his mentor that he had decided to use a travel scholarship to spend a year in Paris in 1948-49.

"Finally, I told him," says Laurent. "He looked at me and didn't say a word for the longest time. I was sure he was going to blow up. But then he said, 'Everybody has to go over there sometime.'"

During his student stay in Paris, Laurent felt the pull of his father's homeland in Brittany. (Robert Laurent came to the United States in 1901 as a child protégé of American painter/art patron Hamilton Easter Field, one of the founders of the original Ogunquit art colony.) Returning to his roots, Laurent woke up after a train journey from Paris and knew instantly he was in Brittany.

"I could smell the land," the artist explains.

Laurent's French heritage has exerted a strong influence on him throughout his life. Today, he can move easily between fluent French and a slightly comic down east Maine patois, both spoken with his distinctive raspy rattle. In 1966, when he won a National Council on the Arts grant, Laurent elected to spend his sabbatical in Brittany. The experience of Brittany marks the next major development in his painting.

In 1967, *Art News* reported that "John Laurent paints Normandy [sic] in a strengthened School of Paris style."

Two Oyster Carriers (1967) in the New Hampshire exhibition documents this stylistic shift. The School of Paris reference suggests perhaps the heavier impastoed surfaces Laurent created in France. The impasto-palette knife technique owes something to another artist important to Laurent, the Russian-born Belgian painter Nicholas de Stael, noted for sculpting pigment on canvas. The heavier surface can also be attributed to a fast-drying putty compound that Laurent discovered in Brittany (and hopes to rediscover when he begins spending more time abroad next spring).

But the most obvious and important influence that Brittany had on Laurent's painting was the expanse of his palette.

"I rediscovered color in a way," the artist explains.

Lively yellows and greens suggested by the cultivated landscape of Brittany make a dramatic appearance. Following the prolonged somber period of dim browns and tinted blacks, the pictures from Brittany arrive like daylight. But these sunny French landscapes soon experience the artist's personal eclipse, an eclipse that Laurent now refers to as "my booze grand finale."

In 1969, Laurent severed his long association with Kraushaar Gallery in New York. In 1970, his father died. In 1971, his mother died. Long a heavy drinker, the artist now found sorrow and self-doubt fueling his alcohol problem. It was taking a fifth of vodka, two six-packs of beer, and untold quantities of wine to get through the day. When he was no longer able to paint, he decided it was time to sober up.

In 1972, John Laurent institutionalized himself for several months to dry out, sober up, and regain control of his life. Except for a brief relapse, he has remained sober ever since and is now an active member of Alcoholics Anonymous, crediting AA with "saving my life."

"I wouldn't want to say I was reborn," says Laurent, "but I certainly got a second chance at life."

It took several years for the artist to recover his powers as a painter, and works from the early 1970s are notably missing from the New Hampshire exhibition.

"After the booze thing," says Laurent, "I started going back to naturalism, observing more carefully, getting my vision back again. I was amazed at how much I had bypassed and had been unable to observe while I was drinking."

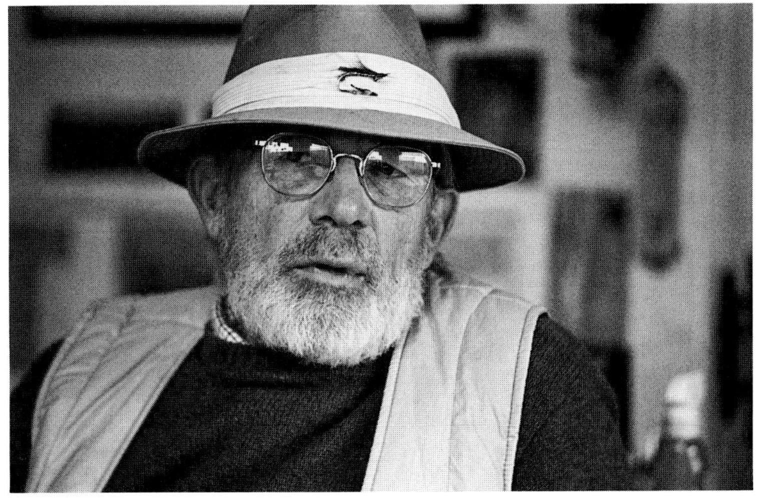

1. *Painter John Laurent. Photo by Christopher Ayres.*

It took several years for Laurent to find himself again as a painter. His return to naturalism initially took the form of broad landscapes, but the large body of beach paintings—straited, horizontal views of Ogunquit Beach and Plum Island Beach—that he did in the mid-1970s are not represented in the retrospective.

The most obvious difference between the paintings Laurent did before and after he stopped drinking is the vitality and enthusiasm he now brought to his familiar subjects. Laurent has always painted the things closest to him—things he has grown and things he has caught—but during his somber period he tended to invest these subjects with the weight of ambition and the weight of art history. Today, he invests these same subjects with the immediate pleasure he takes in them. Where formerly his subjects seemed to possess him, now he possesses his subjects.

It is a curious coincidence that most of John Laurent's favored subjects happen to begin with the letter F: fishing, fly tackle, food, fruit, farm, France, and (to stretch a point) mud flats and tidal flats.

Images of fish and fishing recur throughout his work, and the artist makes the obvious statement that fishing is one of his great passions.

"I probably think more about fishing than I do about painting," says Laurent. "I think

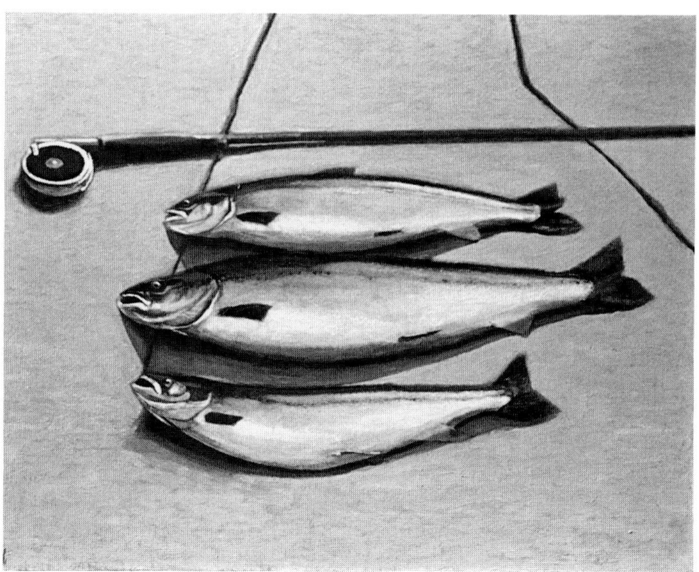

2. *John Laurent,* Three Grilses, *1980. Acrylic. Courtesy of the artist.*

fishing is a great way to get in nature and observe."

Some of the most intense images Laurent has created have resulted from excursions he has taken on the boat of a close friend, a commercial tuna fisherman from Ogunquit. *Boated Tuna* (1979) is a strikingly asymmetrical overhead view of a working fisherman and a huge, bleeding tuna. The contrast between the blood-red of the silvery-blue fish and the deep blue-black of the water is stunning and dramatic. The image itself is riveting. Similarily, in *Tuna Tower* (1984) Laurent takes a bold perspective, isolating four male figures in the rigging of the tuna boat, setting them against the clear blue of the sky. The great open expanses of water in the first painting and the wide open blue of the sky in the second are major aesthetic accomplishments.

But Laurent's real love is fly fishing. And whether wading hip-deep in the Ogunquit River after brown trout or plying the waters of Canadian rives after salmon, the artist in him is always working alongside the angler. The task that Laurent has set for himself is to capture the esoteric excitement and tension of the instant that the elusive fish hits the fly. He attempts this somewhat literally in the oil/acrylic diptych *Salmon at Natashquam* (1980) where the airborne fish leaps out of the water into a pictorial space divided by the taut fly line.

In 1958, an observant *Art News* reviewer commented on how Laurent paints a fish form "that splits the surface vertically with a tempered brutality" and goes on to observe, "This divisionary line reoccurs [sic] effectively even in his abstract panoramic landscapes." This energetic vertical line, a compositional device that divides the picture plane and activates the pictorial space, once belonged to Paul Klee, but Laurent, through constant use, has succeeded in making it his own.

Laurent's 50-acre farm, some six miles inland from the York shore, also provides him with endless raw material for his art. Just as at home on a tractor as he is at the easel, the artist grows just about everything in his vegetable garden except corn (now that he no longer has his dogs, he has a problem with raccoons) and these vegetables often appear in his still life set pieces. Like Kuhn (and Cezanne), Laurent tends to impart thrust and presence to simple arrangements of fruit and vegetable by outlining them in black.

The power of darkness is also key to a series of precisionist barn interior acrylics Laurent executed in 1982. Compared to the hard-edged works of Charles Sheeler in the exhibition catalogue, these barn interiors find Laurent atypically painting against the light to capture the dim intimacy of his cluttered farm building.

Singularly missing from Laurent's work are portraits and figurative paintings. Where human figures do occur, they are used as anonymous elements of composition rather than characters.

"Well, it's very simple," Laurent says, explaining the absence. "I did a load of that stuff in school, with Kuhn [who is most celebrated for his portraits of circus performers], and in Paris

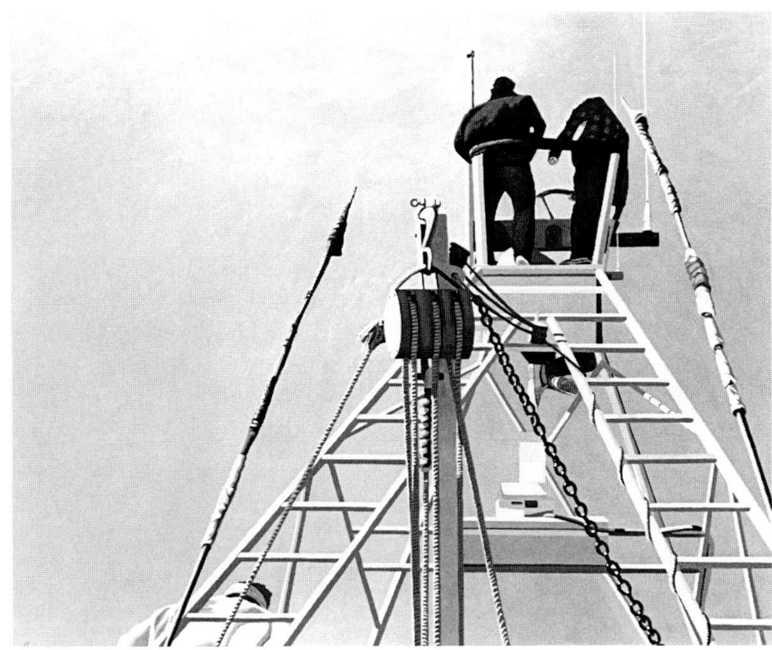

3. *John Laurent,* Tuna Tower, *1984. Acrylic. Courtesy of the artist.*

[where Laurent's professed goal was to draw 200 nudes from life]. The figure does not excite me in painting. I think the human being is the worst animal in the world unconsciously doing so much pollution. Landscape and still life is my excitement."

Of course, there is also the fact that the artist's father is primarily known for his full-bodied female nudes carved from wood and alabaster. Though not consciously rebelling against his father, Laurent says he learned very little from the famous sculptor.

"My father," he says, "never really taught me. He never talked a great deal. He'd just look at my stuff and say, 'Unh-hunh' and 'Ah-hah' and brush his nose with his thumb."

But being the son of a noted artist did have an effect on Laurent, adding to the pressures to achieve and succeed, pressures that may have compounded his drinking problem.

"Sure it did," says Laurent. "When I was drinking heavily I would always compare my career with my father's. I was always looking at myself and asking where Robert was at this age. That bugged me for a long time and certainly had an effect on me."

Coming to terms with himself as a man and as an artist meant in part accepting the fact that John Laurent was not Robert Laurent. Paraphrasing the artist Georges Braque, Laurent says, "The most important thing is to know your limitations."

"I don't have the obsession I had years ago to make it big in New York," confides Laurent. He severed his 14-year association with Kraushaar Gallery when he realized that to really pursue and push his career he would have to be part of the New York art scene, possibly even live in the city, and that he was unwilling to do. His life and his interests were elsewhere.

Recently, John Laurent has told several interviewers that he will be content to be remembered as "a good Maine painter." That reputation already seems assured. His 1982 debut exhibition with Barridoff Galleries (after showing with Frost Gully Gallery for a number of years) was the best-received exhibition of his career, most of the major museums in the state having acquired works from the show for their collections.

"The thing has arrived here in Maine," says Laurent, "that I used to talk about all the time with Tom Crotty [artist-proprietor of Frost Gully Gallery]. There are now three good year-round galleries in Portland. I think that should be a great incentive to young artists. You can indeed make it in Maine."

November 16, 1984

In Hardy Country

Pat & DeWitt Hardy

One night in early spring, the sky above alive with the pulsing of stars and the contrails of jets, the North Berwick Drawing Group gathers in the loft of Pat and DeWitt Hardy's barn to draw the nude. The model, a young male dancer, sits on the floor near the woodstove and talks of Sigmund Romberg operas.

Deployed around him are 14 artists, some of them among the best in the region. Janet Conlon Manyan of Kennebunkport stands working resolutely at her easel. George Burk, a neighbor from just up the road, sits painting on a woodblock in preparation for making a print. Sigmund Abeles, over from New Hampshire for the evening, chats amiably, all the while scratching away on a little drypoint etching plate in his lap. Pat Hardy, whose birthday this is, works quietly on a sanguine crayon drawing, while husband DeWitt, peering now over his half-spectacles at the model, now through them at the paper before him, executes one of his tightly controlled watercolors. A Marian McPartland piano piece plays on public radio in the background. The evening is warm, relaxed, focused. Scenes such as this have been repeated weekly in York County since 1963, the year after Pat and DeWitt Hardy arrived in Maine to pursue art and life together. That they have managed to keep this drawing group—not to mention their marriage, their friendships, and their art—together for better than a quarter-century testifies to a level of commitment which has made the Hardys two of the Maine art community's most solid and respected citizens.

"There are very few people in Maine," notes George Burk, a friend of 28 years, "who have so single-mindedly gone about being artists and been so successful at it on such a sustained basis."

Pat and DeWitt Hardy, both of whom turn 49 this year, originally settled at Perkins Cove in Ogunquit in 1962. As such, they help link the contemporary Maine art scene with the last hurrah of the Ogunquit art colony. DeWitt, in fact, grew up summers in Ogunquit and made his first paintings there while just a teenager.

Because his father was "an academic gypsy," DeWitt Hardy found himself moving a great deal while growing up. Born in St. Louis, Missouri (his father taught history just across the Illinois border), Hardy moved to Maine as an infant when his father took a position at the University of Maine in Orono. While in Maine, the Hardys discovered Ogunquit; even after moving on to Ohio, the family continued to return summers to the arty beach resort. In 1953, at age 13, Hardy made his first adolescent

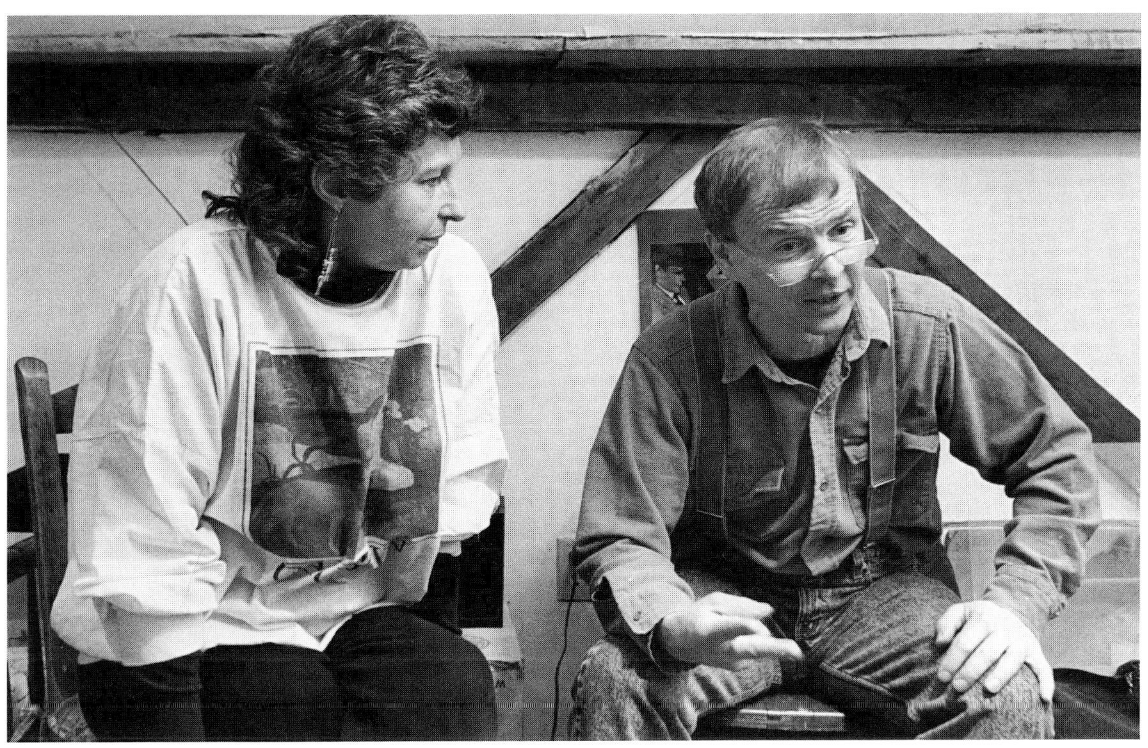

1. *Pat and DeWitt Hardy. Photo by Scott Perry.*

stabs at painting and received "the most helpful criticism I've ever gotten anywhere" from Edward Betts, the noted watercolorist long associated with the Ogunquit colony. "He said I had not considered the contrast of darks and lights at all, that the drawing could be better, and that I had placed too much emphasis on the details and not enough on the basic drama. The next painting I did—an old lobster shack at Cape Neddick—I know if I saw it now would be the absolute seed of what I'm doing today."

After graduating from high school in Hudson, Ohio, Hardy enrolled as an art student at Syracuse University primarily because "a girlfriend was going there." That passion cooled before he ever reached Syracuse, but there in that grungy industrial Athens he met another young woman named Pat Schloz who would keep his interest. Fittingly, since Hardy is much enamored of trains and frequently features them in his work, the couple first met on the train from Syracuse to Cleveland while headed home for the Christmas holidays.

Pat Hardy grew up in Cleveland where her father, who now teaches watercolor in his Florida retirement, was a plumbing contractor with an artistic inclination. One of her strongest childhood impressions was of the drawings her father would make to illustrate the stories he told his children. Encouraged from early childhood to enjoy and create art, Pat took Saturday art lessons at the Cleveland Institute of Art as a teen, but even from the time she was three, she knew "there was no question what I was going to do with my life."

Having thrust them together at Syracuse, fate then pointed Pat and DeWitt back toward Ogunquit. Because painter John Laurent, son of sculptor Robert Laurent, had graduated from Syracuse University, the Ogunquit School of Painting and Sculpture (which the Laurents ran summers at Perkins Cove) offered scholarships to Syracuse students. Encouraged by DeWitt to apply, Pat received a scholarship to study at the Ogunquit School during the summer of 1960, the next-to-the-last year the school was open. John Laurent, himself one of Maine's most accomplished resident artists, calls DeWitt Hardy "one of the top Maine painters and one of our good national painters," but he also recalls that when the Hardys arrived in Ogunquit that summer of 1960 Pat "was a much better painter than he was." And given the work he was doing at the time, Hardy wouldn't argue with Laurent.

Momentarily caught up in the heady rush of '50s expressionism and abstraction, Hardy went through a youthful period of action painting in which he would drip paint onto masonite, shatter the spattered painting with a baseball bat, and then exhibit the fragments. In 1959, not yet 20 years old and still in school, he even hired a vanity gallery in New York to exhibit these smashing works of art. The best criticism he received of that show came from a New York City cop who wandered in, pronounced the paintings "terrible," and threatened to arrest Hardy for his crimes against art.

"When I hung that show," says Hardy, "I realized I really didn't know anything. I also realized that everything since strong abstract expressionism—by which I primarily mean de Kooning—is just mannerism. I realized what I was doing was mannered as well." Rejecting his flirtation with abstraction, young Hardy went looking for "something sufficiently complex to fill up a lifetime." What he rediscovered was realism and the seductive power of the well-drawn line. ("Remember, there is no drawing in the world, there is no line.")

The paintings which have earned DeWitt Hardy a reputation and a living as an artist are studio nudes, figure groups, mill townscapes, and florals rendered in a straight watercolor technique which marries aspects of Oriental art (flatness, stillness) with traditional American qualities (clarity, vigor). If one were looking for an "-ism" to hang upon his art it would be humanism, an art of small-town America conversant with the history of art.

An energetic worker, Hardy paints every day ("I get physically ill if I don't"), often roaming the Maine-New Hampshire border country in the faded gray Chrysler which serves as his mobile studio. Most of the figurative paintings begin with work done during drawing group sessions, and there is nothing Hardy paints with more authority than tones and texture of human flesh.

"When I go and sit in front of the figure I don't just look at the figure," he says. "Memories of the history of art keep playing through my body and they come out in my hand."

Over the years some of Hardy's best work has been done in what he refers to as his "Variations on the enigma" series, self-portraits with attendant female figures which are not so much erotic narratives as lyric essays in form and composition. *A Fancy* is his latest variation on the enigma and one of his finest paintings to date.

A Fancy depicts the artist in typical countryfolk *déshabille*, t-shirt and suspenders over long-sleeve polo or undershirt, being led into the forest by three nude women. His regard is tired and wary ("I always try to make myself look as bad as possible") as though he resents the viewer's intrusion on his private sylvan fancy ("A fancy is a dance, you know.") But while the viewer is free to fantasize about this *al fresco ménage à quatre*, for Hardy this fancy is primarily an hommage to past masters of the nude. The female figure closest to the artist and leading him on is freely drawn from Edgar Degas nudes. The largely obscured figure with the wrapped head is specifically based on Jean Ingres' *Baigneuse de Valpincon*. And the reclining figure in the background was inspired by the nude studies of Aristide Maillol. Having confided all this, however, Hardy backs away from explication with evident distaste.

"I just detest explaining my own paintings," he says. "I love women, so that painting is just an honest explanation of how I feel about them and their bodies. It's because I love art and women, together and in the same way."

For the past five years, Hardy has also been painting subjects from different locations together and in the same place. Realism, he has found, is sufficiently complex to allow him to, say, paint one element of a painting at home in the morning and then transport it to a setting painted elsewhere in the afternoon. In *The Artist and Her Model*, for example, Hardy painted his wife and a model at work in their North Berwick backyard and through the illusionistic fiction of watercolor set the two women before a farmhouse in Eliot.

DeWitt Hardy's is an art, then, of captivating imagery expertly rendered and exactingly laid down, but it does suffer from limitations both self-imposed and culturally conditioned. To begin with, he does his major work in watercolor. His attraction to the medium stems initially from its close relationship with drawing, but he also loves it for its delicate, translucent self.

"It's such a beautiful medium," Hardy says of watercolor. "I don't like oil paint. I don't have to paint in oil paint!"

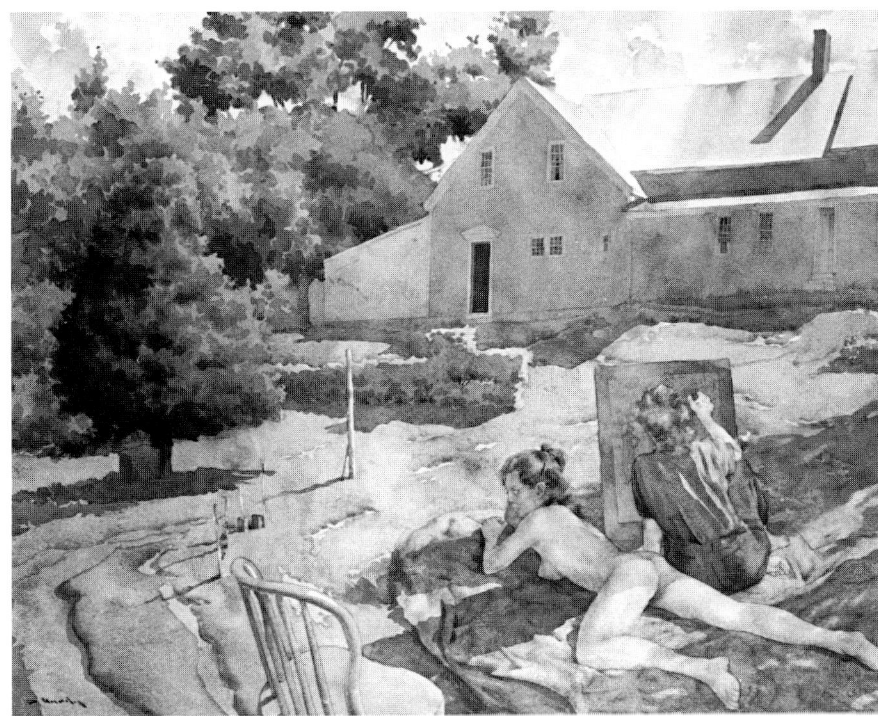

2. *DeWitt Hardy,* The Artist and Her Model, *1988. Watercolor. Courtesy of the artist.*

Yet Hardy knows that art's historical bias in favor of oil painting means that his work is often overlooked when major exhibitions are mounted—watercolor, no matter how fine, being considered a minor art form. Working in watercolor also limits the size of Hardy's paintings in an era when important paintings are big paintings. The size limitation is Hardy's own, imposed because he feels he loses the tones and textures he loves if his paintings grow too large.

And, finally, Hardy believes his choice of subject matter works against him in many cases.

"The thing you cannot do now and enter into the big market is humanism," he says, explaining that by humanism, he means "anything in which a thoughtful human confronts another across the picture plane. Nobody wants it."

Until quite recently, DeWitt Hardy showed regularly in New York, first at the Frank Rehn Gallery and then at the Robert Schoelkopf Gallery, but these days, having divorced himself from New York out of a sense that his work was not being appreciated there, he finds he can stay busy exhibiting at Frost Gully Gallery in Portland, Mast Cove Galleries in Kennebunkport, Blackthorne Gallery in Portsmouth, and the Allport Gallery in Larkspur, California.

"The idea," he says, "is to keep rolling so the shows pile on one another and the deadlines come fast and furious."

Pat Hardy, who shows at Barridoff Galleries in Portland and Allport Gallery with her husband, interrupted her own career to mother twin sons Adam and Harris, now 26, and son Ethan, 24. In the past decade, however, she has regained her aesthetic momentum.

"I think having kids put the fear of God into me," says Pat Hardy. "I was afraid if I stopped, I'd never start again. When you're working all the time, you're leaping ahead; when you're not, you're crawling along."

When she was at home most of the time with her children, Pat naturally tended to paint whatever was at hand around the rambling North Berwick farm she and DeWitt purchased in 1966. Often that meant domestic still lifes featuring seashells or eggs and painted in a watercolor vocabulary similar to DeWitt's. As the boys became more independent and a second car gave her mobility, she moved on to painting lowland landscapes of southern Maine, the tabletop still lifes having been surrogate landscapes for her all along. But neither still life nor landscape completely satisfied Pat Hardy's urge to express herself. Her search for meaningful content has taken Pat along the well-worn artistic path from Maine to New Mexico where she has found inspiration in the native American heritage. "They're trying to preserve their culture while we're busy destroying ours," she says of the Southwest Indians.

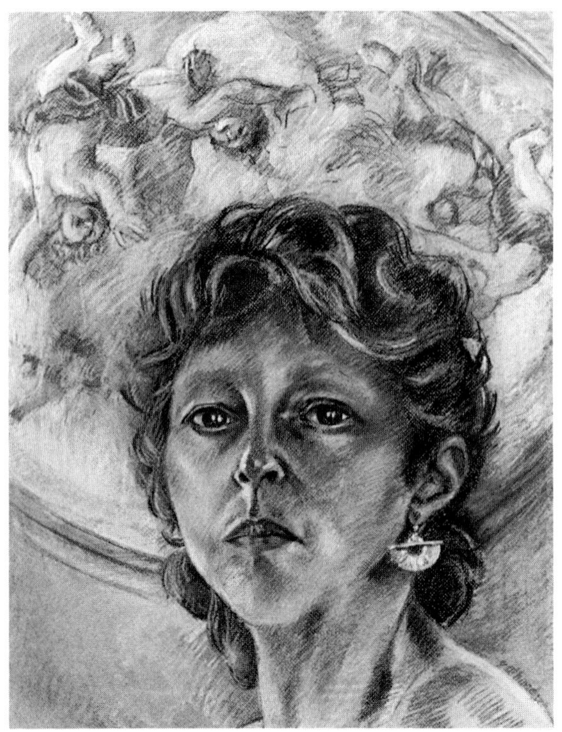

3. *Pat Hardy,* Self-Portrait wth Putti, *1989. Pastel. Courtesy of the artist.*

But even the still life arrangements of Indian rugs and pots Hardy has been working on recently do not get as close to her creative core as her ongoing series of pastel self-portraits.

"I find I get trapped by realism," Pat says. "The struggle has been to find the self in it. My self gets lost [in the still lifes and landscapes]. That's why the self-portraits are exciting to me. I'm trying to get to something much more essential. I feel like I'm a sponge when I'm out there looking. I forget sometimes to simplify it."

Self-Portrait with Putti is a frank work of self-examination and reflection, with a touch of elegance supplied by the artist's fan earring and the halo of cherubim. The circle of putti above Hardy's head could easily be read to symbolize a woman's life of children and art, but, more factually, the decorative angels refer to a painted ceiling Hardy restored in an old Kennebunk mansion.

For the past seven years, Pat Hardy and artist Michael Walek (and, more recently, artist Susan Amons), doing business as Fancy Painters, have been busy restoring ornamental painting and murals, and painting original architectural ornamentation. This fine commercial art venture began when Walek's great friend Robert Beardsley asked the two artists to help restore a Queen Anne-style house he had purchased in Kennebunk, and has since expanded to include everything from painstaking recreations of Victorian freizework to Pop art murals (Elvis, Marilyn, Betty Boop, etc.) for Shape, Inc., in Biddeford and a hi-tech *trompe-l'oeil* replica of a Strategic Air Command control room for a Digital Corporation trade-show display.

"I don't know that it is related closely to what my own work looks like," says Hardy of her fanciwork. "I don't think it's art. To me it's just fun. It's decoration."

Fancy painting may be fun, but it is also hard, time-consuming work, and one of the ways Pat Hardy has found to support the Hardys' common commitment to a life of art (teaching art is another). Except for free-lance stints as set designer for local theater groups, DeWitt Hardy has enjoyed the rare privilege of life completely devoted to painting. It has never been easy and not always lucrative, but Pat Hardy says, "Making a living was never an issue. You just had to distinguish yourself."

In the business of making a painting, you're really in "the miracle business," says DeWitt. "If you don't produce a miracle, nobody wants to look at it. It's a very daunting process, but if you've got to explain it, there is no miracle."

May 5, 1989

Transplanted Visions

Lisa Allen & Mark Wethli

A year from now, the travelling exhibition, *New England Now: Contemporary Art From Six States*, will open at the DeCordova Museum in Lincoln, Massachusetts. From there, the exhibition will make the round of the New England states with stops at the Currier Gallery of Art in New Hampshire, the University of Vermont, Brown University in Rhode Island, the New Britain Museum of Art in Connecticut, and Bowdoin College in Maine (summer 1988). The idea for a major traveling survey of the best of New England art originated with John Coffey, curator of the Bowdoin College Museum of Art, and Amy Lighthill, former curator at the Museum of Fine Arts (MFA) in Boston. Once the cooperation of institutions in all six states had been enlisted (unfortunately, the MFA dropped out when Lighthill left the staff), the curators of each institution began pre-screening the best and the brightest artists in their states.

In Maine, John Coffey listed almost two dozen artists to be considered by his counterparts. Meeting as a group and working from slides, the six curators ultimately selected 27 artists for inclusion in this major, first-of-its-kind exhibition.

The final best includes four artists from Maine. As one of America's premier landscape painters, Neil Welliver was an obvious selection and, along with William Bailey of Connecticut and Gregory Gillespie of Massachusetts, will be one of the few "name" artists in the show. Marjorie Moore is well-known in the region for her playfully intelligent post-Pop creations. But the other two Maine selections may not be as familiar to Maine viewers. They are Mark Wethli of the Bowdoin College faculty and Lisa Allen of the Portland School of Art faculty. Wethli, a realist, and Allen, an abstract painter, differ markedly in the directions their art has taken, but they share a common aesthetic impulse—the liberation from ideology, which is at the root of the new pluralism in contemporary American art.

Wethli: readily accessible, but also sublime

Mark Wethli, 37, appreciates the irony of having arrived in Maine in 1985 as a "West Coast realist" only to be singled out a year later as a New England all-star. Prior to coming to Brunswick last year to direct Bowdoin's studio art program, Wethli had taught for seven years at California State University at Long Beach. Thus, in 1984, two of his paintings preceded him to Bowdoin as part of the traveling *West Coast Realism* exhibition organized by the

Laguna Beach Museum of Art. These two immaculate studio interiors may be the only Wethli paintings Maine audiences have seen to date, for while the artist is in the process of shifting his focus toward the New York art scene, he is still primarily oriented toward Los Angeles. Next spring Wethli will have a one-artist show at the Koplin Gallery in L.A. In the fall of '87, just prior to the opening of the New England invitational, he will be given his first museum exhibition at the Long Beach Museum of Art.

The exhibition catalog of *West Coast Realism* acknowledged, however, that Mark Wethli does not really belong to any regional school of art. "His work relates not at all to a Southern California milieu," wrote curator Lynn Gamwell, "nor to any other place he has lived for that matter, but has a timeless, universal quality that has more to do with Van Eyck and Vermeer than with contemporary variations on realism."

"Moving to Maine was a way of bringing my environment into synch with my art," says Wethli, explaining that the quality of light in his paintings was never the buttery Mediterranean light of California, but always the cool northern light of his native New York State.

Mark Wethli is a quiet, thoughtful, confident young man. As an artist and teacher, he is the product of the homogenizing effect of mobile American society and rapidly transferred American culture. Born in New York but educated in Florida, he has worked in New York City; Cedar Rapids, Iowa; Long Beach, California; and Brunswick, Maine. He has escaped the identifiable imprint of place. In this, Wethli is representative of the new generation of American artists, those maturing after the decentralization of art and the brief flourishing of regionalism (California funk, New York new wave, Chicago grit, Texas brut, New England realism, etc.) that took place in the 1970s in the wake of modernism. This generation is less the product of regions, styles, and -isms than of graduate school educations and instantly transmitted cultural currents. More mobile than most, Mark Wethli got on the artistic fast track early.

When he was in high school, Wethli's family moved from suburban New York to Florida, where he eventually received a scholarship to the University of Miami (BFA, 1971; MFA, 1973). But Wethli escaped the provincial stamp of the southeast because of his father's job.

"My dad was an airline pilot, so I was a world traveler," explains Wethli. "In my junior and senior years in college, I went to New York most weekends. The free pass to fly provided the texture of my life. Between learning the lessons in the classroom and going to see Matisses and Vermeers, there was the sum of the education I was getting. By the time I was 20, I was already in a gallery on Madison Avenue."

While still in school in Florida, Wethli was showing in New York at French & Company, and when gallery manager Nancy Hoffman left to form her own gallery, now a firmly established part of the New York art scene, she took Wethli with her. After completing his MFA in painting at Miami in 1973, Wethli himself moved to New York where he worked as a commercial artist, first as art director of *Film International*, a short-lived cinema journal produced by Stan Lee of Marvel Comics fame, and then designing sheet music for a music publishing company. His nine-to-five routine did not allow Wethli a great deal of time to pursue his own art, but he did manage to have a painting included in the 1975 Whitney Biennial, a show that has launched a great many young careers.

In 1976, in search of time and room to work, Wethli accepted a teaching position at the University of Northern Iowa. In Iowa, he experienced a sort of aesthetic crisis that changed his perspective on art decisively. The crisis was precipitated by a visit from artist Robert Irwin, the conceptual guru who has liberated the creative spirits of a great many young artists in America.

First recognized as a minimalist for his obsessive series of subtly painted stripes, Irwin eventually emerged as the master theoretician of the manipulated environment. Art ceased to be a manufactured commodity with Irwin, becoming instead a public mission to gently force people to become aware of and appreciate "the visual wonderland" all around them. To this end, Irwin has installed strategic scrims in empty gallery rooms to manipulate light and

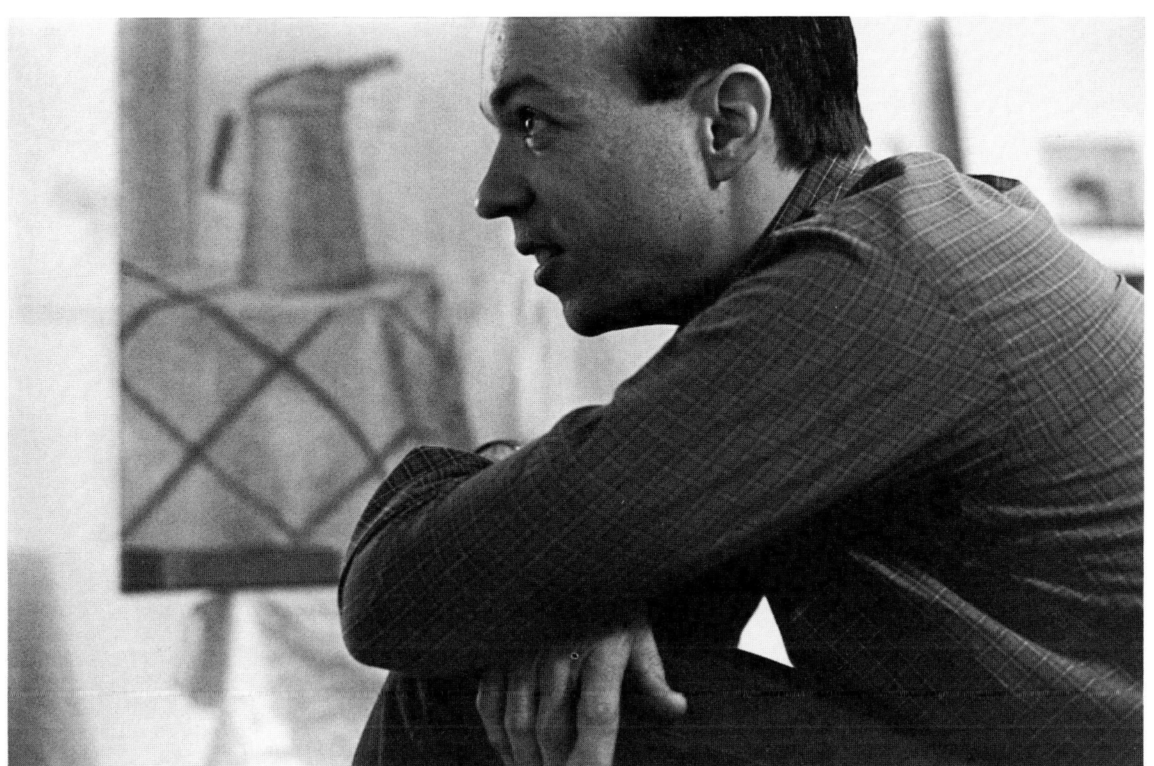

1. *Mark Wethli was a "West Coast Realist" before he moved east and became a New England all-star. Photo by Christopher Ayres.*

space, installed planes of Cor-Ten steel across segments of landscape, and proposed slightly elevating patches of earth to heighten one's experience of place. To an easel painter like Wethli, married to classical realism, such notions were both liberating and inhibiting. How to continue, in good consciousness, making conventional representational paintings when one had seen the light?

"In Iowa," says Wethli, " I really came under [Robert Irwin's] spell, the ideas in his work and that of people like [experimental composer] John Cage and [painter] Jasper Johns. I did a body of work in Iowa that was not representational, but more phenomenological, about conditions arising out of an object. Having been exposed to Irwin, I looked at art entirely differently."

In 1978, Wethli left Iowa for Robert Irwin's home turf, Los Angeles, but by this time he had resolved his international conflicts about making paintings. The resolution came about as the realization that the concepts Robert Irwin stood for were liberating in a total sense. There was really no reason why an artist couldn't bring a heightened conciousness of perception to bear on conventional realist painting. And that has been what Mark Wethli has been about ever since.

"Historically," says Wethli, "realism is the style of certainty, the entrenched, the established, but I try to give it a twist, to use one language to undermine itself."

Use realistic means to undermine realism? Precisely.

In Wethli's studio, a space under the eaves of the Bowdoin mathematics building, is a still life of wilted pink gladiolas in a simple white vase. The flowers and vase are set against the background of a crumbling wall. The subject and setting suggest decaying beauty. The gilt frame enhances the sense of the painting's preciousness, one of life's prizes. Because Wethli works very slowly, this is one of few finished paintings in his studio. And because he wishes to enforce an intimate isolation on the viewer, the painting is small, perhaps eight by ten inches.

"It looks very deterministic," says the artist of the painting. "There is no evidence of doubt or change. My works tend to be very, very confident, finished, resolved. But, in fact, the process they go through is very unphotographic and unrealistic. It is very much a finding process."

Wethli makes a distinction between paintings that are "made" and paintings that are "found." Similarly, he notes critic Robert Hughes' distinction between paintings that are made to be "looked at" (the majority of Western art) and

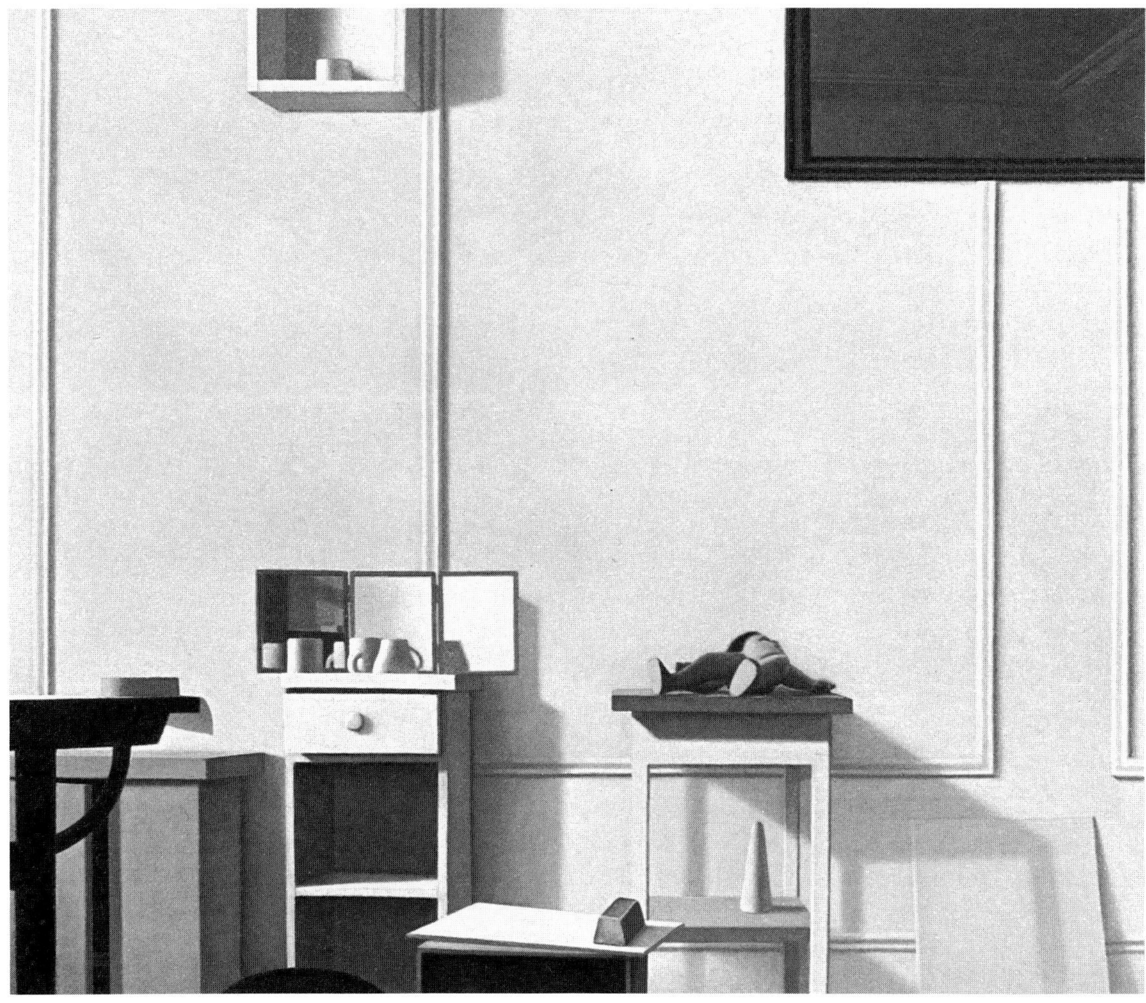

2. *Mark Wethli,* New York Studio, *1985. Oil on board. Courtesy of the artist.*

paintings that are meant to be "scanned" (most contemporary painting). His own work is designed to be looked at. What Wethli is after is a moment of transcendence in which a realistically represented object or image is elevated from simple "likeness" to the sublime. Wethli believes the sublime is only experienced when the viewer is no longer aware of the "artistic maneuver" at work on his perception. He believes it should be just as possible for him to achieve this state through the manipulation of paint on canvas as it is for Robert Irwin to invoke it through the manipulation of phenomenal reality. To illustrate his attitude toward representative painting, Wethli uses the analogy of a Japanese garden.

"In a Western garden," says Wethli, "you have things to look at. In an Eastern garden, things are there to draw your attention to something intangible."

Wethli wants his paintings to point beyond themselves, "to throw your attention off of themselves." When his paintings are successful, Wethli says they "pop the boundaries" between perception and illusion. It is not exactness that accomplishes this breakthrough, but the sensibility the artist brings to work. In a pantheon of personal gods that includes Irwin, Mark Rothko, Philip Guston, Balthus, and Giorgio Morandi, Jan Vermeer reigns supreme. In fact, the only work of his own art that Wethli hangs in his home is a little pencil drawing of Vermeer's *The Girl With a Pearl Earring*, a painting he considers the "the most sublime and most beautiful" he has encountered. What he values in his Vermeer portrait is the way it manages to be simultaneously timeless and instantaneous, an over-the-shoulder glance caught as though at 125th of a second and frozen forever on canvas.

"In one sense," says Wethli, "I'm very Platonic. The essence of my painting is a kind of moment in which the ideal takes residence in a less than ideal form. Unlike a lot of realists, who tend to be empiricists, I tend to come out of the ideal into the object."

Mark Wethli's paintings possess a conventional beauty that makes them readily accessible to the average viewer, yet they also satisfy his own subliminal criteria, the subtext of awareness that informs his intuitive approach to reality.

Allen: Thrashing it out with thick paint

Lisa Allen, 31, is better known in Maine than Mark Wethli, both because she has been here longer and because she has exhibited more frequently. Allen came to Maine from Chicago in 1981 to teach at the Portland School of Art. Since then she has shown in group shows at Bowdoin, Colby, the Portland Museum of Art, Maine Coast Artists, Hobe Sound Galleries North in Portland, and Gallery Sixty-Eight in Belfast. Like Wethli, however, she is not represented on a regular basis by a Maine gallery. Her only one-artist show in Maine was at the University of Maine in Orono last year, but because it took place during the summer, not many people saw it. But if Lisa Allen is not a household name in Maine, it may be because she is an abstract artist in a region not historically friendly to abstraction.

The fact that Allen will be the only nonrepresentational artist of the four representing Maine in the all-New England show next year accurately reflects the predominance of realism in Maine. Of the two dozen artists John Coffey submitted as Maine's best, only three (including Allen) could properly be considered abstract artists. Abstraction is primarily an urban point of view conditioned by the inner directedness required of confined, unlovely surroundings, but Lisa Allen is a country girl at heart, having grown up on her family's farm in rural Illinois. And while it may not be obvious to casual viewers, her bold, expressive abstractions are generally keyed to concepts of landscape and space. Indeed, Lisa Allen is most animated and articulate when discussing the qualities of landscapes she has experienced, whether the hill farm and groves on the edge of Illinois flatness, the monumentality of the desert Southwest, or the watery wildness of Maine.

Lisa Allen began painting as a farm girl in Illinois in part because she envied and sought to emulate her older sisters and cousins who took painting lessons with an artistic aunt. Those childhood impulses were quite naturally directed toward accurately representing whatever she was looking at at the time. The shift toward abstraction came later at the University of Illinois at Champaign-Urbana (BFA, 1977; Masters in Lithography, 1979). At the university, Allen was initially influenced by teachers Bill Briggs, a hard-edged colorist, and Vicky Briggs, an expressionist painter. It was not until she was doing graduate work in lithography that Allen began to find herself as a painter. If the landscape remains central to her thematic content, it is the process of printmaking that most directly impacts her paintings in a material way.

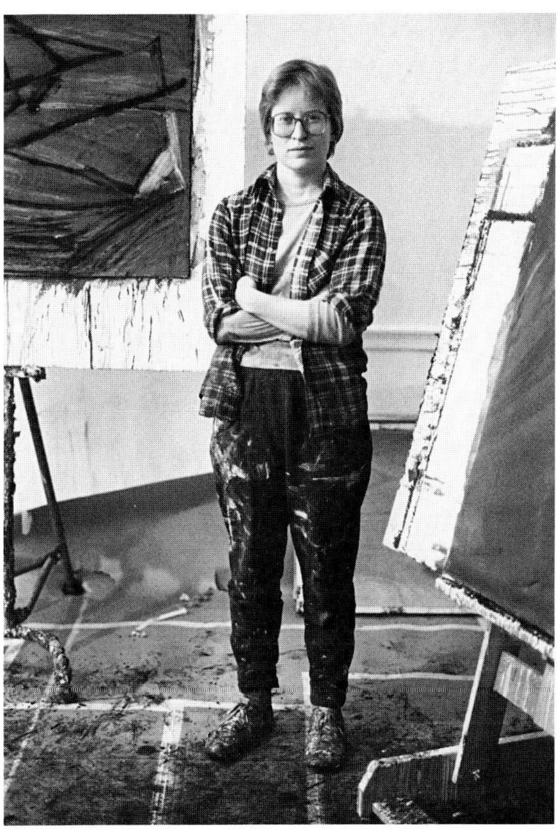

3. *Lisa Allen in her studio. Photo by Christopher Ayres.*

"The influence of lithography in terms of color-layering, physically building a print, was a major influence on my painting," says Allen.

It was not until 1979 that Lisa Allen traveled outside of Illinois, a trip to Arizona being a major eye-opener for her. Stunned by the monumental scale of the landscape and the dramatic forms of desert cactus, she returned to Illinois to produce some of the very few works in her career that contain recognizable imagery.

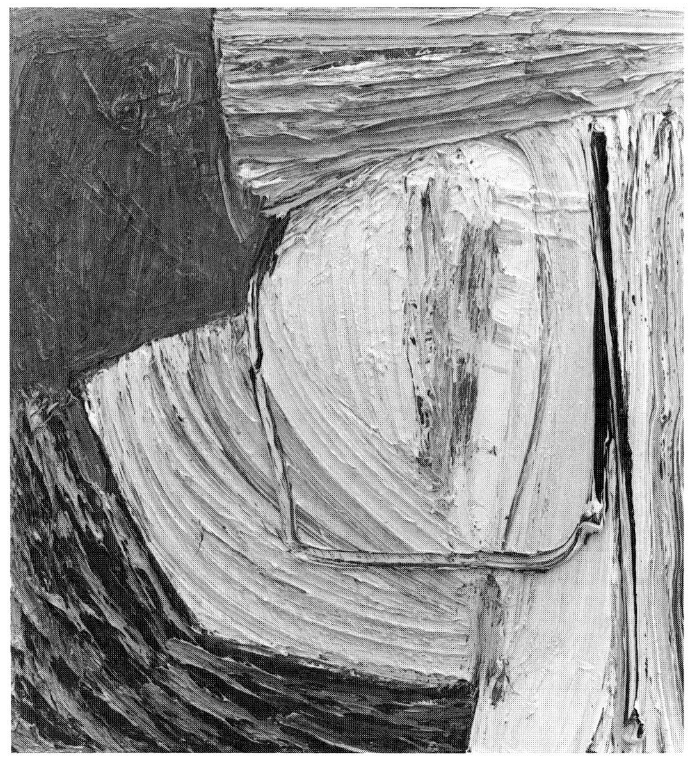

4. *Lisa Allen,* Fold, *1982. Oil on board. Courtesy of the Stephen Rosenberg Gallery.*

"I started applying paint and removing it and these clean, specific, funny images would appear. They had a sense of impending doom and humor all in the same space."

These images of rooms caught in a maelstrom, walls flying apart, apocalyptic cacti bristling from the external ether, disappeared, however, when the artist moved to Chicago.

"I think the city made me aware of my connection with the country," Allen says. "So I started doing these paintings about landscape again. They were about color and space with color becoming a primary, primary interest. The paint got thicker, too."

Lisa Allen's studio is in the Congress Building, a drab urban warren filled with odd medical specialists, nonprofit headquarters, and artists' studios. It is a long narrow room with white sheets at the window, paint spattered everywhere, and large (typically six by four feet) panels densely worked with bright oils. The best Allen abstractions tend to be complex surfaces built up of layers of color (red, black, and a deep forest-green predominating) that only seem to achieve the proper tension and balance once they threaten to drip off the surface. Allen must be one of the few artists ("Oh, you might be surprised") who applies paints directly by hand, wearing latex gloves. This hands-on application results in works that have an aggressive humanity both in size and texture. The runnels and rivulets of her thick surfaces are finger strokes, not brush strokes. The gestural passages of color are exactly that—gestures, movements of the hand, finger, palm.

Just as Mark Wethli waits for the ideal to find residence in the real, Lisa Allen says her work is a matter of "finding the form through the process."

"I find the best way for me to work," says the artist, "is to come in here every day and see what evolves. I try not to have any particular expectations. It's the classic mystery of the thing unfolding in front of you. What I'm looking for is a sense of solidity. What I try to avoid is when something is pleasant, but doesn't have any real substance. I'm not interested in formal ideas; I'm interested in something coming out that's convincing. When they're good, each painting seems to have its own personality. I kind of thrash around a lot is what it comes down to."

This thrashing around results in paintings that have an autobiographical core, paintings that use the structural forces and components of landscape (mass, density, color, form, shape) to convey the internal forces at work on the artist. In this, they might be considered mainstream abstract expressionist works. The obvious comparisons that come to mind are the works of Elizabeth Murray (a fellow Illinoisan) and Gregory Amenoff, a premier Boston-area artist not included in the New England survey, perhaps because he is now working in New York. Allen accepts these associations tentatively, but disassociates herself from the fashionable body of contemporary art referred to as neo-expressionism.

"I feel my process is expressionist," Allen explains, "but when they really work I think they are intelligent paintings also. The neo-expressionists are more about nihilism and crudeness. I'm interested in refinement, but using the materials in an emotional and sensual way, not just throwing it around, but defining it in the end."

There are three major paintings standing against the walls of Allen's studio. (Several other new works have recently been transported to the Stephen Rosenberg Gallery, the New York gallery that recently took on Allen's work.) *Stone Circle* is a powerful rectangle of red, maroon, purple, and yellow shapes orbiting slowly within a matrix of glossy blacks. It was inspired, says the artist, by her experience of stone circles in England and Scotland. It was not her intention to distill the essence of her British travels, but that is what evolved through the process of "thrashing around."

"One day," says Allen of the painting, "it just felt real still—quiet, reserved, yet powerful, like Scotland. There was this sense of containment and power, quiet power."

The other two paintings are *Morning*, a diffuse and dynamic display of color passages which have been smeared, pulled, wiped, and dragged over the surface, and an untitled vertical panel orchestrated around a central fall of pure white surrounded by deep green and black forms. As with most of Allen's paintings, her fingers have left great striations, rifts, and ridges running rhythmically through the paint.

"These paintings are completely about Maine," Allen says. "They are about water and space. That's Maine. They're also about turbulence. Maine is placid, but it is also wild."

Oddly enough, despite the stylistic gulf that separates the precision of Mark Wethli's realist interiors and the turbulence of Lisa Allen's landscape abstractions, the two artists find a common ground in their formative response to the thought and example of Robert Irwin.

"I saw Irwin in Illinois," says Allen, "and he had a real major impact on me. I was impressed by his whole sense of anything being possible, the feeling that art is about the ultimate sense of freedom. He really does open doors, but he's also very intimidating because he's not at all negative. He's totally positive."

When Robert Irwin appeared at Bowdoin last month at Mark Wethli's invitation, many of Lisa Allen's Portland School of Art students attended. With any luck, once this new corps of artists figures out what Irwin was all about, we can expect a liberating influence at least as great as that which helped produce two young artists now deemed to be among the best in New England.

November 21, 1986

Deep in the Dumb

Marjorie Moore

"In Atlantic City," says Marjorie Moore, "there used to be this high-diving act at the Steel Pier. A woman rider all dressed in spangles would get on a horse, climb up a ramp to a 60-foot tower, and then dive off into a tank of water. I saw this when I was eight years old. It was my first trip to the ocean and I was with a favorite aunt and uncle. I've never forgotten it."

Marjorie Moore is talking about the inspiration for an audio-cassette children's book she would like to create. The subject matter may sound a bit bizarre, but then the Famous Diving Horse of Atlantic City has all the ingredients of a great Marjorie Moore work of art—a peculiar animal-human relationship, an element of theater, a sense of humor, and the appropriation of popular culture imagery for fine art purposes.

In recent years, Marjorie Moore has been making "animal art" of increasing visual intensity and imaginative reach. Dogs, deer, moose, and, most recently, elephants animate her art in the most surprising ways. She is certainly the only Maine artist capable of taking Bambi and Dumbo seriously as the stuff of art.

"Ever since I was a kid I've always had a lot of fantasy going on. One reason I do the kind of art I do is that it takes me back to those places, frees up my mind to think about the past and my family."

Moore was born in 1944 in Akron, Ohio, where her father worked as an engineer in a steel mill and her mother, who had studied illustration at Pratt Institute, did fashion illustrating and modeled.

"My mother was very interested in art and took me to museums as a kid. Around the fifth grade or so, we went to see a Van Gogh show at the Cleveland Art Institute. I was blown away! I had never seen paintings like that! From the time I was in junior high school, I knew I was going to be an artist."

In 1962, an eighteen-year-old determined to become an artist but too timid to tackle anyplace as arty as the Rhode Island School of Design, Moore enrolled at Syracuse University where, influenced by her mother, she initially majored in illustration. During the years she was at Syracuse (1962-66), Pop art was blowing abstract expressionism off the New York art map, and illustration, of course, was at the heart of the Pop aesthetic. Pop-meister James Rosenquist, in fact, was a visiting artist at Syracuse, and Pop idioms still flavor Marjorie Moore's art, but she insists that as a student her art was much more instinctive than intellectual.

"It took me years," she laughs, "to come around to thinking about ideas before dealing with a piece of art."

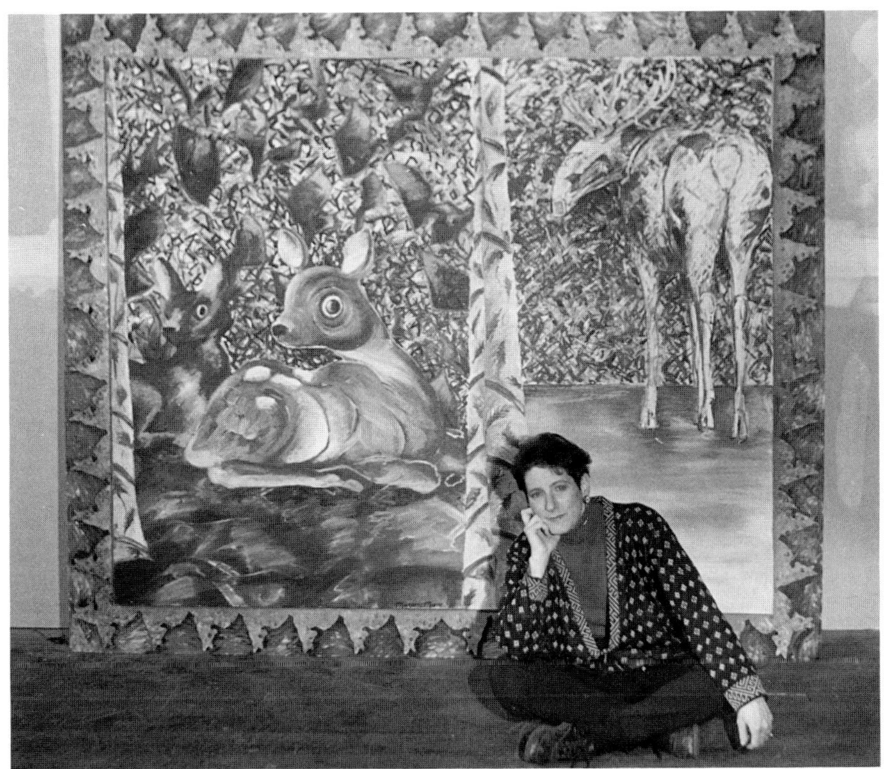

1. *Marjorie Moore seated in front of one of her paintings,* Trouble in the Thicket. *Photo by Scott Perry.*

Another important influence from her Syracuse days was an interest in architecture acquired from a young architecture student named Steven Moore. Steven and Marjorie Moore were married in 1966, and today Steven Moore, a partner in the firm of Moore-Weinrich in Brunswick, is one of Maine's best-known architects.

After college, Steven and Marjorie Moore joined the Peace Corps together and spent the turbulent years of the late sixties in medieval Iran. Moore says the only visible influences of her Iranian experience on her art are obscure at best—the hooded deer which appear in some of her paintings remind her of veiled Moslem women, that sort of thing. But being out of the country during the decisive days of the decade, reading about the race riots, political demonstrations, and assassinations back home in month-old magazines, seems to have permanently warped Moore's vision of America.

"We suffered reverse culture shock," she says. "We missed the years 1967 to 1969 in this culture. We knew peripherally what was going on, but getting off the plane in Washington in the summer of 1969 I thought things were going to be burning before my eyes."

Marjorie Moore is not a nostalgic hippie, but the '60s sensibility does survive in her art, principally in her use of humor as a goad to consciousness—the '60s "goof" as serious art strategy. The handmade aesthetic of the counterculture, however, is more often associated with the potters and weavers of the crafts movement than with the fine arts, and Moore did, in fact, begin her creative life in Maine as a craftsperson.

On Halloween day, 1970, Marjorie and Steven Moore moved to a 125-acre farm at Rumford Point which they had found on a camping trip to Mt. Blue. The original idea was to establish a commune on the farm, but that idea lasted only a few months. Intent on supporting themselves with craftswork, Marjorie began making puppets while Steven designed and made furniture.

Moore's first puppet business proved successful, but the artist incubating in her began to feel constrained by all the construction. ("I felt I was spending my whole life behind a sewing machine.") Her disenchantment with fabric art reached a crisis point during the summer of 1978 when, while teaching at the Haystack Mountain School of Crafts, she experienced what might be called a "material nausea."

"I just saw all this work and suddenly felt 'I can't do this anymore. I've got to stop.' There

was just this proliferation of STUFF! It was like a boutique, too commercialized."

Having moved to Brunswick in 1977, Moore rented studio space in the basement of the old Grant's department store and began experimenting, painting on plywood, making constructions, working in neon. Initially, she worked in the Pop vein with kitsch postcard imagery and vernacular architecture (Moody's Diner, The Half Moon Motel in Freeport, etc.), but soon she began to be seduced by animals.

In 1981, for instance, Moore erected her *Cow Fence* outside Barridoff Galleries in Portland coincident with her *Rural Signs and Billboards* show inside. Her use of Holsteins as billboards was a perfect marriage of her interest in animals and roadside architecture. The real breakthrough in her animal consciousness, however, occurred later in the year, when first prize at the 1981 All Maine Biennial was awarded to an innocuous painting of a deer jumping a fence by moonlight.

Upset that a supposedly sophisticated, out-of-state jury should select an amateur picture of a deer as the best of new Maine art, Moore began drawing and painting deer with a vengeance. Among the first and most literal of her deer works were those in her *Journey to Greenville* series, a group of images inspired by a family ski trip. In a drawing such as *Journey to Greenville II*, for instance, Moore makes a rather blunt comment about the starkness of life in northern Maine by simply depicting a mobile home and a deer in a bleak, wintry landscape.

"When I first started the deer paintings," Moore says, "they were as much about the culture as about the animal, but deep down inside I think the reason I chose deer was my feeling about the animal being manipulated."

From the factual commentary of the *Journey to Greenville* series, Moore quickly took flight into fantasy. In 1984, for example, she satirized the ritual aspects of hunting in a multi-media installation at Bowdoin College entitled *The Artist as Hunter*.

In the 1986 performance piece *Toying in the Woods*, which Moore collaborated on at Portland Museum of Art, and in related paintings such as *Trouble in the Thicket* and *Cervine Mutations*, she appropriated Walt Disney's Bambi as a symbol of man's ultimate manipulation of nature. In Bambi, something with wild integrity has devolved into a figure of absurd banality.

"There's always been an edge to whatever I've done," says the artist, "and that edge is sitting on a bridge between a sense of the absurd and wanting to say something about what's happening to us."

It is not lost on Moore, for instance, that behind Bambi's cartoon cuteness is a tale of mother loss, loss of innocence, coming of age, and initiation into power. Pushing her art and ideas ever farther from the conventional, Moore has more recently seized upon the character and figure of Disney's Dumbo as absurd hero.

"Dumbo," Moore points out wryly, "is an outcast who learns to fly in order to free his mother. These stories are very ancient. They are about the soul of us all."

Bambi meets Dumbo on the road to salvation and deliverance. Absurd? Perhaps. But Marjorie Moore is an artist who is constantly seeking the deep in the dumb, the meaningful in the mundane, the truth in the trite.

The wackiness of Moore's subject matter has a tendency to obscure the finesse of her execution. For all her inventive use of media, she is still primarily a painter. And just as her animal imagery has intensified, so her handling of paint has become more excited and exciting. The early graphic quality of her work has given way to expressionist brushwork, but she does not see herself headed the way of pure abstraction.

"I can't paint without subject matter, and I need the physicality of paint to make the subject come alive."

Moore's painterly influences are diverse—the figuration of Francis Bacon, the abstractions of Willem de Kooning, the Pop imagery of Jim Dine, Robert Rauschenberg, and James Rosenquist—but she reserves a special place in her pantheon of personal greats for Lucas Samaras. Samaras, who has worked in mediums ranging from mirror glass to Polaroid snapshots, is one of the few major artists who has managed to slip the noose of style.

"There's no consistency to his work," says Moore of Samaras, "except that it's all bizarre."

Marjorie Moore's own consistently bizarre art

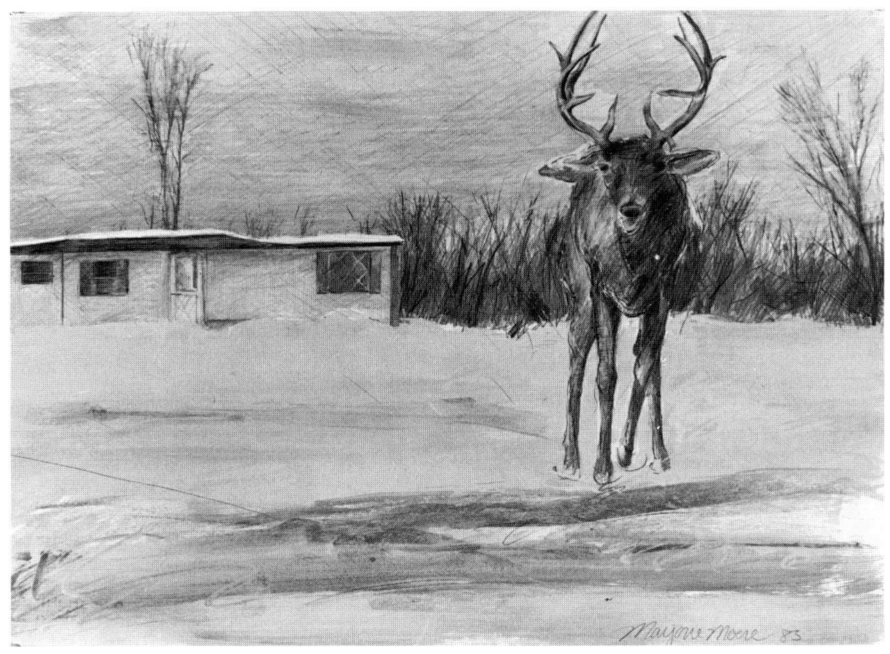

2. *Marjorie Moore,* Journey to Greenville II, *1983. Mixed media on paper. Courtesy of the artist.*

has earned her a growing regional reputation. In 1987, she was selected along with Lisa Allen, Neil Welliver, and Mark Wethli to represent Maine in *New England Now*, a traveling exhibition conceived as an all-star exhibition of New England artists. In 1988, she won a coveted fellowship to the MacDowell Colony in Petersborough, New Hampshire, where she painted a difficult group of paintings she calls her *High-Wired Series*.

The *High-Wired Series* paintings, never exhibited in Maine, depict a strange figure which seems to be Moore's apotheosis of Self. In the solitude of the artists' colony, Moore conjured up a being at once human, canine, and marionette who performs an awkward balancing act in the garish light of a circus tent. In most of the *High-Wired* paintings, this Moore-anima seems in immediate danger of falling, but in *On and Off the Shelf*, a painting now in the collection of the Rose Art Museum at Brandeis University, her doggy other is just sitting there like a lifeless doll.

"One of the things that scares me most," says Moore, "is becoming a Maine artist who gets taken down off the shelf and dusted off once in awhile."

And so 1990 finds Marjorie Moore struggling with the limited horizons Maine can offer an artist. She has done most of what an artist can do here. Now she's beginning to "look for stimulation beyond Maine." Just what form this stimulation might take—relocation, a career move, a new direction in her art—she cannot say, but in her most recent work Moore seems to be looking deeply into her past for signs of her future.

Tacked around the walls of the tower studio attached to Moore's Brunswick home are a series of new works which combine animal imagery and text. One piece seems particularly prescient. It is a diptych in which the left half is covered with a pattern of wolf-like forms while the right contains a picture of a German shepherd named Strongheart staring out a window.

"A wonderful picture of Strongheart," read the words of the children's book from which it came. "Gone for the time is the wild lure of the north. His brother the Wolf calls no more. In place of it all is the even, smooth tenor of civilization, of life among men. Sometimes, I think, there comes a strange loneliness and desire for that life of the far North."

"I don't have to make this stuff up," Marjorie Moore laughs. "It's out there."

February 9, 1990

A Few Rounds with Carlo Pittore

Carlo Pittore

The industrious painter Carlo Pittore, of whom in disorderly passages we are now to speak, has earned modest renown for his whimsical graphic work, but his serious paintings have steadfastly failed to find an audience. In his recent paintings he treats boxers, and through them attempts to prove that to paint the figure with an eye to the third dimension is the rightful pursuit of contemporary art. He is in his way a disciple of the great painters of the Italian Renaissance, laboring not to imitate but to emulate his masters. While working on his boxers, he lives in a yurt in the Bowdoinham woods and maintains the Academy of Carlo Pittore in a former chicken slaughterhouse nearby. Pittore often makes copies after the Italian masters, and on one wall of his studio hangs an unfinished copy of *The Resurrection of the Saved* by Luca Signorelli, whose life as recorded by Vasari begins with a paragraph not unlike this one.

Okay, so everybody knows Carlo Pittore. Eyebrows are habitually raised when his name is mentioned. But do we know him? Really know him, that is? I'm not sure I do.

What I do know is this: Carlo Pittore is a coeval of *Maine Times*, having arrived in Maine from New York in 1968 just as the first issue of the paper was going to press. He was Charles Stanley the writer then, but in Bowdoinham one day he heard a voice, simultaneously internal and external. "Charles," it said, "you were always going to be an artist when you grew up. You've grown up now—you better move your ass." So in 1969 he moved to Portland, where he lived on Portland Pier and attended Portland School of Art, briefly. In 1971, following the good advice of Dean Hogg of the Episcopal Church, he set out for London where he studied at the Chelsea Art School. Shortly thereafter, Stanley moved to Montecielo, a little Italian hilltown where he became Carlo Pittore (Charles the Painter), confirmed Italophile.

"In Italy there is respect for somebody who wants to be an artist," explains Pittore. "In America there is skepticism and contempt."

Carlo Pittore is the avowed foe of all who would exploit artists. In 1975 he helped found the Union of Maine Visual Artists, champions of artists' rights in Maine. All of his battles are about respect—respect for art, respect for artists as members of the community, respect for himself. As recently as last week Pittore was going toe-to-toe with the Portland School of Art alumni association over its policy of charging artists a $5 entry fee to submit work to its annual exhibition. Artists exploiting themselves. The battle of entry fees was fought and won years ago, but as Pittore points out, "The price

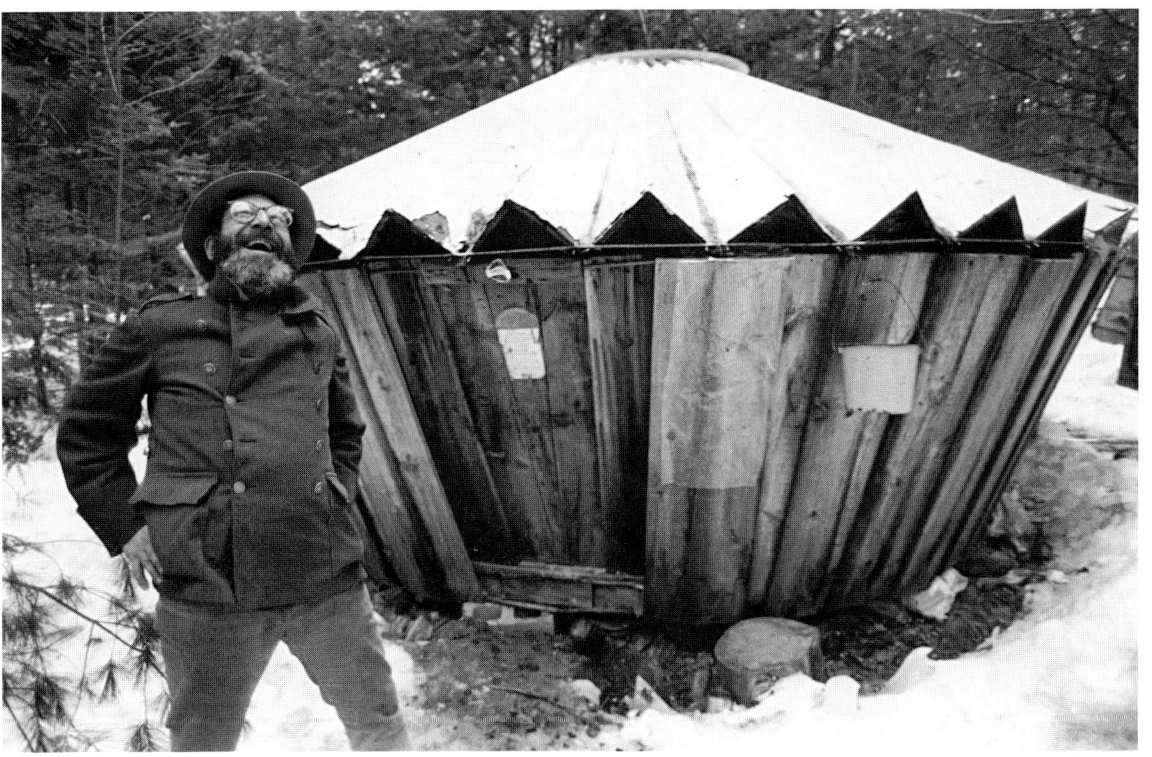

1. *Carlo Pittore has himself a good laugh outside his yurt in Bowdoinham. Photo by Christopher Ayres.*

of liberty is eternal vigilance."

Yes, who in the Maine art world has not received urgent letters written in Carlo Pittore's bold, black hand, letters arguing for support and justice and standards and right thinking, letters covered in the art stamps for which Carlo Pittore is known, if he is known at all? Certainly I have, many, always passionate, always entertaining, always welcome.

Knowing Carlo Pittore only through his letters, I traveled to Orono in 1981 when *The Printed Art of Carlo Pittore* was featured at the university gallery. At the time I read Pittore's autobiographical postcards and stamps as the work of a raving egomaniac, an artist engaged in a cult of Self, said as much, and resolved to avoid Mr. Pittore whenever possible. Very possibly I was wrong, but then I had never met the man or seen any of his paintings. In fact, Pittore hadn't really shown his paintings in Maine since his *Blackwerk* show (all-black paintings inspired both by a need to understand color and by the death of a friend) at Bowdoin College in 1977. Then, in February of this year, he was invited to exhibit his paintings of boxers at the Seamen's Club in Portland. I had every intention of taking this opportunity to see a body of his work, but before you could say "Old Port" another letter in the familiar black hand arrived informing me that Pittore had withdrawn his paintings from the artsy bistro. It seems some diners of delicate constitution had objected to eating beneath paintings of bloodied prizefighters, and restaurant owner Joe Soley, who has been earnestly cultivating his image as an art patron since arriving in town, summarily removed the offending picture. So much for Mr. Soley's credibility as an art lover. Carlo yanked the show.

"It's all right that he found it offensive," said Pittore of Soley's action. "It's not all right that he had no dealing with me or with the woman who put the show up [before he removed the paintings]."

In order to see Pittore's boxing paintings, therefore, I drove out to Merrymeeting Farm, where the artist's great friend and patroness Priscilla Berry provides Pittore shelter in Bowdoinham's fabled yurts and studio space in her former chicken plant. A tendril of a footpath leads through deep snow from the studio across an excellent and pristine field to the yurt, one of eight or nine hidden in a grove of pasture pine. The world there is still and quiet, an ice palace, the snow-domed yurts standing like giant cupcakes in a slightly surreal wood. The artist, who often winters in New York City, has the yurts to himself this winter. His cozy hut is the lair of a solitary, warm with wood heat, littered with books, papers, blankets, and the

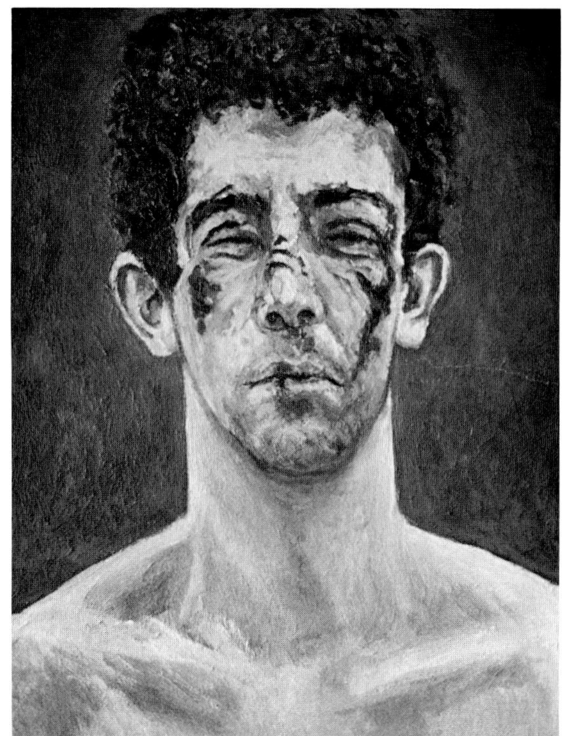

2. *Carlo Pittore,* Battered Boxer, *1984. Oil on canvas. Courtesy of the artist.*

essentials of a spartan existence.

Pittore's studio, the Academy, is utilitarian space enlivened only by the artist's presence and industry. The Carlo Pittore I found there bore a passing likeness to the daffy Toulouse Lautrec/Charlie Chaplin figure of Pittore/Stanley's postal altered ego, but he was decidedly not the madman I had been avoiding all these years. Pittore, 44 and starting to grey, is either an aging hippie or a latter-day beatnik, a theatrical fellow possessed of a whimsical good humor and a burning passion to paint. Though he is capable of ranting and raving with the greats, his most effective locution is the habit of affecting a stage whisper to confide important, but potentially controversial, thoughts such as "I'm 44 and I really don't know anybody who LOVES painting." What I was not prepared for was Pittore's vulnerability, the intimation of deep hurt because his work has not been taken more seriously.

The paintings of boxers I had come to see were stored in an unheated room attached to Pittore's studio. There were images of boxers slumped in the corner of the ring, boxers ducking under the ropes, boxers trying to rise off the canvas (literally and figuratively), boxers taking a punch, throwing a punch, feinting, defiant, exhausted, defeated. "The artist's lot is the fighter's lot," they seem to say. There were about 20 paintings in all, part of a series—now numbering 80—begun in 1981 when the artist wandered into a New York City gym by mistake while looking for a sketch class. All are painted in meaty pinks with green shadows against green-black backgrounds. ("All great painting is based on a red-green axis," maintains Pittore.) The best of the boxer paintings is the very one that was first removed from the Seamen's Club, a full-front head and shoulders portrait of a badly battered fighter, an image of almost iconic simplicity. Pittore says it is his Christ.

When paintings in this series were shown in Chicago last fall, a reviewer for the *Chicago Tribune* wrote, "The painting itself is only workmanlike, but when he treats boxers we feel the heightened degree of his identification." When I confessed that with the exception of the Christ-like portrait, a singular painting in its own right, I tended to agree with the Chicago reviewer's assessment, Pittore said the review had made him indignant.

"I think someone might have looked at Cezanne's canvases and said something like that and then been embarrassed 20 years later."

And so I asked myself, would one call the late paintings of Philip Guston—clumsy compositions of cartooned heads, discarded shoes, cigarette butts—"workmanlike"? Certainly they are awkwardly painted, but the awkwardness is part of the intention. Guston, perhaps more than any other artist of his generation, granted permission to the current generation of painters to paint "badly," to make the difficulty of painting part of painting. ("Guston is the great master of our century," says Pittore.) New York is now filled with young painters who succeed wildly in their deliberate attempts to paint badly. The irony is that Carlo Pittore fails (if not having sold a painting in 20 years except to friends is considered failure) on the same count by trying to paint correctly.

"Paint correctly"?

"THE ACADEMY OF CARLO PITTORE," states the brochure for the art classes Pittore has been teaching in recent months, "is dedicated to reviving the dying art of painting by resuming the explorations of the great tradition of Italian painting, the mural, and the pursuit of the third dimension. Because the 20th Century has essentially eschewed 3-dimensionality, and then, the figure; and as painting has diminished even while it has become more popular & all but ceased to be handmade, the Academy is dedicated to encouraging the process of learning to see and to paint the human figure."

Such a conservative philosophy seemed entirely out of character for such a radical artist, but Pittore insisted his single-minded "pursuit of the third dimension" is radical in this day and age.

"Flat art," argued Pittore, "is graphic art. Fine art can't be graphic. The pursuit of the third dimension, that's the problem of all art, all fine art, and it always has been. Giotto painted the third dimension. Cezanne was so great because he pursued the third dimension. Ingres said, 'Drawing is the probity of art.' If you don't draw correctly, what kind of intellectual fiber do you have?"

Pittore associates flatness in art, the aesthetic legacy of abstraction, with spiritual flatness.

"Society does not need the flat. It's not healthy," he said. "You begin by painting the real and striving for the ideal. Abstraction is just pure escapism."

Having listened to an equally dogmatic abstract painter argue to the contrary that figurative art is dead, that to pursue the third dimension is to pursue an illusion, I suggested to Pittore that painters like Mark Rothko and Willem de Kooning certainly seemed to have captured something spiritual in their paintings. Abstraction was okay in its day, the artist responded, but no longer. He then argued that Rothko painted "rounded forms" with a luminosity that admits of a third dimension. "De Kooning," he said, "definitely achieved roundness."

But it's not just style that offends Pittore's Italianate sensibility, it seems; it's also the commercialism of modern art.

"America is hurting right now," said Pittore, "because we have completely forsaken the spiritual in art. Everything is money, money, money, and success. Who's talking about art for the sake of beauty, aesthetic proportion?"

Pittore plopped down the March issue of *Esquire*, containing a nasty article entitled "The Four Brushmen of the Apocalypse," a chronicle

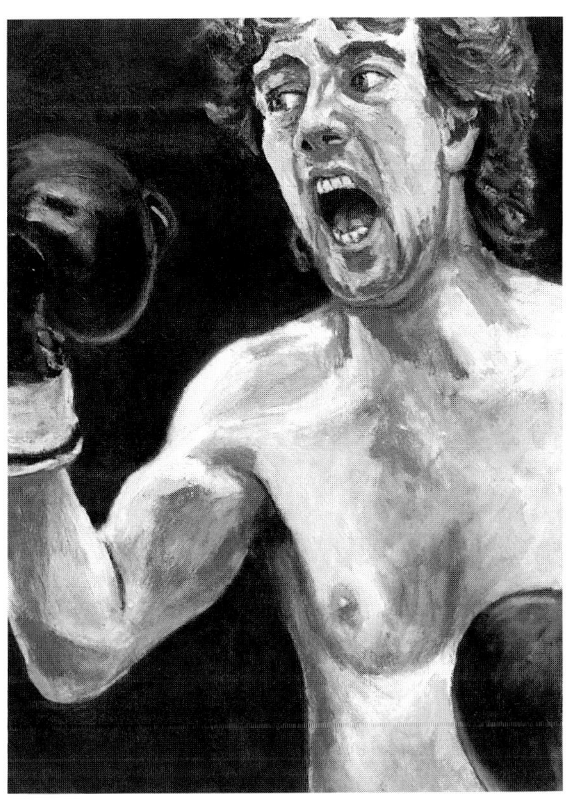

3. *Carlo Pittore,* Mother F. . ., *1984. Oil on canvas. Courtesy of the artist. Photo by Tom Warren.*

of the shallowness, jealousy, careerism and bitchiness of the contemporary American art scene as embodied in the persons of Robert Longo, Julian Schnabel, David Salle and Eric Fischl. Certainly, if this sorry state of affairs is what art in America has become—greed percolated to the highest levels of human activity—then we are all in deep trouble.

"I studied classical art," said Pittore. "I've always thought one should aspire for laurels."

Pittore the uncompromising idealist, then? Not exactly. Perhaps Pittore the uncompromised idealist.

"The fact that I get rejected is probably good," he consoled himself. "I would have sold out, too. But the fact that nobody bought me means I still have my integrity."

Later he defined his dedication in the face of adversity in a lighter way by asking, "How many dentists would still be filling cavities if they hadn't been paid for 20 years?"

Despite the fact that Carlo Pittore adopted an Italian name and identifies so thoroughly with Italian culture ("Italian for me *means* culture") does not necessarily mean that he is a dismissable eccentric intent on living a 20th-century American life as a 16th-century Italian, though Lord knows there are hugely successful American artists living under greater delusions. No,

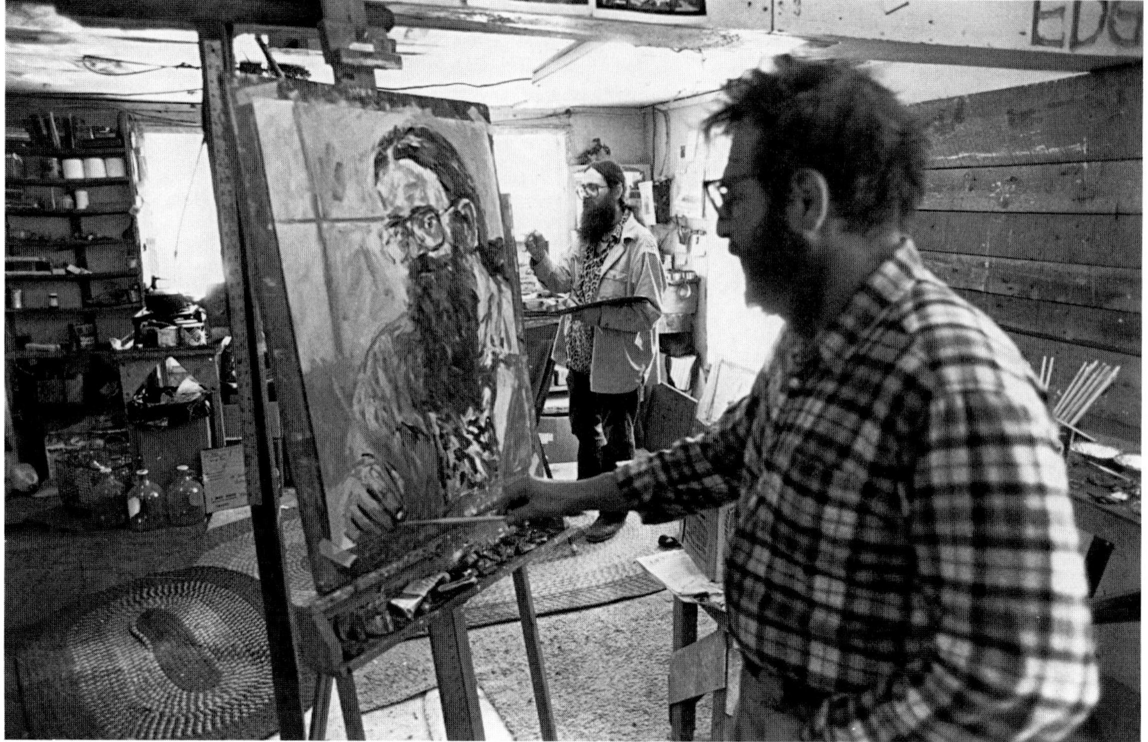

4. *Carlo Pittore painting Stephen Petroff painting Carlo Pittore. Photo by Christopher Ayres.*

his obsession with the Italian Renaissance is more an aspiration for the future than an escape into the past. It is a rejection of fashionable decadence and despair in favor of a more uplifting cultural aesthetic. Unfortunately for Pittore, the very force that urges him to seek solidarity between artists and the community seems to make him the odd man out in a cynical age.

"You talk about progress in art, progress in civilization," Pittore said. "So we have technology. Are we more civilized than the Italians were 300 years ago? No."

And so, back to Italy. I listened and recorded as Pittore extolled the virtues of his ideal. "An Italian peasant appreciates art better, instinctively, than any middle-class American... Michelangelo and Raphael made lines that were better than Nature, but they referred to Nature...If the Met brought the Sistine Chapel to this country, Michelangelo would reign for 100 years as the greatest artist in America." And listening to this paean to Italy, I began to wonder what Giorgio Vasari, architect of the Uffizi, painter of the Palazzo Vecchio frescoes, author of *The Lives of the Most Eminent Italian Architects, Painters, and Sculptors*, indeed the man who gave the Renaissance (*Il Rinascimento*) its name, would make of Carlo Pittore. In fact, I began a draft of this profile with the 475-year-old Florentine trekking through the Bowdoinham snow toward Pittore's yurt just to see how the conceit would work, but then I thought better of it. Artists, most of whom live without financial or critical rewards, at the very least deserve respect.

"So I'll be famous in 300 years," said Pittore. "That's not the goal. The goal is to make good art. Time will judge. Maybe I'm not a great artist. Maybe I'm mediocre. So I've had a lot of other disappointments."

This little speech, which began so expansively, seemed to deflate even as he spoke. That little needle of doubt, popping all our balloons. Yet the last thing Carlo Pittore said to me before I left reassured me that he had gotten his second wind, that he was back to fighting trim.

"I'm going to win, damn it," he said confidently. "I'm going to make a painting the people are going to love, a painting they will be inspired by."

March 27, 1987

Painting on Porcelain

Paul Heroux

In person, Paul Heroux is as fine and brittle as his porcelain. He is wraith-like, intensely thin. Rimless glasses, close-cropped hair, and a sparse bristle of beard contribute to a sense of concentration. If at times he seems uneasy with his own intensity, the pressure is relieved by an unguarded and unpretentious approach to his own work. He is a man blessed with a highly-refined sense of taste in all things. In fact, when art collectors began discovering Paul Heroux's ceramics a few years ago, Maine lost one of its finest chefs.

Paul Heroux, 37, was born in Rochester, N.H., just across the border, and came to Maine 12 years ago from Boston where he received both his artistic and culinary training.

Heroux began working as a waiter in Boston while a student at the School of the Boston Museum of Fine Arts (where he earned a fourth-year diploma in 1969 and a Masters of the Studio degree in 1970).

"I liked what I saw happening in the kitchen," Heroux says of his introduction to the world of fine dining. "I graduated from waiting on table to working on the steam table. They found I had a good eye for arranging food so I started doing some short-order cooking and worked through it like that."

As his credentials at the stove increased, Heroux began doing a little catering on his own. For a time he ran a lunchwagon to Parker 470, an art gallery operated by art dealer and patron Joan Sonnabend. Art and appetite came together as Heroux brought quiches and moussaka daily to the gallery and to the architectural firm housed with it. Joan Sonnabend, who has also operated the Obelisk Gallery in Boston and directed the corporate art collection for her husband Roger's Sonesta hotel chain, has been a major supporter of Heroux's career, but it was quite a few years before she went from eating his quiche to selling his porcelain.

"If you introduce yourself as the cook," says Heroux, "it's hard to be seen as an artist."

After graduating from art school and working as a chef for a few years, Heroux began to tire of city life. In 1972, while serving as a studio assistant in ceramics at the Haystack Mountain Craft School on Deer Isle, he began to think seriously about moving to Maine. When a friend from Haystack offered him room in a large house in Yarmouth, he jumped at the chance, but after applying to "every restaurant in the area" without any luck, he returned to Boston.

Eventually, Heroux spotted an ad in *Maine Times* for people in Auburn looking for a chef. Through well-known Maine chef and caterer

Leslie Land, who was serving as a consultant to the new restaurant, Heroux landed the job as chef at No Tomatoes. During the approximately four years that he was associated with No Tomatoes, he also served as an instructor in pottery at the Craft School in Lewiston. For the first two years, however, Heroux applied himself primarily to cooking and managing the restaurant in order to save enough money to buy some land on which to build a home.

In 1975, Heroux and a friend purchased 23 acres of white pine in the New Gloucester backwaters of the Royal River, and in 1977, they moved into a small shed-roof passive solar home built with the aid of a course at Shelter Institute. The house sits in a clearing in the pine woods like a great birdhouse surrounded by swallow boxes. The interior is simple and rustic, yet slightly exotic in keeping with Heroux's tastes. There is something, for example, in the brilliant red, four-headed amaryllis beside Heroux's bed that lets you know this house is not inhabited by homesteaders.

Heroux's ceramics studio is a small passive solar clone of the main house perched just down the hill, but until last summer he shared studio space in Portland with Jaap Helder, owner of The Vinyard restaurant. The Vinyard chef, Dennis Gilbert, trained under Heroux at No Tomatoes, and together they operated a small catering business for a time. Diners who have sampled Heroux's impeccable sushi and steamy dim-sum know that something was lost when his artistic career began to take off. Heroux occasionally pinch-hits for Gilbert at The Vinyard, but for the first time in years, he does not have to cook to earn a living.

Last year Heroux's porcelain pieces were shown at Barridoff Galleries in Portland, Harcus Gallery in Boston, Convergence Gallery in New York, and Halder/Rodriguez Gallery in Houston. A superb Ming-like Heroux vase has been on display at the Portland Museum of Art since it opened last May. And last summer Heroux completed his major work to date, a twenty-six-by-seven-foot ceramic mural for Deering High School in Portland. The mural illustrates Heroux's ability as a fine artist in an applied medium. In fact, he majored in painting at the museum school until his last year when he switched to ceramics.

"The reason I stopped painting," he says, "is that you spend so much of your time just standing there, looking at the thing, and biting your nails. It becomes too cerebral." Heroux says he enjoys the physical engagement required in working with ceramics.

Heroux likes to throw pots, but if he cared greatly about what other people thought he would probably spend more time making murals. It's plain to see that Paul Heroux is a painter on porcelain, whether the porcelain is in the form of a vase or a mural tile, but as he puts it, "As soon as it's flattened, it's taken much more seriously."

Heroux's porcelain pots are jigger-built in a technique that involves both throwing them on the potter's wheel and slab building. For the most part he has favored very traditional ceramic forms—cylinder vases, Ming vases, ginger jars, platters, and rimmed chargers, while employing a thoroughly contemporary painting style to decorate them. His unusual conical top-shaped vases with irregular stacks on top are an exception to this formal conservatism.

Briefly, Heroux's ceramic technique involves first firing the initial forms to a soft bisque hardness. On the blank bisque pots, he draws with a water-based marker to create major designs. A glaze is then applied and the drawn lines come through the glaze. These lines are painted over with a black oxide that runs on the slick glaze and gives the drawn line a blurred and bleeding character. The pots are then fired in the kiln, resulting in a black and white pot with linear markings. The fired pots are finally painted with China paints and re-fired to bake the color in.

"I really see my work as very decorative…the murals included," Heroux says. "But then I see most art as decorative or as having a decorative function…at least in the time they are made.

"I think I have a lexicon of images that are personal, but I don't want to analyze them or have them analyzed by others."

Heroux's lexicon of images include fan shapes, tables, tops, the saw-toothed edge, and a white pine motif that recurs throughout his work. Lately he has seen his imagery approaching landscape. But though his work is very pain-

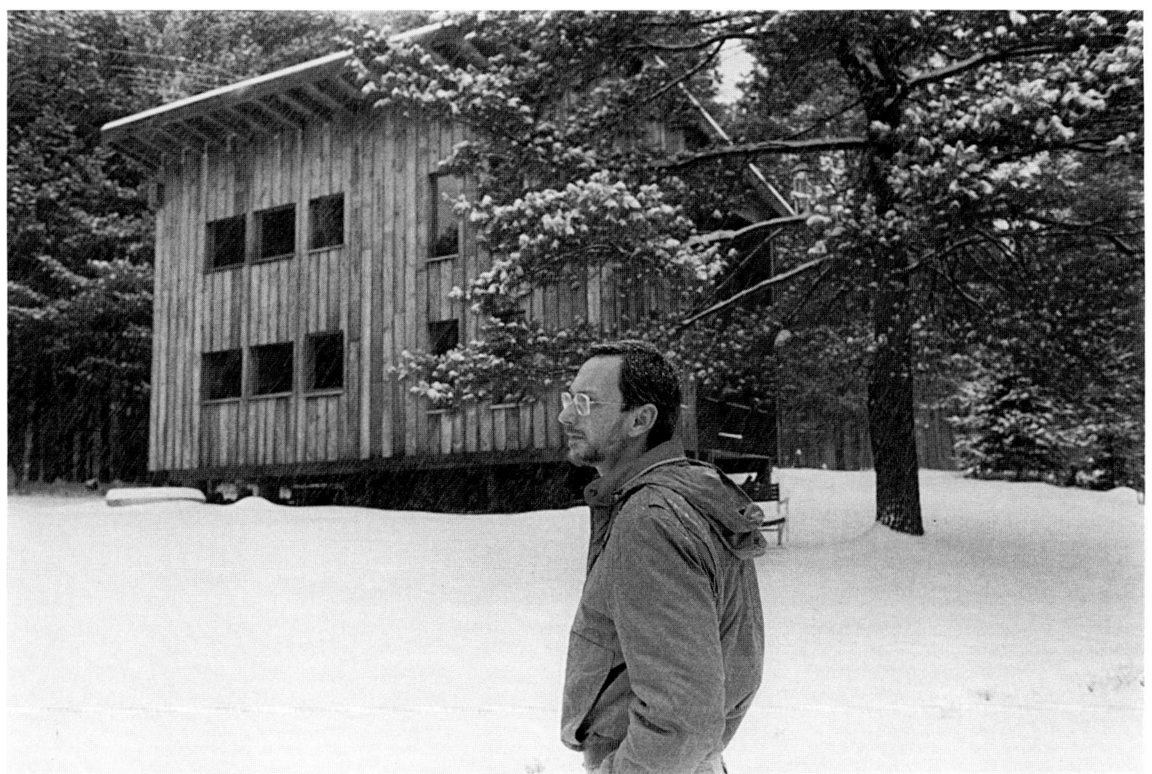

1. *Paul Heroux lives in a Shelter Institute-type house on 23 acres in New Gloucester. Photo by Stephen B. Nichols.*

terly, calling to mind Matisse and the enigmatic Klee, Heroux's greatest influences have been other contemporary ceramists, particularly those of the California funk school led by Robert Arneson, creator of the controversial ceramic bust of slain San Francisco mayor George Moscone for that city's Moscone Center convention complex.

In creating ceramic murals, Heroux has been most influenced by his experiences working with artist Katherine Porter, whom he met through Joan Sonnabend in Boston. Porter is one of this country's foremost abstract pattern painters and is now a resident of Belfast, Maine.

Heroux first worked with Porter making tiles for a mural commission she did for a private residence in California. The two artists next worked together in Porter's own mural project for the Moscone Center, a ceramic abstraction which was ultimately rejected by the center when Porter added a border containing the names of political activists and revolutionaries. More recently Heroux helped Porter create a large ceramic tile diptych which will be installed in a new addition to the Sonesta Hotel in Cambridge next spring.

Heroux's own ceramic mural for Deering High School was an $8,000 commission through Maine's Percent for Art program. The mural occupies a concave wall in an architectural dead space at one end of the pedestrian bridge which connects the old high school to the new building. The mural suggests the creation of the universe in imagery that is at once cosmic and microscopic, terrestrial and submarine, worldly and other-worldly. Heroux would probably just call it "decorative" and let it go at that. But then his work is a perfect blend of the cosmic and the cosmetic.

For the past three years, Heroux has worked exclusively in porcelain because he values the properties of the medium.

"I like the whiteness and the density of porcelain," Heroux says. "And there is something about the way it can warp and still be fine that I like."

But because porcelain limits the size of the pots he can make, Heroux is now beginning to experiment with stoneware. In his New Gloucester studio are two large stoneware pots painted with a white slip. Heroux sees them as variations on his hard-edged top vases (rotating tops or whirling dervishes), but to my eye they resemble nothing quite so much as beehives. Heroux has taken the basic urn shape and dented and distorted it while it was still wet. On a work table is a finished vase in the same manner. Slate-grey finishes are punctuated with

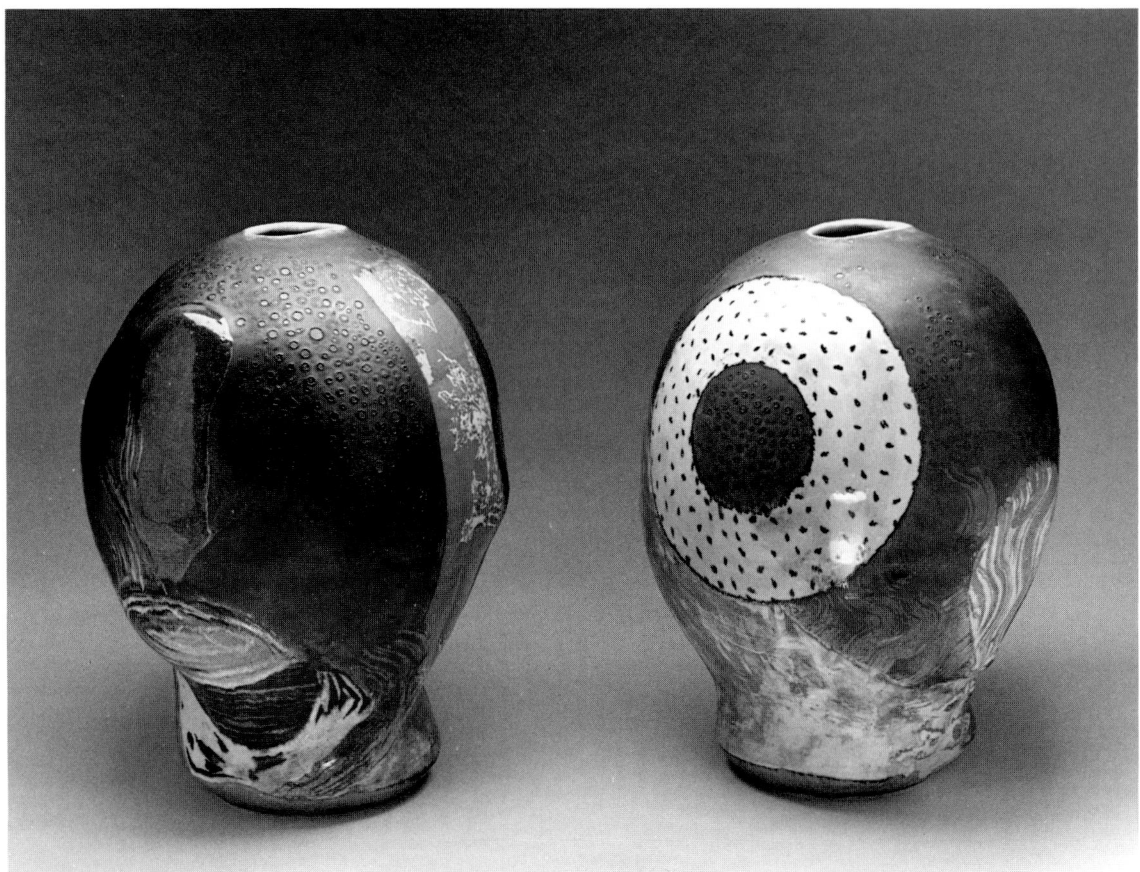

2. *Paul Heroux,* Head Set, *1989. Porcelain. Courtesy of the artist.*

ruby-red glosses. Where previously he has been painting irregular (even wild) markings on regular surfaces, now he seems to be bringing form and finish together, coming down decidedly on the side of the organic and the irregular.

But then Paul Heroux has always been an experimenter, and a snow-covered shard dump not far from the studio attests to his failures.

"I'm not very productive," he says apologetically. "I make about 100 pots a year that I keep. For a potter that's pathetic...100 pots is really bad."

In the art world, where scarcity is often more valued than quality (though not in Heroux's case), less is more even in the marketplace. But Paul Heroux does not console himself for what he sees as his meager output by calculating how supply and demand influence the market for his work. His consolation is at once personal self-deprecation and affirmation of the strength of his work.

"My work is so decorative that one is enough for any family," he says. "I can't even stand having a lot of my own work around. They really need a lot of space."

I am looking at one of Paul Heroux's porcelain vases. It is a pale green ginger jar with elegant gold lightning down one side and brutal black marks disfiguring the other. Paul Heroux is right. This vase commands a great deal more visual space than actual space. But then that's why it's a work of art.

January 20, 1984

An Artist on the Edge

Wendy Kindred

"I still have the feeling that I'm just visiting the U.S. The foreignness I feel in my own country makes our national preoccupations and characteristics appear as startling to me as they would to a visiting Danakil."
—Wendy Kindred, statement in *Contemporary Authors*, 1979

A Danakil is a desert nomad in Ethiopia. Wendy Kindred is a painter in Maine. But as an artist Wendy Kindred inhabits the fringes of her own world, an intensely personal, internalized world with a center in Addis Ababa and a far edge in Fort Kent where she has lived, worked and taught (at the University of Maine at Fort Kent) since 1973.

Over the past five years, as it has become apparent that Wendy Kindred is one of the most original and important artists in the state, observers have been asking: "What is Wendy Kindred doing in Fort Kent?" How does such talent survive so far from the centers of culture? Why does a woman of such vision and sensibility choose to live in a remote border town in Aroostook County? In order to understand what Wendy Kindred is doing in Fort Kent, it is necessary to understand the place Ethiopia occupies in her consciousness.

Born in 1937, Wendy Kindred graduated from the University of Chicago in 1959 with a Bachelor of Fine Arts.

A year later, she married a lawyer who wanted to work in Africa and, in 1965, the couple moved to Ethiopia. Wendy Kindred arrived in Addis Ababa seven months pregnant; two months later, twin daughters, Audrey and Jessica, were born.

Though she had been trained as a printmaker and had taught art in an Illinois high school, Wendy Kindred did not really become an artist until she found herself in Addis Ababa with time on her hands. The Ethiopian class structure insured that the Kindreds were provided with cooks, maids, gardeners, and nursemaids for the babies. Seeing no point in staying home, Kindred took a position teaching woodcut techniques.

In Addis Ababa, the blossoming artist fell under the spell of Ethiopian art, the distinctive style of Ethiopian manuscript illumination in particular.

"Ethiopian manuscripts are essentially Byzantine," she explains. "They have very flat space. Everything is boxed off and highly decorative." She displays reproductions of Ethiopian illuminations in which both figures and spaces bear a striking resemblance to even her most recent work. "This style happened to suit my feelings about my space in the world at that time—wedged into a relationship I wasn't totally comfortable with."

The Kindreds' marriage ended in divorce in 1968 while they were still in Ethiopia.

"After that," Kindred says of her divorce, "my paintings stopped being about people wedged into tight places."

Despite the openness with which Kindred acknowledges certain influences and the willingness (uncharacteristic of contemporary artists) with which she provides insight into her work, her art is as much a product of attempts to avoid influence as it is of derived style or imagery. While still in Ethiopia, for instance, she found that the paintings of the Ethiopian artist Skunder (now at Howard University)—paintings she describes as "a synthesis of French surrealism and African motifs"—were having a profound influence on young artists and students in Addis Ababa. In order to resist this prevalent influence, Kindred looked back more and more to European art. From Rembrandt and Goya, in particular, she took a sense of the psychology of character. In simplistic terms, Wendy Kindred's highly expressive figures set in segmented, patterned spaces can be traced to two sources: the decorative objectivity of the Ethiopian manuscripts and the personal subjectivity of Rembrandt and Goya. Neither influence, however, is obvious.

Following her divorce, Kindred spent a year alone in Ethiopia, during which time her painting became more and more abstract. Then, in 1969, after four-and-a-half years in Ethiopia, she returned to the United States, settling in New York with her daughters.

"In New York," says Kindred, "I was trying to improvise a life—doing children's books, magazine covers, office work, odd jobs."

In 1971, Kindred published the first of her four children's books, *Negatu in the Garden*. The story line was inspired by the friendship of two little American girls with an Ethiopian girl and boy, but in an uncharacteristically (for children's literature) unhappy ending, Kindred drew on the same theme of unsatisfactory male-female relations that she still explores in her painting.

Negatu is unhappy because the three girls exclude him from their play. The girls are playing house. "Can I be the father?" Negatu asks. The little girls consider and reply, "Okay, you can be the father. You go away and pretend you're at work."

In *Ida's Idea*, published a year later, a little girl and her mother systematically devour a maple-sugar candy doll, the little girl saving the head for herself by bribing her mother with a gumball. Curiously, arms and legs—usually awkward, useless, or powerless—have become powerful metaphors for the human condition in Kindred's paintings.

Lucky Wilma (1973) concerns a little girl who learns to enjoy just being alone with her father during one of his Saturday visitations. And *Hank and Fred, Fred and Hank* (1976) is about the friendship between a little black boy and a little white boy.

All four of Kindred's children's books are illustrated with bold, simple woodcuts, a technique she employs now only for illustrations—as in the designs and images she creates for *The Black Fly Review*, UM-Fort Kent's poetry annual.

Three years improvising a life in Manhattan convinced Kindred that it was financially impossible for her to live in New York City, so she took her young daughters and moved to a farm in rural Indiana to be near her own parents.

The year spent in Indiana proved to be a year of troubled silence. She found herself cut off from the social mainstream, spending a great deal of time alone, often going to the grocery store just to have someone to talk to.

"It became clear to me that I needed to get a job."

One day her mother handed her a dog-eared ad she had clipped from *The New York Times*. The University of Maine at Fort Kent was looking for an art teacher.

"Ethiopia was a far-fetched place to go," Kindred says. "I was willing to go to another far-fetched place."

She moved to Fort Kent in 1973 because she needed a job. She elected to stay largely because of her children.

"The kids moved into the area very comfortably," she explains. "Here they could have a lot of freedom to move around on their own that

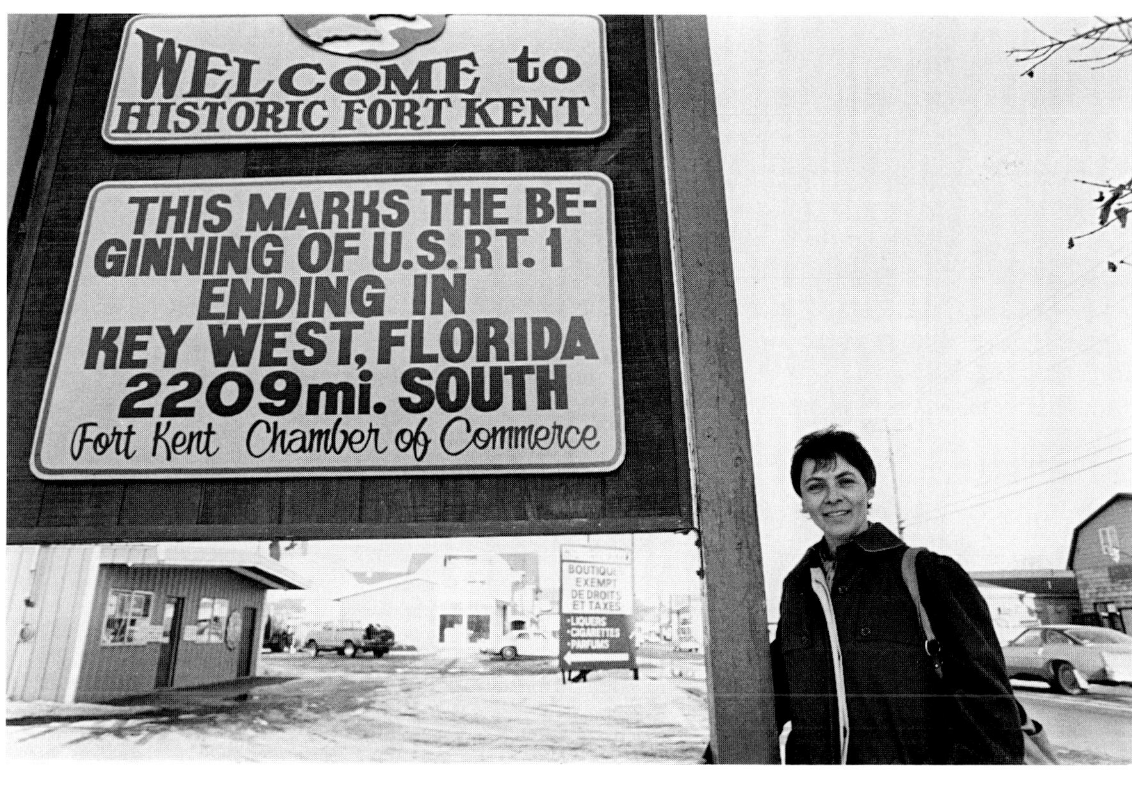

1. *Wendy Kindred stands beside the welcome sign to Fort Kent. Photo by Christopher Ayres.*

they wouldn't have in the city.

"The job allowed me a lot of flexibility—time to paint and scheduling flexibility.

"I had decided to stay here until the kids got out of high school. When they got out (her daughters, 20, are now students at Brown and Bennington), I discovered I had lots more mobility and flexibility."

Although Fort Kent is home now, the seat of Wendy Kindred's imagination is still Ethiopia. She recalls flying out of Addis Ababa in 1969 and looking down from the plane at the house she had lived in.

"The center is still there," she thought. "I didn't take it with me." And after 11 years in Fort Kent she can say, "Here I'm really on the edge...which confirmed my suspicion that the center was back in Ethiopia."

Fort Kent is a friendly Franco-American town situated on the Maine-Canada border at the northern extreme of U.S. Route 1. In deep winter the main street is dreary and gray. A pall of wood smoke from Fort Kent stoves and Canadian cone burners across the St. John River hangs over the town. But the rolling Aroostook potato fields and woodlands surrounding Fort Kent are pristine white and wind-blown—a landscape to rival the more vaunted Yorkshire dales and Scottish highlands, a starkly beautiful landscape that might inspire an artist inclined to paint the environment. But Wendy Kindred does not paint the Aroostook reality. She is driven to paint a reality at once more remote and more immediate.

Still, the physical reality of northern Aroostook does influence Wendy Kindred's art.

"A lot," she says. "It's just not visible."

In some cases, the environment creeps into her work unconsciously, as with a series of collages she did one winter. The collages were all small compositions set in the middle of big sheets of white paper. One day she looked at the bald white hills of the potato land with little pockets of settlement tucked in here and there and realized why.

Then there are environmental influences she is conscious of.

"Up here, you don't see color all winter. Everything is stark contrast," she observes. "My paintings are very colorful. But I feel I have to invent all the colors. The colors I use in my paintings don't relate to any color in real life. I'm not very subtle about color. There are not a lot of nuances. I tend to take it out of the tube straight."

Kindred's isolated, uncomfortable, struggling figures are most often located in bright chromatic space or locked into the pictorial space by color fields and decorative patterns. All of Wendy Kindred's paintings are autobiographical; the struggling figures represent her own personae.

"I do feel very isolated," the artist admits. "I don't get a lot from the area personally, so it throws me back inside myself a great deal. I find myself painting out of the past...which always brings me back to Ethiopia."

But Kindred is careful to point out that the influence of her experience and ideas about Ethiopia do not relate "to what's going on in Ethiopia as any Ethiopian would recognize it."

"What I use out of Ethiopia is very personal," she says. "It's not a link anyone would recognize as coming out of Ethiopia."

The emergence of the strong human imagery in Kindred's recent painting was a slow and painful process.

"A few years ago," she says, "I lost track of what I was doing. When I was painting abstract, I lost the point...the goal of pushing all that color around."

Then one day she came home to find her daughter Audrey drawing and obviously enjoying herself in the exercise of rendering reality in order to discover how the appearances worked. Kindred was envious. She decided she wanted to draw too.

"Out of desperation," Kindred says, "I just sat down and started drawing the thing opposite me." That thing happened to be a chair.

For some time after that Kindred concentrated on chairs as subject matter. One sabbatical in Paris she found herself concentrating on wing chairs with coats casually thrown over them.

"The coats became increasingly human and so did the chairs," the artist explains. "I realized I was drawing coats as caricatures of people, so I decided I should do people."

Gradually, her chairs evolved into four-legged, dog-like creatures, then into human figures. Last summer, as an experiment, Kindred executed a series of realistic portraits of people seated in chairs. These atypical portraits had some folks in Fort Kent (who tend to find the main body of her work "weird") saying, "Oh, so you really can paint."

Yes, Wendy Kindred really can paint, but the strength of her painting is not in the specifics of representation (likeness), but rather in the universality of experience she visits upon her more generalized figures. For while her paintings are autobiographical, visual equivalents of the inner life of the artist, even Kindred acknowledges that her figures are more male than female. In fact, she pursues an aesthetic androgyny out of a sense that conventional female sexual identity excludes women from the human experience.

To this end, Kindred creates figures that are devoid of hair...hair tending to betray sex, hairstyles tending to characterize and classify people. Her figures undergo similar disfigurements to render body, limbs, even clothing asexual at best.

"I want to address an experience that everyone has access to," she explains. But it is perhaps a sign of her gathering strength that Kindred's fictive figures have lately tended to become more and more female. This emergent sexuality can be read in the title of the 1984 painting currently being exhibited as part of the 1985 Maine Biennial at the Portland Museum of Art: *What Does She Want?* The bald, blinded figure in this painting even appears to be wearing a dress.

Asexual, powerfully human, and strongly expressive. For an artist who started painting in the 1950s, the influence of abstract expressionism might be expected. Kindred reports that as an undergraduate art student, "Abstract expressionism didn't filter through to us in Chicago." But the spirit of expressionism has had a more subtle impact on Wendy Kindred's artistic outlook. Very few of us escape the imprint of the age that spawned us.

"I assume," says Kindred of the determining influence of abstract expressionism, "that the way to approach painting is to have some accidents happen on canvas. I always start by smearing some paint around. In the end the painting should look like a lucky accident instead of something tightly controlled."

And always there is that anxiety of influence... easier to avoid, perhaps, in Fort Kent, but nonetheless a perceived danger. Kindred consciously avoids looking at the early figurative work of Richard Diebenkorn, for example; likewise the currently fashionable work of the

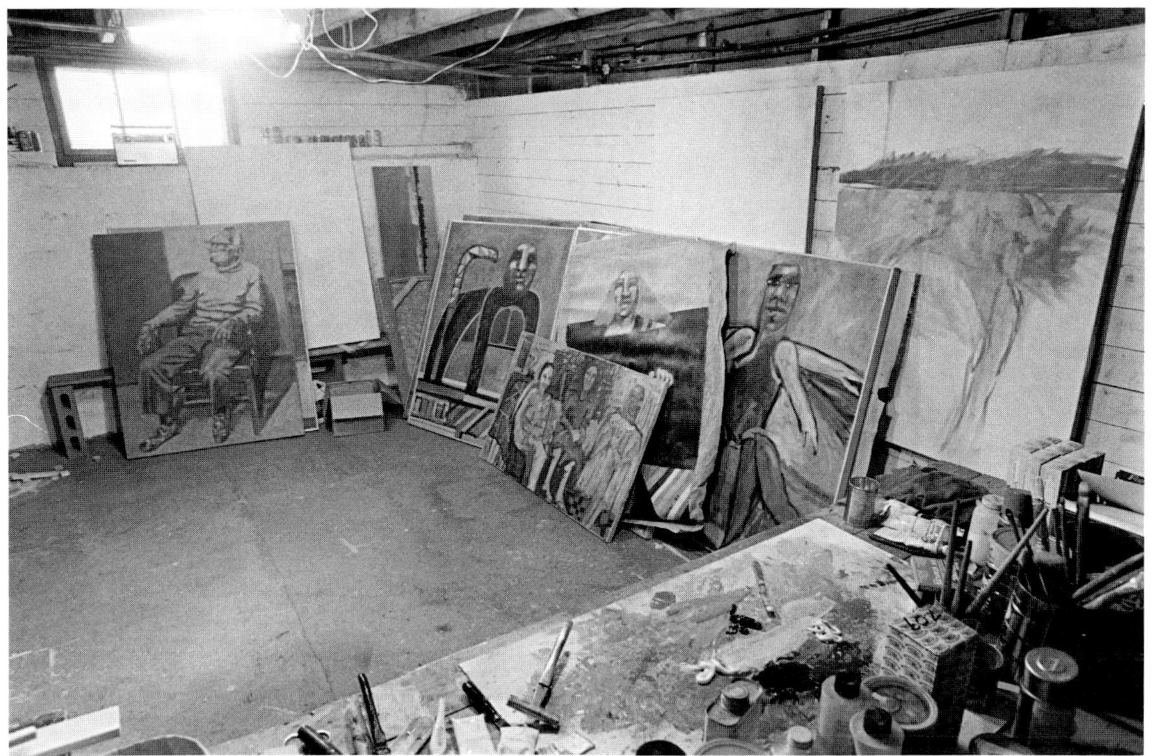

2. *Wendy Kindred's studio in the basement of the UM-Fort Kent Honors Center. Photo by Christopher Ayres.*

young neo-expressionists.

"There's a danger of getting too close to them," she says.

Only in recent years has Kindred made contact with the Maine art scene "downstate," most notably showing at *Spectra II* at UMO in 1982 and Bowdoin College's *Maine Artists' Invitational* in 1983. She shows regularly in the summer at the Leighton Gallery in Castine (now moving to Blue Hill), having befriended artist-gallery proprietor Judith Leighton at a UMO art function. And though she is no stranger to New York (a city as far south from Portland as Fort Kent is north), she has made no attempt to make her mark on the U.S. art capital. Why?

"I'm scared," she says. "It's that simple."

Danger...fear...uncertainty, all states of mind that ironically permeate her very decisive canvases. But ambivalence—the difficulty of choosing, deciding, acting—is one key to Wendy Kindred's art. A pair of exposed heads in the small 1981 oil *One Who Sees What Must Be Done / One Who Sees Nothing To Do* visually embodies this dilemma in her art and life. But now events at the felt center of her life—the famine and political upheaval in Ethiopia—are forcing the artist to do "what must be done."

Two weeks ago, Kindred brought her old

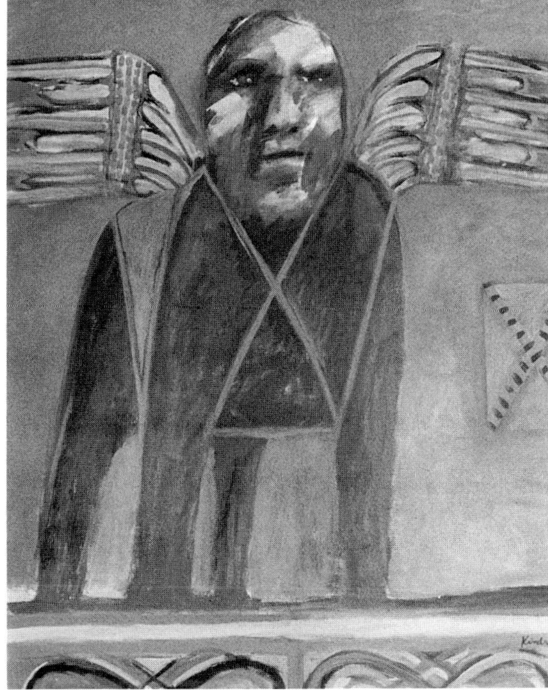

3. *Wendy Kindred,* Guardian II, *1982. Oil on canvas. Courtesy of the artist.*

friend Yonas Deressa, director of the Washington-based Ethiopian Refugee Education and Relief Foundation, to Portland and Fort Kent to speak about conditions in Ethiopia. She has also approached fellow UM-Fort Kent faculty member, Speaker of the Maine House John Martin (D-Eagle Lake), about having the Maine Legislature pass a resolution asking the U.S.

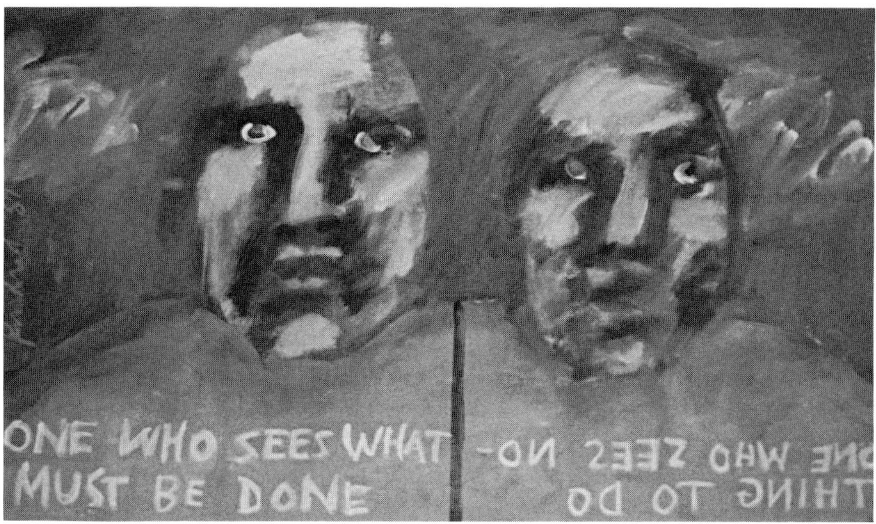

4. *Wendy Kindred,* One Who Sees What Must Be Done / One Who Sees Nothing To Do, *1981. Oil on canvas. Courtesy of the artist.*

Congress to investigate and act upon the political situation in Ethiopia as well as giving humanitarian aid.

Yet even in taking action on Ethiopia, there is a dilemma. The dilemma as Kindred sees it is that providing humanitarian aid to starving Ethiopians also constitutes support of the existing totalitarian regime that has aggravated the famine disaster. Kindred naturally supports aid to starving Ethiopians, but opposes aid that must be funnelled through Ethiopian government hands.

Wedged into tight positions, groping, caught in dilemmas of thought and action, trying to come to grips with the world around them, Wendy Kindred's painted personae express at once her own uncertainties and the moral and emotional dilemmas of every thinking man and woman.

"You ask me why I'm still in Fort Kent. It's that fear of moving."

February 22, 1985

The Island as Universe

Eric Hopkins

A thousand feet above Penobscot Bay, the sea is revealed as translucent glass, bright blue in the distance, bottle-green directly below. The island of North Haven, volcanic rock bristling with evergreens, is a continent at the center of the universe. Above and beyond is space, blue and pure. One hundred miles per hour is nothing at a thousand feet. As the little four-seater banks right, the world tilts and the view changes gracefully as though seen from a kite sheering on the breeze.

"It knocks me out," says Eric Hopkins, gawking at the natural display. "It drives me nuts every time I think of it. We're on a big blue ball!" He falls silent to take it all in for a moment. The window is open and the air rushes in over the drone of the engine. "Okay," he continues, "we're at 1,000 feet. The glacier was 5,280 feet thick. So figure that out. There was ice 4,000 feet above us!"

No doubt about it, Eric Hopkins is in his element. This is his inspiration. You can almost hear the shutter on the artist's internal camera clicking. Days, weeks, months later, he will close his eyes and screen these visions again. Then he will begin to paint, rendering scenes that shimmer in the ether between image and imagination.

"I really can see stuff with my eyes closed," he says. "I really want to catch on canvas what you see with your eyes closed...with your eyes open. If that makes any sense."

Charlie Jones brings the Cessna U-206 down on a pasture airstrip at Oak Hill on the north end of North Haven. Parked beside the field is Hopkins' white Dodge Tradesman van which has been attacked by New York graffiti artists. A stenciled likeness of pop star Grace Jones adorns the rear doors. Anarchistic slogans (most whited-out) run all around the truck. Inside, a hyperactive mutt named Dutchess and an aged, deaf (and dearly loved) dog named Polly wait impatiently and patiently for the master's return. Soon Eric Hopkins' island road show is rocking and rolling at a snail's pace down the road to town.

Eric Hopkins, 34, is an angular, bespectacled islander, described by one friend as looking very much like a great shore bird. A handsome Ichabod Crane? A homely Sam Shepard? There is something undeniably compelling about this young man, about the way he converses intelligently about art in a downeast accent, about the tension in him between insularity and sophistication, worldliness and other-worldliness. A few years ago he was well on his way to a successful career as a glass artist, showing his singular hand-blown sea shells on

Madison Avenue. Today, having retreated to the island of his childhood, he seems bent on remaking himself and his art from a more complete vision.

In 1981, Hopkins had an exhibition of his shells at the prestigious Heller Gallery in New York. Uptown openings and all the hype. A show that would have launched most artists' careers seemed to send Hopkins into retreat. He couldn't see himself making glass shells for the next 20 years. One Saturday he was sipping cocktails in Manhattan with collectors, the next he was back on North Haven swigging beer and listening to country music with his cousins.

"Hey," he says, "there's reality and then there's REALITY." Reality was a bauble; REALITY was a big blue ball whirling in space.

But the immediate reality is the village of North Haven as the rattling van pulls into the parking lot at the ferry terminal. Dutchess jumps out and hightails it up the street. Polly plods faithfully toward the compound of Hopkins family buildings that back up to Fox Islands Thorofare, which separates North Haven and Vinalhaven.

"Big hit today," Eric says, retrieving three fresh eggs from a coop containing five barred Rock hens and a mixed-breed rooster. Beside the North Haven wharf, he has started a sculpture garden of distinctive stones carted from all over the bay islands. His lobster shack hangs thick with "funk folk art"—red buoys daubed with white patches. Casually kicking open a side door, Hopkins reveals the spacious interior of his painting studio, which once served as a grain shed. Upstairs, Eric's mother, June Hopkins, runs a summer gift shop and art gallery in the old Hopkins storefront. Next door in the former carriage house, Eric maintains a sculpture studio. A nearby ice house (complete with granite floor) serves as a place to make "pyrographics"—fire drawings created by whipping lines of molten glass across primed, often sky-blue particle board.

"You ever draw on your toast with honey? Two-thousand degrees...same thing...bigger scale."

The pyrotechnics, trajectories, contrails, orbits through space, are fusions of Hopkins' work as a glass artist and painter, just as his fusions of native rock with ice-green molten glass manifest the glass artist and the sculptor. Hopkins' methods are as varied as his sources, but beneath the diversity is a hidden wholeness that makes all this—the art, the place—his own.

Eric Hopkins was born in Bangor while his father was in a submarine stuck in the mud off the coast of New Jersey. He was brought up in North Haven and attended junior high and high school in Rockland, where his father, William R. Hopkins—pilot, boatman, writer (a novel, *Freeman Cooper*, and a collection of letters, *Better Than Dying*)—taught English.

"I was always very connected to North Haven," Eric says. "I didn't want to go to the mainland. It was like being in a city, believe it or not."

Hopkins traces his earliest artistic inclinations quite literally to the sea around his island.

"My father ran a party fishing boat when I was a young boy," he wrote in notes to a show last year at Rockland's Caldbeck Gallery. "I'd jump at any opportunity to go in the boat with him. At first I was kept in a bait barrel so I wouldn't fall overboard. Finally I graduated to a fishing line and pulled a flipping, fresh, brightly colored codfish from the deep blue sea. By the time I got the fish home the colors had faded, so I took my poster paints and painted directly on the fish. After three days my mother made me throw it away. I then learned I could paint 'fish' on paper. I've been doing so ever since."

As a senior in high school (class of '69), Eric applied to and was rejected by Rhode Island School of Design (RISD). Then one fateful Saturday during classes to make up for snow days, Eric jumped at the opportunity to chauffeur two students to interviews at the University of Maine's Gorham campus. He decided to apply, too, and when a headlight ring fell off his old Cadillac, he spit on it, shined it up a bit with his bandana (these were the hippie days of the late '60s, after all) and presented it with his portfolio as "skulpcha."

As a fledgling art student at Gorham, Hopkins worked in the art gallery under Juris Ubans. His vision of art was propelled up and out from there as a result of a traveling exhibition he helped uncrate. There before him were Miros, Picassos, Dalis.

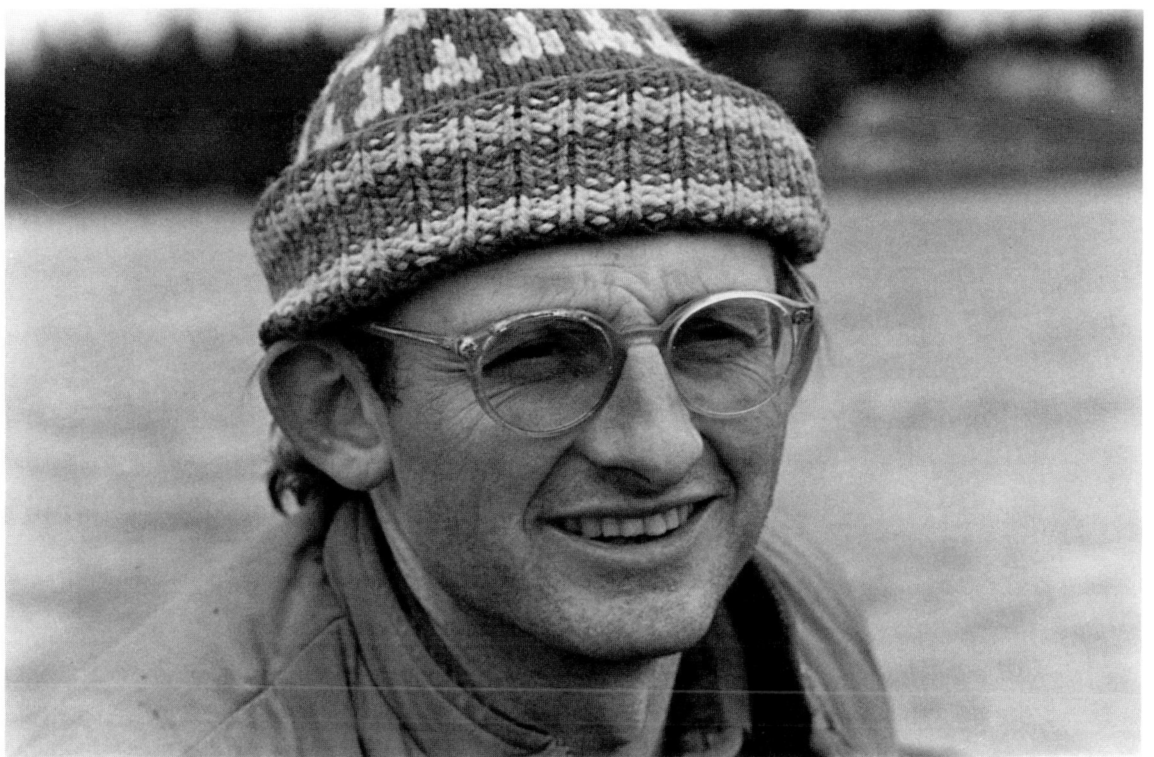

1. *Eric Hopkins looks to the sea. Photo by Christopher Ayres.*

"It really opened my eyes," he says. "I really responded to the colors, the shapes, the images. I thought, 'Hey, this is okay to do!'"

From Gorham, Hopkins embarked on a checkered career as an art student, with stops at Montserrat School of Visual Arts in Massachusetts and Marlboro College in Vermont. After bumming around the country a bit, he eventually wound up at the Haystack School of Crafts on Deer Isle as a night watchman. It was there that he first encountered (well, almost) the allures of glass.

"As kids on the island," he explains, "we used to build huge bonfires and melt thick Coke bottles in them. Then we'd poke them with sticks.

"Glass-blowing was the most exciting thing there," Hopkins says of his stint at Haystack. "I'd never seen it before." Naturally, he gravitated toward the excitement. And glass-blowing was the most exciting thing going on at Rhode Island School of Design at the time, too. With the backing of his Haystack friends, he applied and was accepted this time.

Eric Hopkins, Glass Artist, was in the furnace. He spent time at the Pilchuck Glass Center in Washington, served as a studio assistant to world-famous glass artist Dale Chihuly and sculptor Italo Scanga, and after graduating from RISD, took his mobile Molten Glass Unit—a glass furnace mounted on a flatbed trailer—on a gypsy tour of demonstrations and performances.

What had always excited Hopkins about glass was its primitive, organic nature. He was often more intrigued by the by-products of glassmaking—spills, shards, burns, squiggles on the studio floor—than by the products—goblets, vases, etc.

"I remember being down on the rocks at Haystack," he says, "and thinking how all these things (rocks, fissures) paralleled things I saw in the glass shop—cracks, molten forms. I didn't know what to do with it then, though. There was still pressure to make things."

Though Hopkins may have been more interested in dropping molten glass off four-story buildings, the things he made recommended him to public attention. The things were shells, forms rooted in his native experience, elegant spirals he took to breaking with hammer and pliers to suggest the destructive as well as creative forces at work in nature.

"The shells," he explains, "were basically a switch-off on an old technique." Where traditional art glass had long taken blown forms and wrapped rods of glass around them as embellishment, Hopkins took a solid rod of glass and wrapped a bubble around it, blowing

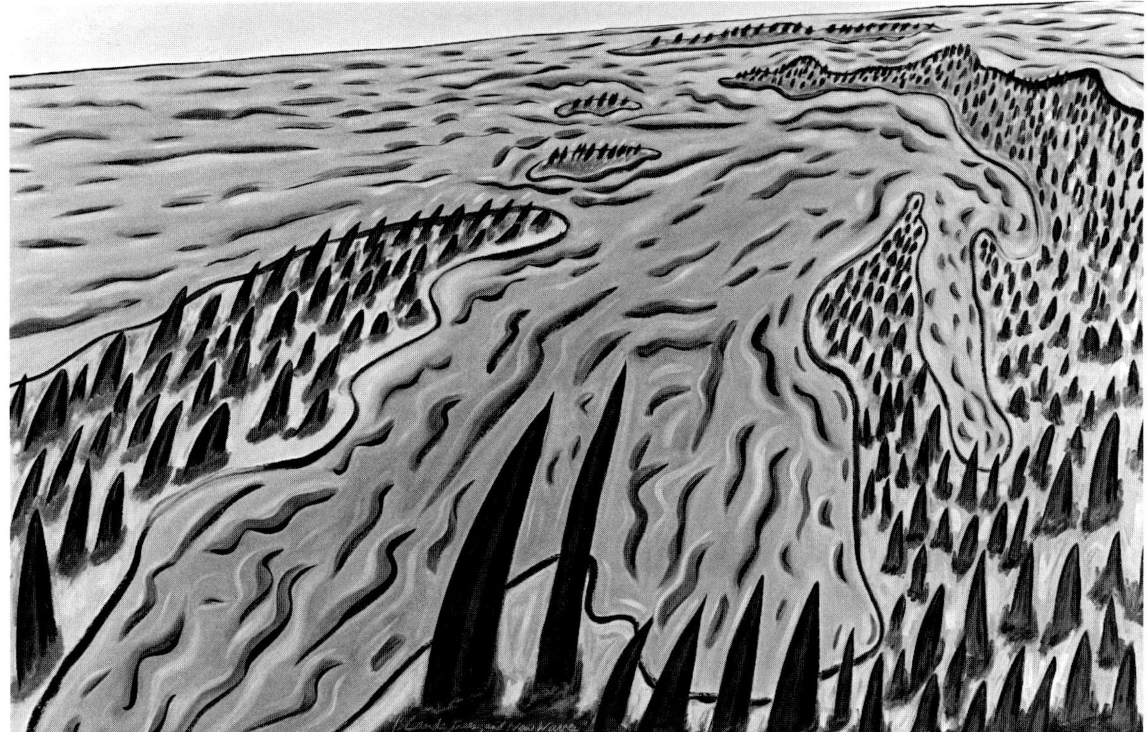

2. *Eric Hopkins,* Islands, Trees, and New Waves, *1983. Oil. Courtesy of the Barridoff Galleries.*

at the same time. "That made the shell. Then I'd break them."

But Hopkins hasn't made glass shells since 1982. He is cautious about his disaffection with the glass art movement, but he does find, if not satisfaction, then something like confirmation of his own doubts in articles like "Americans in Glass: A Requiem?" which appeared in the March issue of *Art in America*. The article speculates on the imminent demise of the art glass movement, crushed by the weight of its own preciousness.

"The glass world," observes Hopkins, "is filled with a great many people who are very, very skilled, but there's not much content. The content is glass."

And so Eric Hopkins has turned his attention from baubles to the big blue ball. At home on North Haven, content is everywhere he looks.

In summer, however, everywhere Hopkins looks there are people. North Haven is an old New England upper-crust resort, and the big cottages on the island (significantly, edited out of his aerial views of the island world) fill with summerfolk. The waterfront outside his studio (where only a handful of working watercraft are tied up at this time of year) fills with pleasure boats. Fortunately, Hopkins has a retreat within his retreat.

In the 1950s, William Hopkins (constantly and affectionately referred to as "the Old Man" —a nautical term of respect, not an adolescent term of disrespect) purchased 40 acres at the head of Southern Harbor. It is there that Eric Hopkins lives in a one-room shack on the water's edge. The shack is reached on foot or at one's vehicular peril over a twin rut of a road.

"The shack's down here," Hopkins says as the Dodge van creaks and veers through the overhanging branches like an aging subway car in a tight turn. "And this is where we die down here."

Eric's father, who died of cancer in 1979, and a younger brother, who drowned in 1960 at the age of five, are buried in the Hopkins family plot behind the shack. The burial site is marked by a pyramid of granite salvaged from Fiddlers Monument off Crabtree Point after the Coast Guard replaced the marker cap with plywood. "I've got an uncle, a grandfather, and a couple of dogs down there," he adds, gesturing beyond the marker.

The shack comes into view over the last rise before the sea. The hut has its back to visitors; its front is an expanse of glass panes staring straight down Southern Harbor. The central structure of the shack was once the Bell House, a ferry shelter on the Vinalhaven side of the

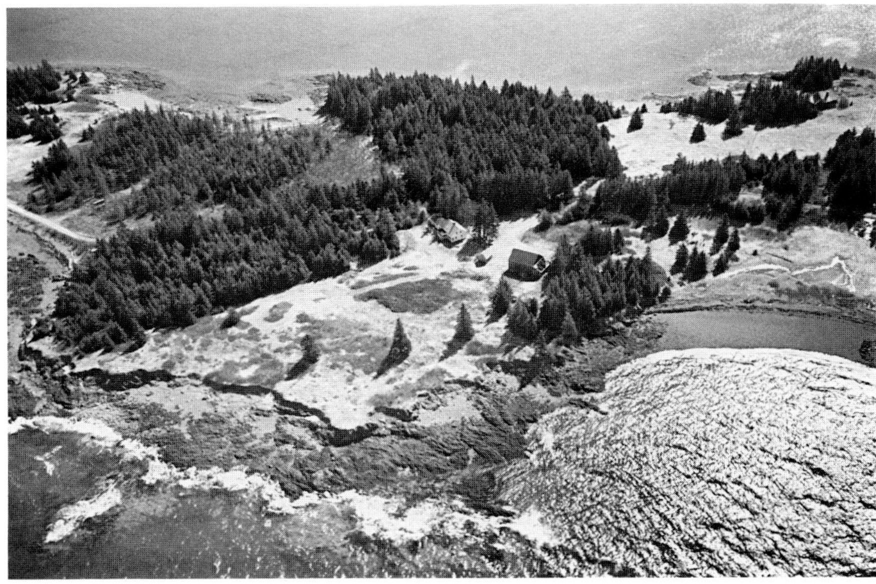

3. *North Haven Narrows between Wooster Cove and Crabtree Neck. Photo by Christopher Ayres.*

Thorofare. Eric's father hauled the little shanty over here and Eric added the shed wings during his hippie era. The west wall of the shack is a rosy window of blown glass.

"I really wouldn't want to live anywhere else, to tell the truth," Hopkins says.

The dogs chew up white steamer clam shells mounded outside the door. Crows mob a bald eagle in the distant sky over the Dumpling Islands.

"There is a real, pure force somewhere," Hopkins says, "and it's right here. You can see it. I guess when you have time to think about it...when you make time to think about it..." and he loses himself for a moment in the pleasure of being here. "We go around the sun. The moon goes around us. That's pretty good," he enthuses. "And it sounds so simple."

"As soon as I started taking flying lessons [which he did two years ago with $300 worth of returnable cans and bottles he saved up on the North Haven Wharf]," says Hopkins, "I started painting more."

What he saw flying this morning will no doubt find expression in the aerial paintings that have brought the artist to new public attention. He stresses over and over again that he has only just begun to paint seriously, but Hopkins has created a lot of excitement and come a long way for someone who has only just begun. His distinctive oils were first exhibited at his mother's gallery on the island, then made their way over to the Rockland mainland. This year they were shown at Congress Square Gallery in Portland, and this summer (June 28-July 27) they will be featured at Barridoff Galleries in Portland.

The aerial paintings began as sweeping, tilted bird's-eye views of island landscapes, but they have gradually become more cartographic, overhead views of island land masses reduced to simplest terms and purified. Only recently have roadways begun to appear on Hopkins' islands, the first traces of human habitation in the artist's recapitulation of natural history. Yet Eric Hopkins' subject—the content he has found on North Haven—is ultimately man's place on earth, on this planet, in this universe, in this mysterious space. Such a quest cannot help but become spiritual in nature.

"One thing the Old Man said while he was dying," Hopkins says. "He said, 'You haven't seen the last of me yet. You might be riding down the road and screech on the brakes. There's the Old Man. We'll stop and shoot the breeze. How're you doing, that sort of thing. And when it's over you'll wonder, Is that real?'

"He was reading the script on the ceiling... meaning there's more to it than what you see right here."

April 19, 1985

True Native Vision

Celeste Roberge & Dozier Bell

Metal sculptor Celeste Roberge lives at the beach with a man who deals in scrap metal. Landscape painter Dozier Bell lives up the river with a man who does landscaping for a living. A queer coincidence of love and labor, perhaps, but with this loose mental stitch we begin to baste together the lives and works of two young women who, though they have never met, have emerged in recent years as two of Maine's most important artists. For while Andrew Wyeth and Neil Welliver are still the primary suppliers of Maine art images to the outside world, Celeste Roberge and Dozier Bell are among a new generation of artists giving Maine something it hasn't had since the death of Marsden Hartley (1877-1943)—a true native vision.

Artists, of course, have been long attracted to Maine by its natural beauty, but the native artist of the new Maine is less interested in the picturesque than the primal qualities of the local landscape. Both Roberge and Bell, for example, are more concerned with the idea of place than with the look of a place. Theirs is the art of the internalized landscape.

Roberge's 1987 *Northern Archive: Walking Cairn*, in fact, is a quite liberal rendering of this idea of humanized place—a nine-foot-high steel cage self-portrait filled with beach stones the artist gathered in walks along the coast. Her bodily apprehension of space is also apparent in the 1984 *Geographies*, a trio of "heads" (one being lead and two being open steel grids filled with stones and waste wire, respectively) which prefigured her 1987 *Northern Archives: Geographies* (a trio of much larger "heads," one of lead, one stuffed with stones, one with charred wood).

"I'm really into the idea of something walking across the landscape, coming across objects in that field for contemplation, and figures doing things that are extremely mundane like getting up, walking, lying down, the basic human stances," says Roberge.

Where Roberge is an empiricist who would ingest and objectify geography, Dozier Bell is more of a mentalist conjuring places out of pure consciousness. Roberge is mind made metal. Bell is soil in her soul. The stark, ashen landscapes she paints arise in what she calls her "genetic memory," a kind of neural map of ancestral experience. Bell's oil on linen landscapes (of which the 1988 *A Hundred Years* currently on view in the Farnsworth Museum's juried exhibition is a perfect example) are often little more than horizon and atmosphere punctuated with vertical "marker" lines, focal crosshairs, and corner brackets. They do not

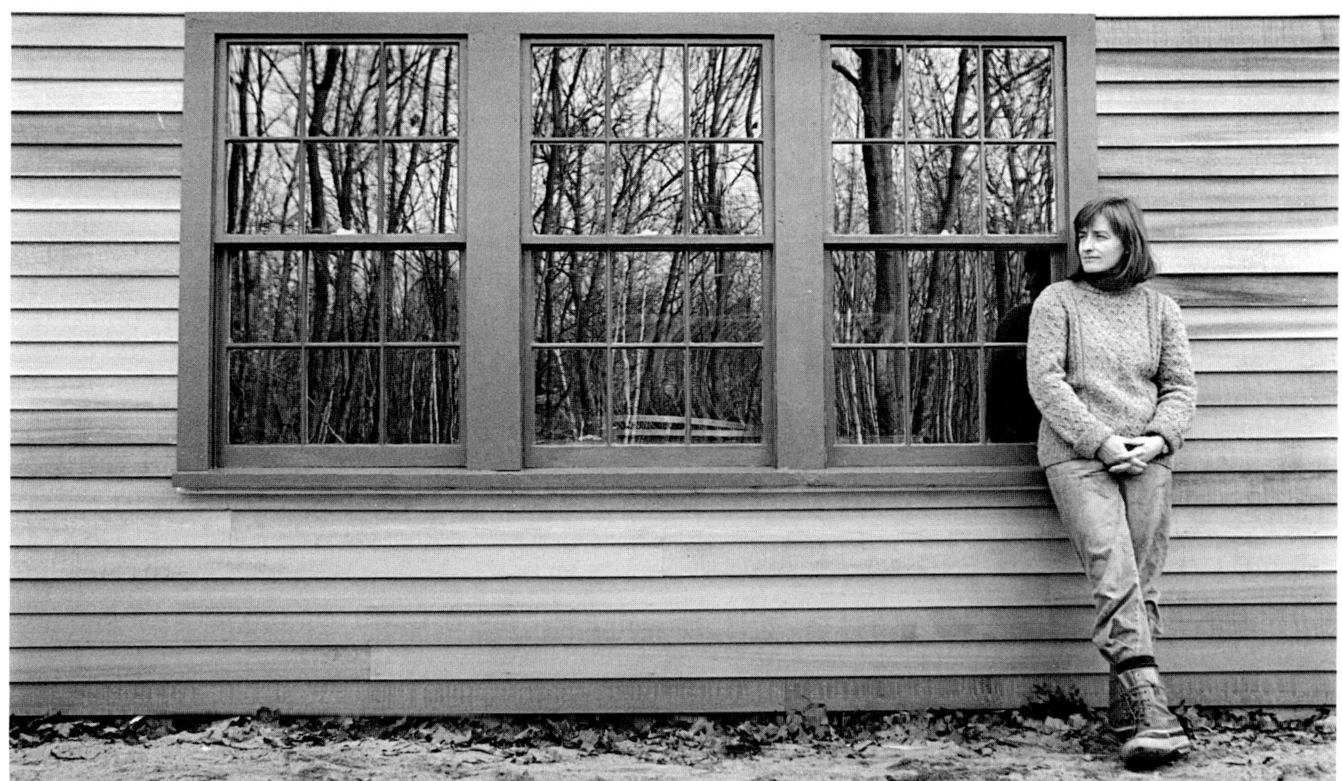

1. *Celeste Roberge outside her studio in Biddeford. Photo by Scott Perry.*

correspond to any particular Maine landscape, but rather a collective experience of place. When Bell's paintings are populated, it is not by human beings but black dogs, beings at once domestic and wild.

"Animal consciousness, the total, acute awareness of place and the moment, is the basic source of genetic memory," writes Bell in an artist's statement. "The dog images represent this, as well as something as yet undefined in my own orientation to consciousness."

Art as exploration of place, art as locational devise, art as orientation—the aesthetic ideas uniting Roberge and Bell evolved out of individual experiences with several points of similarity.

Celeste Roberge, 37, was born and raised in Biddeford. Fourth of nine children in her family, she was educated in parochial schools until her final two years of high school. As a child, she showed little interest or aptitude for art, her exposure to culture being limited to piano lessons with the nuns and singing in the choir. Dozier Bell, 31, was born in Lewiston, raised in Bath, and graduated from Kents Hill School, but her ancestral roots are on a farm the Bell family still owns in South Waterford. Unlike Celeste, Dozier did demonstrate a talent for painting and drawing as a child, but her serious interest in art did not surface until her third year in college. Indeed, both women began their undergraduate educations in more academic fields.

Celeste Roberge earned her bachelor's degree in sociology in 1975 from the University of Maine in Orono where she was the first editor of the *FAROG Forum*, the Franco-American student publication. (FAROG stands for Franco-American Resource Opportunity Group and is a not-so-subtle pun on the ethnic slur, "frog.") Family ties and her interest in her cultural roots led Roberge to spend her junior year at L'Université de Sherbrooke in Quebec, an important formative experience on the road to becoming an artist.

"The genesis of it," Roberge says of her interest in art, "was when I went to Quebec. My roommate, my cousin Sylvie, who became an opera singer, was studying visual art. She let me use her paints and I helped her solder things. My other cousin, Nicole, got me into theater and I started designing sets. In Quebec, there was this sense of possibility. I was living in a new country. I didn't have a history. I could do anything."

After graduating from Orono, therefore, Roberge decided to enroll at the Portland School of Art.

Dozier Bell was a junior at Smith College

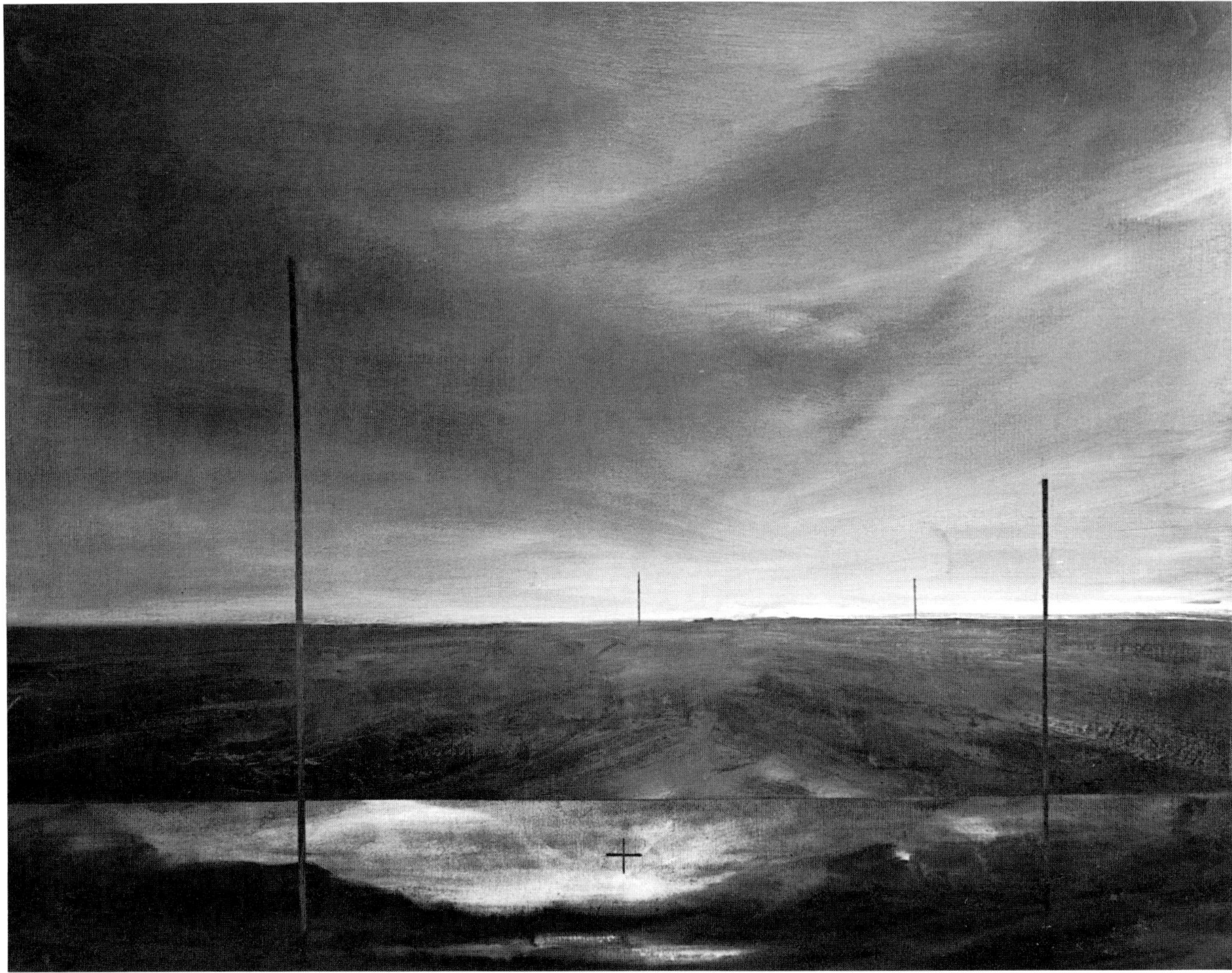

2. *Dozier Bell,* A Hundred Years, *1988. Oil. Collection of the William A. Farnsworth Library and Art Museum. Courtesy of the artist.*

when she made the decision to major in art.

"I was a philosophy major at Smith," she explains, "but I started spending a lot of time in art classes. I realized that the experiences I was trying to get at through philosophy were more direct, more apparent in the art work."

The experiences Bell was trying to get at through philosophy involved issues of animal consciousness, animal rights, and morality. Rather than pursue these ideas through the inscrutable arcana of obscure philosophical journals, Bell decided she could communicate her feelings about the phenomenal world more effectively in art.

"What animal consciousness is, how human consciousness takes part in that, that's sort of where my painting comes from right now," she says. "That and a really intense awareness of place."

Celeste Roberge's sense of place is less localized than Bell's, stemming less from growing up in Maine than from travels undertaken after she graduated from the Portland School of Art in 1979. Those travels included a stay in western Scotland where the bleak, windswept terrain inspired her *Botanical Series* of steel and wire trees, and the years (1984-86) she spent in "New Scotland" acquiring an MFA at the Nova Scotia College of Art and Design.

"I don't know as Maine per se is that important in my art, but the area—call it the North Atlantic, Nova Scotia, Scotland—is," Roberge says. "I don't think I really became aware of my physical space until I experienced Nova Scotia and Scotland. It was really those landscapes, more dramatic than Maine in a raw sense, that made me aware of place. It's not really landscape though that's important. Landscape is simply the metaphor, a mental condition. What interests me is the psychological state that corresponds to the landscape."

This last is a statement Dozier Bell could have

made. After graduating from Smith in 1981, she spent two years living and clerking in Portland before entering the University of Pennsylvania to do graduate work. Having grown up in small-town Maine, however, Bell found herself totally unprepared for the physical and psychological vicissitudes of big city life in Philadelphia. During her first year of graduate school, she suffered from what she calls "visceral disorientation," a stressful state of confusion and dislocation that upset her stomach constantly and caused her to regularly fall asleep in her studio. This unnerving urban experience was epitomized for Bell by the loud vastness of Philadelphia's 30th Street Station, the "hell on earth" she had to pass through getting in and out of the city. To confront and conquer her anxieties, she forced herself to draw and paint the disorienting interior of the crowded terminal. Still, the experience was profoundly upsetting.

"I spent the whole summer letting it blow over," says Bell, "and then in the fall Neil was there."

Neil, of course, is Neil Welliver, America's most important landscape painter, head of the University of Pennsylvania graduate art program, and a resident of Lincolnville, Maine. Welliver had been on a leave during Bell's first year at the school, but when he returned his presence had an enormous impact on the sensitive young artist.

"I think Neil Welliver is the only person who is an artist who I would say had an influence on me. He probably saved me years of work by pointing out to me what I was doing. That second year he and [painter] Raphael Ferrer really vaulted me ahead."

Unlike many Welliverites, however, Dozier Bell never took to imitating Welliver's instantly recognizable style of schematic landscape painting. What Welliver was able to offer Bell was insight into her own paintings, at that point paintings of seashells.

"Neil said they weren't specific enough to who I was. Then I saw that anyone could have done those paintings, which was very threatening for a while."

At a loss as to how to proceed, Bell took to making simple charcoal marks on paper, working blind and blank until she discovered

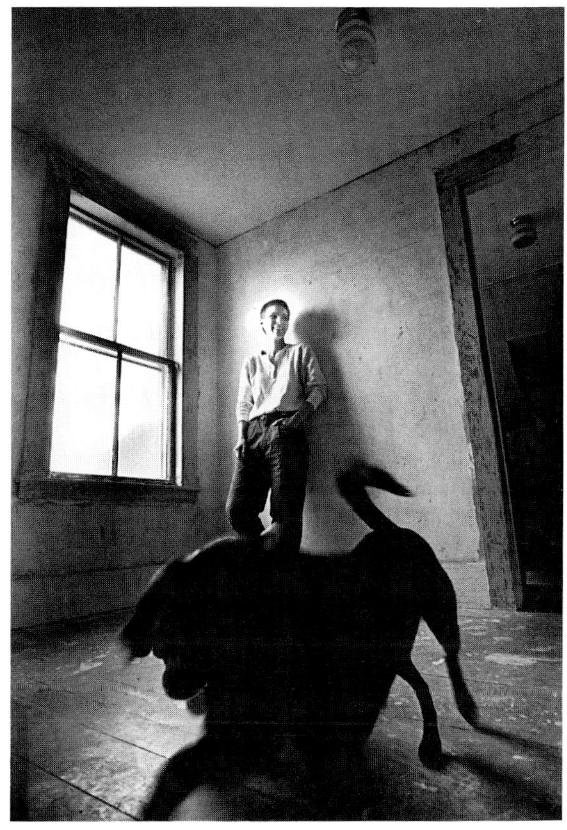

3. *Dozier Bell at home in Richmond. Photo by Scott Perry.*

the landscape of her own territorial imagination.

Celeste Roberge's major influences are not always apparent, nor exclusively visual. Asked for an artist she feels close to, she names Albrecht Durer (1471-1528), whose 1514 engraving *Melancholia*, a scholar contemplating the ineffability of the existential sphere, was the inspiration for her 1985 *Geography's Body*, a steel cage and waste wire figure contemplating a globe of welded rods. A great many artists feel connections to the great artists of the past, but the mental ease with which Roberge makes the 500-year leap to Durer is very indicative of her approach to art.

"I see it very historically, I guess. Because I've read a lot of art history and social history, I see my art within a context much broader than my own life. So, in that sense, the work is not that personal. It has its own function."

This statement hints at a philosophical detachment in Roberge which connects her to another of her primary sources, the writings of the late Marguerite Yourcenar. *Northern Archives*, the series title of Roberge's most recent works, was inspired by Yourcenar's untranslated autobiography, *Archives du Nord*. Perhaps it is not surprising that Madame

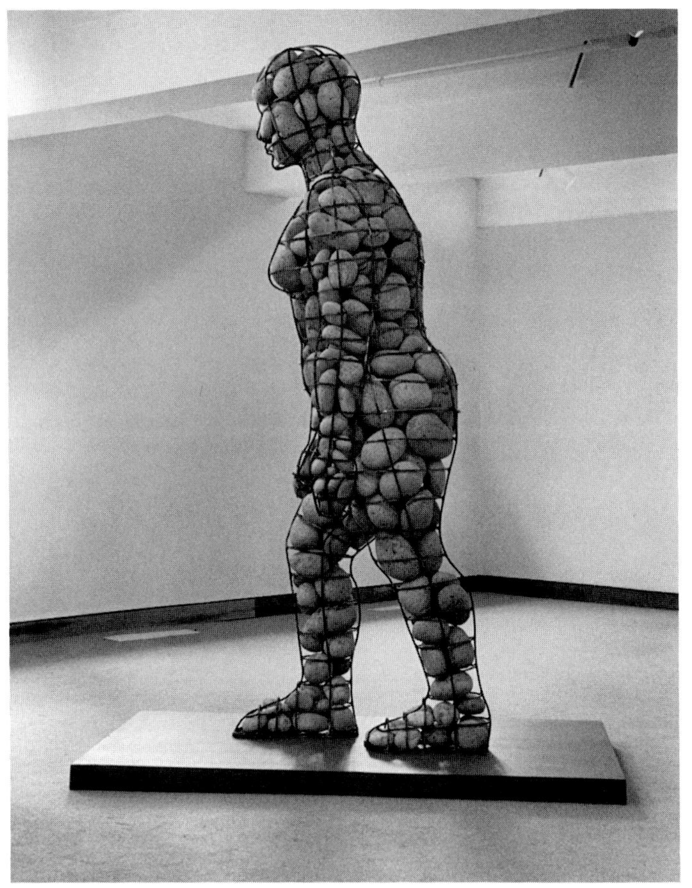

4. *Celeste Roberge,* Northern Archive: Walking Cairn, *1987. Galvanized steel and granite stones. Courtesy of the Runny Mede Sculpture Farm.*

Yourcenar, an intellectual woman of French heritage living in Maine (Yourcenar lived in Northeast Harbor for many years), should serve as a role model for a brilliant young Franco-American woman, but Celeste Roberge says it is less the facts of Yourcenar's life and writings than a certain quality of mind that appeals to her.

"In some way I have yet to figure out, the way she thinks about things, the way she chooses to write about the things she writes," says Roberge, groping in the present tense to describe her attachment to the late novelist. That Roberge should respond strongly to "a way of thinking" is appropriate, for she is an artist whose work finds its coherence not so much in manifestations of style or materials as in conceptual unity.

Dozier Bell, too, professes a literary influence perhaps as strong as any visual stimulus.

"Thomas Mann is a big influence for me, the way he thinks about his life and his work, the way he melds his art and his life," says Bell. "I read *Magic Mountain* in college and it became a focal experience for me."

What intrigues her about Mann is the fact that he was so intimate with human nature in his work, yet so distant from his family in real life.

Family closeness and the intimacy of a people with the land they inhabit and inherit are crucial to Dozier Bell's art. The disorientation she felt when she was away in the city disappeared when she returned to Maine in 1985.

"It was a great relief to be back here," she says. "The theory I've come up with to explain why I have to be here is 'genetic memory,' a culmination of the perceptions of generations of ancestors seeing the same landscapes and responding to them. In my family, the landscape really formed everyone. We're very much of a type."

That first summer back from the University of Pennsylvania, Bell attended the Skowhegan School of Painting and Sculpture, just as Roberge had done in the summer of 1979 after graduating from the Portland School of Art. The experience of America's premier finishing school for artists had a similar effect on both women. Bell says her Skowhegan summer built up her professional confidence and enabled her to "see myself as an individual among individuals." Roberge speaks of the Skowhegan experience enabling her to "take myself even more seriously because I was with others who took me seriously." Roberge, in fact, was the only native Maine artist included in the Skowhegan School retrospective on the occasion of its 40th anniversary in 1985.

Celeste Roberge is a very frank, articulate, and self-confident woman. A powerful and grounded artist, she sometimes seems to have attained a stature and a measure of respect out of proportion to her accomplishments. Four years out of art school, for example, she was jurying her peers in the 1983 Maine Biennial and the following year she was a juror in the Skowhegan School's Maine scholarship program. Perhaps because in recent years she has taught full-time at Cape Elizabeth High School, her artistic production has tended to be quite limited. Though she has not sold a work of art in three years, Roberge's rewards have always tended to be more honorary than monetary.

During this current 1987-88 academic year, Celeste Roberge is a fellow of the Mary Ingraham Bunting Institute, the feminist think tank at Radcliffe College. There she is at work on

more environmental sculptures in her ongoing *Northern Archives* series. On the weekends, she comes home to the cottage at Fortunes Rocks she shares with junk dealer/environmentalist Sam Zaitlin and works on the new studio she has built in the Biddeford woods. Her life and her art remain, as ever, grounded in thought.

"When you talk to physicists, you think of their ideas objectively, but when you talk to an artist it always becomes personal," says Roberge. "I object to that in a way. I am trying to create an image of an historical moment or an image of thought. If the work were personal, I couldn't exhibit it. I experience the work on an abstract level. I don't emote. I never feel like I'm expressing myself when I'm working. My art has very little to do with me. I have no choice. I have to do it. As painful as the process is, as lonely as it is, it is far more satisfying than anything else I can imagine doing."

And Dozier Bell says, "My paintings have a very separate existence from me. That makes me feel a real sense of awe. And that's why I paint—for that feeling."

Bell, a young woman as vulnerable and wary as a wild animal, lives in an old house up the Kennebec in Richmond with her husband, landscaper Patrick Bard. A bumper sticker on her '69 Chevy pickup advocates a veal boycott. The yard around the house is all fenced in to provide a secure run for Freida and Joey, the little mongrels who live with Bell and Bard. Even as she speaks of her continuing exploration of animal consciousness and internal landscape, her most recent paintings are being shown at the Schmidt Bingham Gallery in New York where they are selling well and beginning to attract attention from major museums.

Selling paintings is the way the ideas and images get out into the world, Bell says, but that's not what her art is ultimately all about.

"For me, these paintings are a way of orienting in reality and a way of anchoring myself in the underlying layers of experience. I find them very calming. Usually the people who buy them get that sense of calm, too," she says. "It's about this place and my family's connection to it. I feel I'm the member of my family who can make the family psyche visible—not just my family, but all the people who have lived in Maine."

December 2, 1988

Color Plates

2

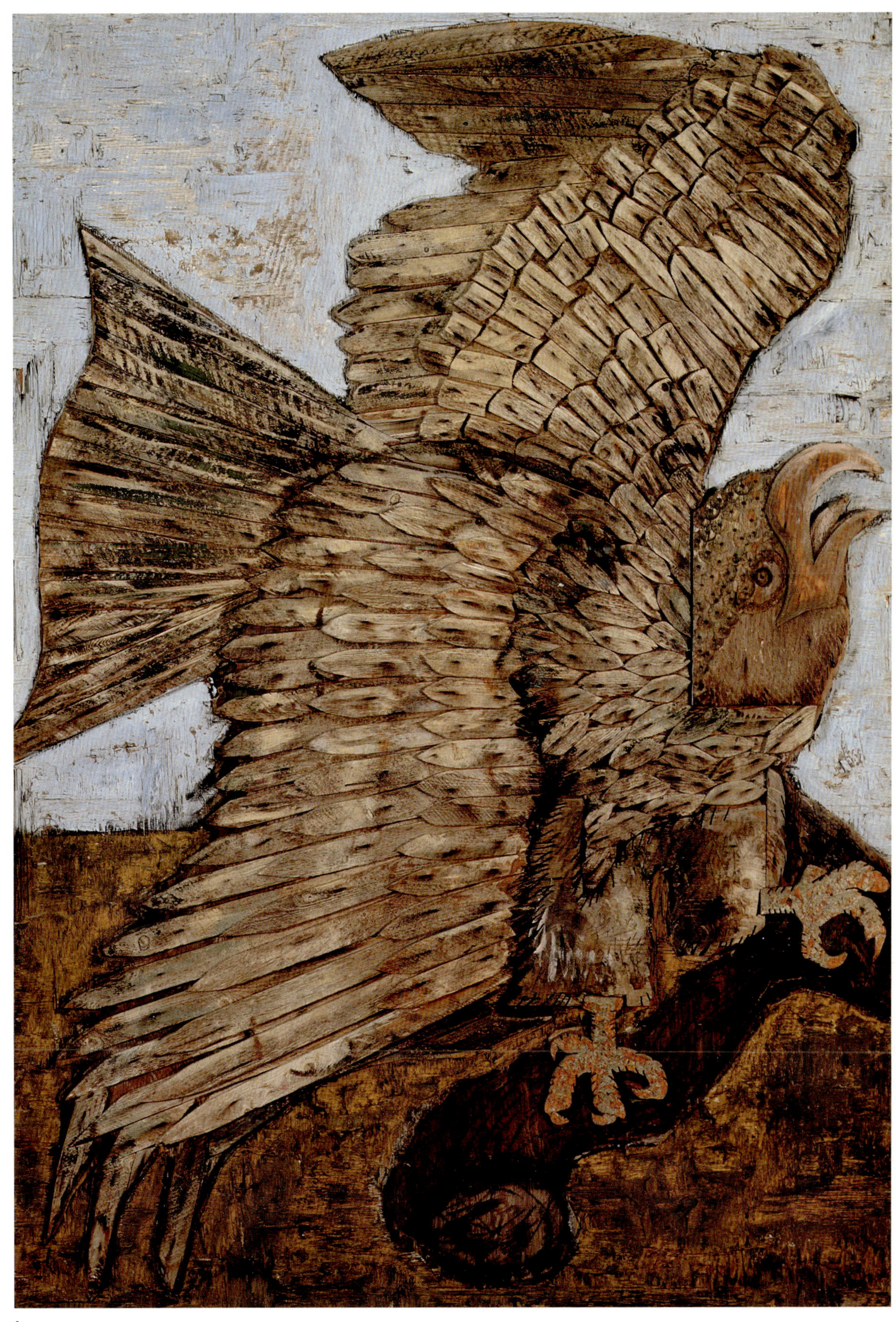

1.

1. Bernard Langlais, *Hawk*, c.1964, wood relief, 72 x 48.
Courtesy of the Maine Savings Bank. Photo by Stretch Tuemmler.

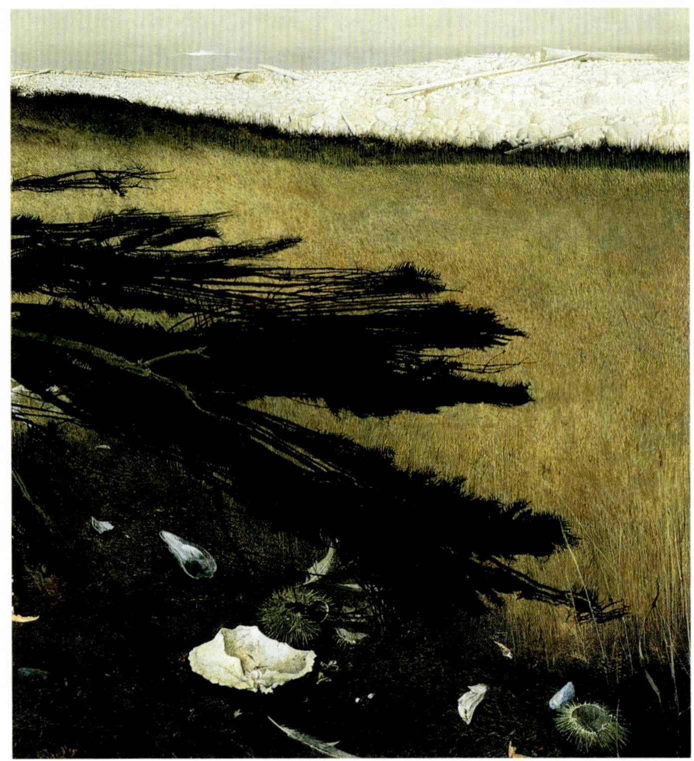

2.

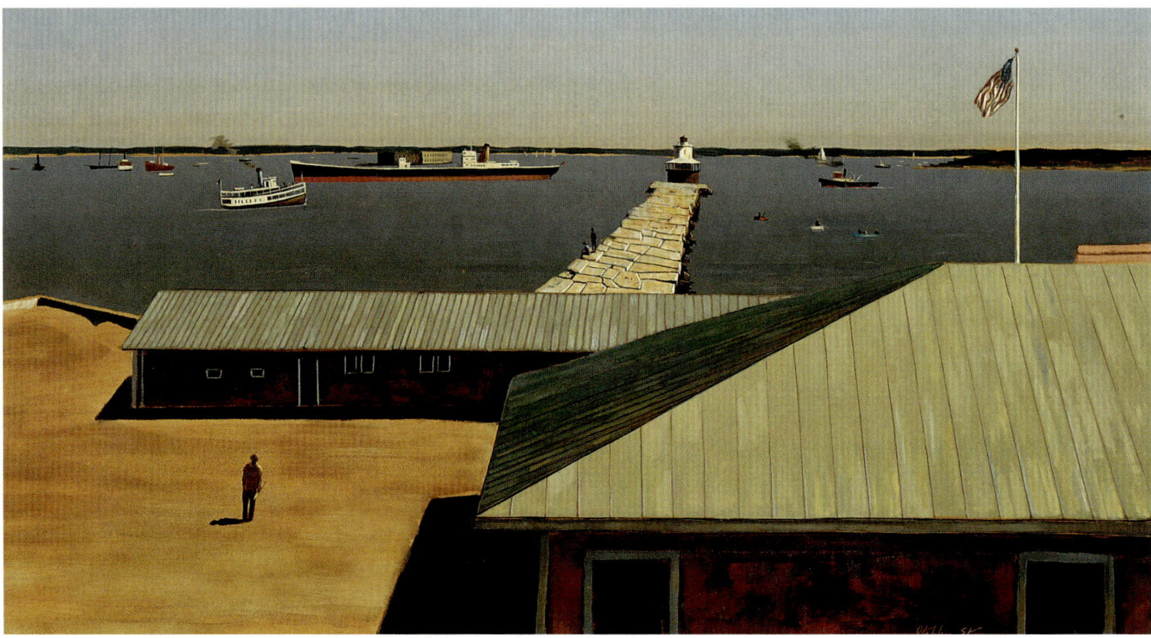

3.

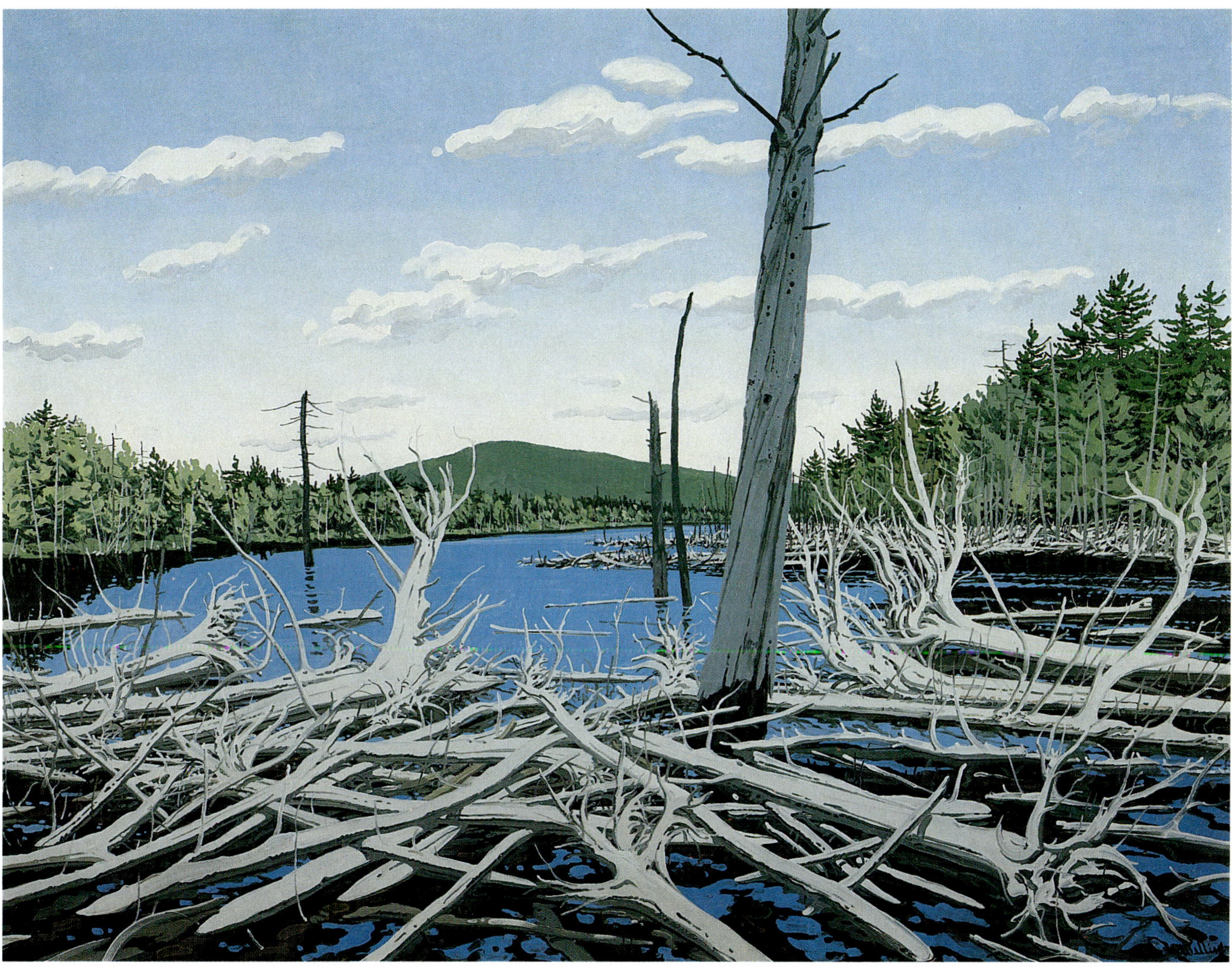

4.

2. Andrew Wyeth
Raven's Grove, 1985, tempera on panel, 31 x 27 3/4. Promised gift to the Portland Museum of Art from an anonymous donor. Photo by Peter Ralston.

3. Stephen Etnier
Portland Harbor, oil on masonite, 22 x 36. Courtesy of the Maine Savings Bank. Photo by Stretch Tuemmler.

4. Neil Welliver
Drowned Cedar, 1980, oil on canvas, 96 x 120. Courtesy of the Marlborough Gallery.

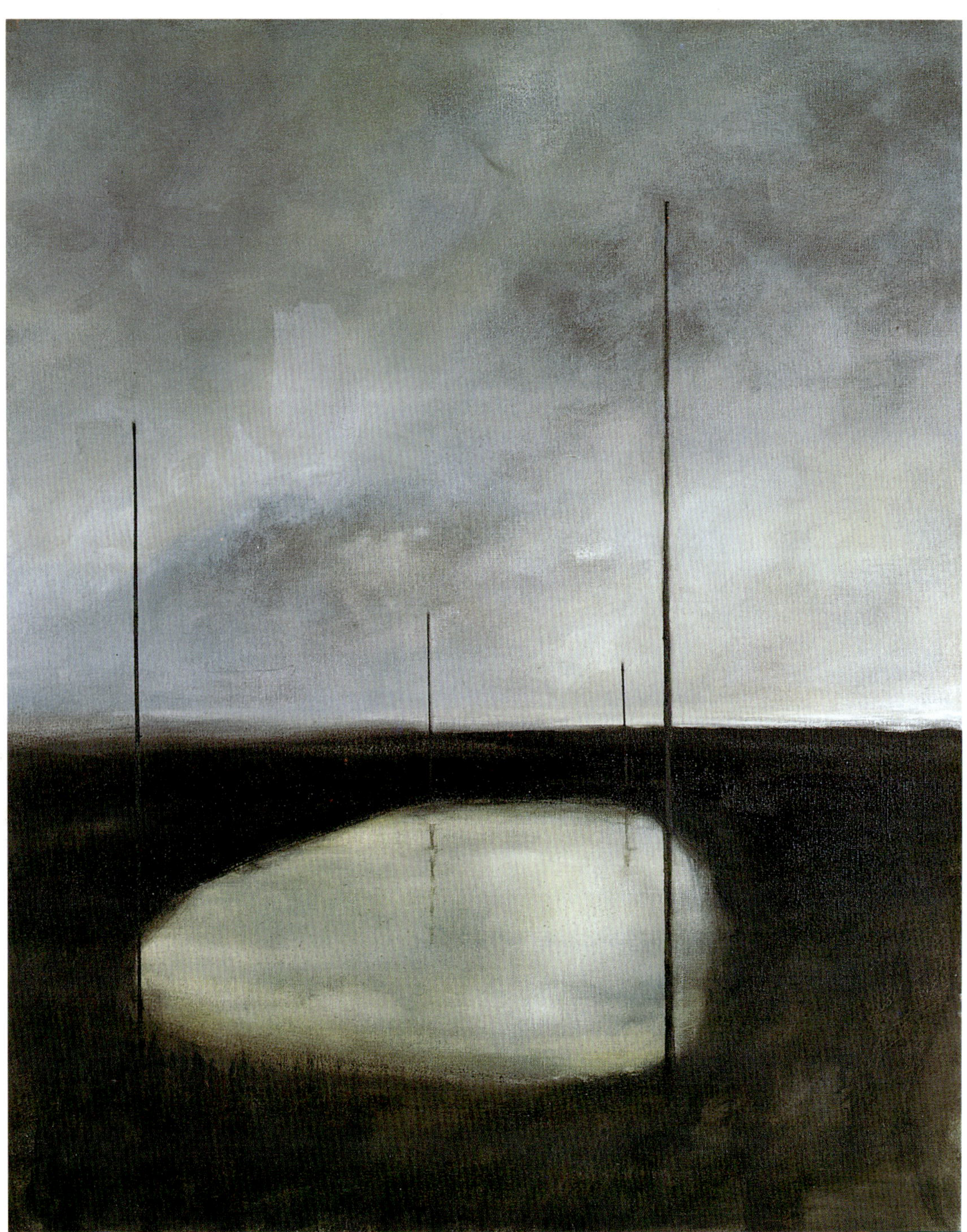

5.

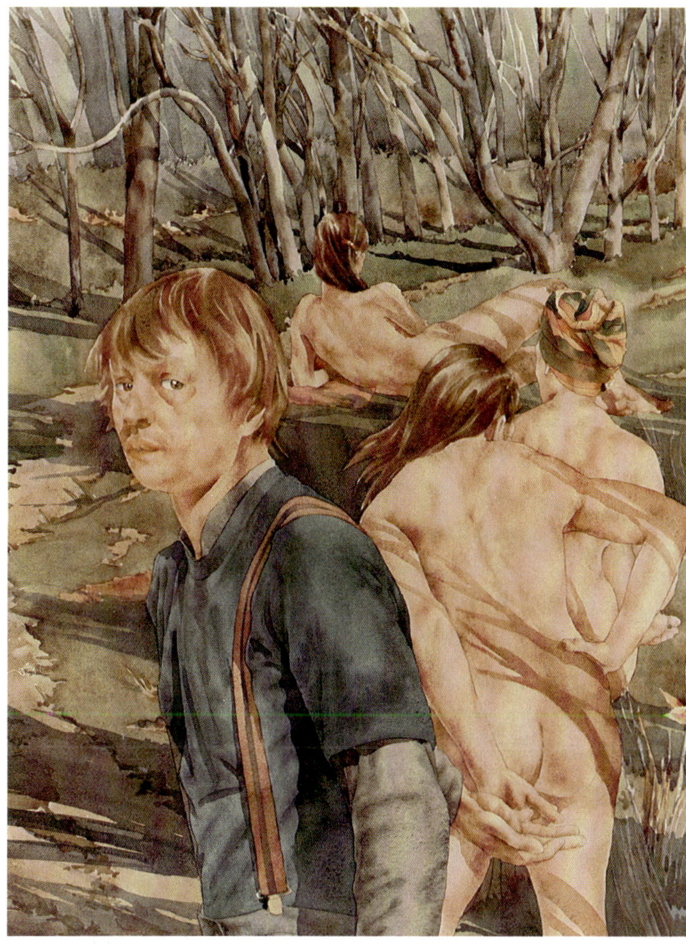

6.

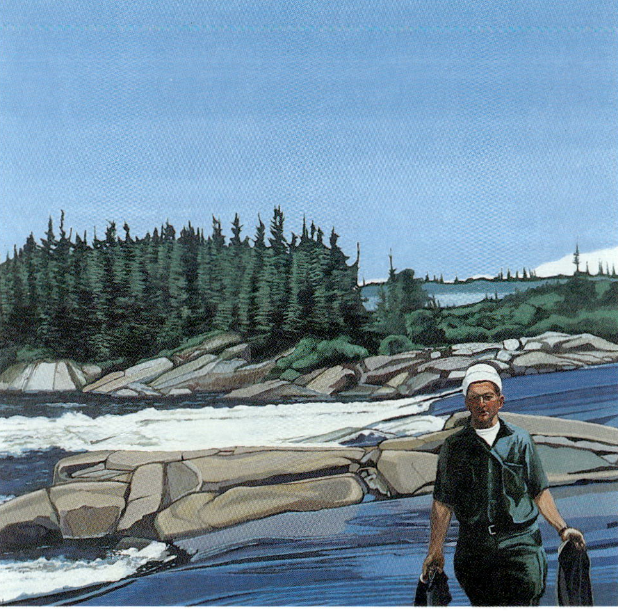

7.

5. Dozier Bell
Pool with Four Markers, 1987, oil on linen, 36 x 28.
Courtesy of the Schmidt Bingham Gallery.
Photo by Adam Reich.

6. DeWitt Hardy
A Fancy, 1989, watercolor, 22 x 32.
Courtesy of the artist. Photo by Scott Perry.

7. John Laurent
Marcel, Salmon, First Fall, Natashquan,
1987, acrylic on board, 48 x 48. Courtesy of Peter Jacobs and the Barridoff Galleries. Photo by Jay York.

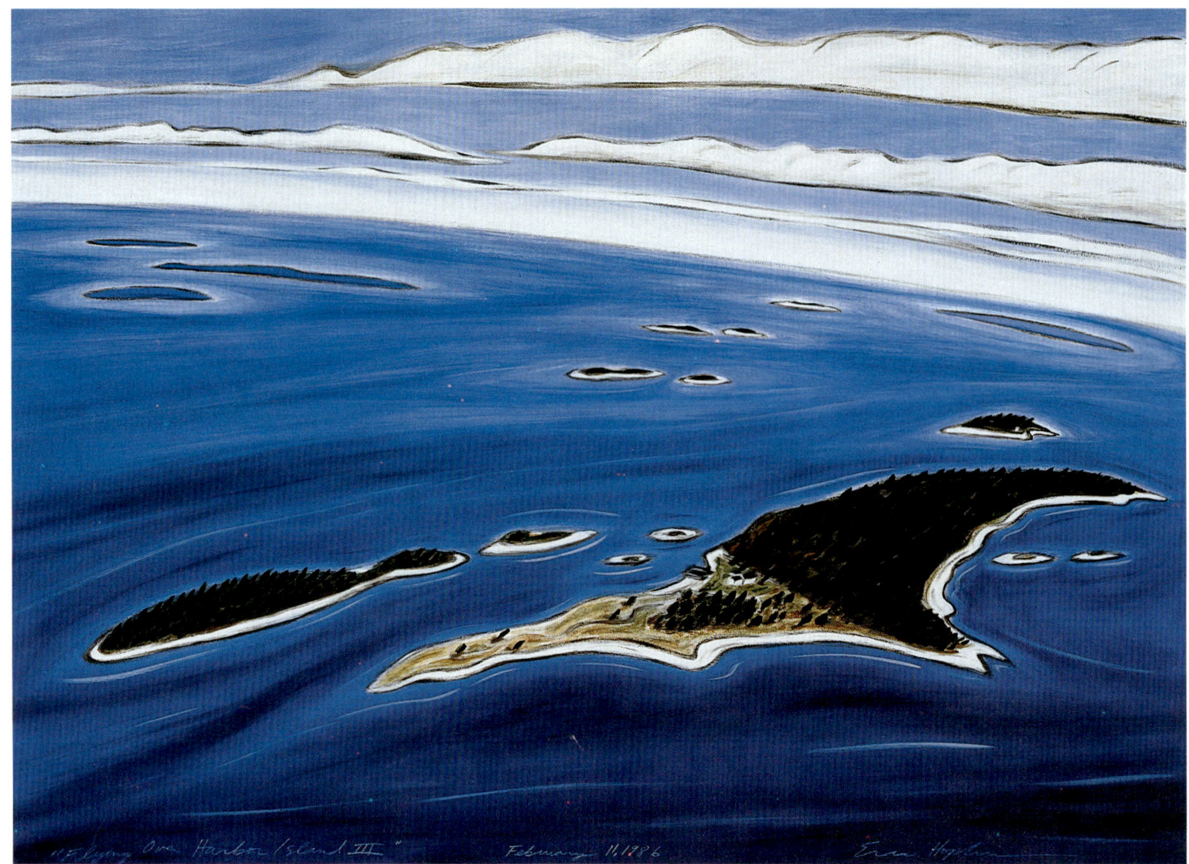

8.

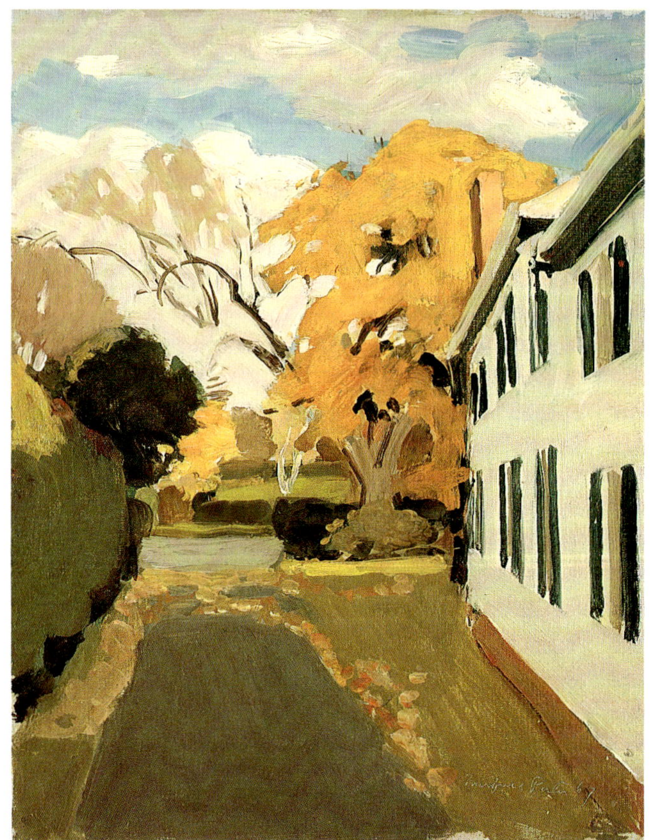

9.

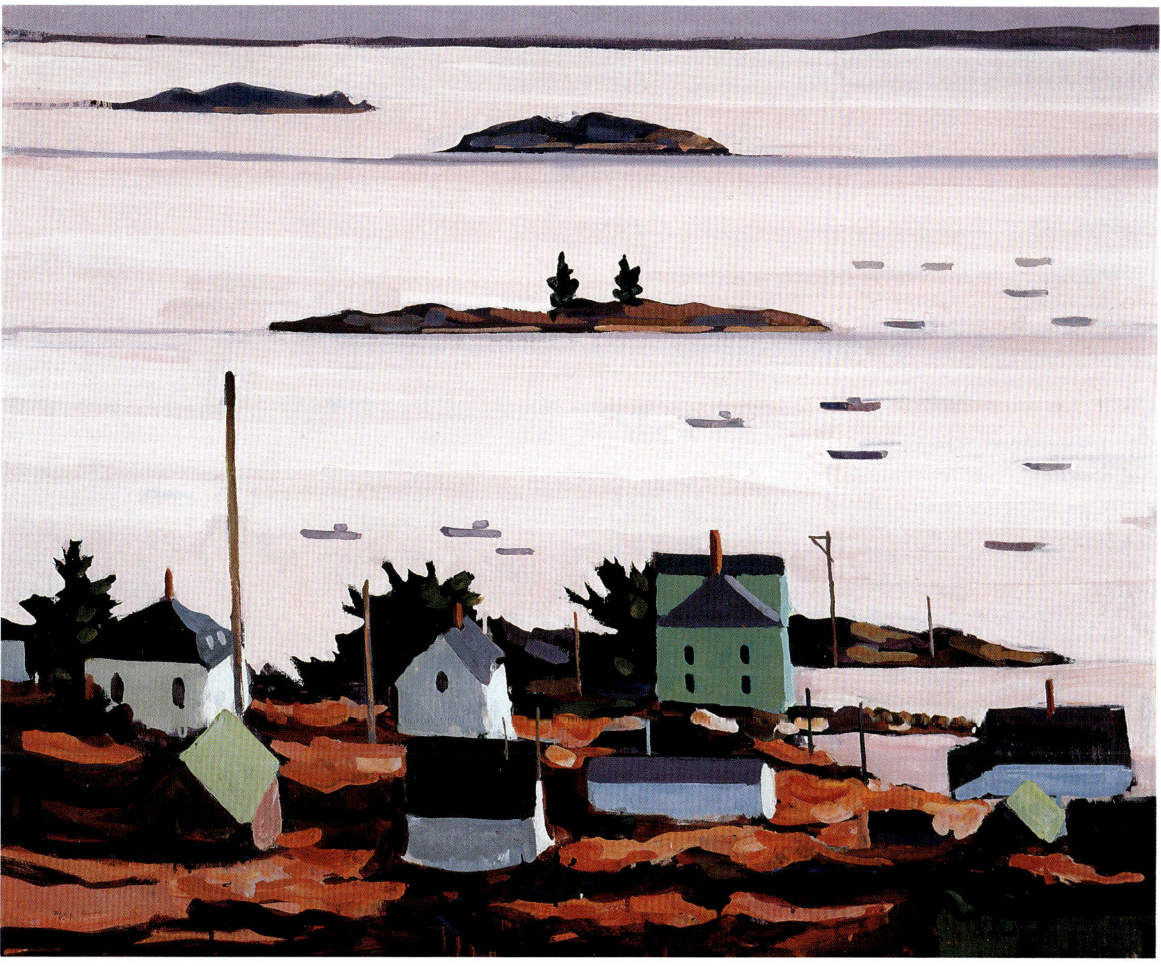

10.

8. Eric Hopkins
Flying Over Harbor Island, III, 1986, oil on canvas, 36 x 48.
Courtesy of the Barridoff Galleries. Photo by Jay York.

9. Fairfield Porter
The Driveway, 1967, oil on canvas, 20 x 15.
Courtesy of the Hirshl & Adler Modern.
Photo by Zindman/Fremont.

10. Alfred Chadbourn
Stonington - Autumn, 1985, oil on canvas, 30 x 36.
Courtesy of the Maine Savings Bank.
Photo by Stretch Tuemmler.

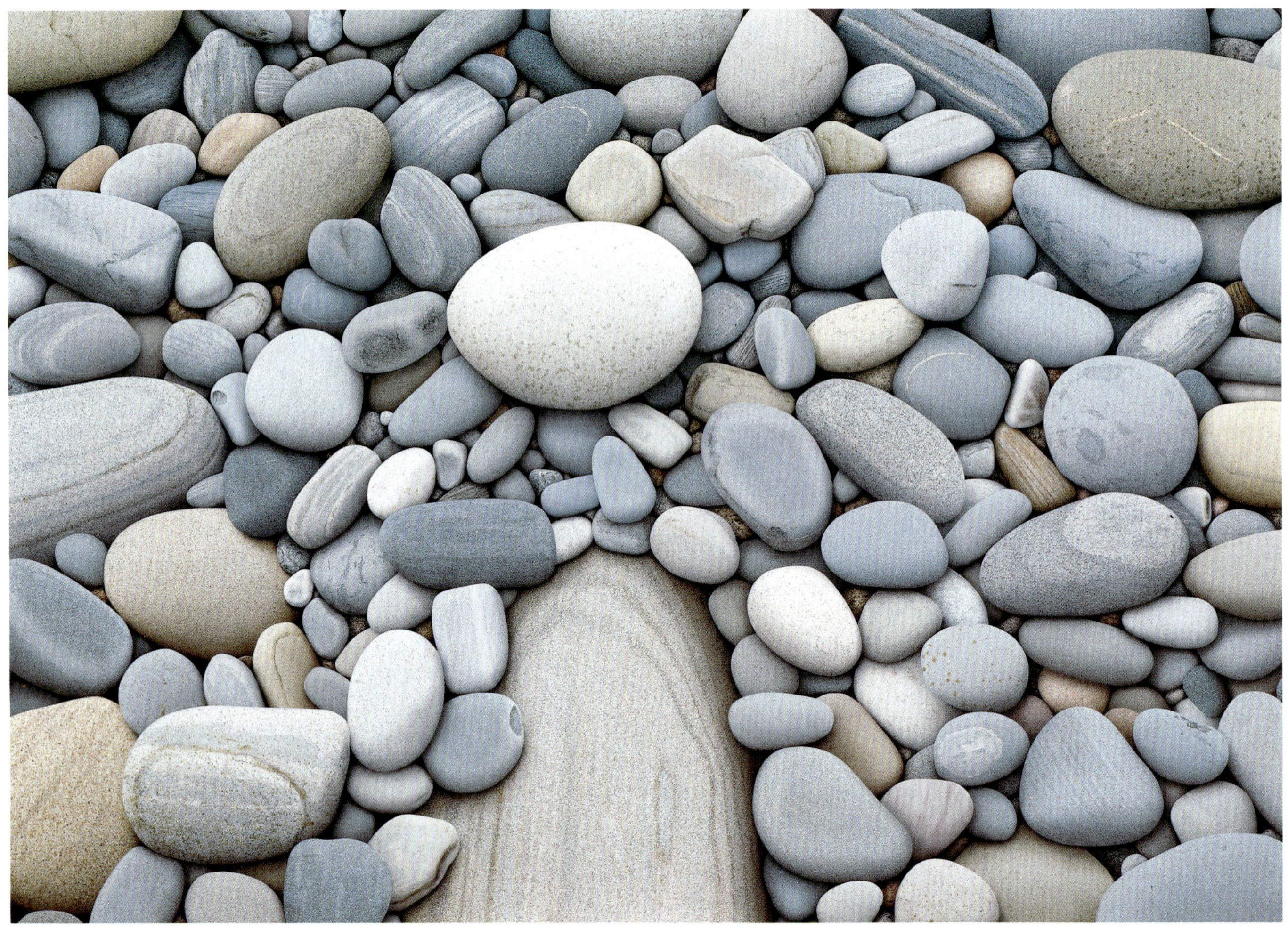

11.

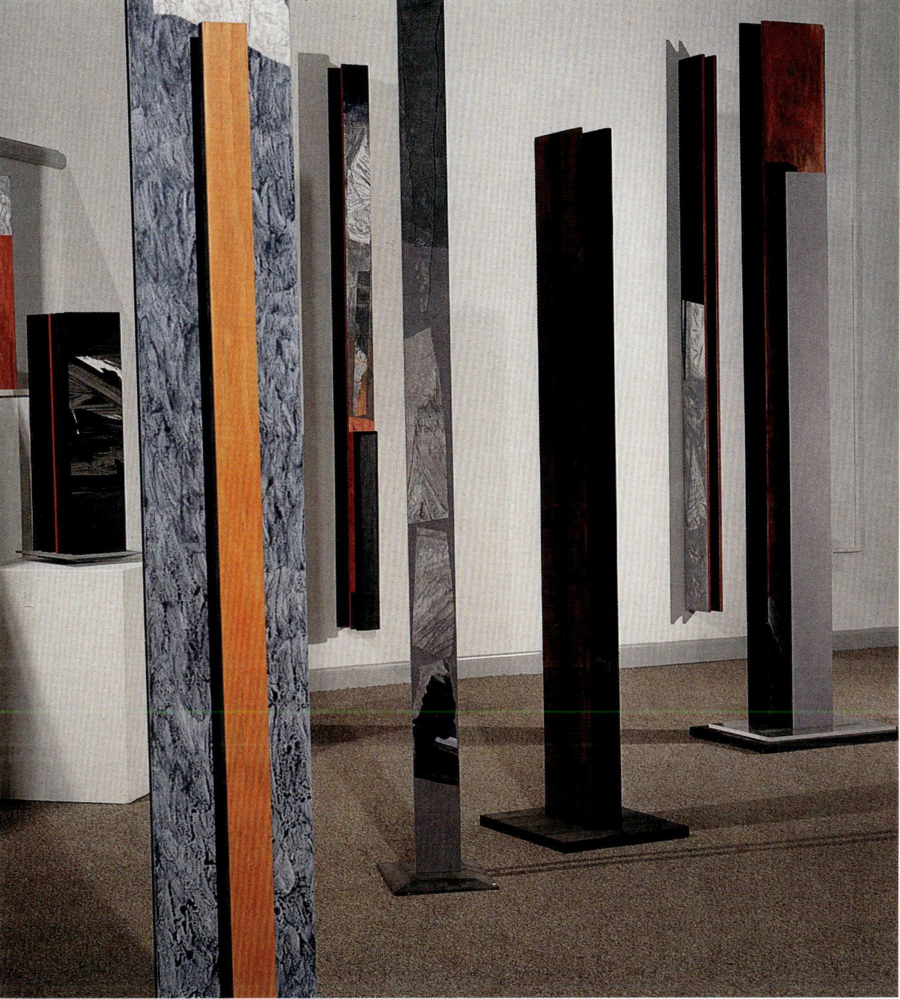

12.

11. Alan Magee
detail of *The Orrery*, 1985, acrylic on canvas, 60 x 96. Courtesy of the artist. Photo by Peter Ralston.

12. William Manning
Installation view of free-standing and wall pieces, 1988, mixed media. Courtesy of the Barridoff Galleries. Photo by Jay York.

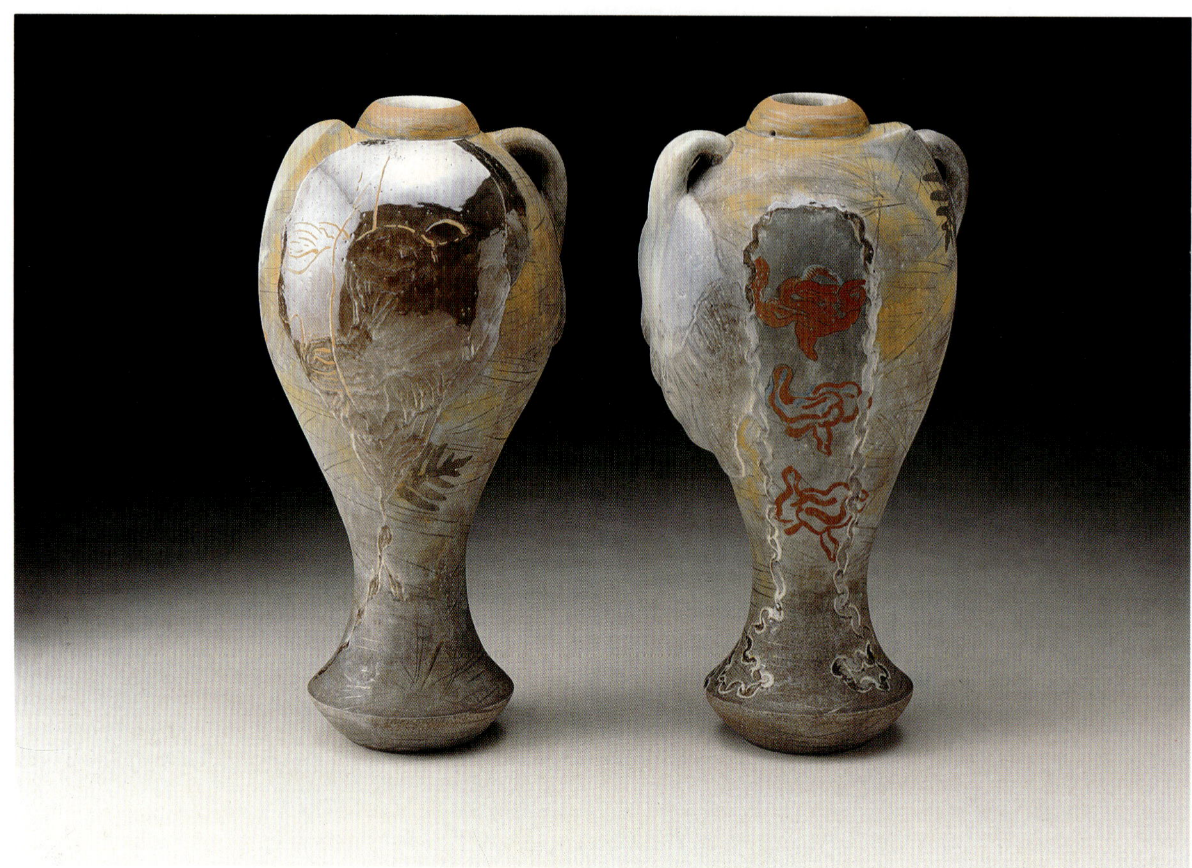

13.

14.

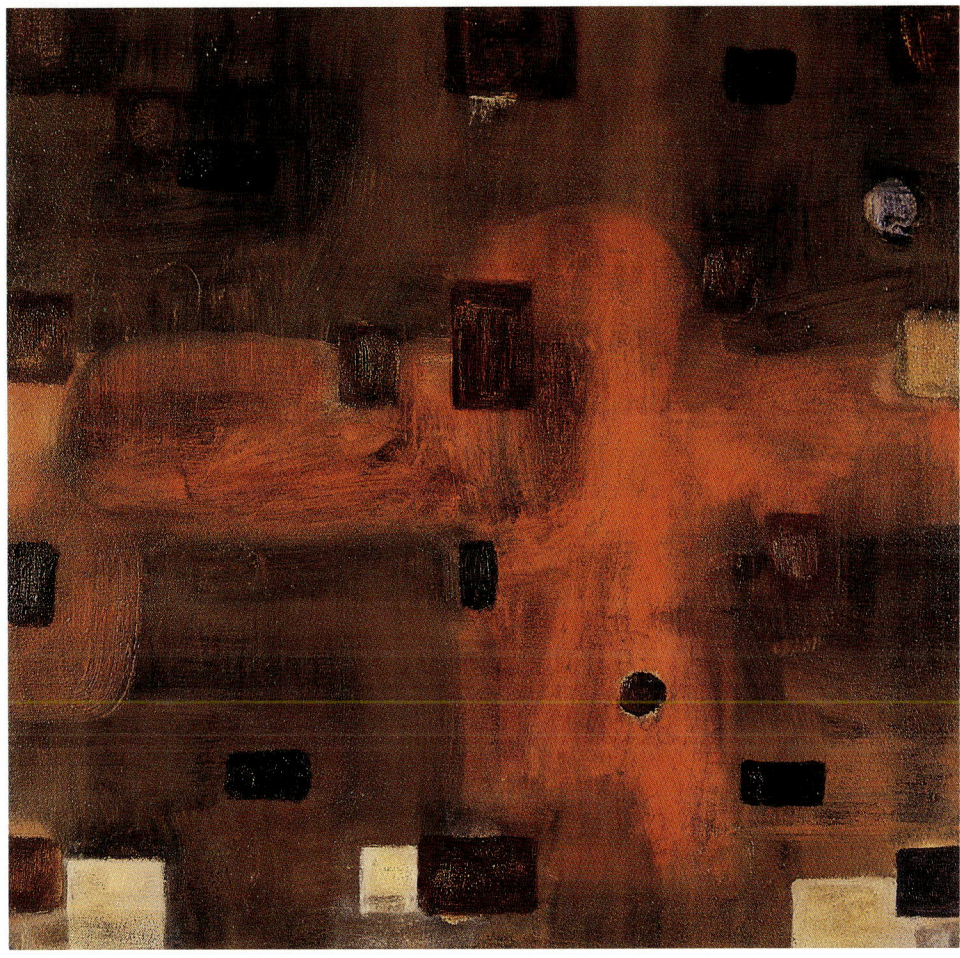

15.

13. Paul Heroux
Urns, 1988, acid etched stoneware, 20 1/2 x 10.
Courtesy of the Barridoff Galleries. Photo by Jay York.

14. Johnnie Ross
Untitled, 1988, acrylic and mica/iron on canvas, 60 x 78.
Private collection. Courtesy of the Barridoff Galleries.
Photo by Jay York.

15. Katherine Bradford
Night Fall, 1989, oil on canvas, 22 x 22.
Courtesy of the Victoria Munroe Gallery.

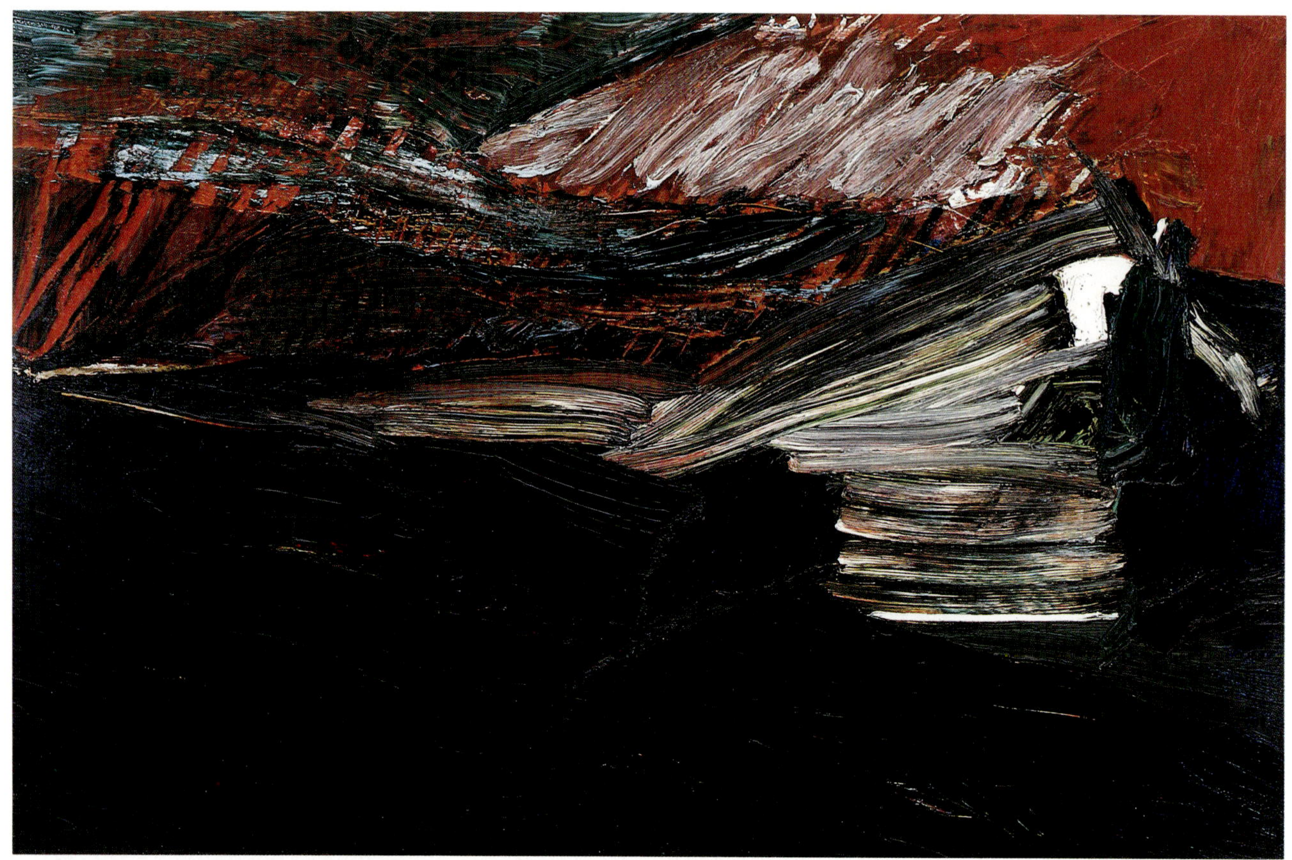

16.

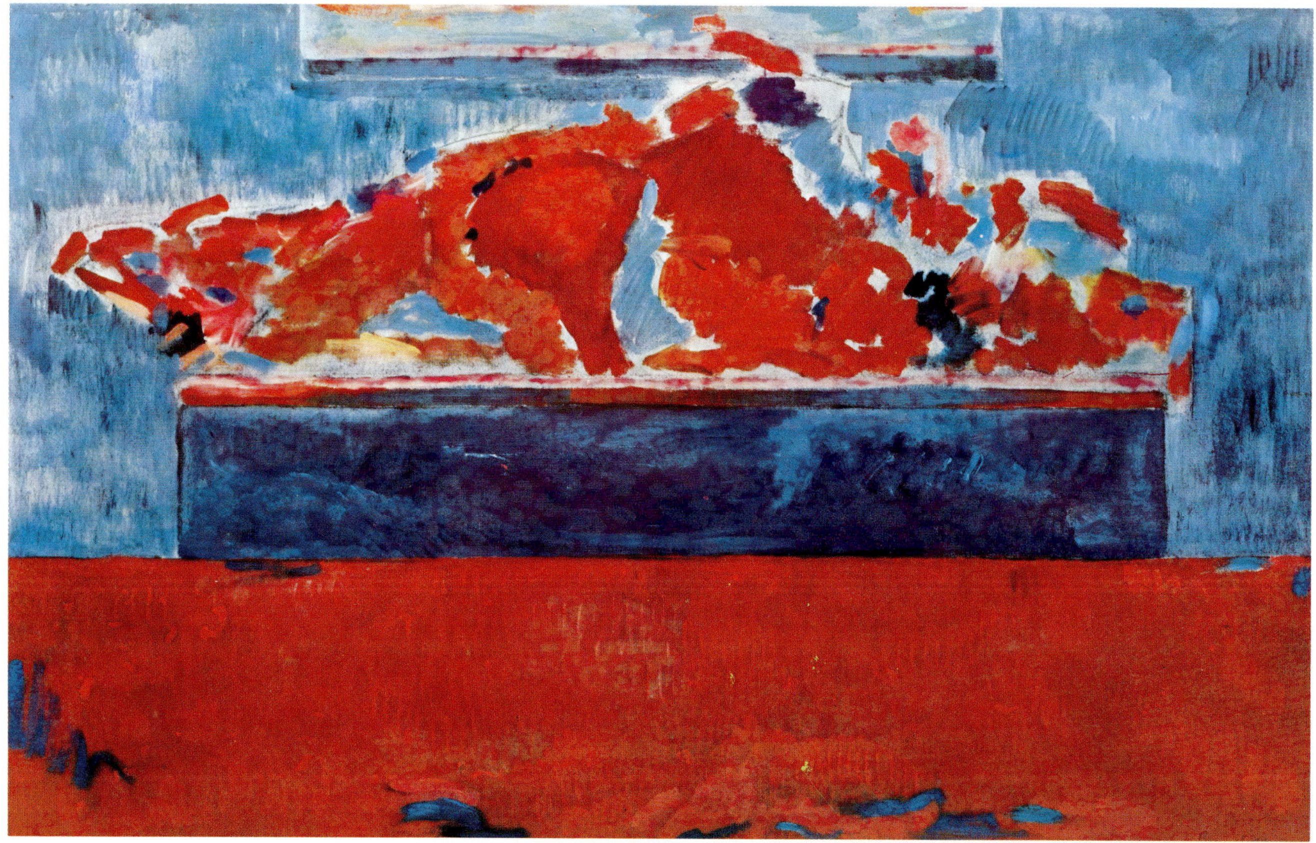

17.

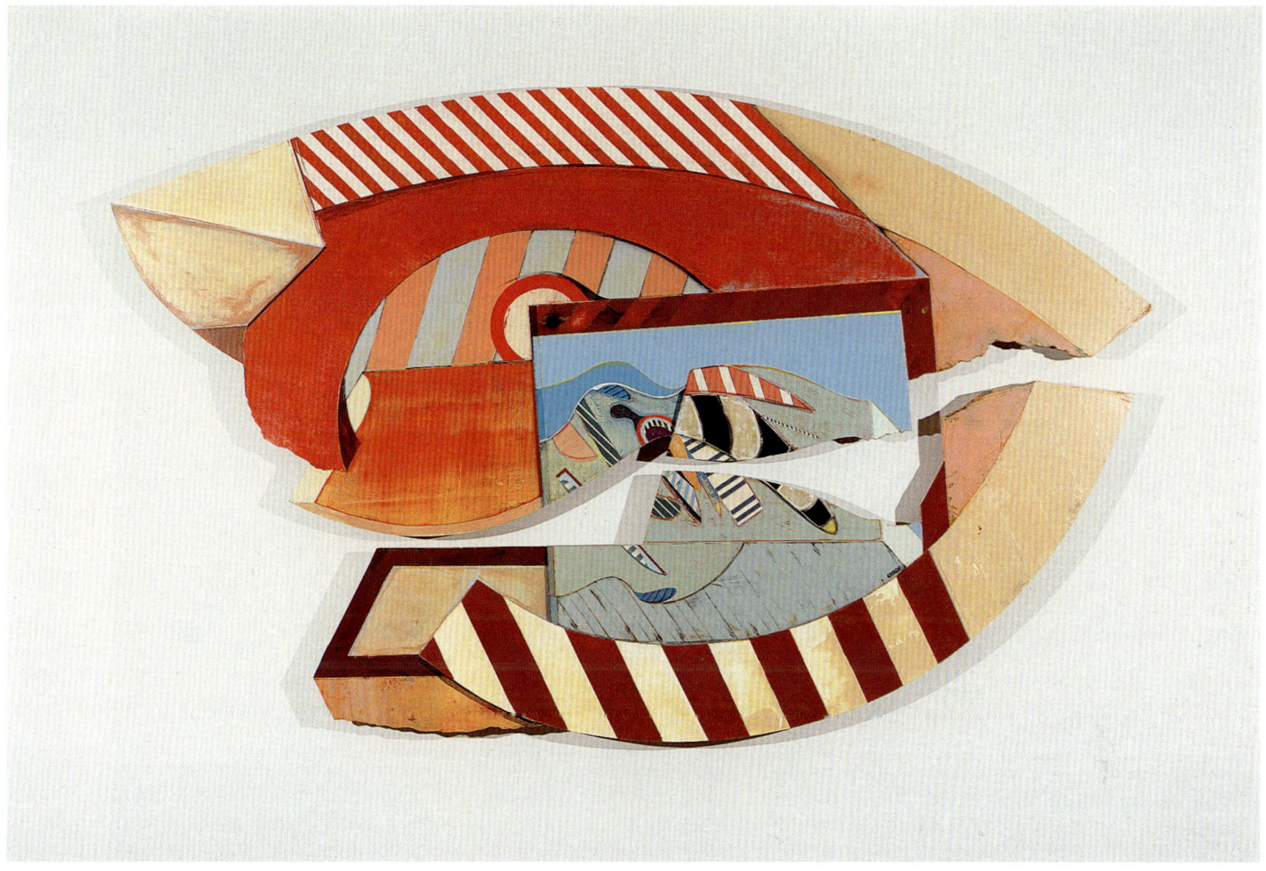

18.

16. Lisa Allen
Restless Night, Rushing Night, 1987, oil/oilstick/casein on paper mounted on birch plywood, 48 x 72. Courtesy of the Stephen Rosenberg Gallery. Photo by Stretch Tuemmler.

17. William Kienbusch
Autumn Island Stillscape #1, 1974, casein, 27 x 41 1/4. Private collection. Courtesy of the Kraushaar Galleries.

18. Frederick Lynch
Carnivore, 1988, acrylic on panel, 58 x 78. Courtesy of the Barridoff Galleries. Photo by Jay York.

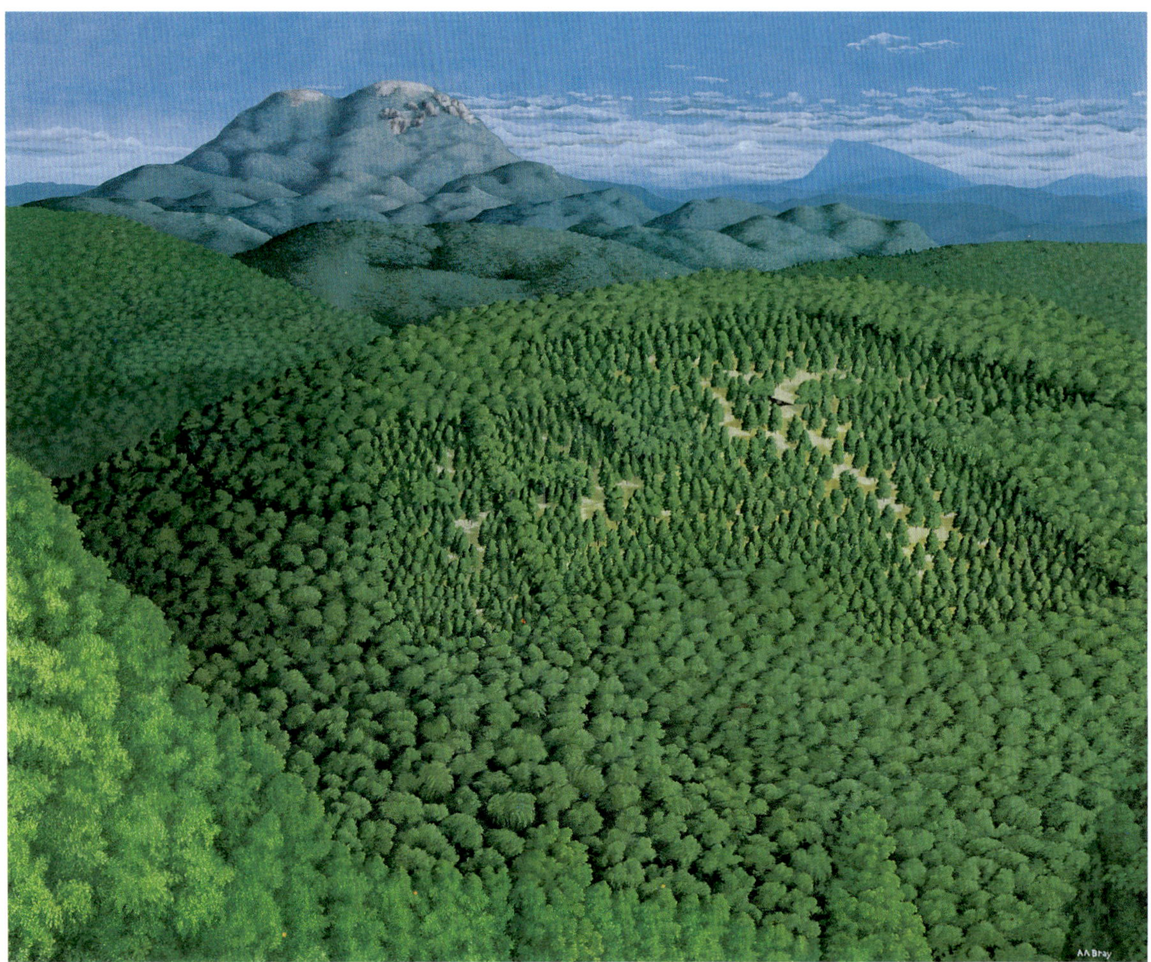

19.

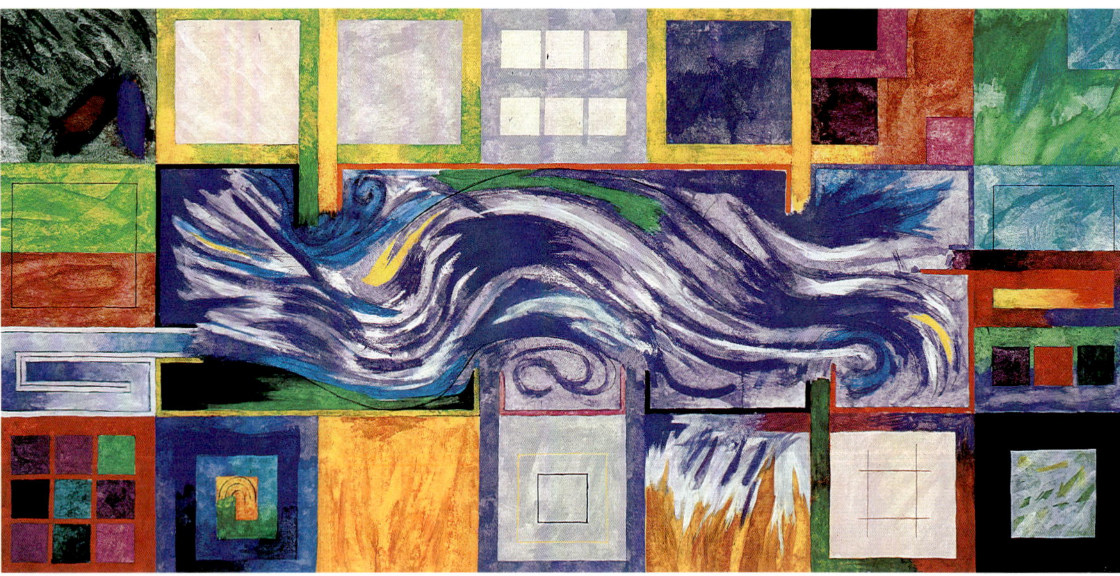

20.

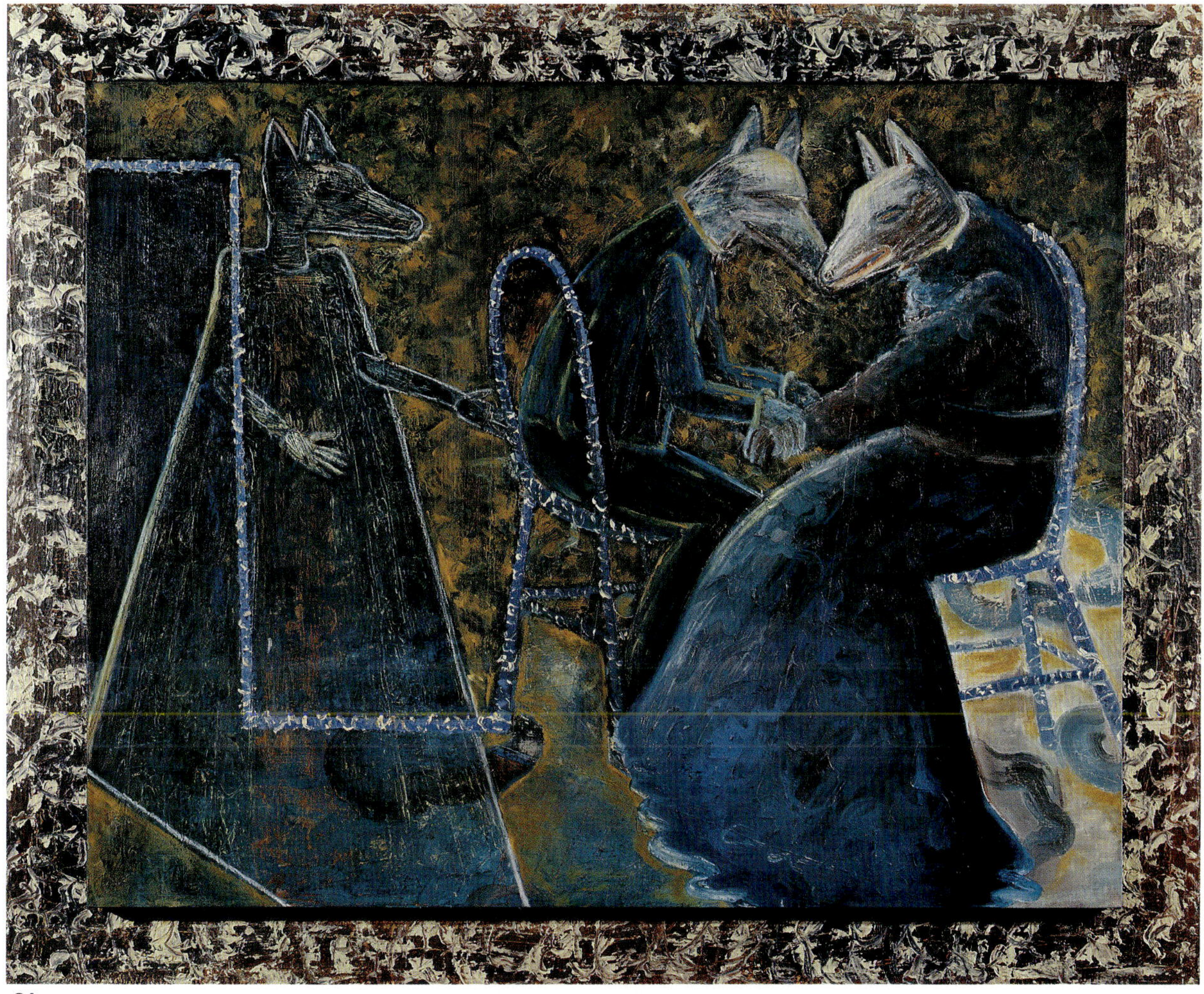

21.

19. Alan Bray
Ghost on Flanders Hill, 1982, tempera on wood, 20 x 26.
Courtesy of the Maine Savings Bank.
Photo by Stretch Tuemmler.

20. Abby Shahn
Anna Livia, 1987, tempera, 60 x 119.
Courtesy of the Hobe Sound Galleries North.

21. Marjorie Moore
Conjuring Up the Faith, 1988, oil on linen, 50 x 70.
Courtesy of the Barridoff Galleries. Photo by Jay York.

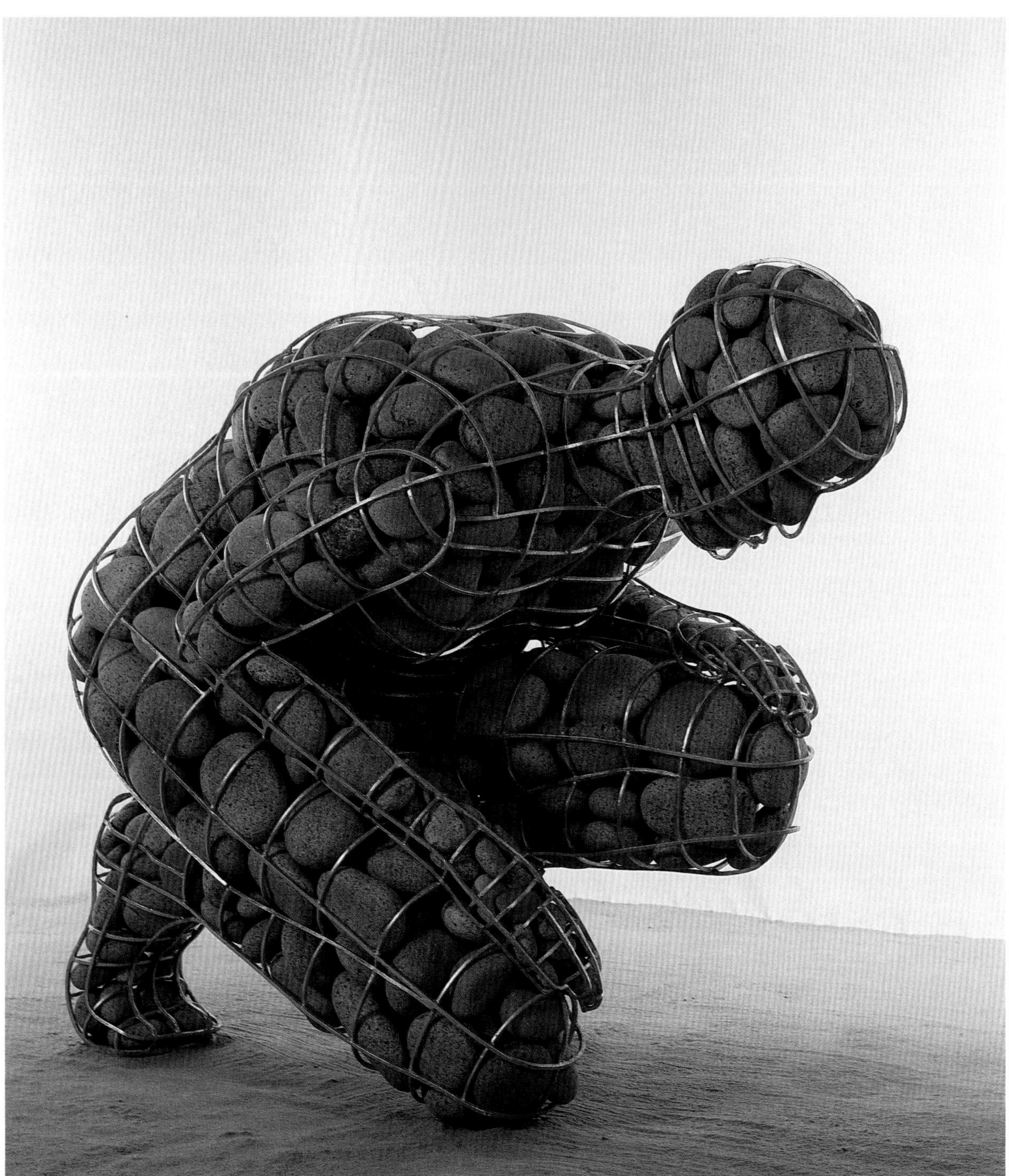

22.

22. Celeste Roberge
Northern Archives, Rising Cairn, 1989,
galvanized steel and granite stone, 54 x 58 x 40.
Collection of the Runny Mede Sculpture Farm,
Woodside, California. Photo by Jon Bonjour.

Scenes

3

The Maine Art Scene

An Appraisal

The Maine art scene as it is presently constituted involves a community of perhaps 500 artists and 5,000 viewers united by works and events of art exhibited and staged by perhaps a dozen private galleries and a dozen art institutions. The Maine scene is, then, a very human-scale and manageable little subculture. It is also a relatively new one.

Painter Thomas Crotty established Maine's first year-round commercial art gallery, Frost Gully Gallery, in 1966. Since that time, serious galleries have proliferated all along the coast — Mast Cove in Kennebunkport; Barridoff, Congress Square, Greenhut, Gallery 127, and Dean Velentgas in Portland; O'Farrell and Hobe Sound Galleries North in Brunswick; Anne Weber in Georgetown; Franciska Needham in Damariscotta; Caldbeck in Rockland; Artfellows, Gallery Sixty-Eight, and Frick Gallery in Belfast; Judith Leighton in Blue Hill; and the Turtle Gallery on Deer Isle. And with but one or two exceptions, all of these galleries opened during the expansive decade of the 1980s.

The important point to note here, of course, is that the artists came first. Prosperity follows population. During the late 1960s and early 1970s, Maine experienced an inmigration of new population. Then, during the 1980s, the same expansive economy which triggered a development boom threatening the very nature and character of Maine also financed a period of cultural growth and advance. The growth in the number of art galleries in the state, for example, is coincident with the growth in the number of architects, designers, movie theaters, theater companies, dance troupes, and restaurants.

As we stand poised on the cusp of the 1990s, we are witnessing a downturn in the economy—banks foreclosing on developers, empty condos all over the state, a slowdown in new construction, architects looking for work—which may bode ill for anything as consumable as art. My guess is that whatever artistic growth lies ahead in the immediate future will be seen in the development of individual artists rather than in any further expansion of the Maine art community.

To say that the Maine art scene is in a period of transition may be trite (the present is always in flux for those of us trapped in it), but the wholesale changing of the guard at Maine art institutions would seem to support that conclusion. In the summer of 1989, the nonprofit Maine Coast Artists gallery in Rockport hosted a symposium, "New Voices, New Vision," at which the panel consisted of a dozen Maine curators and directors, all new to their jobs within the past two years, most within a matter of months. The new arrivals tended to characterize the change in command as a turnover natural to their profession, but those of us who had been around awhile understood the change as a function of an era of new and greater expectations.

The Portland Museum of Art, Maine's putative flagship art institution, provides a good example of how raised expectations create pressure for change. In 1977, when millionaire industrialist Charles Shipman Payson promised his collection of 17 paintings by Winslow Homer to the Portland Museum of Art, the museum was principally an historic house museum with an attached gallery. By the time its new $8.2 million Charles Shipman Payson Building opened in 1983, however, the Portland Museum of Art seemed to have pretensions to being a major regional art museum. No matter that the museum had neither a major art collection nor money for major acquisitions and exhibitions; it had a world-class building by Henry Cobb of I.M. Pei & Partners. When, inevitably, the programming expectations raised by the new building could not be met, the trustees gave the director the sack in 1987.

The old Portland Museum of Art had a reputation for neglecting contemporary Maine art and artists, a situation exacerbated by the fact that the museum seemed to go through curators like cheap nylons. Under the new leadership, the museum has made more of an effort to become part of the Maine art community, its *Perspectives* series highlighting some of the best artists in Maine.

Ironically, however, where Maine artists may have suffered institutional neglect a decade or so ago, the problem today may actually be one of too much attention. The impulse to support emerging Maine artists and to celebrate distinguished ones may be healthy and natural, but Maine's new enthusiasm for art has resulted in a situation where the principal art institutions—Bowdoin, Bates, Colby, Westbrook College's Payson Gallery, the Farnsworth Museum, Portland School of Art's Baxter Gallery, the University of Maine galleries, Portland Museum of Art, Maine Coast Artists, and the Barn Gallery—all tend to show the same artists, and indeed the same artists the commercial galleries are showing. It is perhaps inappropriate to say so in a book about Maine art, but what Maine really needs now is more exposure to contemporary art from the rest of the world.

Another thing the Maine art scene needs is more and better criticism. In the 1970s, it was possible for one writer to see and write about virtually all of the exhibitions in Maine that deserved attention. By the early 1980s, it was still possible for one person to see all the important shows, if not to write about them all. Today, the quantity, quality, and frequency of serious shows is such that one critic can't even see every show that should be seen.

From 1978 to 1981, Maine was blessed with *VISION*, a quarterly review of Maine art begun by the Union of Maine Visual Artists. The nonprofit *VISION* folded, however, when volunteer efforts and federal funds flagged. Then, in 1986-87, we were treated to the lavish, full-color pages of *AM* (*Artists in Maine*). The audience simply was not there, however, for a quarterly Maine art slick. What Maine needs and could support is a monthly publication reviewing and reporting on *all* the arts.

Finally, despite the growth in the number of artists, the number of galleries, the audience, the market, the activity, and the consciousness of art in Maine, the Maine art scene is still more active in the summer than it is the rest of the year. The Skowhegan School of Painting & Sculpture, Haystack Mountain School of Crafts, and the Vinalhaven Press print workshop will probably always be seasonal operations, but Maine will not reach cultural maturity until key summer galleries such as Maine Coast Artists and the Barn Gallery (these two being the closest Maine has to non-collecting institutes of contemporary art) can operate year-round.

The articles and essays gathered here deal with a few of the issues on the Maine art scene. They all concern what I would call matters of aesthetic commerce.

Art as Business

Art Market

When Ray Farrell heard that Kathryn Begg was having a Neil Welliver show, his blood began to boil. He phoned everyone he could think of to complain and sent his invitation to the show back with a note scrawled across it asking Begg whom she was going to steal from next.

A lot of people (including myself) found it somewhat laughable that Ray Farrell should think that he had a Maine exclusive on Neil Welliver, an artist of international status long before he ever exhibited at the O'Farrell Gallery in Brunswick. But the way Farrell looked at it, he had given Welliver his first one-artist show in a commercial gallery in Maine, was close to Welliver, and had spent a lot of money promoting not only his own Welliver show, but Welliver in general. Now here was this new kid on the art scene—Begg—whose Gallery 127 opened in Portland just this summer, stealing his thunder. Even though he had no contractual relationship with Welliver, Ray Farrell felt wronged.

Since pioneering a year-round art gallery in Brunswick in 1984, Farrell has consistently sought to distinguish his gallery ("I'm always looking for a competitive advantage," he says) by exhibiting big name artists such as Welliver, Alex Katz, Robert Indiana, Louise Nevelson, and Andy Warhol. In fact, Farrell does have an exclusive on the sale of Warhol prints in Maine.

"My obligation to these artists doesn't stop when I take down a one-person show," says Farrell. "I have spent and I do spend a great deal of money advertising all of the artists I have an association with. Therefore, I think it's unfair when you advertise and promote an artist very, very heavily and someone else comes along and doesn't have to advertise and promote because you've gotten the word out already."

Kathryn Begg doesn't know why Farrell is so upset. She represents artist Graydon Mayer, an old friend of Welliver's, and simply wanted to show the two artists together. She called Welliver to ask if she could show his work, Welliver told her that Marlborough Gallery in New York handles all of his business, she called Marlborough, and Marlborough sent her some paintings. It's as simple as that.

"I never gave Ray Farrell serious consideration," says Begg. " The show wasn't done for any reason except to have a show of Graydon and Neil's work. I did it for Graydon."

"The whole damn thing is very confusing for me," says Welliver. "I'm sure these things happen in places like Kansas City and Waco all the time, but I never hear about them."

Welliver attended the opening at Gallery 127,

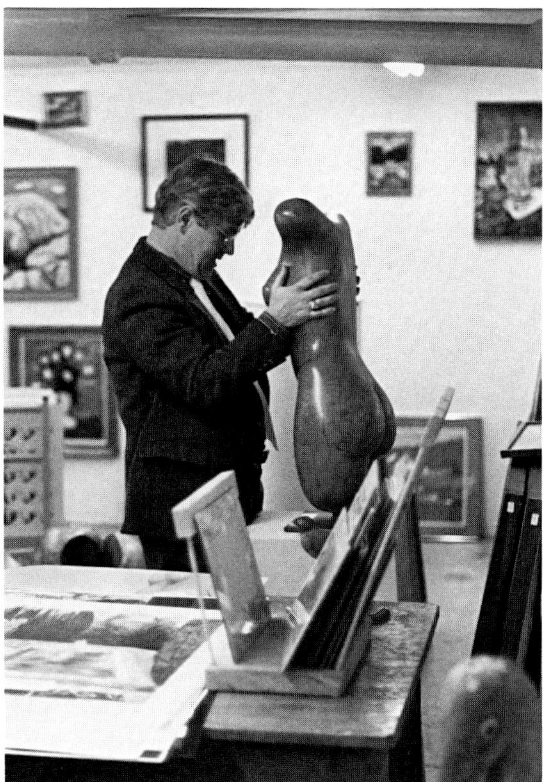

1. *Ray Farrell, owner of O'Farrell Gallery, in Brunswick. Photo by Christopher Ayres.*

but he understands why Ray Farrell is so upset and says, "he should be." Welliver figures that the folks at Marlborough just didn't realize how close Brunswick and Portland are. To make amends, Marlborough has promised Farrell a big Welliver show next year. *Fini.*

Now the fact that one art dealer may have stepped on another's toes is not in itself news-worthy, but what this minor territorial dispute underlines is the rapid proliferation of art galleries in Maine and the competitiveness that comes with growth. Twenty years ago there wasn't a single gallery in Portland. Today there are, well, let's see, Frost Gully, Barridoff, Posters Plus, Hobe Sound North, Congress Square, Pine Tree, David Hitchcock, Elwyn Dearborn, Dean Velentgas, Wellin Gardiner, Peter Rolfe, and Gallery 127, not to mention crafts galleries and the host of restaurants and banks that regularly exhibit art. Nor is this gallery boom restricted to Portland. The *Maine Times' 1987 SummerGuide* lists 92 galleries statewide. Most of these galleries have opened within the last ten years and last week's mail brought news of two more gallery openings—Central Place Galleries in Bangor and Sarah Elizabeth Look Fine Arts in Ellsworth.

So what does all this art market activity mean? Certainly it means a lot of people are interested in showing and selling art. It means artists have a better chance of showing their work in Maine than ever before, and art lovers have a better chance of seeing art in Maine than ever before. Just what the boom means to the dealers, however, isn't quite so clear.

Gretchen Schaefer, director of the Congress Square Gallery, for instance, doesn't see the market expanding with the galleries.

"There are so many more galleries now," says Schaefer, "but the business doesn't seem to have increased that much."

Judith Leighton of the Leighton Gallery in Blue Hill agrees.

"I think every other gallery is going to fold in a couple of years because there aren't that many art dollars around and there aren't that many good artists. The year I opened up, three galleries in this area closed."

"I'm sure the pie is getting sliced thinner," says Peter Bullock, director of Hobe Sound Galleries North, "but I've always subscribed to the theory that the best place to have a hot dog stand is right across the street from another stand."

"If the number of galleries increases and the galleries that are showing art are good ones," says John Ames, owner of Gallery Sixty-Eight in Belfast, "then the fact that there are a few more galleries isn't going to hurt anyone. It just puts pressure on the galleries to be clear about what they do. It forces you to focus on a customer's perspective of your gallery."

To a certain extent, Maine galleries have established individual identities for them-selves—Gallery Sixty-Eight concentrates on prints and drawings; Dean Velentgas focuses on difficult, adventurous work by both Maine and New York artists; O'Farrell goes for name artists, etc. But when you come right down to it, most Maine galleries do pretty much the same thing—show and sell art by Maine artists.

"With a good artist," says Hobe Sound's Bullock, "I don't think it matters whether he's with Barridoff or me or Crotty." Tom Crotty owns Frost Gully Gallery.

If it really doesn't matter which of the better galleries a good artist is with (though there has been enough movement of artists between and among these "big three" galleries to suggest it does), then perhaps one ought to ask what gallery representation means to an artist in Maine. What is the artist-gallery relationship?

In the best of all possible worlds, every good artist would have a relationship with a gallery such as Neil Welliver has with Marlborough. He makes his art and, in exchange for an international exclusive and a 50 percent commission, Marlborough, in Welliver's words, "does everything else." "Everything else" means Marlborough picks up Welliver's paintings in Lincolnville, transports them to New York, frames them, insures them, photographs them, documents them, publicizes them, places them in shows, exhibits them, and, of course, sells them. But then Welliver's major paintings now fetch $50,000 to $60,000, and he is just one of many bankable artists that Marlborough represents. No Maine gallery could afford to do all this for its artists. In fact, it appears that Maine galleries don't even make a living for most of the artists they represent. In Maine, the dealers make the money, not the artists.

Rob Elowitch, who operates Barridoff Galleries with his wife Annette, believes that his gallery probably sells more contemporary art than any other Maine gallery, approximately $250,000 worth in the last year. Barridoff, which once represented as many as 40 artists, cut its roster drastically when it sold its original building and now, in new quarters, represents 21.

"Our top ten artists," says Elowitch, "can almost earn a living."

By "almost" Elowitch means that ten Barridoff artists net $10,000 or more from gallery sales with the top seller netting $50,000. Both Hobe Sound North and O'Farrell (without citing actual figures) report total sales close to Barridoff's $250,000 and Frost Gully reports sales approximately half that figure, but very few artists make a complete living from any of these galleries. Jean Briggs of Mast Cove Galleries in Kennebunkport reports sales of approximately $175,000, but this figure represents the sale of 250 works by more than 60 different artists. And Judith Leighton, who believes she could probably sell $250,000 worth of art if she moved her gallery from Blue Hill to Portland (a move she is not about to make), sees the potential for some artists making a living out of her summer gallery in the near future.

"In five years," says Leighton, "I can see several of the artists in the gallery making a living out of this gallery in the time it's open."

Currently, however, those artists in Maine who manage to make a living from their art primarily do so by showing in a variety of galleries both in-state and out, and by selling from their studios. No one Maine gallery seems to be in a position right now to guarantee its artists an honest living.

"If you're not making a living for an artist," says Kathryn Begg, "you can't make demands on him."

But Maine galleries do make demands on artists. Exclusivity is one of them, but the boundaries of exclusivity vary greatly from gallery to gallery.

Perhaps it was inevitable that Ray Farrell should be the first to get his toes stepped on, because his gallery is the only Maine gallery I could find that asks for statewide exclusivity. Farrell is also one of the few Maine dealers who asks artists to put this promise in writing. Most Maine galleries do not have written contracts with their artists. Barridoff used to insist on statewide exclusive rights to sell an artist's work, but recently relaxed its policy to cover only southern Maine, Brunswick south. Frost Gully and Congress Square describe an area of exclusivity within a 50-mile radius of Portland. And Hobe Sound North identifies its exclusive market as an area bounded by Bath to the north, Lewiston to the west, and Kennebunk to the south. (The Kennebunk cut-off is to accommodate gallery artist Michael Palmer who operates Ps Gallery in Ogunquit during the summer.)

Galleries in outlying areas of the state generally have much more lenient prohibitions on showing with other galleries. Jean Briggs, for example, only asks that artists showing at Mast Cove not show anywhere else in Kennebunkport. Judith Leighton asks that artists showing in her gallery not show anywhere else in Hancock County at the same time they are showing in Blue Hill.

The other major and more necessary demand that galleries make on artists is the commission a

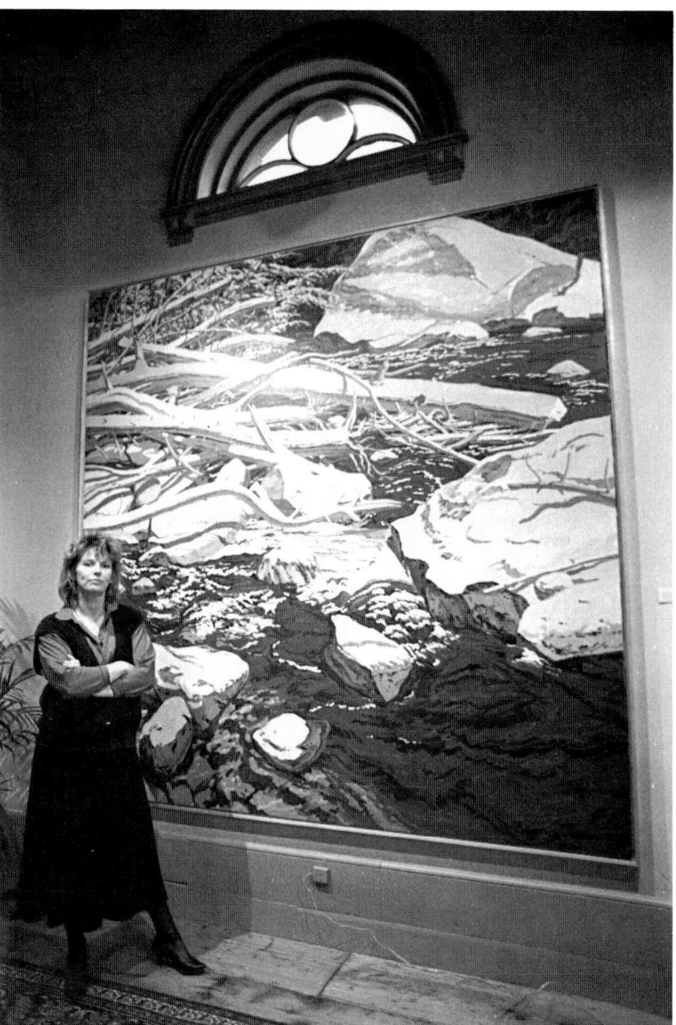

2. *Kathryn Begg, owner of Gallery 127, in Portland. Photo by Christopher Ayres.*

gallery takes on the sale of an artist's work. Here again the policy varies from gallery to gallery. Barridoff, Hobe Sound North, and Congress Square all take a 50-percent commission, the norm in the national art market. O'Farrell, Frost Gully, Leighton, and Gallery 127 work on a 40-percent commission. Dean Velentgas only takes a 35-percent cut because his gallery is only open 14 hours a week. And Jean Briggs gives artists an even more generous share of the income, taking only 30 percent from sales at Mast Cove. She explains her generosity by noting that since her gallery is in her home, she has less overhead than many other galleries.

Tom Crotty at Frost Gully says he fought to hold the line at 33-1/3 percent commission, but finally upped his commission to 40 percent a year and a half ago.

"The market in Maine," insists Crotty, "is so hard-nosed and tight that when you jump from $1,000 paintings to $2,000 paintings, you've changed your market. You cut down your market drastically by going up in price to cover commissions. When I lost the 33-1/3 battle, the whole art market in Maine inflated."

Crotty, an artist himself, started the state's first serious contemporary art gallery at his Freeport (Frost Gully) home back in 1966 and moved to Portland in 1973. At that time he represented 50-odd artists. Today, he represents 19, only six of whom (Crotty himself, George DeLyra, DeWitt Hardy, Dahlov Ipcar, Laurence Sisson, and the estate of the late Stephen Etnier) remain from the original Frost Gully roster. Most are either no longer showing in Maine or have moved to other galleries. Crotty, a maverick who seems to take a minority view on most matters in the Maine art world, is of the opinion that more often than not when an artist is unhappy with a gallery, it is the artist's work, and not the gallery, that is at fault. But as in baseball, when the team isn't winning, the easiest thing to do is replace the manager. Crotty is also of the opinion that the artists call the shots in Maine.

"It's the artists who create the world of galleries almost entirely," says Crotty.

If this is so, then perhaps it would be profitable to consider the gallery experiences of some representative Maine artists, beginning with an artist who seems to agree, in principle at least, with Crotty on the artist shouldering responsibility for his/her own fate.

"It's pretty clear," says painter Howard Clifford, "that you can't expect any gallery to make a living for you from your painting. You can't count on anybody but yourself. You have to look to yourself and build your own thing for the long term."

Clifford, an artist who works just as hard at promoting his art as he does at making it, was briefly represented by Barridoff Galleries a decade ago, but has primarily made his way alone, establishing a market for his art by himself. Other artists are often envious or incredulous at the prices he now commands for his work, particularly considering that he isn't paying any commissions.

"I can sell paintings out of my studio now for $16,000 each," says Clifford, "so it's like I'd be crazy to lock myself into something where I'd have to pay someone $8,000 to sell a painting."

Which made it all the more surprising then the name Howard Clifford turned up this summer on Kathryn Begg's Gallery 127 list. But then Clifford explains that while Gallery 127 gets a 40 percent commission on anything it sells, he is still free to sell out of his studio without giving the gallery a cut. ("I'm taking Howard on his terms," says Begg.) Why, if he can sell his work himself, has Clifford joined Gallery 127 at all?

"Belonging," says the artist. "I've felt like an outsider long enough."

Eric Hopkins is another largely self-made artist, one whom some people on the Maine art scene consider to be overexposed at this point. Hopkins burst onto the scene back in the summer of 1984 with a terrific show at Caldbeck Gallery in Rockland and since then seems to have shown just about everywhere—David Hitchcock, Congress Square, Barridoff, Leighton Gallery, Turtle Gallery on Deer Isle, Huston-Tuttle Bookstore in Rockland, Art for America in Newcastle, and the University of Southern Maine, just to name the places I can recall.

"I think Eric Hopkins is a neat guy, but because he sells himself so well he is overexposed," says John Ames, whose Gallery Sixty-Eight is one of the few places that has not shown Hopkins. "Eric is a classic example of an artist who, if they are generally available and perceived to be everywhere, the last thing they need is another gallery."

"I don't think I've been very exposed lately, nor have I been very productive lately," says Hopkins, who has been spending a great deal of his time at home on North Haven clearing land for a new studio. From Hopkins' point of view, what looks like overexposure to dealers who want to sell his work (and to reviewers who get around a lot) is just good business. It's like fishing; the more lines one puts out, the more fish one catches. Since the bulk of Hopkins' sales are made directly from his island studio, showing in mainland galleries is a way of advertising.

"I make 100 percent of my living from my art," says Hopkins, "but I could only make lunch and part of supper out of one gallery."

Eric Hopkins was with Barridoff for a few months, but he was dropped when the Elowitches sold their building and cut their roster. Perhaps not surprisingly, Hopkins says he was relieved to be cut because, at the time, Barridoff had a statewide exclusive in force and it was killing him to honor it. Now Hopkins is back with Barridoff, but the Brunswick south exclusive allows him to stay in business for himself on North Haven. What the Barridoff connection means to him is prestige.

"A gallery gives you credibility," says Hopkins. "The fact that I was at Barridoff impressed people."

John Laurent, one of Maine's best-known painters, currently has paintings hanging in Portland at Barridoff (a small still life of mussels), Hobe Sound Galleries North (a large landscape) and Frost Gully (a large still life of a sea bass), all three of which have represented him at one time or another. When Frost Gully was the only show in town, he showed there. When Barridoff opened, he saw it as a more active, energetic gallery and moved there. Then, when John Payson, owner of Hobe Sound galleries in Maine and Florida (where Laurent had been showing all along), purchased the Midtown Galleries in New York, Laurent left Barridoff and went with Hobe Sound Galleries North.

"I guess it was an ego trip for me to get back into New York," says Laurent, who for 14 years was represented in New York by the Kraushaar Gallery.

Laurent's return to New York proved something less than triumphant, however, and today he is back with Barridoff. In the case of Laurent, Peter Bullock is right: it probably doesn't matter where he shows, his audience will find him.

Then there is the case of a brilliant young artist who found an audience and decided it made her too uncomfortable. Anne Gresinger was fresh out of art school last year when Ray Farrell took on her work at O'Farrell Gallery. To just about everyone's surprise (since Gresinger's art is deeply personal and not in the least commercial), Gresinger's paintings fairly flew out of the gallery.

"Anne made a good living when she was here," says Farrell. "I was selling paintings as fast as she could make them, but I think it was too much, too fast for her."

"I felt myself being very visible," explains Gresinger. "There was a lot of interest in the work, but when I started painting with the feeling of people watching me, it inhibited me."

When Farrell asked Gresinger to stay on at O'Farrell, she declined. She didn't like feeling pressured, "selling, being a commodity, doing my taxes, being a business." This summer Anne Gresinger felt more comfortable showing her work at the Dean Velentgas Gallery. Currently, she is working as a waitress and waiting until she has new work that she feels good enough about to exhibit. Now Farrell is pushing a young artist who is ready to be pushed, painter Dozier Bell, a former student of Neil Welliver's who will have her first New York solo show next February at the Schmidt-Bingham Gallery.

Last year was a big year, too, for Johnnie Ross, but in a different way. The audience for abstract art in Maine is still not great, so it is perhaps not surprising that several of Maine's best nonrepresentational artists such as Ross, Lisa Allen, and Susan Groce have not been associated with local galleries. In Ross' case, he simply didn't want to be until now.

"My philosophy," says Johnnie Ross, "has been that it takes a certain amount of energy and time to put together a show and make inroads in a gallery, no matter which gallery it is. I decided I wanted to start up close to the top with New York galleries. I wanted to get my foot in the door in New York and then work back."

Ross' strategy paid off last year with an important show at the Stux Gallery, one of New York's hottest galleries, and now he has prospects of showing in Dallas, Chicago, and Los Angeles. This validation on a national level made Ross more comfortable about showing locally, so this fall he signed on with Barridoff. And according to Barridoff owner Rob Elowitch, it was just as well that Ross tackled New York first, since the stigma of being a "Maine artist" would have followed him all over Soho.

"The most provincial place in the entire world is New York," Elowitch says. "If you don't have your own branch in New York as Hobe Sound does, forget it. A Maine gallery can't help an artist get a New York gallery. It's better for an artist to go in cold. What's happening in New York is what's happening in New York."

The Maine art scene has undergone some startling changes in the past 15 years—more galleries, more artists, more public interest, more sales, more competition—but as Howard Clifford suggests, beneath it all what has changed the most is the attitude of the artists.

"When I first started painting," says Clifford, "I always wanted to make a living as a painter, but at the time I felt there was a double standard. That's changed now. But back then, everyone wanted to make a living from their work, but you couldn't talk about it. You were supposed to put yourself above that. For a long time, a lot of artists felt like second-rate citizens in our society, but the artist of the '80s is an artist who not only paints, but has a good self-image, feels good enough about his art to sell it, and feels good about selling. People bitch about the commercialism of artists in New York, but they're making the work they want to make and they're selling it. That's the bottom line."

November 27, 1987

The Most Beautiful Painting in Maine

Vincent Van Gogh's Irises

"But I am sure that many rich people, who for some reason or other buy expensive pictures, do not do so because of the art value they find in them—for such people the difference which you and I see between a tulip and a picture, is not visible. They, the speculators and 'pochards blasés' *and many others, would buy tulips now just as formerly, if it were but fashionable."*

—Vincent Van Gogh, in a letter to his brother Theo, December, 1883

The afternoon before Vincent Van Gogh's *Irises* went on the auction block at Sotheby's, a stout little old lady in a threadbare cloth coat approached one of the two armed, uniformed guards posted inside the red velvet ropes separating the curious from the precious.

"How much do they think it's worth?" asked the old lady.

"Between 40 and 50 million dollars," answered the guard authoritatively.

"They don't know who will buy it, do they? Probably a museum?"

"A museum couldn't afford it," replied the guard.

"Probably an Arab or the Japanese."

"Probably. This is supposed to be the most expensive painting ever sold in the world, more expensive even than *The Pietà*. Tomorrow night someone will pay for this one picture what they would have to pay Michelangelo today to do the Sistine Chapel."

"Well, it's a national treasure," concluded the little old lady. "I hope some museum gets it and not some individual."

"I'd hate to have to pay the insurance on it though," quipped the guard.

During the last 10 years, anyone resourceful enough to overpower a student attendant at the Joan Whitney Payson Gallery of Art, a little International Style bunker jammed up against a cemetery at the rear of the Westbrook College campus in Portland, Maine, could have easily made off scot-free with Van Gogh's *Irises*. But now, on the eve of its commercial execution, the painting—a wind-blown flutter of irises, radiant blue and one white, lashed by sword-like blades of too-green leaves—was heavily guarded. And well it should have been, for *Irises*, fresh from a publicity tour of Tokyo, London, Geneva, and Zurich, would be hammered down the following night at $49 million ($53.9 million including the 10 percent premium Sotheby's charges buyers), a world record for any work of art sold at auction. Yet even as it awaited its uncertain fate, *Irises* glowed with a defiant beauty. A showroom full of attendant Monets, Renoirs, and Picassos paled in comparison. Any fool could see that this painting was too beautiful, too important, and too valuable to remain hidden away any longer in Maine, a sleepy hinterland where the stars shine at night and pickup trucks roam the back roads.

There are no stars or pickup trucks in Manhattan. Distant worlds are obscured by the city's own nocturnal aura, a vaguely sinister incandescent gloaming through which cruise schools of menacing yellow taxis and silvery shoals of predatory limousines. On the evening of November 11, Veterans' Day, the taxis and limos all converged on Sotheby's (Founded 1744) New York headquarters, attracted by the bright bauble momentarily lodged there. In waves they came, platinum blonds in uptown minks and gobs of gold, stately dealers, sundry heirs and various entrepreneurs, celebrities and wealthy exotics (known locally as "Eurotrash" and to Van Gogh as *pochards blasés*—literally "jaded sots"). They stepped briefly into the night from the luxurious confines of chauffeured limos, braved a gauntlet of glaring camera lights and entered the auction house, there to be ogled and occasionally identified by lesser lights. Bianca Jagger, rock courtesan, about as inconspicuous in her little red riding jacket and Ray-Bans as an organ grinder's monkey at a state funeral. The guy in the beret who looked like he had set out for Madison Square Garden and wound up at Sotheby's by mistake was unmistakably movie madman Jack Nicholson. And who was that in the baseball cap and safari jacket? Woody Allen? No, just screenwriter Buck Henry. Who?

There was an undeniable and irresistible element of intrigue in the air. How much would *Irises* fetch? (Sotheby's estimated $20 million to $40 million, but did the security guard have insider info?) Who would buy it? (The Japanese? The Getty Museum?) Would it sell at all after the stock market crash-and-burn of Black Monday? (Sotheby's North America chairman John Marion, reputedly America's best auctioneer, vowed "it will sell and sell well.") Was Sotheby's prestige on the line, then? After all, rival Christie's had sold the previous big ticket Van Goghs in London earlier in the year, *Sunflowers* going for $39.9 million in March, *The Bridge at Trinquetaille* for $20.2 million in June. ("No, we're way ahead of them in sales," said John Marion.) And what about Sotheby's upcoming stock offer? Could the performance of *Irises* affect investor confidence? ("Sotheby's is bigger than one painting. We have $100 million worth of art for sale tomorrow night," said Marion on the eve of the auction.) Still, the world press and SRO crowd of 1,000 chic bidders and gawkers didn't show up at 1334 York Avenue just to look at pretty pictures. They smelled the ozone spark of disposable income. They smelled money.

Vincent Van Gogh (1853-1890), everyone's archetype of the stark-raving, starving artist, painted *Irises* (*Les Iris*) in May, 1889, in the garden of the asylum at Saint-Remy, France, where he had voluntarily committed himself. Fifty-eight years later, having passed through the hands of five collectors and three galleries, it was purchased in 1947 by Joan Whitney Payson for $84,000. When Mrs. Payson, best known as the owner and number-one fan of the New York Mets baseball team, died in 1975, she left *Irises* along with 26 other paintings to her son John Whitney Payson with the understanding that they would form the nucleus of a collection to be housed in a gallery to her memory. The gallery would be located at Westbrook College in suburban Portland.

From the outset, Westbrook College was a strange choice to be graced with the Joan Whitney Payson Gallery of Art. A professional and business school primarily noted for training dental hygienists, Westbrook College had no demonstrable interest in art, but John Payson's first wife, Nancy Lawler Payson, was both an alumna (class of '60) and a trustee of the school, so Westbrook it was. The gallery opened in 1977 with *Irises*, the showpiece of the collection, ensconced on a wall specially designed to show it off to the 10,000 or so diehards who managed to find the little modernist cube at the rear of the brick and leaf campus. Yet even with the gallery a reality, some people still felt the collection was wasted on Westbrook, and an effort was launched by the director of the Portland Museum of Art and a local art dealer to have the collection moved to the Portland museum. When John Payson got wind of the negotiations, however, he was furious. Thus, Van Gogh's asylum irises would quaver quietly at Westbrook College for the next 10 years, traveling only occasionally to attend major exhibitions such as the Los Angeles County Museum of Art's *A Day in the Country* (1984-85) and the Metropolitan Museum of Art's *Van Gogh in Saint-Remy and Auvers* (1986-87).

Then, on September 2, 1987, John Payson called a news conference to announce that he was putting *Irises* up for auction, citing the enormous prices paid for *Sunflowers* and *The Bridge at Trinquetaille* and the resultant burden of insurance and security costs for *Irises* as the primary reasons for the sale. The announcement caught many people, those who assumed Payson had given the painting to Westbrook 10 years before, off guard. In fact, despite a letter of intention "to either donate or bequeath those of my paintings which are currently in the permanent collection of the Joan Whitney Payson Gallery of Art," *Irises* was only on "permanent loan," a slippery oxymoron at best.

"Ownership was never clear and I never pursued it," said the Payson Gallery's original director, Martin Dibner. "Ownership was a problem for the president, who at that time was James Dickinson. I didn't want to get into the legalese of it, but, of course, the term 'permanent loan' had some flaws in it. It's a question of semantics."

Though rumors began to circulate in the weeks following the sale announcement that someone was bringing suit to block the sale, no one with standing in the matter ever opposed the sale or attempted to enforce John Payson's letter of intent.

"It wasn't ours to keep. We have to be respectful of Mr. Payson's wishes," said John DiMatteo, chairman of the Westbrook College board of trustees during the sale negotiations and president of the Guy Gannett Publishing Company, publishers of Portland's daily and Sunday newspapers.

Given the fact that John Payson had announced his intention to donate 12.5 percent of the sale price of *Irises* to the college's endowment and another 12.5 percent to a charitable foundation in his parents' names which would also benefit the college, it was not surprising that Westbrook College officials didn't fight to keep the painting. Indeed, the college had never made any serious commitment to art. The lone Payson Gallery cube was meant to be the first of a modular cluster that never developed. The school offered no art major. A printmaking workshop had been dismantled and sold over the objections of local artists and the school's active photography gallery was recently displaced by a student lounge. Clearly, the financially troubled college had every reason to prefer Payson's money to his painting.

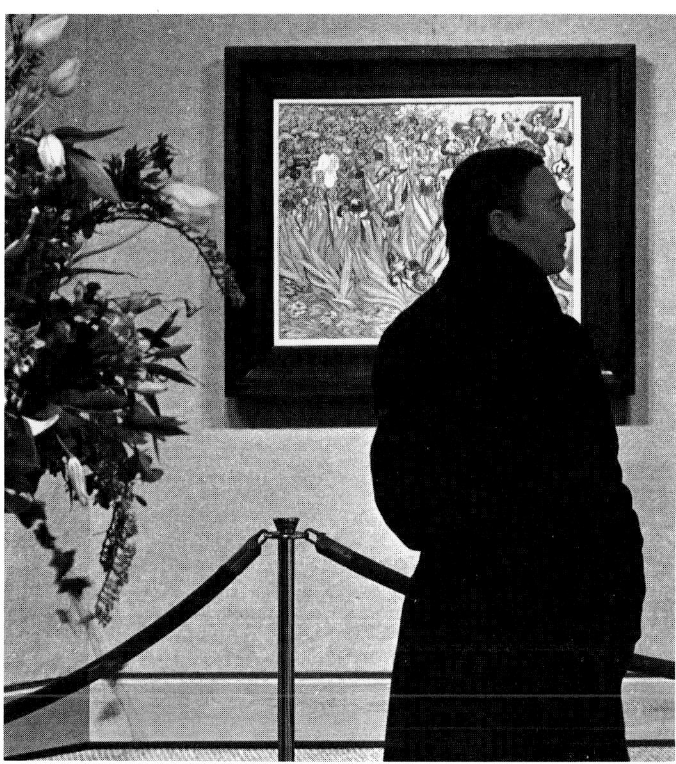

1. *Vincent Van Gogh's* Irises *on display before auction. Photo by Christopher Ayres.*

"That was never a real question, because we didn't own it," replied John DiMatteo when asked whether trustees would rather have *Irises* or the money from its sale.

"That's an impossible question to answer," echoed college president Dr. William Andrews. "We never had that choice."

Nancy Lawler Payson, who is the sole reason *Irises* came to Westbrook College in the first place, is still a college trustee, but she stayed out of the sale negotiations entirely. Trying to block her ex-husband's sale of the Van Gogh was "not my style," said Nancy Payson, declining to comment on what she thought of the plan other than to say that she would not benefit personally from the sale.

In blaming increased insurance costs for

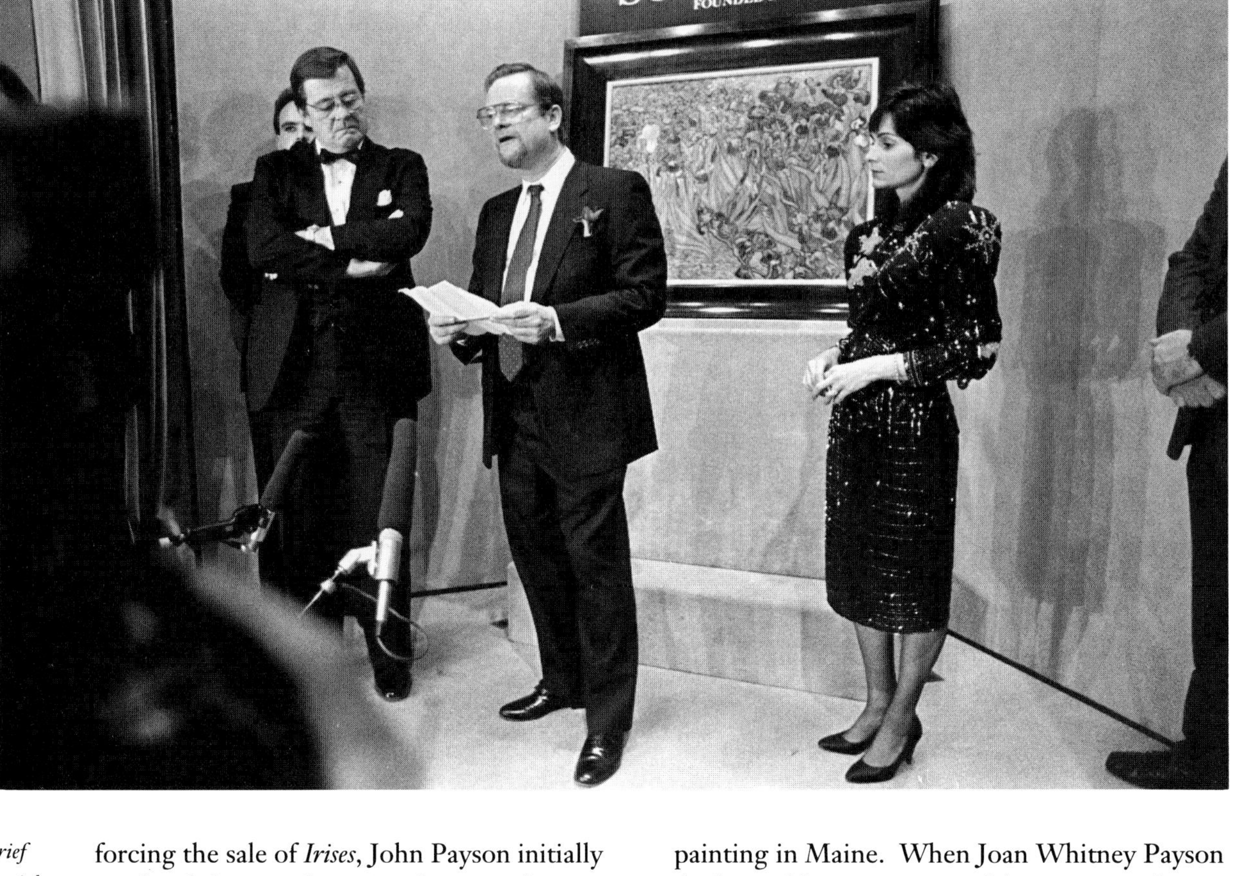

2. *For a brief moment the night of November 11, the world's attention was focused on Van Gogh's* Irises *and the man who was forced to sell it. Photo by Christopher Ayres.*

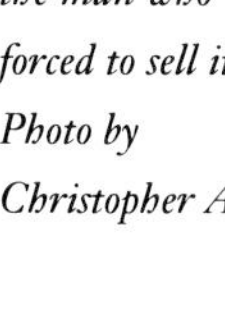

forcing the sale of *Irises*, John Payson initially confused the issue by citing the cost of insuring the painting when it traveled to other institutions. But insurance, an insidious institution which has brainwashed society into believing that all loss must have a monetary pay-off, is a real spoiler in the art world as elsewhere. According to one of the major American insurers of fine art, it might cost Westbrook College 17 cents per hundred dollars of valuation a year to insure *Irises*. At $53.9 million, that factors out to an annual premium of $91,630. But according to Dr. Andrews, Westbrook College has a rate of 25 cents per hundred. Thus, the $9 million worth of art (12 works) that John Payson has given the college as part of the *Irises* deal could cost the school $22,500 a year to insure at full market value. The *Irises* at that rate would cost an exorbitant $134,750 to insure. Obviously, these outrageous costs are one reason that many major art institutions can't afford to insure their entire collections.

Overlooked in the initial announcement and press coverage, however, were a number of other circumstances contributing to John Payson's decision to sell the most beautiful painting in Maine. When Joan Whitney Payson died, in addition to some of the paintings from her collection, she left her son $7.5 million from her $100 million estate. The bulk of her fortune went to her husband, industrialist Charles Shipman Payson. John Payson and his three sisters were given to believe that when their father died they would inherit another $5 million apiece, but when Mr. Payson died in 1985, the Payson children were shocked to discover that he had left them only a few more paintings and Stonecroft, the family's Maine estate on Falmouth Foreside. Charles Shipman Payson had left $70 million to his second wife, Virginia Kraft Payson.

In March, 1987, just as Van Gogh's *Sunflowers* was stunning the world with its inflated value, the Payson children and their stepmother were beginning a bitter legal battle in Nassau County, New York, Surrogate Court over Charles Payson's will. The children charged that their stepmother was a fortune hunter who had exerted undue influence on their father in securing a will favorable to her. Their stepmother countered that Charles Payson didn't leave his fortune to his children because they were spoiled and he was ashamed of them. "I can't imagine them going out and earning a living," Virginia Kraft Payson told reporters from *Forbes* magazine. The court found in favor of Mrs. Payson.

In addition to the loss of an anticipated inheritance, John Payson had also suffered other financial setbacks prior to the decision to sell *Irises*. *Warrior*, a 60-foot, $2.5 million luxury fishing yacht he had commissioned in 1981, sank in 1985 before it was even completed, leaving Payson embroiled in legal suits. Then earlier this year, a Falmouth car dealership he was involved in went out of business. The family well was running dry, so the Van Gogh had to go.

Those familiar with John Payson's personal financial situation found it suspicious, even insulting, then, when the Portland newspapers failed to mention that Payson might have anything other than insurance and philanthropic motives for selling *Irises*. The fact that Payson had been allowed to handpick the reporter, popular columnist Bill Caldwell, to tell his story to only added to the appearance of a whitewash.

"I told the college I would agree to an in-depth interview provided it was Caldwell. I like his writing and I believe in him," said Payson. "It was strictly my request."

Despite all the background noise, however, the story leading up to the Sotheby auction was fairly clear and just about everyone got the message. *Irises* was John Payson's to do with as he wished. Clearly, it was too valuable now to stay in Maine. Better to sell the jewel than lose the crown. Poor John Payson was a well-meaning man caught in a web of unfortunate financial circumstances.

Irises by Vincent Van Gogh was lot 25 on the evening of the auction. John Marion, chewing gum to keep his throat moist, warmed up for the big event by disposing of various lesser impressionist works for sums ranging from $190,000 for a Fantin-Latour floral to $2.3 million for a Monet landscape. As the countdown to lot 25 progressed, cameramen took last-minute light readings, sound technicians did sound checks, and reporters jockeyed for the best view of the revolving auction block: Chairman Marion and his evening-wear-clad cadre of bid-takers and spotters, and the big currency board where dollar bids are translated into pounds, yen, Swiss francs, marks, French francs, and lire. Finally, at 8 p.m., John Marion, preferring the proper Dutch pronunciation, called *Irises* by Vincent Van "Gokh" to the block.

"Who'll say 15 million to start it?"

An art auction, despite pretensions to being a subtle, nuanced cultural affair, is really just a commodity exchange carried on like a television game show. If only the suave John Marion had begun the disposition of *Irises* by blurting out, "Vincent Van 'Go', come on down!" And what if a haggard, red-bearded little man with one ear missing (the right) had clambered forth, babbling about the corruption of artistic values by money, and comparing (as he did in his letters) the art market to the wild speculation in tulip bulbs that swept Holland in the 17th century?

"Trade is old-fashioned and…thrice decayed," he would shout. "There must be renovation, for the old systems do not work well any longer. The prices, the public, everything needs renovation, and the future is to work cheaply for the people!"

Then perhaps, as old Van Gogh was being hauled off by Sotheby security guards, someone else would find the courage to speak out against this elegant display of wretched excess. Pandemonium breaks out among the beautiful people as the TV cameras turn on the intruder who rushes the podium to denounce the betrayal of the people of Maine.

"There is nothing comparable to the *Irises* anywhere in Maine!" he yells. "No amount of money can substitute for the loss of true greatness in our midst! This auction isn't about art, it's about greed!"

I might have, but I didn't. Instead as John Marion tolled the mournful numbers…"Twenty on my left. Twenty-one on the phone in front. Twenty-two. Twenty-three on the far side. Twenty-four in the center"…I thought of something Arthur Danto, art critic for *The Nation*, had told me earlier in the day. He had likened hearing that Van Gogh's *Sunflowers* had sold for $39.9 million to the news that Jacqueline Kennedy was marrying Aristotle Onassis.

"Some myth had been shattered. A lot of

illusions were destroyed," Danto said. "With *Irises*, it's almost like anything goes now."

So what's the use?

Now whether there were any real bidders in the room is open to question. Perhaps in the early going John Marion was just bouncing bids off the wall or, as they say in the auction world, "bidding off the chandelier" (perfectly permissible under New York auction laws until the high estimate for a piece is reached). From $25 million on, however, all the attention was focused on Sotheby's David Nash and Geraldine Nagler, seconds in a long-distance telephone duel of million-dollar parries and thrusts. When the $40-million high estimate was reached, the strong murmurs in the room erupted into "ooohs" and applause. At $42 million, nervous laughter. And up it went.

"There's 48 million for it. Forty-nine against you in the center. Forty-nine million on the far phone. All done at 49 million dollars? Are you still there, Geraldine? SOLD for $49 million!"

Upstairs in the glass booth reserved for the Payson family and beneficiaries, John Payson was reportedly euphoric. And why not? He had been hoping *Irises* might fetch between $32 million and $34 million. Seventy-five percent of $49 million, even after taxes, would go a long way toward filling the depleted family coffers. And the remaining 25 percent would make some headline-grabbing, double-dip philanthropy possible. Once sold, twice given.

Down on the auction floor, Westbrook College trustee Owen Wells quickly calculated the college's share of the proceeds at something slightly in excess of $8 million ($6.125 million toward the general endowment and $1.96 million over five years for the art gallery out of the $6.125 million Joan Whitney and Charles Shipman Payson Charitable Foundation). Roy Leaf, executive director of the Skowhegan School of Painting and Sculpture, was equally pleased about the $1.2 million his favorite charity would be receiving from the foundation over the next six years. And somewhere, unknown supporters of the Gulf of Maine Aquarium ($100,000 over five years) and the American Tall Ship Syndicate ($75,000 payable next year) were celebrating too.

Down in the basement where reporters were lined up five and six deep at the pay phones, John DiMatteo paused long enough on his way to the men's room to say he wasn't surprised that *Irises* had sold for $49 million. He had guessed $50 million in the insiders' pool and had walked off with the $25 prize money for coming closest to the actual sale price.

Even Payson Gallery director Judith Sobol, who had been so upset at the loss of *Irises* that she declined to attend the initial announcement press conference at Sotheby's back in September, even she was smiling brightly now.

"If it's gonna be sold," said Sobol, "$49 million is better than $20 million."

Better for Westbrook College maybe, but was it really good for a single work of art to command such an astronomical price? Wasn't the Payson Gallery losing *Irises* precisely because a Japanese insurance company had inflated the Van Gogh market by paying $39.9 million for *Sunflowers*? Upon more sober reflection (back in her Portland office, where calls from Maine artists about the foundation money were already coming in), Judy Sobol qualified her remark.

"As long as it had to be sold, the outcome of that sale making great philanthropy possible, better $49 million than $20 million. The downside of that is it makes it very hard for museums to continue to collect great works of art and to borrow from other museums and collectors works of art for others to see because insurance costs become so prohibitive."

Just imagine, for instance, what Van Gogh's *The Starry Night* must be worth now. $100 million? Why not say a jillion dollars? Imagine what the Museum of Modern Art must pay in insurance premiums, assuming, of course, they carry insurance on *The Starry Night*. After all, it is irreplacable.

Disturbing implications? Yes. Exaggerated concern? Maybe. But within days of the announcement that *Irises* was to be sold, Rob Elowitch of Barridoff Galleries in Portland received a call from a New York art dealer asking whether the Winslow Homer paintings that Charles Shipman Payson gave to the Portland Museum of Art might be for sale. They aren't, but then again, there is nothing in the bequest to prevent the museum from selling the Homers if times got tough enough and someone were willing to pay serious money.

"The image that we in Portland gave the world," said Elowitch, "was that we were for sale ...or that our art was for sale."

Of course, the big question as far as the international press is concerned is "Who bought *Irises*?" Who in the world would pay $53.9 million for a painting? At press time, all Sotheby's was saying was that *Irises* was purchased by "a European dealer buying on behalf of an anonymous collector." Rumor around the auction floor had it that industrialist Armand Hammer was the big spender and that Australian financier and yachtsman Alan Bond, rumored to have been the underbidder on *Sunflowers*, was also the underbidder on *Irises*. But rumors are just that. There was also a rumor that androgynous pop star Michael Jackson was the underbidder. Note that the buyer of *The Bridge at Trinquetaille* has never been identified. The night of the auction, Judith Sobol thought she knew who had purchased her lovely *Irises*, but no appeal to her sense of justice could pry the name from her. A bribe perhaps? Or torture? (Eventually, when he was unable to pay Sotheby's the money he had borrowed from them to purchase *Irises*, it became known that Alan Bond was the top bidder.)

On the night of November 11, Sotheby's unloaded $110,022,000 worth of art, despite the fact that 25 of the 100 pieces did not sell. With the history-making sale completed, the dignitaries and luminaries disappeared back into the night, fleeing to bistros and boudoirs all over Manhattan. As she prepared to leave, the ravishing Bianca Jagger was approached by a stranger (always a tense moment in New York) and was asked what she thought of someone paying $53.9 million for a painting.

"It's insane," she replied.

And the stellar Mr. Nicholson? Would he have paid $53.9 million for *Irises*?

"Not a penny over 32."

But before the day was through, the *Newsday* electronic marquee in Times Square was telling midnight cowboys, lounge lizards, peep show freaks, and downtown johns something they probably already knew...that everything and everybody has a price. Someone had actually paid $53.9 million for Vincent Van Gogh's *Irises*.

At the news conference following the sale, John Payson, who had visited his mother's grave before deciding to sell *Irises*, again invoked the dead in support of the sale.

"That a man could paint a painting not 100 years ago and it could do so much good for young artists is wonderful," said Payson. "I really think Vincent Van Gogh would be happy for these young artists."

John Payson is a decent, well-meaning man who was caught in a web of unfortunate financial circumstances. And perhaps he is right. Perhaps Van Gogh, who agonized all his brief working life over the inequities of the art market, would be pleased that a portion of the proceeds from the sale of one of his paintings would be used to support artists working today. But then, finally, there is this from a letter to his brother Theo found on Van Gogh's person the day he died of a self-inflicted gunshot wound:

"Well, the truth is, we can only make our pictures speak. But yet my dear brother, there is this that I have always told you and I repeat it once more with all the earnestness that can be given by an effort of a mind diligently fixed on trying to do as well as one can—I tell you again that I shall always consider that you are something other than a simple dealer in Corot, that through my mediation you have your part in the actual production of some canvases, which even in the deluge will retain their peace.

"For this is what we have got to and this is all or at least the chief thing that I can have to tell you at a moment of comparative crisis. At a moment when things are very strained between dealers in pictures of dead artists, and living artists.

"Well, my own work, I am risking my life for it and my reason has half-foundered in it—that's all right—but you are not among the dealers in men so far as I know, and you can still choose your side, I think, acting with humanity, but what's the use?"

November 20, 1987

Popular Painting

Crowds Love It

Let us begin with the proposition: All Art Is Good. After all, considered on the broad scale of human behavior from murder to martyrdom, painting a picture is a relatively harmless, even praiseworthy thing to do. Whether the result is a modern masterpiece or sidewalk-art-show schmaltz, the act of making art is creative and ought to be encouraged. Why is it, then, that when faced with art we do not like or, worse, do not understand, we tend to react with the sort of moral indignation more appropriately reserved for child molesters, drug dealers, and terrorists? I mean does the word "bad" have any real meaning when applied to a good thing like art?

As one who writes regularly about art, I find it a continuing source of paradoxical amusement that the majority of artists in Maine seem to consider the majority of artists in Maine to be little better than hacks. Just as everyone makes fun of yuppies, but no one ever admits to being one, no artist ever considers himself or herself a hack. Maine is full of artists who enjoy enormous popularity despite being regularly found deficient by the art establishment, the "serious" artists, critics, collectors, dealers, and curators who call the shots in the polite world of art. The aesthetic deficiencies of this popular art are well known and well chronicled. Over the past 10 years or so, I myself have called it conservative, traditional, derivative, old-fashioned, anachronistic, sentimental, nostalgic, romantic, decorative, slick, commercial, illustrative, irrelevant. And when the good ship Popular Art still refuses to go down, we haul out the big gun, Not Art.

Lately, however, I have grown both weary and uncomfortable with this sustained attack. Though motivated by an earnest desire to educate and elevate taste and appreciation, I have begun to question both the necessity and validity of pronouncing the judgment "I know what good art is and this isn't it." For the purposes of challenging some of my own assumptions and perhaps educating myself (and others) in the ways of popular art, I recently visited three Maine artists whose work I find difficult to appreciate. My intention was not to make them whipping boys or to ask them to defend their art, but rather to hear what they had to say for themselves and their art. Knowing in advance why I was calling, all three agreed to discuss their approaches to art. In my estimation, Peter Rolfe, Don Stone, and John Gable are all successful and talented enough to withstand this kind of scrutiny. Their art is good enough to be problematic.

Peter Rolfe, outsider

Peter Rolfe, 45, is a self-taught artist who lives and works in a studio overlooking the Sheepscot River in Edgecomb. There he paints country landscape, garden, village, and street scenes in a style of latter-day French and American impressionism, brushy oils in warm colors suffused with a soft, natural light. What distinguishes Rolfe in my mind, however, is not his art but his approach to it. For Peter Rolfe is a complete outsider, a loner who is not only self-taught, but who, with one or two exceptions, has never exhibited except in his own gallery. In the 16 years that he has been painting, he has fashioned an audience and a market for his art independent of the established gallery and museum systems.

Born and raised in Portland, Rolfe studied engineering at the University of Illinois, earned a master of business administration degree from the University of Pittsburgh, and worked in engineering supervision and management for Westinghouse Electric before dropping out of corporate life in 1971 in order to return to Maine and paint.

"I've always looked at painting," says Rolfe, "but I thought painting was something out of the question. It wasn't something you do for a living."

Frustrated with his business career and armed with a set of watercolors (a gift from a girlfriend), Rolfe took a painting vacation in 1971 and decided it was time to change his life.

"The reason that I began painting," he says, "was so that I could live life on my own terms."

Initially, Rolfe sought advice from painter Laurence Sisson, one of Maine's most popular artists, now living and working in New Mexico. Sisson advised the novice to forgo art school and just paint. Accordingly, in 1972, Peter Rolfe opened his own gallery on Route 1 in Wiscasset, where he quietly and steadily sold paintings for 12 years. In 1984, his partner and girlfriend Caroline Denham (whose professional background is in marketing) moved the Peter Rolfe Gallery to Newcastle, and in 1985 moved it again to its present location on Exchange Street in Portland. Today, Peter Rolfe's pleasant paintings sell briskly at prices ranging from $250 to $25,000, with the most popular being twelve-by-sixteen-inch oils in the $1,200 to $2,800 range.

Since Peter Rolfe has never had any exposure outside of his own gallery, it seems fairly obvious that the people who buy his paintings aren't buying his name. They simply like what they see. Rolfe's canvases are very pretty, restful pictures. What they lack, from my prejudiced position as a culturally conditioned critic, is a strong personal vision or intellectual underpinning, but then Peter Rolfe subscribes to a disarming theory of emotional needs.

"I only know art in a narrow range of art," explains Rolfe. "To me it's the emotional impact that's important and that's all there is. When someone says they like something and then apologizes because they know it's 'bad,' I don't understand it. Anyone's emotions are as valid as anyone else's. That's the way they feel...What they're saying if they're looking at my work and don't like it is 'This gives me no feeling.' That's all they can say about it."

When I express reservations about what I perceive as an absence of theoretical substructure, Rolfe responds, "What you're intimating is that this kind of painting has to do with knowledge. The more you learn about a painting, the more important it becomes to you. But if it's knowledge, it's not emotion. There are no theories to what I paint."

So here I am up against the "I don't know what's good, but I know what I like" approach to art. In fact, a few days later Caroline Denham reinforces this argument in Rolfe's Portland gallery by observing that art buyers in the East are always apologizing for their lack of knowledge, while collectors and buyers in the Southwest know what they like and buy it confidently. Peter Rolfe may be something of a *naif* in the art world, but he has been able to determine that the real market for his style of art in not in New York, but in Santa Fe.

To me, as one who has apparently bought into the precepts of the East Coast intellectual elite, the "I don't know what's good, but I know what I like" approach sounds like an aesthetic dead end, admitting little room for meaningful discrimination or increasing sophistication. Good taste is only recognized by those who share it, but to each his own. If a lot of people like cowboy-and-Indian art, so be it. In Peter Rolfe's view, I just have different (but not necessarily higher) needs than the person who responds to art immediately and emotionally.

"I paint these paintings just because of my needs," says Rolfe. "Now here is the result. It turns out that it has a big impact on many people. Why? I really don't know why. But here are the kinds of comments I get." And Rolfe proceeds to describe a letter from one of his collectors, a laboratory technician or scientist who has come home from a rough day at work to be refreshed by looking at Rolfe's paintings. What the collector values in Rolfe's art, then, is the calmness it communicates.

"I suspect there are people," says Rolfe, "who have a need for that kind of image or that kind of feeling. That's a different need from those people whose lives are dull and want to add action [which is how Rolfe understands people who buy provocative contemporary art]. I think it is just as valid to add action as to add calmness to your life."

Perhaps because both our intellect and our educational system are weighted so heavily in favor of the verbal over the visual, people who enjoy reading pulp fiction (say, Harlequin romances) know they are not reading great literature, while people who enjoy popular art (say, LeRoy Neiman's sports prints) don't always seem to realize they aren't looking at great art. To me, a person is just as culturally impoverished if he can't distinguish between the art of LeRoy Neiman and the art of Jasper Johns as he is if he can't distinguish between the writings of Barbara Cartland and the writings of Saul Bellow. To my amusement, however, Peter Rolfe rejects this argument.

"I think it's much more difficult to say what is good music or good art than it is to say what is good writing," says Rolfe.

I wonder, then, whether Rolfe makes any critical distinction between his art and that of Julian Schnabel, the wunderkind of cracked crockery.

"We're not in the same business," says Rolfe of Schnabel and himself. "Those people who buy that art and who paint it have entirely different needs, but I'm not saying one is more valid than the other."

Don Stone, insider

Don Stone, 58, is an award-winning painter who lives and works half the year in a spacious modern home overlooking the Webhannet Golf Club in Kennebunk Beach and the other half in a cottage on Monhegan. Stone employs a style of traditional realism to create scenes of rustic Americana and family life. The paintings that hang in the living room of Stone's Kennebunk home are fairly typical of his subject matter—girl and dog sitting on seaside rocks, a team of draft horses standing by as three men tap sugar maples in the woods, a young boy with his sled at the foot of a snowy hill, the family cat reclining atop a woodpile. Pictures like these have won Stone a host of awards and established him as a true insider, an artist widely recognized in the separate world of "popular" American art.

Don Stone is a pure product of rear-guard American art, that school of local realism that chose to ignore the tenets of modernism when they arrived from Europe back around the turn of the century. By birth and choice, he is steeped in an art world that has always run along its own course, oblivious to "modern art."

Born and brought up in Gloucester, Massachusetts (where he went to high school with the noted art critic Hilton Kramer), Don Stone studied commercial art at the Vesper George Art School in Boston and worked as an illustrator and cartoonist before moving to the Rockport, Massachusetts, art colony and committing himself totally to painting. From Rockport, he eventually moved to the Ogunquit art colony, still comfortably within the ranks of the rear guard. By the early 1960s, he had begun to win prizes and awards regularly. Today, his paintings, which range in price from $1,200 watercolors to $26,000 oils, earn Stone the distinction of being one of the two best-selling (in dollar amounts), living artists in the Hobe Sound Galleries North stable. (The works of the late Bernard Langlais are Hobe Sound's biggest money-makers. Stone and painter-printmaker John Muench are the gallery's most profitable living artists.)

Scanning the list of Don Stone's prizes and awards (two typewritten pages, single-spaced) makes it clear to me that there are two distinct art worlds in America, each with its own system

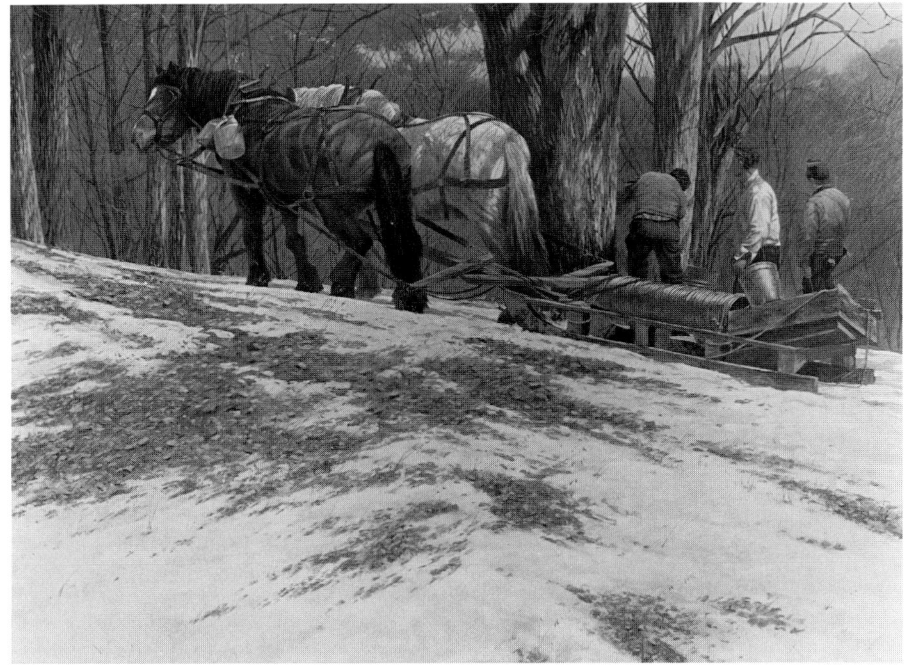

1. *Don Stone,* Tapping, *1986. Egg tempera. Courtesy of the artist.*

of validation. The art that I value is reported in journals like *Artforum*, *Art in America*, and *Art News*, and the artists who make it are rewarded and acknowledged with prizes from the Guggenheim and MacArthur foundations and exhibitions at the Guggenheim Museum, the Museum of Modern Art, and the Whitney Museum of American Art. The art Don Stone values and makes is reported in journals like *American Artist* and *Southwest Art*, and the artists are rewarded and acknowledged with prizes from the American Watercolor Society and National Academy of Design and exhibitions at places like the National Academy and the Butler Art Institute of American Art in Youngstown, Ohio. The two arts regularly meet in the pages of the major art slicks where the serious art gets all the ink and the popular art appears in ad copy.

I have never heard of the prizes Stone has won, and I have never heard of the contemporary artists he admires—Donald Teague, Ogden Pleissner, and Edward Seago. Nor, come to think of it, had I heard of Peter Rolfe's favorite artist, Richard Schmid. Different worlds, different art, different artists.

"I don't think," acknowledges Don Stone, "[the Whitney Museum of American Art] will ever come knocking at my door or Peter Rolfe's or Jack Gable's."

True enough, but I am interested in why Stone thinks this is so.

"Because," says Stone, "my art doesn't upset the apple cart. It doesn't disturb enough people. I don't want my paintings to disturb people. I want them to get a kind of warmth from them, as though when they have one of my paintings they have me hanging on their wall and I'm a nice guy to have around."

The central concerns of "mainstream" American art in the 20th century have been the examination and expression of Self and the self-referential inquiry into the nature of art itself. In short, a quest for new knowledge. The central concern of "popular" art is the reaffirmation of established values, the known. In this Don Stone is correct. The one is about the business of questioning, the other about the business of comforting.

"It's nice to be liked," says Stone, "but it isn't important."

John Gable, crossover artist

John Gable, 43, is an intense man who until recently lived and worked in a large, shingled cottage in the heart of the Kennebunkport summer colony. In the eight short years he has been painting for a living, Gable's technical facility with watercolors and his sense of dramatic lighting have allowed him to progress with amazing velocity from lobster boat and lighthouse kitsch through images worthy of a Norman Rockwell American folk celebration, to portraits and scenes of the good life (the Old

Port at night, sailboat races, rowing contests) that aspire to something higher than the feel-good warmth of most popular painting. Jack Gable is a crossover artist, one who entered the world of fine art "through the side door" and is still finding his way around.

Born an identical twin in Louisville, Kentucky, Gable was from birth an aggressive competitor. Grandson of a doctor and son of a hospital administrator, he initially planned to enter medicine, but after a year of pre-med studies at the University of Kentucky, he transferred to the Art Center College of Design in Los Angeles, where he studied industrial design. A lifelong fascination with power led him to draw automobiles in art school, an academic exercise that steered him toward his first career. From 1966 until 1979 (with time out to serve as a combat illustrator in Vietnam), Gable worked as an automobile designer for General Motors (GM) in Detroit. Having seen some of the show car designs he did for GM, I can say that Gable's auto art was as slick, sleek, and powerful as his subjects.

In 1979, disillusioned with life in the auto industry fast lane, Gable (like Rolfe) dropped out of the corporate world and came to Maine to paint.

"My theory was that I wanted to come to Maine, get away from the crazy social environment of Bloomfield Hills, paint the seagulls, walk the beach, and find my center. The tools of how to paint were no problem."

What to paint has been part of Gable's problem as far as I'm concerned, but in the process of painting his way through and out of a number of artistic clichés, Jack Gable became an overnight success. Talent, which Gable has in obvious abundance, is just the starting point for serious artists, but all too often is an end in itself for popular artists. Obviously possessed of a marketable talent, Gable no sooner embarked on his painting career than shows, prizes, and commissions came his way. As he puts it, his reception into the art world was like "being pulled along by a freight train."

"You're a fool if you don't realize how people get their exposure," says Gable. "I think what happened to me was, having been in business life, I wasn't afraid to talk to people."

What happened to John Gable was that he was commissioned to paint a series of watercolors of *Freedom*, winner of the 1980 America's Cup Race, was invited to show at Coe Kerr Gallery (where Andrew and James Wyeth show) in New York, and was featured in a four-page spread in *American Artist*, all within four years of beginning his new career. Subsequently, he has painted commemorative pictures of the 1983 and 1987 America's Cup winners, executed a series of watercolors of the 1987 12-Metre World (sailing) Championship in Sardinia, completed a very folksy portrait of former Senator William Hathaway for the State House rotunda in Augusta, and become the top money-maker at Barridoff Galleries in Portland, fetching prices of $8,000 to $20,000 for his virtuoso watercolors.

Having conquered what I have called the rear-guard art scene, Jack Gable seems poised to cross over into the realm of serious art. I got the distinct impression that Gable is an artist whose work will grow in strength as he learns more about what is expected of serious contemporary art. He is, for example, resentful of being discussed in an article with Peter Rolfe (who, coincidentally, owns a Gable watercolor). Gable, unlike Rolfe, does make critical distinctions in art. He distinguishes, for example, between his commission work ("tickets to life experiences") and the main body of his art. He also seems prepared to disown some of his earlier work, for instance, a 1981 painting of a jolly jazz band playing atop an antique fire truck.

"I wouldn't do the guys on the fire truck anymore," he says. And he follows this admission with a statement of his own aesthetic aims.

"The most wonderful value about any kind of art," he says, "is if the artist is given the opportunity to go through his own form of self-expression. What should be critiqued ultimately is only one thing—that is quality. Not technical quality, but the quality of perception, the quality of sincerity.

"When I think about what I do, I don't think about being conservative or leading edge or anything else. Ultimately what creates a fine piece of work is the spirit with which it is taken on. My form of realism I think will always exist.

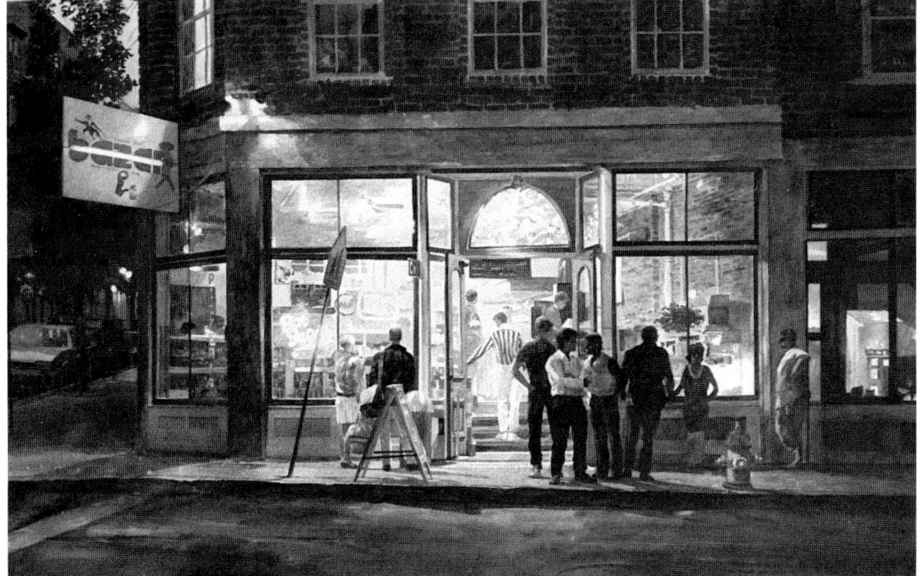

2. *John Gable,* Portland at Night. *Watercolor. Courtesy of the artist.*

I'm not trying to duplicate nature. I'm trying to deal with power and look at life in terms of the way I see it."

When Gable asks why I have difficulty relating to his art, I have to tell him that, with the possible exception of his most recent work (most notably a powerful self-portrait of the artist as an angry young man), his paintings seem to have very little to do with life in 1987. Gable is appropriately offended by this. He tells me he would rather be thought a cynical hack who turns out paintings he knows will sell, rather than be judged a sincere artist who is out of tune with his times.

As Jack Gable and I sit in the rain discussing our differences, I find myself wishing that I could embrace Peter Rolfe's non-judgmental philosophy of art. How much easier life would be. But here is Jack Gable earnestly trying to convince me not that I shouldn't judge, but rather that my judgment is wrong. I am finally back on familiar, though disputed, artistic terrain. It's nice to be liked, but it's not important.

August 28, 1987

The Portrait Painters

Portraiture

In 1930, when Gardner Cox, one of America's premier portrait artists, graduated from the Boston Museum School, "Portrait painting was the glamorous thing to do...it was very prestigious, perhaps the most prestigious branch of painting. At that time I greatly admired [John Singer] Sargent [who had died only five years earlier]. Sargent had a big retrospective at the Met in New York. The Sargent show equalled or surpassed the excitement and publicity of the Picasso show."

But during the next 50 years, the portrait went into a steady decline, supplanted commercially by the more economic means of the photograph and surpassed aesthetically by waves of impressionism, abstraction, and expressionism. Objective painting lost currency. Portraiture tended to be diminished to a minor art form, a rear-guard institutional appendage. Through all of this, Gardner Cox persevered.

Gardner Cox, 79, stands in a direct line of descent from John Singer Sargent. A summer resident of North Haven since 1947, Cox is the dean of New England portrait painters. His Fenway Studio in Boston is a venerable art institution, a great brick block of 48 studios that has housed artists since 1902.

Cox's studio is dingy and cluttered with years of work. Thin, gray light streams in through the towering windows that overlook the expressway. At either end of the big room stand commissions in progress—a portrait of Tufts University president Jean Mayer and a portrait of Harvard Law School professor Louis Loss. The portraits seem less in the Sargent society tradition than in the more expressionistic vein of Graham Sutherland, one of the last of the great English portraitists.

Standing in the middle of his studio, Gardner Cox is a portrait artist's dream. Even a child could capture his likeness. Wavy white hair beneath a blue wool slouch hat, wild, bushy eyebrows above gold-rimmed glasses. Jaunty green bow tie, fire-engine-red suspenders and matching socks, yellow and black checked sports jacket with a red bandana stuffed casually in the breast pocket. Brooks Brothers bohemian, Boston Brahmin *déshabille*, an artist and a gentleman.

Cox estimates that in the past 50 years he has executed some 300 portraits. These days, he commands $12,000 to $20,000 for a portrait, but at this point in his career he takes very few commissions. He has been called "the court painter of Harvard University" and a *catalogue raisonné* of his portraits would show a decided inclination toward lawyers and jurists. He has painted seven Supreme Court justices, a dashing portrait of Felix Frankfurter being one of his most noted commissions. Dean Acheson and Dean Rusk, Robert Kennedy and Robert Frost all sat for Cox. He was also commissioned to do a posthumous portrait of John Kennedy, but found that working from photographs, "I couldn't get it right."

Another portrait Cox didn't get right (at least in the eye of the sitter) was Henry Kissinger. Commissioned to do Kissinger for the State Department, Cox came up with a portrait that the White House curator rejected in 1978 because "it didn't capture his character." Rumor had it that Kissinger felt Cox's portrait made him look "dwarfish." (By many accounts, Kissinger *is* dwarfish.) But in rejection, Cox joins about every portrait artist who has ever lived. Remember LBJ's distaste for Peter Hurd's portrait of him? Winston Churchill's disgust at (and destruction of) the portrait Graham Sutherland did of him?

Gardner Cox is a methodical, studious portrait painter. He begins by just hanging around with his subject and making numerous sketches, absorbing the subject's mannerisms and personality. By the time the subject arrives for sittings (an average of two hours each for as long as it takes), Cox has a pretty good idea what the pose should be. He often takes indistinct black and white Polaroids of the sitter for formal reference, but he paints from life. Painting from photographs doesn't interest him.

"Photography, of course, is a big item," Cox says, "but it can't compete in the last analysis with a painting. A painting is editable a great deal more." In a painting, says the artist, "You can get two or three expressions in a face that are never really there at one time." He demonstrates his point by covering half of Felix Frankfurter's face in a photograph of the Felix Frankfurter portrait. Sure enough, one side of the judge's face looks genial and impish, the other is cold and calculating.

Marvin Sadik, former director of the National Portrait Gallery, now a private art dealer in Falmouth Foreside, recommended Cox to the State Department for the Kissinger portrait. Sadik underscores Cox's observation about the limits of photography in portraiture.

"One of the things that is critical," says Sadik, "is that the camera has monocular vision. It doesn't see the way you and I see."

"You hope they are going to like it," says Cox of a sitter's portrait, "but if you try to think what they're going to like you really get lost very quickly. You try to make [the painting] *feel* like them to you. That's the best you can do."

Actually, the best you can do is make both a good portrait *and* a good painting. In pursuit of a good painting, Gardner Cox employs a number of artistic tricks. For example, though he is left-handed, he will sometimes paint with his right hand to get looser, more spontaneous strokes. He also tests every painting to tell when he's finished. If the painting looks right through a reducing glass, in a mirror, and in a photograph, he's done.

Since the explosion of Pop art in the 1960s, realism (or objective painting, as Cox prefers to call it) has gradually returned to respectability on the world art scene. Gardner Cox knew it would. He quotes Henry James to the effect that literature (and by extension all art forms) grabs an audience by arousing the emotion of recognition and/or the emotion of surprise. Objective painting, Cox asserts, is capable of arousing both. That's what a portrait is all about—recognition and surprise.

"The young, talented people are going to want to be original and have an impact," says Cox, "and non-objective art is not the way to do it at present."

"Painting portraits…a successful portrait is not necessarily a work of art," says Claude Montgomery, Maine's most noted portrait artist. "It can be and should be, but the portrait artist has an instinct toward something other than the aesthetics of painting. It's a special instinct. I have a lot of artist friends who've tried portraits. Their paintings please, but come to a portrait and they're abysmal failures. It's an instinct."

Claude Montgomery, 73, is a ruggedly handsome graybeard cut in the romantic mold of a portrait painter like Augustus John. He is perfectly content to be associated with the English school of portraiture. Portrait painting has been good to him. A Portland native, he now lives and works in semi-retirement on the Georgetown shore. His studio is possibly the

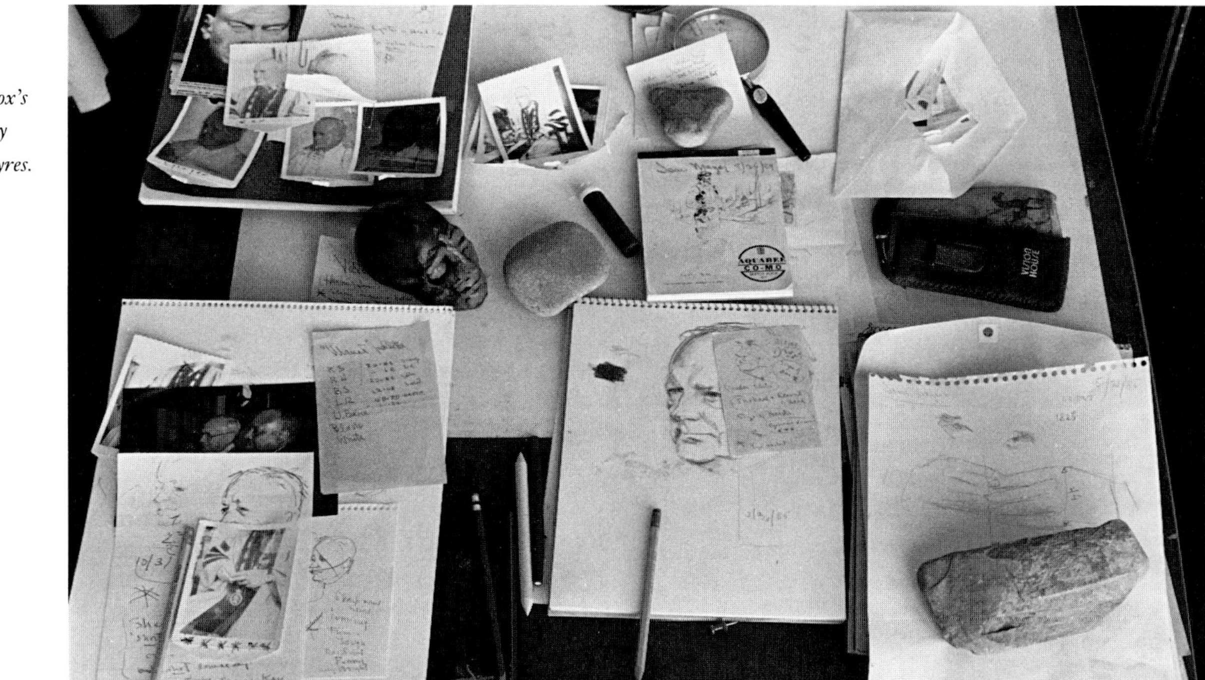

1. *Gardner Cox's studio. Photo by Christopher Ayres.*

most human space in Maine. Ash and burnt logs spill from the great stone hearth. The walls are cluttered with portraits of friends and family. Books mount to the ceiling a dizzying height away. North light skylight, ocean view picture window. A grand piano and a grand array of artistic impediments—a bouquet of brushes here, Winslow Homer's old easel there—command the floor.

After graduating from the Portland School of Fine Art, Montgomery followed the conventional career path to New York City and then Europe. Though he has pursued parallel careers, executing Homeresque landscapes in watercolor and English school portraits in oil, portraiture has been his meat.

"I think in many respects you make your own market," says Montgomery. "Seeds fall on fertile soil." With portraiture in the cultural sloughs most of his working life, Montgomery sowed his seeds in fertile backwaters of art. His portrait career really began in Mexico.

"I went to Mexico right after the war. I painted Mexicans and a number of vacationers saw my paintings. They'd say, 'Would you be interested in painting my daughter?'"

The Mexican connection led Montgomery to Tulsa, Oklahoma, where he soon had so many commissions from the oil-rich society of the Southwest that he bought a home there. Of the approximately 750 portraits he has painted, Montgomery estimates that 350 were done in Tulsa, another 100 or so in Texas. The rest are scattered around the world.

Among the first portraits Montgomery ever painted were those of Hildegard and Phyllis Thaxter, daughters of Judge Sidney Thaxter and Phyllis Schuyler Thaxter. Some 50 years later he painted Hildegard's husband, Judge Edward Gignoux, for the federal courthouse in Portland. Other well-known Montgomery portraits in Maine include Charles Shipman Payson at the Portland Museum of Art, Gov. Edmund Muskie and Gov. Kenneth Curtis at the State House in Augusta, and the posthumous portrait of L.L. Bean (executed last year) at the Maine Medical Center.

Claude Montgomery's naturalistic portraits are exactly what businesses and institutions tend to think of when they want a portrait of a founder, retiree, or benefactor. A conservative traditionalist as a portrait painter, Montgomery the man is a progressive liberal. Though he commands $6,000 for a head and shoulders likeness and $12,000 for a three-quarter length portrait, he, like Gardner Cox, now takes only the commissions he wants. In semi-retirement, Montgomery and his wife Louise prefer to spend their time and energies on another instinct, the instinct to help others. Currently, the Montgomerys are overseeing the conversion of a house they purchased on Brackett Street in Portland into a free shelter for the homeless. If Friendship House succeeds, it may well become Claude Montgomery's most important work.

As established portrait painters like Gardner Cox and Claude Montgomery slow down and representational painting accelerates towards new importance, the possibilities of portraiture are attracting a new generation of painters.

"That segregation [of portrait painting from pure painting] that occupied portraiture for the last 50 to 75 years is going out," says portrait expert Marvin Sadik. "I think the portraits of the next half-century will be done by artists who are well-rounded—there are a great number of contemporary artists who do really marvelous portraits who are not part of the portrait establishment and who are not part of the avant-garde establishment."

George Delyra is one of those artists.

Delyra, 56, is a friendly, thoughtful, and extremely exacting man. There is something vaguely monkish about both his personal and professional habits. He has had what he refers to as a tripartite career: creating paintings for exhibition, executing commissioned portraits, and working as a graphic designer. Because he works very slowly and meticulously (rarely producing more than 10 paintings a year, sometimes finishing none, once going four years without completing a painting), the two dozen or so portraits he has done constitute a significant portion of his total work. And though he says of painting, portraiture, and graphic design, "the differences between them are less significant than what they have in common," Delyra does maintain a fundamental distinction.

"The focus is on the sitter," says Delyra of a portrait, "not on the artist. For me, that body of work is clearly outside my main body of work."

Because he works so slowly, sometimes working on one painting for years at a time, Delyra began doing portraits in acrylics about 10 years ago. (Oil paints bond to dried surfaces mechanically, resulting in cleavages; acrylics bond to themselves completely, permitting the artist the freedom of time.) Oil portraits by Gardner Cox and Claude Montgomery tend to have a material and emotional "warmth" which is in part due to the oil medium. Delyra's acrylic portraits tend to look cool, clinical, detached, even ruthlessly objective. If a Delyra portrait looks somehow more "modern" than a Cox or Montgomery portrait, it is part medium, but also part attitude. Delyra's harsh realism is closer to the dominant sensibility of contemporary art. Delyra's portrait fees are in the $10,000 range, with double portraits going as high as $20,000.

Three of Delyra's eye-popping public portraits hang in Wing Lounge at Westbrook College: past college presidents Edward Blewett and James Dickinson, and Dorothy Healy, longtime college administrator, now curator of the college's Maine Women Writers' Collection. The Healy portrait is, in fact, the second painting Delyra did of her. The first, done from photographs in order to surprise the subject, was stolen some years ago during a panty raid. Delyra didn't mind too much; he never cared for the picture anyway. He's much happier with the likeness of Healy he did from life, though some find the portrait cold and unforgiving.

Like many easel painters, Delyra does not like to work from photographs. A case in point is the nearly completed posthumous portrait he is doing of one-time Maine Governor Lewis O. Barrows, the only Maine governor without an official state portrait. The primary photograph Delyra had to work from was a formal portrait done by a famous photography studio. In looking at candid snapshots of Barrows and through talking with his friends and family, Delyra discovered that the close-up photo had erased powerful lines from the man's face.

"It makes a rugged man look like a pretty boy," says Delyra.

While the artist maintains an intellectual distinction between his portraits and his personal paintings, there are definite signs that the two are approaching union. In recent commissions like the double portrait of art dealer John Payson's children, Delyra has taken to including extraneous landscape elements that have nothing to do with the subjects, but have personal meaning for him. In his little Richmond studio is a painting in progress of a

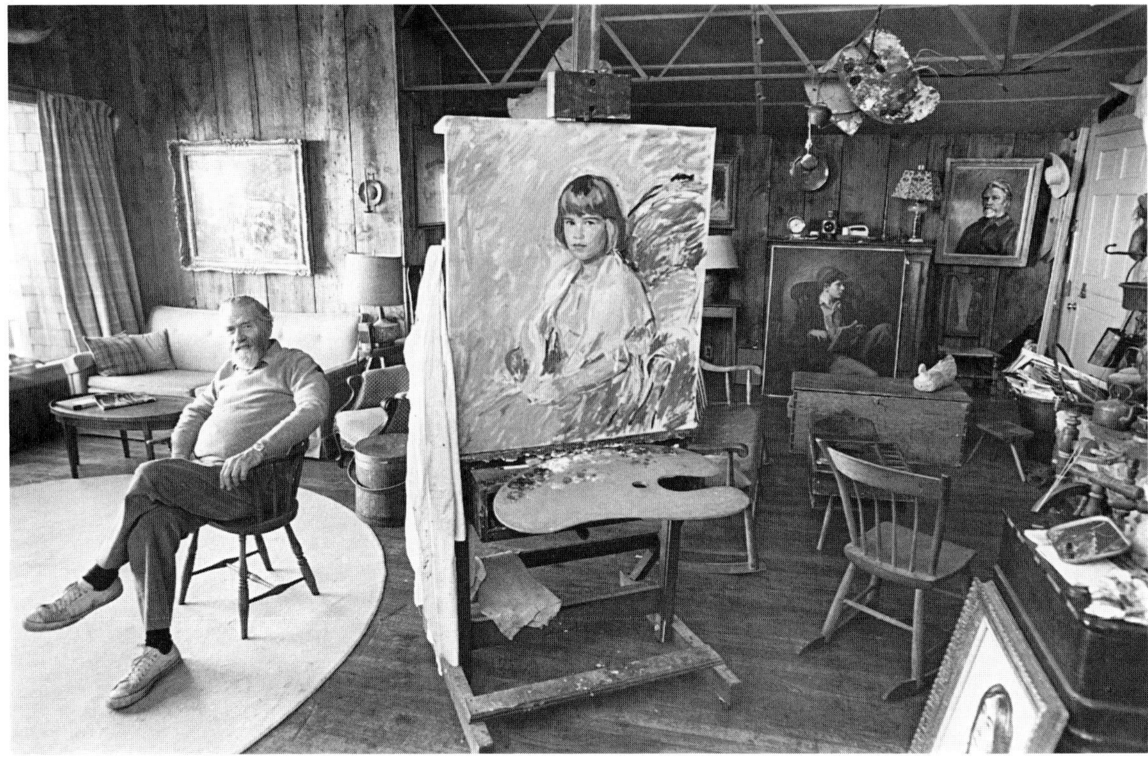

2. *Claude Montgomery, Maine's best-known portrait artist, says portrait painting is an instinct. Photo by Christopher Ayres.*

young woman that differs in style and format from the portrait commissions only in the fact that the girl is fictional.

Given the obvious craftsmanship and painstaking realism of Delyra's portraits, it is curious to hear him say things like "Details don't signify that much" and "Likeness is more than just getting the features right." What he is getting at, of course, is the often overlooked fact that human beings recognize one another by other than facial details. Gestures and postures communicate a great deal. Delyra has even had viewers fail to notice that a portrait had no face because the subject had been as well captured in other bodily forms.

Still, George Delyra says, "Portraiture is the ultimate realism. A really probing study into somebody's persona as evidenced in the outer layers of the body is the ultimate push in that direction in the arts."

"Doing a head is technically the most difficult thing any representational painter tackles," insists Joseph Nicoletti. "Every viewer, even if they don't know anything about art, is extremely sensitive to heads. It's the thing we look at most in the world. Any little inaccuracy will show up as awkwardness."

Joseph Nicoletti, 37, is generally regarded as one of the state's best representational painters. He is a master of landscape, still life, and even self-portraiture, but to date he has really only painted one serious commissioned portrait, that of his Barridoff Galleries dealer Annette Elowitch. Among those who have seen it, Nicoletti's portrait of Annette Elowitch is nothing if not controversial. Some maintain that it is a good painting, but not a good portrait. Some say it is neither. Others insist it is both. One recent viewer concluded simply that Nicoletti "missed," that the proportions were wrong. But then the same viewer also repeated John Singer Sargent's famous definition of a portrait as "a likeness in which there is something wrong about the mouth."

There are slight distortions in the Elowitch portrait, but the subject is definitely Annette Elowitch. If there are problems with Nicoletti's first foray into portraiture, they may have resulted from the fact that he took much greater risks than most seasoned portraitists would. For one thing, hands are often just as hard to paint as faces, and most portraitists charge more if hands are to be included. Nicoletti took the daring tack of painting Mrs. Elowitch with her hands at her temple. The distortion about the left eye, on close scrutiny, is actually the result of the pose. Further, Nicoletti chose to play with positive and negative spaces by painting

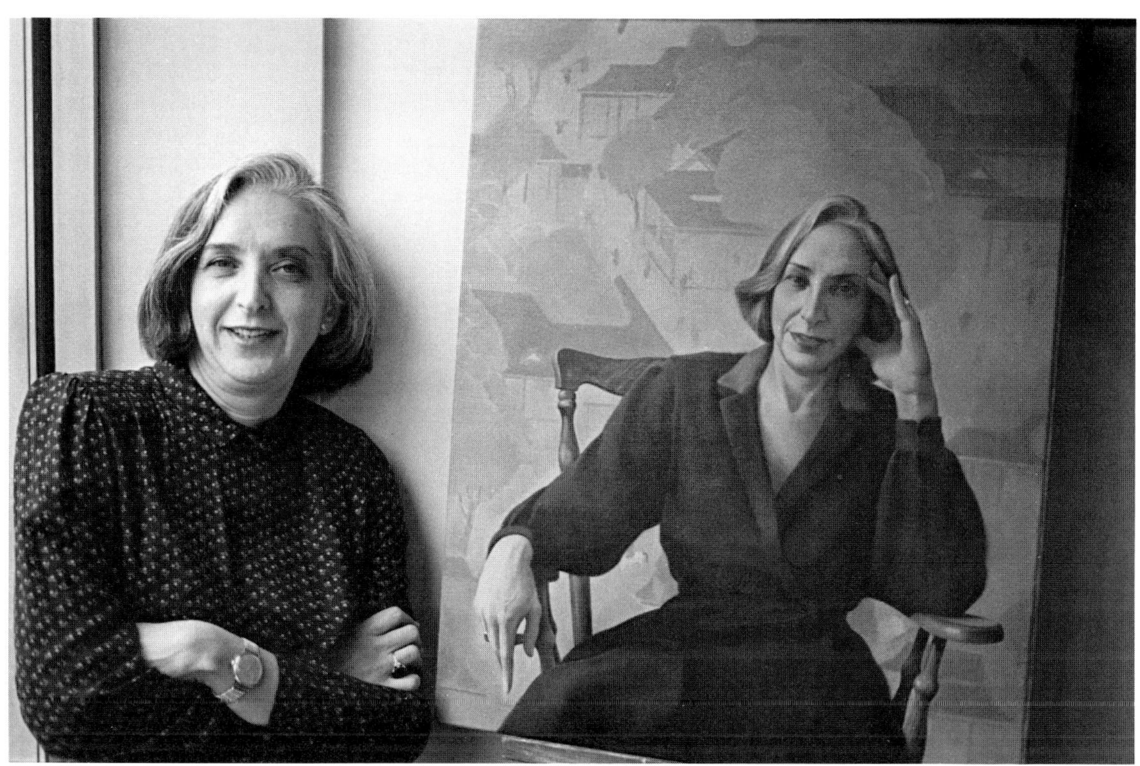

3. *Art dealer Annette Elowitch and her portrait by Joseph Nicoletti. Photo by Christopher Ayres.*

Oriental wallpaper as a background.

"I suppose I could have just done a head against a neutral background," says the artist, "but if you play it safe, hedge your bets, you might as well do something else."

In other words, Joseph Nicoletti is a contemporary realist who is unwilling to make compromises in order to paint a successful portrait. A portrait must be a good painting first, a good likeness second.

Joseph Nicoletti is an artist who could benefit from a new kind of portrait patron, the kind of visually sophisticated person who commissions a portrait by Andy Warhol, Philip Pearlstein, Neil Welliver, or Alex Katz. For with the rebirth of realism in art has come a new market for portraiture, the serious collector who is more interested in the artist's work than in a definitive self-image. You don't want a Katz portrait, for example, to look exactly like *you* ("Exactitude is not the truth," as Matisse put it), you want it to look exactly like a Katz. The focus is on the artist and the art, not the sitter.

"There was a soft notion," says Nicoletti, "that portraiture is something a good artist doesn't do, but then you think that people like Katz and Welliver are doing straight commission portraits now.

"I think there's a real [desire for] mediocrity [among traditional institutional patrons for portraits]. They want the *regular* thing. It's an institution making a decision, not an enlightened patron. Maybe that's the problem, a lack of patrons who will say, 'Do me in one of your paintings and that will be a portrait of me.'"

Marvin Sadik puts the quest for new, enlightened portrait patrons in even harsher terms.

"It's astounding," says Sadik, "how people who are eminent in business are utterly unsophisticated in art. Look at the buildings they put up, the houses they live in, and what's in those houses. Their admiration for painted portraits that look like photographs is childishly naive. They mistake the most banal for a miracle."

Annette Elowitch, who is thrilled with her portrait, estimates that a portrait by Joseph Nicoletti will sell for between $6,000 and $8,000.

Of course, despite the new art market for portraits, the traditional market still endures. And in many respects Donald Drake, a 31-year-old artist who maintains a studio adjacent to a Westbrook appliance repair center, is both heir to that tradition and a rarity among his generation of painters—an artist who wants above all else to be a good portrait painter.

"Ever since I was a kid," says the youthful

Drake, "I drew portraits. I did all the JFK photos, all the astronauts. After six years of school [BFA from Boston University, MFA from American University], I was doing still lifes and landscapes, but they were not interesting me too much. I guess I was looking for what excited me."

Portraits excite Drake. In the past four or five years he estimates he has done 50 to 75 portraits in pastels and in oils. He will do a pastel head for as little as $150; oils range from $750 to $2,000. His major commissions to date have been a posthumous portrait of L.L. Bean (done from the same photograph as Claude Montgomery's portrait of Bean), which hangs in the company's Freeport offices, and a full-length portrait of Mrs. G.G. Monks, mother of Robert A.G. Monks.

When it comes to capturing a likeness, Drake has amazing facility. His struggle now is to mature as a serious artist. To that end he has sought out men like Gardner Cox, Claude Montgomery, and Marvin Sadik (of whom he did a pastel portrait) for advice.

"There are two classes of portrait painters," says Drake. "First, there are guys who can get a likeness. Then there are, like Marvin says, guys who have a vision."

For his 50th college reunion (Harvard '28), Gardner Cox was asked to deliver a 10-minute talk on the past, present, and future of art. In that remarkably compressed history, he spoke of the history of art as "a long, undulating, horizontal line" whereas he envisioned the progress of science as a vertical rise. To make his point, Cox told his classmates, "If I had a brain tumor and Hippocrates was around, I would walk right by him and go to our classmate, Dr. Lawrence Pool. On the other hand, if I was going to have my portrait painted and Rembrandt was available, I certainly wouldn't hesitate to go to him."

Many of the greatest paintings of the western art world are portraits. It now seems possible that some of the greatest paintings of the future will be, too.

November 15, 1985

Public Art

Always Controversial

When Maine's Percent for Art program first tried to get off the ground last year, the question it raised was, "How can a state arts agency attempt to educate and elevate taste without appearing to dictate taste?"

Now that the program is in full swing, the broader question has become, "What is the proper role of government in support of art?"

Under the 1979 law, one percent of the total construction cost of any building erected with state funds, or $25,000, whichever is less, is to be spent on the purchase of art. The law applies only to buildings costing more than $100,000 and does not apply to inappropriate buildings such as state warehouses and garages. Public schools have the local option of participating in the program.

In an effort to control quality, the Maine State Commission on the Arts and Humanities (MSCAH) helps set up a selection panel and find an artist, either through direct selection or competition. It was this effort at quality control which contributed to the first Percent for Art project's being a disaster from beginning to end.

Because of lack of information and guidance, owing in part to the fact that MSCAH had not yet appointed anyone to direct the program, the Poland Community School jumped the gun, holding 18 meetings and arriving at a selection before the commission was brought into the picture. The work of art that the Poland committee had selected was a thoroughly amateurish woodland mural, and the commission felt it had no choice but to veto the selection. Tempers flared on both sides.

Paul Dupuis, chairman of the Poland school board, the building committee, and the art selection committee, angrily charged that the commission was on an ego trip and claimed that members of his committee had been characterized as "visual illiterates" by one MSCAH representative. State Senator Frank Wood (D-Springvale), one of the original sponsors of the Percent for Art legislation, was at the meeting when MSCAH turned down Poland's request.

"I was appalled by the arrogance of the commission," says Wood. "It seemed to me we had created an elitist program that we had never intended. If a program like this is going to gain community acceptance, you have to make allowances for local tastes."

Wood agreed with Paul Dupuis that MSCAH's final approval should be eliminated. He and Rep. Libby Mitchell (D-Vassalboro), the prime mover behind the original bill, promptly introduced an amendment that would have done just that had it not been killed in committee. Wood now says he is taking a wait-

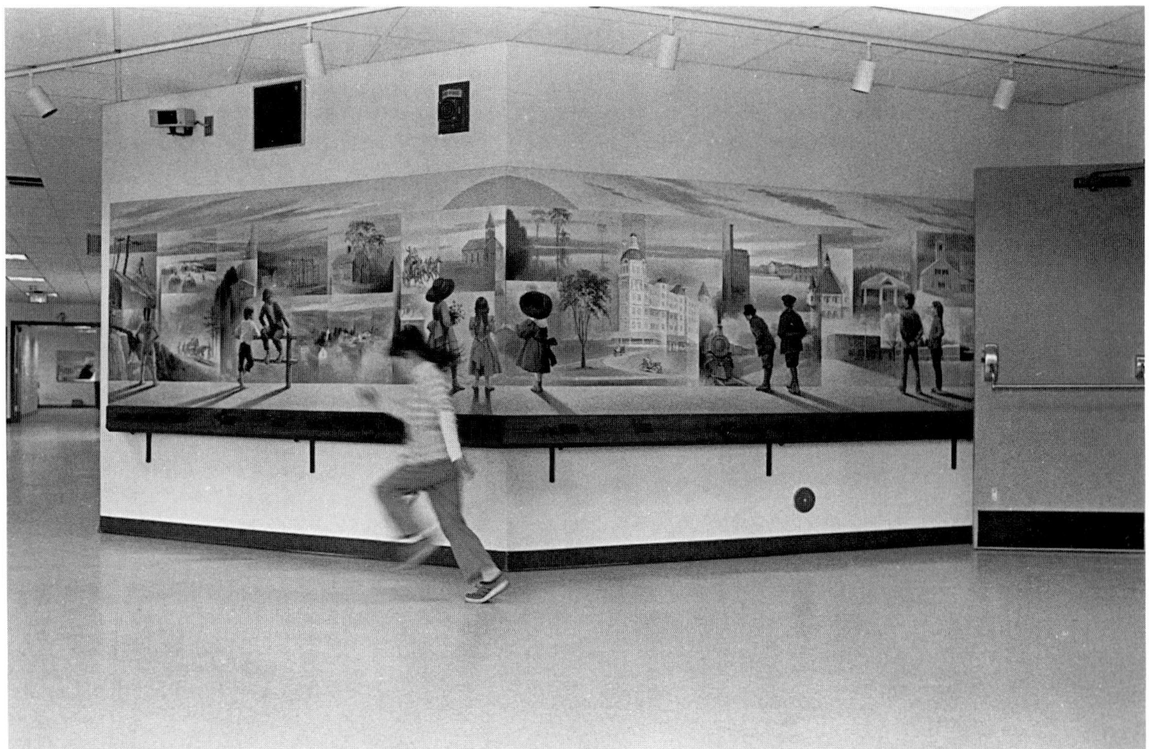

1. *This mural by Alan Lehtis finally adorned the walls of the Poland School, after the artist originally chosen by a local group was rejected by the state. Photo by Stephen B. Nichols.*

and-see attitude to re-introducing the amendment.

"It appears that the commission has cleaned up its act since the Poland incident," Rep. Wood says.

Unfortunately, the second Percent for Art project met with similar frustration, this time from the other end. After the selection committee for the Maine Veterans Home had decided on works by two of the top young artists in the state, Tom Higgins and Abby Shahn, the home's board decided they didn't like the choices. They apparently had something more patriotic in mind and are now awaiting approval of a parade mural by Martha Buck.

In order to facilitate the selection process, MSCAH maintains a registry containing slides of works by 530 artists, all but 100 of them from Maine. One potential problem with the use of this registry is that anyone may submit slides to it. The slide registry, which is used for other things than just the Percent for Art program, is non-juried, so it is possible for a local committee to select an artist from it who will ultimately not be acceptable to the commission. Though the artist who submitted the vetoed Poland mural was not identified through the registry, he is included in it.

What Poland eventually ended up commissioning was a mural depicting town history as seen through the eyes of a child ($11,000) by Alan Lehtis, a painting of chickadees ($500) by Richard Field, a wood carving of the school's panther mascot ($4,000) by Antoinette Schultz, and an animal mural by veteran muralist Dahlov Ipcar. While Ipcar's personal style and subject matter is perfectly suited to school environments, the Lehtis mural (not technically a mural, rather a large, two-panel painting) points out another difficulty with the program.

When working on his own free paintings—large, tight-focused nudes—Lehtis is one of the state's top painters. But when trying to work down to his audience, attempting to please someone other than himself, his work is diminished. His historic mural is competent, but undistinguished.

"There is a great difference between commissioned work and a free work of art," says sculptor Clark FitzGerald. "Commissions are always loaded with compromises."

A few summers back, FitzGerald was commissioned by the Portland Parks and Recreation Department to be an artist-in-residence in Deering Oaks. Under the commission, he created an uncharacteristically graceless milkweed pod sculpture which now stands in the city's Winslow Park. The artist attributes the failure of the piece to the constraints he had to work under. There was a limited budget. The choice of material (a tree trunk) was made for him. And he was hired primarily as a "performing" artist to create art while children watched. Placing the pod in the park was a secondary consideration.

"So help me," says FitzGerald of the awkward milkweed, "I did the best I could under the circumstances."

FitzGerald had much greater success in creating a strangely beautiful brass and copper pumpkin seed sculpture ($7,500) for Wilton Academy under the Percent for Art program. Wilton Academy also commissioned a free-form corkscrew-and-eyelet-carved wood column ($5,000) from Gary Ambrose, and two brass relief murals—animals in a school bus and a moose confronting a blueberry picker—($9,500) by Barry Norling.

Gary Ambrose has also been commissioned to carve a column of wood into a pleated accordian form ($5,500) for the Solon Elementary School. Jil Gilman, who directs the program for MSCAH, says that the commission would like to spread the work around, but if local sites share similar tastes, nothing currently prevents any artist from monopolizing the program.

"Percent for Art is not a support system for artists," says Gilman. "It is an art acquisition program."

But while there is currently about $250,000 tied up in approved and proposed Percent for Art projects, no one is getting rich off the program. Jil Gilman says that at a recent meeting the commission calculated that most of the participating artists are actually working for a minimum wage after the cost of materials has been deducted and the time involved has been figured in. And while the price tags attached to commissioned works may seem high to those unfamiliar with the art market, they are not sufficiently high by national standards to attract the most successful Maine-connected artists. Artists like Neil Welliver, Alex Katz, Louise Nevelson, Katharine Porter, Robert Indiana, and Alan Magee have not bothered to submit slides to the MSCAH registry. On a national scale, the amounts involved in the Maine program are modest. For example, artist

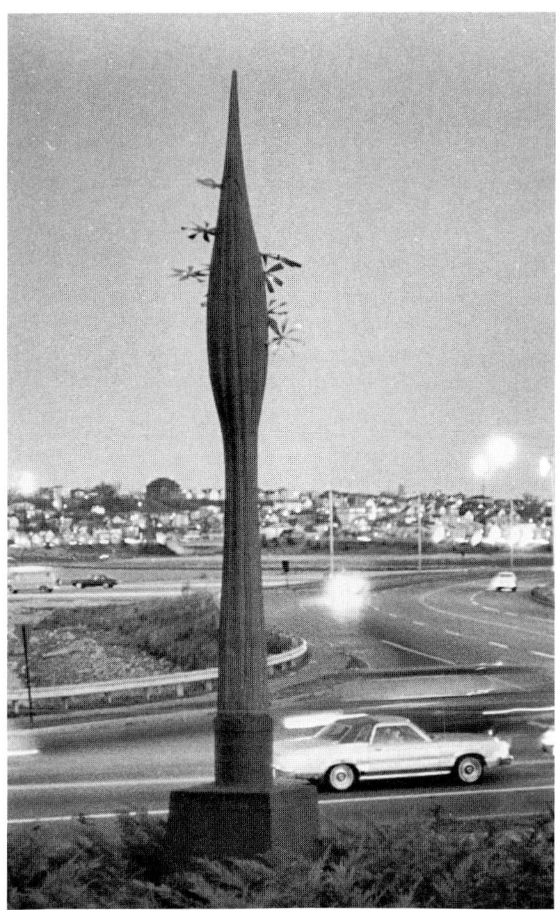

2. *Clark Fitz-Gerald's milkweed pod overlooking Back Cove in Portland didn't satisfy anyone, least of all the artist, who cites the inherent problems of public art. Photo by Stephen B. Nichols.*

Yvonne Jacquette, a Maine summer resident, received $40,000 through the National Endowment for the Arts for her grand aerial triptych, *Autumn Expansion*, in the Bangor Federal Building. By comparison, the largest Percent for Art commission so far recently went to sculptor James Skinner for a cast concrete monument ($17,000) at Southern Maine Vocational-Technical Institute.

Because Maine's art community is relatively small (about 800 artists typically respond to major open competitions) and isolated, Percent for Art is going to have an impossible task avoiding the appearance of conflict on interest, cronyism, and cliquishness. An artist appointed by MSCAH to a selection committee may well be in the running for a commission at another site. And in one recent project, the two commission appointees, one semi-finalist, and the eventual winner all had close ties to the same school. Charges of conspiracy (or at least a lack of impartiality) might have been leveled but for the fact that the selection committee made a good choice.

After the rough start that Percent for Art had,

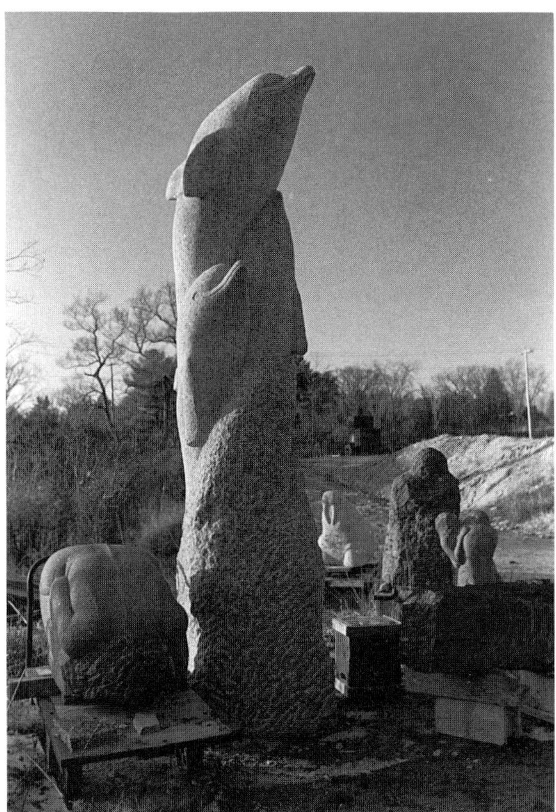

3. *Cabot Lyford's dolphins were to have been part of a fountain in front of the Portland Museum of Art, but after the museum rejected it, it eventually found a home in Portland's Old Port. Photo by Stephen B. Nichols.*

Jil Gilman isn't looking for any more major confrontations, but she can foresee a number of potentially troublesome situations. What happens, for example, if the completed work of commissioned art turns out to be unacceptable to the local site? Or, worse still, what happens if the finished piece is substantially different from what had been commissioned? Nationally, there are precedents for both cases.

The most notorious case of an unacceptable work of public art is Richard Serra's *Tilted Arc*, a wall of rusted steel which bisects the plaza of the Jacob Javits Federal Building in Manhattan. More than 1,000 area office workers signed a petition asking that the work be removed as a nuisance and an eyesore.

Closer to home, Katherine Porter, a Maine resident, was commissioned to create a $30,000 ceramic mural for the George Moscone Center in San Francisco. The completed mural was rejected because the artist had added a border to the mural not included in the original proposal. The border contained a list of politically charged names such as Cesar Chavez, Che Guevara, and Martin Luther King. Porter's political statement was overshadowed, however, by a more celebrated rejection at the Moscone Center—that of Robert Arneson's irreverent, graffiti-encrusted bust of the slain San Francisco mayor for whom the center was named.

Paul Heroux, the ceramic artist who assisted Katherine Porter in creating the Moscone Center mural, has recently been chosen to create his own ceramic mural ($8,500) for Deering High School through the Percent for Art program. Heroux offers his assurances that the Deering mural will not become politicized. "I'm not as political as Kathy is," he says.

The Deering High School project is one sign that the Percent for Art process is beginning to work well. A blue-ribbon selection committee made up primarily of art professionals recently decided to commission, in addition to the Heroux mural, a realistic painting of basketball action ($7,500) by Joseph Nicoletti, five drawings interpreting the local neighborhood and architecture ($3,500) by Marjorie Moore, and sixteen photographs ($4,000) by C.C. Church.

The Deering selections are all fairly sophisticated, but saying so begs the question of local taste. Portland is Maine's largest city and the site of the most energetic art scene. If a small town decides that it wants a carving of the school mascot, who is to say that their taste is any better or worse than Portland's? No one can fault MSCAH for wanting to help towns and schools get the best art for their money, but then who's to say what's best?

Says Frank Wood, "If the selection process works well and the commission works closely with the community, then at some point you have to trust local judgment."

One way that the state might possibly assure that funds will be spent only on high-quality art would be to establish an Art Bank such as has operated in Canada for ten years. An Art Bank would amount, in effect, to pre-selecting art for public places. A qualified (but then who's qualified to judge art?) and changing panel would purchase the best works they could find in Maine and then local sites could select works (possibly on a rental basis) from the bank. Such a program is only a remote possibility, but Gilman has been studying the successful Canadian program and has compiled a report on it.

A visit to the sites at Poland and Wilton where Percent for Art projects are in place demonstrates, however, what little impact a few pieces of art have on harsh institutional environments. Even $25,000 worth of art doesn't go very far toward humanizing an otherwise uninspired and dehumanizing interior. If the intent of the Percent for Art program is to enhance the quality of public space, perhaps the money would be better spent on interior designers.

Finally, there are those, even within the arts community, who argue that government has no business subsidizing art in the first place.

"The government shouldn't be in the business of collecting art," insists painter Tom Crotty. "Tax money shouldn't be used to purchase art."

Crotty is the proprietor of Frost Gully Gallery in Portland and a man with strong opinions on just about everything—especially where art is concerned.

"It's a case of the tail wagging the dog," Crotty says of state-subsidized art. "The incentive and motivation for creating art becomes that the money is available. It becomes a matter of looking for something to spend money on rather than looking for quality in art. We're already beginning to see a group of artists in this state developing a proficiency at that kind of project. Government just has a corrupting influence on art."

Past controversy

This is a tale of three troubled fountains, two public sculptures, and a mural in need of a home, offered simply to illustrate the misfortunes that plague public art.

The story begins in 1960 with the painful history of sculptor William Zorach's fetching *Spirit of the Sea* fountain in Bath's city park. Zorach, the internationally celebrated artist who had summered at nearby Robinhood for 40 years, had offered a fountain, in the form of a fulsome seven-foot female figure, as a gift to the city, and the Bath Garden Club had begun to raise the $15,000 necessary for the black Labrador granite basin and pedestal, transportation, installation, and landscaping when the ghost of McCarthyism appeared in the maritime city.

A campaign of innuendo swept over the city after someone tipped the local Smith-Tobey American Legion Post off to the fact that the name William Zorach appeared on the black lists of the House Un-American Activities Committee. Zorach, like other Maine-connected artists Ben Shahn, Leon Kroll, and Yasuo Kuniyoshi, had once supported leftist causes such as Spanish Relief, Relief for the Foreign Born, and British Relief. But as Zorach pointed out in his autobiography, *Art is My Life*, "They didn't mention the Red Cross and the War Orphans."

It was a nasty personal attack, and though Zorach was never openly charged with anything, he was forced, in a long statement to the Bath paper, to declare:

"Let me say in the first place I am not a Communist, have never been a Communist, and have never had any dealings with the Communist Party, nor have I supported any causes that I suspected of being Communist. In fact I am not and have never been politically minded. I am art minded; art is my life, and all my contacts with people are in relation to art."

This "Are you now, or have you ever been?" denial added a shameful chapter to Bath history and caused such anguish to those involved that even 20 years later they prefer not to talk about it.

"We'd just as soon not drag the whole thing up again," commented one prominent local citizen who fought for the statue.

Even the artist's daughter, painter Dahlov Ipcar, preferred not to discuss the controversy, saying that the people involved had long since "done a complete reversal and apologized." When it was suggested that forgetting about things that were over and done with argued against the writing of any history, Dahlov Ipcar insisted, "It's not history yet. Most of the people involved are still living. There may be a lesson to be learned, but not yet."

Within more recent memory is the case of the 1979 Samoset chainsaw massacre of sculptor Bernard Langlais' ill-fated fountain. Langlais' fountain for the Samoset Resort in Rockland seemed doomed from the outset. The 24-foot construction of wood pilings graced with carpentered shore birds and a seal never actually became a fountain because of financial troubles. The original Samoset owners went through

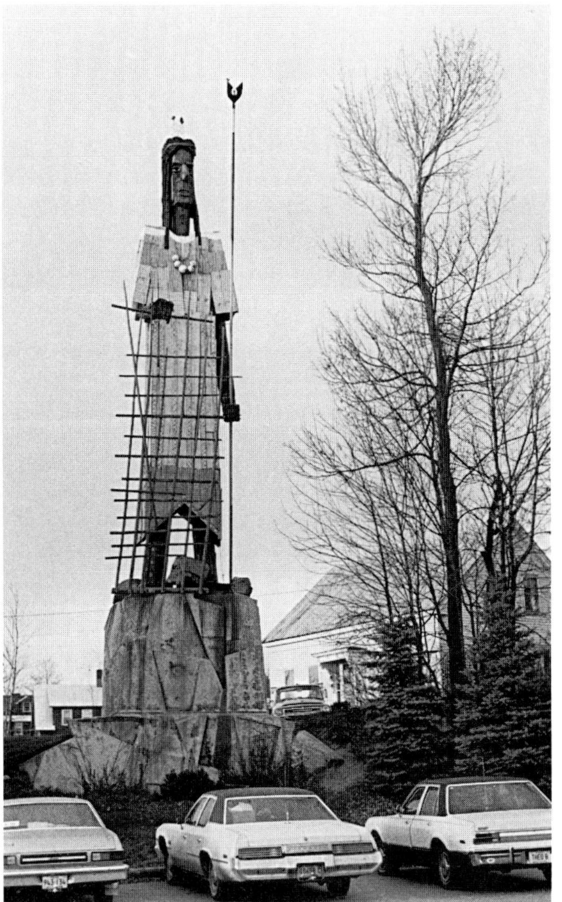

4. *Bernard Langlais' Indian has become a landmark in Skowhegan despite its rather odd location between parking lots. Photo by Stephen B. Nichols.*

bankruptcy and never paid Langlais.

In December, 1977, Bernard Langlais died unexpectedly and in the summer of 1979, the new owners of the Samoset set about re-designing the resort, in the process dismantling Langlais' fountain. The daily press had a field day with the fact that a chainsaw had been taken to a work of art. In actual fact, the fountain was carefully taken apart piece by piece. The chainsaw was only used to saw through the base of timbers which had been sunk in concrete.

The Samoset executives first tried to sell the fountain, then, briefly, offered to give it to the artist's widow. Ultimately it wound up in the possession of the Portland Museum of Art.

Langlais, who is probably best known in Maine for his 60-foot Skowhegan Indian, left a legacy of arts legislation in his wake. It was his passing and the testimony of Helen Langlais which led to the passage of a law which now enables artists' heirs to pay estate taxes with works of art. The Langlais rhinoceros on the Gorham campus of the University of Southern Maine is there in lieu of taxes. The Samoset incident led Rep. Merle Nelson (D-Portland) to sponsor an Artists' Moral Rights bill which would have prohibited the defacement, alteration, or destruction of works of art had it passed, but the measure was killed in committee when no artists appeared to support it. Nelson plans to re-introduce the bill.

One nearly forgotten work of public art which might have needed the protection of such legislation had it not been rescued by the Portland Museum of Art is Waldo Peirce's mural for the Westbrook Post Office. Peirce, who died at age 85 in 1970, was the hard-living Bangor-born painter who came to be known as "the American Renoir" during the first half of this century.

Peirce's mural, executed in the 1930s for the Works Project Administration (WPA), depicts four loggers in the deep Maine woods felling trees and stripping bark. One of the loggers is believed to be Peirce himself. The mural was painted on canvas and mounted with beeswax around a doorway in the old Brackett Street Post Office. In 1978, when the Post Office moved to new quarters, the Peirce mural was left behind in the vacant building.

That's when the Portland Museum stepped in and removed the painting from the walls. Since the Post Office is prohibited from selling or giving away federally-commissioned property, the mural is now on "permanent deposit" at the museum.

Other works of WPA art have not been fortunate enough to find homes, however. There is an often-repeated horror story of WPA paintings being sold to painting contractors for use as drop cloths, and Dahlov Ipcar, who painted two WPA murals herself, reports that a mural which her mother, Marguerite Zorach, did for a courthouse in Fresno, California, has disappeared from the face of the earth.

When a work of art is committed to the public trust, it is consigned to an uncertain fate. Witness the case of Victor Kahill's *The Maine Lobsterman.*

Kahill, a Lebanese-born sculptor, created *The Maine Lobsterman* for the 1939 New York World Fair. Though hardly a great work of art, the lobsterman was enormously popular. But since there was never enough money to cast the plaster model in bronze, only the plaster

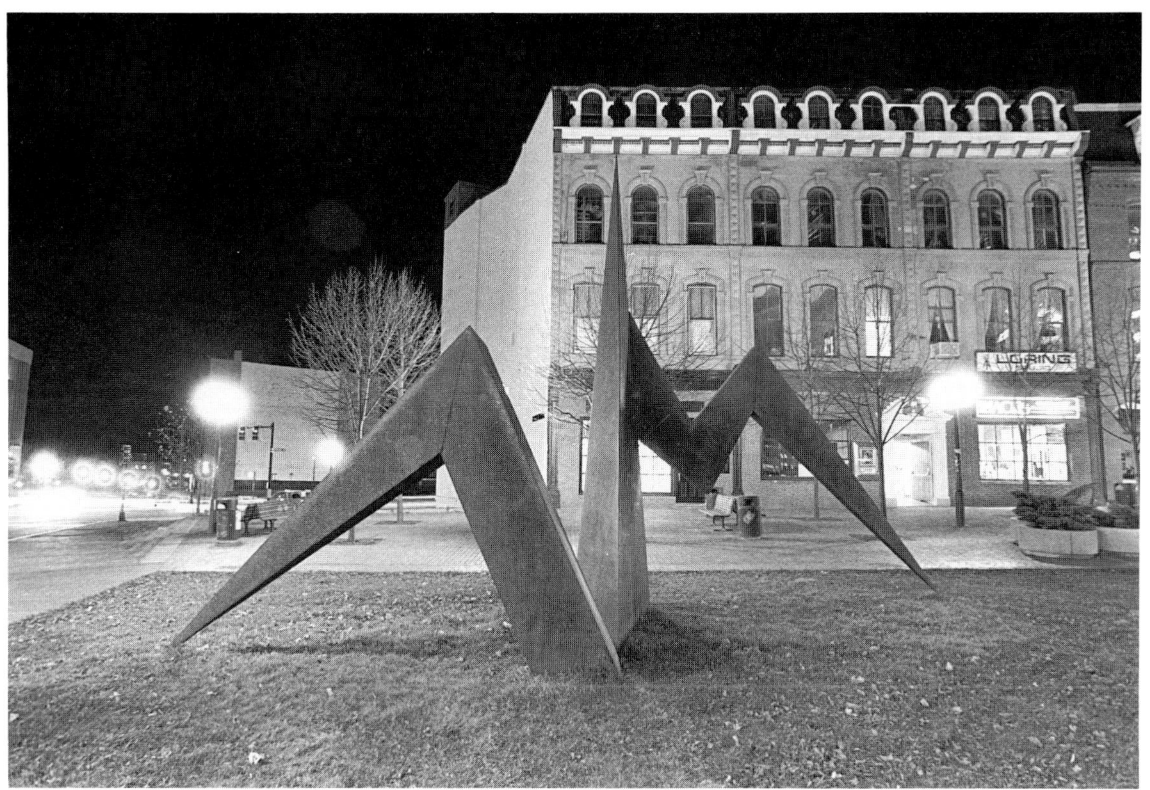

5. *John Raimondi's sculpture* Michael *raised quite a stir when it was installed in downtown Portland. Photo by Stephen B. Nichols.*

original was exhibited and that was repeatedly vandalized. In 1941, Kahill left Portland and left his paean to the common man to the city.

In 1962, Congressman Stanley Tupper proposed having the damaged model cast in bronze and installed on Maine Avenue in Washington, D.C., but no funds could be found to support the project. Then, in 1973, Elroy Johnson, the model for *The Maine Lobsterman*, died on Bailey Island. Public outrage that the statue was stored in a Boothbay warehouse led to the legislature appropriating funds to have the lobsterman cast in bronze.

Currently, there are three bronze castings from Kahill's plaster model. One is situated at the tip of Bailey Island. One is located in downtown Portland near Canal Plaza. And the third reposes in the Maine State Museum, along with the original. It seems that the museum's lobsterman may, finally, be destined for Washington.

For the past two years Ruth Heiser and her Cundy's Harbor Campfire girls have been raising money ($14,000 to date) to have *The Maine Lobsterman* installed in Park Five between Maine Avenue and the Potomac River. Having raised the money and shepherded the idea through the Maine legislature, the U.S. Congress, and the Department of the Interior, Mrs. Heiser and the girls are now waiting for a local architect to finish plans for the base, which is to be made of Deer Isle granite.

"We hope the statue will be in place by the time Congress recesses for Christmas," says Mrs. Heiser, but given the history of *The Maine Lobsterman*, she is not making any promises.

Perhaps it is the curse of the Golden Triangle which has befallen *The Maine Lobsterman*. The Portland copy does rest precariously close to that star-crossed plot in the darkest heart of the city, an area that has been notoriously unfriendly to art in the recent past.

In 1975, 27-year-old John Raimondi caused a bit of a stir in downtown Portland with his $10,000 Cor-Ten steel abstraction called *Michael*. The angular metal construction was commissioned by Canal Bank, fabricated with the help of SMVTI students, and donated to the city in a ceremony on May 29, 1975. A little plaque on the ground in front of *Michael* bears the inscription, "So Our Children Will Know the Difference"—implying, apparently, the difference between good art and bad art.

But there is nothing quite so mysterious as the power of modern art to disturb people, particularly people who have no real interest in art. It is

fair to say that a great many people did not like *Michael* in 1975. The Portland papers reported the sculpture "caused something of a flap among local politicians, educators, business people, and art critics." When a telephone kiosk infringed on *Michael*'s territory (Canal Square, where *The Maine Lobsterman* now kneels), Rob Elowitch, owner of neighboring Barridoff Galleries, consented to having the troubled art work moved to the esplanade in front of his gallery.

John Raimondi, after a rocky start, has since gone on to bigger and better things. In 1976, he was one of nine American sculptors invited to create a work for the Nebraska Interstate Highway. In 1977, after having purchased a Lincoln Continental and a mansion on Portland's Western Prom, he filed for bankruptcy.

"I don't come from money," Raimondi explains. "I just didn't know how to handle success so young. The same thing happens to movie stars and sports figures."

In 1977, Raimondi landed on his feet with a major commission from Blue Cross-Blue Shield in Milwaukee. Since then he has consistently been winning commissions from corporate giants like IBM and Levi-Strauss. His public commissions have brought as much as $200,000 and his limited edition bronzes fetch $7,000.

The intervening seven years have not been as kind to *Michael* as they have been to John Raimondi. Intentionally and heavily oxidized, partially obscured by saplings, and violated from time to time by graffiti, *Michael* has become Portland's invisible sculpture. Passersby who were once provoked are now mostly indifferent. Other targets have been found for the curse of the Golden Triangle. When Barridoff exhibited the raw metal sculpture of Ken Greenleaf on the lawn beside the gallery, city officials ("They look like they blew off the roof") tried to have the works removed as a public menace. And when Marjorie Moore erected her fanciful *Cow Fence* on the same spot, vandals quickly dismantled it for her.

And, finally, in these annals of the perils of public art we have the case of The Fountain That Never Was.

Sculptor Cabot Lyford of Exeter, New Hampshire, was commissioned to create a fountain for the Congress Street plaza in front of the new Charles Shipman Payson Wing of the Portland Museum of Art. Well, the Lyford Fountain is not to be...at least not in front of the museum.

The story goes that John Payson noticed that the plans for his father's museum called for an ornamental fountain and went ahead on his own to commission Cabot Lyford to create it. Lyford carved seven tons of Deer Isle granite into a 12-foot column in the form of three dolphins rising out of the rock and water. John Payson then attempted to present the fountain to the museum, but to no avail.

Museum director John Holverson explained that the museum had not been consulted beforehand, terming the fountain "not appropriate." Lyford says that architect Henry N. Cobb changed his design, replacing the fountain with a ring of silver birches. The artist says that the fountain may find a home one day on the revitalized Portland waterfront, but in the meantime there is a fountain in Exeter and a hole on Congress Street that looks suspiciously like there ought to be a fountain in it.

November 19, 1982

Down West

The Maine-New Mexico Connection

Could two places in one country possibly be more different? Maine, Vacationland, a mat of thick evergreen and blue waters flowing down from the forested mountains to the drowned coast and the green sea beyond. New Mexico, the Land of Enchantment, a chaos of monumental mountains and threadbare, pinon pine-studded foothills marooned high and dry and brown as suede on a shelf in the Rockies. Maine and New Mexico, united only by the clear blue ether and a punctuating red which in one place is the color of steamed lobsters; the other, the color of hot chili peppers. Yet these contrasting landscapes, the closed New England landscape of Maine and the open Southwest landscape of New Mexico, have another connection, a cultural connection in the attraction each place holds for artists, often the same artists. And, so, a winter's journey from Maine to New Mexico in search of contrasts and aesthetic commerce.

"The obvious reason artists, particularly sculptors, would go to New Mexico is the space sensation," says Carole Hanson, a sculptor who returned to her native Maine last year after nine years in Santa Fe, Taos, and Tucson. "The confrontation of the self in those spaces is tremendous. The most freeing experience of my life was when I entered New Mexico. It was like the feeling you get when you cross the Portsmouth bridge, that breath of relief. But it was even more intense—like crossing the Portsmouth bridge and suddenly being on top of Cadillac Mountain."

The panoramic summit of Cadillac Mountain, however, stands only 1,500 feet above Frenchman Bay. When you're on the ground in Albuquerque, you're 5,000 feet above sea level and still looking up at the Sandia Crest which rises another 5,000 feet above the city. So pile up four or five spiritual Cadillacs, place them not against the North Atlantic but upon a dried-up, ancient sea bed, and there you have Carole Hanson's analogy. Welcome to New Mexico.

When Carole Hanson first arrived in New Mexico in 1978, she headed straight for Taos, the storied artists' colony sequestered high in the Sangre de Cristo Mountains of north-central New Mexico.

"I'm a big fan of D.H. Lawrence, so I wanted to go to the shrine where he is buried," she explains. "Taos was my real goal, but I didn't have the courage to tackle it, so I settled in Santa Fe which is easier and lighter. Taos is unbelievably hostile. It's like some towns in Maine where, if you're not from there, you're from nowhere."

As a stone carver inspired by pre-Columbian

and primitive art, Hanson found a feast for the eye in the Indian and Mexican art forms of the region and in the dramatically sculpted landscape itself, but what called her to New Mexico in the first place was not so much the promise of a picturesque geography as the romance of Taos and Santa Fe, the siren song of a Bohemian Shangri-la first heard as a girl growing up in milltown Westbrook.

The colonization of Taos and Santa Fe by artists commenced at the turn of the century with reports of the colorful Indian life there carried abroad by painter Joseph Henry Sharp who had scouted the area in 1893. In Paris in 1895, he described the rich natural and cultural resources of the area to painters Ernest Blumenschein and Bert Phillips, who visited Taos together in 1898. These three artists, along with painters like Oscar Berninghaus, Irving Couse, Henry Dunton, Victor Higgins, Walter Ufer, Martin Hennings, and Kenneth Adams (who arrived later), formed the Taos Society of Artists, which flourished from 1915 until it was disbanded in 1927.

In the 1920s, five artists attracted to Santa Fe—Willard Nash, Josef Bakos, Will Shuster, Walter Mruk, and Fremont Ellis—banded together as *Los Cinco Pintores* (The Five Painters), a group which exhibited together from 1921 until 1926. The early Taos artists and *Los Cinco Pintores* were essentially local-color painters sharing a common aesthetic interest in painting the life of the pueblos and the Hispanic community. Their artistic instincts were primarily romantic. During the teens, however, another group of artists discovered Taos and Santa Fe, and with them came both the modernist aesthetic and the Maine connection.

In 1916, Robert Henri, founder of New York's Ashcan School and a man perhaps more important in art history as a charismatic teacher than as a painter, came to Santa Fe at the invitation of Dr. Edgar Hewett, founding director of the Museum of Fine Arts there. A prime mover and shaker on the American art scene of the day, Henri was responsible for attracting to Santa Fe some of the most important artists of the day, among them John Sloan, George Bellows, and Edward Hopper. Just prior to coming to Santa Fe, of course, Henri had planted "the art spirit" in the thin soil of Monhegan, the rugged Maine island he introduced to the likes of Rockwell Kent, Bellows, and Leon Kroll (who also painted in Santa Fe). So one of the primary Maine-New Mexico currents runs through the person and personality of Robert Henri. Indeed, Andrew Dasburg, who was to become a mainstay of the New Mexican modernist community, was a student of Henri's and painted on Monhegan in 1913.

Dasburg, however, was initially enticed to New Mexico by the legendary Mabel Dodge, Bohemian hostess to the Taos counterculture. Mabel Dodge's enthusiasm for surrounding herself with interesting people (D.H. and Frieda Lawrence being her most luminous houseguests) was responsible for introducing three of the most important early modernists—Marsden Hartley, John Marin, and Georgia O'Keeffe—to New Mexico. O'Keeffe, who visited New Mexico briefly in 1917, returned as a guest of Mabel Dodge in 1929 and thereafter become the high priestess of Abiquiu, the small town where she settled permanently in 1949. Her ascetic spirit still hovers over the more mystical aspects of art in northern New Mexico.

Hartley, Maine's one true native genius, was in the midst of his modernist vagabondage when he sampled New Mexico in 1918 and 1919. Marin visited a decade later in 1929 and 1930. Yet while neither artist lit for long in Taos and Santa Fe, and both are more closely associated with Maine than New Mexico, the influence of Hartley and Marin on the New Mexican art scene was profound. Hartley's heavy-handed expressionist oils and Marin's more dashing and ethereal cubist watercolors brought European modernist strains to bear on the Southwest and helped define the polarities from which that landscape could be seen and depicted. Where other artists came to New Mexico in a simple search for subject matter, the more internationalist Hartley and Marin were always more concerned with how to paint than what to paint. The future of art in America, as we now know, was with process, not pictures.

From common modernist roots in the works of artists like Henri, Bellows, Hopper, Hartley, and Marin (and even O'Keeffe, who painted in Maine briefly in the 1920s), both Maine and

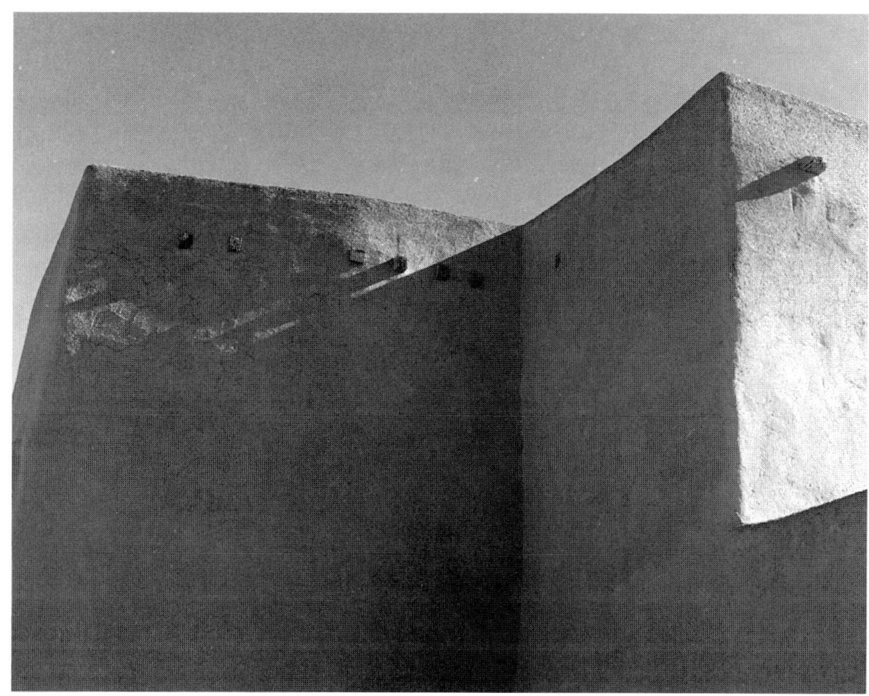

1. *Jane Gilbert,* Rancho de Taos, N.M. *Photograph. Courtesy of the artist.*

New Mexico evolved distinctive regional art scenes. The Maine scene was focused along the coast in summer art colonies like Ogunquit and Monhegan; the New Mexican scene focused year-round on the mountainous principalities of Taos and Santa Fe. Circumstances conspired, however, such that New Mexican regionalism developed a much more concentrated and commercialized core.

Santa Fe—tourist town, trade center, and capital of New Mexico—is a soft, handmade city of low, uniform adobe and stucco buildings. It is a city of mud that has been shaped up out of the earth like a giant sandcastle. Perhaps because it is a tourist town—a favorite summer watering hole of oil-rich Texans who are now being replaced by hi-tech Californians—Santa Fe has evolved as an art market as well as an art colony. In this city of 50,000 there are in excess of 150 art galleries. By comparison, Portland, which has only recently become an art market of sorts, is a city of 65,000 with fewer than 20 art galleries. But then red-brick Portland has not had the benefit of being a tourist town, the state capital, or an art colony.

Today, where the regional art of Maine is awash in rowboats and lobster pots, lighthouses and splashy seascapes, the galleries of Santa Fe are primarily burdened with an excess of stylized Indians and a surfeit of silver and turquoise jewelry. And if the ready-made abstraction of the Rancho de Taos Church has been done once, it has been done to death—not unlike Maine's Portland Head Light. Of the 150-plus Santa Fe galleries, only four or five—Munson, Linda Durham, Janus, Gerald Peters, Elaine Horwitch—seem to show artists who participate in a contemporary idiom. For example, Linda Durham, who has spent many summers in Georgetown, Maine, shows an adventurous selection of emerging New Mexico artists, many of whom flavor prevalent international styles with local imagery. The Munson Gallery might be termed "conservative contemporary," not unlike Portland's Hobe Sound or Barridoff Galleries. Larry Munson, who has operated a gallery in Cape Cod for 34 years, opened his Santa Fe gallery 10 years ago and has periodically shown work by Maine artists.

"Ninety percent of what we sell," says Larry Munson, "we sell to visiting people. Of that 90 percent going out-of-state, more than half—maybe 60 percent—goes back east to Boston, Connecticut, New Jersey, New York, Washington, and Philadelphia. There is almost no Texas market now [there is a downturn in the Texas oil economy]. The Texas market has been replaced by more sophisticated New England and East Coast buyers.

"When I first came out here, I put together a very strong New England show including people like Andrew Wyeth and Robert Eric

Moore, but I didn't sell a thing, not one picture. There wasn't the slightest interest here in New England art."

Regionalism inevitably begets a degree of provincial chauvinism, but in at least one important respect historical attitudes toward local art differ radically between Maine and New Mexico. In Maine, artists have tended to be ignored; in New Mexico they have been actively encouraged. Beginning in the 1880s, for example, the Santa Fe Railway provided free passage to artists headed for New Mexico and used their paintings of the Southwest as promotional devices. The Museum of Fine Arts, which opened in 1917, also provided artists with a warm welcome to Santa Fe.

On the advice of Robert Henri and John Sloan, the new museum established an "open door policy" toward exhibitions which remained in force until the 1950s. Instead of curating or jurying exhibitions, the Santa Fe museum simply opened its doors to any local artists who wished to show there. In many cases, artists simply walked in and hung their own shows. And there were also numerous instances of the museum providing newly-arrived artists with a place to work.

"Santa Fe may do the rare thing and become itself," wrote Henri in 1917. "The painters are all happy. The climate seems to suit well both temperaments—to work or not to work—and here painters are treated with that welcome and appreciation that is supposed to exist only in certain places in Europe."

Twenty years later, Dr. Edgar Hewett would write, "There has been no jury, no favoritism for any theory or 'school' of art. The Director's idea was to provide all the facilities possible within our means, then keep out of the way and give art a fair field."

Thus, where most eastern art museums function as critical standard-bearers, the Santa Fe museum was founded as an artists' support system. While the museum does exercise a good deal more curatorial judgment today, its traditional *Alcove Shows* (now by invitation, but still seeking the unknown) were reinstated in 1986 after a 30-year hiatus.

Open landscape, open minds? Perhaps because many of the artists who settled in New Mexico did so to escape the conventions of the East Coast art establishment, and perhaps because they found there institutions willing to aid and abet them, an aura of non-critical acceptance still pervades the Santa Fe art scene. Whether this attitude is read as less discriminating or simply more liberated obviously depends on one's own turn of mind. Still, the question of quality in art is a real and difficult one, particularly when complicated by matters of regionalism.

Questions a long way from home. Would Alfred Morang, the Portland Bohemian who became the Toulouse Lautrec of Santa Fe, ever have found the sort of validation in Maine that he found in New Mexico? His heavily impastoed impressionist scenes—paintings of questionable quality at the very least—hang in galleries and museums all over New Mexico. But had he not moved to Santa Fe in 1937, had he remained in Portland where he was largely regarded as an eccentric and a figure of fun, would Alfred Morang still be ignored in the annals of Maine art? It just seems possible. And there are potential Morangs aplenty painting in Portland today.

"The attitudes are just so different. It's a Southwest phenomenon," says artist Thomas Crotty, proprietor of Frost Gully Gallery in Portland. "There's a tendency on the part of people there that if they like something, they buy it. Here if they like it, they think it ought to be in a museum. In general, the Santa Fe art scene is more alive, more spontaneous, and more progressive. Here it's more conservative, tight, and Yankee. People down there were way ahead of us in recognizing great artists like Marin, Hartley, and O'Keeffe."

Crotty is one of the many contemporary artists in Maine who have worked in New Mexico in recent years. Among the best-known are Robert Solotaire, Alfred Chadbourn, John Muench, Stuart Ross, Johnnie Ross, Pat Hardy, Patt Franklin, Sharon Townshend, Kevin Donahue, Peter Rolfe and Gina Werfel. Crotty made his pilgrimage in 1986 at the urging of Laurence Sisson, a popular painter of the Maine scene who moved to New Mexico in 1978.

Laurence Sisson seascapes—rhapsodic, vaguely Japanese fantasies of the Maine shore—

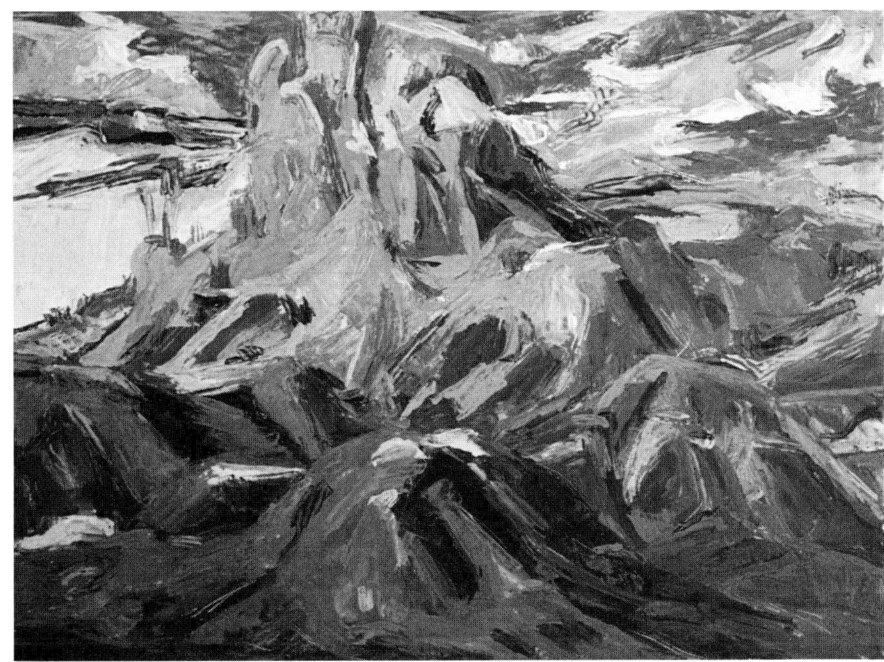

2. *Gina Werfel,* Red Hills, *1988. Oil on linen. Courtesy of the artist.*

hang behind the desks of bank presidents and CEOs from Portland to Boston, but these days Sisson (who lived in Boothbay from 1950 until 1970) is a mainstay in the Santa Fe art scene. His Yankee roots and his commercial success have earned him a reputation out West as the cashmere cowboy of Nambe. Where sculptor Carole Hanson relates to New Mexico first as space, Sisson responds to the region's remarkable light.

"Everything here depends on light," says Laurence Sisson. "Maine is gorgeous when it's gray. I didn't like Maine on sunny days. But here, without the light, you lose all the color, the contrasts, and the vibrancy of the landscape."

The shift of landscapes from Maine to New Mexico is dramatic and elemental, but Sisson found he had little trouble adjusting his vision from the foggy North Atlantic coast to the intense clarity of the big sky over New Mexico's mountains and mesas.

"I'd been in Santa Fe no more than a day," he explains, "when I realized that not only had I never seen such light, but that it was like being in the middle of the ocean looking back at the land. I felt I was at sea. I felt I was at home. Suck the water out of a seascape and you have the desert."

So nine years after leaving New England, Laurence Sisson is comfortable painting the pebbles of Southport into the arroyos of Chimayo.

When he was working in Boothbay and Boston, Sisson was the nearest thing to a best-selling Maine artist, but his market back East was nothing compared to the commercial success he has experienced since moving to New Mexico.

"I haven't had a critique since I moved here, but my dealer sells just about everything I paint," says Sisson. "I've made a fortune out here."

While Laurence Sisson is striking it rich up in Santa Fe, Lisa Allen is "on the grant" down in Roswell.

Two hundred miles of high plains—a surreal natural vacancy thinly populated by cattle and antelope—separate chic Santa Fe from gritty Roswell to the southeast. An oil and ranching city of some 40,000 souls, Roswell is more of a West Texas town than a New Mexican town, and it is probably better known as a bus manufacturing center (Greyhound and GMC both make buses here) than as an art center. Yet it is here, to a stucco compound on the edge of town, that Lisa Allen came to work.

Lisa Allen, a faculty member of the Portland School of Art and one of Maine's most serious painters, arrived in Roswell last summer for a year of painting under the aegis of the Roswell Artist-in-Residence Program. Her PSA colleague Johnnie Ross had been "on the grant" in 1974-75 and Allen applied five times before

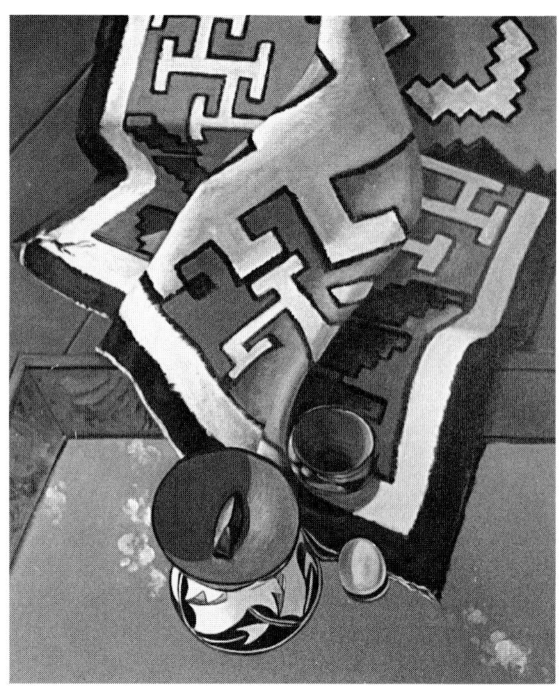

3. *Pat Hardy,* Navajo Sky Mirror, *1989. Oil on canvas. Courtesy of the artist.*

being accepted.

"What the program is," says Lisa Allen, "is Donald Anderson's dream."

Donald Anderson is a shy, generous man, a self-taught painter and an entirely unlikely oil tycoon. Twenty years ago, desiring the company of other artists in remote Roswell, Anderson began sponsoring an artist-in-residence program administered through, but independent of, the Roswell Museum and Art Center. Artists accepted into the program receive the use of a free house, a free studio, $8,000 for materials, and $500 a month for living expenses. That's six months or a year of freedom—no strings attached, no teaching, no studying, just working. Since 1967, 100 artists have been the beneficiaries of Donald Anderson's "gift of time."

Though Lisa Allen is well aware of New Mexico's artistic heritage and of the aesthetic connections between Maine and New Mexico, she does not see herself or her work as participating in any ongoing regional tradition. Allen is an abstract painter who internalizes landscapes before expressing her response to them. Working with fistfuls of paint (she has already spent her $8,000 materials budget after just seven months), she creates powerful gestural paintings in which the physical and psychological realities of her environment merge. A passage of brilliant red may, however, have more to do with the chili pepper fields on the edge of Roswell than with a particularly intense emotion. Since coming to Roswell, Allen has sensed her paintings becoming more open, broader, freer, and more colorful than her dense, tightly woven evocations of Maine.

"I think a lot of what's going to happen in my work will be after-the-fact," says Allen. "The first time I came out to the Southwest was to Tucson in 1979. It just blew me away. These high plains strike a strong chord in me. I'm finding a recurrence of themes. It's like Maine has been a long sojourn in between the flatness of the Midwest [where she grew up in rural Illinois] and the flatness of the Southwest."

Still, reminders of home are surprisingly easy to come by even out here in the vastness of the high plains. On one wall of Donald and Sally Anderson's rambling Roswell home, for example, there hangs a large painting Anderson did of Mount Desert Island. It's like crossing the continent and suddenly being on top of Cadillac Mountain. And the reverberations of Maine become even stronger at the Roswell Museum and Art Center.

Just visible in the obscurity of an unlit, unopened gallery is a landscape by Alfred Morang. Out in the main gallery are Marsden Hartley's 1920 oil *Landscape: New Mexico* and John Marin's 1930 watercolor *Near Taos—New Mexico.* And one entire gallery of the Roswell Museum is devoted to work of Henriette Wyeth Hurd, widow of artist Peter Hurd, sister of artist Andrew Wyeth, and a resident of San Patricio in the nearby Hondo Valley. The most arresting painting in the room is the 1937 *Portrait of My Father*, in which the stern figure of N.C. Wyeth is seen seated before his own painting of a Maine island funeral.

"It feels like a Maine museum to me," says Lisa Allen.

March 18, 1988

The Politics of Art Criticism

Lucy Lippard & Hilton Kramer

It is understood by now that all art is ideological and all art is used politically by the right or left, with the conscious or unconscious assent of the artist. There is no neutral zone. Artists who remain stubbornly uninformed about the social and emotional effects of their images and their connections to other images outside the art context are most easily manipulated by the prevailing systems of distribution, interpretation, and marketing.

—Lucy Lippard in a catalogue essay for the 1984 *Art & Ideology* exhibition at the New Museum of Contemporary Art in New York

Bad art is bad art, whatever its political purpose, and only the most zealous supporter of the "no neutral zone" doctrine could seriously believe otherwise.

—Hilton Kramer in *The New Criterion*, April, 1984

Lucy Lippard and Hilton Kramer are two of America's most noted art critics. Lippard, activist darling of the populist left, has distinguished herself in the field of art criticism primarily by making connections—between issues and images, people and ideas, one culture and another, art and politics. Kramer, Olympian lawgiver of the neo-conservative movement, has made a name for himself principally by making distinctions—between high art and popular culture, good art and bad, art and politics.

Since one of the few things Lucy Lippard and Hilton Kramer have in common is summer residence in Maine—a state where the art dialogue is rarely elevated above the level of "Do you like it?"—there seemed an instructive purpose to be served by having them go head-to-head here in these pages. For not only are the two critics poles apart in their social and aesthetic values, they also adopt very different personal styles and professional strategies. Kramer, for instance, is very much a stand-and-deliver critic given to withering critical broadsides. Lippard, whose monthly column in *Zeta* magazine is called "Sniper's Nest," is more of a hit-and-run critic whose guerilla art tactics are not as well served by direct confrontation.

"We exist in different spaces," says Lucy Lippard. "I'm not in competition with Hilton. I don't want to do anything he does and I don't want to be anything he is…except a good writer."

Still, this exchange—between a woman who fervently believes that art must be integrated with daily life and a man who adamantly insists that artistic standards must be maintained—is a contest of equals.

Lucy Lippard, 52, grew up in New York City, New Orleans, and Charlottesville, Virginia, but

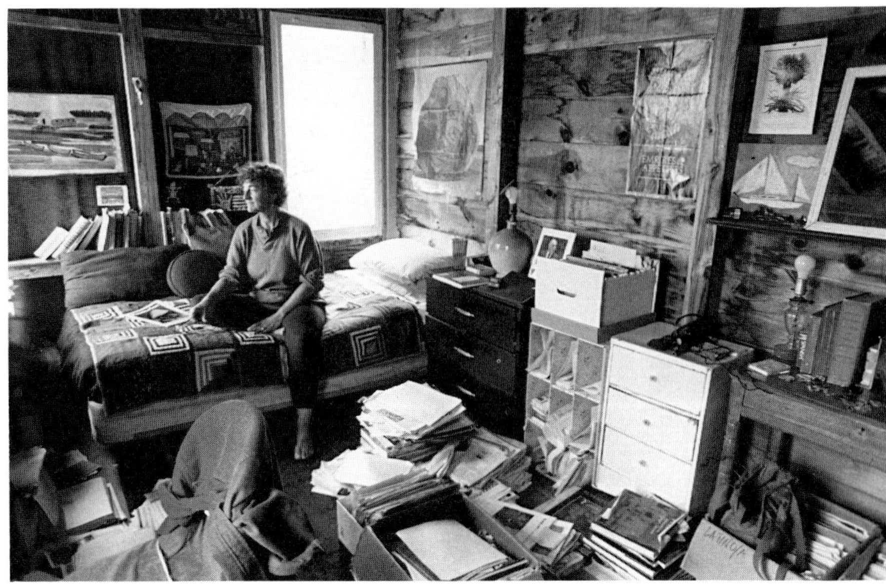

1. *Lucy Lippard has summered at Kennebec Point in Georgetown all of her life. Photo by Christopher Ayres.*

"home" has always been Kennebec Point in Georgetown, Maine, where her grandparents began summering in 1914. These days she divides her time between Boulder, Colorado (where she occasionally teaches at the University of Colorado), a loft in New York City, and a cottage in Georgetown. While in Maine she observes a strict schedule of writing from seven a.m. until noon, after which, when the tide is right, she sails her 12-foot gaff-rigged catboat *Rosita* (named for a victim of political repression in Guatemala and for German Marxist agitator Rosa Luxemburg) around Sagadahoc Bay.

The author of 14 books, chief among which are *From the Center: Feminist Essays on Women's Art* (1976), *Overlay: Contemporary Art and the Art of Prehistory* (1983), and *Get the Message? A Decade of Art for Social Change* (1984), Lippard is devoting the summer of 1989 to finishing a book entitled *Mixed Blessings: Contemporary Art and the Cross-Cultural Process*, about...?

"It's very elusive. It's hell to figure out. The art is all by artists of color, but it's not a survey of artists of color and the book is not just about the art." (Note: "artists of color" is the politically correct term for non-Caucasian artists.)

Hilton Kramer, 61, grew up in Gloucester, Massachusetts, a fishing port with a visual culture similar to that of coastal Maine—Fitz Hugh Lane, Marsden Hartley, and a plethora of local scene painters. After having risen through the critical and editorial ranks of *Arts*, *The Nation*, and *The New Leader*, Kramer was for 17 years (1965-1982) the art critic for *The New York Times*, meaning he was essentially the art critic for the nation. Since 1982, his base of power has been the influential conservative journal, *The New Criterion*. His writings on art have been collected in two books—*The Age of the Avant-Garde: An Art Chronicle of 1956-1972* (1973) and *The Revenge of the Philistines: Art and Culture, 1972-1984* (1985).

Regular Maine summer visitors since 1964, Hilton and Esta Kramer, residents of Westport, Connecticut, purchased a small cape on the main street of Waldoboro as a summer retreat in 1987. This summer Kramer is devoting his time in Maine to finishing a book entitled *Abstract Art: A Cultural History*.

"Basically, it's a history of the ideas that have shaped abstract art from the beginning to now."

By and large, the art that interests Hilton Kramer holds little interest for Lucy Lippard. On the evening of July 14, for example, Lippard gave a slide lecture at Bowdoin College, sponsored by the Union of Maine Visual Artists and devoted to works by feminist, activist, and community artists—"the snipers and moles of modern art."

Lippard's show of activist art included street theater, murals, performances, protests, and more conventional works of art concerned with a gamut of social issues including pornography, rape and sexual discrimination, reproductive rights, U.S. involvement in Central America, homelessness, AIDS, aging, racism, the arms race, Hiroshima, and the labor strike at the International Paper mill in Jay. Lippard's "slide blitz" of political art prompted one woman in the Bowdoin audience to ask her the obvious question: "Do you think that art that is not political has value?"

"This is what I'm involved with. This is where I've put my life," replied Lippard diplomatically. "This is what I do, but it doesn't exclude every other kind of art."

Her purpose, she said, is not to attack the art she doesn't value, but to seek respect for the art she does. Her tolerant response caused some in the audience who have known Lippard for years and who expected her to take a harder line against "art for art's sake" to observe that she seemed to have mellowed, to have softened her stance.

"It's partly that I realize audiences get bizarrely alienated when I talk about this art," explains Lippard, "so I try to be very kind to all kinds of art."

All kinds of art. The much booed and ballyhooed artistic pluralism of the 1970s and 1980s reads as progress to the liberal-minded, and permissiveness to conservatives. Whether good, bad, or indifferent, every card-carrying critic feels compelled to weigh in with a theory to explain the "anything goes" climate of the current art scene. Arthur Danto in *The Nation*, for instance, argues an "end of art" theory and happily credits pluralism as the freedom which results once "the time for next things is past." Robert Hughes in *Time* blames post-modern pluralism on "the suction of a colossally expanded art market" willing to validate anything in order to have something to sell. And Hilton Kramer, of course, calls what happened in the wake of modernism "the revenge of the philistines," a subversion of seriousness which he blames on an ironic shift of left-liberal mindset.

"One of the principle effects of the '60s counterculture, not only in the art scene, but in the whole cultural world," maintains Kramer, "was to eliminate, or at least diminish, distinctions between high art and popular culture. It was also one of the consequences to eliminate, or at least diminish, the role of critical thought, because critics who make distinctions based on quality were considered elitist. From elitism it's a short step to saying it's authoritarian and from there to totalitarian. But you're still left with the problem, if you're interested in art, that some things are better than others."

In her Bowdoin talk, Lippard specifically rejected the word "quality" as one too class-bound to be useful in talking about art. She preferred instead "aesthetic integrity."

And in a 1980 essay entitled "Some Propaganda for Propaganda" reprinted in *Get the Message?*, Lippard wrote, "'Quality' in art, like 'objectivity' and 'neutrality' belongs to them ['the ruling/corporate class']. The only way to combat the 'normal' taken-for-granted propaganda that surrounds us daily is to question their version of the truth as publicly and clearly as possible."

"She regards it [quality] as a residue of bourgeois formalism," says Hilton Kramer. "But, alas, there is such a thing as quality in art just as there is quality in human relationships. Even to want to abandon the concept of quality in art is to surrender to a certain kind of social barbarism."

"Of course there is such a thing as quality. Some things are better than others," counters Lucy Lippard. "But I do not think there is one single quality that people who are good at it can see and people who are not good at it can't see."

Lippard objects, then, to a standard of quality "handed down from above by the ruling class."

"One man's quality," she says,"is another woman's poison."

The achievement Lippard says she is most proud of is getting "information out and models for art making and living in the world out that are not those the establishment have laid very heavily on us." The "models" she refers to are, as she explains in the 1980 essay, "Sweeping Changes: The Contribution of Feminism to the Art of the 1970s," essentially techniques borrowed from "revolutionary socialist practice—techniques on which the Women's Movement itself is based: consciousness-raising, going around the circle with equal time for all speakers, and criticism/self-criticism.

"These models, I repeat, are not new ways of handling the picture plane, or new ways of rearranging space, or new ways of making figures, objects, or landscapes live; they are inclusive structures or social collages."

The collage metaphor, piecing bits and pieces

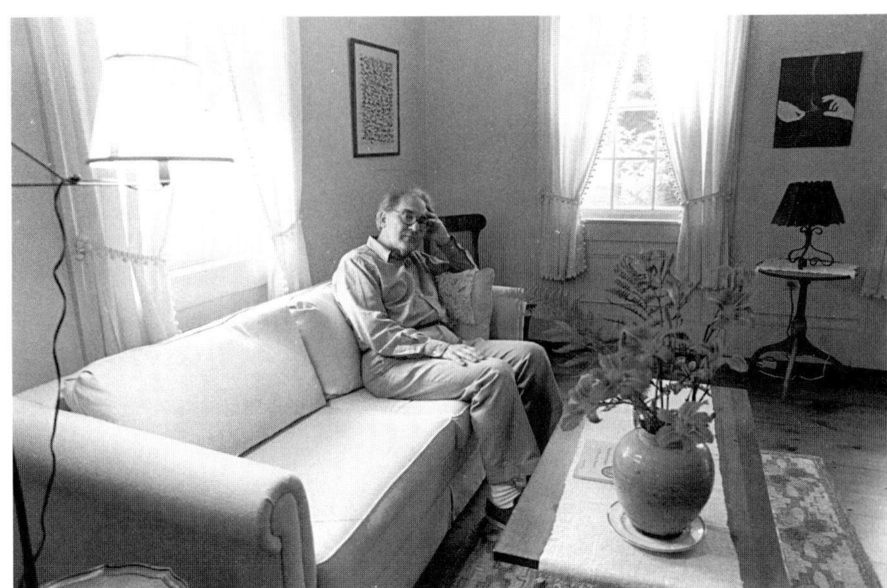

2. *Hilton Kramer purchased a renovated cape in Waldoboro as a summer home in 1987 after having vacationed in Maine ever since 1964. Photo by Christopher Ayres.*

of the culture together in hopes of creating a more beautiful whole, is central to Lippard's thought. Her basic thrust is, again, to include, to connect. For her, politics and art are inseparable.

In November, 1982, Lucy Lippard attended a celebration dinner following the opening of artist Louise Bourgeois' retrospective at the Museum of Modern Art. Because Bourgeois' work deals with female sexuality and because Lippard believes the Women's Movement helped bring Bourgeois to wider public attention, she proposed a toast to the artist from the Women's Movement. When she did, she heard a loud noise at the other end of the table. It was the sound of Hilton Kramer hissing.

"I did hiss that remark," admits Kramer, "because I have a great respect for Louise Bourgeois as an artist and I like her tremendously as a woman. I felt that it was a coarse and vulgar act for Lucy to attempt to reduce what was a high moment in Louise Bourgeois' artistic career to a political campaign that Louise supported but had not made any effort to identify her exhibition with."

Indeed, Hilton Kramer has been periodically hissing Lucy Lippard now for some 20 years. In 1986, in fact, reviewing Kramer's *The Revenge of the Philistines* in *The New Republic*, Robert Hughes makes reference to "the only critic Kramer detests more than Susan Sontag, the Marxist feminist activist Lucy Lippard."

Susan Sontag, of course, is the intellectual who articulated the notion of Camp, that modern attitude of irony which, in Kramer's words, "confers legitimacy on what it pretends to ridicule." Thus, in Kramer's view, Sontag opened the floodgates of popular culture which pollute high art today. But what did Lucy Lippard do to earn Kramer's enmity?

"Obviously," says Lippard, "he feels betrayed at some deep level."

"I think she betrayed her best self," says Kramer. "The reason for that, I think, has nothing to do with art. She underwent this political conversion and art just happened to be the ground she was standing on when the conversion took place."

The political conversion Kramer refers to occurred at the height of the counterculture movement when Lippard, who had been "raised a caring liberal," rediscovered her social conscience.

"It surfaced again on a jurying trip to Argentina in 1968," she writes in the preface to *Get the Message?*, "when I was forced to confront and reject corporate control and met for the first time artists who had committed themselves to militant social change, feeling that isolated art for art's sake had no place in a world so full of misery and injustice."

Fired with a new commitment to social change, Lippard's task became the integration of art and politics. Married at the time to white-on-white monochrome minimalist painter Robert Ryman, Lippard's first art political act was to co-curate "a beautiful minimalist show" at the Paula Cooper Gallery for the benefit of

Vietnam Veterans Against the War. As her political activity intensified, however, she began to pursue forms of artistic expression which not only benefitted her political interests but embodied them as well.

To Hilton Kramer, who prefers his art free of obvious political motive, Lucy Lippard must seem the embodiment of everything that is wrong with contemporary art.

"Lucy is an interesting case," says Kramer, "because she has deconstructed her own views over the course of time. She began as a big champion of minimalism. She wrote good books on [painter Ad] Reinhardt and [sculptor Eva] Hesse. She edited two excellent anthologies on Dada and surrealism. Then she suffered a political conversion. It was in the nature of that political conversion that the whole realm of aesthetic experience had to be eliminated."

"I have never disavowed any of that," objects Lippard. "I continue to write about abstract art. Dada and surrealism have always been my models for everything."

As Lippard points out, all of the books Kramer approves of were written after 1968 and one of her most popular, *Overlay*, is "a completely romantic book about art."

Still, asked who she considers to be the most important contemporary artists (a request she only reluctantly accedes to, since she does not like to think of art as a competition to determine who's best), Lippard names feminists, activists, and artists of color: Adrian Piper, Leon Golub, Nancy Spero, May Stevens, Hans Haacke, Houston Conwell, Amalia Mesa-Bains, Jerry Kearns (her partner in many art activities), Judy Chicago, Suzanne Lacy, and Juan Sanchez.

"These are artists," she says, "who are taking in the world the way it is and at the same time doing very personal art."

As an afterthought, Lippard adds the name of her former husband, Robert Ryman, to her list.

"I still adore his work, though it doesn't have anything to do with politics. He doesn't even know the world is out there."

Hilton Kramer has no reservations at all about naming his MVPs (most valuable painters).

"Right now," says Kramer, "probably the best living American painter is Richard Diebenkorn. Of the younger generation, there is Bill Jensen."

Kramer also values the landscapes of a lesser-known painter named Sonia Gechtoff and the abstract stain paintings of Helen Frankenthaler.

"I'm a great admirer of Helen Frankenthaler," Kramer says. "I think she's a marvelous painter now being underrated. I was astonished that her retrospective [currently at the Museum of Modern Art] was violently attacked by Kay Larson in *New York* and Peter Schjeldahl in *Seven Days*. I think they're really attacking her admirers, like Clement Greenberg and myself."

Most of the artists Lucy Lippard names operate outside or on the fringes of the mainstream art scene, whereas the artists Hilton Kramer nominates—Richard Diebenkorn and Helen Frankenthaler—are among the reigning princes and princesses of the art world. Yet one of the few things Lippard and Kramer seem to agree upon is that the contemporary art scene is not rich in talents and geniuses.

"I still go to about 20 galleries a week," says Lippard, "and I see an awful lot of empty art."

"I don't think this is a particularly wonderful period for painting," echoes Kramer. He, too, mentions seeing 20 shows a week, often without being moved to comment. "It's pretty grim not to see anything you even want to attack."

One of the developments in current American art that Kramer might be expected to attack and Lippard to applaud is the new respectability accorded openly political art in the art market. Back in 1980, Lippard observed, "There is a pervasive belief, in the United States at least, that art with political subject matter is automatically 'bad art.'" Today, message artists such as Jenny Holzer, Barbara Kruger, Sue Coe, Leon Golub, and Tim Rollins and KOS (Kids of Survival, a group of South Bronx schoolkids Rollins collaborates with) are bankable artists. Lippard, however, says most of what passes for political art in the market is sanitized—"veiled, ironic, and ambiguous."

"People say, 'Oh, we have political art. It's in all the museums,'" says Lippard. "But it's not political art. It doesn't name names. It neither alienates nor instigates."

And while Hilton Kramer rails against the liberal bias of the art culture, Lucy Lippard insists, "The right wing have owned the art world since I've been around. They own the context.

"The only person who really believes the left is powerful," Lippard says, "is Hilton Kramer."

"It amuses me to have Lucy say I'm the only person who thinks the left is powerful," counters Kramer. "Try getting a book published at Pantheon, Knopf, Viking, or Random House that is conservative in its outlook. You'll find it extremely difficult. Try getting a job teaching English at a college or university if you're known to have anti-liberal views. The whole academic culture is primarly a left-liberal culture. The media—from *The New York Times* to the *Maine Times*—is basically a left-liberal culture. The left can exert a tremendous influence on the cultural world and on the media, but the one thing they can't do is elect a president. That's because there is a real split between the common sense of the American voter and the privileged illusions of educated liberals."

Ironically, Hilton Kramer once regarded himself as an educated liberal. He now answers to the neo-conservative calling and subscribes to Irving Kristol's definition of a neo-conservative as "a liberal who has been mugged by reality."

"Basically, my views haven't changed since I thought of myself as being a liberal. What it meant to be a liberal in the '50s now constitutes being a neo-conservative," says Kramer. "You believe in advancement by merit. You believe in the laws of the land being colorblind. It's a basic tenet to be anti-totalitarian and to believe that democracy is the best political/social system under which to live. In the late '60s, when liberalism took a sharp turn to the left, embracing totalitarian regimes in place like North Vietnam, Cuba, and China, and the philosophy of civil rights deteriorated into the reverse discrimination of affirmative action, liberalism went left and I stayed in the same place."

In the February, 1989 issue of *The New Criterion*, Kramer delivered a ringing indictment of the arts and humanities as taught in U.S. colleges and universities in which he warned his conservative confreres against "the temptation to emulate our enemies in subordinating art to politics." Yet his own hectoring of the left and left-liberal institutions would seem to constitute politicking in and of itself.

"Why isn't my position as political as Lucy's?" asks Kramer. "Because I don't believe that all cultural phenomena are reducible to politics and Lucy does."

"Oh bullshit," responds Lippard in frustration. "I don't reduce everything to politics."

No, this is not a game Lucy Lippard wanted to play at all. She and Hilton Kramer have so few assumptions in common that the words "art" and "politics" mean all but different things to them.

So Hilton Kramer writes, "Art, as I wish to understand it—and this includes scholarship, too—must be defended and pursued and relished not for any political program it may be thought to serve but for what it is, in and of itself, as a source of spiritual and intellectual enlightenment, as a special form of pleasure and moral elevation, and as a spur to the highest reaches of human aspiration."

To which Lucy Lippard responds, "I would agree with all of that if you took out the little part about the political. I don't separate the political and the spiritual."

There is no neutral zone.

August 4, 1989

Reviews

4

Criticism

A Personal Note

As I understand it, the work of art is the search for meaning. No matter how sensual the means or how emotional the urge, the creative act is essentially a philosophical undertaking. Even the simplest imitation of nature by the making of marks or the making of shapes is a form of exploration, an attempt to apprehend the miracle we inhabit—our blue ball in black space, our bubble in time.

Where art cannot discover meaning, it can itself supply meaning for life. From the first primitive cave paintings through the highest celebrations of faith in the Renaissance to the desperate posturings of post-modernism, art has always been about the business of helping the human identify and locate Self in relation to the rest of the phenomenal world.

On a more social level, I hold the greatest value of art to be its insistence on upholding the individual over the mass, the one over the many, the particular over the general. Art is an elitist activity to the extent that it values most highly that which is unique, one-of-a-kind. Where most of the cultural forces at work in our lives—economics, politics, education, technology, media—mitigate toward social conformity and uniformity, great art maintains the integrity of the individual being and the individual act.

I subscribe, then, to artist/critic Fairfield Porter's dictum that art (though he was writing specifically of painting at the time) "is a way of expressing the connections between the infinity of the diverse elements that constitute the world of matters of fact, from which technology separates us in order to control it and control us."

We conspire in this culture to convince ourselves that certainty can be captured in the net of scientific rationality, but, ultimately, it cannot. The net is empty. Art, when it is good and strong and true, reminds us of this ineffable truth—that it is miraculous and mysterious beyond belief that we are here at all. The miracle is that we are; the mystery is that once we were not and soon will cease to be. Art marks our passing.

As a newspaper art critic, I realize that much of whatever value my writings may have falls into the category of boosterism. A critic in Maine, a state still developing an audience and a market for art, must function somewhat as a cheerleader and a shill for art—good art and good artists, certainly, but mostly for the value of art as a form of knowledge and of experience.

Essentially, I assume my words operate somewhere in the highly charged space between the audience and the work of art. As Arthur

Danto, philosopher and art critic, has pointed out, a good critic functions much like an actor, criticism being primarily an interpretative art.

"The space between the viewer and the work," writes Danto, "is filled with the impedimenta of ignorance, of bad theory and prejudice, and faulty perception. The critic, like the actor, must make this space transparent. Nothing could be a greater perversion of the critic's art than to clog this space with wrong theories or obscure prose, or to draw attention to the critic himself."

Of course, I like to think that as a critic I am being helpful, but I am sure I am often less than transparent, sometimes even just in the way. Having been invited (by editors, publishers, art dealers, and even a few artists) to insert myself into that space between the art and the audience, my major endeavor is always to make myself the best possible audience for an artist's work. I want to be the one person the artist can count on to look, look hard, take seriously, consider carefully, and respond honestly.

The function of criticism as I see and practice it is, first, to elevate the discourse on art above the level of taste. Everyone knows what he or she likes. But to achieve the higher level of appreciation, you must be able to understand the qualities and accomplishments of the good art you don't like.

Secondly, a good critic can, where relevant, help a viewer understand what a work of art means and how it seeks to achieve that meaning. The arrogance many people ascribe to the critic lies, of course, in the critic's presumption that he/she knows what a work of art means. All I can offer in my own defense is a decade of daily experience which tells me that artists whose works get praised thank the critic for his brilliant insights, while those who get panned think the critic is a fool.

Thirdly, the critic can, when and where possible, provide some historical and theoretical context for understanding what an artist is doing. One of my obvious shortcomings in this regard is the lack of a rigorous formal training in the history of art. Philip Isaacson, the Lewiston lawyer who is Maine's senior art critic, believes that the passionate amateur has an advantage over the schooled professional in that he/she is innocent of orthodoxies, has no allegiance other than to quality and authenticity. I'd like to think he's right.

The one thing I'm fairly sure I'm right about is the value of criticism as a written record in response to an artist's work. Nine years as a librarian and ten as a journalist have convinced me of the reference value of documentation. So I derive satisfaction from knowing that—thanks largely to the thankless labors of periodical indexers—the artists I have written about will not be entirely lost to recorded history should their art not secure for them the immortality they deserve. And it is in this modest spirit that I have selected a chronology of 60 reviews from among the nearly 500 I have written to preserve here in *Maine Art Now*.

Joseph Nicoletti

Joseph Nicoletti has done something very fine. He knows it. I know it. And you will know it too when you see his recent works at Barridoff Galleries. His studio self-portraits are undoubtedly the most powerful visual images I have ever seen exhibited in Maine. They are so powerful that for me they overpowered and diminished his very accomplished little landscapes, which hang about the balcony as if in attendance of the masterworks. The inconsistency between the disturbingly beautiful self-portraits, which are executed with such a subtle distortion of angle that the images seem to fall out of the picture plane, and the safe beauty of the landscapes, which seem to be charming travel notes, bothered me immediately. It continued to bother me for two weeks until I called Joseph Nicoletti and discussed it with him.

"One of my chief pleasures in painting is experimenting. I experiment a lot. I even accuse myself of inconsistency."

Clearly the artist knew what he was about. He knew what could be explained and what could not.

"I don't think you can expect as much out of a landscape as far as a multiplicity of layers. The reason I am a representational painter is that I like the multiplicity of layers and possibilities in a painting."

But what was the relationship of the landscapes to the self-portraits?

"I don't think I know that myself."

Nicoletti is a teacher on the faculty of Bowdoin College and I was going to indulge one of my pet peeves—artists and writers who teach—to explain the inconsistency, but that wouldn't have been fair. Joseph Nicoletti is acutely aware of the pitfalls of academia. It can make an artist lazy. Too comfortable. As Nicoletti sees it, it is a constant trade-off. Teaching provides security and time to work and with it goes a kind of freedom, but that freedom is the freedom of ease. What is missing in the academic equation is often a driving force—the compulsion to create in order to survive. Nicoletti knows this and guards against it.

"The danger in teaching is that you can end up believing that what you are saying is the

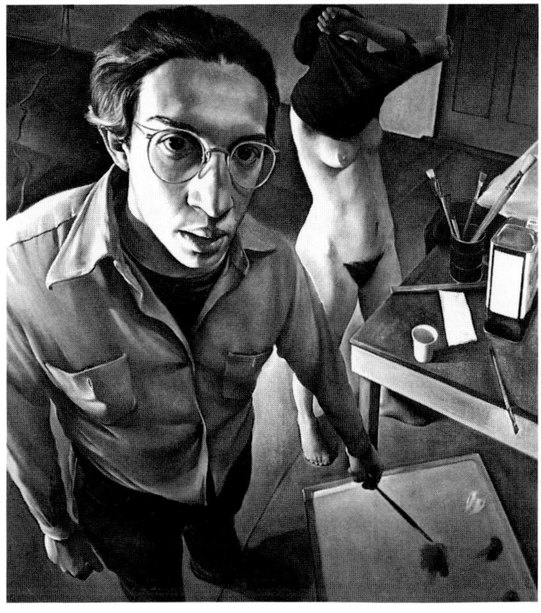

1. *Joseph Nicoletti,* Studio self-portrait, *1979. Oil. Courtesy of the University of Southern Maine Art Gallery.*

truth. Unfortunately in teaching you have to try to get at one medium through another, so you end up resorting to analogy and metaphor."

In defense of inconsistency, Nicoletti expressed his own pet peeve—exhibits that have a "forced consistency". "Consistency can become a marketing issue—producing a consistent product."

"I like painting that is annoying, paintings that are available to change." What he is talking about is good art. Good art has a life of its own. In order to produce good art the artist must ultimately deal with himself without holding back. Joseph Nicoletti knows that his self-portraits are premier performances and if he has held anything back, I can't imagine what it could be. It's all there on the canvas for the world to see—talent, intelligence, power and vision.

My only question is whether the level of intensity evidenced in Nicoletti's self-portraits can be sustained in any circumstances. Probably not comfortably. Perhaps that explains the inconsistency I sensed. Perhaps not.

Nicoletti's one-man show will hang at Barridoff until the end of May.

May 18, 1979

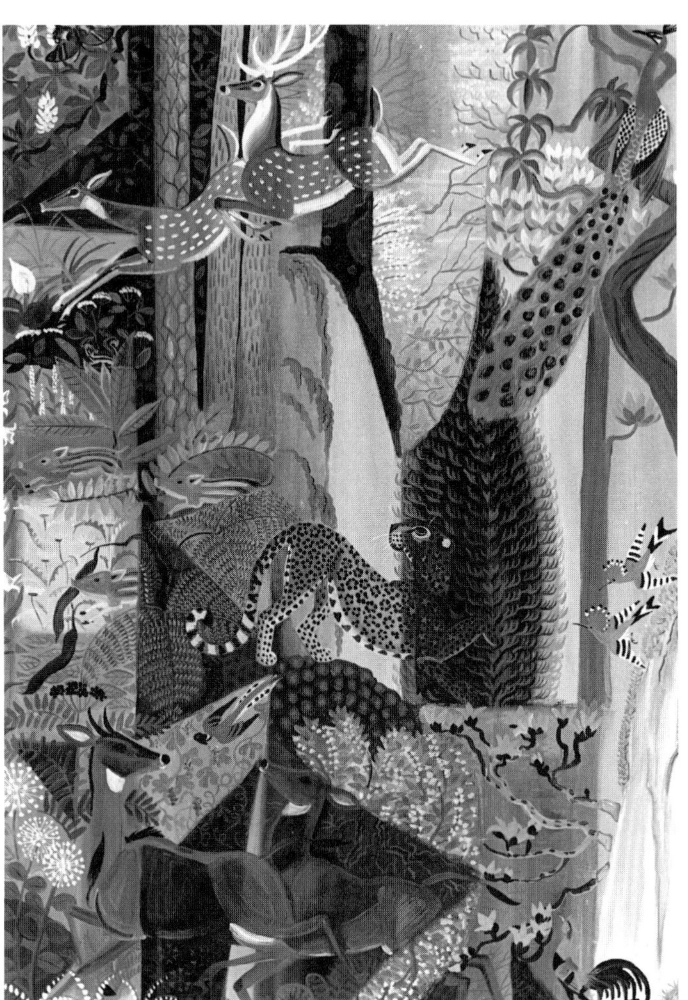

1. *Dahlov Ipcar,* Hill Forest of Kumaon, *1976. Oil. Courtesy of Charles Ipcar.*

Dahlov Ipcar

The enchantment of childhood was not wasted on Dahlov Ipcar. The daughter of artists William and Marguerite Zorach, Ipcar mines the depths of the fanciful and the feral in populating her fantastic landscapes with a menagerie of fabulous beasts. The jungle, the barnyard and the world of myth serve as settings for vivid, stylized oils that are sophisticated enough to appeal to adults, yet ingenuous enough to delight a child. In addition to being a painter and sculptor of distinction, she is also the author and illustrator of thirty children's books.

The William A. Farnsworth Library and Art Museum in Rockland has mounted a showing of Ipcar's recent paintings and sculpture which will hang until March 2, 1980. Though predominantly new works, the show includes a selection of pieces from 1969 to the present. Twenty-six oils and fourteen soft sculptures give the viewer both insight and perspective on her wonderfully imaginative work.

Ipcar's paintings share the enchanting flatness of fine tapestries and have the flavor of fable and allegory. They are ingenuous, but not naive. Elegant, colorful, lush jungle and wilderness settings are carefully designed around visions of wildlife. In *Sumatra Jungle*, for instance, a floral and foliated background comes alive with wildebeest, monkeys, a panther, a lizard, peacocks and tapirs. The style is deceptively two-dimensional, giving the paintings a look of flatness and exploded perspective, but in many cases this flatness is a result of the startling prismatic effect Ipcar achieves by fragmenting light and colors into a patchwork of surface areas.

In *October Farm Garden*, she has employed a friezework technique to present horizontal bands of animals. The effect is one of textile design, almost folk art, but never primitive.

Dahlov Ipcar is said by some to have invented "soft" sculpture, and the gay fabric animals in the show are as impressive for their workmanship as for their conception and modeling.

Lest anyone think them merely "stuffed animals," it can be noted that her sculpture—bulls, pigs, giraffe, birds, fish, jack rabbit—all achieve a remarkable animation. They are alert and lively. Their poses are active and the delicacy with which they stand upon their mountings is superb.

Dahlov Ipcar's work is an imagined wilderness tamed by artistic vision. Interestingly, the one painting which shows a human form, *Adam Naming The Beasts*, depicts a naked man who blanches in comparison to the vividness of the animal life. Man does not fit well in her natural panorama.

If Ipcar has stylistic debts they might be to the noble savagery of Gauguin or the exacting primitivism of Henri Rousseau. But in her works, as with dreams and myths, what is important is not what they mean, but what they are.

January 1980

George Delyra

George Delyra is back. After a prolonged absence from public view, George Delyra has finally delivered up a feast of new paintings that show him once again to be a technical master and a wizard of pure imagination. Delyra is a realist, but his brand of realism is more like surrealism without the distortions and absurdities. My dictionary says that surreal means "having the intense, irrational reality of a dream." George Delyra's acrylics and gouaches have an intense reality, but it is the reality of imagination. It is not irrational; rationality seems simply to have been numbed for the moment, as in a fever.

The work for which Delyra was best known before he stopped painting for a few years was characterized by ominous, anonymous humans or human forms peopling stark and obscure landscapes that, if they were not hopeless, were at best bleak. His new paintings have a different quality of light to them, a colorfulness and compositional variety, but his figures remain enigmatic. Where once they often had no eyes at all but merely shadows, now they have eyes fixed in blank stares or gazing raptly, distractedly off canvas. The change in mood is subtle but distinctive.

Passing Through is one of the finest new paintings. A red-headed young man in aqua jacket and purple tie stares over his right shoulder through an opening where a portion of an airplane's red and white tail can be seen. Behind him, to his left, a woman stands at a bar. The exterior shaping of the composition suggests an airplane window with its rounded corners. When we travel, we abandon ourselves. We are anonymous, vulnerable. Delyra's characters—for that is what they are—are real fictions. They are not representations or imitations of reality; they are wholly created and imagined fictions. They suggest Magritte without the trickery.

The Other Side of the Mountain depicts a lone bureaucratic or executive figure (many of Delyra's characters suggest bureaucrats in their suitcoats and ties and in their etherized, Kafkaesque expressions) standing before a dark range of mountains. A stylized wall and lawn run immediately behind. The bald, authoritative figure has a curious look in his eyes. Unlike earlier Delyra creations, the effect here is not sinister; it is one of relief.

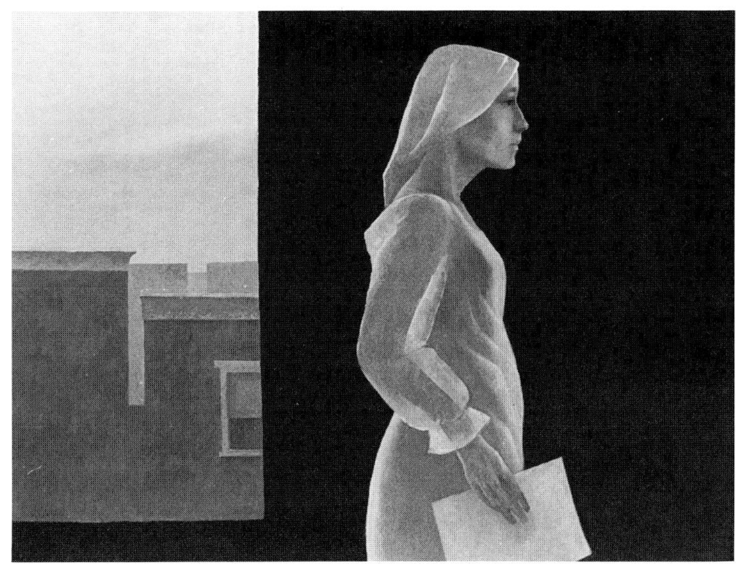

1. *George Delyra,* Woman in White. *Oil. Courtesy of the Frost Gully Gallery.*

One of the most beautiful and unearthly (meaning divine) paintings in the show was *Spring Comes To a Desolate City*. An ethereal female in loose white gown shaded with blues stands in the center of a horizontal canvas. Behind her is a wall composed of bands of modulated purples. To either side are windows looking out over an empty cityscape done in pastels. The design, the colors, and the execution are riveting.

George Delyra paints with a precise, dabbling stroke, building up brilliant textures out of flecks of color. He paints very, very slowly, producing perhaps ten paintings of modest size in a year. For all the painstaking deliberation, his works have a supple ease.

Delyra's superb new paintings, along with representative older works, were on view at the Frost Gully Gallery as well as in a show at the ADA Gallery in Hanover, New Hampshire.

December 1980

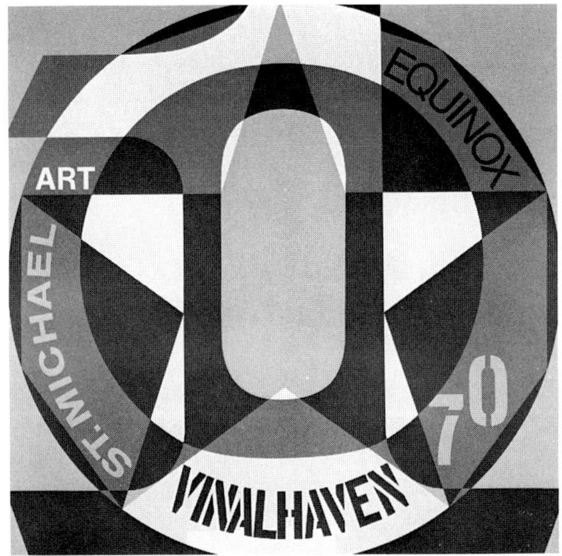

1. *Robert Indiana,* Decade, Vinalhaven Suite, No. One. *Serigraph. Courtesy of the Colby College Museum of Art.*

Robert Indiana

Robert Indiana's campaign of artistic self-advertisement has recently added a Maine chapter with the publication of his *Decade: Autoportraits, Vinalhaven Suite*, a series of ten 26 3/4-by-26 3/4 silkscreen logos now on display at the Colby College Art Museum. The prints are visually handsome and esthetically problematic—nothing new for Indiana.

Robert Indiana was born Robert Clark in 1928 in New Castle, Indiana. As an artist he discarded his family name and took the name of his home state in a self-promoting, but oddly anonymous, move which has parallels in his art. As Robert Indiana he became one of the stars of the Pop art scene in the 1960s and early 1970s on the strength of his hard-edged, even commercial, designs. The most famous of his images are his LOVE logos which became ubiquitous in the seventies, appearing first as a painting and quickly proliferating as print, sculpture and 330,000,000 eight-cent postage stamps.

In 1978 Indiana moved permanently to the former Odd Fellows building, Star of Hope, on Vinalhaven in Penobscot Bay. The suite he has designed to commemorate his decade of summer and year-round residence in Maine is a kind of verbal and visual shorthand, combining impersonal geometry (a star within a decahedron within a circle within a square overlaid with numerals) with personal references to people and places that have figured in his life. All are done in the classic Indiana style of bright primary colors with sign motifs. The prints have a distinctly nautical look, a flotilla of gay lifesavers cast on the public seas from a floating circus.

Handsome. Decorative. But is it art? Critics have been asking this question of Indiana's work from the very beginning. And, of course, it is art, but art which presents distinct problems.

The first problem that has to be overcome is the slickness. Indiana's designs have the commercial impersonality of corporate logos. The problem is only compounded by the obvious personal references, and Indiana has obligingly supplied an explanation for the verbal symbols he employs in the suite. "Vinalhaven" is obvious, as is "70" (for 1970) in the first print, which is done in black and white and grey. "ART" is self-explanatory, but "ST. MICHAEL" and "EQUINOX" are not.

"On a trip to visit the composer Virgil Thomson in New Hampshire I saw Mount Equinox for the first time with a friend named Michael," Indiana explains in his notes to the series. Simple enough, but the question arises whether the audience should have to read an explanation of a visual experience. Can the work stand on its own with full meaning or must it be propped up verbally? This is essentially Tom Wolfe's objection to much of modern art in his iconoclastic *The Painted Word.*

Well, Indiana's autobiographical signs do stand on their own, but not at full value without verbal clues. And, of course, his use of lettering and numerals has ample historic precedent in art. His Vinalhaven suite calls to mind the numerical paintings of Marsden Hartley from his pre-World War I Berlin days. Numerals as personal symbols publicly shared. And his use of signage finds precedent in Stuart Davis's social abstractions. Indiana has done a numeral series before (a series hangs behind the reception desk at the Colby gallery), but not with the overt personal references.

Robert Indiana is a major American talent, and perhaps it is just his ability to make a manufactured, consumer style uniquely and recognizably his own that accounts both for his importance and the Americanness of his art.

May 22, 1981

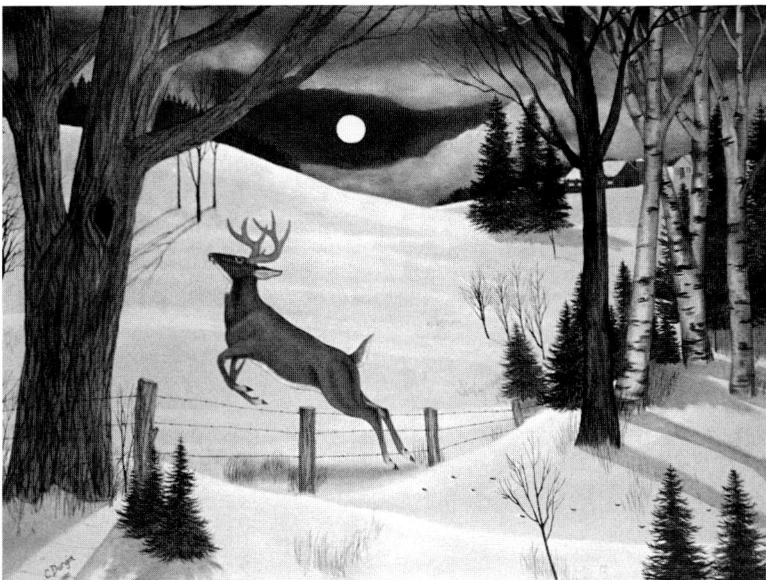

1. *Carol Durgin,* Moonlight Flight, *1980. Oil. Courtesy of the artist.*

1981 Maine Biennial

The 1981 All Maine Biennial looks like it was mugged by a sidewalk art festival. How else to explain the hanging of trite paintings of lighthouses, fishing boats, cowboys, outdated and tasteless psychedelics and the awarding of a first prize to a romantic little oil of a deer jumping a fence by moonlight, presented in a plastic, imitation wood frame?

The inclusion and rewarding of overtly amateurish works is a great disservice both to more serious visual artists and to the viewing public, but what is most unfair is the position in which it puts amateurs—holding them up to ridicule by elevating unpretentious art to a status it does not deserve.

The second Biennial is not a major exhibition of new art, emerging art or established talent. More than anything else, it looks like a show which was not juried at all. Of course, the show was juried—by Texas sculptor James Surls, California artist Vija Clemins, and Rhode Island publisher Bruce Helander.

In trying to discover why the '81 Biennial is the major disappointment (disaster?) that it is, I came to the conclusion that the judges were just too sophisticated for their own good and actually overestimated the value of some amateur art, mistaking the stiffness of underdeveloped skills for important naive folk art. There is a national vogue for "bad" or "dumb" art—art which is intentionally vulgar and unsophisticated—and it seemed a real possibility that the jury read "intention" where they should have read "accident."

I had the opportunity to speak with jurist Vija Clemins in Skowhegan recently and she expressed genuine surprise that the show should cause any controversy. The jury's choices, she assured me, were made in deliberate good faith. In self-defense, however, she did say that the jury found very little challenging art to choose from.

"You'd have to have seen the whole show (meaning the over 700 submitted works) to understand our choices," she said.

Asked specifically about the first prize awarded to Carol Durgin's kitschy deer painting, *Moonlight Flight*, Vija Clemins insisted that all three jurors saw "something magical" in it. She used words like "genuine," "honest" and "pure" to describe it.

The 1979 Biennial at Bowdoin College was criticized for not including artists on the jury. In light of how the '81 Biennial has turned out, it has been suggested in some quarters that perhaps artists don't make good judges after all. But if Vija Clemins is right and there is something magical, honest, and genuine to be seen in Maine genre art, then perhaps there is another possibility which ought to be considered. That possibility is that "serious" Maine artists (and critics as well) suffer from a conditioned response which immediately dismisses pictures of lighthouses and fishing boats. In any case, I must confess to being blind to what the judges saw in many of their choices.

In 1979 the Biennial consisted of 167 works by 141 artists and was considered too crowded. This year there are 149 works by 149 artists with only 39 repeaters. Because of the limited space in the Gorham campus Art Gallery, the show has been divided between the main gallery and Center Gallery in the university's dining center. The smaller Center Gallery exhibition consists mostly of photographs and works on paper, and, on the whole, provides more visual consistency than the main exhibition.

The first prize of $500 was split between Carol Durgin's *Moonlight Flight*, the controversial fence-jumping deer, and another daring choice, Julie Coxe's untitled SX-70 *trompe d'oeil* snapshot of a figure in tropical shirt seated against lush foliage. The photograph was included in last spring's Portland School of Art Senior Show (I counted at least 15 Portland School of Art-affiliated artists in the Biennial).

The award of a one-person exhibition at the University of Southern Maine gallery was made to J. Thomas R. Higgins on the basis of his large oil on linen, *Autumn Pond*, a painterly landscape which Vija Clemins said struck the jurors as one of the few paintings in which the artist was "really looking." A conservative choice, but a reasonable one given the fact that Higgins is probably one of few artists in the show with enough quality work to fill a major gallery.

Thomas Nadeau was designated the artist to provide visual continuity between the '81 Biennial and the '83 Biennial. Nadeau's *C Series—Parable of the Cave* is a heavily symbolic, tightly composed oil which uses Plato's famous allegory to question both the nature of reality and of perception.

The works of eight other artists were singled out for honorable mention.

Second-guessing the judges, I found Judy Valentine's brutal collage, *Velocity*, to be the single most compelling work in the show. Large, nasty and raw, stuck through with T-pins, protruding nails and contained within a border of menacing tacks, Valentine's antithetically beautiful image seemed to be elbowing aside all of the prettiness in the room to get at a vision beyond simple appearances.

I would also note Henry Nigl's huge rhoplex/acrylic monochrome, *No Song for Butter*, which features a two-inch paintbrush embedded in the ground. It is a post-modernist exploration of smooth and melting color and texture.

Along with Rick Randolph's outlandish coffee table, John A. Sabasteanaski's *Sled*, a clear-glass replica of a Flexible Flyer, was one of the most intriguing objects in the show. The transparent sled has a kind of memorial beauty to it, but it's a shame that it wasn't more sturdily constructed. A number of glued joints had already come apart the second time we saw it, and I had to wonder whether it would survive until September 18 when the show closes.

Of the 24 photographs submitted this year, I found C.C. Church's *Young Woman* to be the most refined. The image of a nude woman (sheepishly biting her lip) posed next to a plaster statue of a nude has that stunning clarity one gets from a view camera, and a kind of classical beauty borrowed from antiquity.

The 1981 All Maine Biennial catalogue provides statements by each of the jurors, but they are singularly unhelpful, running mostly to pleasantries and generalizations. Sculptor James Surls does say, however, that he would have preferred spending his three days in Maine hanging all of the submitted works "woven together to make the spiritual cloth of our society. Then we could come look, dance all night, and when the sun came up we could look the other way and start again."

So look away and start again. The 1981 Biennial was a sincere and dedicated effort on the part of the organizers, particularly director Juris Ubans, to provide an open, democratic forum for exploring what art in Maine is. The lesson here is that art is not a democratic activity. Almost any single, discerning individual could have selected a more meaningful exhibition. The case has been made, it seems to me, for trying something other than a juried exhibition in 1983.

If the Biennial is to survive as an important exhibition of either the best or the new, someone will have to find the courage to sanction either a curated show or an invitational show. Otherwise, James Surls's suggestion starts to make real sense. Just open the doors every two years and hang everything in sight.

July 24, 1981

William Kienbusch

I wish now that I had never used the word "exciting" before so that I might apply it fresh and undiluted to the works of William Kienbusch. For not only should Colby College's Kienbusch retrospective (through October 11) provide most viewers with an exciting visual experience, excitement itself is at the heart of the man's art. Kienbusch, a long-time summer resident of Great Cranberry Island who died last year at age 65, is represented at Colby's Jette Gallery by 43 uniformly and consistently excellent works which add up to the most satisfying exhibition in Maine so far this year.

William Kienbusch worked primarily in casein on paper, and with few exceptions his poetic abstractions begin with a response to landscape and environment. What is everywhere apparent in this exhibition is that Kienbusch saw with an excited eye and painted with an excited hand. His paintings seem to be happening right before your eyes, which is the best definition of "moment" in art I can think of. His works have that immediacy which speaks of retinal nerves newly stimulated.

If I dared, I would limit my written response to Kienbusch's art to three words of my own choosing—excitement, immediacy, nerve—and to printing a poem by Rainer Maria Rilke entitled "The Panther." For as I moved from one Kienbusch painting to another, I began to think of the artist as Rilke's caged beast. In his poem, Rilke sympathetically shares the great cat's enforced solitude and isolation, imagining the panther as "dazed" and "stunned," "a great will" encircled by bars.

"But there are times," Rilke tells us, "the pupils of his eyes / Dilate, the strong limbs stand alert, apart, / Tense with the flood of visions that arise / Only to sink and die within his heart." And so Kienbusch's paintings seemed to me to be of this kind, "Tense with the flood of visions," alert to recollections of a primal power and wildness. But Kienbusch, being both human and an artist, did not have to suffer the death of such visions in his private heart; he could share them visually.

As sentient beings we have all been struck from time to time by those acute and fleeting perceptions of specific and often ineffable beauty and awe, visions of transcendence and oneness in nature. Some artists attempt to recapture "an impression of" such moments by painstakingly recreating the scene which produced the emotion. Others, like William Kienbusch, attempt to "respond to" such moments by abstracting the dynamic quality of the vision. It is sad, then, that all too often the living value of art gets lost in dense, esoteric discussions of aesthetic issues peripheral to the experience and of interest only to other artists. Kienbusch, however, despite his abstraction, is never far from the experience. He was not an academic painter, nor a decorative painter, but a profoundly human one.

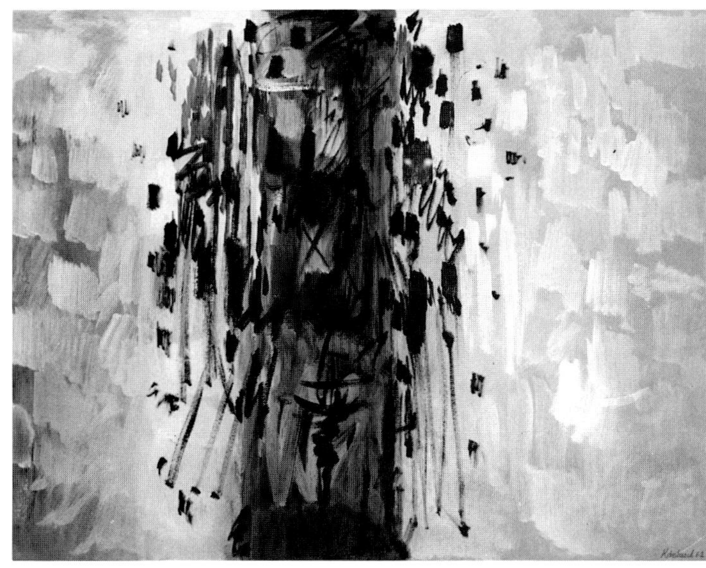

1. *William Kienbusch,* Sound of the Gong Buoy, *1962. Casein. Courtesy of the Colby College Museum of Art. Photo by Geoffrey Clements.*

Abstract Expressionism, a cerebral response to emotional stimuli, is a curiously American habit of mind inherited from a northern European tradition—Franz Kline, Vassily Kandinsky, Hans Hofmann, Willem De Kooning—and passed along to Kienbusch by Arthur Dove, Marsden Hartley and John Marin. Kienbusch seems to have inherited Hartley's eye for structure and Marin's dashing brushwork, both of which come together in works like *Autumn Island Stillscape #2*, freely adapted from Hartley's *Sea Window, New England.* Flame red-orange curtains bracket a window view of the sea, but where Hartley had placed a highly modeled and outlined arrangement of fruit, Kienbusch has substituted a riot of colorful forms.

Although there is often as much color in Kienbusch as the eye can stand, his preferred palette was a cautious, almost reverential mixture of blacks, whites, greys and blues. Works such as *The Edge of the Spruce*; *The Pass, Winter, Colorado*; and *The Sound of the Gong Buoy* show him working his magic within these self-imposed limitations.

Kienbusch was at the height of his powers in the 1960s, and in these works you are most likely to find his colors aflame. In the early works of the late forties and early fifties—*Dirigo Island* is a good example of this—you find him working in somber black and autumnal gold, deriving his brand of abstraction from a diagrammatic approach to realism such as one associates with Paul Klee.

In the late paintings of the mid-seventies, before his health began to fail, he had again returned to a more ordered and premeditated approach to composition. Works like *The Island in the Spruce* and *From the Porch, Cape Split #3* demonstrate the sublime rationality of the later works.

Linked as they are, beginning to end, by the return of decorum and geometry, Kienbusch's life work assumes the aspect of a closed circle, a circle which the gallery layout and chronological arrangement reinforce. In view of the power he generated within this circle, William Kienbusch's paintings form both his aesthetic cage and his spiritual key to escape.

"His weary glance, from passing by the bars, / Has grown into a dazed and vacant stare; / It seems to him there are a thousand bars / And out beyond those bars the empty air."

August 28, 1981

The Camden Hills Site Show

The alteration and transformation of the environment, both accidentally and intentionally, has always been a by-product of life on earth. No creature fails to leave its mark in passing, from the worm's imperceptible hole in the ground to the spruce budworm's defoliation of entire forests. Man, however, goes about this business of alteration and transformation with particular ardor.

Currently at Camden Hills State Park, Vision Publications and the Union of Maine Visual Artists are staging a unique art exhibition, *The Camden Hills Site Show*, comprised of installations, environmental art, earthworks and site-specific pieces which deal directly with man's physical experience of place. The results run from controversial to sublime but are never less than thought-provoking.

Site-specific art, developed on the spot and because of the spot, is late in coming to Maine, perhaps because of the state's natural conservatism. Works of this kind have already found a permanent place in art history from Robert Smithson's paradigmatic *Spiral Jetty* in the Great Salt Lake to Walter De Maria's cosmic *Lightning Field* in New Mexico. The former is a bulldozed curl of rocks and earth projecting into the lake; the latter is 400 steel rods arranged in a one-mile-by-one-kilometer rectangle on the desert floor. And there is, of course, the enigmatic Christo's 24.5 mile-long *Running Fence*, which has to be one of the major artistic statements of this or any other age. But while none of the Camden pieces is as grand either in concept or execution as its progenitors, each nonetheless serves the same function, altering our perception both of the landscape and of what art can be.

The most conservative of the Camden site-specific works might be Natasha Mayers's simple, associative *Snake Roots*, in which the artist has transformed a system of exposed roots in a pine grove into brightly colored snakes. Henry Nigl (Richard Leeman) also works close to the classical concerns of art in his *Dew Laps Night into Day*, creating the illusion of ground water on the forest floor with camouflaged sheets of aluminum.

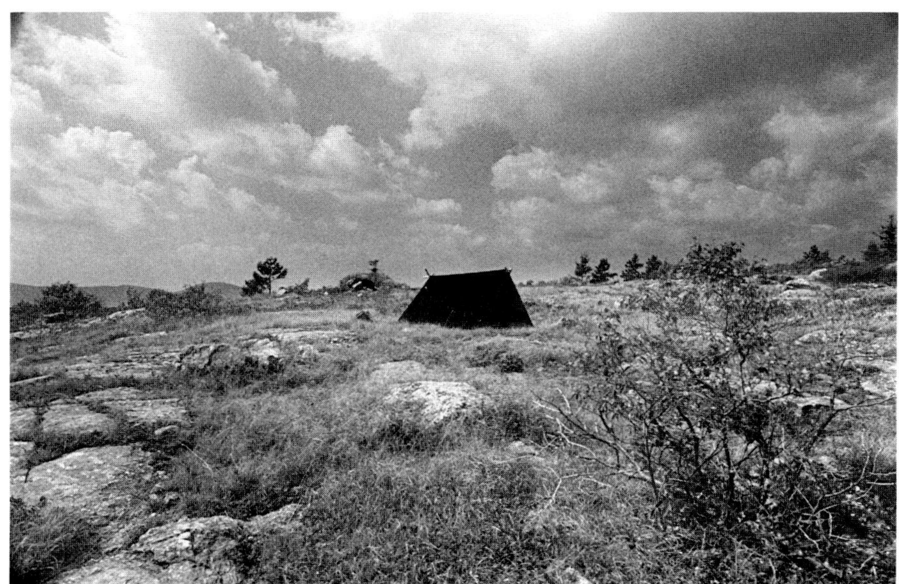

1. *Leslie Bowman,* Black Velvet Tent, *1981. Velvet, wooden dowels and rawhide thongs. Photo by David N. Hingston.*

In most cases the works at Camden do not reject the notion of easel art, but simply extend the possibilities and context of studio art. What most site-specific art does reject, however, is the traditional practice of marketing art works. Art in the environment is more fact and less product (merchandise) than art in the gallery.

Vision editor Darrah Cole supplied perhaps the quintessential earthwork in *Mark to Mark*, a 60-foot line created by removing stones from the shore out into the water toward Mark Island in Penobscot Bay. Cole's mark (and the making of marks is what all two-dimensional art is about) "indicates" the island. Within hours of its creation, the line had already begun to decompose, erased by the force of tides. A most benign gesture.

The most controversial work in the show (and like Cole's, very close to traditional drawing) is Bill Coyne's huge, white felt handprint pinned on the face of the Mt. Megunticook Ocean Overlook. Local residents feared that it was painted on, the work of vandals. All of the Camden installations are designed to be removed after the October 4 closing of the show, but Coyne's hand does point up the relationship of art to vandalism, cave painting to subway graffiti; all public art being in some way a defacement. The same point is made by Wally Warren's crushed and painted cans nailed to cedar stakes which serve as markers for each installation. Warren's art is borderline litter: beautiful, but disposable, like so much else in a consumer society.

Perhaps the most unnatural work in the show is Leslie Bowman's *Black Velvet Tent* on the top of Mt. Battie. Bowman, the admissions director at the Portland School of Art, has fashioned a luridly black pup tent out of velvet, wooden dowels and rawhide thongs. Seen from the Mt. Battie observation tower, it seems almost to be a negative space. Up close it is an incredibly erotic venue.

The piece which comes closest to the very definition of site-specific is Pat and Tony Owen's *No Boundaries*, a bright red door and a bright red window frame installed on top of Mt. Battie. The door gives entrance to a ledge clearing and the window dramatically "frames" a view of neighboring hillsides. The door and window determine a very particular (specific) point of view.

Ideally, site-specific works are anonymous and work their intrigue best when encountered by chance. This is the strength of David Brooks' *Stone Sun Dial* constructed atop Mt. Megunticook. Brooks is a dedicated environmental artist, and even viewers who have gone looking for his sun dial have failed to locate it after the one-hour hike.

The cumulative effect of viewing the Camden Site Show is that the viewer begins to see the hand of man on the landscape anew. Highway cuts, power lines, cultivated fields, stone walls and buildings all take on the aspect of art, man's doodling on the landscape. It is a simple, but important heightening of awareness which is at the very heart of art making.

September 4, 1981

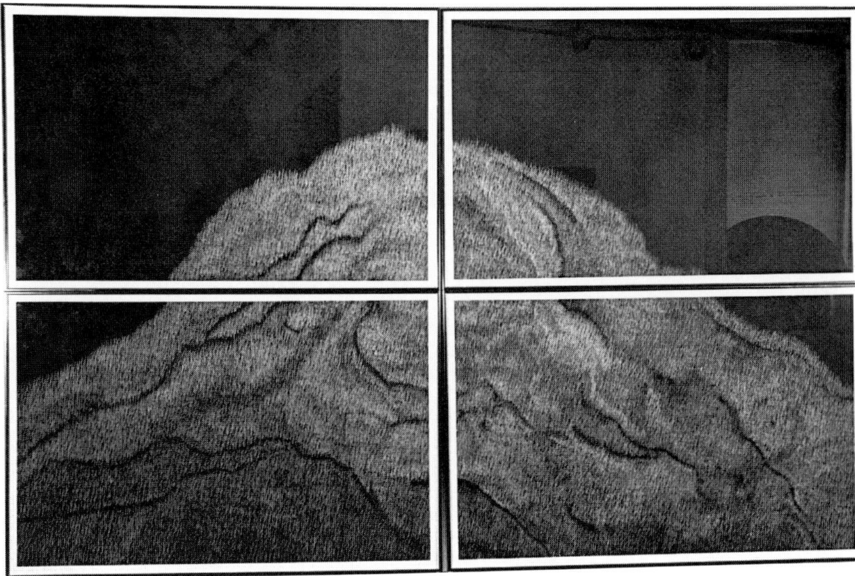

1. *Patt Franklin,* Night Escapes IX. *Pastel. Photo by Christopher Ayres.*

Contemporary Drawings from Nature and Artists' Selections from the Joan Whitney Payson Collection

With *Contemporary Drawings from Nature and Artists' Selections from the Joan Whitney Payson Collection* (pause for breath), Judy Sobol of the Payson Gallery at Westbrook College has taken a refreshing approach to curating an exhibition. From solicited submissions, Sobol has selected eight artists to 1) show their drawings, 2) select a masterwork from the gallery collection to hang with their drawings, and 3) contribute a statement explaining the affinities between the works they have created and the works they have chosen. The result is a supremely intelligent and instructive show in which the idea and the company of great masters tend to elevate the contemporary works above what they might achieve on their own.

Looking for the perceived connections between contemporary drawings and masterpieces has a way of deflecting the viewer's attention from the works at hand, but trying to see what and how the artists see ultimately adds to the experience. Not surprisingly, the connections the artists make tend to be heavily technical, many artists having a disconcerting tendency to be seduced by materials, process, and technique to the detriment of purpose.

Shannon McArthur, for example, shows three multiple charcoal drawings, strong formal field renderings that look like aerial survey maps, in connection with Degas' *La Leçon de Danse*. In her statement she writes of responding to Degas' ballerinas as "old friends," but in enumerating her responses she lists Degas' diagonals, muted colors, use of space, and sense of impending movement. Her initial response is social, but her articulated responses are all internal to the art.

Christopher Willard, a recent graduate of Portland School of Art (you would know by his drawings even if you weren't told), also chose to show his eight colorful natural abstract pastels with the Degas dancers. "Not because of the literary quality," Willard writes, "but because of structural aspects." Willard, too, responds to line, space, and color, rather than subject matter, spirit, or expressed concern.

In some cases the visual connection seems tenuous at best, as between Antionette Browning Jackman's illustrations and Maurice Prendergast's watercolor, *Rhododendrons, Boston Public Garden*. Jackman feels an affinity for Prendergast's "exquisite control" of color, composition, content, and passion, and her own drawings, the best being strong linear renderings of cornstalks, a dead mouse, and rotted tomatoes, are controlled to the point of being stylized. But the Prendergast lives in its sense of human and natural society, where Jackman's drawings are skillful still-life autopsies.

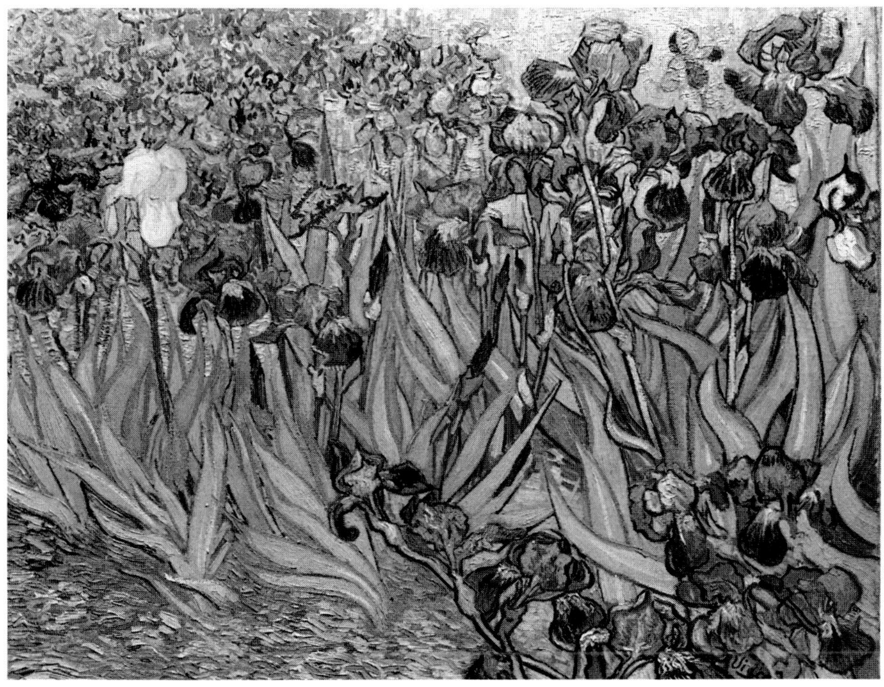

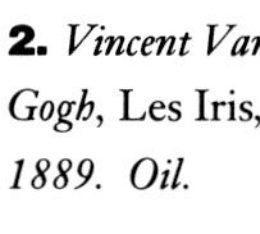

2. *Vincent Van Gogh*, Les Iris, *1889. Oil.*

The most obvious congruence of form, attitude, and materials is between Michael's Walek's four large pastel landscapes and the Whistler pastel, *Venice at Sunset*. Both artists work to achieve romance using color as light.

But if the Walek display is the most obvious, Patt Franklin's is the most convincing and powerful. Franklin shows her dramatic pastel *Night Escapes IX*, four individually framed quadrants which form a domed mountain of the imagination, with Van Gogh's *Les Iris*, arguably the most beautiful painting in Maine. An unmistakable shock of recognition exists between Franklin's turbulent drawing on midnight-blue paper and Van Gogh's tortuous flowers. The shock is one beyond art; it is the shock born of expressed and shared pain.

As Franklin writes, "He (Van Gogh) speaks about his life and the risk-taking that causes so much pain." Here, at last, we feel some real emotional investment in art. The Van Gogh is as fresh and vibrant as if it had been painted yesterday, and Franklin's drawing pulsates in response.

Elizabeth Knox's *Mt. St. Helens Series: Dreams and Ruminations* draws on an isolated natural event in the same way Winslow Homer's *The Backrush* does, but there is a telling difference. Both artists seek dynamism, but Knox, working from photographs, achieves a highly mediated response, while Homer, working from experience, achieves moment. There is the suspicion that Knox misreads Homer's painting when she writes of his wave's "crushing caress" and "dashing against rocks." The backrush is not a moment of impact, but of withdrawal and dissipation. The lesson seems to be that to succeed with "drawings from nature," an artist first must go to nature.

Gina Werfel's six black and white landscapes, bold and blunt, are teamed with Soutine's pastoral gaggle of geese, *Paysage*. The sympathy as Werfel sees it is rooted in "the transformation of feeling into form."

Donald Lent's anatomical renderings of trees are associated with Monet's *Springtime in Argentueil*. Lent writes of drawing and painting as records of physical action, but his drawings come off as a static second to Monet's lively grove. Unfair, perhaps, but the comparison is, after all, invited.

May 7, 1982

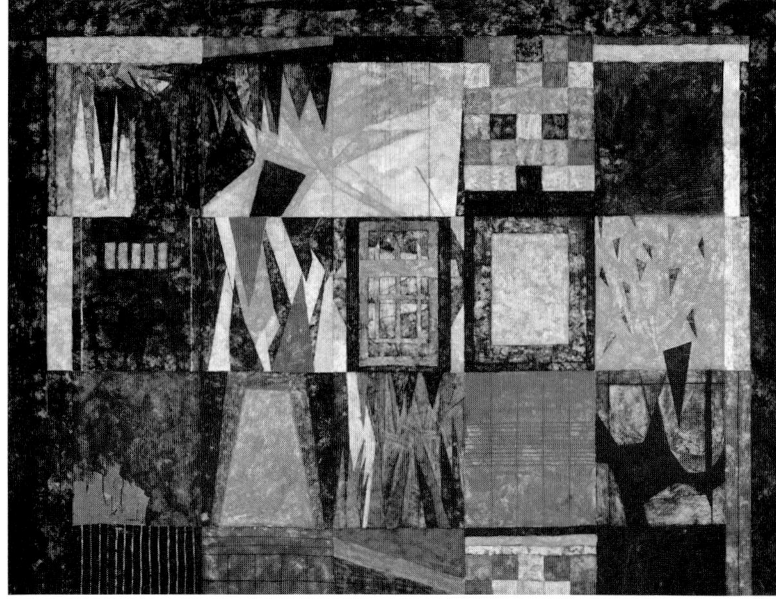

1. *Abby Shahn,* El Salvador. *Egg tempera. Courtesy of Hobe Sound Galleries North.*

Abby Shahn and Natasha Mayers

The naked eye can discern at least four magnitudes of art. Art in the first (and by far the most common) magnitude involves only what everyone sees. Art of the second magnitude concerns what the artist sees. Rarer still is art of the third magnitude, which lets one see not only what the artist sees, but what the artist thinks and feels as well. Abby Shahn and Natasha Mayers are artists of this third magnitude, which means that they are at but one remove from the fourth and highest magnitude where art actually changes the way we think and see. The way to the fourth magnitude is one of ever-increasing purification and simplification, and there are indications that both artists are on the right path.

Abby Shahn and Natasha Mayers have a great deal in common. To begin with, they are good friends. But they are also forceful women, committed artists, members of the Union of Maine Visual Artists, and out-of-staters who have chosen to live and work in rural Maine. Abby Shahn is from South Solon; Natasha Mayers from North Whitefield. Through July 9, both women are showing their recent works at Barridoff Galleries.

The similarities end in the gallery. For while both artists employ art as a way of understanding the world, they do so in distinctly different manners. Abby Shahn might be called an expansionist since, through her art, she merges self with the larger world of history and culture. Natasha Mayers, on the other hand, is an intimist seeking to extract universal significance from the specific, thereby reducing the phenomenal world to personally manageable visual units.

Abby Shahn's tempera paintings are characterized by the use of luminous color arrayed in decorative patterns—woven bands, serpentines, interlacing fretwork. The masterwork of her Barridoff exhibit, *Mamma Occlo*, looks as if it belongs behind an altar, and draws its sense of visual order from Shahn's reading of Inca civilization. Mamma Occlo names the feminine principle of creation identified with the moon and things lunar. The painting is a huge T-construction made up of 14 painted panels. The panel in the top middle features a silvery moon while the others display their colors in step-linked folk patterns. The effect is positively sacramental.

Mamma Occlo also provides the organizing principle through which to approach Shahn's other works. Thus we see in a wall of miniatures how the artist works out color and design problems. Shahn's major paintings are block-building constructions made up of individual painted panels.

In *Sampler*, a single panel painting based on quilt patterns, we see the technical working out of color and design for their own sake. Then, in the large six-by-eight-foot free-hanging tempera on paper *El Salvador*, we see how an artist with a head on her shoulders as well as eyes in her head can elevate the domestic decorativeness of the patchwork motif to infuse color and form with symbolic social significance.

El Salvador is as disturbing and anguished as *Mamma Occlo* is hopeful. Shahn thoughtfully provides a crib sheet to *El Salvador* indicating her thought process and use of symbols, but the crib sheet is hardly necessary except for a close textual reading. The unguided eye will surely see the clear blue and lush greenery of the old natural order. But then there are the prison bars, the suddenly gunmetal skies, the peace shattered by explosions of fragmented, colored shards, the brilliant red which is the blood of the people. *El Salvador* is just color and form, but it is an unmistakable evocation of social chaos.

The majority of Shahn's new paintings are based on a serpentine form of undulating bars of color. The snake paintings can be viewed as simple visual exercises or as records of emotion and sensation charted through prismatic progress. One entitled *Abby Goes to the State House*, for example, seems to be a chromatic chronicle of a journey at the heart of which is a red-hot coil, the angriest use of red I've seen in a long time.

The beauty of Abby Shahn's art is that it operates at many levels simultaneously, from the purely ornamental through the personal and social on to the spiritual. Having developed a visual vocabulary of color and design, Abby Shahn is well-equipped to entertain, invoke, inveigh, and comment at one and the same time.

Natasha Mayers' work is more obviously personal than Shahn's. All of the mixed-media (primarily oil-based crayon) drawings on display are in her *Mapping* series of childlike, ideographic projections aimed at expressing the way the world seems to the artist.

Natasha Mayers began drawing "maps" about 18 months ago on the occasion of her first pregnancy. Through the making of maps she sought to center herself, discover her true relation with the world. Her maps are bold, colorful, primitive charts drawn in a cunningly childish scrawl. Most delimit the world of North Whitefield and the world of Mayers' childhood in Croton, New York. In distorting perspective in accordance with personal values and a felt sense of space, Mayers has produced maps which bear a temperamental, if not stylistic, likeness to Saul Steinberg's now-famous *New Yorker* map of the United States.

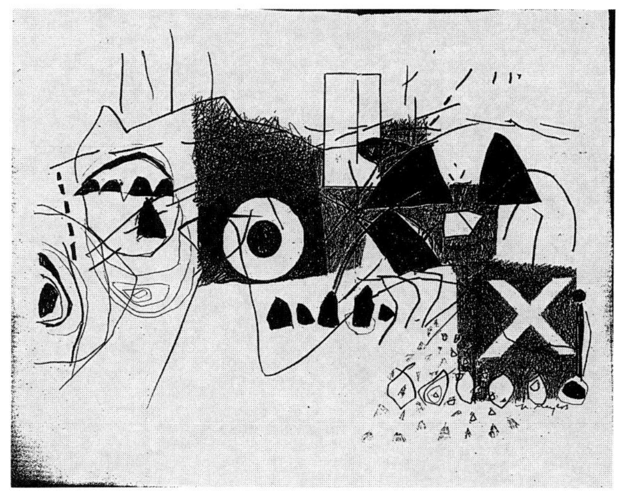

2. *Natasha Mayers*, The Artist at the Center of Her Universe Before the Baby Comes and Knocks Her Off Center (first map). *Colored pencil. Courtesy of the artist.*

Some of the cartooned maps, such as *Map to Commemorate a Backroad Trip to New York*, are literal enough to actually be followed, but most are joyously distorted and illustrated with private landmarks—the topology of fields, the scheme of a garden plot, aerial perspectives, the piecing together of visually disconnected road segments.

One particularly witty map, *Across the Street and Around the Block*, delineates a short walk in primitive perspective which has the houses and trees across the street drawn upside-down in that flat, two-dimensional kind of perspective anthropologists often find in the drawings of primitive peoples.

Nor does Mayers restrict her mappings to the terrain. She also provides a *Pregnancy Map* which charts the fetal development of her son, Noah.

Natasha Mayers' maps bear a striking resemblance to the earliest maps known to mankind: Babylonian maps inscribed in Sumerian and dated to 2500 B.C. Thus we are reminded that each individual's life recapitulates human history. And Mayers' free-spirited use of color and foreshortened perspective also remind us of Henri Matisse's admonition that the artist "has to look at life as he did when he was a child and, if he loses that faculty, he cannot express himself in an original, that is, personal way."

Abby Shahn and Natasha Mayers seem to have found the child within. Two talented ladies, two stars on the ascendant.

June 11, 1982

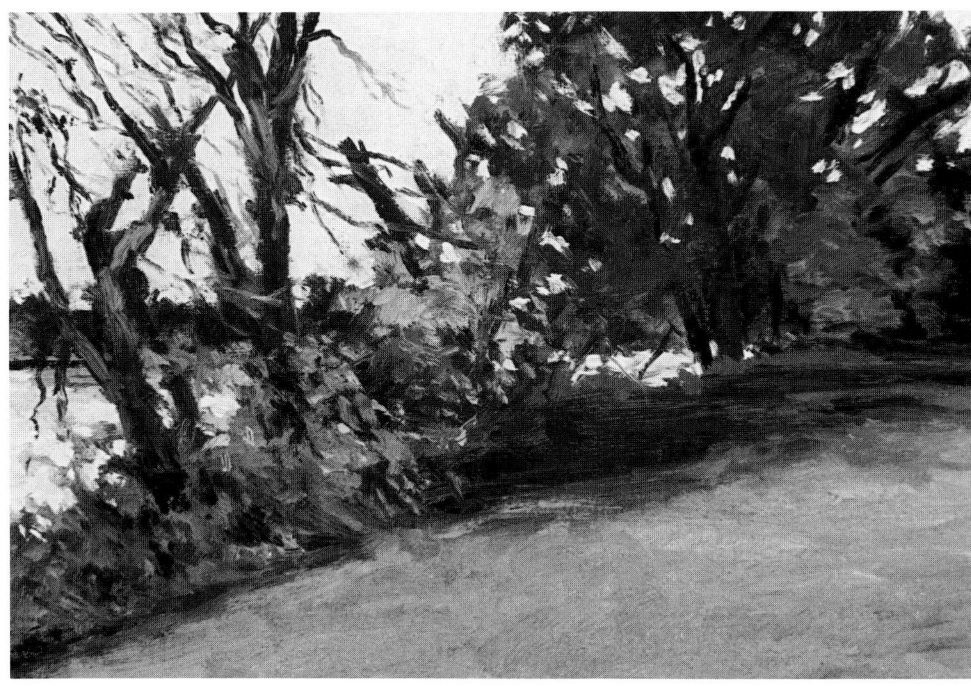

1. *J. Thomas R. Higgins,* View of the Kennebec in Autumn. *Oil on panel. Courtesy of the Barridoff Galleries.*

Tom Higgins

Upon viewing *J. Thomas R. Higgins, Paintings of the Last Decade*, one of Maine's most knowledgeable collectors declared, "The Biennial has been vindicated." Tom Higgins, who lives in Skowhegan and teaches at the University of Maine in Farmington, was the winner of a solo exhibition at the controversial 1981 All Maine Biennial. As I recall, at the time, I wrote that Higgins was a fortunate choice because he was one of the few artists in the Biennial capable of filling the USM Art Gallery in Gorham with quality work. Well, fill the gallery he has, but the Higgins retrospective is not so much a vindication of the Biennial as an example of splendid timing.

As the 73 works in Gorham show, Tom Higgins has always been a good artist with plenty of talent and promise. What is more important, however, is that Higgins' art seems to have reached full maturity just in time for this singular exhibition. It is heartening to be able to report that Tom Higgins' most recent paintings are unquestionably his best, reconciling as they do both art and nature.

If the Higgins paintings in Gorham were hung in chronological order, I think viewers would easily see the visual progress he has made. In major early oils such as *Lazy Panorama* (1973) and *Emerald Green Is Cool* (1973) all of the elements of his mature style are there, but they have not established equilibrium. Both share a kind of brushy naturalism flirting with Impressionism. The colors are subdued, flat and active. Yet in approaching the Maine landscape, Higgins has not found a balance between painting and picture. His subjects never quite achieve parity with his painting; brushwork and pigment triumph over imagery.

On a number of occasions I have heard accomplished painters voice vague problems with wholehearted endorsements of Higgins' work, and in surveying this decade of painting I think I know what the problem has been: a seeming indifference to the visual interest of his chosen subjects. Particularly in paintings like *Edge of the Wood* (1975), a stand of trees before an open field, one senses that the artist has been so intent upon solving personal stylistic problems that he has overlooked the fact that the subject is not particularly interesting or dramatic in nature. Happily, in most of his new work, indifference ceases to be a problem.

Through the middle 1970s Higgins seemed to have worked in two representational veins, one suggestive of Wolf Kahn's broad-patterned approach to domestic landscape, the other closer to Fairfield Porter's brand of sun-dappled realism. *Color Field* (1977), *Barn with Sheds* (1980), and *Late Summer Light* (1977) share Kahn's aesthetic concerns for the monumental in nature. *Camp at North Pond* (1975), *Near the Sandy River* (1976), *Backyards, Norridgewock* (1976) and *East of Skowhegan* (1975) are all painterly Porteresque. These are all good paintings and not at all badly derivative, yet they wrestle with and fail to resolve the problem of realism versus representationalism. Realism subverts painting to nature, making paint look like something it is not, while representationalism, in its loosest sense, merely makes nature a point of departure for painting.

Now what seems to have happened about two years ago is that Higgins discovered spaciousness, the value of vacancy that had missed the mark as indifference in earlier works. Thus we have in *January Without Snow* (1980) and *Space Near Madison* (1980) a new expansiveness in Higgins' work, a sense that he is painting not only what is before his eyes, but also the totality of nature as represented in the fragment before him.

In the superb 1982 paintings *Woods at Long Pond*, *Bog at Norridgewock*, *Overcast Day*, and *Crowell Pond from Berry Hill*, Higgins has at last achieved the reconciliation his art has been headed toward. In all three, art and nature—painting and image—are balanced. One may see the landscape first, but it is impossible to forget that any of these paintings is canvas and pigment before it is an illusion of reality. The hallmark of maturity has been reached. These paintings are simultaneously pictures *of* nature and works with integrity of their own as painting.

Woods at Long Pond, for example, is a dancing, symphonic forest interior lifted above the commonplace by the simple, but ingenious device of painting in the shards of blue sky over the already painted trees. The effect this has is dazzling to the eye. The sky seems to wink and pulse as it does when seen through a dense tangle of branches (nature) and yet the undisguised obviousness of the blue brushstrokes proclaims that this is paint (art).

Except for a few experimental aberrations, Tom Higgins' work has a surprising consistency over the years. It is a consistency of palette above all. Whether painting the dead of winter or the brightest summer day, Higgins prefers between-season colors: muddy browns, yellowed greens, muted grays.

I was recently taken to task in a letter for issuing a blanket indictment of a group show as displaying a wretched and ill-conceived use of color. Well, what I meant by that was that modern artists, given the emancipation of color since Fauvism, have a tremendous freedom to employ color which they use at their own peril. Color has meaning, embodies meaning. Tom Higgins, in choosing to restrict himself to quiet, sober, between-season colors, exhibits his maturity by using color responsibly. One of the most obvious signs of growth in his painting is that where color choices sometimes seem arbitrary in early works, color selection and placement in his best works are both thoughtful and deliberate.

Perhaps Tom Higgins' greatest technical strength is his ability to work large expanses of canvas without sacrificing vitality. Far too many of the paintings I have seen around Maine in recent years suffer from dead spots when artists attempt to cover large fields of vision. Half a Higgins landscape, for example, *The Dunlap Farm* (1980), may be devoted to a relatively featureless expanse of pasture, but his lively brushwork and divining of pattern save these passages from dullness.

This is a landmark show in the career of one of Maine's best young artists. It will hang at the USM Art Gallery in Gorham through October 7.

September 24, 1982

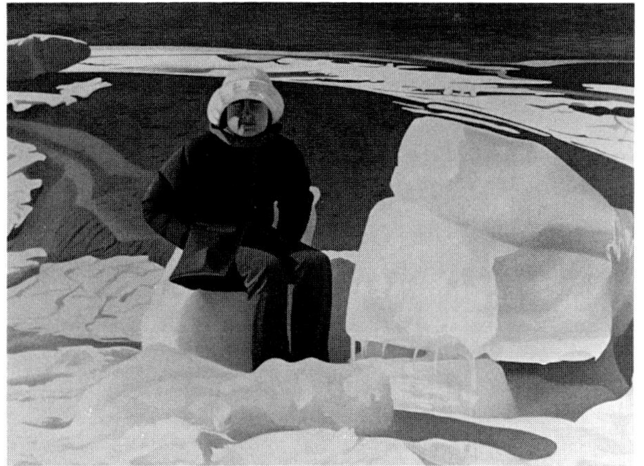

1. *Lesia Sochor,* Winter. *Oil. Courtesy of the artist.*

Spectra-2

Spectra-2...There's no good reason for it, but it's a wonderful show.

Without belaboring the point, there is no good reason why, in 1982, 150 Maine women artists should feel the need for an exhibition restricted to women. Women are not discriminated against in the arts, not in the galleries, and not by the critics. Most thoughtful women artists admit this. Even Spectra-2 director, photographer Anne Elzas-O'Keefe, says she has her doubts whether an all-woman show is called for. She feels the biggest obstacle facing female artists these days is a reluctance to be assertive, to promote one's own work.

That said, I now enthusiastically endorse the second edition of Spectra, the month-long (October) festival of feminine art at the University of Maine at Orono. Rationale aside, Spectra-2 is a strong showing for a great diversity of women artists. The first Spectra event was held at Westbrook College two years ago, so it is fitting that this second show, juried by Haystack director emeritus Fran Merritt, painter Beverly Hallam, and sculptor C. Regina Kelley, should be held up north. Unfortunately, the Orono site, coupled with the worst publicity I have ever seen (or not seen) surrounding a major exhibition, will probably mean that Spectra-2 will not get the public exposure it deserves.

Two galleries in Carnegie Hall are jammed over-full with work, the Hole-in-the-Wall Gallery in Memorial Union is being dedicated to the work of one woman per week, and the lobby of Hauck Auditorium is ringed with paintings. As stated, there are 150 women represented in Spectra-2, and you really have to penetrate to the bottom third of the order before you run out of quality. There are probably fifty women showing in Orono who produce work of a sufficient quality to warrant solo exhibition spaces.

In the first week of the exhibition, when I visited, the Hole-in-the-Wall Gallery was devoted to the work of Wendy Kindred. Over the past few years Kindred has developed into one of the most powerful image makers in the state. The boldness of her brushwork matches the riveting simplicity of her images, the best of which is a series of three oils entitled *Guardian*. The *Guardian* paintings depict an anthropomorphic, yet mythified winged dog which could easily be a creature from the collective unconscious. There is both horror and beauty in Kindred's work, as there is in the work of English painter Francis Bacon. Kindred shares Bacon's ability to unsettle by giving visual form to a state of mind.

Much of the best painting in the exhibition is representational. Lesia Sochor's *Winter*, a portrait of a woman muffled in cold blue sitting at the ice-strewn shore, has an Arctic stillness about it that speaks volumes about isolation. Her *Stepping Out*, an horizontal oil portrait of a pair of high heels and a pair of white bucks, melds commercial art with social recording.

Three Girls by Penny Oliphant is an Alex Katz-like portrayal of three young women seated on a wooded hillside. Oliphant is the mistress of the flat, billboard realism popularized by Katz. The effect of this technique is to render human beings as objects. In *Closing Time*, Oliphant uses the same deadpan technique to capture a couple seated in an immaculately deserted restaurant. Again, there is a sense of isolation and loneliness, with humans as the furniture of painting.

Cicely Aikman stretches the techniques of the new realism in *November Dream*, three trees, two ducks, and a dog, to achieve a kind of drawn oil which is part expressionist (emotion) and part impressionist (vision). Her style of free color use and bold outline has become very popular in Maine.

Lisa Allen, whose outrageously juicy oils overpowered the recent Maine Festival exhibition, shows the savage oils here, but also turns her hand to more subdued, but equally dynamic lithographs. *Miss J. Steps Out* and *Storming the Midwest* are quasi-realistic studies in vertigo: rooms, furniture, and figures about to fly apart in the teeth of a devastating force.

Sculpturally, Spectra-2 is strong on constructions as opposed to carved or modelled pieces.

Shallow Victory by Gemma and Dennis Morrill-Dreher (a male presence does invade the show) is an intricate construction of painted wooden balls and coils of stainless steel wire that has about it a scientific elegance and beauty. The colored balls are cradled in geometric conformation within the matrix of steel in such a way that the eye apprehends shifting color relations and formal relations as it moves around the piece. *Shallow Victory* looks like a molecular model and acts like a kaleidoscope.

Luda Borysenko contributes two constructions in wood and wire, *Ebb Tide* and *I Could Have Danced All Night*, which bear an unmistakable family resemblance to Russian constructivism. Natural process and human figure are reduced to mechanical components and suspended in space.

But the most fanciful and decidedly feminine objects in the exhibition are Jenifer Jane Tift's hanging assemblages, *Bo Peep Benedictus* and *Cat Death Rattle*. The former is a sheep skull mounted on a yellow cane wrapped in blue ribbon; the latter, a cat skull atop a red velvet pillowed dome surrounded by dangling, etched egg shells. Both have the appearance and force of ritual fetish objects, embodiments of an at-once naive and frightening aspect of the female sensibility.

The weakness of the show is the relative absence of successful abstract painting. Nancy Earle's *Four Corners*, an acrylic and sand creation which looks like a lesson in Buddhist geometry, is the only analytic abstraction of any note.

In trying to assess the overall impact of Spectra-2, my only thought was that the best work in Orono gave evidence of art as a way of coping. That evidence seems to indicate that women artists in Maine are coping very well, thank you.

October 22, 1982

Fairfield Porter

Would Fairfield Porter (1907-1975) have approved of calling his major retrospective at the Museum of Fine Arts, Boston (through March 13) *Fairfield Porter—Realist Painter in an Age of Abstraction*? Very doubtful. For while Porter was certainly instrumental in maintaining the integrity of realistic painting at a time when abstraction was all the rage, he was an artist and critic of extremely catholic tastes and, like all true artists, knew that labels and categories are meaningless. The painting is the thing.

"The important thing for critics to remember," according to Fairfield Porter, "is the 'subject matter' in abstract painting and the abstraction in representational work."

Fairfield Porter was the least doctrinaire artist and critic I know of. He was capable of enthusiastically embracing the gestural and figurative abstractions of DeKooning without feeling the need to veer from his own course of painterly realism. Porter's long-time friend, the painter Neil Welliver, recently said, "The thing about Fairfield was that he didn't care what anyone thought of his work." Welliver did not mean to imply that Porter was arrogant; simply that he was a man of independent judgment, secure in what he was doing.

A sense of this personal and artistic security pervades the galleries where 144 of Porter's works are hung. Fairfield Porter did not look far for the truth; he found it staring him in the face, in the faces of his friends and relatives, in the rooms he inhabited, and in the places like Southampton, Long Island, and Great Spruce Head, Maine, which he made his own. In Fairfield Porter's world it is eternally summer; everyone and everything is smothered in light and love. Porter was an intimist, no questions asked.

In the early paintings, dating to the late 1940's, we see Porter working out domestic and studio interiors with a limited palette of somber greys, putty, and mustard. In the portraits, the figures begin somewhat stiff, posed, and uncomfortable, and remain so from the '40s to the '70s. What becomes freer and easier as Porter matures is his use of color and his brushwork. A painting like *Lunch Under the Elm Tree* (1954)

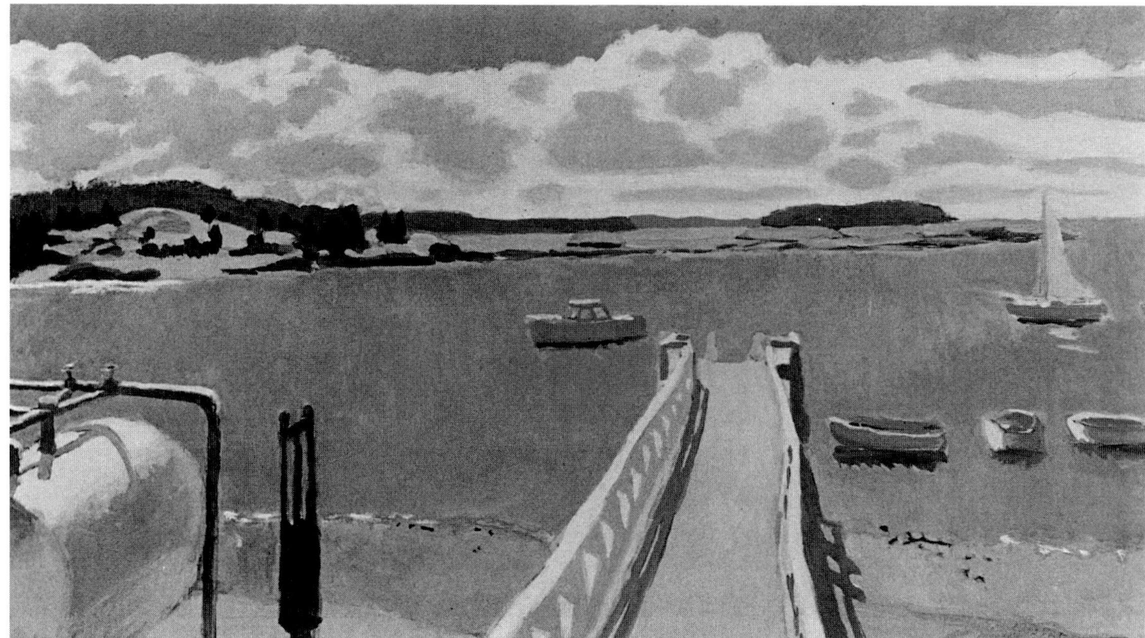

1. *Fairfield Porter,* The Harbor—Great Spruce Head, *1974. Oil on canvas. Courtesy of the Barridoff Galleries.*

prefigures his later pastoral celebrations; the elements are all there—civilized nature, *al fresco* activity, deep shadows—but the colors are opaque and muddy, the light less dramatic.

Through the years, Porter's colors become bolder and less localized, his approach to subject flatter. We see him performing in manners later brought to maturity in the work of friends and contemporaries like Welliver (strong, inclusive backgrounds) and Alex Katz (flat, reductive figures). But always there is that transported, initial and intimate joy of the European, of Vuillard and Bonnard, Mary Cassatt here and there.

The consummation of Porter's vision comes, suitably, near the end of his life with the 1970s. *Lizzie and Bruno* (1970), a vertical masterpiece, is quintessential Fairfield Porter. Daughter Lizzie, barefoot on the porch, surrounded by small paintings, the golden retriever Bruno at her feet, is shown in cut-off blue jeans and dark blue sweatshirt. She looks wealthy, intelligent, and wary. It is the summer of the good life.

Under the Elms (1971-72) is where Porter was headed in 1954 with *Lunch Under the Elm Tree.* A young girl (also Lizzie?) dominates the foreground with pink face and figured smock, while the background is deep in green shadow or else bursting with sunny pools of yellow-green light. A painting like this says that the real and the everyday are magical, and though Porter once objected when a critic referred to his painted world as "enchanted," the conclusion is inescapable.

No viewer really needs any critical help to enjoy Fairfield Porter's art. For while he was an intellectual (critic for *Nation* and *Art News*, ardent environmentalist, staunch foe of technology), his paintings are not intellectual. Porter's paintings are not about ideas, but about the real, the immediate, and the beautiful. I don't think I've ever seen paintings that look less at home in a museum. These are paintings to be lived with, not visited. The only real point of a notice such as this is to say *that* these paintings are and *where*, not what and why.

Fairfield Porter—Realist Painter in an Age of Abstraction begins in Boston, and, after traveling to Greenville, South Carolina, Cleveland, and Pittsburgh, will spend the summer of 1984 at the Whitney Museum in New York. The Porter retrospective, like last year's traveling Welliver exhibition, is exactly the kind of show we should hope to see in Maine once the new Payson Wing of the Portland Museum of Art opens. Until then, Boston.

February 4, 1983

Alfred Chadbourn

Alfred Chadbourn paints bestsellers. His boldly colorful canvases are among the most popular in the state. One of his dashing panoramas of the Portland skyline was adapted as the poster for last year's Portland 350 celebration. And at the current (through March 31) exhibition of his *Recent Paintings* at Barridoff Galleries, 12 of the 25 new oils were sold by opening night.

As a friend of his, I know that this popularity tends to worry Chip Chadbourn. He worries that he will somehow manage to saturate the small Maine market before he is through painting, but the evidence is still to the contrary. He also worries that his popularity will prevent fellow artists from taking his work seriously. But because he worries most that his painting may not be all that it could be, Alfred Chadbourn's art remains fresh and vital without appearing to change drastically from year to year. In an art world that often overvalues the new and the ground-breaking, Chadbourn's art is like bedrock, solid and reassuring.

Alfred Chadbourn is a thorough-going sensualist. The secret of his popularity is the obvious pleasure he extracts from the world and shares through his paintings. It is with Chadbourn as Robert Hughes writes in a chapter entitled "The Landscape of Pleasure" in his landmark *The Shock of the New*: "One of the projects of art is to reconcile us with the world, not by protest, irony, or political metaphors, but by the ecstatic contemplation of pleasure in nature." A Chadbourn painting is always a feast then, a feast of food and sunburned beaches, of village life and city celebrated, and always, always of color.

Years ago Chadbourn seems to have given himself the assignment to get as much color and light into his painting as possible, but while his use of color is free and enthusiastic, it is rarely gratuitous. His salmon skies, rose-pink beaches, and deep purple oceans have a chromatic logic all their own. Although each daub of paint has a corresponding reference—house, head, boat, tree, etc.—in reality, Chadbourn's painterly strokes fight free of imitation to become records not only of what has been seen, but also of what has transpired on canvas.

His images are by now familiar; his own beginning with a masterful little *Self-Portrait* —the mustachioed maître, hand on hip, at ease at the easel, bathed in fleshy pink backlight. From the self we move to favored subjects such as working harbors—five views of Stonington alone, two of Portland, one each of Port Clyde, Round Pond, Boothbay, and Five Islands. The best of the Stonington views is an eccentric, off-balance angle on a sweep of houses held together by the deep purple and blue band of the horizon. The Chadbourn palette is set dark and deep looking for stark contrasts—bruising blues against creamy whites, hot pinks and salmons against rich reds and pulpy orange.

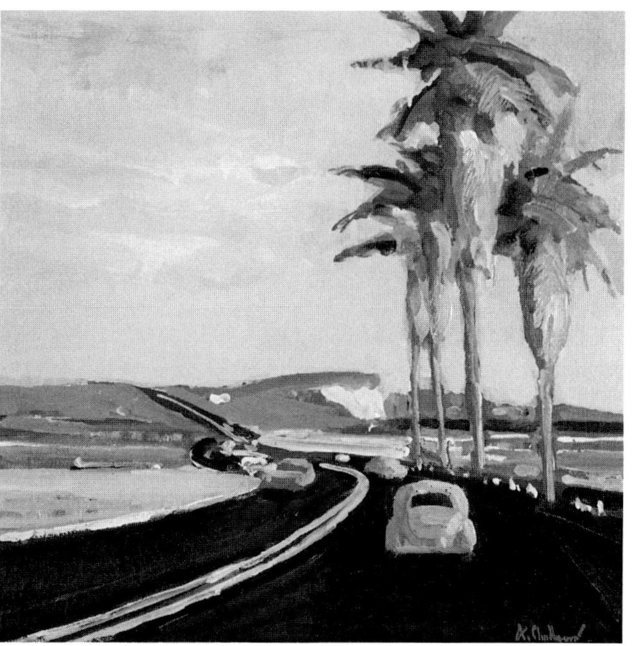

1. *Alfred Chadbourn,* Coastal Highway, CA. *Oil on canvas. Courtesy of the Barridoff Galleries.*

Chadbourn is most at home on the beach, where sun and surf bathers are painted in barbecue reds upon hot pink sands. Light is heat. Heat is color. There are five beach scenes in the current collection covering Maine, Florida, and Cape Cod. Chadbourn renders groupings of bathers with the same riot of colorful strokes he renders groupings of buildings.

For the gourmet and the gourmand, there are market windows from Paris hung with duck, cheese, fowl, and sausage; crates and flats of produce in a Boston North End market; and a sumptuous dish of mussels, mussel blue-black being Chadbourn's signal color, the rich garlicky flesh of the mollusks suggested in a few deft strokes of mustardy oil.

The anomalies of the show are the Vermont scenes: a large, too-too green canvas of a Ver-

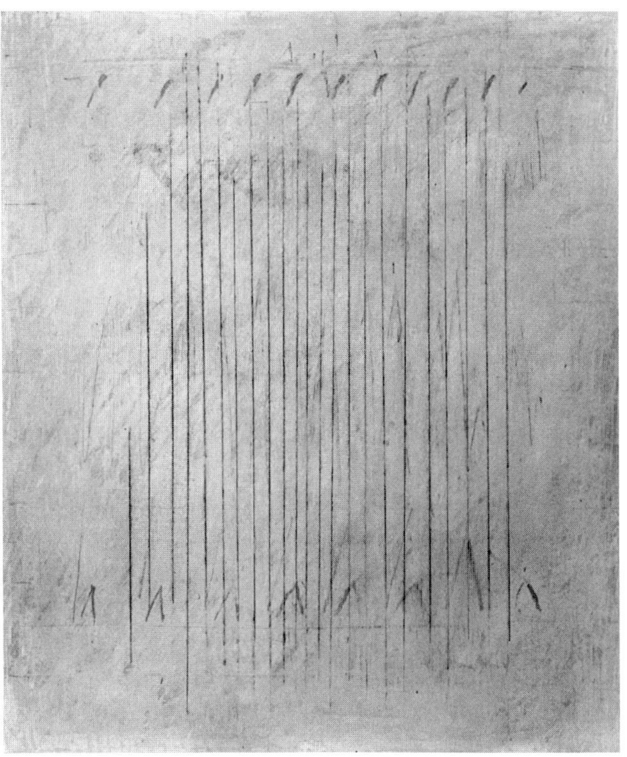

1. *Leonard Craig,* Cantos I Series: Hylochichla Mustelina II, *1983. Encaustic and charcoal on canvas. Courtesy of the artist. Photo by Scott Davis.*

mont village and a small, anxiously dark view of a herd of Vermont cows. The black and white cows blend into one another to become pure pattern, the cow painting being more abstraction than not.

Chadbourn's vulnerable spot appears when he appears to work too fast, and as he works larger, his paint seems to become thinned. In a painting like *Boats, Five Islands*, the masts of sailboats become spittles of paint. This device works well when masts are but details in a larger composition, but trickery is not enough to support an entire canvas. When Chadbourn makes an error, however, it is an error of enthusiasm.

Alfred Chadbourn paints from the skin out, his hand awaiting the pleasure of his eye and stomach. A strong, sensuous show of affection and assurance.

March 11, 1983

Leonard Craig

Unity College art faculty Leonard Craig, Gretchen Lucchesi, and Jonathan Taylor are showing *New Works* at the college gallery through April 28, but to be more exact, Lucchesi and Taylor are showing new works while Leonard Craig is showing a new Leonard Craig. The new Leonard Craig is a man inspired. No doubt about it.

In a new series of encaustic paintings entitled *Canto Series*, Craig has undertaken to explore visualizations of sound, or, as he puts it in the show notes, "My intention lies in creating drawings and paintings about life music..." What Craig has in his *Cantos* is a brilliant reconciliation of conceptual art with easel art. Other artists have attempted to paint sound, but Craig seems intent on pursuing the idea beyond purely artistic limits.

Beginning with the tape-recorded sounds of birds and animals, Craig translates his natural "music" into spectrographs and sonographs on which he then bases the drawings and paintings. Eventually, Craig is talking about trying to devise a method to get a computer reading of his sonograph-spectrograph generated surfaces, translating his art into a digital code that can be retranslated into new music. This new music, based on patterns in art derived from patterns in nature, might then be played back to the birds and animals and their reactions observed and recorded.

Obviously, this line of inquiry leads to a point of intersection between art and science. What Craig is after is art as a form of knowledge. The question he is raising is, "Are there certain universal patterns that are meaningful to both humans and non-humans?" Fortunately, Craig's paintings are not subverted to the idea. Even if one dismisses Craig's *Cantos* as exercises in interspecies communications, the paintings still hold up.

Naturally, it helps to know that in a painting like *Canto Series: Hylocichla Mustelina II* the artist is attempting a visual translation of the song of the wood thrush, but the painting can be enjoyed without this knowledge. The pale grey surface is dense, richly worked and subtly nuanced. This aural space is then modulated by a series of vertical black lines accented near the top with orange cues. Without knowing that the painting is about either birds or sound, the thoughtful viewer will still realize that Craig is dealing with intervals, frequencies, and mensuration—the imposition of rational order on seemingly irrational nature. This is an extremely fertile and exciting line of inquiry, and Craig's preliminary results positively reverberate with newfound energies.

Craig has created *Cantos from Mimus Polyglottos* (the mockingbird), a whole mini-series from *Spizella Passerina* (the chipping sparrow), and two small, but piercingly beautiful recordings from the shrill *Cicadidae*. All take the form of linear and graphic mediations on the experience of natural sound. Line becomes frequency. Color becomes tone. And surface becomes the matrix of silence. Craig's new sonic abstractions strike a deep and resonant chord.

April 15, 1983

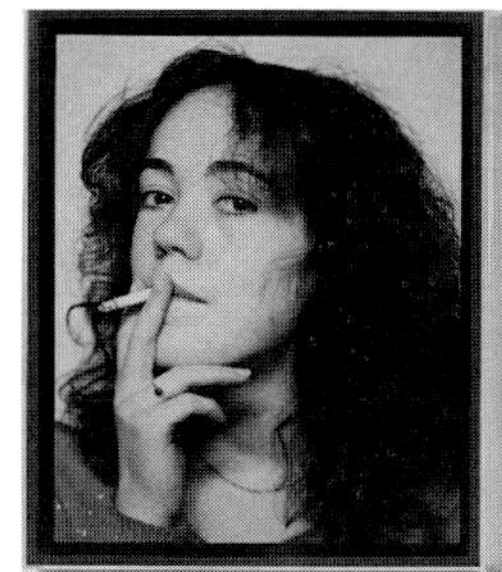
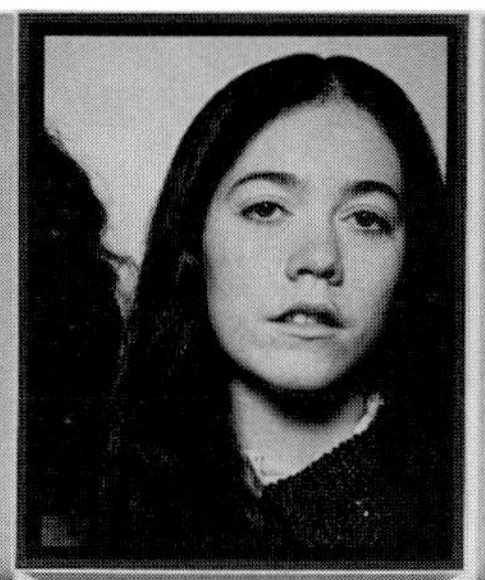
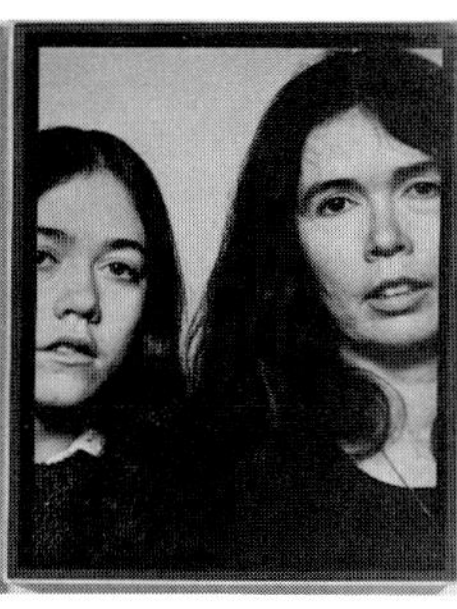

1. *Karen Smiley*, Tracy and Cindy Pinkham, Linda Townsend, two sisters and their mother. *Cibachrome photographs. Courtesy of the artist.*

1983 Maine Biennial

Years from now when I think of the 1983 Maine Biennial (at Colby College Museum of Art through October 2), I'm sure I will remember three things: sculptor Guy Williams' marvelously daft *Prototype for a Lunar Disk Harrow*; photographer Karen Smiley's eye-popping Cibachrome serial family portraits; and that 1983 was the year of the Portland School of Art Biennial.

Unlike the previous two biennials, which were wide-open, democratic artistic free-for-alls, the Colby exhibition is a sort of invitational. After looking at 300 to 400 submitted slides at the slide registry of the Maine State Commission on the Arts and Humanities, and after making 40 to 45 studio visits, a four-artist jury selected 16 Maine artists to exhibit several works each.

The jury—or curatorial selection committee—consisted of photographer Bruce Kidman and sculptor Celeste Roberge, both Portland School of Art (PSA) graduates, painter Johnnie Ross of the PSA faculty, and printmaker Susan Groce from the University of Maine at Orono. Eight of the 16 artists chosen are from Portland, six by way of PSA. The PSA contingent includes painter-printmaker Lisa Allen, painter Edwin Douglas, painter Veronica Benning, and photographer John Eide, all faculty members; and printmaker Donna Evans and sculptor Williams, both graduates.

Colby museum director Hugh J. Courley III believes that the preponderance of Portland artists in the show reflects the fact that a great deal is happening in Portland. Juror Susan Groce says she is not uncomfortable with the heavy Portland concentration, insisting, "It would be a falsehood to suggest (the judging) was 'who you know.'"

More likely, the high PSA count is the result of who the jurors knew about and who knew about the new biennial format. The fact remains, however, that the 1983 biennial is tainted by the jurying process. If a curated exhibition with a definite point of view on what's happening in Maine art is what the biennial decides to become, then perhaps some thought should be given to letting one individual curate the show. As it is, the 1983 Maine Biennial is a four-juror version of what John Coffey has been doing with the Maine Festival exhibition at Bowdoin College the last few years...and Coffey does a better job by himself.

That said, what have the four jurors selected? The 1983 Maine Biennial consists of neo-expressionist prints and oils filled with big, emotional gestures by Lisa Allen; dark dirge-like utterances and incantations in black castle paper by Baychar Morris; Androscoggin River abstractions by Veronica Benning; wild mixed-media cartooning in Billie Bowman's ongoing adventures of the green dragon; painterly abstractions based on cemetery landscapes by Ed Douglas, who is a master of compression; urban exotica in black and white by photographer John Eide; wonderfully whacky little woodcuts by Donna Evans; gouache pattern abstractions by Ron Ghiz; funky, surreal ceramics by Mark Huff; geometric color abstractions in pencil and crayon by Janice Kasper; finely detailed landscapes in black and white by photographer John McKee; tents and fabric sculpture by Bill Moss; ethereal color photographs of the seashore by Richard Procopio; Karen Smiley's high-impact portraits; Guy Williams' speculative contraptions; and sculptor Christine Woelfle's extremely delicate constructions in basswood and rice paper, brass and bronze.

In general, there is a nice diversity of materials and concerns within the three-dimensional work, a thoughtful diversity of points of view within the photography, but a bit too much kinship in the painting. Both Douglas and Benning are first-rate painters, but they have similar enough concerns within natural abstraction so that one of them might have been eliminated to good advantage. Aside from the photographic images, realism and representationalism are not represented this year. The only way the figure gets into the show is in distorted caricature form—Bowman to Evans to Huff.

The Colby museum space is dominated by Williams' *Prototype for a Lunar Disk Harrow*, a machine half farm implement and half space robot which seems the perfect intercourse between the 19th and 21st centuries. The lunar harrow comes with a control panel that performs a countdown, flashes warning lights, and then activates the great, useless machine which rotates in the middle of the floor. Williams also contributes a *Device for Catching Flying Objects from Space*, a metal monster that opens its three claws (jaws?) when rotated and then, as the rotation slows, tips each claw (jaw?) back delicately into a waiting spring...tink, tink, tink.

Williams says that he came to his interest in building art machines out of a background as a geometric color-field painter, learning to view a painting as a kind of machine made up of related parts. Williams earns an A for form and an A for content.

Karen Smiley's photographic triptychs and diptychs all take the form of larger-than-life serial portraits of family groups. Each of the head-and-shoulder shots pops out of a deep, black surrounding space to confront the viewer head-on the way a Chuck Close portrait does. There is something emotionally distressed and distressing about the scale and the degree of scrutiny in these superhuman visions, but they are absolute knockouts.

The other find of the 1983 biennial is Christine Woelfle, a recent arrival on the Peaks Island art scene. Like Williams, Woefle is a builder. *Emitting a Sound* and *Primary Circuit* are lightweight wood and paper constructions about two feet high, both of which look like attempts to build a model of Marcel Duchamps' *Nude Descending a Staircase No. 2*. Her *Swift-Shooting Presence* takes the form of a brass rack about six feet high with little organic bronze configurations like ears sprouting from the brass rod ends.

We have come to expect the Maine Biennial to be a controversial show. The 1983 edition is and the 1985 edition, to be held at the Portland Museum of Art and to concentrate solely on painting and decorative arts, promises to be. But then controversy is healthy, and so is the Maine art scene.

July 29, 1983

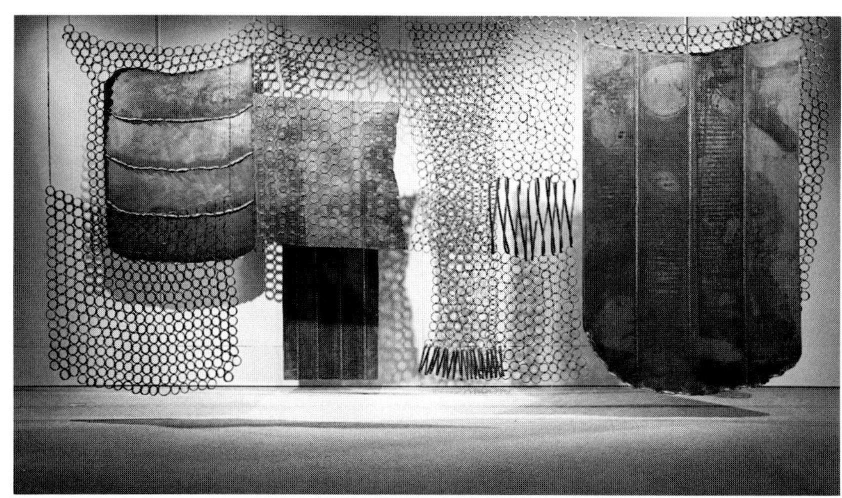

1. *Celeste Roberge,* The Cellular Structure of My Reptilian Brain, *1981. Steel. Courtesy of the artist. Photo by Abe Morrell.*

Maine Artists Invitational

The weakness of the 1983 Maine Biennial (reviewed last week) at Colby College is the way it was curated; the strength of the 1983 Maine Artists Invitational (July 29-September 4, in conjunction with the Maine Festival) at Bowdoin College is the way *it* was curated.

The 16 artists in the Biennial were selected by a committee of four artists. The nine artists in the invitational were selected by John Coffey, curator at Bowdoin. The works at Colby do not communicate one to another; the works at Bowdoin do.

"Our goal," says Coffey, "was to find people who hadn't received as much exposure as they deserve and to challenge other people to do things they hadn't had a chance to do before."

The freewheeling format of the festival show, united only by Coffey's taste, results in a sustained excitement where the Biennial only has its moments.

To begin with, the Maine Artists Invitational features work by two of the hottest painters in the state: Wendy Kindred and Gary Buch. Both artists paint for 1983, right now, but that said, it would take a small book to explain.

Wendy Kindred, who teaches at the University of Maine at Fort Kent, paints in the gap between figure and pattern where her eye and imagination create bright, primitive portraits. She paints personas, not persons. I am told she acknowledges the influence of years spent in Ethiopia, but I find her stiff, distorted figures and strong, fist-like patterns devoid of specific culture…like the haunted visions of Francis Bacon.

Gary Buch, who lives in Portland and starred in a recent Hobe Sound show, paints the wilderness of his imagination in boiling hot colors. In *A Living Dog is Better Than a Dead Lion*, for example, a red dog slinks through a hot pink jungle, a perfect vision of visceral cowardice and caution.

Demonstrating just how conservative New Wave painting can be, William Rand of Blue Hill contributes two large oils in black, white, and greys which want to be seen as archly punk, but come away looking oddly old-fashioned, as staid in their way as Morandi bottles.

Natasha Mayers is not necessarily underexposed or underappreciated, but the Bowdoin show gives her a chance to indulge herself, which she does with a wonderfully whacked-out installation with many titles including *Armagarden* and *Map of the War Zone*. Mayers' vision of her North Whitefield garden as a war zone—invading sheep, snails, cherry bomb radishes, surrendering gourds, self-devouring carrots—is a rural Red Grooms. Playful panic, but then Mayers is always finding new ways to show us the art of play.

Robert Katz, of the University of Maine at Augusta, has been given a wall which he has come off of with *Intensive Care Unit*, a grotesque medical vision made up of antique wheelchairs, a dead bird attached to monitors, and 40 boat-caulking cones displayed to suggest intravenous feeding on a massive scale. Terminal art.

The straighter sculpture in the show is by Celeste Roberge and Duncan Hewitt. Hewitt, of USM, is best known for his cast concrete forms, but here is represented by carved and painted wooden butterfly wings, one in conjunc-

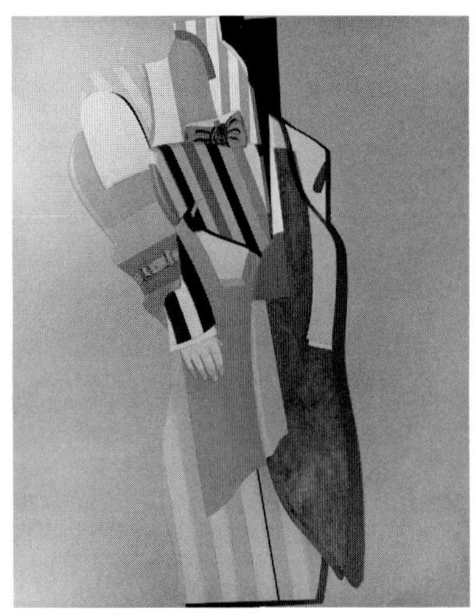

1. *Frederick Lynch,* Male Figure. *Acrylic on pine. Courtesy of the Barridoff Galleries.*

tion with a large wooden segmented box, the other pinned and clamped by angles of steel.

Maine's first lady of steel, Celeste Roberge, continues to thrill with the delicacy she imposes on brute metal. The major attraction of the Maine Festival show is surely her *Cellular Structure*, nine hanging units of sheet steel and ring-looped falls like chain-mail armor. *Cellular Structure* (which was created in 1981 but has never been displayed because of lack of space) is a formal synthesis of the organic and dramatic. It would make a great stage set, or backdrop for dance.

Joshua Nadel, who is rarely seen outside the University of Maine at Augusta despite being one of the most ambitious ceramists in the region, shows a small selection of brightly ornamented glazed earthenware pieces—slab cups, turned vases—which are conservative by his standards, but wild compared to the work of all but a few potters in the state. As John Coffey says, "It looks like California funk, but Josh has been doing it here for so long it's now Maine funk."

Finally, Bernie Vinzani, who is in the process of setting up a state-of-the-art papermaking studio way down east in Whiting, shows handmade papers collaged with metal screen and plastic mesh. His exquisitely colored abstractions are nice overlays of organic fiber and geometric grid.

This is probably the best exhibition of contemporary Maine art you are going to see this year. It would be instructive to view the invitational with the Biennial if at all possible...just to see what *is* possible.

August 5, 1983

Frederick Lynch and Paul Maddrell

The recent works of Frederick Lynch and Paul Maddrell are currently (through August 31 at Barridoff Galleries) engaged in a visual *DIALOGUE* (the show's title), the subject of which is appearances (as in apparent reality), the language of which is construction, the vocabulary being pattern, with the accent on sexuality.

To begin with, there is a nice material congruity between the works of the two artists.

In this dialogue, Fred Lynch reports and comments on the external reality of social life while Paul Maddrell reports and comments on the internal reality of emotional life. The shared metaphor of this dialogue is fashion. Lynch makes use of fashion to satirize socialized man. Maddrell uses fashion as a visual equivalent of emotional events.

For almost 10 years now Fred Lynch has been exploring manifestations of fabric striping as a metaphor for human civilization, in the process constructing a visual logic which constitutes an argument for existence based solely on appearances. In his recent work, Lynch carries this visual logic into three dimensions (almost).

Inclined Paddle is an acrylic on pine board construction, something like a large cutting board with two oar-shaped protrusions. The painted imagery on the paddle is of female cleavage in blood-red bodice, disembodied crotch in pale blue shorts, a wrist wearing watch, and, as always, shirt-striping patterns. *Inclined Paddle* is accompanied by a maquette, *Small Inclination with Tiles*, mounted on masonite painted with a tile motif, and a gouache, *Paddle*. This kinky triple play reveals that the strength of Lynch's art is now, as it always has been, his drawing. Line is at the heart of his creation. That the line in the form of the stripe should become emblematic of Lynch's work is poetically justified.

Where Lynch's and Maddrell's works are positioned so as to converse most directly, it becomes equally obvious that Maddrell's strength is as a designer. Maddrell's cantilevered wall construction, *Romance May Be Dangerous*, consists of a rectangle, the right half of which is given over to bold blue and white diagonal stripes, the left half being scumbled white with blue under, a hook or beak lifted off the surface. *Romance May Be Dangerous* is set diagonally across from Lynch's *Leaner to the Right*, a wall construction which employs equally bold wavering blue and white stripes. Lynch seems to use the stripe as decoration; Maddrell to use it as an end in itself.

Maddrell's other major piece in the show, *Seduction of the Sublime*, is similar to *Romance*, but uses diagonal purple and orange stripes that really make the retinas dance. His maquettes, called *Flaming Groovies*, are wicked little shooting flames studded with sharp, spiked forms. The shooting flame recurs as a motif throughout his works on paper, aggressive mixed-media studies with suitably nasty titles like *Tablet Violation*, *Violation of the Archetype*, and *She Hit Me and It Felt Like a Kiss*.

Male-female symbology is strong in the work of both these men, Lynch approaching the sexual with fact and decorum, Maddrell pushing on toward the violent edge. Just look at Lynch's *Male Figure* all dressed up and on the prowl. Then look at Maddrell's *D.O.L.* with its three-pronged male-female coupling uncoupling. Lynch says keep up the appearances. Maddrell says do it. Because Maddrell seems to be exploring the mysteries of his own personal felt reality while Lynch is exploring the conventions of human behavior in general, Maddrell's art pushes Lynch's nicely in this debate. Lynch, more of a classicist, insists on some etiquette; Maddrell, a romantic, obeys the dictates of the moment. Maddrell's art is his personal style. Lynch's art has very little to do with the man personally; it is about style in general.

All in all, this two-man show is nicely balanced, for where Maddrell's work is more difficult, Lynch's work is more fully realized. The works of these two artists converse, but, in the end, they do not speak the same language.

August 12, 1983

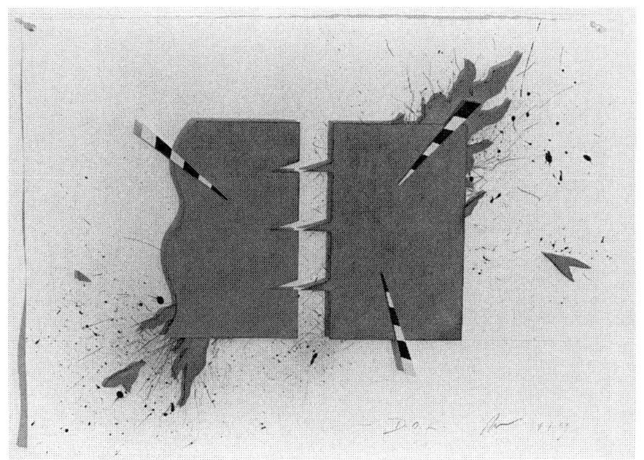

2. *Paul Maddrell,* D.O.L., *1983. Acrylic and graphite on paper construction. Courtesy of the Barridoff Galleries.*

Roger Majorowicz

Roger Majorowicz was born in 1931 on a ranch in Sioux country, Little Eagle, South Dakota, where he learned to work with metal from his blacksmith father. He has been moving East ever since. In 1958 he got a BFA from Minneapolis School of Art, between 1961-65 he taught at the University of Illinois, and from 1965-83 he was in Baltimore teaching sculpture at the Maryland Institute.

First exposed to Maine as a student at the Skowhegan School of Painting and Sculpture in 1957, Majorowicz has been summering in Maine since 1970, and, two years ago, moved permanently (80 tons of tools and materials equal permanent) to Whitefield.

Currently (through November 11) the University of Maine at Augusta is exhibiting *Sculpture of Roger L. Majorowicz*, a major exhibition of 50 works spanning a period of some 20 years of the artist's career. Though the works vary greatly over time, Majorowicz is consistently baroque (referring to style, not period) in marrying the picturesque, wild and fantastic to the well-ordered.

Greeting visitors outside Jewett Hall is *Sunset Chariot*, the first piece Majorowicz made in Maine. The welded iron-and-steel bit of monumental whimsy takes the form of a mutant farm implement. Seated high in the tractor seat of the chariot, the charioteer is able to control the sunset and the movement of clouds with knobs at either hand.

Also outside is *Galdolph the Magician*, a totem figure in granite and iron which is closer in spirit to the monumental works travelers along Route 218 in Whitefield are used to seeing in Majorowicz's field. *Shogun*, a brightly painted red steel piece inspired by the book and by

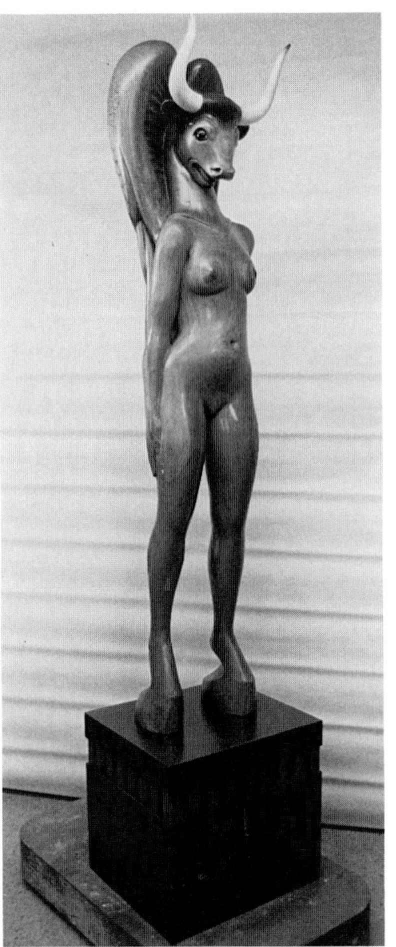

1. *Roger L. Majorowicz,* Queen Tut, *1977. Cherry wood carving and epoxy. Courtesy of Forum-A, the University of Maine at Augusta.*

Japanese culture, graces the entrances to the hall and takes its lines from Japanese armorial design.

Inside, the work runs the gamut from Majorowicz's customized woodstove (*Knight for a Stove*) featuring an aluminum plume, an altar-like installation of highly polished aluminum inspired by South Dakota windmills (*Watering Hole*), and abstract cast bronzes to a set of doors created for a Baltimore high school, a series of mythic bronze figurines, and a hooved and horned *Queen Tut* carved out of cherry and epoxy.

The baroque sensibility and the fascination with the winged form holds these diverse forms together. The abstract bronzes, for instance, are turbulent folds and flourishes about branch-like forms. Majorowicz calls these his Indian bronzes because, asked for titles, he simply named them with Sioux numbers.

"I once told a reviewer they were inspired by grouse flying up out of the prairie bush, but they're really more about the material than anything else," confides the artist.

Door I and *II* are sepia-toned epoxy impressions taken from the molds for *Six Bronze Doors* Majorowicz did in 1974-75 for Greenspring High School in Baltimore. Characteristic of his work, the doors are both light and heavy at once, substantial yet with an ethereal sense, imagination trapped in metal and material. One door contains the emerging figure of a winged baby (cherub). Separately, there is an impression of a bull in relief. Large areas of the doors are patterned as though the artist had been drawing with a plaster trowel.

My favorite pieces in this expansive show were the seven-foot eight-inch bull-headed *Queen Tut*, her epoxy horns seamlessly wed to her cherry head, and *Nam Mercury*, a cast bronze winged foot fashioned from propellors. The *Queen Tut* (1977) and the *Nam Mercury* (1966) seem best to capture the Majorowicz spirit, his controlled flights of fancy, the irregular, the accidental, the mythic reined in by a baroque cowboy.

September 23, 1983

Ghost Dance

Ghost Dance, an exhibition of works by 11 artists being held at the University of Maine-Farmington gallery through December 15, is a spiritual, if not always an artistic success. *Ghost Dance* is a tribalistic event straight out of the 1960s with all the big virtues and all the big faults of that apocalyptic decade. *Ghost Dance* is art as action, artist as avatar.

"The Ghost Dance religion, which swept through the Plains Indian tribes in the late nineteenth century," states the exhibition poster, "was a visionary response to a terribly desperate situation, imagination vs. annihilation."

Well, the Indian nation was annihilated and now all nations face a similar global fate. The artists' statement goes on to say, "As artists, we take our link with the Ghost Dance to be that continuous thread of consciousness that responds to despair with individual conceptions of ritual & art."

Abby Shahn organized the exhibition and her *Ghost Shirt In Five Pieces* is the purest expression of the show's messianic theme. Five luminous color squares of unframed paper are united by an armature of branches, cruciform arrangement bound in brown twine. Shahn's work is a shamanistic scarecrow, the gorgeous, flayed remains of civilization.

Abandoned by Margaret Leonard is a mixed-media work in which two ravenous grey wolves roam through a barren wasteland. A pair of human hands are wrapped about a central pole like scraps of humanity. You get the idea. The Ghost Dance was a death cult.

The most graphic representation of the threat that *Ghost Dance* responds to is *Bomb Lovers* by Nancy Marstaller and David Brooks. A plaster likeness of Marstaller sits astride a plaster likeness of Brooks on a bed of bleached bones and hawk feathers. A large black bomb is suspended above the lovers' heads. This is clearly a vision of the last act.

Brooks even manages a little gallows humor about the eschatological mess we've gotten ourselves into...or rather about those who have helped to make the mess. His *American Chiefs Staff* is a gay, particolored wooden crook made

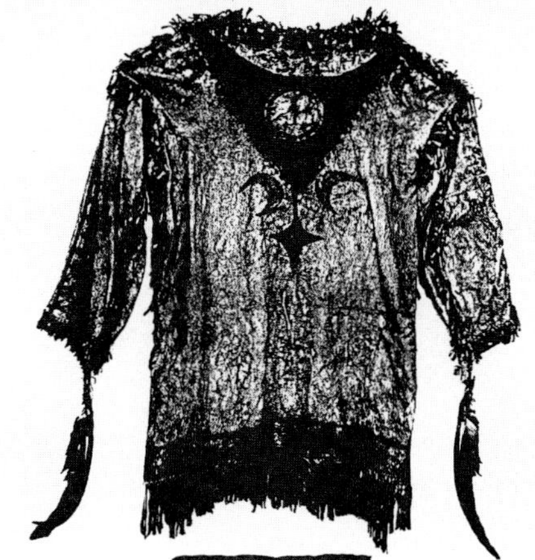

1. *Stephen Petroff,* Ghost Dance, *exhibition poster (detail), 1983. Pen and ink. Courtesy of the artist.*

of parts from a spool bed. From the tip of the staff hangs a fall of conservative neckties. Brooks' *Hail to the Chief* is a garish wooden war mask adorned with a fringe of swamp leaves.

One of the more ghoulish works is a collaboration between Judith Valentine and Baychar (Morris) called *Basket Heads.* In the crude grass basket the pair have placed four shrunken heads made of paper. Fetish magic runs through all of the assemblages Valentine and Baychar contribute.

The most flat-out angst and anger in the *Ghost Dance* exhibition comes from James Fangboner, an artist who does business as APIU (which, I am told, stands for Anti-Police Infiltration Unit). Fangboner's *Clip Board Series* consists of multiple messages and images attached to five hanging clipboards. The central clipboard holds a collaged image of Ronald Reagan as B-movie cowboy advertising "Build Your Own Monster."

Fangboner also contributes a series of box assemblages arrayed with none-too-subtle warnings about science, violence, and militarism. *Just a Second to Wave Bye-Bye*, for instance, consists of an image of an atomic accelerator in front of which stands a toy likeness of Yoda and a photograph of Rasputin.

"This is a political art," explains the exhibition poster, "but not politics-as-usual, no smugness, no hectoring, no more joy in having located a villain. We might be defined as those who would make art if we were the last people on earth—that is, we feel useful here and now."

November 11, 1983

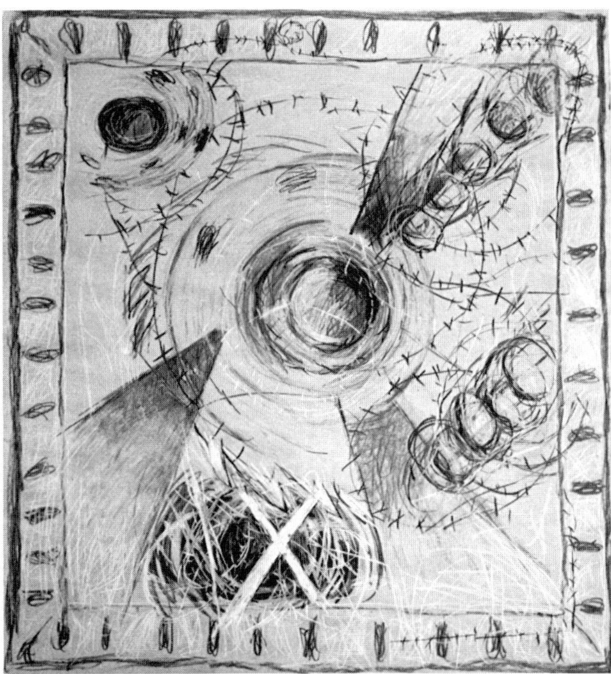

1. *Katherine Porter*, Untitled, *1981. Charcoal and pastel on tan wove paper. Courtesy of the Portland Museum of Art. Gift of Yvonne Jacquette, 1983.*

The Maine Drawing Biennial

The Maine Drawing Biennial at Portland Museum of Art (through February 26) is a show that raises a great many questions about how an exhibition such as this ought to be conceived and carried out, but first things (art) first.

What is a drawing? In trying to answer this questions, the Maine Drawing Biennial takes the traditional approach that a drawing is a linear composition, preferably in a dry medium such as graphite or charcoal; but there are many exceptions even to this rule.

In the case of Hans Moller, for instance, a drawing is a strictly linear outline. Moller has five drawings in the show, one of the best being an untitled Socratic head with profile and full-front views superimposed.

To Jay Kuhlman a drawing is a finished product. Kuhlman supplies three excellent formal portraits in pencil.

Then, of course, there's abstract artist William Manning, whose six ink, watercolor, graphite and wax crayon works show convincingly that a line can be a trail left in chromatic space and a drawing can be an act.

Elena Jahn's oil pastel and graphite landscape, *Evening path, Monhegan*, is a finished work, painterly in its execution. So are the 25 separate drawings that make up Natasha Mayers' oil stick and crayon *Toward a Town Map* series.

Drawing as pattern? Katharine Porter's untitled charcoal and pastel is an aggressive (even angry) pattern abstraction with formal border. Porter's drawing was given to the museum by Yvonne Jacquette, who is herself represented in the drawing show by a pastel, *Fly By Night I*, an aerial night view obligingly donated to the museum by Porter.

Alan Magee has the most subtle and involving drawing in the exhibition with his super-real colored pencil and watercolor, *Irony of Observation*, in which a woman's braided hair is superimposed over an addressed envelope (to Dr. George Magee in Philadelphia) and surrounded by anatomical drawings of human bones. For Magee, drawing is an exercise in the hand overcoming the eye...a revelation.

And Joseph Nicoletti, as though to demonstrate how a revelation is realized, gives us in *Studio Nude, Standing* a graphite sketch of a female torso which is then partially fleshed out in gouache.

So you begin to see the richness of possibilities? Whether drawing is end product or preliminary phase to creation, an artist who can't draw has his or her hands tied.

Now to the hard part. PMA director John Holverson and museum curator Michael Preble selected 103 drawings by 57 artists out of a field of 100 artists for the museum's first drawing biennial. The biennial started out as an invitational exhibition, but somewhere along the line was opened to juried submissions. The museum, apparently, did not get the word out wide and far that the biennial would be an open competition. Compare, for example, the 100 artists considered to the 800 or so artists who ordinarily turn out for the All Maine Biennial.

The Maine Drawing Biennial appears to be an exhibition made up of works by artists the museum officials knew about and artists who knew about the show. What this translates into are four distinct groupings: Portland area artists, well-established artists, a few artists discovered at museum portfolio review days, and the artists connected with Monhegan Island, where museum director Holverson spends time each summer. To its credit, the museum has defined "Maine" in the broadest possible context to

include summer visitors.

The museum also specified that all works in the show had to be available for sale and has itself purchased seven drawings from the exhibition for the permanent collection. The sales provision, according to Holverson, deterred artists Andrew Wyeth and Neil Welliver from showing in the biennial.

Lots of little problems, then, plague this drawing exhibition. Some artists invited, some artists juried, many artists who didn't hear about it. Twelve of 57 artists connected with Monhegan. Three museum employees in the show. No clear criteria established for what a drawing could be, but works rejected as not being drawings. Most of the drawings created in the last two years (as one would hope from a biennial), but several dating from the 1960s.

So what is the Maine Drawing Biennial? A flawed attempt to present an underappreciated art form in a meaningful context. Inclusion in a museum exhibition should accord an artist's work a certain distinction, but in this case, because of the irresolute manner in which the exhibition was carried out, it does not. Fortunately, the drawings in the exhibition are meaningful, even if the Maine Drawing Biennial is not.

January 13, 1984

Gretchen Langner

Artist Gretchen Langner moved to Maine in November, 1982, after spending the better part of 10 years in the Boston art scene. She came to Portland looking for a new start personally and professionally, and apparently the change of scenery did her some good; in the past year Gretchen Langner has emerged as one of the freshest, most vital talents in the state.

Currently (through March 30) a small selection of Langner's oil on paper drawings is hanging in the Attorney General's office in Augusta under the auspices of the Maine State Commission on the Arts and Humanities. Previously, Langner's works were exhibited at Union Mutual headquarters in Portland and a drawing was included in the Maine Drawing Biennial at the Portland Museum of Art, but soon Langner should be finding a wider Maine audience. Barridoff Galleries has recently contracted to represent her, and a generous selection of her works can be seen there in the basement gallery.

Langner's drawings at Barridoff are visions of innocence tempered with the wisdom of experience. The most lasting impressions are made by pictures like *Rois* (pronounced Rose) and *The Magic Rope*, both of which are visions of childhood. *Rois* is a double portrait of the artist's daughter with flowers. *The Magic Rope* is a triptych of colorfully attired children at play, each child captured at a moment of high energy and linked to the others by an invisible rope of vitality. This same childhood innocence and freshness informs a drawing of *The Beast*, a very childlike rendering of what appears to be a buffalo.

There is a more idyllic innocence at play in other Langner works which do not deal directly with childhood. A graduate of the Villa Schifanoia graduate school of fine arts in Florence, Langner sometimes draws on images recollected from time spent in Italy. *Memories of Stromboli* (an island off the coast of Sicily), for instance, isolates a romantic female figure against a dramatically simplified Mediterranean landscape. *Soft Breezes* isolates a woman's black arm highlighted by a gold bracelet and set against the brilliant pink of her skirt.

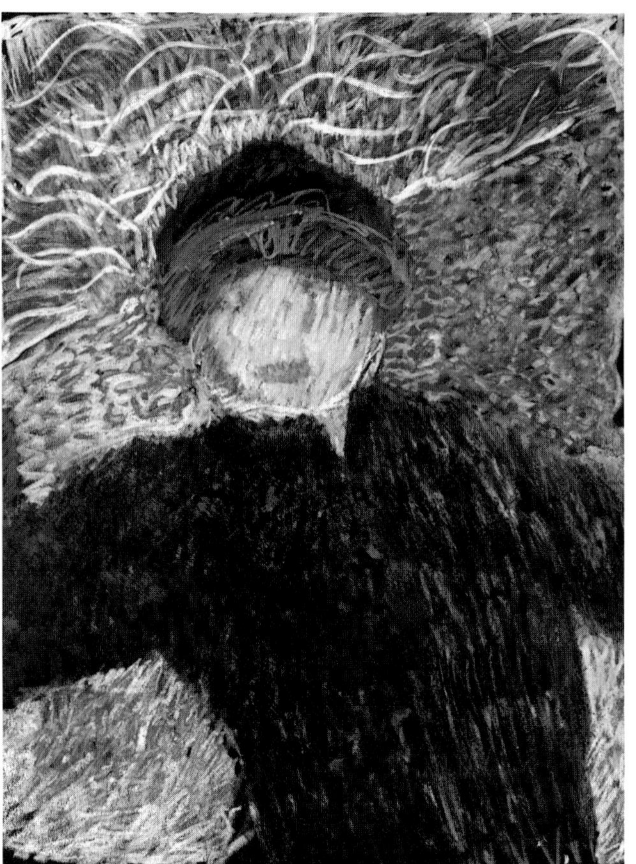

1. *Gretchen Langner,* Magic Rope, *triptych (detail). Oil on paper. Courtesy of the Barridoff Galleries.*

In all except her most recent work, Gretchen Langner has employed a use of color (simple, direct, pastel, and lyric) similar to Milton Avery and an approach to representation (flattened and reduced) akin to Alex Katz. Her method of composition is often to crop an otherwise realistic scene in such a way as to render it first as abstract color areas and only second as a constituted reality.

This principle of eccentric composition is everywhere evident in the works on exhibit at the Attorney General's office. Blood-red peonies burst from the frame against the background of a yellow vase. The green fronds of a spider plant rake down through a composition grounded by a red vase. A child's yellow head projects into a picture of a bather. In all of these pictures, the strong, uni-directional strokes speak to post-Impressionism and pointillism. The best of Langner's work in Augusta is a floral wallpaper-pattern abstraction heavily redolent of Matisse and showing the artist's roots quite clearly.

But if Gretchen Langner's work does find origins in the romance of French Impressionism, it is clearly headed toward German expressionism along with most of contemporary American painting today.

A visit to Langner's Congress Street studio revealed that, as her energy heats up, her imagery and execution are becoming more liberated. Compare, for example, the sedate and studied air of *Anticipation of Anja* to the keyed-up female figure of *On the Terrace for a Breath of Fresh Air*. Langner, along with artists like Billie Bowman, Richard Baron, and Gary Buch, is one of those bringing New Wave kink influences to art in Maine. The cultural constant in the art of the '80s is a sense of menace, frenzy, and hysteria, and Langner is capable of portraying this nervous energy from neurasthenia to mania.

All of Langner's art is infused with a feminine aesthetic and female point of view. She brings a kind of tenderness and gentleness to the wildness of contemporary neo-expressionism. And in some of the works she has not exhibited yet—color-charged abstractions that look like Punk fried eggs, multi-panel figures, figures buried under gaudy quilts—she makes a strong entry into the terrain of decorative pattern painting pioneered by women. Through all of these rapid developments, however, Gretchen Langner manages to remain her own woman.

March 16, 1984

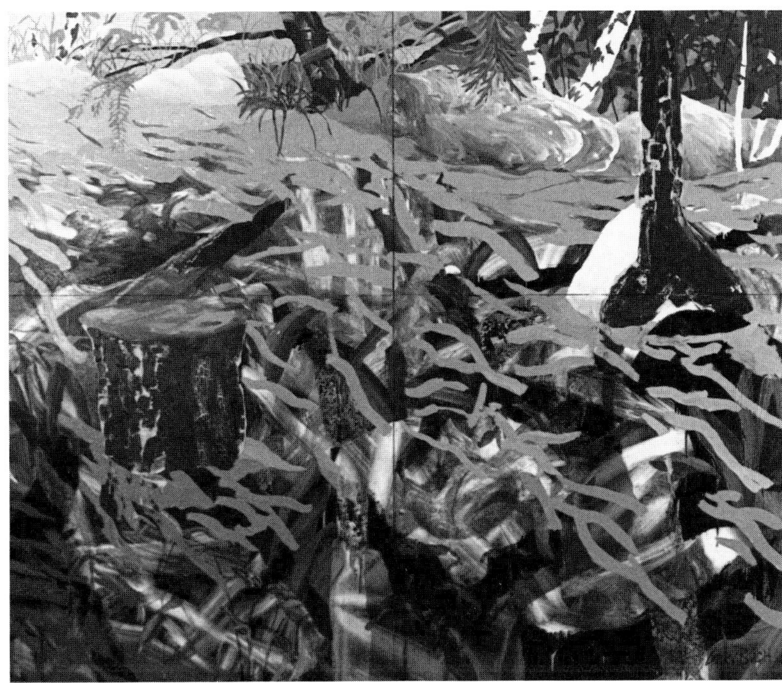

1. *Gary Buch,* The Illusion is deep as the night. *Oil on panel. Courtesy of Hobe Sound Galleries North.*

Celeste Roberge and Gary Buch

Just five years out of art school, sculptor Celeste Roberge has captured most of the artistic terrain Maine has to offer—a scholarship to the Skowhegan School, exhibitions at Bowdoin, Maine Coast Artists, Spectra, the Barn Gallery, a juror's role at the 1983 Maine Biennial. Her current exhibition at Hobe Sound Galleries North (with painter Gary Buch through April 7) establishes Roberge in my mind as the most talented sculptor Maine has produced in at least a decade.

Celeste Roberge works in steel—honest, straightforward welded steel—at a comfortable human scale. At Hobe Sound she is showing one work, *Casanova Swing*, which was previously exhibited at Rockport, and two new sculptures in a *Botanical Series*. *Casanova Swing*, an enigmatic draping of rusted wire over a suspended armature, has been my candidate for the most original three-dimensional work produced in Maine since I first saw it, but it is also difficult for the general public to respond to. In her *Botanical Series*, Roberge has successfully rendered her sculpture more accessible without sacrificing much in the way of formal integrity.

Botanical Series: English Hawthorne is a green and coppery painted steel tree inspired by a trip the artist took to Scotland. The steel tree reaches out with naked branches swept away as though bent by years of fighting the wind and elements. Like a great deal of the best in art, Roberge's sculptures have that elemental quality which comes from reducing nature to simplest forms.

Botanical Series: Daphne 2 is an oxidized steel tree created out of piping and crimped wire. Daphne, saved from the rape of Apollo by being turned into a laurel tree, seems caught in mid-metamorphosis—the bent, blunt trunk of pipes giving way to crimped upper branches as thick and streaming as a full head of hair. Roberge's art is patently feminine in a way no other artist I know of anywhere has managed in steel.

If Celeste Roberge is the best, then Gary Buch is a leading candidate for the brightest. His super-charged landscape oils escape from a brilliant palette of colors so hot these paintings are almost thermo-chromatic, having the distinct look of infra-red thermography.

Buch's unblinking use of Day-Glo oranges and yellows, garish greens, and glaring blues presents such a challenge (assault?) to the eye that I have a feeling there is no middle ground between loving and hating them. The viewer is either put off or bowled over. I'm bowled over every time. In the past I have tended to interpret his use of color as the feverish result of an overheated imagination, but Buch suggests his electric palette is really more about painting than hallucinating.

"Using all of these kinds of industrial, junky

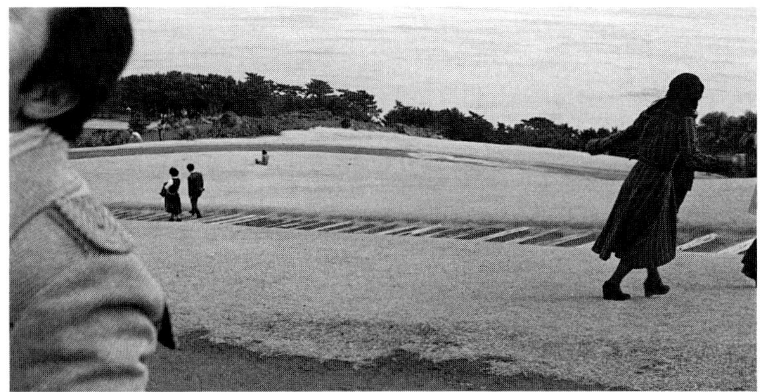

1. *John McKee,* Kawashiri, Japan, 1976. *Black & white silver print. Courtesy of the artist.*

apartment colors," Buch says, "I'm trying to use really ugly colors to make them exciting and maybe not ugly anymore."

Buch landscapes, until recently, were inhabited or haunted by roaming, crazed animals like dogs and penguins, but only one painting at Hobe Sound North contains animal figures. *Keep the river on your right*, a pulsating forest landscape with an inky river flowing through it, is prowled by two ghostly grey dogs (wolves?) that all but disappear into the forest surroundings. This merger of animal figure and ground is just as intentional as the banishment of the figure from the remaining landscapes.

Buch reports losing interest in the narrative quality of his paintings, feeling that figures (even animal figures) provide focal spots "at the expense of the whole painting."

"I'm not interested in illustrating," Buch says. "I'm interested in painting." For that reason, he believes he must "subordinate detail to mass."

Buch's landscapes, thick with the adventure of painting one's way out of a wilderness, often bear literary titles—*There must be other deeper forests for me*, *Searching for an herb of forgetfulness*, etc.—which Buch says are incidental and often interchangeable. One title, however, seems to me to speak to the kind of impact Buch has achieved in his painting: *The jungle either accepts you or rejects you*. These paintings are on you before you have a chance to judge them.

Gary Buch has just won a scholarship to the Skowhegan School and Celeste Roberge is turning her attention to graduate school (the spawning ground of contemporary art stars). Their art works have the power and drama to stand up to one another in this gallery context, and to recommend both Roberge and Buch to a much wider audience.

April 6, 1984

John McKee

Last week photographer John McKee spoke to some 50 friends, colleagues, and admirers at the Bowdoin College Museum of Art on the occasion of his grand retrospective, *John McKee Photographs 73-83* (through May 27).

Among other things, McKee told the gallery gathering that for the past 10 years he has been interested in photographing places where neither man nor nature is dominant, but where the two exist simultaneously, or "interface," to use McKee's term. The majority of the prints in the 100-picture exhibit, then, depict barren European landscapes, stony places where the ribs of earth show through. But these are civil wilds, places where centuries of human passage have marked the land in benign ways…a stone wall here, a twist of ancient roadbed there.

Recently, Maine has had a feast of McKee. Best known until now for his landmark *As Maine Goes* exhibition at Bowdoin in 1966, McKee seemed (at least to me) to be dormant in recent years. Then last summer these brilliant, empty landscapes emerged at the 1983 Maine Biennial and reappeared later at Barridoff Galleries' first photographic exhibit. If, then, one thinks of John McKee as the crusading environmentalist of *As Maine Goes* (images of coastal clutter, litter, development, and decay), *Photographs 73-83* celebrates a more mature vision, indeed a spiritual vision.

Many of the best photographs in the Bowdoin show were taken on the Causse Mejean plateau in France where McKee has lived for part of the year over the past few years. In this bleak, limestone landscape McKee seems to have found a spiritual home.

"This was a place in the world that could serve as the center of the universe," McKee told his listeners.

Thus, it is with reverent stillness that McKee photographs this solemn, almost sacred landscape.

"John McKee is a classic landscape photographer," critic Philip Isaacson tells us in his sensitive and appreciative introduction to the show's catalogue. McKee's landscapes say this too.

Not all of the prints in the exhibition are

landscapes, however. Some of the liveliest are oddly peopled places photographed in Japan in 1976. There, too, McKee was often drawn to "sacred sites"...temples and shrines, Zen gardens of raked sand and still stone islands. In these Japanese photographs, McKee often appears to be following the snapshot school of thinking, clicking off quirky views for no obvious reason other than to capture a moment on film. Figures move into and out of the picture frame in seemingly random fashion, creating skewed patterns in which people are but elements of design. Here McKee seems more concerned with "seeing" (the artist as subject) than with the subject at hand. But McKee confesses that some of the odd angles in his Japanese photographs are created by temperament, rather than design. John McKee is a shy man and he finds it difficult to point a camera at strangers.

All of the photographs in the show are black and white prints. Asked why he prefers black and white to color, McKee replied, "I like black and white because it is expected that you are going to produce something other than a second-rate version of the real thing."

McKee also told the audience that he most often photographs abroad because away from home, "I have no other object." Since his whole reason for being in a foreign land is to photograph, McKee finds it easier to concentrate and focus. As artists through the ages have often found, exile (or travel) can produce a wonderful singularity of purpose.

McKee spoke of the need for photographs to be at once "deliberately difficult" in order to involve the viewer and "immediately appealing" in order to engage the viewer's attention in the first place. All of John McKee's photographs have a rich complexity of detail, but if they are vulnerable on any count it might be (particularly in an exhibition setting where there are so many ostensibly similar photographs) on the matter of "immediate appeal." McKee is not always a grabber. You have to look into and around in a John McKee photograph, but if you take the time and care, you will always be rewarded.

April 27, 1984

Jamie Wyeth

When respected art critic Hilton Kramer (in Portland to deliver a lecture on Gaston Lachaise) recently dismissed Jamie Wyeth as "a terrible painter" and "a slick illustrator," I was reminded with a wince just how glib and vicious we can be in pronouncing our judgments on artists. Coming from a critic of Kramer's status, it almost sounds as though Wyeth has no right to exist, his paintings being so offensive as to present an affront to the refined sensibility. Most critics (myself included) have an unfortunate habit of responding to work judged inferior or unworthy with language that makes it seem the artist involved is a bad person, a criminal, worse.

When Jamie Wyeth came to town last week for the opening of *Jamie Wyeth: An American View* at the Portland Museum of Art (through September 9), I asked him his response to Hilton Kramer's dismissal. Wyeth replied that he feels some people are blinded to his work because they can't see past his commercial success and his family name.

"If you have any degree of success, that's the kiss of death in the critics' eyes," said Wyeth. He said that Kramer in particular among critics "spends most of his time speaking about my family" when reviewing his work.

Artists like Jamie Wyeth do present a real problem for intellectuals. There seems to be the feeling that the popularity of such accessible artists blinds the public to richer visual experiences, impoverishing the culture in general, and frustrating more serious artists in particular. If you believe that Norman Rockwell or LeRoy Neiman is the most important artist of his day, is there any way in the world you can get anything out of Willem DeKooning?

Certainly I understand what Hilton Kramer means when he pegs Wyeth as an illustrator. The comparison I would make is to a writer of well-researched historical romances. There is absolutely nothing wrong with such romances. Some of them are very fine and very intelligent. It's just that you wouldn't want one of these period pieces confused with serious literature, nor would you want to read them exclusively.

In viewing the Wyeth exhibit at the Portland

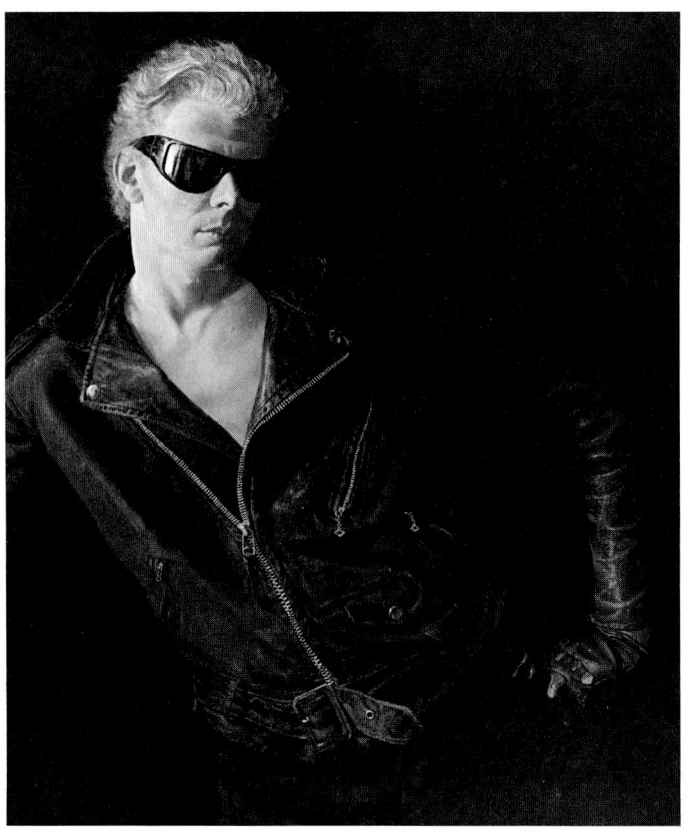

1. *Jamie Wyeth,* Draft Age, *1965. Oil on canvas. Courtesy of the Brandywine River Museum.*

Museum of Art, it was immediately clear to me that it was as a portraitist that Jamie Wyeth distinguished himself. I say "was" because the works that most deserve to be taken seriously in this 32 painting mini-retrospective covering work from 1963 to 1984 are the portraits, several painted in the 1960s, some in the mid-1970s.

Probably the richest single work in the exhibition is Wyeth's oil *Portrait of Andy Warhol* in which America's premier art star gazes out at us with his patented zombie stare. Warhol, red-eyed and pale, clutches a miniature Dachshund that is as sickly as he is.

In his portraits of John Kennedy (1967), Andrew Wyeth (1969), Shorty (1963), and in the powerful figure of rebellious youth in *Draft Age* (1965), the young Wyeth (and he was only 19 when he painted *Draft Age*, remember) brings a contemporary idiom to a traditional approach to portraiture that follows in a direct American line from Gilbert Stuart and Rembrandt Peale to Thomas Eakins.

It is when Wyeth indulges his affection for animals—pigs, cows, dogs, geese, and chickens all inhabit Wyeth's world—that he verges on cuteness. But it is in paintings like *Wicker* (1979), a young woman in straw sunhat lost in a sea of white Victorian wicker, and *Excursion Boats* (1982), the same young woman in an ornate wicker wheelchair looking out over a party of little boats, that Wyeth goes overboard.

I asked Wyeth whether he realized he was laying himself open for criticism by painting such frothy period pieces. He replied that these scenes were not anachronistic (the very word I was searching for), that they exist on Monhegan Island where he has always spent his summers. I could only conclude then that it is Monhegan that is the anachronism, for these paintings clearly do not speak to our age. They are filled with nostalgia and sentimentality. But Wyeth defuses this criticism by admitting that he is a sentimentalist.

"I hope they say I'm sentimental," said Wyeth.

Wyeth's brief comments and this small exhibition persuaded me of a suspicion I have harbored in recent years that rather than dismiss the Wyeths as popularizers, we must regard them as a special case. There is obviously a private, magical world—sometimes vaguely mystical and sinister, sometimes just too well-loved and privileged—that is inhabited only by Wyeths. Just look at *Kleberg* (1984) and tell me this is not true.

Kleberg is a mutt with a perfect ring (*à la* Our Gang) around his left eye. He is posed next to a great beehive. Behind him are shelves of books. The books on Wyeth's dim background shelves speak to us of his world. *The Stray*, a children's book by his mother. Robert Louis Stevenson's *Treasure Island*, illustrated by Wyeth's grandfather. Pyle's *Book of Pirates*. Monographs on Degas and Eakins. John Fowles' mind-bending reality trip, *The Magus*. And Alain-Fournier's *The Wanderer*, the book about a youth's search for philosophical truth that inspired Fowles.

Jamie Wyeth is a young man lost in a magical world. He knows it as reality. I guess some critics just don't believe it exists.

June 29, 1984

Inside/Outside

Inside/Outside, the 1984 Maine Artists Invitational co-sponsored by Bowdoin College and the Maine Festival of the Arts (through August 19), is an exhibition with a simple premise that leads to a marvelously rich and complex visual experience.

Curator John Coffey's "thin thematic veneer" is that the works of the 16 artists he has selected all express "the character of space, the territory within and without us." All works of art deal in one way or another with space, but the imaginative diversity of spatial concerns taken on by these particular artists is remarkable challenging and satisfying.

Painter Frederick Lynch and fabric artists Gayle Fraas and Duncan Slade involve the viewer with the real space of the Bowdoin art gallery. Lynch's *Corner Piece* is a wood construction painted in acrylics. Its real planes and edges and painted planes all work on and in the gallery corner for which they were designed. Lynch defines space both pictorially and literally, tucking his painted elements into the corner of the construction and wrapping the entire two-part work around its assigned corner.

Fraas and Slade have transformed the stairwell that connects the two exhibition galleries into a decorative passageway which is (as they have suggested) half Egyptian tomb entry and half Coney Island funhouse entry. *Entrance, Exit, and the Forgotten Link* begins with an elaborate geometric door surround that leads into a stairwell painted with tumbling little triangles, all of which ultimately call attention to a panel on the lower level upon which is painted an archetypal arch. The installation can be enjoyed both as a kind of funky Art Deco escalator decor and as a celebration of the negative space that separates and connects one perceived space to another.

Susan Groce and James Linehan both create intricate spatial illusions. Groce's mixed-media triptych drawing has the viewer flying over a bent and folded maze, an idealized space that is at once mental and architectural. Linehan's *Southern Exposure* is a 20-foot, four-panel *tour de force* that on its simplest level is a studio interior with white table and chair and *trompe l'oeil* photographs taped to the...but where are the walls? The walls are everywhere and nowhere in this exploded blue and green space. Linehan's is one of the most exciting paintings I have seen in a long time, surrealism that is somehow more factual than fantastic.

Beverly Hallam's large floral still lifes contain technical manipulations of pure space as defined by light, shadow, and reflection. *Goldenrod*, for instance, is a simple sprig of golden weed in a clear glass vase imprisoned in a cage of bars created by light and shade coming through a venetian blind. Painted from photographs, these elegant paintings create a magical space at once real and ethereal.

Perhaps the works that fit the inside/outside theme with the greatest conceptual economy are DeWitt Hardy's watercolors, both of which show interior scenes with exterior landscapes visible through windows. *Scene from a Trip to the West* is a refreshing departure for Hardy, being a self-portrait of the artist on a berth in a train compartment with a rugged Western landscape flashing by out the window. Inside, outside, moving through space.

Christine Woelfle's intense and precise plywood and glass constructions define open architectural spaces and arrive to the eye in their intricacies like fanciful houses of the mind. Elena Jahn partitions and obstructs real space with a five-panel folding screen, *Ocean/Sky—Looking West from Monhegan*, a piece of interior furnishing upon which is painted a morning-to-night sequence of seascape. Pat Hardy's horizontal watercolor landscapes (a departure for her as well) subtly play with perspective in space by giving us a 360-degree panorama forced into a single plane. Gretchen Langner also exerts pressure on real space by pushing it up flat against the picture plane so that perceived realities (decorative patterns from domestic interiors) become painted abstractions.

In David Crowley's immensely still oils—cubes and rectangles of what look to be quarried pink granite—the outside (stone) has been brought inside to sit for portraits that are ultimately minimal abstractions which bring to mind the deep chromatic meditations of Mark Rothko.

Sculptors Lin Lisberger and Harriet Mat-

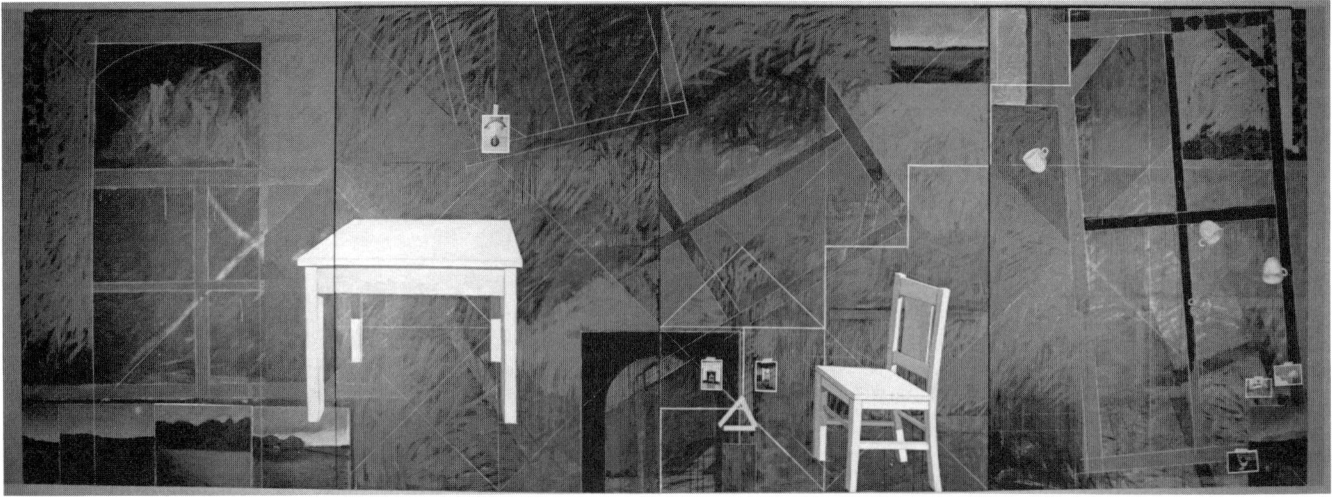

1. *James Linehan,* Southern Exposure, *1984. Oil and acrylic on canvas. Courtesy of the artist. Photo by Dennis Griggs.*

thews use the obvious advantages of three dimensions to exploit the inside-out properties of fantasy. Lisberger's little carved and constructed popular piece, *Sunday Supper*, is like a child's fancy in which a tree evolves into a house. Matthews' welded steel *The Old Gypsy's House, In the Clouds* is a kind of organic celestial dome broken open to reveal perfect stars peeling from the inside of the sphere. The ripe universe in the clouds is supported by a ladder to the stars in this cosmic construction.

The works in the exhibition with the thinnest relation to the show's thematic veneer are three paintings by Kevin Donahue. Donahue's paintings of a studio still life and a house in Brunswick satisfy the inside and the outside, but the cameo portrait of a young woman placed between them seems out of place in this context.

Now for the most ambitious and one of the most inspired creations of *Inside/Outside*, Marjorie Moore's *The Artist As Hunter*. Borne ever onward by her enduring obsession with Maine's rural society, Moore has constructed an ersatz see-through log cabin about the size of a toolshed in the Bowdoin gallery. Inside the log cabin is a fireplace. In the hearth is a television monitor. On the monitor plays a video tape of Marjorie Moore as deer hunter. The tape is a satiric, black comic drama in which the artist stalks and shoots one of her own paintings of a deer. Blasting the stylized stag with a stick rifle, Moore lights up the painting which is then consumed in flames. The artist-hunter scoops up the ashes and places them in a vase, the same vase which now sits on the mantelpiece above the hearth monitor. The drama done, the viewer is treated to a few minutes of cool fire as flames flicker on the screen.

Art is a brave front thrown up in the face of death. *The Artist as Hunter* is a performance not to be missed.

July 6, 1984

Alan Bray and Nancy Wisseman-Widrig

Very few of the best artists working in Maine are natives of the state. Alan Bray is one of the brightest exceptions. Born in Waterville and brought up in Dover-Foxcroft where he still resides, Bray honed his very personal vision of Maine in isolation, away from both the centers of artistic influence and the centers of Maine culture. He is by no means a naive talent, yet the Maine reality he conveys through his magical paintings is infused with a primitive sense of the landscape as inhabited by an intelligence or animus of its own.

Because Bray is a painstaking and not very prolific painter, the selection of seven *New Paintings* on exhibition at Portland's Barridoff Galleries (through August 11) constitutes a rare opportunity to see a body of his work. These seven paintings reveal an artist who has penetrated the deep structure of the Maine reality in a now lucid, now visionary style that stands in brilliant contrast to the usual visions we are treated to by artists in the state.

The same day that I viewed Alan Bray's exhibition, I also viewed an exhibition of *Maine Paintings* by Nancy Wisseman-Widrig at Hobe Sound Galleries North (also through August 11) and the contrast between the competing visions of Maine was nailed down for me. Wisseman-Widrig is a highly accomplished and highly respected painter who works in Cushing in the summer and New York the rest of the year. While I do not wish to suggest that her view of Maine is superficial compared to Bray's, I do submit that it is a limited view and one generic to artists who primarily experience Maine as Vacationland. Her Maine is the world of the summer coast, a pretty world of privilege, idleness, and ease. Bray, on the other hand, experiences the interior Maine, the internal Maine. He has internalized his environment. Summerfolk play in theirs.

The most ambitious of Wisseman-Widrig's paintings is a large acrylic, *Top of the Cove*, which depicts a stretch of water and a spit of land bracketed between tree trunks. In the distance a sailboat with pristine white sails moves sunnily across the scene. In *April-May* a lone figure rests in a lawn chair and contemplates the early spring greenery of a world of off-season pink and browns. A sailboat lies moored at anchor ready to take the figure cruising through his recreational world.

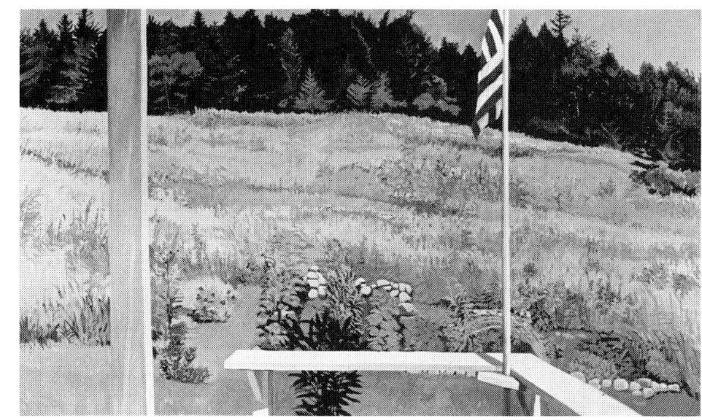

1. *Nancy Wisseman-Widrig,* American Field. *Oil. Courtesy of Hobe Sound Galleries North.*

The summer world is safe, pretty, pleasant, romantic, innocent. The reality lies elsewhere.

Every single one of Alan Bray's seven casein paintings invoked in me that same uneasy, slightly threatened feeling I experience when straying too far from the urban-suburban Maine I know well into the backcountry. There is, for instance, *Right of Way*, a fairly straightforward rendering of what I take to be a powerline clearcut through dense woods. Man has made this mark upon the earth, but man is not safe here. The beauty of the trees and of the barren, bouldery earth is too impersonal, too unmindful of man. Bray paints these simple natural elements as though they possessed a mind of their own. The very modeling of the foliage and rock structures suggests brain whorls.

In *Blowdown*, a dense mass of bare trees lie dead and tangled, barring passage. In *Quarry Point*, six nimble birches protrude from a stark landscape crazily concatenated of slabs of drill-striated slate. The major slab thrusts itself up like a stone zebra rearing into view. This is not a place we want to be.

Bray's sense of menace and the ominous is quite literal in *Calamity*. A dressing table and dining table with toppled chair rest in a bare patch of lawn in a snowy landscape presided over by naked trees. The narrative explanation is probably house fire, but these trees have the presence of a coven of witches and seem somehow to be witness to/even responsible for the calamity. You know this Maine?

But the masterwork of Bray's septet is *An*

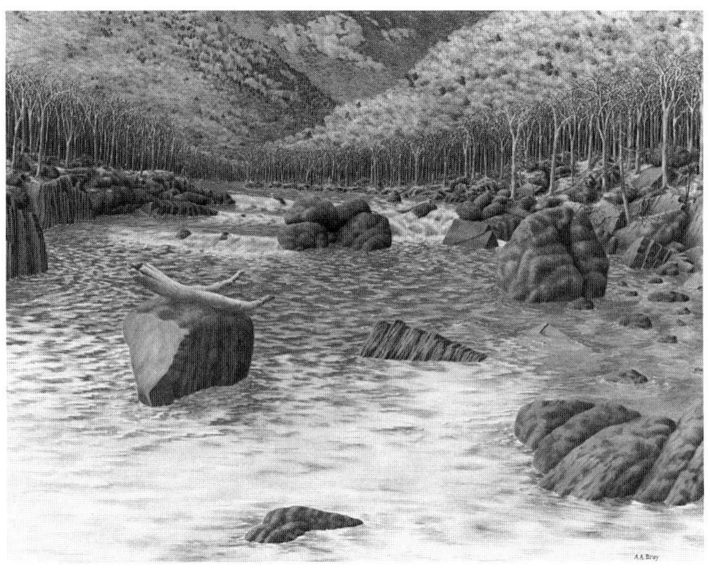

2. *Alan Bray*, An Interval, On the Death of My Father, Jan. 12, 1984. *Casein on panel. Courtesy of the Barridoff Galleries.*

Interval, On the Death of My Father, Jan. 12, 1984. The viewer is placed midstream looking upriver at waters strewn with erratics. The focus of the painting is a boulder upon which a dead limb has been left stranded. Bare trees sprout from the river banks like whiskers. The world is suffused with unnatural pinks and purples over its sullen greys and browns. Even without the emotional direction of the title, this would still be one of the loneliest paintings I have ever seen in my life. We may not know this place, but we all know this reality.

July 27, 1984

1985 Maine Biennial

If you look to the Maine Biennial exhibitions to be showcases for the best art in the state, you will be disappointed in the 1985 edition (at the Portland Museum of Art through March 3). But if you look to the biennial to give exposure to new talent, you will be delighted by the 1985 Maine Biennial, *Paintings by Maine Artists*. In my case, I found 30 of the 64 artists in the show were previously unknown to me. The undeniable energy of the '85 Biennial is the energy of discovery.

The show-stealers of the exhibition, however, are by one of Maine's best and best-known artists, Abby Shahn. Shahn's large (55 x 92 inch), vibrant, twinkling egg tempera color square compositions, *The Blanket of the Night* and *Ground Cover*, impose a kind of rational aesthetic grid over chaotic natural phenomena. In recognition of her achievement, the Portland Museum of Art has purchased *The Blanket of the Night* for its permanent collection.

But in keeping with the new talent excellence of this biennial, the museum has also purchased *The Gardener*, a loose and lively image of a young woman hoeing her garden, by Douglas Frati, an artist who graduated from Portland School of Art only two years ago.

Familiar names on the Maine art scene are conspicuously absent from the 1985 Maine Biennial. Among the few well-known painters represented are John Laurent, Fran Merritt, Johnnie Ross, Stuart Ross, and Wendy Kindred. Kindred, in fact, is one of only five artists (Rufus Coes, John Heagen Eames, Thaddeus Macy, and Barbara Peakes are the other four) who have been selected to exhibit in all three open juried biennials (1979, 1981, and 1985—the 1983 Biennial at Colby was an invitational show).

The question on everyone's lips at the opening of the 1985 Maine Biennial was "Who are these artists?" The fact of the matter is that many of the artists in the show have never exhibited in Maine before...some have never exhibited their works, period.

Katherine Allen, who contributed three gouache on paper collages, is a relative newcomer to Maine, the wife of Ray Allen, the new dean at the Portland School of Art. Diane

Dahlke, whose acrylic of three ducks explored white in terms of the unexpected colors that inform the absence of color, arrived in Cumberland only two months ago, but she is a trained artist who has shown frequently in Connecticut galleries. Cliff Gallant, who had an oil-based wax on paper male figure study accepted, is a South Portland salesman who has never exhibited before. Anne Gresinger, represented by a powerful expressionist self-portrait of art student as soulful sufferer, is a student at the Portland School of Art. Joe Klofas, who painted a haunting nocturne of his former home in Bridgton, is an English teacher at Sanford High School who has painted since childhood but has never shown before. Margaret Libby, a Colby art grad who returned to Maine after giving New York a try, found inspiration for her wonderfully witty *Hiroshima Day Sale on Chicks* (a tableau of soft-porn nudes interwoven with advertising graphics) in encounters with male chauvinists while on the job as a waitress in Waterville. Theodore James Murphy, whose three surreal landscapes are sleepers in this exhibition, is an Orono artist who came to my attention just last year with a flaming yak he contributed to a juried competition at the Farnsworth in Rockland. And Peter L. Sheldon, represented by two fine little precisionist acrylics, is a retired English professor from St. Joseph's College in Windham who has been a long-time supporter of art in Maine, but who surfaces here (after being rejected from the two previous juried biennials under a *nomme de brosse*) with works that show the distinctive influences of his discovery of Italian Futurists as a student in Rome back in 1960-61.

And these are but a few of the talented unknowns brought to light by *Paintings by Maine Artists*.

Curiously, the 1985 Maine Biennial is weak where Maine art is traditionally strong—in landscape paintings. J. Thomas R. Higgins' painterly oil, *Norridgewock Farm*, looks rather lonely and out-of-place in an exhibition dominated by works of high color and high-keyed emotions. If there is a distinct bias in the judging of the show, it is a bias against traditional realism. In fact, the designers of the show seem to have been sensitive to this bias, hanging the few academic realist pieces in a hidden alcove of the gallery.

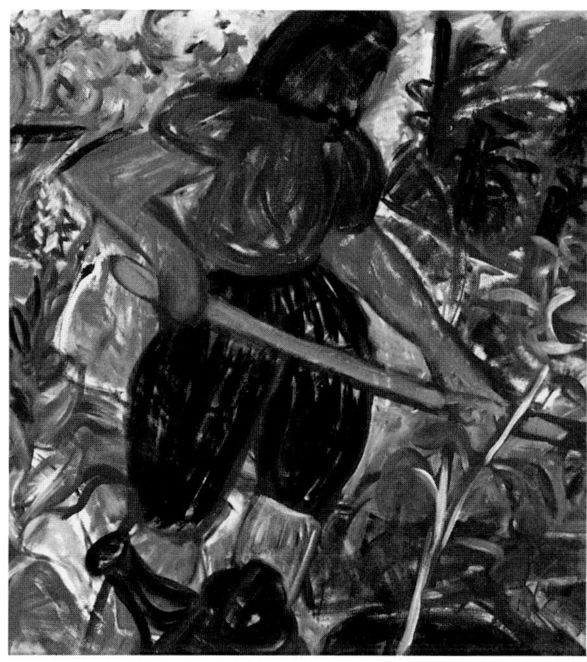

1. *Douglas Frati,* The Gardener, *1984. Oil on canvas. Courtesy of the Portland Museum of Art. Purchased in part with gifts from Joan B. Burns, Annette and Rob Elowitch, Alison D. Hildreth, Dr. and Mrs. Harold L. Osher, Horace K. Sowles, Jr., Roger and Katherine Woodman and one anonymous donor, 1985.*

The jurors for the 1985 Maine Biennial were art dealer and print publishers Brooke Alexander and Diane Villani, and painter Judith Rothschild. Asked in the midst of their jurying how Maine submissions differed from what they might find in a similar show in New York, the jurors cited a preponderance of realism in the Maine paintings and a certain freedom from fashionable influence...which I interpreted as a scarcity of neo-expressionist images. To my eye the only true fashion-conscious work in the exhibition is a large (96 x 96) two-panel encrusted creation by Richard Baron entitled *Recognition of Baelitz*. I assume the title is a misprint of the name of German art star George Baselitz, who, like Baron in this case, paints human figures upside-down.

The predictable discussions of who got in and who didn't are essentially meaningless in this competition, the choice of 84 works from 1098 submitted reflecting solely the tastes of three individuals. Three other equally qualified judges might well have selected an entirely different show of equal quality. It should also be remembered that looking at 1098 works of art in one day is a less than ideal situation for exercising critical judgment. That the judges should have settled on high-impact paintings while possibly overlooking works of subtler qualities may be a natural result of the judging process.

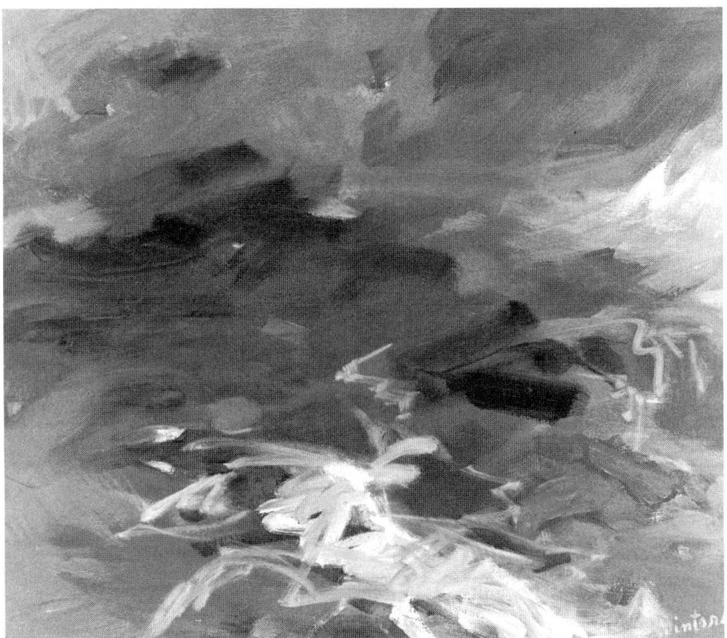

1. *Denny Winters*, Roiling Sea. *Oil. Courtesy of Lew Dietz.*

To their credit, however, the judicial trio did manage to keep the 1985 Maine Biennial quite free of both the sweet romanticism and decorative styles that weigh so heavily on the summer art season in Maine. The judges seem to have preferred evident struggle to effortlessness and facility, rewarding perseverance over polish.

What we see in *Paintings by Maine Artists* is the maturing of the Maine Biennial. The inaugural event in 1979 drew 812 submissions from 438 artists in all media, and resulted in a very crowded exhibition at Bowdoin College of 167 works by 141 artists. The 1981 democratic free-for-all at the University of Southern Maine drew 689 submissions from 394 artists and resulted in a very unsatisfying exhibition of 149 works by 149 artists in a variety of media. Surprisingly, the 1985 Biennial, limited to painting, drew 1098 works by 422 artists, resulting in a very selective show of just half the size of previous biennials—84 works by 64 painters.

Very selective. Very fine. The 1985 Maine Biennial should serve as a model for state-sponsored shows to come.

January 25, 1985

Denny Winters

If realism dominates the art of Maine, the subdominant strain is natural abstraction. Few, if any, artists working in Maine have ever produced pure abstractions, free of associations with the external reality, but many have made emotional and stylistic abstractions based on personal responses to the land, the light, the sea. One of the best was Denny Winters (1907-1985).

Denny Winters: A Commemorative Show (recently concluded at the Leighton Gallery in Blue Hill) honored the memory of a woman whose strongest responses were to the atmosphere of the Maine coast, not the big forms, textures, and colors, but the quality of specific moments in time marked by the passing of clouds and the ebb and flow of the tides. Her best works were painterly, lyric atmospheric abstractions, light canvases fulminating with amorphous color.

But since Denny Winters clearly saw with her heart, she was occasionally guilty of loving Maine too well. At least this is one way to account for the inconsistency of her vision. At her strongest—as with paintings like *Touch of Class* (1982), *Rock-Strewn Beach* (1980), *Ocean Floor* (1980)—Winters produced symphonic, Turneresque responses to place and time. Paintings like these are distillations of air, water, and light in which the world is kept poetically out of focus...as though in a haze of memory and reflection. Unfortunately, when Winters brought the world into sharper focus, she was capable of committing rather corny romantic cliches.

A painting like *Cloud Reflections* (1979) is spoiled by the needless inclusion of strolling beachcombers. The effect is somewhat like having cartoon characters inexplicably strolling through a Rothko painting. Entirely inappropriate. Invariably, whenever figures appear in the midst of her atmospheric abstractions, the painting is diminished and a kind of disturbing Simbari romanticism takes over.

Yet, though Winters had lapses in taste, she clearly understood that time was the essence of her art. This is why her best work is shapeless and formless, coming to us as orchestrations of

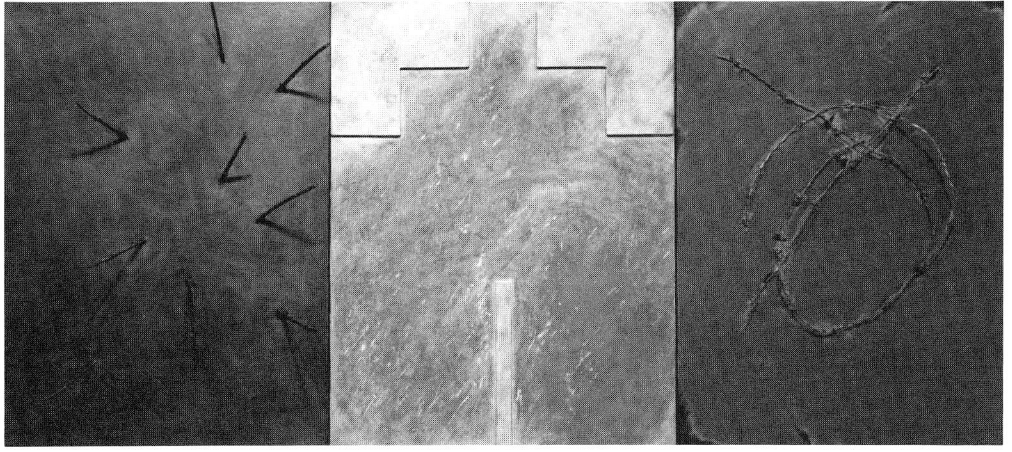

1. *Paul Maddrell,* Mystery Grace and Desire *(triptych), 1985. Acrylic. Courtesy of Maine Coast Artists. Photo by Richard Weatherwax.*

loosely applied colors capturing the momentary vision. Movement is everything in a Winters painting, and when her surfaces cease to move (as when bathers suddenly appear), they fail...they die.

The temporal underpinnings of Winters' art are graphically revealed in the late collages the artist created dealing with time in its most measured form. *Fragments of Time* (1984) and *Half Time* (1983) depart from the atmospheric to explore the chronometric in compositions keyed to the faces of clocks. Time passing. Time running out. Yet all time eternally circular...like the rotation of the globe that sends the clouds whirling around the earth, like the orbit of the moon that determines the rhythm of the tides.

June 21, 1985

Abstractions

Nine artists are represented in Maine Coast Artists' *Abstractions*, among them several of the state's best non-representational artists. But if the field were just twice as large, the Rockport show might actually include *all* of the abstract artists in the state worth considering.

Maine, the realists' haven, has never been strong on abstract art. Where nature presses so heavily on the senses and sensibilities, even abstractions tend to be rooted in the concrete realities of the external world. So it is a bit surprising to see in this coastal gathering of hardcore abstract artists that the nucleus of Maine's best non-representational painters are working not in the natural, organic, expressive tradition, but rather out of a cool, rigid, analytic aesthetic...imposing an Apollonian sense of order on the Dionysian rush of physical and psychic phenomenon. Maine's best abstract artists seem to share a predisposition for tight constructions, shaped canvases, color squares, grids, hard edges...a rather architectural approach to building a painting.

William Manning is probably the state's best-known and most accomplished (as well as long-suffering) abstract artist. His wall-mounted acrylic on wood constructions project from the wall into the viewer's space like baffles. All sides, edges, and interstices are painted and painted upon, creating new and surprising "looks" with every shift in the viewer's position. The best of these, *Tribler* (1985), is a triptych of paired, thrusting slats, the narrow slits between boards flashing intense pinks and purples, oranges and yellows as the eye passes.

Manning's art is more about the experience and dynamics of seeing than about anything seen.

Frederick Lynch's dazzling wall constructions play with ideas about real and illusionary space through the cunning interplay of actual and painted planes. Lynch's characteristic strong patterns (stripes, etc.) and his habit of painting a cluster of objects crammed tightly into a small space on his *trompe l'oeil* surfaces contribute to the multi-dimensional quality of these beautifully impure abstractions.

Johnnie Ross is rightly celebrated as a colorist, but in the asymmetrical canvases *Persuasion/ Night Boat Back and Persuasion/Monhegan Early* he seems to be moving uncannily toward overt representation. The tilted lines where his color fields meet read obliquely as horizon lines. Color and form still dominate his austere aesthetic, but there are signs that the Maine reality is finally creeping into Ross' art.

Paul Maddrell is perhaps Maine's most soulful artist. His acrylic triptych *Mystery Grace and Desire* (1985) embodies all of his intense emotional and psychic range—from the black spiked darkness of Mystery, to the high green temple of Grace, to the elegant, but violent, eroticism of Desire. This last third of the contiguous whole features coils of barbed wire on a sensuous purple ground with sexy pink bleeding through beneath the metal thorns.

Quint-Rose encloses the large, free-form fan of her paint on paper collage *Fantal* in a pristine plexiglass box. A few years ago she might have been out of her depth in this present company, but recently she has forsaken beauty for its own sake in favor of an art that is more lasting in its pleasures.

Michael Loew is the most mathematically analytical of the artists in the exhibition. His acrylic and watercolor on linen *Monhegan Mosaic* (1983) is a superb example of Loew's use of color squares and color bars on a white ground to create idealized geometry out of observed reality. The physical direction and inspiration of Monhegan passes through his intelligence and is translated into rigidly controlled paintings that make Loew the Mondrian of Monhegan.

Abby Shahn takes a similar rational approach to re-ordering nature into color square grids, but within each square unit Shahn is often quite painterly. The emerging strength of works like her unframed diptych *Ice Out* is Shahn's acquired ability to preserve the presence and spirit of natural phenomena within the narrow, unnatural limitations of the grid.

Tim Van Campen's airbrush acrylics *Eggplant Blocks* and *Turnip Columns* are the show's greatest departures. Van Campen verges on the decorative in these most architectural of paintings, paintings that look like cerebral stage sets.

Kathy Bradford's abstractions are the most modest and painterly of the exhibition. *Green Shadow* (1985), *Rim* (1984), and *Hearth* (1984) are intimate, murky little works that reduce perceived reality to the residue of essentials, allowing Bradford to spend as much time painting as seeing.

In conjunction with the *Abstractions* show, through July 10, the Rockport gallery is showing a large selection of new works by Stew Henderson. Henderson's latest efforts are very showy and very ambitious hybrids that overlay a lingering concern for representational realism (white clouds floating in blue skies) with the abstract playfulness of shaped canvases, superimposed imagery, and pattern painting. One finds in Henderson's new work correspondences (if not outright references) to many of the distinctive features of the art in *Abstractions.* A fitting end to a meal for the mind.

June 26, 1985

1985 Maine Photography Biennial

The 1985 Maine Photography Biennial opened quietly on Sunday, July 21, to the strains of harp music. The sedate opening seemed fitting as the photography biennial (at the USM Art Gallery in Gorham through August 29, reopening September 15 to October 10) has somehow lacked the pre-exhibition excitement of last winter's painting biennial. Just why this juried photography show seems something less than a major event is not quite clear to me because the biennial certainly has all the trappings of an important show...opening, catalogue, prizes, posters, a blue-ribbon jury.

A jury consisting of Museum of Modern Art photography curator Susan Kismaric, photographer Todd Webb of Bath, and California photographer Henry Wessel, Jr. considered 304 prints (178 black and white, 126 color) by 144 Maine photographers and selected a tight little show of 33 works (20 black and white, 13 color) by 31 artists. Or are they artists?

Oh no! Is this clown going to suggest that photography is not an art form? Of course not. But after viewing the jury's selections and prize-winners I am forced to consider the possibility of intentional artlessness in contemporary photography. You know, the so-called Snapshot School.

The prize of a solo exhibition was awarded to Portland photographer Katie Fagan for her untitled color print of an adolescent girl wearing striped bathing suit and glasses standing self-consciously in the woods. It is an affecting, almost affectionate image, and among the simplest in the exhibition. It's a dumb, deadpan pose, such as one might find in every family album.

One might suspect that the jurors were responding to something (I have no idea what) other than the snapshot sincerity of the image if it were not for the selection of numerous other prints with the same offhand, artless snapshot quality. Craig Blouin's Cibachrome image of father and son afield, *Hunters, New Sharon, Maine*, for instance. Tom Brennan's untitled shot of a family group with dog. Robert Kelley's slightly more didactic silver print,

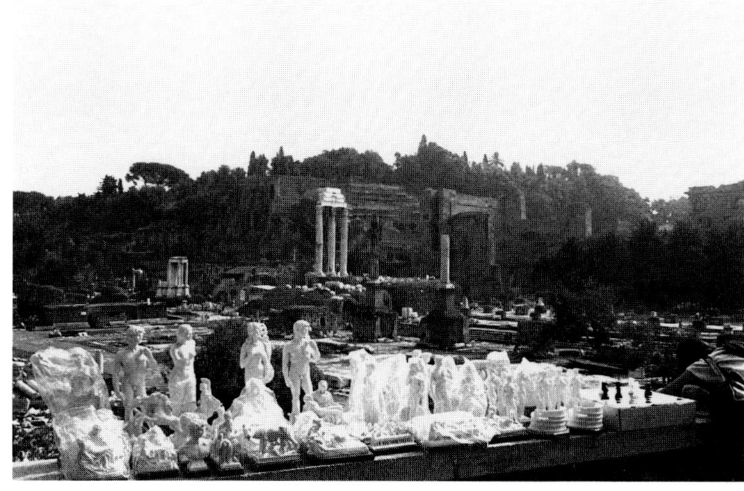

1. *John Eide,* Untitled. *Gelatin silver photograph. Courtesy of the artist.*

Love & Jealousy, an unposed family group at the table. Marjorie Mills' color print *Man's Best Friend*, a barking dog in a suburban backyard seen through a chainlink fence. And there are yet other prints that share this sense of deliberate casualness.

Photography long ago won respectability as an art form, but one senses a lingering inferiority complex (or perhaps identity crisis) among some photographic artists. For one thing, there's that curse of democracy...not everybody paints or sculpts, but just about everybody takes pictures. Then there's the bothersome fact that unknown amateurs rather often come up with photographs that are every bit as good as the professionals'. The modern vogue for awkwardness in serious photography seems to be a response to this dilemma. If shutterbugs can accidentally make art, then why can't artists intentionally make "snapshots"? The banal elevated to the sublime.

Not all of the prints in the show, of course, participate in this fashionable inferiority. William Thuss' black and white portrait of Cicely Aikman, one of a series of artists in their studio environment, is a more formal, composed print, more obviously thought-out, for example. Thuss received a $100 cash prize for his effort.

To my eye, the most interesting and compelling photograph in the exhibition is an untitled gelatin silver print by John Eide. The foreground of the picture is taken up with a collection of marble statuary, apparently set aside during the restoration of a European temple site. The background is richly detailed with the reassemblage of the classical landscape. This is one of the very few photographs in the biennial

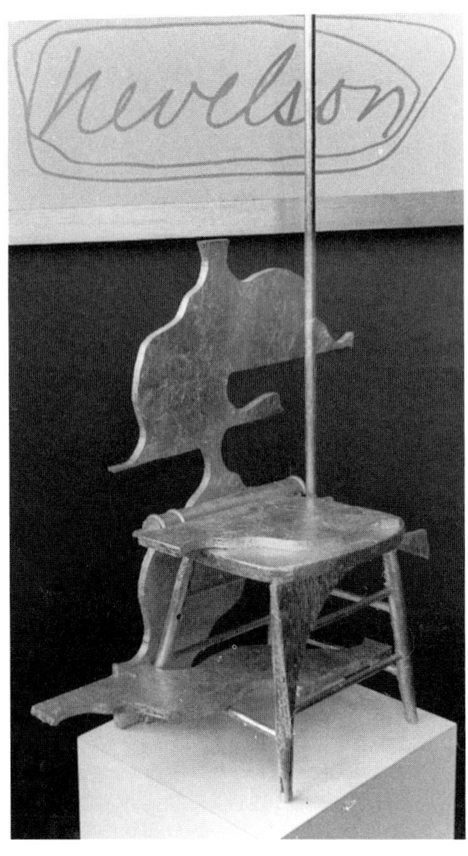

1. *Louise Nevelson*, Gold Throne I. *Gilded fiberboard. Courtesy of the William A. Farnsworth Library and Art Museum.*

that you can actually get involved with, get inside and look around.

With the exception of *Lou's Legs* by Peter A. Scarpaci, there are no nudes in the show. There is also a notable absence of natural history and straight landscape photography. As I understand it, Todd Webb, a classicist with a camera, was outnumbered and out-gunned by the two young jurors from New York and San Francisco. So Webb probably deserves no credit or blame for this most artless of art shows.

Todd Webb's complete juror's statement in the catalogue reads, "I fought hard, but I lost."

July 26, 1985

Louise Nevelson

Louise Nevelson elevates the lowest to the Most High, the base to the precious. She is a sorceress, an alchemist. In the kingdom of modern art, she plays the Black Queen of sculpture to Georgia O'Keeffe's Dowager Queen of painting.

Entering the exhibition *The Gifts: 1985, Nevelson at the Farnsworth* (in Rockland through November 19) is like entering a throne room. Black and white banners made from the same cloth Nevelson designed for the robes of the demon chorus in Gluck's *Orfeo and Euridice* hang like royal tapestries on either side of the gallery entrance. The two gilded thrones (discarded chairs done up with fiberboard and painted gold) command the center of the gallery. In the rear alcove stands *The Endless Column*, a black wooden wall assembly once known as *The Black Wall* (when it graced the dining room of The Thorndike Hotel in Thomaston), now reassembled as a vertical altarpiece. To either side stand sentry panels, creating an art holy triptych.

The lighting is dramatically subdued, imparting a sacred atmosphere to the gallery. In glassed cases repose the Nevelson crown jewels, abstract wooden pendants the size of tea saucers, abstract wooden pins the size of bars of soap. Gold and silver surfaces have been added to the lowly blocks of wood—the Nevelson touch. No one ever said Louise Nevelson wasn't theatrical.

Around the walls are hung a a dozen brand-new collages from a series entitled *Volcanic Magic*. The three-dimensional wall collages are elegant tableaux of picture frames, furniture parts, raw wood, and metal debris that erupt into the gallery space like exploding paintings.

In the auxiliary gallery is a selection of rather stale paintings by Louis Eilshemius (1864-1941), an obscure artist the great lady apparently looked on with favor. From easygoing early landscape watercolors through allegorical idylls to tortured late paintings of personal torment, the paintings are recommended to public attention because Nevelson collected and approved of them.

In a basement gallery are assembled a collection of immature Nevelson works, memorabilia, and gifts of art to the Farnsworth from the artist and her brother, the late Nathan Berliawsky. Dominating the basement gallery are a dozen black terra cotta sculptures, most anthropomorphic abstractions in the manner of Picasso and Moore, that Nevelson donated to the museum. In the memento case are little curios, such as an untitled clay muffin man Louise Berliawsky created as a Rockland high-school girl, that attest to the fact that Louise Nevelson was once a mere mortal. The most curious of these archival pieces (which set in the context of her High Art take on the aspect of religious relics, the bones of a saint) is a design drawing of two chairs, the carving and turning of the legs and backs speaking directly to the thrones and disembodied chair parts of the mature constructions upstairs.

The Gifts amounts to Louise Nevelson's self-coronation, in which both the artist and her raw materials transcend their common origins through the power of imagination. Art with a capital A.

October 25, 1985

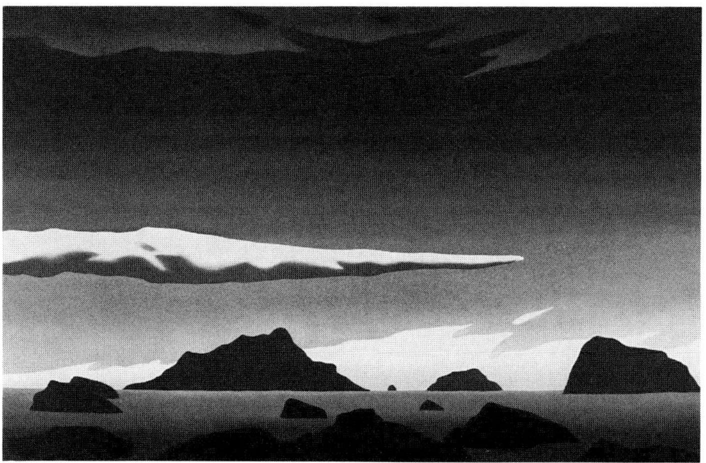

1. *Howard Clifford,* Surface Series IV, *1985. Oil on canvas. Courtesy of the artist.*

Contemporary Works from Maine

Howard Clifford missed his calling. He should have been a curator. *Contemporary Works From Maine*, the eight-artist exhibition he put together for the University of Southern Maine Art Gallery (in Gorham, through February 13) is probably the meatiest little group show you're likely to see in Maine. But then Howard Clifford only hangs with the best.

A couple of years ago, looking for a space to show his own paintings, Clifford approached USM's Juris Ubans. Ubans suggested Clifford consider asking a few other artists to show with him. Clifford elected to invite the cream of the crop.

"I chose people's work I liked," says Clifford. "I chose people's work that challenges me, people whose work I find myself chewing over for a long period of time."

The seven artists Howard Clifford invited to show with him are painters Beverly Hallam, John Laurent, Frederick Lynch, Joseph Nicoletti, and Johnnie Ross, and sculptors Celeste Roberge and John Ventimiglia. There are probably seven other artists in the state Clifford could have invited without diminishing the quality of the exhibition, but he could hardly have done any better. With one exception, each of the artists is represented by four pieces, and Juris Ubans has created an unusually successful arrangement by hanging three of each artist's works together and one apart. It's an interlocking exhibition with hardly a weak link. And to my mind and eye, the eight artists constitute four pairs.

Howard Clifford and Beverly Hallam do a dance of light and shadows. They both work large and are both concerned with atmosphere—Clifford with the big, primal forms of land, sea, and sky; Hallam with the intimate atmosphere of the elegant interior. Mr. Outside-Mrs. Inside.

Clifford is obsessed with the histrionics of nature. His ongoing *Cloud Series* sails cement clouds through increasingly colorful skies, but on a fishing trip last year to Iceland, Clifford apparently found a landscape to match his grand conceptions. Two of Clifford's four huge oils depict raw Icelandic mountains jutting up into his iceberg-cloud skies.

There is also a surface relation between Clifford's thin, flat oils and Beverly Hallam's airbrushed acrylics. Both are purifiers. Hallam's serene, floral still lifes play with light and shadow and glassy, reflecting surfaces with a mechanical purity, while Clifford's elemental forms seem to have been thought rather than brushed in place.

John Laurent and Joseph Nicoletti are the painterly realists of the exhibition. In two new bravura oils, Laurent attacks the figure with a swiftness that in one case verges on abstraction. *Umpire* and *Nordique* are both inspired by hockey, *Umpire* being the headless residue of the zebra-striped official and *Nordique* a more fully realized player of uniformed menace. The hockey figures are a dramatic departure for a master who refuses to gel.

Joe Nicoletti's two pencilled still lifes and two still life oils (arrangements of cups, vases, bowls on table tops) are ethereal, exquisitely wrought images of the mundane and contrived, elevated through sheer painting to the sublime. There are none better.

Frederick Lynch and Johnnie Ross share primary concerns for shape and color. Lynch, fresh from the best single-artist show Barridoff Galleries ever mounted, shows four shaped wooden panels from his *Satellite Series.* And while Lynch orbits his brightly patterned and aggressively social panels through public space, Johnnie Ross continues to probe the mysteries of murky, interior chromatic space with his shaped canvases. Four is the magic number in this exhibition, and Ross' four canvases are eccentrically divided into color quadrants. Each painting looks as though it is desperately trying to achieve the square, the interior color squares battling to bring the irregularly shaped canvases back into line. These are tense and powerful paintings by Maine's master color theorist.

Celeste Roberge and her former Portland School of Art mentor John Ventimiglia bring art out into full three-dimensions. Ventimiglia is an abstract formalist, his glowing *Comets* consisting of folded planes of burnished brass defining and creating volume where there is none. But for me, the thriller of the show is Celeste Roberge.

Celeste Roberge is quite simply the most important and most exciting sculptor working in Maine today. Just one of the things that excites me about her art is that it doesn't have a *look*, it has a *mind.* Where other artists have a continuity of style, Roberge has a continuity of thought...and this is one tough-minded lady.

In *Dreamhouse*, Roberge plays off several of her previous metal sculptures in creating a tabletop tableau, a miniature self-portrait with miniaturized sculptures. Roberge is unequalled in her ability to give physical form to ideas, not just to express an idea, but to *embody* an idea in metal.

The knock-'em-dead work of this show of shows has to be Roberge's *Geographies*, an arrangement of three skull-sized pieces set on the floor. Two pieces are cage-like structures (a catcher's mask comes to mind), one enclosing egg-sized stones, the other hairy bundles of wire. The third piece is a solid form like a mummy wrapped in steel. *Geographies* is as graphic and compelling as a beheading. But then Celeste Roberge metaphorically beheads herself with every work she makes.

It is possible we're having the show of the year in January?

January 24, 1986

Cabot Lyford

When I first started looking seriously at art in Maine a dozen or so years ago, it seemed to me the state had only three sculptors. There was Blackie Langlais, the mad carpenter who pieced together a humorous menagerie of wooden beings from his wild imagination. There was Clark FitzGerald, the formalist who often fought the properties of wood and metal to force them into idealized forms. And there was Cabot Lyford, the naturalist who seemed to extract human and animal forms from wood and stone with equal ease. Blackie Langlais is gone now, but FitzGerald and Lyford are still chipping away masterfully. There still aren't more than a handful of good sculptors in Maine, so the chance to see a body of work by any one of them is a rare treat.

To mark his retirement after 23 years of teaching, Phillips Exeter Academy in Exeter, New Hampshire, has mounted a Cabot Lyford retrospective at the school's Lamont Gallery (through March 12). *Cabot Lyford—Sculpture* consists of 28 pieces (plus a small selection of watercolor sketches) executed between 1961 and 1986. More than half the pieces were created in the last five years, but there are enough earlier works to see where Lyford has been.

Cabot Lyford is a carver and a chiseler. His art is about as straightforward and direct as you're ever going to find. He seems to respond equally to subject matter and material, finding sculptural images in wood and stone while maintaining their inherent integrity. In this he is a conservative sculptor, a traditionalist in love with natural forms and natural materials.

The earliest piece in the Exeter show tells you exactly what Lyford is about. *The West Wind* (1961) is a jagged block of slate into which Lyford has carved a mask-like female face. Most of the black rock is left in its raw, natural state. The woman's face is an artifice. Clearly, Lyford loves what the slate *is* as much as he loves what he can *make* of it. As his work matures, he manages to overcome the natural resistance of stones and wood to the point where the man-made and the God-given exist in much greater harmony.

In *Leviathan* (1962), Lyford uses a much lighter touch, shaping and polishing a chunk of slate that already suggests an epic whale form. Here he merely accentuates the stone to approximate a whale, or rather *the* whale. Of the 38 works in this show, six are whale forms and 14 are female figures. Cabot Lyford is a sculptor with one idea (like most good artists)—balance art and nature. His vocabulary is rock and wood. His themes are whales and women, both of which supply him with powerful and sensuous forms to explore.

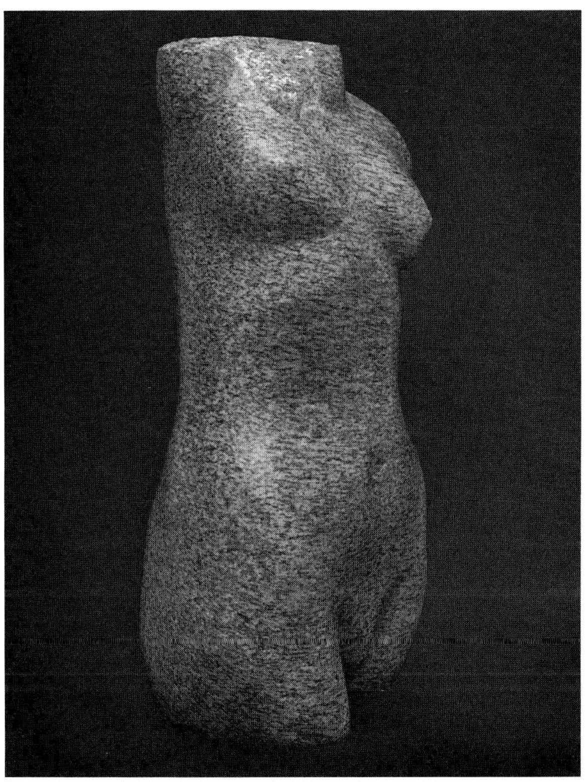

1. *Cabot Lyford,* Brown Skin Gal. *Oklahoma granite. Courtesy of the Midtown Galleries, Inc., New York. Photo by Nathan Rabin.*

In two pieces, *Childe Roland To The Dark Tower Came* (1968) and *Lear's Daughters* (1971), Lyford experiments with narrative abstractions in cast metal, but these heady departures are unconvincing. Lyford is a physical artist. In the late sixties and early seventies, he seems to have been diverted by the pervasive cosmic "cool," but even the representational work of this period like *All American Girl* (1968)—a wooden female nude doing a yoga headstand while wearing brass boots—and *Shades* (1973)—a basalt head with sunglasses—are out-of-date hip.

The works of the eighties show what the mature Lyford does best—whales and women *au naturel*. The fully modeled mahogany *Finback*

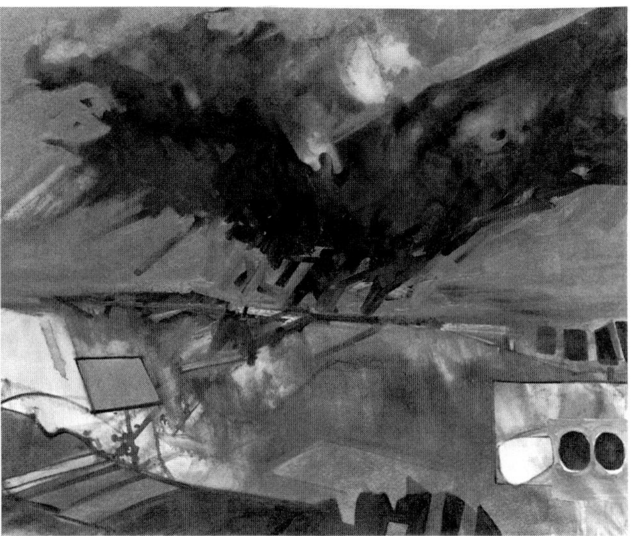

1. *John Hultberg,* Demon Cloud, *1965. Oil on canvas. Courtesy of the artist. Photo by Mike Fischer.*

(1981), the vertical mahogany *Sounding Whale* (1983), the black granite *Surging Whale* (1984), and the pine tail flukes of *Farewell* (1984) are Lyford the naturalist pure and simple. The untitled black granite torso (1983), the reclining form of the laminated mahogany *Mrs. Montessori* (1983), and the emerging black granite figure of the *Contessa* (1986) are Lyford in love.

Complex, Lyford is not. When he tries to be clever, his sculpture tends to become contrived...as in the five interlocking geese of the 25-foot *Mt. Sunapee Summit Sculpture* (1964), a model of which is on display at Exeter. When he strays from the grace and majesty of marine animals and the female body, his pieces often taken on a folk art look. So wedded is his vision to the amorphous shape of the whale that even his granite *Black Rooster* (1982) at first appears to be a whale.

Whales are life itself. Women are love. These are all Cabot Lyford needs to explore big themes in a most basic and direct manner. Lyford's recent sculpture will be on exhibit during April at the Midtown Gallery in New York City.

February 28, 1986

John Hultberg

Since September 1984, when I visited painter John Hultberg on Monhegan, the efforts to rehabilitate his reputation, which ascended with the second wave of expressionism in the late 1950s and plummeted with the arrival of Pop art in the 1960s, have been gaining momentum. Just a year ago, *John Hultberg: Painter of the In-Between*, a retrospective of his work from 1953 to 1984, debuted at Hamilton College in Clinton, New York. In June of last year, Barridoff Galleries in Portland exhibited a selection of Hultberg's recent paintings. All last summer, seven of Hultberg's paintings hung in the National Gallery of American Art in Washington as part of the *Martha Jackson Memorial Collection*, Martha Jackson having been Hultberg's dealer and patron from 1955 until her death in 1969. Now through May 4, the Hultberg retrospective, which made an interim stop at the Westmoreland Museum of Art in Greensburg, Pennsylvania, is being featured at the Portland Museum of Art. Next month, an exhibition of Hultberg's recent work will be mounted at the Anita Shapolsky Gallery (formerly Arbitrage Gallery) in New York's Soho district.

This sudden flurry of activity on behalf of John Hultberg is by and large the work of Grant Jacks, who curated the retrospective and designed its excellent catalogue, and his wife Shirley, who contributed the catalogue's extended and insightful essay. Jacks, a former associate of Martha Jackson, is now a free-lance catalogue designer. Grant and Shirley Jacks moved to Portland from the Philadelphia area just two months ago.

As any visitor to the Portland Museum of Art will see, the need to rehabilitate John Hultberg's reputation is not a reflection on the quality of his art, which has remained consistent in vision and values for 30 years now; rather, it is a function of the ebb and flow of style (taste) in contemporary art. In the 1950s, Hultberg bucked the abstract mainstream of expressionism as it flowed inexorably flatter and flatter, banishing all subject matter until it ran dry on the barren plains of minimalism (monochrome paintings that were *nothing* except paint on/in canvas).

Instead, Hultberg clutched his apocalyptic visions of personal, social, and cosmic disintegration and kept painting pictures that were *about* something. For the past six or seven years now, a new generation of painters has been turning back the pages of contemporary art history to pre-abstract chapters with the result that pure abstraction now looks curiously outdated, and old war horses like John Hultberg are being rediscovered. There are a host of young neo-expressionist painters who have stylistic and thematic affinities with Hultberg's work, but few have a vision that communicates the kind of authenticity and commitment that Hultberg achieves.

In a sense, John Hultberg is a one-trick pony. For 30 years, his best paintings have all been variations on a single painting. In general, Hultberg creates a panoramic view of deep space, dividing the picture plane in two, about one-half to two-thirds up the canvas. The viewer is given a soaring perspective over a compartmentalized landscape that recedes into oblivion beneath a turbulent, almost cataclysmic sky. The velocity with which one is sucked into the Hultberg world is frightening and exciting. These visionary landscapes (in between dream and reality) are populated by humanoids and human blanks, corpses and rising souls, ghosts and descending angels. The atmosphere is charged with horror and fascination, revelation and revulsion, anxiety and anticipation. Hultberg paints nothing less than the highest moments of the human soul, the social epiphany, the cosmic last gasp. It's a trick worth getting right.

The Hultberg retrospective gives the viewer just an inkling of where the artist was coming from before he hit the fast-forward button and launched himself into deep space. *After De Chirico* (1953), the earliest picture in the show, is an atypically static composition, a claustrophobic interior space (yet with the box-like cubes that continue to serve Hultberg as vessels of civilization) with just a peek into the beyond. This painting and *Parenthetically Poetic Heads* (1955), which is Hultberg painting over an abstract canvas by Sam Francis, have a flatness that will never again characterize Hultberg's work.

It is rather unfortunate that a key painting in Hultberg's career and development, *Yellow Sky* (1954), could not be included in the retrospective, as originally intended. It was this painting that first attracted Martha Jackson and, in 1955, won Hultberg the top purchase prize at the Corcoran Gallery of Art biennial (as the catalogue points out, "In competition with de Kooning, Kline, Larry Rivers, among others.") *Yellow Sky* (which the Corcoran would not loan for insurance reasons) is the transitional piece between the surreal still-life composition on *After De Chirico* and the panoramic visions that were ever-after to follow.

The apotheosis of the Hultberg panoramic vision is the huge (98 x 158 inches) *Twilight: Down the Drain* (1975). Here Hultberg has painted a blue symphony set in what looks like the mission control center from which the end of the world might be directed. As with many of Hultberg's best paintings, this picture is animated both by the sheer grandeur of the receding space and by passages of brilliant red emerging here and there from screens and monitors on the floor of civilization. This above all Hultberg paintings belongs in a major museum collection, but, like over half the 40-odd paintings in the show, it is owned by the David Anderson Gallery (David Anderson being the son of Martha Jackson).

So as not to stereotype John Hultberg as a painter of deep space, I should add that my favorite painting in the show is a small (20 x 30 inches) figurative acrylic, *Robot Dancer* (1980-83), that isolates a deep-blue winged robot (activated by orange outline) against a bright red background. This painting, a generous selection of black and white drawings, and perhaps the oil *Demon Cloud* (1965)—a black angel form against a red sky—suggests a profitable future direction for Hultberg in concentrating on the figure as well as the firmament.

John Hultberg clearly deserves the attention he has been getting on the outskirts of the art scene. Let's hope someone is paying attention when he hits New York next month.

March 28, 1986

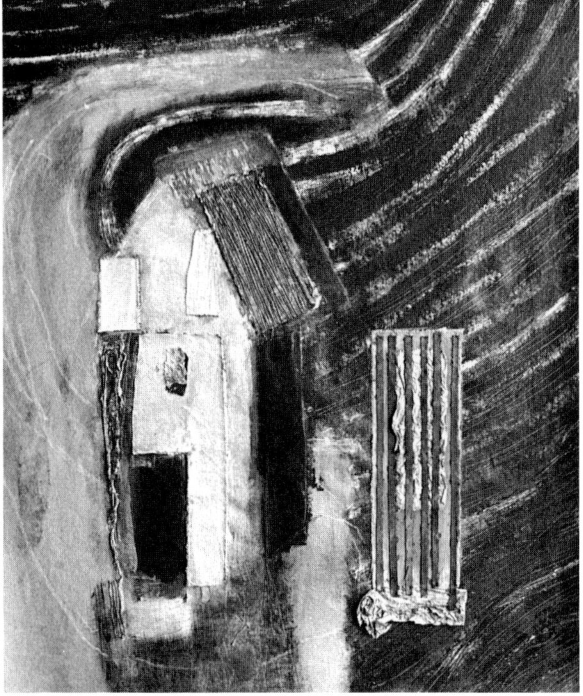

1. *Anne Gresinger*, No Fear of External Forces. *Acrylic on canvas with mixed media. Courtesy of the O'Farrell Gallery.*

Anne Gresinger

Anne Gresinger's very private, very beautiful paintings have been "something of a sensation" at the O'Farrell Gallery in Brunswick, in the words of gallery owner Ray Farrell. Since Gresinger began showing there a year ago, O'Farrell has sold 32 of her works. Currently (through June 14), 31 of Gresinger's colorful acrylics are being featured in a solo exhibition. It is a show of quiet sensations.

What one notices first about Anne Gresinger's paintings is her use of the unrestricted palette so popular among today's young hard-chargers. But unlike so many of her free-color contemporaries, Gresinger seems to have her dynamic palette under control. There is a logic to her use of garish coppers, bright aquas, and blood reds. The logic comes through in her handling of the paint, the skillful way she applies jarring hue to jarring hue without producing paintings that scream and howl.

The paintings at O'Farrell belong to three distinct cycles—moody self-portraits, explorations of formal structures such as doors, windows, and houses, and what the artist calls "subliminal" themes. The subliminal works operate like a kind of personal iconography obsessed with pattern, yet clearly "about" the inner life of the serious young woman portrayed in the self-portraits. All of the paintings ultimately come back to the self as subject, but they avoid solipsism by virtue of their generous superficial beauty. Gresinger seems to be involved in a process of painting her way out of a closed little world and into the light of a larger, more expansive one.

What I find most arresting and involving about Anne Gresinger's art (indeed, what I find most meaningful about the art of most talented young artists today) is her appropriation of existing styles and manners. As the art world learns to deal with the new pluralism in the wake of post-Modernism, we find ourselves in a period of cultural backwash. Even those artists who try to forge ahead seem to become immersed in a reinterpretation and recapitulation of the past. Anne Gresinger's work, at once her own and yet heavily indebted to established idioms, makes me wonder once again whether the process of influence is a conscious one, or whether the "new" art of the 1980s is simply a product of everything that's in the gene pool of modern art.

You look at Anne Gresinger's self-portraits and you know you're in the company of an Expressionist. In *Self-Portrait with Bird* and *Self-Portrait with Ochre Hair*, color is emotionally laden and psychologically charged. A sense of deep hurt, something slow and sad like heartbreak, comes through the self-portraits. A little painting like *Self-Portrait with Supporting Frame*, a full-figure portrait of the artist supported by what looks to be a lounge chair, bridges the gap between the self-portraits and the more analytic structural paintings. Yet this little gem is almost erotic in the way it bares itself while withholding so much.

The structure paintings and the subliminal abstractions owe debts going back to the cave walls and have overtones of the kind of public-private symbolism developed by painters like Marsden Hartley and Stuart Davis, but the most obvious influence is the contemporary style of pattern painting that emerged with the women's movement as a way for female artists to make use of "women's work" (quilts, needlepoint, stitchery) in a new women's art. An artist like Miriam Schapiro appropriated the merely

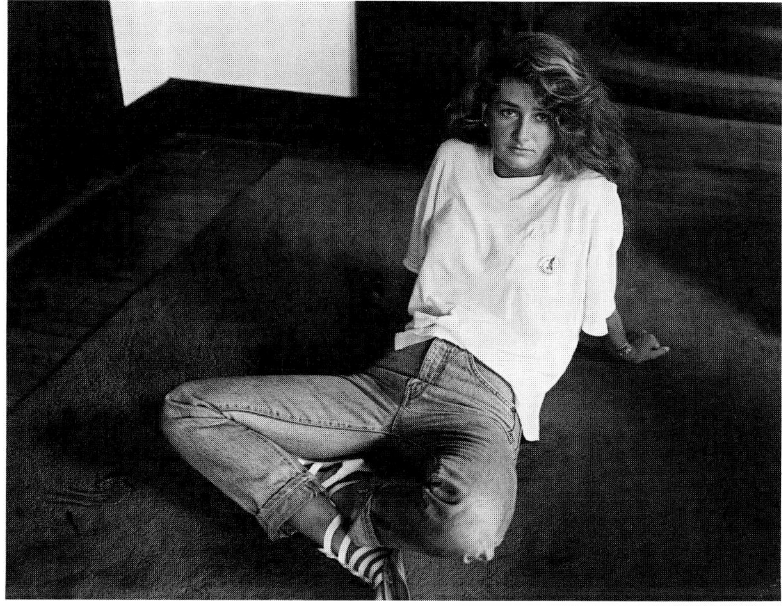

1. *Katie Fagan,* Patty, *1987. Cibachrome. Courtesy of the artist.*

decorative as a way of celebrating feminine creativity. Katherine Porter, a more overtly political artist, managed to render pattern as polemic. Anne Gresinger's loose, expressive patterns fall decidedly between the celebratory and the hortatory.

In two of the best paintings in the show, *This is My Friend Lisa* and *Birth Painting*, Gresinger lavishes and layers attention on purely decorative motifs (border prints, stripings, linked arcs, geometric shapes, etc.) while ultimately achieving a very poetic "likeness" of persons and phenomena. These paintings have both real presence and a sense of passage and the transitory. I came away from Anne Gresinger's exhibition thinking of her as a solemn princess dressing up her deepest responses in gaudy raiment in order to act out a painful personal drama. These are very affecting works.

May 16, 1986

Katie Fagan

Of the current generation of photographers emerging in Maine, Katie Fagan is one of the best. Her prints are as bright as an eyeball and as deceptively simple as a snapshot. Yet as her current exhibition at the University of Southern Maine (USM) Art Gallery (in Gorham through March 26) shows, in working hard to appear casual, Fagan's photographs speak directly to the spirit of the 1980s.

Fagan's exhibition of 47 color prints begins with the untitled backyard portrait of a little girl in glasses and a red-and-white striped bikini that won the 1985 Maine Photo Biennial at USM. Seemingly as awkward and offhand as an image from any family album, this print is elevated above the mundane both by the quality of Fagan's printing (she makes prints for Portland Photographics) and by the artist's sensitivity to the relationship between figure and setting, between people and the places they inhabit. Over half the show is devoted to portraits in a similar vein of Fagan's friends and relatives. While the posed people are the ostensible subjects of these photographs, the real subject of Fagan's art—indeed, the proper subject of photography—is time, in her case time as captured in the tension between the human moment (people) and the historic context (place).

Most of Fagan's subjects are her contempo-

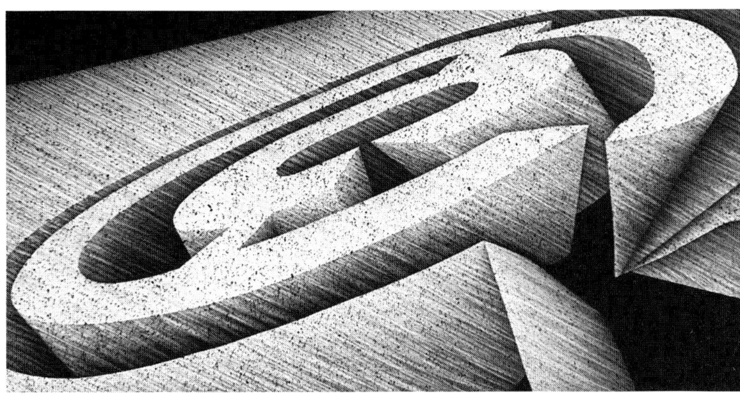

1. *Susan Groce,* Swirl. *Mixed-media drawing. Courtesy of the artist.*

raries—bright young people (many artists themselves) alert and alive to the styles and manners of the 1980s. Most of the settings in which Fagan finds her contemporaries, however, are remnants of the past, 19th- and early 20th-century interiors that mirror the age of Portland. We live in the eternal present, but we inhabit the places of the past. Fagan's portraits have a 1980s look, but what do the 1980s look like? They don't "look like" anything; they are an attitude toward living, not an aspect of it. Casual people formally posed, once elegant interiors now cheaply furnished and stylishly disheveled, mismatched kitchen chairs, old stuffed chairs wearing contemporary camouflage, interiors in the midst of renovation—all speak to the way human beings appropriate and transform spaces by living in them. These are the good old days.

Fagan's friendly portraits are complemented by a suite of a dozen photographs taken on a 1985 trip to Europe. While they seem to bear little pictorial likeness to the local portraits, the images from Italy and Spain—mostly candid shots of people in public places—reinforce the central metaphor of Fagan's images: mortality. America has youth, Europe has age. Thus the theme of people living now in the spaces of the past acquires both clarity and depth. My favorite of the European images shows two elderly Italian women, oblivious to one another, alone together in a sculpture court. One kerchiefed lady sits resolutely on a folding canvas stool and scowls. Her crutch lies beside her. The other old lady studies the romance of a marble figure. Gnarled vines cover the wall of the court. Even the eternally young sculptured figure is covered with dust. A perfect picture of aging.

March 27, 1987

Susan Groce

One of the standard conceits of 20th-century art is the appropriation of images and forms from prior ages and foreign cultures for purely visual purposes. Images and forms that, in their day and place, were fraught with social, cultural, and spiritual meaning are resurrected in this age of disbelief as contemporary artists attempt to drag meaning up out of obscurity and bring it to bear on the present moment. Susan Groce, a consummate artist and a member of the University of Maine art faculty, does this with spiritually laden architectural forms borrowed from the cultures of ancient Rome and ancient America, specifically the Anasazi culture of the desert Southwest. Groce's exhibition of large-scale drawings and aquatint prints at Westbrook College's Joan Whitney Payson Gallery of Art (through April 26) is a bravura performance in which technical mastery is brought to bear on the culturally loaded to purely visual ends.

Purely visual ends? Yes, for it is not necessary to know anything of the dead meaning of the maze-like architectural forms of the Anasazi to appreciate the aesthetic experience afforded by Groce's grand drawings. And grand they are, some running to 21 feet in length, inspired mixed-media drawings in which architecturally altered landscapes take fantastic flight. Ancient ruins, perspectives in Escher-ish distortion, swoop, swirl, glide, and hover in intellectual orbit like granitic geometries launched into deepest, blackest space. The stony surface quality, a product of sanding and airbrushing, is illuminated by a thin, unearthy light, the product of subtle striations of orange to yellow colors. Groce's images read like earthy monuments suddenly sucked into the black hole of another dimension where the laws of physics are twisted into a strange new logic. Stone folds like paper. Things of great weight have none. Drawing takes on the illusion of sculpture. Thrilling!

Susan Groce's is the art of time travel. Her prints—discrete images of sundials, bleached skulls, and clockworks executed in rusty, metallic oranges and greens—deal directly with the corrosiveness of time. Her drawings amount to an archeological exploration of inner space. In notes to the exhibition, Groce is quoted as saying that her *Landformations* series is all about "the intrusion of man into the landscape—what we build, what we destroy, how we relate to the land and how we use it." She claims not to "judge," but merely to "present." In fact what she does is appropriate and transform. Her drawings are transcendental landscapes lifted out of all context.

Ordinarily, unless an exhibition is so poorly hung or mounted as to be distracting and detracting, I rarely comment on the installation of a show. In this case, however, the fit between exhibition space and art is so seamlessly fine that it demands mention. First, the Payson Gallery cube is the perfect setting from Groce's architectonic drawings, the lines and forms (even the textures) of the gallery being perfectly congruent with Groce's forms and images. Beyond this, the installation by Peter Simmons is superb. He has encased the artist's drawings in ingenious plexiglass frames and hung them so that the drawings occupy the gallery space the same way Groce's *Landformations* occupy illusionistic space. The total effect is sublime.

April 3, 1987

Christine Woelfle

When a young person dies, we grieve over the loss of fullness. Wrapped up within our own skins, we sense an injustice in the arrested potential. What might this life have become? What might this person have achieved? Not fair. Not right. And when that young person is an artist, our sense of tragedy is particularly poignant. For what is the pursuit of art if not the mitigation of mortality? *Ars longa, vita brevis.* But surely not this brief. Doesn't it take a complete lifetime to shape our answer, to word our message to eternity?

When Christine Woelfle, a sculptor of exquisite sensibility, died last year at age 36, I found myself wondering what would become of her art. Where would her intricate, complex, still, and silent constructions—base plywood ennobled by spare applications of gold leaf and clear glass—find space to survive in the world? Had she accomplished enough to establish a place for her art in the history of things, for herself in the history of ideas? Could creative seeds lightly planted in the thin cultural soil of Maine take root and flourish? Unanswered questions.

Christine Woelfle came to Maine in 1982 after receiving her Master of Fine Arts degree from the University of Pennsylvania. Quickly and quietly, she assumed center stage in the Maine art scene. In 1983, she began teaching at the Portland School of Art, and the same year she was among the select group of artists invited to show their works at the Maine Biennial held at Colby College. In 1984, she showed at Bowdoin and the Farnsworth; in 1986, at Hobe Sound Galleries North and Maine Coast Artists. With each exposure the appreciation of her work and the respect she commanded from other artists grew. Christine Woelfle was a young woman of uncommon talent, rare perceptions, great promise. Then, on September 6, 1986, she drowned when a car she was riding in plunged into Belfast Harbor.

Naturally unprepared for the artist's sudden death, the Portland School of Art made room in the full schedule at its Baxter Gallery for a memorial retrospective. *Christine Woelfle, Sculptor* (May 3-13) was as brief as her career,

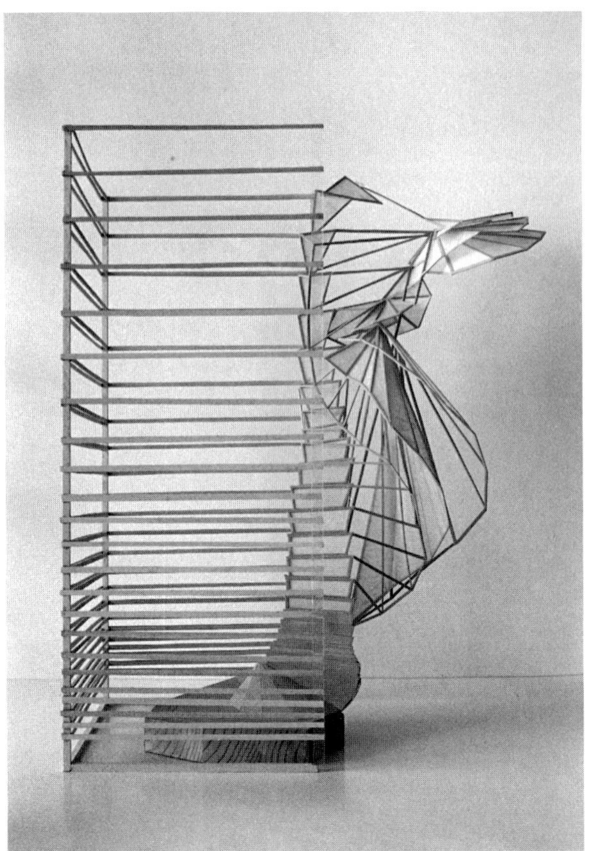

1. *Christine Woelfle,* Emitting A Sound. *Basswood, plexiglass and rice paper.*

and yet it was a full and important exhibition. Whether this first step in the preservation of the artist's work and reputation will lead outward to a wider audience and into posterity is uncertain, but when one considers what Christine Woelfle's art was all about, material and professional survival seems somewhat less urgent.

Christine Woelfle was a graduate of Maharishi International University and a Transcendental Meditation adept. She practiced *kundalini* yoga. Her entire adult life involved the othering of experience. Her art was an expression of the search for meaning in a transcendent reality. Her sculptures never aspired to fame and fortune; they were and are part of the spiritual ladder she climbed up and out of illusion. We can only hope that these beautiful and intriguing objects served their purpose and, left behind, may be of use to others.

In the copious journal quotes and letter excerpts accompanying the excellent exhibition catalogue (the verbal and pictorial record of the artist's passing) we find a great deal to illuminate our understanding of what Christine Woelfle was after in constructing the elaborately latticed, maze-like architecture of her art. Just below a photograph of the artist, for instance, is printed the following:

From sculpture notes. From darkness into light never losing it for an instant as light reveals its fullness and roundness—that is the sculptural ideal.

-a monumentality which is not earthbound
-to command the air
-calligraphical quality
-melodic phrases

This cataloguing of qualities is an insightful précis of Christine Woelfle's art. Her visual task, inspired by the seminal work of Robert Irwin, was the provocation of heightened awareness. Her spiritual task, pursued through meditation and art, was a transcendental enlightenment. In her sculpture, energy becomes matter, briefly, perhaps forever. The correspondences between physical forms and the experience of spiritual energies are quite specific and personal, therefore, difficult to read exactly. What I found most curious and compelling, however, was that standing in a balconied gallery surrounded by Christine Woelfle's soulful, cerebral art, I experienced a peculiarly sensual kind of beauty. In plywood, glass, and gold leaf were the beauty and presence of a young woman, an ash blond wearing gold jewelry.

May 15, 1987

Made in Maine

Made in Maine, an exhibition which celebrates the works of eight artists born and educated in Maine, is an outgrowth and expansion of a show Juris Ubans, director of the University of Southern Maine (USM) Art Gallery, curated last year for the College of St. Rose in Albany, New York. That show consisted of art by Alan Bray, Eric Hopkins, and Richard Wilson. The expanded version (which hangs in Gorham through August 13 and will re-open from September 20 to October 8) also includes work by Wolcott Dodge, Allen Grindle, Thomas Nadeau, and Pola Shoppe. All eight artists are USM alumni.

Of this native Maine art show, Ubans, himself a native of Latvia, says, "My point is that an artist has to be grounded and the New York art market can't be that ground; it's not a real connection." Ubans believes that the art and artists in *Made in Maine* are "connected to real life" and have "an original point of view."

What one clearly sees in *Made in Maine*, however, is that "an original point of view" does not necessarily mean a "Maine point of view." The artists themselves may have been "made in Maine," but the art could have been made anywhere. Indeed, some of the invited artists specifically downplay the importance of Maine in their art, backpedaling away from the provincialism of the old Maine.

"If there is something intrinsically 'Made in Maine,'" writes artist Richard Wilson, a Sanford native, "it may be that native spirit that you develop growing up in the isolated environment that Maine has always been and is becoming less and less."

Richard Wilson's own art is a pictorial narration of a universal, karmic tragi-comedy, the central principle being a male-female spirituality that is more Far East than down east. To pick just one choice example, the large oil *Unnatural Act* depicts a young male bather about to throw a large rock into a body of water, the surface of which shimmers with tiny female nudes. Though many of Wilson's paintings contain suggestions of sexual exploitation and violence, Wilson explains that *Unnatural Act* was inspired by his accidentally hitting a seagull while throwing stones at the beach. What the painting means to him is that "everything is alive."

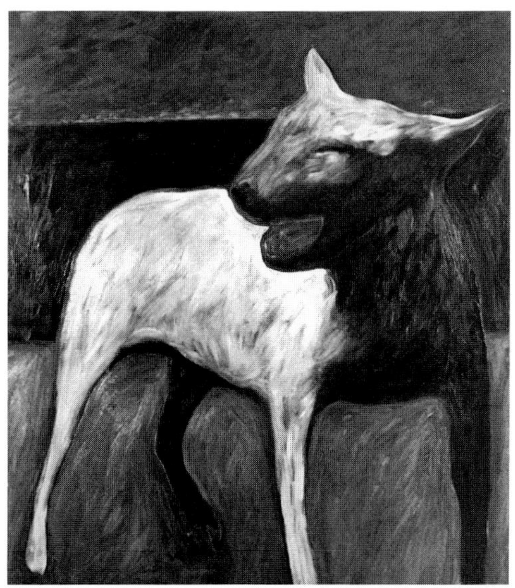

1. *Allen Grindle,* Fire on the Horizon, *1986. Oil.*

Eric Hopkins grew up on North Haven and, perhaps because of the more intense isolation of island life, his art is the most closely connected with the physical forms and processes of Maine. The preponderance of works in this show, however, apply the artist's singular style of active, exaggerated landscape painting to the mountains of Washington State, where he studied at the Pilchuk Glass Center and where he frequently returns to refresh his bi-coastal vision.

Alan Bray, who grew up in the Dover-Foxcroft area, is an artist of the cold interior, of places inhabited by the incubus of a potentially hostile nature. In the 1977 tempera *Incident in Wilson Gorge*, for example, a dead moose lies in the black and icy maw of a slate quarry. Bray's art might be thought of as survivalist surrealism.

Allen Grindle, of Milo, and now of Albany, New York, paints large, discrete, and disturbing images, heads and dogs stony in composition, yet placed in fiery pictorial space. In the 1986 oil *Fire on the Horizon*, for example, an iconic bull terrier stands illuminated by night fire, making Grindle's an art of mute finality, dumb-struck apocalypse.

Wilson, Hopkins, Bray, and Grindle all came of age in the Maine of the 1950s and early 1960s; in other words, before the social revolutions of the 1960s and the emergence of Maine from cultural depression to social desirability.

Three of the younger artists in the show, Wolcott Dodge, Marc Pelletier, and Pola Shoppe, matured during the media explosion of the 1960s and 1970s. Their art, consequently, is more a product of the times than of the place they were born.

Wolcott Dodge, of Portland, is an emerging artist who, at this point in his young career, is taking advantage of the permissive pluralism of the 1980s to re-explore modernist conventions, abstracted forms in cubist space, collaged landscapes of symbolic content.

Marc Pelletier grew up on the same Lewiston street where Marsden Hartley (Maine's premier native genius) once lived. And just as Hartley experimented with most of the stylistic trends of his era, Pelletier's grotesque oil paintings are pure and primal neo-Expressionism. *The Hunter's Nightmare*, for example, is a powerful image of an deathly hunter embracing (or is he making ghastly love to?) the bloody carcass of a deer. Pelletier has brought the ubiquitous, mutant humanoid of 1980s art home to the cold, dark, outer limits of Maine.

Pola Shoppe, a Bangor native, makes intentionally crude works of stitched and unstretched canvas painted in fast, brushy acrylics. In wavy strokes of paint and strips of sewn canvas, she conjures a watery world suspended in air.

Thomas Nadeau, who grew up in the mill-town Westbrook of the 1920s and 1930s, is the wise old man of the *Made in Maine* show. His untitled oil of a female nude, flesh with the solid presence of sculpture, is also the most refined and resolved work in the show. Nadeau's muse stands in his studio, her delicately stippled body and dark, rich hair at once sensual and sublime. Thomas Nadeau came of age in Maine at a time when both the aesthetic and economic horizons for an artist working in Maine were limited. He has pursued his vision through decades of changes (a cubist painting from 1947 is included in the show), independent of the mainstream art world, indeed independent of even the emerging Maine art scene. Having made the transition from the old Maine to the new, Nadeau no longer experiences Maine as fundamental to his art.

"At this stage," he writes, "I believe that Maine has done for me and to me all that it can. I could probably work anywhere with about the same results. But I enjoy these surroundings. My roots are here."

The designation "Maine artist" may carry the stigma of picturesque amateurism into the near future, but a new native (neo-Native?) Maine artist has emerged from the cultural debris of the past to stand individually and equally among the ranks of contemporary artists. What artists in Maine share is a lifestyle, not an artistic style. Thus the greatest service that *Made in Maine* can perform is to demonstrate once and for all that an exhibition of native Maine artists, like an exhibition of women artists, is no longer necessary.

July 17, 1987

Katarina Weslien

Transformations and Other Everyday Events, an exhibition and installation by Katarina Weslien at Westbrook College's Payson Gallery (through December 13), extends the concept of weaving from humble, utilitarian craftsmanship to sublime, inspired artistry without losing the thread of methodology which gives the concept its meaning. Weaving is essentially the interlacing of parts to form a unified whole, and this is the structural grid which underlies the art of *Transformations*, one of the best-conceived and best-executed exhibitions to appear in Portland in recent years.

Katarina Weslien is a Swedish-born, American-educated artist who has been living and working in Portland for the past three years. Her background is in fiber art, having graduated from the Cranbrook Academy of Art in 1980, and her limited exposure in Maine has tended to identify her with the crafts tradition. In 1984 and 1986, she contributed woven collages to the Maine Crafts Association *Makers* exhibitions. Last year she collaborated with Tony Montanaro's Celebration Theater Ensemble on a stage set, and this year she will be collaborating with choreographer Daniel McCusker on a set design for the Ram Island Dance Company. But neither weavings nor stagecraft adequately prepares one for the physical and conceptual manipulation of space which is *Transformations*.

On the first floor of the Payson Gallery, Weslien has hung a selection of her woven collages, subtle and elegant art weavings of acrylics on paper with rayon warp and lurex weft. The collages consist of abstract paintings which have been cut into thin strips and woven together on a loom, intercutting distinct images and patterns to form a coherent whole of several elements on the same plane. Visually, Weslien's collages look like highly decorative and refined tatami mats or venetian blinds, but in their integration of imagery they participate in one of the major trends in contemporary art, the simultaneous presentation of multiple images, a trend manifest in various ways: for instance, in the spliced paintings of James Rosenquist, the radical juxtapositions of John Baldassari, and the overlays of David Salle. What this trend

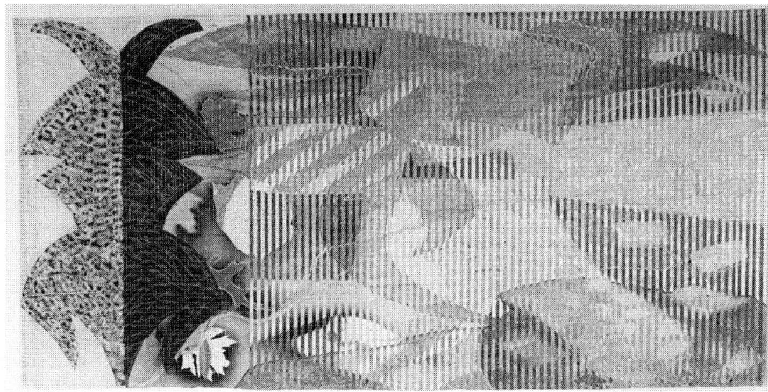

1. *Katarina Weslien*, When We Walk We Talk. *Woven collage. Courtesy of the artist.*

responds to and calls attention to is the way in which the modern being is constantly bombarded with undifferentiated sensory information. Typically, artists translate this sensory overload into art which is jarring and confusing in a very calculated way, but Katarina Weslien synthesizes the raw material of perception into one comprehensible unit. She weaves a net of consciousness out of competing information, thus integrating individual stimuli into a cognitive whole which is greater than the sum of its parts.

The second floor of the Payson Gallery is devoted to an installation which explodes Weslien's visual weavings out into a real time, real space experience. The artist refers to the *Transformations* installation as a "walking narrative," an art environment which the viewer walks into and through; a collage of three-dimensional structures, two-dimensional projections, light, shadow, and sound which would be disorienting if not for Weslien's calm intelligence and ability to control chaos.

Walking into *Transformations* is like entering a dream. The dramatic hi-tech space of the Payson Gallery has been transformed into a visionary white room, the centerpiece of which is a small symbolic house of wood and scrim which fills in the gallery overlook. In the house are a bird cage, a table set for tea, a chair and a bench; all white, all distorted and off-balance in a surreal suggestion of vertigo. Three corners of the room contain small auxiliary houses and the walls between are lined with an odd assortment of objects—sleds, tricycles, rakes, shovels, brooms, windows, branches, and mysterious cardboard cut-out figures, all painted white. Over this whole assembly plays a symphony of images, 640 slides in eight projectors, some set to dissolve quietly, others flashing on and off at various intervals. An hour-long audio-collage of taped voices and music (woven sound) contributes background noise to the white room. One wall suddenly goes up in projected flames while another is frozen in ice and snow. Images of the artist's face in clown white alternate with images of exotic New Guinea tribesmen in ceremonial regalia. Fragments of a conversation, meaningless to the auditor, are overheard. Pixilated light renders the floor beneath your feet suddenly infirm and unsure. Your steps become more considered, your progress more deliberate.

If all this sounds hallucinatory and disorienting, the marvel is that Weslien has managed to modulate the experience such that it is not. What she has created is a synthetic simulation of everyday existence which, despite its complexity, can be assimilated and made sense of. In its artificiality, Weslien's installation heightens our awareness of the complex of experiences we sort through routinely. It asks us to pay attention to the immediacy of our ongoing experience and our faculties for dealing with it. "In all this chatter," asks Katarina Weslien, "can you find the heartbeat?"

Katarina Weslien's hugely sensitive installation is a sort of maximal statement of perceptual manipulation, the minimal pole of which might be the subtle manipulations of light and space carried out by Robert Irwin, the guru of art as awareness. The only time I have had an experience similar to that created by Weslien's white room was when I stepped inside Lucas Samaras's *Mirrored Room* at Buffalo's Albright-Knox Art Gallery. But where Samaras reflects the simple Self into complex infinity in an act of expressionist narcissism, Weslien locates the Self within projected complexity. That she should do so with weaving as her conceptual foundation is really quite remarkable.

November 13, 1987

Inside/Outside: Private Art

Would we as a society be healthier and happier if all that is private were made public? Would a more just and free and caring culture result from a communal soul-bearing, a cathartic confession of our deepest fears, desires, and guilts? Would the truth really set us free? I have a tendency to think so, yet when faced with an exhibition aimed at just this sort of truth-telling and revelation, I found myself unexpectedly repulsed. But then the value and importance of *Inside/Outside: Private Art* may lie in the challenges it presents to some of our most cherished assumptions about life and about art.

Inside/Outside (at the University of Southern Maine's Area Gallery in Portland through Dec. 31) is an exhibition which integrates paintings and drawings by three dozen professional Maine artists in an undifferentiated and largely anonymous format with those of 100 prison inmates, mental health clients, and sheltered workshop participants. Conceived and curated by artist/activist Natasha Mayers, *Inside/Outside* "attempts to show where the need to create art comes from, to demonstrate that we all have the creative potential to make art and translate our feelings into visual metaphors." What Mayers wants to ask is, "what are we afraid of revealing? Why are we so hesitant to reveal ourselves?" One partial answer suggested by the visual experience of *Inside/Outside* might be that what we reveal about ourselves is not always pretty.

Plastered all over the walls of the USM lounge gallery are images, most childlike and raw, which set up a kind of collective howl of execration. Everywhere we are faced with expressions of anxiety, alienation, torment, dread, anger, fear, repression, revulsion, confusion, guilt, loneliness, and distress. The point seems to be that the same psychic irritants which produce social and mental illnesses also produce art, but there is a danger in this symptomatic identification, the danger of mistakenly concluding, for example, that Vincent Van Gogh's genius was a function of mania rather than lucidity.

In terms of a liberal, humanist agenda, *Inside/Outside* advances a number of laudable arguments: that the true value of art exists apart from the economics and elitism of the art market; that artists are as much outsiders in a corrupt, conformist consumer society as criminals and "crazies"; that art can be an agent of political and personal liberation; that the truth recognizes no cultural or class identities—we are all one in our humanity. These and many more points are eloquently made by Mayers, critic Lucy Lippard, artists Stephen Petroff and Nancy Coyne, art historian Margot Clark, and writer Bunny McBride in catalogue essays accompanying the exhibition. But what does the exhibition itself have to tell us?

The first and most obvious (so obvious as to be easily overlooked) fact is that despite its radical intent, *Inside/Outside* is a very conventional exhibition, completely respectful of the idea of art as an image contained within a rectangle. No matter how outraged and outrageous the content may be, each image passively accepts the straitjacket of the rectilinear, testifying once again to the frame as the fundamental artistic reality.

Next, the anonymous format, meant to subvert the conditioned response of looking at "names" rather than at the thing-in-itself, seems to have backfired on Mayers. I was relieved to hear from her that I was not the only viewer sucked into the identity game, viewing the show in an attempt to discern which images were made by "artists" and which by "amateurs." The invitation to discriminate is the implicit, if unintentional, challenge of this egalitarian exhibition. Could I, as someone who has been paid for the last 10 years to look at art in Maine, pick out the artists from the others? In the vast majority of cases I could not. In the few cases where I could detect or identify an artist at work, the telltale factor was usually a certain stylistic polish. Had I not previously seen Alan Magee's macabre cartoons (a fat slob dining on a roast baby, for instance), I think I still would have recognized the finesse of execution as that of a trained artist, though not necessarily Magee. The same is true of the pieces by Janice Kasper, Fred Lynch, Marjorie Moore, and Diane Bowie Zaitlin. Sophistication betrays them. Then, too, certain cultural affectations, such as inscribing paintings with messages in German, suggest a professional familiarity with current fashions. But, as I have said, for the most part I could not tell the professionals from the amateurs.

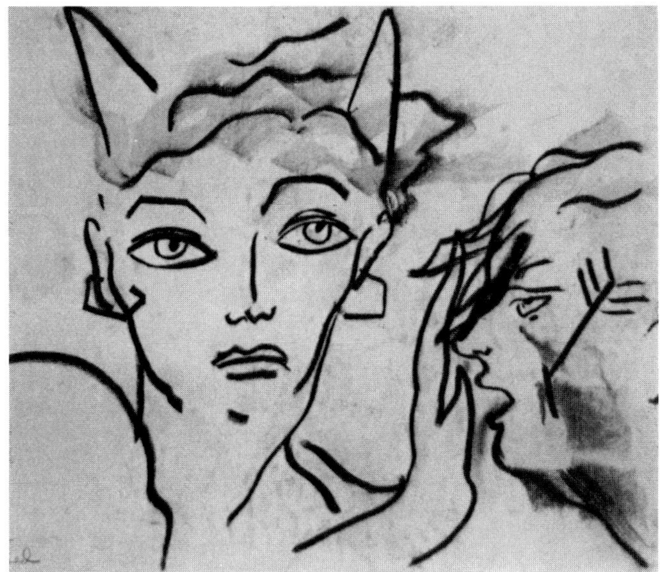

1. *Anonymous,* Sigfried. *Pastel. Courtesy of Natasha Mayers.*

Must I conclude then that there is no qualitative difference between the art of the amateurs and the art of the professionals? I don't think so. To begin with, Natasha Mayers purposefully asked artists for very personal, "private" works which they might not ordinarily show. What this accomplished was an exhibition in which equality is achieved at the expense of quality, similarity as the lowest common denominator. I know, I know, there's loads and loads of bias here, but for the most part, I would have to say that the art in *Inside/Outside* has more therapeutic value than aesthetic merit.

The dominant characteristic of the art in the exhibition is a childlike primitivism of execution. One could view this quality of rawness as evidence of honesty, directness, and authenticity, but I sense something else at work. For the serious artist, naivete is a strategy, one of many employed to aesthetic ends. For the naive, naivete is unavoidable and unintentional, a given. Since I am firmly convinced that *intentionality* is the only thing which distinguishes a work of art from any other made object (even an object exactly like it, as with Duchamps' urinal), I believe we must honor the intended over the accidental in art.

Some of the essayists commissioned for *Inside/Outside* suggest that the art of the "outsiders" is

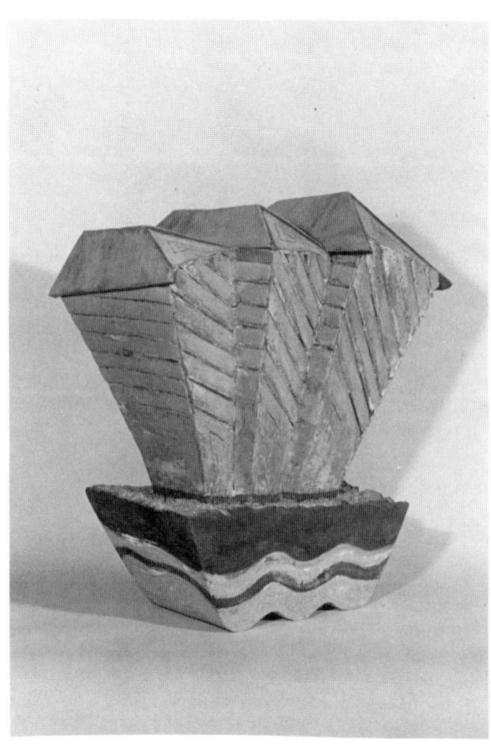

1. *Abby Huntoon,* Townhouses by the Sea, *1987. Glazed earthenware. Courtesy of the artist.*

somehow more honest and more powerful for being unfettered by learning, conditioning, or stylistic concerns. But is style really dishonest, a pretense which must be stripped away before the truth can be revealed? I don't think so. Style is simply *the way* of art, it is what makes communication possible, it is reason made visible. If the power to disturb were the criterion for artistic honesty, then snuff films would be the height of contemporary art. Confusing art with illness is a dangerous thing to do. *Inside/Outside* does not make this mistake, but it flirts dangerously close to the edges of confusion.

Finally, I could not help thinking that if the motivation for *Inside/Outside* was truly "to demonstrate that we all have the creative potential to make art," a better and more positive conjunction could have been made between the art of professional artists and the art of children. The truth is not always awful, nor beauty necessarily terrible. Still, *Inside/ Outside: Private Art* is a profoundly provocative exhibition. Your response to it may reveal more about you than you wish to know.

November 27, 1987

Four Clay Sculptors

Earth is the basis of all art. The sculptor's stones and metals, the painter's pigments, the printmaker's ink, all begin as earth. Art is alchemy, dirt transformed and transcended. Perhaps because of all the intellectual hot air and economic hard cash we invest in art, we sometimes lose sight of this essential truth—that art, like man in Christian cosmology, is earth with value added. I was reminded of this last weekend when I visited the Dean Velentgas Gallery in Portland to see the works of three clay sculptors (through January 3). Ceramics is one of the earthiest of art forms, being in all its myriad manifestations essentially clay plus heat, but the fact that I was made mindful of sources here—and not two weeks earlier while viewing the porcelain soup tureens at the Portland Museum of Art—says something, I think, about the material integrity of the artists Abby Huntoon, Nancy Nevergole, and Sharon Townshend. All three ceramicists, who share studio space in South Portland, work close to primal sources.

Abby Huntoon, whose functional works were featured last month at Viewpoints in Wiscasset, is an artist who takes an architectural approach to clay. Each of her earthenware constructions is a form of totem shelter, a vessel containing a peculiarly human spirit. Visually, she finds inspiration in everything from the replicated forms of domestic townhouses to the exoticism of Islamic mosques, but in all cases she seems to see shelter not only as an enclosed space, but a space set apart. *Haven*, for example, is like a primitive hut on stilts rising safely above a storm of coppery-green corrugated waves. *Townhouses* is a trio of tottering gray towers which seem to have sprouted from their common base, itself painted in a watery motif. And *Sahelian Mosque Pot*, as dry and drab as desert sand, stands on its four legs like an extracted molar set upon its roots. In both her functional ceramics and her sculpture, Abby Huntoon possesses an intuition of the precarious which is both keen and exciting.

Nancy Nevergole, working in stoneware, creates organic forms which, in her own words, are "soft and repulsive; anxious and relaxed;

beauty and beast." To this binary catalog, I would also add "earthy and erotic." Most of Nevergole's pieces in this show are biomorphic abstractions which look like...what? mutating croissants? copulating sweet potatoes? three-headed maggots? tumescent tubers? The strange forms themselves are about as attractive as (I imagine) a bowel resection, yet, in their surface treatment and sense of subhuman drama, Nevergole's freakish sculptures stand up as somehow vulnerable and painfully self-conscious, even brave.

Sharon Townshend's earthenware sculptures are both narrative and figurative. Inspired by a canoe trip during which she sought out the petroglyphs of aboriginal Mainers, Townshend takes the viewer on a kind of terra cotta odyssey in clay canoes powered by Indians, some of whom appear to belong to the same tribe as Gumby. When Townshend gets too literal, she tends to get too cute, but her best work in the show, *Story Tree*, is a sublimely simple and convincing piece, a ceramic trunk inscribed with personal pictographs.

For those (other gallery owners?) who keep track of such things, I am well aware that this makes the fifth time I have reviewed a show at the Dean Velentgas Gallery since it opened last February. Unfair? Perhaps. But as long as the most compelling and adventurous art in town keeps showing up here, I don't see that I have any choice except to keep coming back.

In the interest of fair play, however, it should be noted that Maine's premier art potter, Paul Heroux, is currently showing a new selection of porcelain pieces at Barridoff Galleries. His new work finds Heroux, whose vases and platters are more functional paintings than decorative pots, caught in a battle with the beautiful. His vases bulge and sag in a misshapen rebellion against ideal form, but his exquisite taste and painterly sensibility triumph over even intentional ugliness. What matters, most, of course, is that the master keeps pushing the possibilities. And to think, when you come right down to it, it's all just mud.

December 18, 1987

New England Now

Neil Welliver should be more careful about the company he keeps. After the images, names, and experience have all faded in memory, that is what I imagine I will remember most about *New England Now*, the New England all-star show currently (through February 14) at the DeCordova and Dana Museum in Lincoln, Mass., and scheduled to come to Bowdoin College this summer (June 30-September 4). For what impressed (or depressed) me most about the exhibition as hung in the DeCordova mansion was how singularly out-of-place and forlorn Welliver's *Drowned Tree*, a gnarl of bleached dry-ki on a field of coll blue ripples, looked in the company of so much—no, not lesser work, just *different* work.

Originally conceived as the *Minus Manhattan Project*, *New England Now* is intended to recognize and give exposure to the wealth of artistic talent resident in New England, the tacit assumption being that the best, most important "New England artists" are every bit as good and sophisticated as "New York artists." True. To that end, curators from six New England institutions (The DeCordova in Massachusetts, the Currier Gallery in New Hampshire, the Bell Gallery at Brown University in Rhode Island, Bowdoin College in Maine, the New Britain Museum in Connecticut, the the Fleming Museum at the University of Vermont) got together and came up with an exhibition of works by 25 New England artists, 18 men and 7 women ranging in age from 33 (Portland's Lisa Allen) to 62 (Dartmouth College's Varujan Boghosian), only eight of whom are New England natives, only five of whom still reside in the state they were born in. Not surprisingly, therefore, the curators, in their joint statement, "found no unifying theme, no attitude, no *look* that could be called *New English*." And the fact that at least 16 of the 25 artists have already had solo shows in Manhattan leads me to wonder, "What's the point?"

"The dizzying eclecticism of this exhibition mirrors the diversity of the contemporary visual arts in the region," state the jurors. "It is the intention of this show to celebrate that diversity."

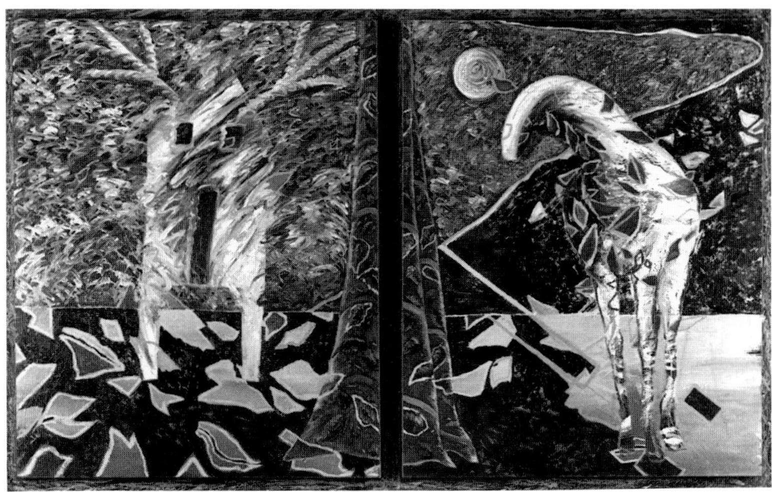

1. *Marjorie Moore,* Forest Eyes, *1986. Oil on canvas and wood. Courtesy of the artist.*

Well, happy diversity, ladies and gentlemen. But isn't it strange how we can mourn the loss of regional identity when Suburban Everywhere looks just like Suburban Everywhere Else, and yet celebrate the cultural homogeneity of diversity in art? But then, perhaps not so strange. For while our feet are planted on particular earth, our heads operate in universal space.

Admitting a degree of chauvinism, I'm pleased to report that Maine acquits herself well in *New England Now*. Welliver, while not the star of this particular show, is the best-known artist in the exhibition. The fact that he is not represented by a major painting is a shame, but apparently *Drowned Tree* was the only painting the curators could borrow. (The difficulty in getting a gallery to commit work by a bankable artist to a 14-month traveling show is reportedly also the reason that Yale's William Bailey is not among the Connecticut contingent.) At the DeCordova, Marjorie Moore's *Forest Eyes*, an expressionistic diptych evocative of wild intelligence, is accorded center stage between two major oils by Jonathan Imber (Massachusetts), a narrative nude and a brooding, boggy landscape. The Portland School of Art's Lisa Allen (currently working in New Mexico under a Roswell Foundation grant) contributes a dynamic, heavily impastoed abstraction, *Willow*, which speaks the same language of immediacy as Vermont artist Phillip Wofford's densely worked abstraction *Second Transmigration*. And Bowdoin's Mark Wethli, who first showed in Maine as part of a West Coast realism exhibition, whispers on about the sublime with three small oils of classical quietism.

The pluralistic diversity of *New England Now* generally resolves itself into five categories—representation, abstraction, expressionism, photographic manipulations, and installations. For me, the most distinguished piece in the show is a Duchampian construction by Malcolm Cochran, a New Hampshire artist currently teaching at Ohio State. Cochran's *Song Without Words (for Amy Beech)* consists of a room-size brass and glass conservatory housing a derelict spinet piano upon which are mounted nine functional electric table fans. His hothouse of memory and imagination hums a hymn which is but mechanical wind trapped in an isolation chamber.

The deficiency of this exhibition is a function of its birth by committee. A single sensibility could have done a far better job, perhaps intuiting or imparting a point of view, but not one of these six small museums had the resources to mount such a wide-ranging regional show. As an exercise in collaboration, *New England Now* is a useful experiment, but a definitive exhibition of contemporary art from New England is still out there to be done.

I intend to review *New England Now* again when it comes to Bowdoin, where it will be a slightly different show. Bowdoin, for instance, has commissioned an environmental installation (the preliminary drawings for which are exhibited at the DeCordova) from Michael Timpson, one of the most adventurous young artists working in Massachusetts. Timpson, I might add, is from Ireland. That's *New England Now*.

January 22, 1988

Sigmund Abeles

Sigmund Abeles, unexcelled draftsman, realist and tragedian, frequent border-crosser, has retired from the University of New Hampshire faculty after 17 years of teaching. To honor the man, the teacher, and the artist, UNH has mounted *Sigmund Abeles: a Retrospective*, a most satisfying exhibition (University Art Galleries in Durham through March 6) consisting of more than 80 drawings, prints, pastels, and sculptures produced over the last 27 years. While the exhibition concentrates heavily on the art of the past decade, sufficient earlier work is included to enable the viewer to chart the progress Abeles has made in mining the darker veins of the humanistic tradition.

Like fellow humanists Leonard Baskin, Philip Pearlstein, and the brothers Soyer, Sigmund Abeles is married to the human figure as the embodiment of life and the foundation of art. But where Baskin finds in the human vessel a point of departure for mythic flights, Abeles remains empirically rooted in this world. Where Pearlstein treats the female nude as a de-spirited object for formal scrutiny, Abeles declines to strip his women of personality and individuality. And where the Soyers based an art of social alienation on the face and figure as public mask and shell, Abeles is passionately engaged with and by the private self. His is a sensual art made in response to the mystery of mortality. For while family, friends, female models, and the mirrored self-image are his immediate subjects, death animates and informs all of Abeles' art. Aging parents stand between us and eternity, children are the fragile repositories for our dreams of innocence and immortality, women provide the moments of intimacy and beauty which make life bearable, and with the study of self comes the powerful sense of identity which, like a prism, reflects the light of our lives out into the darkness of unthinkable, inevitable nothingness.

Sigmund Abeles: a Retrospective chronicles a solitary quest for knowledge which begins in fear and ends in faith. Abeles' early works tend to be hard, black, and graphic, angrily, even defiantly rendered. The 1963 etching *Self-Portrait with Cats*, for example, is a disturbing piece in which the artist confronts his feline phobia by surrounding himself with the loathsome beasts. Art as exorcism. There is a ritual quality, too, to the 1964 etching *In My Studio*, a stagey piece of work in which a sleeping woman is posed amid images of death and menace—a stuffed fox suspended from the ceiling and the skulls of a human, a steer, and a ram. The most menacing of these early, Baskinesque images, however, is the 1973 lithograph *Self-Portrait with Saddles*, where the artist glowers out at the viewer over an organic abstraction which only on close inspection resolves itself as the lines and forms of English riding saddles.

One of the curiosities and limitations of Sigmund Abeles' career is that he has chosen to do his major work in pastels. An expert draftsman, he left off painting in the 1960s in favor of mediums closer to pure drawing. (Word has it, however, that Abeles picked up the brushes again just this year.) Viewers who do not know Abeles as a sculptor will find surprising evidence of a workmanlike skill at modeling figures, but it is in his pastels, drawings which want very much to be paintings, that he distinguishes himself. The best of these bravura pastels are brooding works concerned with a single figure and the mastery of perspective. *Midnight* (1986-87), a female nude balled up in a pink chair, and *Change of Seasons* (1985), a nude in an orange canvas sling chair viewed from behind and above, show off the artist's virtuoso skills at capturing the foreshortened anatomy, but they are like performance pieces compared to the pastels which carry, in addition to messages of skillfulness, a psychological and narrative burden. *Late Night Phone Call* (1981), for instance, appears to be about more than an unclothed young woman posing for an artist. Her seated, cross-legged pose is no doubt directed toward technical problems-solving, but her dazed expression as the phone on the bed rings and the shadowy figure of her dog in the background add an air of expectancy and urgency, a sense of contextual reality which is missing in some of the set pieces. Still, as minor masterpieces like *The Peach Robe* (1982, reworked in 1984 after a fire) and *Voyeur, A.M.* (1985-86) show, Sigmund Abeles bows to none in the ability to render both the substance and

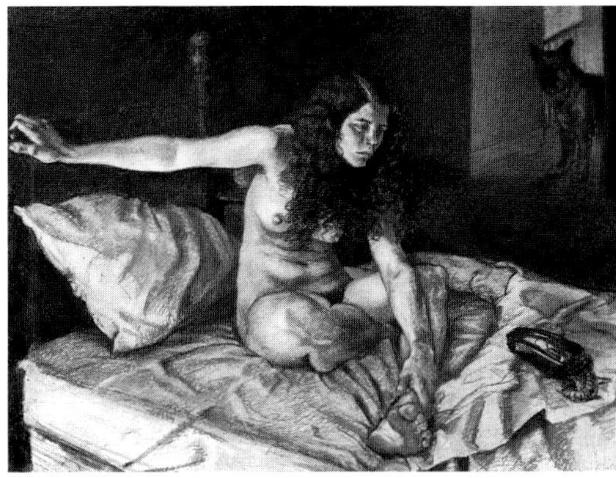

1. *Sigmund Abeles*, Late Night Phone Call, *1981. Pastel. Courtesy of the Babcock Gallery, New York, New York.*

essence of Woman.

The tension between love and death is the greatest strain in most human lives and is the operative force in the art of Sigmund Abeles. How one ultimately handles this strain tends to define a person. Some people seem able to bear up stoically, comforting themselves, if at all, with absurdities. Some people simply snap. The majority of us, however, seek release from this tension in an appeal to a higher, transcendent power. In 1983, hit within months by the death of his mother, the destruction of his work in a New York gallery fire, and the precariously premature birth of his son Max, Sigmund Abeles found himself embracing his Jewish heritage. Thus, the centerpieces of his UNH retrospective are three pastels devoted to scenes of Hasidic life—*Five Lubavitchers at Morning Prayer* (1986-87), *Morning Prayers at 770 Eastern Parkway, Brooklyn* (1987), and *Morning Prayers, Three Generations* (1987).

In many obvious ways, these images of piety are dramatic departures for Abeles, yet even in admitting the spiritual dimension to his life and art Abeles remains faithful to this world of appearances. What he shows us are the outward signs of religious purpose—shawled and bearded figures at worship, a boy binding phylacteries to his arm. A realist still, but perhaps no longer a humanist. And in this spiritual departure, Abeles is presented with new problems and new opportunities. On the one hand, his Hebrew pastels seem so artlessly absorbed with the literal as to flirt with illustration, yet, on the other, the compositional complexities, tonal variations, and detailing of these pictures suggest the door back into painting may be opening once again for Sigmund Abeles. This is a retrospective with a prospective thrust.

February 26, 1988

Michael Waterman

Michael Waterman paints in a studio not much larger than a closet, a little 6-by-10-foot cubicle overlooking Congress Street from the fourth floor of a seedy Congress Square office building. A small, spare man, 41 years of age, Waterman looks as though he might have just stepped out of a painting by Raphael Soyer. His nondescript, utilitarian work clothes and the corncob pipe clenched in his teeth add to the impression of premature age. He seems at once sad and content, neglected and alive. Michael Waterman is a painter of Portland past—which is why I'm pleased to see him painting now. What Portland was not long ago rarely finds its way into the art of the new Portland.

Twenty-two years ago, when Waterman graduated from Portland High School, he was already a practicing artist. His first teacher was his father Alfred Waterman, now a retired baker with a studio directly across Congress Street from his son's. Bankrolled by a scholarship he won in a *Scholastic* magazine art competition, Waterman spent two years after high school studying in New York, first at Pratt Institute, then at the Art Students League. While in New York as a student, he also had the unusual distinction of being represented by a gallery. Today, he says he was simply too young to appreciate the opportunities he let slip past him.

When Waterman returned to Portland in 1968, he rented a $25-a-month studio in Middle Street amidst a motley array of shoe and watch repair shops. But eventually urban renewal leveled the block and took the eccentric curve out of Middle Street. Today, One City Center stands where Waterman's studio used to be.

Anyone interested in art who happened to be in Portland between 1969 and 1975 no doubt recalls Waterman selling his drawings and paintings door-to-door. (In fact, I tend to consider anyone who doesn't an *arriviste*.) At the time, his work took the form of simple, expressionistic images of people and animals.

"My idea was to sell paintings for $5," says Waterman. "I usually sold about 25 a week at $5 apiece. My idea was that the galleries were corrupt, so I'd paint in the daytime and sell in the evening door-to-door."

Toward the end of his Portland peddling period, however, Waterman's art became increasingly minimal, often reduced to little more than three or four strategic lines on bare canvas. As his art became more severely restricted, Waterman himself seemed to disappear from public view. For six years, during which he sometimes claimed no longer to be painting, he worked as a custodian at the Portland Public Library.

"I just wanted to work as a janitor and paint privately. I ignored myself as a public painter and it really helped me to grow. I began building pictures as though they were only for me—no message, no calculation."

What he found as he painted only for himself was that his years of non-objective painting served him well for creating a structure and a surface upon which to project images from his imagination, images having to do with growing up and coming of age in Portland. So when Waterman re-surfaced last year at Gallery 127, it was as a representational painter interpreting his local experience in an idiom loosely related to the social and aesthetic concerns of the Ashcan School.

"The Ashcan School," maintains Waterman, "failed in its attempt to invent a reasonable surface for their themes to come out. Their surfaces were locked in with an Italianate type of palette. I like the motives of the Ashcan School, but I wanted a way of not locking in the images in an antique way.

"I try to paint everything into one picture as though it were going to be my last painting," says Waterman. "They are summations, summing up and estimating as much as I can about what I recall and what I am made aware of now."

Michael Waterman's new paintings will be featured at Gallery 127 in June. There are tentative plans for a retrospective of his work this fall at the University of Southern Maine. What one sees in these new paintings are characters from Waterman's imagination cast in sullen dramas set against a backdrop of low-income Portland, a city of harsh realities which the bright hues of prosperity have not yet touched. Waterman's colors are the colors of old Portland, a sombre palette of brick browns and reds, granite and foggy grays, cloudy blues, and harbor greens. His surfaces are patched and scaly like the walls of an unrestored tenement of warehouse. These are blue-collar paintings of a fading Portland, difficult, unlovely, but honest. Some fail openly, but others achieve an authentic vision of Portland such as no other artist has managed.

"These people [in his paintings] are to me very much ancient people," says Michael Waterman. "Portland isn't really in the world. It's an autonomous region with its own funny history."

April 1, 1988

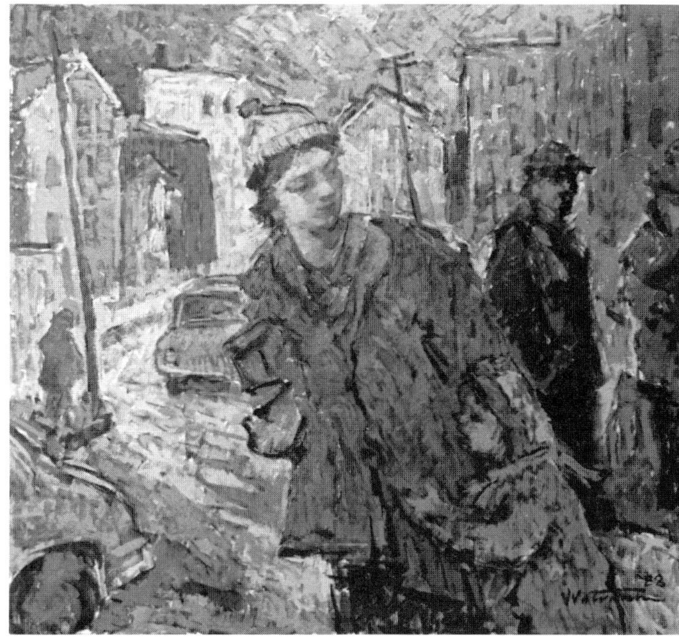

1. *Michael Waterman,* No, That's Your Uncle. *Oil. Courtesy of Gallery 127.*

1. *Greg Parker,* Interstices, *1988. Graphite, charcoal and litho crayon. Courtesy of the artist. Photo by Joan Brown.*

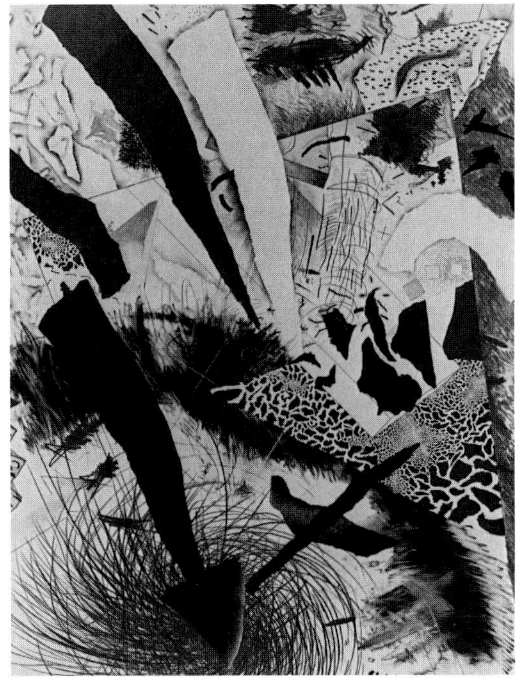

Maine Coast Artists' 10th Annual

Maine Coast Artists' 10th Annual Juried exhibition serves three primary functions. It signals the beginning of another Maine summer art season. It provides exposure for new art in Maine. And this year, for the first time, it adds much-needed credibility to the Barn Gallery in Ogunquit, where it will travel (July 2 through August 13) after it finishes its run in Rockport (through June 26).

This year's edition of Maine Coast Artists' juried show was selected by a trio of judges—Dana Friis-Hansen of MIT's List Visual Arts Center, former Portland School of Art gallery director Steven High, and Pat Nick of the Vinalhaven Press printmaking workshop—who sorted through 1,300 submissions by 450 artists in order to put together an exhibition of 98 works by 58 artists. What they have come up with is necessarily an eclectic exhibition lacking any single animating idea or direction, but it is nonetheless a lively selection from which a number of conclusions might be drawn.

First, the Rockport annual has become, whether intentionally or *de facto* (I'm not sure), a showcase for emerging artists. What this show is *not* is a survey of the state of art in Maine. Being relatively unknown would seem to be a positive factor in getting in. Of the 58 artists represented, 24 were previously unknown to me, at any rate. This strikes me as a good thing, unless of course it means that eventually *only* unknown artists will submit.

Second, painters are not well-represented in the Rockport show. There are a few solid little paintings such as those by Alan Bray, Alfred Chadbourn, and Richard Wilson, but most of the painting is either slack or merely competent. Only Dozier Bell's *Dogfight*, a large oil previously exhibited at O'Farrell Gallery, carries the authority of a serious artist doing major work. By and large, the best works in the show are drawings.

Third, unless representational painters have stopped submitting to Rockport or the jurors simply culled them out, the critical tide seems to have turned against the traditional Maine landscape. The few that showed look serenely out of place in the company of so much nervous expressionism and latter-day shamanism.

Painters Bell, Bray, Gary Buch, Chadbourn, James Linehan, and Wilson, and ceramic artists Paul Heroux, Abby Huntoon, and Mark Kuzio are among the familiar artists represented, but the day rightly belongs to the unsung. When I close my eyes and mentally re-scan the two floors of art, the works of eight artists flash through my visual memory.

Emily Brett's three mixed-media *Rock Form* drawings stand out as strong, simple images handily drawn and nicely differentiated by surface texture. They work both as representation and act.

Susan Dexter Camp's paper, wood, and rusted spike constructions *The Columbus Myth* and *Woman Vessel II* participate in the naturalistic magic artists today so often throw up in the face of a hi-tech culture.

Walter K. Hanson's untitled silver print of a truck at the Dragon Cement plant is an arresting image and the best of the handful of photographs in the show. Hanson manages to lift the buglike dump truck out of the industrial mundane and into the exotic sublime.

The most highly intellectualized of the works at Rockport are Joan Mobarry's acrylic and iron *Dividing Line* threesome. Mobarry gives formal expression to ideas about physical and psychological space, using an oxidized metal bar to establish relationships between and among canvas panels painted to a cement-like finish.

Greg Parker's three black and white graphite, charcoal, and litho crayon drawings abstract a turbulent sensibility using torn, fragmentary forms, allusions to geographic and imaginative space, and animal hide patterns in a complex, controlled chaos.

Dennis Pinette's pair of chalk pastel drawings, *Substation* and *Road to Wiscasset*, use the ironic beauty of Maine Yankee imagery to make powerful visual statements about nuclear power, but they are gorgeous, glowing drawings before they are propaganda. Pinette seems to be under the influence of Yvonne Jacquette, not a bad influence at all.

Gregory Welch's pastel/collage drawings *Kaw* and *Relic* are mute, meditative pieces with an otherworldly feel as powerful as Pinette's more representational apocrypha.

And Jack Welch's raw combines employ architectural and furniture debris in sculptural poems which seem to be about history and salvation. If he painted his combines black, Welch would be accused of imitating Louise Nevelson. As it is, he is something of a down east Rauschenberg trying to salvage beauty from the ruins of civilization.

Big juried group shows can be quite confusing and scattered, but Maine Coast Artists' 10th Annual manages to hold itself loosely together by the simple device of including more than one work by many of the artists. All in all, a fairly well-behaved assembly as group shows go.

June 10, 1988

Works-On-Paper

Take a trip to Gorham, stop in at the little white chapel that is the University of Southern Maine Art Gallery, look at each of the 49 *Works-On-Paper* that constitute the 1988 All Maine Biennial, and then ask yourself this question: "What do these pictures represent?"

Taken together, of course, these 49 pictures represent the combined judgments of the three jurors—Farnsworth Museum director Chris Crosman and artists Martha Diamond and Italo Scanga—about what was best and most interesting among the 362 works submitted by 199 artists to this year's biennial. Individually, they represent the time and talent of 49 Maine artists. Beyond that, they are 49 unrelated works of art that live and die according to what the artists put into them and what you get out of them. Some you will like, some you will not, but more important than personal taste is the measure shows like this (with all their obvious flaws of partiality) afford of the status of art in Maine today.

If you have been looking at art in Maine for awhile, some of the names attached to the pictures (Alan Bray, DeWitt Hardy, Eric Hopkins, Frederick Lynch, Natasha Mayers, Richard Wilson) will be familiar to you, and some (John Baird, Sarah Bartlett, Lynn Bouchard, Carolyn Gurley, Maret Hensick, Martha Miller, Kristin Nelson-Baird, Katharine White) may not. If you saw the annual Maine Coast Artists juried show at Rockport, you may notice that of the 58 artists in that show and the 49 in this one, only eight—Baird, Bouchard, Bray, Camille Cole, Blaine Grindle, Alice Steinhardt, Gregory Welch, Wilson—made the cut in both. This is perhaps significant only as an indication of the diversity of the Maine scene at the moment, but the cumulative effect of open juried shows (which by their nature tend to attract many young, ambitious artists) is to persuade one that the pursuit of serious art in Maine is both vital and growing. I cannot imagine that there were ever as many good artists working in Maine as there are today. And new artists seem to be arriving or emerging monthly.

Recently, it was suggested to me (by someone

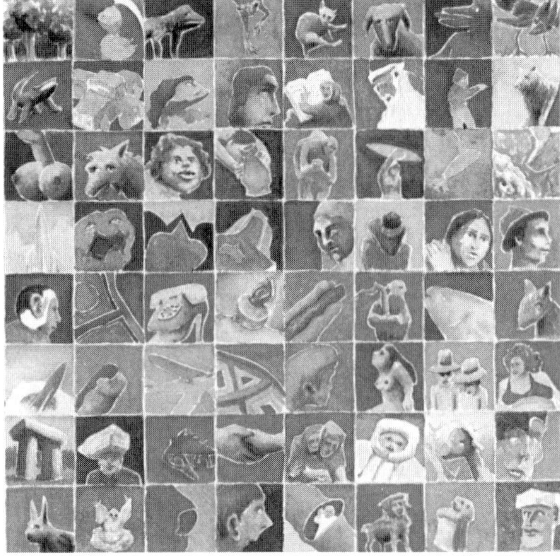

1. *Richard Wilson,* On My Mind *(detail), 1988. Watercolor. Courtesy of the University of Southern Maine Art gallery.*

whose opinion I respect enormously) that the much-heralded regional renaissance in art never actually occurred, that the great things we expected of new art in Maine have not happened. Well, maybe they haven't happened at an institutional level, but down at the grassroots there has been a gradual evolution in the visual arts which, today, adds up to an enormous change. Consider, for example, the fact that there are not more than a half-dozen works in the 1988 All Maine Biennial which, were they exhibited in New York or Los Angeles, would betray their Maine origins. From Cole and Church to Homer, Hartley, and Marin, Porter, Welliver, and Katz, there is an identifiable Maine-ness (whether of subject matter or aspect of light) that pervades the art produced in Maine. That quality has all but been eradicated from the work of the latest generation of artists in Maine.

While recent Maine literature has tended to place a heavy emphasis on regional identity, insisting on the value of the local, new Maine art has tended to flood into the international mainstream where "visual" art has become less a matter of looking at the world than of making something for the world to look at. The painting or drawing of scenes has been replaced by the act of the visual imagination, seeing displaced by being seen. Certainly, many artists are still inspired by Maine's natural and cultural environment, but you wouldn't know it by looking at the works-on-paper singled out for special merit by the biennial jurors.

John Kimball, better known as an art dealer than as an artist, was awarded a solo exhibition on the basis of his mixed-media *The Saturday Afternoon Simon Bussey*, a cartoony, warped rendering of a crowded ferry boat (not, to my knowledge, one that operates in Maine waters). Where some might see clumsiness and error in Kimball's crude craft, the jurors obviously rewarded awkwardness as a sign of honest effort, effort being one hallmark of art as act.

Richard Wilson's *On My Mind*, a *tour de force* watercolor consisting of 204 discrete images arranged in an overall grid, won the design award. Details from this mental mosaic were used to illustrate biennial invitations, catalogue covers, and the exhibition poster. The fact that Wilson makes prints for juror Italo Scanga might raise a few eyebrows, but *On My Mind* is just too good to dismiss.

Honorable mentions went to Lynn Bouchard for *Holy Prison*, an experssionist vision of apocalypse; Alan Bray for *Three Story Landscape*, a strange vertical graphite drawing that might best be described as landscape-as-tire-track; Eric Hopkins for his ink and oil *Shell #4*; Janice Kaspar for *Maine Dogs, Winter*, one of her wonderful canine adventures and the only "winner" recognizably about Maine; Scott Murray for *Too Soon to Tell*, a narrative figuration; Kristin Nelson-Baird for *Showtime*, a surreal corral filled (fittingly enough) with hobby-horses; Scott Redfern for his figurative abstraction *God in Man*; R. Keith Rendall for *Fish Monger*, a heavily drawn and patterned expressionist tableau; Marguerite Robichaux for a large, washy mountain landscape entitled *April 3—Vermont*; and Gregory Welch for *Tilt*, a black and white formal abstraction. I am tempted to suggest the jurors overlooked the exquisite subtleties of Anne Ayvaliotis' mysterious charcoal *Pasture*, the nocturnal glow of Alice Steinhardt's charcoal *10-12-87*, and the disturbing prevision of Katharine White's colored-pencil *Bird with Hands*, but then they did see fit to include them in the first place.

The 1988 All Maine Biennial, then, represents a series of individual acts and scenes on paper, with acts far outnumbering scenes. What this says to me is that, while conservative representationalism still commands the Maine art market, the wide-eyed army is in revolt.

July 22, 1988

Natasha Mayers and Kathy Bradford

The artists in this show remind us that there are no contradictions between politics and the spirit except those artificially imposed in societies that rule by division.

—Lucy Lippard, *Acts of Faith: Politics and the Spirit.*

Katherine Bradford and Natasha Mayers, two extremely intelligent and committed artists, have been friends for years. Bradford's art hangs in Mayers' home and Mayers' art in Bradford's; both have been active in the Union of Maine Visual Artists; and, until recently, they have felt close professionally as well as personally. But now both sense that an aesthetic estrangement has crept into their relationship. Bradford, skeptical about the ability of art to embody anything meaningful politically, is troubled by the overt social content of Mayers' images of oppression in Central America and elsewhere. Mayers, insistent that art can make a moral difference, finds Bradford's paintings increasingly private and divorced from reality.

"Natasha wants her art to mean something to her neighbors," says Bradford. "She wants them to be moved by it. Her subject matter is disturbing, but her language can be understood. My audience is the art community of New York."

"I want my audience to be everybody," says Mayers. "I don't want my work to be just about paint. I don't want it to be about paint at all. I have an inclination to make my work more public—maybe posters, xeroxes, or graffiti."

Private/public, contemplation/commentary, art about art/art about activism—the lines of divergence seem cleanly drawn. Thus, it seems somehow appropriate that in the exhibition curated by Lisa Petrucci for Hitchcock Art Dealers (through September 3), Kathy Bradford's dense, intellectual abstractions occupy one room of the Portland gallery while Natasha Mayers' visual lament for *Los Desaparecidos/The Disappeared* fills the other. Like ex-lovers finding themselves at the same party, Bradford's art and Mayers' contrive uncomfortably to avoid one another.

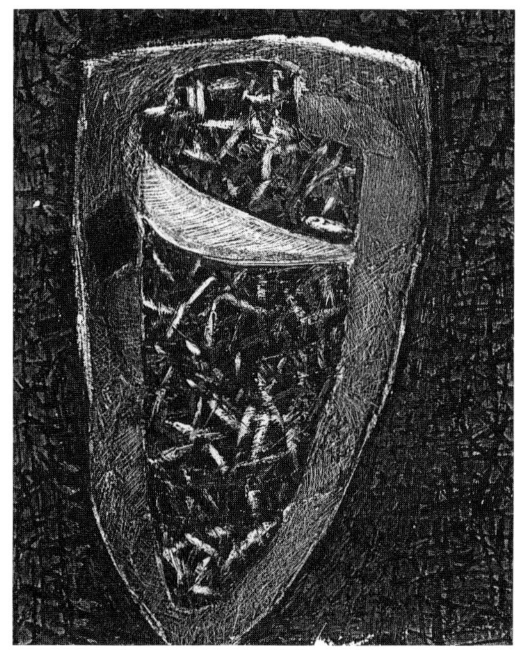

1. *Natasha Mayers, from* Los Desaparecidos/ The Disappeared Series. *Mixed-media. Courtesy of the artist.*

Bradford's eight oil paintings in the Hitchcock show are very slow, locked-in abstractions based upon ambiguous, intuitive forms that well up out of the depths of paint and upon plane geometric forms that sit upon the surface like uncomprehended facts. *Pharaoh*, for instance, focuses on a large, dark, hornlike U ringed and vibrating in space the color of desert sand. *Melville* consists of white circles on fields of gray in each of the four corners of the canvas, this structure defining a huge black cross which dominates the painting. These are paintings about the search for visual language and often seem to function below syntax and grammar at the level of perceptual surds and phonemes. They are paintings in search of relations and, as such, are the artistic equivalents of pure mathematics, theoretical physics, or perhaps ascetic mysticism. While they often appear disengaged from the empirical world, they are inescapably about the search for meaning in human experience.

Mayers' paintings and drawings take her experience of the experience of others and express pain and sorrow, outrage and loss through bound, often barely human forms. Mummified humanity, muffled and silenced, victimized, disposed of—the missing and the dead speak through her art. Hers is the art of conscience, and Mayers wants her audience to be moved to action by what she shows them. These images also represent Mayers' most successful resolution of politics and art to date.

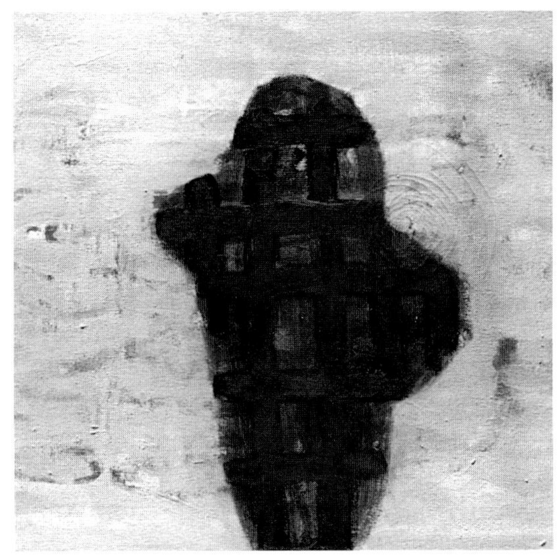

2. *Kathy Bradford,* Patriot. *Oil on canvas. Courtesy of the artist.*

The paintings and drawings possess their own formal integrity apart from referential and didactic values, meaning that one can, if one so chooses, appreciate them as artful images apart from their message.

Despite their diverse purposes, the art of Bradford and the art of Mayers have strong material sympathies for one another—coincidences of mark-making, a common sombre palette, and even affinitive shapes. Bradford's blunt form in the little blue *Patriot*, for example, could belong to one of Mayers' "disappeareds." For that matter, Mayers' figures could just as easily become vases in the absence of titles and texts.

While Bradford tends to regard her paintings as discrete objects added to the world ("I like to think of works of art as having the same drawing power as the lighted hearth in a kitchen or the lone cross in the corner of a monk's cell"), Mayers pursues an art of social action ("I'm not interested in making votive objects. I want my images to move people to feel a sense of loss and responsibility.") Yet, on the spectrum of contemporary art—from pretty decorations to acts of nihilism—Bradford and Mayers are so close they're touching. Whether they know it or not, they are speaking the same language. Kathy Bradford uses that language to pray silently and Natasha Mayers uses it to protest aloud, but there are no conflicts in this, only differences.

One of the most thoughtful, balanced, and provocative exhibitions of this or any other season.

August 5, 1988

Abby Shahn, Fred Lynch and Jack Welch

Abby Shahn, Fred Lynch, and Jack Welch have more in common than five-letter surnames and current one-artist shows in Portland. All three are abstract artists who have developed unique ways to humanize geometry, to make structure tell a story.

Abby Shahn (Hobe Sound Galleries North through October 1) works flat, on paper. Imposing on her luminous egg temperas the rigid order of the minimalist grid, she then proceeds to make her squares sing with prayers and protests. Often she does this through color and texture alone, arranging mottled, monochrome squares such that the fires of hell and the light of heaven seem to show through. More often in her recent works, she uses the rectilinear structure either to contain discrete, symbolic forms or to explode out of with furious, painterly zeal.

El Salvador, a seven-by-eight-foot tempera painted in 1981, is an example of the former strategy, a painting in which the artist's reactions to violence and oppression in El Salvador are contained within the grid. Each square contains its own moment and feeling. Some contain sharp shards that speak of shattering violence, others bleak bars that suggest imprisonment, some pure passages of form and color which provide the context and mood for considering what is happening in this place.

Strolling in Babylon, a large triptych (end panels 60 by 60 inches, center panel 60 by 112 inches) from 1987, employs the opposite strategy. The flat grid itself is shattered by apocalyptic strokes of fiery paint. The flames are fanned from the left panel onto the central panel which is fully involved in the firestorm, bits and pieces of the grid scattered by the power of the blast. The panel on the right contains the ashes of order.

Frederick Lynch (Barridoff Galleries through September 20) works with illusionistic space. Having pulled back from three-dimensional wall constructions, Lynch is now concentrating on producing similar complexes on shaped wooden panels. Coming in cold on Lynch and seeing the extravagant uses he makes of stripes, an art-wise viewer might take him as a former minimalist taking the stripes of Noland and Stella to extremes in the maximalist Eighties. However, Lynch's striped patterns did not begin as exercises in formalism, but as fabric striping in his figurative work of a decade ago. From the standpoint of pure decoration, there are no more sumptuously beautiful paintings coming out of Maine than Lynch's, yet beneath the virtuoso performance of planar illusions and bold patternings these are very social works of art.

Using little more than color-bright principles of plane and solid geometry, Lynch succeeds in evoking a complex universe of human values and vanities. His fragmented, shaped paintings have about them a bodily scale and weight that make them extremely sensuous. And his representational roots still show in the little pockets of recognizable objects (often jackknives, razors, palette knives, or other tools close at hand in the studio) Lynch paints into his pieces as if to give viewers a handle on the nature of his work.

Jack Welch (Dean Velentgas Gallery through October 9) works in real space with found objects. Seeing the way Welch has put together bits and pieces of architectural and domestic debris, viewers will be reminded of Robert Rauschenberg's combines and their predecessors, the ready-mades of Marcel Duchamp, but where Rauschenberg and Duchamp both made witty, ironic use of found objects, Jack Welch plays it dumb and deadpan in his best pieces.

Boat Piece, a strip of old, blue, flowered linoleum married to a tarred boat bottom with pieces of a green shutter attached, strikes an amazingly contemporary attitude in a piece that makes mute poetry of the banal and boring. In *Lost Suppers*, a pair of cheap, discarded prints of Da Vinci's *Last Supper* are spliced together, mounted above a louvered door, and artificially extended into 3-D space with an offset cut-out that mimics the window trinity in the background of the masterpiece.

The worthless is elevated to the art historical in Welch's simplest, straight-faced combinations. He does best when he simply supplies a structure and lets his materials speak for themselves. When he tries to become more extravagantly and loquaciously expressive, slathering paint and graffiti all over the broken bones of civilization, his art loses its eloquence and slips quickly into churlish excess.

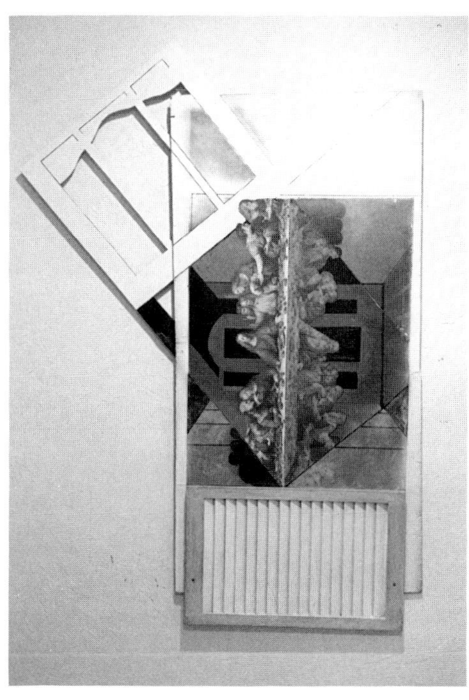

1. *Jack Welch,* Lost Suppers, *1988. Found objects and paint. Courtesy of the artist.*

Abby Shahn and Fred Lynch are both mature, mid-career artists who have learned the importance of restraint, the volume of meaning that comes with an economy of means. Jack Welch, a 1985 graduate of Portland School of Art, is an exciting young artist who still needs to break all the rules before he discovers which ones he ought to obey. If he is as good as his best work indicates, he will respect his limitations once he figures out what they are.

Taken together, the Shahn, Lynch, and Welch exhibitions constitute the most powerful coincidence of shows I can ever recall in Portland. Were there a larger market for serious, non-representational art in Maine, all three would now be getting fat for winter.

September 16, 1988

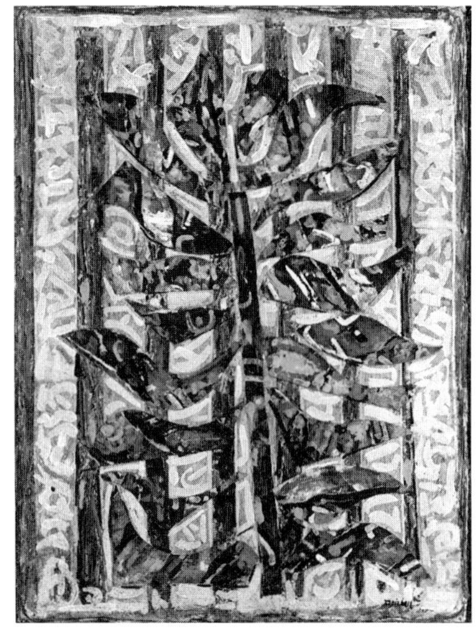

1. *David Driskell,* Pines on Fire, *1988. Encaustic and collage. Courtesy of the artist. Photo by Benjamin Magro.*

David Driskell

David Driskell, a summer resident of Falmouth, is one of the very few black artists working in Maine. (Ashley Bryan on Islesford is the only other black artist I am aware of in the state.) A faculty member of the University of Maryland, Driskell is one of America's preeminent authorities on Afro-American art and he is generally credited with helping to raise public consciousness about the contributions black artists have made to American art.

In 1976, for example, he curated *Two Centuries of Black American Art* at the Los Angeles County Museum of Art, and in 1987, he co-curated *Harlem Renaissance: Art of Black America*, the Studio Museum in Harlem exhibition recently featured at Bowdoin College.

Currently (through February, which is Black History Month), David Driskell's own art is the subject of an exhibition at the Colby College Museum of Art co-sponsored by the college and the Waterville Martin Luther King Celebration Committee. Given Driskell's commitment to black art and culture, one might expect to see some evidence of the influence of African and Afro-American art on his own painting, but if the evidence is there it is not at all obvious. Of course, suggesting that Driskell's art does not look like black art begs the question: What does "black" art look like?

I realize I am on very precarious ground here, but inquiring into the relationship between race and aesthetics seems important enough to risk falling on my face. To begin with, I am confident that most people viewing the Driskell show at Colby would not know the artist is a black man just by looking at his art. By this I suppose I reveal a prejudice that one can tell from looking at the works of, say, William H. Johnson, Romare Bearden, or Jacob Lawrence that these artists are black. Certainly the work of these artists often depicts black people and elements of black culture, but, by the same token, so does the art of Leon Golub, who is not black. And what of Jean Michel Basquiat, the graffiti kid who became Andy Warhol's sidekick? Basquiat was called "the black Picasso," but in terms of African influences Pablo Picasso's art was at least as black as Basquiat's.

No, we do not see in the art of David Driskell any overt references to African tribal masks, nor the sort of primitive folk realism one might conjure to stereotype black art. Working primarily in encaustic and collage, Driskell creates colorful patterned abstractions, field paintings at once highly structured and internally free. The formal structures upon which he builds his paintings seem to be inspired by things in his immediate environment—ladderback and Shaker chairs, patchwork quilts, pine trees, and the rhythm of music. With these simple forms as foundation, Driskell then weaves a dense surface out of calligraphic brushstrokes. His paintings thus have a centered formal strength while being as organically complex as leaf litter and as brightly celebrational as a handful of confetti.

If there is anything even vaguely African about these paintings, it may be the manner in which Driskell individuates his brushstrokes, placing paint in ornamental daubs which might have roots in tribal masks and face painting. I was wrong, however, to expect black art from a black artist. For, as Driskell wrote in his catalogue essay for *Two Centuries of Black American Art*, "The Black artist is no different from any other in his struggle to express his own individual sensitivity to order and form and at the same time relate to the cultural patterns of the time and place in which he lives. Art has no racial barriers."

January 13, 1989

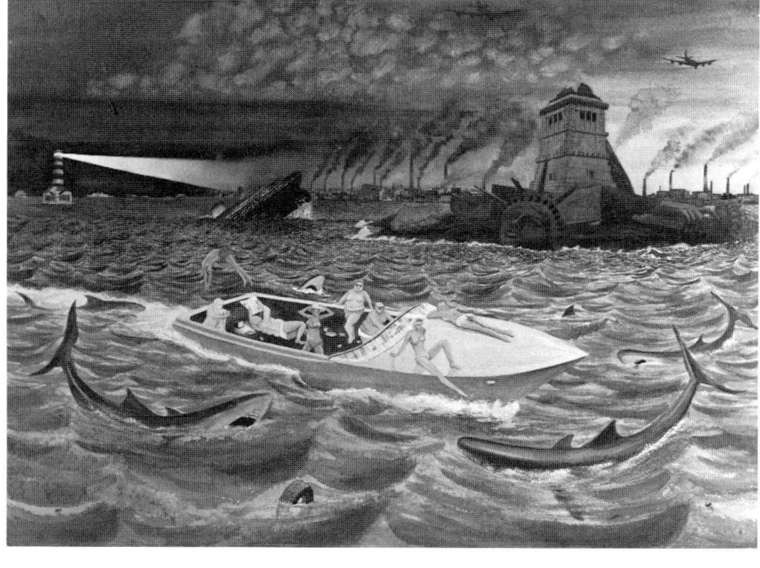

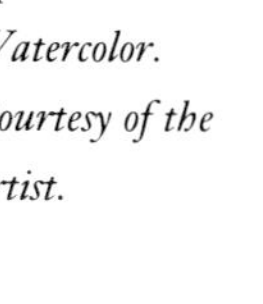

1. *Seaver Leslie,* Speedboat. *Watercolor. Courtesy of the artist.*

Seaver Leslie

Seaver Leslie's art is about as subtle as a bulldozer. Where the majority of painters make of watercolor something delicate, evanescent, and washed-up, Leslie makes vitriolic use of the medium in paintings which rise above satire to pure outrage. The targets of Leslie's wrath are the displacement of America's native and natural peoples and the despoilment of the environment by those who have dispossessed them.

Leslie, who lives and paints and farms in Wiscasset, is currently (through March 12) being featured at the DeCordova and Dana Museum in Lincoln, Mass., in that museum's *New Work/New England* series. Entitled *Tradition Is the Enemy of Progress*, Leslie's DeCordova show issues an unqualified indictment of modern America for crimes against the earth and her people, including, but not limited to, clear cutting, strip mining, real estate speculation, agri-business pollution, and the generation of nuclear power for profit. This acidic little show consists of a dozen watercolors, three oils, two prints, and tempera, and it takes its title from one of the oils, a picture of two traditional Indian women in a desert Southwest landscape being invaded by bulldozers. The title of the picture comes from a sign which once stood outside a Navaho Indian reservation: "Tradition Is the Enemy of Progress."

The benign, spiritual relation Hopi and Navaho people have with Mother Earth is the paradigm Seaver Leslie holds up against the consumer capitalist paradigm of domination and exploitation. There is no moral ambiguity anywhere in sight as Leslie pits tribal against capital, cyclical against linear, feminine against masculine, good against evil, life against death in an art of high indignation.

Three of Leslie's major pieces, a pair of watercolors and an oil, deal with the forced relocation of Navaho people from Big Mountain in northeastern Arizona. Under the series title *A National Sacrifice Area*, Leslie shows us a panorama of Big Mountain being strip-mined into oblivion as Navaho weavers watch from their looms. The creative technology of the Indian has been replaced by destructive technology of the White Man.

In *Intrusion: Shutterbug*, the artist envisions Navaho people being pursued by an airborne paparazzo, a scene inspired by accounts of an Albuquerque news photographer hiring a helicopter to get shots of a sacred ceremony the Navaho would not allow photographed. Profane media violates sacred tribal life.

And in pictures such as *Forward Looking: A Modern View* (gauche tourists outside an Indian compound) and *The Real Estate Ball* (a trio of bewildered Navaho women at a champagne gala) Leslie draws the clearest possible distinction between the native American and the ugly American.

Leslie himself appears as a fist-shaking figure in two of his works, the watercolor *Railing Against the Progress Myth* and the woodcut *Railing Against Nuclear Power*. The former is a rather Gatsbyesque New York City nocturne about a world of unconscionable excess; the latter was prompted by word that a dairy farmer in Wiscasset had been advised to stop selling milk because of excessive levels of strontium-90.

Leslie does not pull his punches, so when it comes to living with Maine Yankee he offers up a vision of Apocalypse Wiscasset. *In a Maine Town* is an almost frighteningly folksy watercolor in which Leslie's fellow townspeople spill out of their snug, smug Greek Revival homes to die in the street of radiation sickness.

Seaver Leslie has the force of moral rectitude on his side, but his painterly crusades are not calculated to win him popular or commercial success. Indeed, there is only one painting in this angry exhibition which abandons the polemical for the sublime. *Night Moon*, a small 1988 oil, shows Leslie's Three Navaho Graces standing back-to, contemplating a moonlit desert landscape. All around is peaceful.

You have to go back in Maine art to Rockwell Kent before you find another artist as maddeningly uncompromised as Seaver Leslie.

February 3, 1989

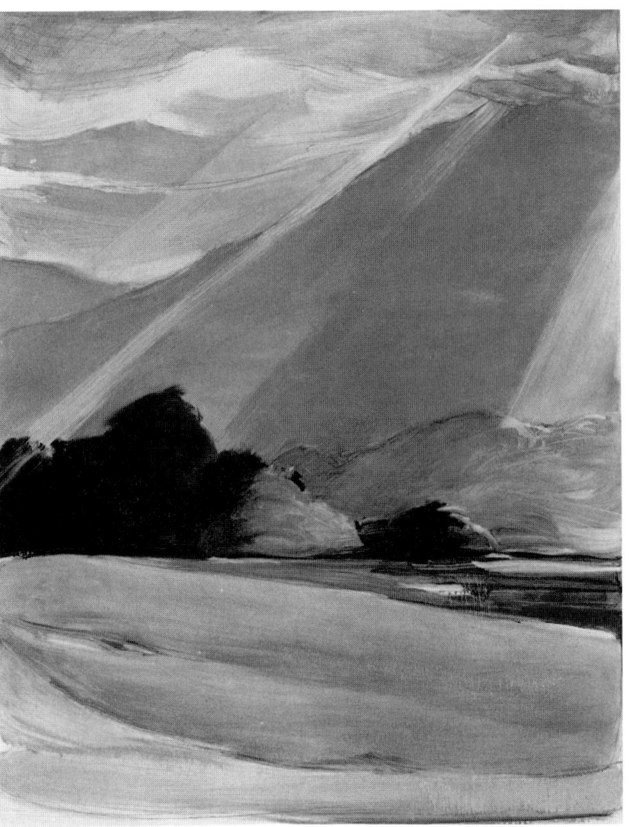

1. *Marguerite Robichaux*, April 10, *1988. Oil on paper. Courtesy of the O'Farrell Gallery.*

Marguerite Robichaux

Last year at this time Marguerite Robichaux retreated from the mountain fastness of the Carrabassett Valley to spend a grant-supported month painting at the Vermont Studio Colony in Johnson, Vermont. While at the Vermont artists' colony, Robichaux produced a series of some 30 watercolor landscapes, several of which she subsequently writ large in oil upon returning to Maine.

These paintings, 33 *plein-air* watercolors and eight studio oils, constitute Robichaux's *April Journal* exhibition now (through May 27) on view at the O'Farrell Gallery in Brunswick. *April Journal* is a ruralist landscape symphony, a body of work that reminds us how very fine and how often overlooked Marguerite Robichaux is.

Robichaux's watercolors (which, like her oils, are identified only by date) are sure, mature, serene paintings in which the artist seems content to faithfully set down the major forms and features of land and sky. They are a fluid following of the rock and roll of geologic ground swells, treelines, mountain tops, and early spring atmospherics. Effectively presented in groups of two to eight paintings, the watercolors are uniformly mounted in whitewashed wooden frames which are a perfect vernacular response to the nature and culture of rural New England.

Marguerite Robichaux knows mountainous northern New England well, but the visual remove from Maine to Vermont was obviously a revelation to her and a catalyst to her art.

"There is something very seductive about the Vermont landscape this time of year," she says. "The Vermont landscape has been cleared by centuries of farming, so you really *see* the land more than you see it here in Maine. I found the buff gold color of the land very sensual."

Her thin, turpy oils keep faith with her watercolors not only in the wash and flow of imagery, but also in the consonance of color. A visual sweep of the gallery takes in a constant harmony of sandy browns, deep evergreens, purplish highlights, and misty grays. These muted impressions of earth speak of a place of thoughtful and tranquil repose, the immemorial hills standing still for their portrait.

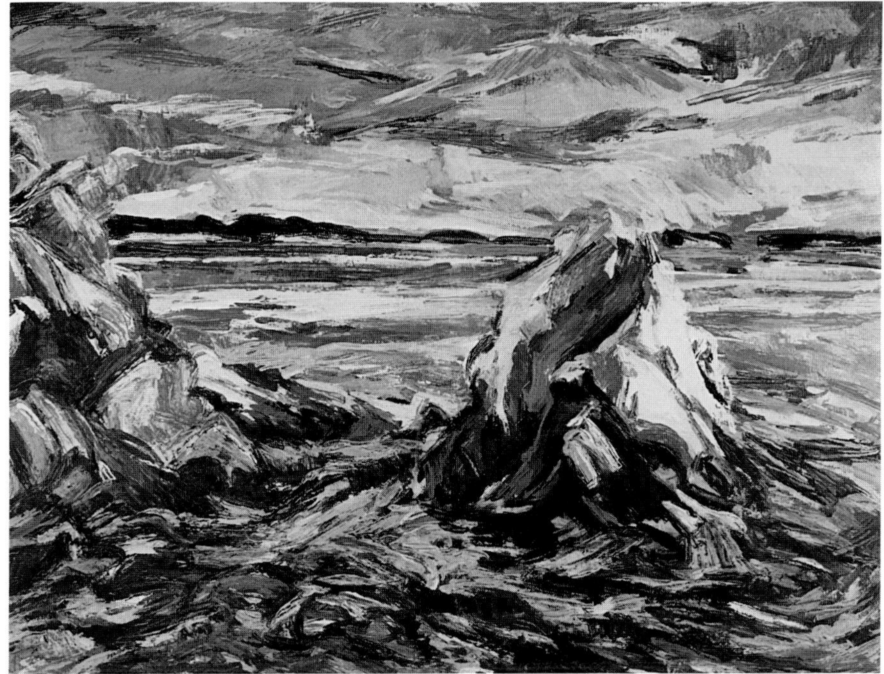

1. *Gina Werfel,* Rocks at High Tide. *Oil on linen. Courtesy of Gallery 127.*

Though Robichaux does not flinch from spectacle and majesty, portraying celestial shafts of sunlight without becoming overly picturesque, her best instinct is to capture soft moments of quietude. My favorite image, for example, is a gentle overlay of hills titled in both watercolor and oil *April 4*. The shoulder of a buff hill inclines across from right to left striped with pale green indications of tire tracks. Another hill scissors in behind from the left wearing a stand of bleak trees as a halo. Through the trees we see the crimson profile of a distant ridge. The effect is one of stability and rest produced with an economy of means.

Landscape, of course, is fundamental to the human experience; it is the *where* of our terrestrial existence. Since most major artists are now urban creatures, inhabitants of man-made spaces, landscape painting no longer figures as prominently as it once did in the American cultural mix, but in Maine, where the landscape remains complete, landscape painting is still the most of art. It is this simple, but profound wholeness that Marguerite Robichaux finds and communicates in and through her mountains. Here is painting as modest, noble, and nurturing as farming.

April 7, 1989

Gina Werfel

Gina Werfel winces at the thought that she might be considered a landscape painter, so she would probably faint dead away at the suggestion that she also paints wonderful seascapes. Nonetheless, Werfel's *Recent Work* exhibition currently (through May 10) on view at the Colby College Museum of Art in Waterville does feature several of the most thoughtful modern seascapes you are likely to see here in Maine or anywhere.

Werfel's reluctance to be seen as a landscape artist is, of course, perfectly understandable. Before coming to Maine to teach at Colby, she studied and worked in New York City where "landscape" as it modifies "art" is, if not exactly a pejorative term, at least a limiting conditional connoting an old-fashioned and probably rural art form. Werfel approaches landscape with a thorough grounding in the New York school of painterly gesture as practiced by Willem DeKooning, Philip Guston, and, most particularly, the late Gretna Campbell, an influential New York painter who spent summers on Great Cranberry Isle. Werfel is, in fact, a stable-mate of Campbell's son Henry Finkelstein at the Prince Street Gallery in New York, where this Colby show originated.

It is difficult to say in a few words what the difference is between an artist who paints the Maine landscape with a working knowledge of modernism and abstract expressionism, and one who paints it as though art in Maine stopped with Winslow Homer. Simply put, however, Werfel's art is as much about the act of painting as about any likeness or sense of place. She participates in and extends the expressionist landscape tradition of Marin and Hartley and, like those two modernist giants, this exhibition finds her working in both Maine and New Mexico.

Clear evidence of the primacy of the painted surface over the landscape perceived in Werfel's art is the fact that her New Mexican landscapes have the same weight and authority as her Maine landscapes. Many of the Maine artists who make the pilgrimage to the Southwest bring back paintings which, because they are more familiar with the closed Maine landscape than with the wide open spaces of New Mexico, have a tendency to be anemic and unconvincing when compared to their Maine work. Such is not the case with Werfel. She is faithful to the canvas, not the geography.

Of her New Mexican paintings, *Red Mesa*, which loosely depicts a view from Georgia O'Keeffe's backyard in Abiquiu, is one of the finest, and its finest feature is the tempestuous purple of the unsettled sky. Most of the exhibition, however, is devoted to Maine paintings, and most of these are seascapes in which Werfel brings her excited brush and keyed-up palette to bear on calm moments along the Islesboro shore.

The chief characteristic of Werfel's work is that she treats all elements of a scene equally such that rocks and seeweed, sky and water, trees and clouds all have the same consistency. She makes no attempt to differentiate the substantial from the insubstantial, because she is not after an illusionistic representation. In fact, the most frequent observation about her paintings is that the image tends to disintegrate as the viewer approaches.

In *Rocks at High Tide*, for example, the shore rock and protruding ledge seem no more solid than the swash of blue water and golden rockweed at their base. The rhythm of the land, sea, and sky are one in a painterly dance of strokes and licks. And time and again, in paintings such as *Gooseberry Nubble*, *Boat Basin*, *Islesboro*, and *Tidal Pools*, Werfel ignores the more majestic vistas of Penobscot Bay in favor of the close-at-hand view. What matters is the immediate and the intimate.

Gina Werfel's paintings are physically beautiful, internally coherent, and immensely thoughtful. This impressive body of new work will move to Gallery 127 in Portland (May 16 to June 6) after its stay in Waterville.

April 28, 1989

Jeff Kellar

Jeff Kellar possesses a sensibility rare among artists working in Maine. Here in the raw Northeast where naturalism flows through even abstract art as incessantly as rivers rush to sea, Kellar's sculpture resists natural forces with almost classical restraint.

Indeed, I would go so far as to suggest that Kellar is unmatched in Maine for the degree of value his art places on order, discipline and material refinement. This preference for the Apollonian over the Dionysian may have something to do with the peculiar path Kellar's aesthetic journey has taken.

Jeff Kellar comes to sculpture from furniture-making, having made a name for himself as a designer/maker of furniture with strong, simple, elegant, memorable forms. A self-taught cabinetmaker, he studied English and film-making at the University of Pennsylvania, and his experimental films, he tells me (I have not seen them), had the same austere, emotional quality his furniture and art have. Four years ago, he began building transitional pieces (furniture, furniture as art, art as furniture, art) and for the past two years he has concentrated almost exclusively on making sculpture.

Last year at this time, Kellar was one of the 10 Maine craft artists selected to exhibit in the *10* crafts cross-over exhibition at the Portland Museum of Art. His *New Sculpture* show at Barridoff Galleries (through June 10) consists of 15 objects which carry on the evolution away from cabinetmaking while at the same time preserving that respect for the well-made which is at the heart of craftsmanship.

The pieces which speak most obviously and directly to Kellar's furniture-making background are a quintet of four-legged sculpture which might be mistaken at a distance for tall tables. In fact, they are viewing boxes meant to be looked down into, and Kellar has simply solved the presentation problem by making the pedestal part of the art. *Transit*, for example, is a black box on legs with wire mesh covering a recessed compartment in which is a 3-by-3 square of nine gold wedges.

The pedestal pieces are related formally to a series of small wall-hung boxes and strategically

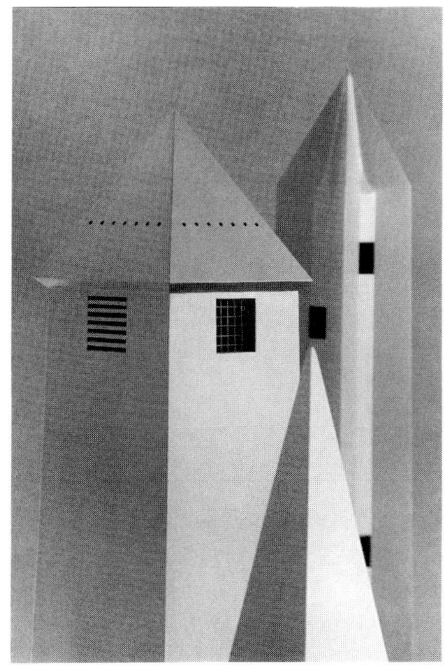

1. *Jeff Kellar, detail of three standing sculptures. Wood, magnesium paint, chalk, and gouache. Courtesy of the Barridoff Galleries.*

to a quartet of free-standing structures which resemble spires, towers, and pyramids. *Standard*, a particular favorite of mine, is a sleek seven-foot tower at once futuristic and medieval. Tucked away at the top in which might be a belfry or dovecote is a little yellow house on bright blue stilts which, should you get down on your knees to examine the base of the piece, you will find extend all the way to the floor.

All of Kellar's new works are constructed of wood painted either with copper leaf, resulting in an aged, green patina, or black magnesium paint which has been rubbed with chalk and washed to a deep, rich sheen. Hiding the process and labor of their making beneath highly finished surfaces, Kellar's sculptures look as though they were conceived rather than constructed.

Architecture often seems to be the point of departure, if not the inspiration, for Kellar's art, and several of the pieces contain miniature houses as elements of the internal composition. In fact, Kellar manages to combine aspects of the real and the abstract in each piece. Just as his chairs and tables were *about* placing real objects in domestic interior spaces, his new sculpture is about looking at objects in public space. The way his art works is by calling attention to the highly structured, ritual way of seeing that routinely goes on in art galleries and museums.

The consummation of this perceptual manipulation is Kellar's installation entitled *Comings and Goings*, a copper-green and gilt chamber perhaps eight feet high. Built up against a gallery wall, *Comings and Goings* admits only the eye through its two-inch vertical gaps. Inside one sees a golden bowl set upon the floor and the suggestion of a door leading into the wall. This is sculpture with the presence of an ancient sepulchre.

The strange combination of a sense of antiquity with the sensibility of a contemporary is, of course, the stylistic calling card of the neo-classical impulse currently sweeping through the art and architecture of America. Jeff Kellar is, however, one of the first and the few to bring a taste for this new order to Maine.

May 19, 1989

Johnnie Ross

Johnnie Ross is as tough as painters in Maine get. He pursues the most extreme form of pure abstraction in paintings devoid of both illusion and allusion. The typical Johnnie Ross canvas is as hard, harsh and elegant as a Formica tabletop and nearly as impenetrable. Recently, however, Ross has subjected himself and his art to a thorough reexamination and, as a result, has made some substantial changes which, in subtle ways, may make his work more accessible to the average viewer.

Johnnie Ross has been a remote presence in Maine since he arrived here 13 years ago from Texas to teach at the Portland School of Art (PSA). His remoteness has been both literal, in that he has tended to show more often in Boston and New York than Maine, and conceptual, in that few other artists in the state share his formal concerns. To understand this Rossian aloofness, it helps to know that Ross grew up in St. Louis where (like former PSA director William Collins and long-time PSA painting professor Edwin Douglas) he studied art at Washington University. WashU was a heavily Abstract Expressionist school under the lingering influence of Max Beckmann, but Ross was even more severely inclined toward the abstract as a result of working in a St. Louis gallery which showed minimalist sculptors Carl Andre, Donald Judd, Ellsworth Kelly, Richard Serra, and Joel Shapiro. What Ross responded to in the works of these modern masters was the power of reduction, the ability to reduce visual information to bare essentials.

"I saw their success," says Ross, "in terms of making work that transcended itself beyond the surface quality of the time we live in and dealt with the root or core quality of the culture."

Because his point of reference was minimal sculpture, it is not surprising that Ross' paintings have long had a sculptural quality both in their shapes and their surfaces. Working most often on shaped canvases geared to circle sections, Ross has built up surfaces of dozens of layers of pigment and then sanded and polished them to a hard shell finish. While nuances of place—elements of light and color as well as a keen awareness of being on the edge—sometimes crept over a Ross canvas, they have always seemed primarily about the vocabulary of color expressed through the grammar of geometry.

Ross worked on this reductivist impulse for almost 20 years before seriously reconsidering the direction his art was taking. Last year, however, he began to question some of his fundamental assumptions about painting, in the process reaffirming many but modifying some. Primarily what he found was that his rigorous concentration on materials and process was resulting in paintings that were very physical and sensual. Thus he undertook a renewed effort to capture in art the same quality of transcendence which had originally inspired him.

The results of Johnnie Ross' attempt to apprehend a more metaphysical element in his art were on view recently (April 24 to May 20) at the Akin Gallery in Boston's South End. Far from constituting a rejection of his past direction, the nine untitled paintings in Ross' Akin show demonstrate how a mature artist makes a mid-course correction without losing aesthetic ground.

Geometry and materials are still fundamental to Ross, but in these new paintings he has replaced the circle with the square and has added a great deal of weight to his pigments. He has elected the square format, he says, because the square kills any figure-ground relationships, thus giving the same pictorial weight and immediacy to all elements of a composition. The new pigments, which Ross developed with a technician at the Golden Paint Company, contain iron rust, corten steel, copper, bronze, and graphite—elements that give these new paintings the evolving patinas of metal sculpture.

The key compositional element in all of the paintings is the cross, a device used for both its symbolic value and its organizational utility. As a simple intersection of lines, the cross divides the pictorial space into chromatic units; as crucifix, it divines the same space. The symbolism does not read literally in a Christian sense by any means, but these new paintings are more obviously open to spiritual possibilities than some of Ross' earlier pieces.

In some cases, as in the large (60-x-60-inch) painting reproduced here, Ross uses the cross and the square to set up grids which speak back through Albers' color squares to Mondrian's Cubist block paintings and Russian constructivism. The bright yellow *éclat* of the small square in the lower left quandrant reads both as Mondrian monad and as a window of palpable light. In other pieces, Ross uses overlapping crosses to create bars and stripes and even constructs crosses from the canvases themselves.

This formal and material shift—from curves and strong colors to squares and earth tones—moves Ross' art away from the lyrical and toward the historical. Lyricism is fine, but Johnnie Ross aspires to paintings that have the quality of a symphony, not just a song. Paintings without imagery, he points out, should be no more inaccessible than music without words.

May 29, 1989

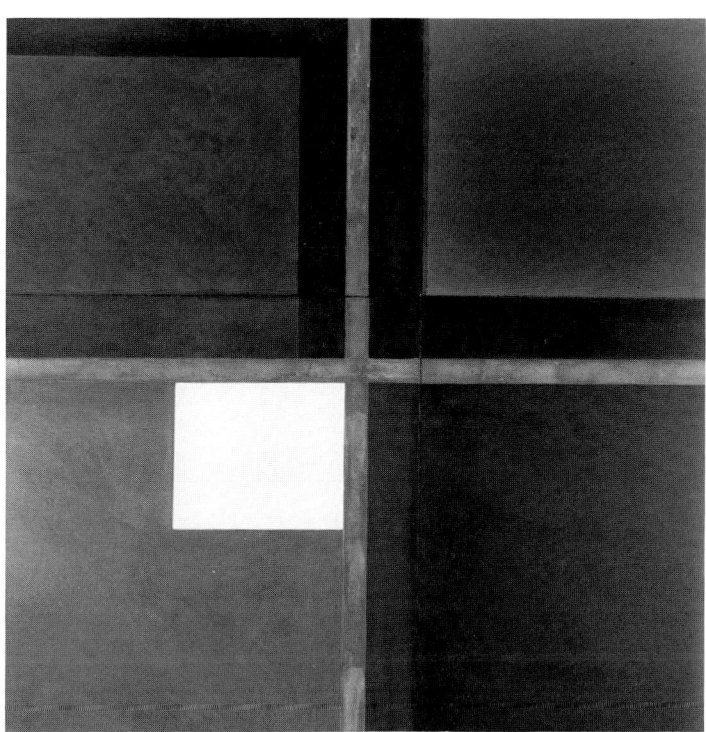

1. *Johnnie Ross,* Untitled, *1989. Acrylic on canvas. Courtesy of the artist and the Akin Gallery, Boston.*

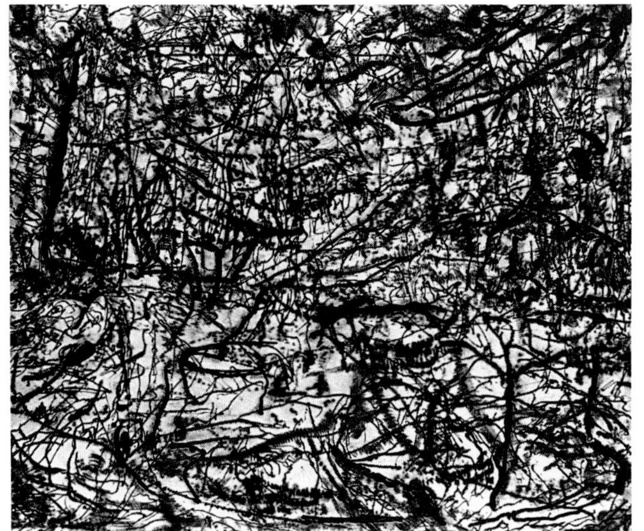

1. *Alice Steinhardt,* Web, *1989. Drypoint. Courtesy of the artist.*

Alice Steinhardt

Alice Steinhardt's paintings announce their seriousness at first sight by challenging the viewer to discover the hidden beauty in the thick, dark mass of paint encrusted upon the canvas. Boggy blacks and swampy greens backed up by mauve undertones and here and there enlivened by licks and islands of red, her palette is nothing if not lugubrious. Yet applying the colors of organic decay to impastoed, imagined landscapes, Steinhardt succeeds in leading us out of ugliness into the beautiful.

Steinhardt, whose *Recent Works* are showing at Dean Velentgas Gallery in Portland through June 11, is married to painter Mark Wethli of the Bowdoin College faculty, but one would be hard-pressed to relate these two fine artists stylistically. Where Wethli uses precise, illusionistic means to point at aspects of reality and beyond, Steinhardt buries the viewer in paint and insists that the painting is the really real.

In her exhibition statement, Steinhardt writes that her paintings concern "creating a sense of place that is tangible and yet unfamiliar, connected to the experience of landscape and yet independent of a specific site or location."

I would suggest that Alice Steinhardt's paintings, by virtue of specifying spaces with their own particular topography and gravity, *are* places. What is more, in this excellent exhibition, the artist provides a detailed map of how she got to these wonderfully mysterious places in the form of supporting prints and drawings.

Though they are not displayed, Velentgas has in the backroom of his gallery a selection of the charcoal nocturnes which began Steinhardt's recent explorations. Quiet, dark, and dim, the charcoal drawings reduce place to ghostly silhouettes against a night sky. The beginning point in the exhibition itself, however, is a series of small ink drawings, just a few black lines of demarcation on the flat, white landscape of paper. I saw the ink drawings as schematic, the orientation seeming to be that of a cartographic overview.

Elements of density and dimension are then discovered and added in a suite of gestural drypoint etchings every bit as bitterly alluring as the drippings of Jackson Pollock or the scribblings of Cy Twombly. Depth and texture of space is created in the prints by webs and tangles of lines scraped, scratched, zipped, and stuttered across the surface. As elegant as Oriental calligraphy, yet as random as a scattering of smashed atoms, the traceries and trajectories of the drypoint prints point the way directly to the paintings.

For the most part, Steinhardt's oils make only the most essential references to landscape—a few smudged verticals suggesting trees, a blur that might be a horizon, that's about it. Beyond that, Steinhardt simply builds and builds with paint until she finds her way out of the picture, leaving us in a place overgrown and mossy, moonlit and wild.

The titles of many of the paintings—*Nomad, Walkabout, Beacon, Here, Near and Far, Return*—suggest not so much landscapes as movement through a landscape, literally finding one's way. In this approach to art as *locus* and the making of art as locational, Alice Steinhardt's work has clear sympathies with that of some of the best young artists in Maine—Dozier Bell, Kathy Bradford, Mary Hart, Larry Hayden, Celeste Roberge—the company she deserves to keep.

June 2, 1989

Dennis Pinette

Dennis Pinette paints and draws industrial installations, both recollected and invented, that have all the bang, sizzle, hiss, crackle and roar of a paper mill going full tilt on the third shift. More often than not, Pinette's hot, noisy paintings are nightscapes illuminated by the infernal, internal glow of the factory. Steam, fire, heat, light, glare—the hellish spectre of the modern world brought to bear on paper and canvas, the hideous beauty of the post-industrial apocalypse laid down in (most fittingly) oils. At least that's the way I interpreted Pinette's art, until I read his statement in the Maine Coast Artists' 11th Annual Juried Exhibition catalogue.

"I am attracted to industrial things and places," Pinette wrote, "because I find them peaceful and harmonious."

So instead of intending his art as an indictment of industry for spewing forth its foulness into the atmosphere, Pinette simply finds factories by night "the armature over which I can drape my painting concerns." The irony of making beautiful paintings of ugly subjects, however, is not diminished by the artist's lack of intent; rather, it is doubled, since Pinette not only *paints* industry as beautiful, he *sees* it as beautiful.

Having taken top honors just weeks ago in the Maine Coast Artists show, Pinette is now being featured in an one-artist exhibition at the Frick Gallery in Belfast (through July 16), and his statement on this occasion is equally clear.

"I have always been absorbed by the History of invention, progress, evolution, and thought. My paintings are about a particular facet of man's presence, occupation, or domination of our planet, and how that presence is harmonious with nature. I do not intend, nor am I interested in, any kind of political statement or judgment about the tangle we are in today."

Of course, neutrality does not exist any more than objectivity does; Pinette's "harmonious" is just as judgmental as my "hellish." But we get the point. Dennis Pinette, like a number of other fine artists who work in Maine (Marsha Donahue, Rackstraw Downes, Yvonne Jacquette, Robert Solotaire), finds the industrial

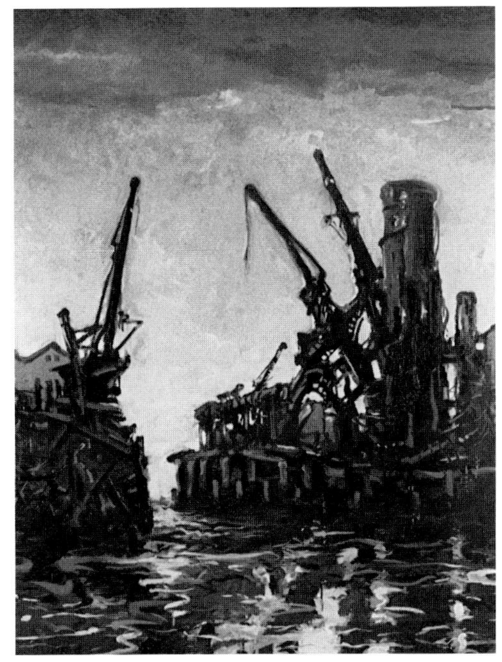

1. *Dennis Pinette,* Cove, *1989. Oil on canvas. Courtesy of the Stephen Rosenberg Gallery and the Frick Gallery. Photo by Peggy McKenna.*

workscape *interesting*. And his interest is more visual than editorial.

The speed, power, and formal complexity of industrial machinery has inspired generations of artists, but where, say, early modernists such as Charles Sheeler and Charles Demuth responded to mechanical precision with paintings of their own iconic precision, Pinette treats electromechanical subjects to some pretty poetic brushwork.

Cove, for instance, is a nocturne of waterfront cranes, derricks, and smoke stacks in which Pinette's excited performance on canvas convinces us that black water and brown skies are beautiful on their own terms.

Pinette says that memories of industrial landscapes in New Jersey as well as elements of local plants such as an old fertilizer mill in Brooks and a defunct feed mill in Thorndike inform the mostly invented shapes in his paintings, but a pair of small triptychs, *Backwater* and *Bend in the River*, were inspired by the industrial banks of the Penobscot River at Bucksport.

Pinette's best pieces, however, tend to be those in which machinery rather than landscape are primary. A painting such as *Night Voltage II*, for example, with its fire-breathing stack and electric blue coils flashing sparks and energy, delivers us straight into the soul of the machine. Whether this soul is marvelous or monstrous is

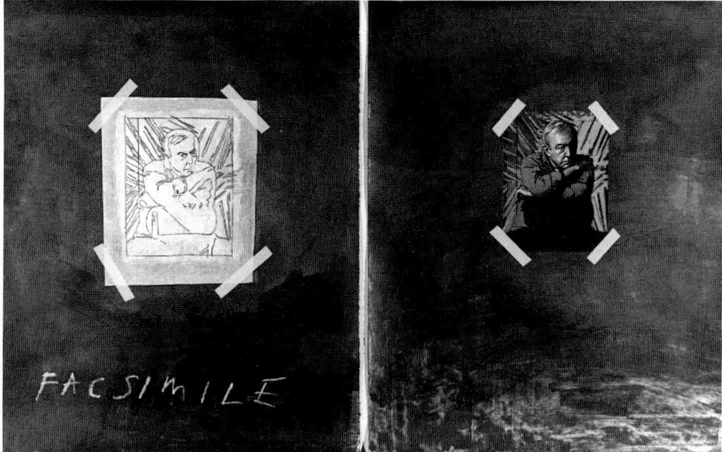

1. *James Linehan,* Facsimile, *1989. Acrylic on paper. Courtesy of the artist. Photo by University of Maine at Orono.*

at least debatable. But Dennis Pinette still insists, "My paintings are about painting."

Pinette was an abstract painter before moving to Maine from Rhode Island five years ago. When he returned to painting after taking a year off to move and get settled in Belfast, he discovered that "my invention process had stalled with abstraction." His working solution was to begin using bridges and other industrial structures as form-givers in his paintings. That strategy obviously worked both personally and professionally, because Pinette and his paintings have really heated up over the past three or four years.

Along with *Dennis Pinette: New Work*, the Frick Gallery is featuring *Works on/of Paper* by a dozen artists, among the most interesting of whom are Libby Lyman, Martha Miller, Scott Redfern, and Richard Wilson. Both shows are further evidence of the Frick Gallery's commitment to showing tough, serious, high-impact modern art.

June 30, 1989

James Linehan

James Linehan has been sending dispatches from the periphery of the Maine art scene ever since he arrived here from North Carolina in 1983 to teach at the University of Maine in Orono. In a distinctive personal style which is a fusion of Pop realism and ideographic abstraction, Linehan has been exploring ideas and asking questions about *place*. A sense of restlessness and dislocation have informed all the Linehan paintings I have seen over the past five years in group shows at Bowdoin, Bates, Portland Museum of Art, and Maine Coast Artists. Now, with *The Meaning of Travel* (at the O'Farrell Gallery in Brunswick through September 2), James Linehan has truly arrived.

The Meaning of Travel, Linehan's first commercial one-artist show in Maine, has roots in a similarly titled, five-page "site-specific" commission Linehan did in 1987 for the now-defunct *AM* (*Artists in Maine*) magazine. While Linehan's opening statement in the *AM* piece is "Travel isn't a metaphor for anything—it's just anxiety in motion, hard work, and painful self-examination per diem," it seems fairly obvious to me that travel *is* a metaphor for Linehan, a metaphor for the mysterious journey of life. Scrawled in the text of that visual essay, at any rate, are two fundamental questions every earnest traveler through reality asks sooner or later: "Why am I here?" and "Shouldn't I be accomplishing something?"

In an enormous mixed-media piece which covers one whole wall at O'Farrell, Linehan seems to have found some answers to his questioning. "The meaning of travel begins and ends with the home," writes the artist in/on *Home Dada*, an installation-on-paper inspired by Linehan's two-year-old daughter Flynn. Fatherhood provides purpose.

In *Home Dada*, the central image of a radiant, child-like house is flanked by a photo-likeness of the artist's daughter and is surrounded by a decorative border of stylized pine trees. As in many Linehan paintings, there is a handwritten text across the surface of the work. The house is "drawn" in Linehan's signature *trompe l'oeil* masking tape. Linehan's *faux* tape device simultaneously makes reference to the display and illusion of art and, in its utilitarian look, connects the viewer with the studio where the illusion on display was created. The studio, of course, is the artist's *place*, and Linehan, an avid world traveler before the birth of his daughter, has found that he can travel extensively within his studio as well.

Linehan's travels—nicely unified in technique, idea, and idiom—take the form of 12 acrylic on paper paintings which combine painted postcard images of places from New Zealand to Stonington with abstract passages which record qualities of color, texture, and light in those places. The realistic postcards are "taped" in the middle of the white paper with the abstract bands, which function as value registers, painted down the left-hand side of the picture.

Linehan also uses his unique combination of precise realist illusion, painterly abstract gesture, and painted words in a pair of partial self-portraits and in a series of paintings which pay homage to artists Jasper Johns, Edvard Munch, and Jan Vermeer, and writer James Joyce.

Backing up the postcard and homage pieces are a series of five bold abstract paintings based on places Linehan experienced in 1986 when he spent six weeks in New Zealand. Linehan often paints direct representations of landscape into his complex compositions, but in this 1988 series he registers an interpretive response to what he calls "the hyperbolic landscapes of New Zealand." The paintings all bear titles taken from the native Maori language and are overpainted in simple "tape" images—for instance, a boat form in *Tangaroa (The Vast Oceans)*—which give the paintings what might best be called a look of Pop primitivism.

The Meaning of Travel is an exhibition which engages the viewer at several different levels—from the perceptual to the personal—and I applaud James Linehan for having the courage and confidence to reveal so much about the source and substance of his artistic ideas. The only way *The Meaning of Travel* might be improved would be to show it in the studio rather than a gallery.

July 28, 1989

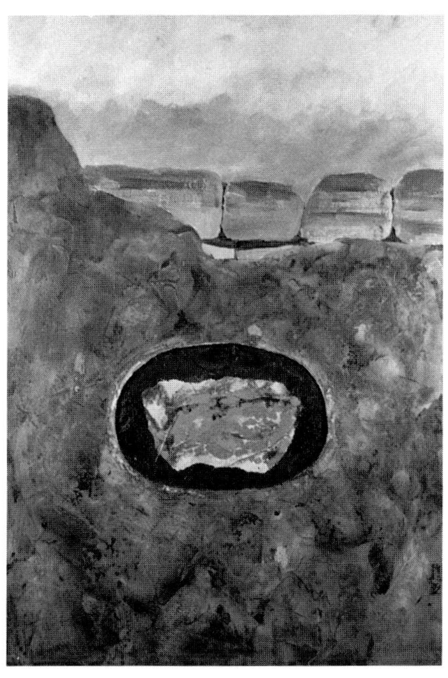

1. *Jack Muench,* How Still the Treasure Lies, *triptych (detail). Mixed-media with gold leaf. Courtesy of Hobe Sound Galleries North.*

John Muench and William Manning

John Muench and William Manning are both artists who have aged well. Colleagues 30 years ago at the Portland School of Art (where Muench was director from 1958 to 1963 and Manning was on the faculty between 1959 and 1969), they have evolved along entirely different aesthetic lines to a point where their disparate interests seem to have converged. A concurrence both of formal concerns and current exhibitions recommends this critical coupling, but the important thing to note is that Jack Muench and Bill Manning are rare among mature artists in that their work has not petrified into a set of conditioned responses. Both men continue to explore, evolve, and grow in their art.

Muench, who went on from the Portland School of Art to teach printmaking at Rhode Island School of Design and Westbrook College, is best known for his history paintings and prints and for his lyrical interpretations of the Maine landscape, but his *Recent Paintings* show at Hobe Sound Galleries North in Brunswick (through September 24) features a series of mixed-media paintings inspired by the culture and landscape of New Mexico. Muench is one of those artists (like Beverly Hallam and John Laurent) who moves comfortably back and forth between representation and abstraction, and his

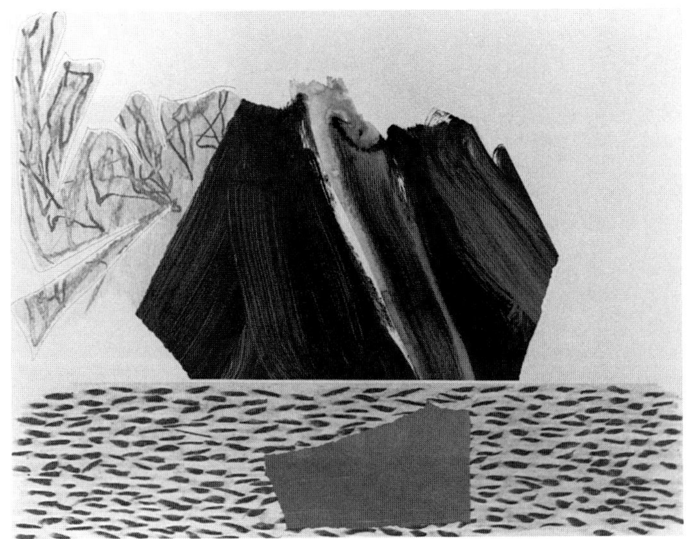

2. *William Manning,* Untitled, *1988. Mixed-media collage on paper. Courtesy of the Barridoff Galleries.*

new paintings are what might be called "geological abstractions."

Executed in rosy hues of desert light and terra cotta tones and textures, Muench's New Mexican paintings explore the subterranean strata of the desert world in search of the precious. Veins of gold leaf, silver leaf, and deposits of turquoise gems are unearthed, petroglyphs discovered, totemic symbols revealed. In some cases, Muench's use of the natural and cultural wealth of the desert seems a bit too literal, but his better pieces are mysterious treasures from the Land of Enchantment. A printmaker to the bone, Muench makes paintings that are as layered with elements and information as a lithograph.

Canyon Mystery and *Marker*, for instance, are both paintings which lift symbols from Southwest Indian culture and place them in an art historical context. Whenever one quotes from the iconography of another culture, of course, the result is as apt to be pure decoration as new meaning. Still, the spiraling arrow which is the focus of *Canyon Mystery* and the golden signpost which stands at the heart of *Marker* are strong, primal shapes which relieve Muench's sensuous surfaces of much of their preciousness.

A generation ago, Bill Manning, a maverick who left the Portland School of Art to co-found Portland's short-lived (1969-73) Concept School of Visual Studies, was one of the very few serious abstract painters working in Maine. The paintings in his *Aurora and Temple Series* show at Barridoff Galleries in Portland (through September 30) continue his formal re-ordering of the natural shapes, colors, textures, and patterns to be found around and upon Monhegan Island.

With the exception of five two-dimensional paper collages, all of the works in Manning's exhibition are three-dimensional sculptural paintings and wall reliefs. Despite their existence in the round, however, Manning's complex, interstitial constructions insist upon being paintings rather than sculpture. No matter how erect they stand, they are less about their form than about their painted surfaces.

Manning tends to work with vertical formats, fragmented forms, and overlaid shapes—all strategies which allude to human form and human perception. It is almost as though the artist has sliced through one's immediate perceptions and reassembled them to suit his own sense of how the world behaves.

The most frequently recurring shape in his work is a trapezoidal chunk which seems both the primal shape of the upthrust island and its mineral essence. In and over this blunt, broken shape he plays a symphony of natural colors and patterns: fog and granite grays, vegetative lines, oceanic surges, crystalline formations, traceries of clouds, bright auroral reds and oranges.

Temple #11, for example, reads like a cross-section of marine landscape, with a splashing black wave tightly contained within Manning's primordial quadrangle. The background layers run red to orange and down to an oozing grey at the bottom, where fossil-like shards have sunken into the muddy matrix. Providing the painting with a certain holy rectitude are two upright panels set out in relief from the painted surface. The first is a deep blue board with carefully beveled edges, the other a slate-grey plank with sharp edges. Whether Manning intends these raised elements to serve as sighting devices or human surrogates, I cannot say, but they add a ceremonial seriousness to an otherwise lyrical abstraction.

What Muench and Manning share in their separate responses to separate landscapes, then, are a preference for the highly structured, a tendency toward the textured surfaces of Tachisme, and sensibilities attuned to the refractory nature of deeply embedded forms.

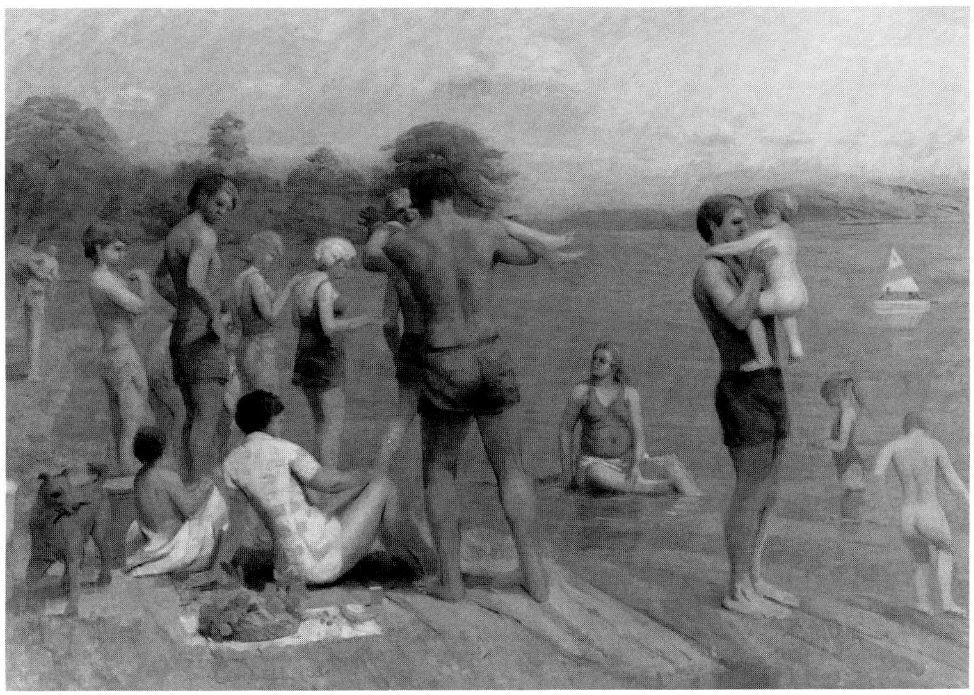

1. *Thomas Cornell,* Bathers V, *1988. Oil on canvas. Courtesy of G.W. Einstein Company, Inc.*

They are after the hard stuff, that which matters and is matter below the level of appearance. They are very solid painters, very sure of themselves as they open new veins in the well-worked aesthetic mines of Santa Fe and Monhegan.

September 15, 1989

Thomas Cornell

Painter Thomas Cornell has been a member of the Bowdoin College faculty since 1962, and his presence there has set a tone of classical realism for the school's art department which has been seconded in recent years by painters Joseph Nicoletti, Kevin Donahue, and, currently, Mark Wethli. But while Cornell's presence has been acutely felt at Bowdoin, it is his peculiar absence that is more apt to be noticed on the wider Maine art scene. Like Leonard Craig at Unity College, Donald Lent and Robert Feintuch at Bates, and Ron Ghiz at Orono, Tom Cornell tends to be something of an academic no-show.

The last time Cornell showed a significant body of work in Maine was in 1977 at Barridoff Galleries. Prior to that, his most substantial Maine show was an exhibition at Bowdoin in 1964 consisting chiefly of prints and drawings. As a mid-career artist, Cornell has concentrated his efforts on attracting national attention, a mission he has quietly accomplished in a variety of ways.

Throughout the 1980s, Cornell has regularly exhibited in New York. In 1985, he was commissioned by the John Hancock Life Insurance Company to execute a four-panel painting of the *Four Seasons* for the company's Boston headquarters. More recently, Cornell's work has been pictured and discussed in *Post-*

Modernism: The New Classicism in Art and Architecture by Charles Jencks, post-modernism's chief spokesman. And this fall Cornell was selected by critic Donald Kuspit as one of 32 artists to exhibit in a Soviet-American relations show entitled *American Painting After the Death of Painting*. The show's title was meant ironically, of course, but if painting were to have a life after death Tom Cornell's Elysian visions would surely qualify.

History—indeed, antiquity—has always been important in Cornell's art. His 1964 Bowdoin show, for instance, consisted primarily of portraits of figures from the French Revolution and the American Civil War rendered in a graphic style strongly influenced by Rico LeBrun and Leonard Baskin. In May, 1990, Bowdoin will mount a major exhibition of Cornell's paintings, but Cornell's current (through December 2) one-artist show at the G.W. Einstein Gallery in New York is fairly indicative of the classical direction his allegorical figure paintings have taken.

In his exhibition statement, Cornell proposes that his art champions "a Nature-centered rationality" which he calls "Dionysian Classicism."

"These paintings celebrate eros and earthly values," writes Cornell. "They propose a new ethos based on psychoanalytic and ecological values. They propose a material 'spirituality' in sympathy with Green political values. Thus they are a critique of instrumental rationality and supernatural illusions. They propose to sublate and transform Judeo-Christian values and ground rationality in Nature. In their celebration of joy in life, they are a critique of Postmodernism and the necromantic chic and cynicism of black New York fashion."

In short, Tom Cornell is an old-fashioned humanist. The paintings and drawings in his *Bathers* series (which are the focus of the New York show), for example, present a pastoral (littoral?) vision of human beings harmonized with Nature. As opposed to the sombre palette "of black New York fashion," Cornell paints in sun-baked, almost Mediterranean pastel hues. Up against the despair and defeatism of urban apocrypha, he presents *al fresco* tableaux of Arcadian simplicity and gentle paternalism. His family of man (in the generic sense of the word) romps on the shore in happy carnality, joined now and again by figures from classical antiquity (a Greek *kouros* statue, for example) which they closely resemble.

Cornell's idyllic *Bathers* are supported in the Einstein show by an oil entitled *Clamdigger*, which depicts a pony-tailed clamdigger at Simpson Point in Brunswick simultaneously in three different poses. The painting suggests both the dignity of hard work close to nature and the temporal nature of art. These figurative feature pieces are themselves offset by a pair of backyard landscapes, *Early Spring* and *A New Planting*, which use gardening as a metaphor for the harmonious union of nature and culture.

"Maine should have its own view," says Thomas Cornell. "Living closer to nature, Maine artists should have a healthier view of the world than the parochial notions of the city."

The sense that Maine occupies a special place in the world of art and that life here embodies a set of naturalistic values which are expressed in Maine art is pervasive, but Tom Cornell's version of the Maine eco-aesthetic is stylistically unique. Where the majority of artists in Maine respond to the power of this place with realistic representations, romantic impressions, and lyrical abstractions of land and sea, Cornell addresses the Maine experience in an antique, even archly didactic manner. His purely perceptual paintings are more easily approachable than those generated by dogma, but his application of classical figuration to contemporary convictions is ultimately very convincing. Perhaps, then, it is not important that Cornell show his art often in Maine. In New York he is ministering to the soul-sick of the city; here he would be preaching to the converted.

November 3, 1989

Index

(Bold numbers indicate pages containing illustrations.)

Maine Art n o w

Design: Ratta Design Communications, Portland, Maine

Production consultant: Jack Leether

Imagesetting: High Resolution, Inc., Camden, Maine

Printing (text) and binding: Thomson-Shore, Inc., Dexter, Michigan

Printing (color plates, cover and jackets): Western Maine Graphics, Norway, Maine

Editorial and production assistance: Robert Saunders, Nessa Burns Reifsnyder, H. Jeremy Wintersteen

Editorial and artistic direction: Mark Melnicove